# Communications
# in Computer and Information Science     1885

## Rationale

The CCIS series is devoted to the publication of proceedings of computer science conferences. Its aim is to efficiently disseminate original research results in informatics in printed and electronic form. While the focus is on publication of peer-reviewed full papers presenting mature work, inclusion of reviewed short papers reporting on work in progress is welcome, too. Besides globally relevant meetings with internationally representative program committees guaranteeing a strict peer-reviewing and paper selection process, conferences run by societies or of high regional or national relevance are also considered for publication.

## Topics

The topical scope of CCIS spans the entire spectrum of informatics ranging from foundational topics in the theory of computing to information and communications science and technology and a broad variety of interdisciplinary application fields.

## Information for Volume Editors and Authors

Publication in CCIS is free of charge. No royalties are paid, however, we offer registered conference participants temporary free access to the online version of the conference proceedings on SpringerLink (http://link.springer.com) by means of an http referrer from the conference website and/or a number of complimentary printed copies, as specified in the official acceptance email of the event.

CCIS proceedings can be published in time for distribution at conferences or as post-proceedings, and delivered in the form of printed books and/or electronically as USBs and/or e-content licenses for accessing proceedings at SpringerLink. Furthermore, CCIS proceedings are included in the CCIS electronic book series hosted in the SpringerLink digital library at http://link.springer.com/bookseries/7899. Conferences publishing in CCIS are allowed to use Online Conference Service (OCS) for managing the whole proceedings lifecycle (from submission and reviewing to preparing for publication) free of charge.

## Publication process

The language of publication is exclusively English. Authors publishing in CCIS have to sign the Springer CCIS copyright transfer form, however, they are free to use their material published in CCIS for substantially changed, more elaborate subsequent publications elsewhere. For the preparation of the camera-ready papers/files, authors have to strictly adhere to the Springer CCIS Authors' Instructions and are strongly encouraged to use the CCIS LaTeX style files or templates.

## Abstracting/Indexing

CCIS is abstracted/indexed in DBLP, Google Scholar, EI-Compendex, Mathematical Reviews, SCImago, Scopus. CCIS volumes are also submitted for the inclusion in ISI Proceedings.

## How to start

To start the evaluation of your proposal for inclusion in the CCIS series, please send an e-mail to ccis@springer.com.

Jorge Maldonado-Mahauad ·
Jorge Herrera-Tapia ·
Jorge Luis Zambrano-Martínez ·
Santiago Berrezueta
Editors

# Information and Communication Technologies

11th Ecuadorian Conference, TICEC 2023
Cuenca, Ecuador, October 18–20, 2023
Proceedings

Springer

*Editors*
Jorge Maldonado-Mahauad ⓘ
Universidad de Cuenca
Cuenca, Ecuador

Jorge Luis Zambrano-Martínez ⓘ
Universidad del Azuay
Cuenca, Ecuador

Jorge Herrera-Tapia ⓘ
Universidad Laica Eloy Alfaro de Manabí
Manta, Ecuador

Santiago Berrezueta ⓘ
CEDIA
Cuenca, Ecuador

Technical University of Munich
Heilbronn, Germany

ISSN 1865-0929        ISSN 1865-0937 (electronic)
Communications in Computer and Information Science
ISBN 978-3-031-45437-0        ISBN 978-3-031-45438-7 (eBook)
https://doi.org/10.1007/978-3-031-45438-7

This Springer imprint is published by the registered company Springer Nature Switzerland AG
The registered company address is: Gewerbestrasse 11, 6330 Cham, Switzerland

Paper in this product is recyclable.

# Preface

Welcome to the eleventh edition of the Ecuadorian Congress of Information and Communication Technologies (TICEC 2023). Hosted in the historic city of Cuenca from October 18 to 20, 2023, this event adopted a hybrid mode at the campus of Universidad de Cuenca (UC).

TICEC stands out as a pivotal conference in Ecuador dedicated to the advancements of Information and Communication Technologies (ICTs). Annually, it assembles a diverse group of researchers, educators, professionals, and students from across the globe, fostering an environment to share research findings and engage in enriching academic endeavors. These collaborations aim to pave the way for innovative ICT applications across various sectors.

This year, the event's organization was masterfully executed through a partnership between the Universidad de Cuenca and the Corporación Ecuatoriana para el Desarrollo de la Investigación y la Academia (CEDIA). The conference featured insightful oral presentations of scientific papers, spanning three primary domains:

- Data Science
- ICT Applications, and
- Software Development

As testament to its growing global influence, this edition witnessed submissions from 245 authors hailing from 12 countries. Ensuring the integrity and quality of our proceedings, all manuscripts underwent rigorous similarity checks and were subjected to a meticulous double-blind peer review by our esteemed TICEC 2023 Program Committee. This committee comprised 150 renowned researchers from 40 countries, with each manuscript evaluated by a minimum of three experts. From this rigorous process, we are proud to present 31 accepted full papers out of 120 received papers, marking an acceptance rate of 25%.

October 2023

Jorge Maldonado-Mahauad
Jorge Herrera-Tapia
Jorge Luis Zambrano-Martínez
Santiago Berrezueta

# Organization

## Honorary Committee

| | |
|---|---|
| Cecilia Paredes | CEDIA, Ecuador |
| María Augusta Hermida | Universidad de Cuenca, Ecuador |
| Juan Pablo Carvallo Vega | CEDIA, Ecuador |

## General Chair

| | |
|---|---|
| Jorge Maldonado | Universidad de Cuenca, Ecuador |

## Program Committee Chairs

| | |
|---|---|
| Germania Rodriguez Morales | Universidad Técnica Particular de Loja, Ecuador |
| Efrain R. Fonseca C. | Universidad de las Fuerzas Armadas, Ecuador |
| Marcos Orellana | Universidad del Azuay, Ecuador |
| Juan Pablo Salgado | Universidad Politécnica Salesiana, Ecuador |
| Jorge Herrera-Tapia | Universidad Laica Eloy Alfaro de Manabí, Ecuador |
| Jorge Luis Zambrano-Martínez | Universidad del Azuay, Ecuador |
| Santiago Berrezueta | CEDIA, Ecuador and Technical University of Munich, Germany |

## Organizing Committee

| | |
|---|---|
| Karina Abad | Universidad de Cuenca, Ecuador |
| Doris Suquilanda | Universidad de Cuenca, Ecuador |
| Lilian Tapia | Universidad de Cuenca, Ecuador |
| Sonia Balcázar | Universidad de Cuenca, Ecuador |
| Fabian Vélez | Universidad de Cuenca, Ecuador |
| Gabriela Parra | Universidad de Cuenca, Ecuador |
| Ana Isabel Ordoñez | CEDIA, Ecuador |
| Micaela Ferrari | CEDIA, Ecuador |
| Santiago Ruilova | CEDIA, Ecuador |
| Francisco Toral | CEDIA, Ecuador |

| Paúl Arévalo | CEDIA, Ecuador |
| Laura Malache-Silva | CEDIA, Ecuador |

## Program Committee

| Adam Wojciechowski | Lodz University of Technology, Poland |
| Agustin L. Herrera-May | Universidad Veracruzana, Mexico |
| Agustín Yagüe | Universidad Politécnica de Madrid, Spain |
| Alex-F. Buitrago-Hurtado | Universidad Externado de Colombia, Colombia |
| Alexandros Liapis | ESDA Lab, Greece |
| Alexandros Spournias | ESDA Lab, Greece |
| Alvaro Llaria | University of Bordeaux, France |
| Alvaro Suarez | Universidad de Las Palmas de G.C., Spain |
| Ana Gabriela Nuñez Avila | Universitat Politècnica de València, Spain |
| Ángel Alberto Magreñán | Universidad de La Rioja, Spain |
| Angel Hernandez-Martinez | Universidad Nacional Autónoma de México, Mexico |
| Ankit Maurya | Indian Institute of Technology Roorkee, India |
| Antonio Mogro | Tecnológico de Monterrey, Mexico |
| Arash Arami | University of Waterloo, Canada |
| Arcangelo Castiglione | University of Salerno, Italy |
| Artur Rydosz | AGH University of Science and Technology, Poland |
| Belen Bermejo | University of the Balearic Islands, Spain |
| Belen Curto | University of Salamanca, Spain |
| Benoît Parrein | Ecole polytechnique de Nantes, France |
| Bugra Alkan | London South Bank University, UK |
| Carlos Abreu | Instituto Politécnico de Viana do Castelo, Potugal |
| Carme Quer | Universitat Politècnica de Catalunya, Spain |
| Cecilio Angulo | Universitat Politècnica de Catalunya, Spain |
| Chaker Abdelaziz Kerrache | Université Amar Telidji de Laghouat, Algeria |
| Chao Min | Nanjing University, China |
| Che-Wei Lin | National Cheng Kung University, Taiwan |
| Christos Antonopoulos | University of the Peloponnese, Greece |
| Christos Mourtzios | Aristotle University of Thessaloniki, Greece |
| Christos Panagiotou | ESDA Lab, Greece |
| Claudia Ayala | Universitat Politècnica de Catalunya, Spain |
| Claudia Marzi | Italian National Research Council, Italy |
| Coral Calero | Universidad de Castilla-La Mancha, Spain |
| Corina Namaj | University of Istanbul, Turkey |
| Cristian Vasar | Politehnica University of Timisoara, Romania |

| | |
|---|---|
| John Castro | Universidad de Atacama, Chile |
| Jorge Parraga-Alava | Universidad Técnica de Manabí, Ecuador |
| José Daniel Padrón | Universtat Politècnica de València, Spain |
| José Martinez-Carranza | Inst. Nac. de Astrofísica, Óptica y Electrónica, Mexico |
| Jose Huertas | Tecnológico de Monterrey, Mexico |
| José Olivas-Varela | Universidad de Castilla-La Mancha, Spain |
| José-J. De-Moura-Ramos | University of A Coruña, Spain |
| José-Juan Pazos-Arias | Universidad de Vigo, Spain |
| José Fernán Martínez | Universidad Politécnica de Madrid, Spain |
| Jose Tenreiro Machado | ISEP University, France |
| Josip Music | University of Split, Croatia |
| Kester Quist-Aphetsi | Ghana Technology University College, Ghana |
| Khalid Saeed | Bialystok University of Technology, Poland |
| Kiril Alexiev | IICT – BAS, Bulgaria |
| Konstantinos Antonopoulos | ESDA Lab, Greece |
| Krzysztof Bernacki | Silesian University of Technology, Poland |
| Kwan-Ho You | Sungkyunkwan University, South Korea |
| Lidia Lopez | Barcelona Supercomputing Center, Spain |
| Liyanage Kithsiri Perera | USQ, Australia |
| Loredana Stanciu | "Politehnica" University of Timisoara, Romania |
| Lucian Pislaru-Danescu | INCDIE ICPE-CA, Bucarest |
| Luis Martin-Pomares | Qatar Environment and Energy Research Inst., Qatar |
| Luise Wolfshagen | Universität Heidenheim, Germany |
| Lukasz Sobaszek | Lublin University of Technology, Poland |
| Lydia Schawe | Hochschule Bremerhaven, Germany |
| Mahendra Babu G. R. | Karpagam Academy of Higher Education, India |
| Marcin Ciecholewski | University of Gdansk, Poland |
| Marcin Górski | Silesian University of Technology, Poland |
| Marco Zappatore | University of Salento, Italy |
| Marco Antônio P. Araújo | UFJF, Brazil |
| Maria Francesca Bruno | Politecnico di Bari, Italy |
| María Cristina Rodriguez | Rey Juan Carlos University, Spain |
| María-Luisa Martín-Ruíz | Universidad Politécnica de Madrid, Spain |
| Marian Wysocki | Rzeszow University of Technology, Poland |
| Marija Seder | University of Zagreb, Croatia |
| Mario Miličević | University of Dubrovnik, Croatia |
| Mariusz Kostrzewski | Warsaw University of Technology, Poland |
| Marlon Navia | Universidad Técnica de Manabí, Ecuador |
| Martín López-Nores | Universidad de Vigo, Spain |
| Massimo Donelli | University of Trento, Italy |

| | |
|---|---|
| Massimo Merenda | Università Mediterranea di Reggio Calabria, Italy |
| Michał Tomczak | Gdańsk University of Technology, Poland |
| Modestos Stavrakis | University of the Aegean, Greece |
| Mohiuddin Ahmed | Edith Cowan University, Australia |
| Natasa Zivic | University of Siegen, Germany |
| Noman Naseer | Pusan University, South Korea |
| Noor Zaman | Taylor's University, Malaysia |
| Omar Abdul Wahab | Université du Québec en Outaouais, Canada |
| Oscar Alvear | Universidad de Cuenca, Ecuador |
| Panagiota Yota-Katsikouli | Technical University of Denmark, Denmark |
| Patricio Galdames | Universidad del Bio-Bio, Chile |
| Paul Nicolae Borza | Transilvania University of Braşov, Romania |
| Pietro Manzoni | Universidad Politécnica de Valencia, Spain |
| Piotr Borkowski | Maritime University of Szczecin, Poland |
| Prasanta Ghosh | ICEEM, India |
| Przemysław Mazurek | West Pomeranian University of Technology, Poland |
| Raúl Antonio Aguilar Vera | Universidad Autónoma de Yucatán, Mexico |
| Robert Dobre | Politéhnica University of Bucharest, Romania |
| Roberto Murphy | INAOE, Mexico |
| Roemi Fernandez | Universidad Politecnica de Madrid, Spain |
| Rosaria Rucco | University of Naples Parthenope, Italy |
| Rostom Mabrouk | Bishop's University, Canada |
| Rui Zhao | University of Nebraska Omaha, USA |
| Ruoyu Su | Memorial University of Newfoundland, Canada |
| Saleh Mobayen | University of Zanjan, Iran |
| Samuel Ortega-Sarmiento | University of Las Palmas de Gran Canaria, Spain |
| Santiago Gonzalez Martinez | Biogeco, France |
| Sara Paiva | Oviedo University, Spain |
| Shaibal Barua | Mälardalen University, Sweden |
| Shernon Osepa | Internet Society, The Netherlands |
| Silvia Grassi | Università degli Studi di Milano, Italy |
| Stavros Souravlas | University of Macedonia, North Macedonia |
| Stefano Mariani | Università degli Studi Modena e Reggio Emilia, Italy |
| Sule Yildirim-Yayilgan | Norwegian University of Science & Technology, Norway |
| Sunday-Cookeyn Ekpo | Manchester Metropolitan University, UK |
| Thomas Usländer | Fraunhofer, Germany |
| Tomasz Bieniek | Institute of Electron Technology, Poland |
| Tuan Nguyen-Gia | University of Turku, Finland |
| Utkarsh Singh | Depsys SA, Switzerland |

Valerio Baiocchi            Sapienza University of Rome, Italy
Vera Ferreira              Federal University of the Pampa, Brazil
Vinayak Elangovan          Penn State Abington, USA
Vladimir Sobeslav          University of Hradec Králové, Czech Republic
Wojciech Zabierowski       Lodz University of Technology, Poland
Xavier Franch              Universitat Politècnica de Catalunya, Spain
Yanhua Luo                 University of New South Wales, Australia
Yu Huang                   Chinese Academy of Sciences, China
Zoltán Ádám Tamus          Budapest University of Technology, Hungary

# Contents

## ICTs and their Applications

## Software Development

# Data Science and Machine Learning

# Uncovering the Effects of the Russia-Ukraine Conflict on Cryptocurrencies: A Data-Driven Analysis with Clustering and Biplot Techniques

Leo Ramos[1,2,3]($\boxtimes$) (iD), Mike Bermeo[1] (iD), and Isidro R. Amaro[1,2] (iD)

[1] School of Mathematical and Computational Sciences, Yachay Tech University, Urcuquí 100119, Imbabura, Ecuador
{leo.ramos,mike.bermeo,iamaro}@yachaytech.edu.ec
[2] Numerical Analysis and Data Science Research Group, Yachay Tech University, Urcuquí 100119, Imbabura, Ecuador
[3] Kauel Inc., Houston, TX 77098, USA

**Abstract.** This paper examines the impact of the Russia-Ukraine armed conflict on cryptocurrencies, focusing on the period between December 2021 and April 2022. Utilizing data from platforms monitoring the cryptocurrency market, the study evaluated fluctuations in major cryptocurrencies in relation to various variables, aiming to understand how the conflict has influenced them. Clustering and HJ-Biplot techniques were employed in the analysis. The findings revealed a decrease in valuation across all cryptocurrencies in 2022, with a particularly sharp drop in February, the month when the conflict started. Although there was an increase in valuations from March onwards, the analysis indicates that cryptocurrencies have not recovered to their value at the end of 2021, and they continue to be valued less overall.

**Keywords:** Cryptocurrencies · Data analysis · Cluster analysis · HJ-Biplot · Machine Learning

## 1 Introduction

Wars have historically been events that exert both direct and indirect influence on various aspects of society, including public health, commerce, and economic organizations. The recent armed conflict between Russia and Ukraine is no exception, having caused numerous human losses and instigating shifts in several economic sectors globally. Within the economic repercussions, there have been noticeable increases in the prices of oil, gas, and various food items [11,13].

In recent times, cryptocurrencies have become a standard tool for economic transactions. Both individuals and organizations are adopting cryptocurrencies

J. Maldonado-Mahauad et al. (Eds.): TICEC 2023, CCIS 1885, pp. 3–21, 2023.
https://doi.org/10.1007/978-3-031-45438-7_1

as official currency. For instance, El Salvador has become one of the first countries to recognize Bitcoin as legal tender. In a similar vein, the Center for Strategic and International Studies (CSIS) reports that Ukraine leveraged cryptocurrencies to solicit donations and procure military equipment. Conversely, Russia has explored cryptocurrencies as a means to circumvent Western-imposed sanctions. Since cryptocurrencies are not controlled or regulated by a specific institution, they have become an attractive option for conducting transactions without the need for intermediaries like banks [6].

Within the spectrum of fields affected by the Russia-Ukraine conflict, cryptocurrencies have not remained untouched by its consequences. The market is known for significant fluctuations in the value of cryptocurrencies [10], leading to considerable losses or profits in mere minutes for traders [16]. Therefore, this paper intends to explore the effects of the armed conflict between Russia and Ukraine on cryptocurrencies. Employing multivariate statistical analysis techniques such as HJ-Biplot and Cluster Analysis, the goal is to categorize some of the world's most prominent cryptocurrencies and discern the variables influencing their classification. Additionally, the study aims to analyze how these variables and cryptocurrencies have fluctuated within a time frame encompassing two months before and two months after the official invasion.

This work is organized as follows. Section 2 describes the data set used for this study, the data processing methods, and the data analysis methods used. Section 3 describes the technical procedure and the software used in this work. Section 4 shows the results obtained from our analysis and classification numerically and visually. Section 5 analyzes and contrasts the results obtained in search of inferences. Section 6 addresses the conclusions of the work.

## 2   Methodology

### 2.1   Data Set Description

The data set used was retrieved from CryptoCompare[1] and CoinGecko[2]. CryptoCompare allows the utilization of its API to extract the data and save it in various formats, while CoinGecko enables direct downloading of the data in CSV format. 11 cryptocurrencies were analyzed, as shown in Table 1. These are among the most widely used and recognized in the world, representing around 80% of the market's trading volume. The period studied spans five months, from December 2021 to April 2022. The variables selected for analysis were chosen based on existing literature [2,3,12], as they were deemed most suitable for examining the cryptocurrency market. Six variables were analyzed, and they are listed below:

- **High**, is the highest price on a given date.
- **Low**, is the lowest price on a given date.
- **Open**, is the opening price on a given date.

---

[1] https://www.cryptocompare.com/.
[2] https://www.coingecko.com/.

- **Close**, is the closing price on a given date.
- **Volume**, is the volume of transactions on a given date.
- **Market cap**, is the market capitalization in USD.

**Table 1.** Cryptocurrencies addressed.

| Crypto | Code |
|--------|------|
| Bitcoin | BTC |
| Ethereum | ETH |
| Tether | USDT |
| USD Coin | USDC |
| BNB | BNB |
| XRP | XRP |
| Cardano | ADA |
| Solana | SOL |
| Dogecoin | DOGE |
| Polygon | MATIC |

## 2.2   Data Preprocessing

Since the initial data set contains all the data in a single file, it was necessary to divide it according to each month studied. In this way, five sub data sets corresponding to December, January, February, March, and April were obtained from the initial data set. Likewise, since the sources from which the data was obtained provide a daily frequency, each month's average was taken to obtain a monthly estimate. Finally, it is necessary to mention that the data was scaled before being used through min-max normalization.

## 2.3   Analysis Techniques

**Cluster Analysis.** Clustering is a technique that groups data based on the search for patterns or similarities [9]. It is considered an unsupervised learning technique since it works from uncategorized data. Clustering techniques can be classified into two groups: hierarchical and partitional [8].

**K-means** is a technique belonging to partitional clustering techniques. K-means assigns n data points into k groups by grouping the data points that share similar characteristics [9] and minimizing the intra-cluster distance [1]. To choose the optimal number of clusters, a criterion function is used. To begin with, k centroids are defined randomly or from a priori information. Then each pattern in the data set is assigned to the closest cluster. The centroids are then recalculated concerning the associated patterns, and this process is repeated until convergence is achieved [1,15].

**HJ-Biplot.** Biplot methods are considered the multivariate analog of scatter plots [14]. This way, it can detect important elements such as patterns or outliers. The classic Biplot methods were initially proposed by Gabriel [7] and allow interpretation of the relationship between points and vectors.

The HJ-Biplot is a variant of the classical methods [5]. It is considered an exploratory method that allows describing the rows and columns to search for hidden patterns or relationships in the data [4,5]. Mathematically, it consists of displaying a multivariate matrix $X_{nxp}$ using vectors as points called markers $g_1, g_2, g_3, \cdots, g_n$ for each row and vectors called markers $h_1, h_2, h_3, \cdots, h_p$ for each column. Each row represents a subject, and each column is a variable [4]. The markers are obtained from the singular value decomposition (SVD), defined as:

$$X = UDV^T \tag{1}$$

where $U$ is the matrix whose columns are the eigenvectors of $XX^T$, $V$ is the matrix whose columns are the eigenvectors of $X^TX$, and $D$ is the diagonal matrix of singular values $\lambda_i$ of $X$. Therefore, the HJ-Biplot decomposes a data matrix $X$ such that:

$$X = AB^T \tag{2}$$

where $A = UD$ and $B = VD$.

The interpretation of the HJ-Biplot combines the rules of other multidimensional representation techniques [5]. The distance between rows (points) allows identifying similar clusters. The length of a column (vector) approaches its standard deviation, columns with acute angles between them are associated with high positive correlation, almost right obtuse angles are related to high negative correlation, and right angles show no correlation [4].

## 3   Procedure

First, an exploratory study was carried out to analyze the behavior of the variables throughout the period studied. For this, the accumulated values of each variable were taken, and a line chart was made.

Then, we focus on the study per month. For this, HJ-Biplot was first performed to obtain the data representation in plane 1–2. The PyBiplots[3] library was used in this stage. Then, the clustering was performed using the Biplot coordinates obtained from the HJ-Biplot. For clustering, K-means was used through the Python scikit-learn[4] library. To obtain the optimal number of clusters, the elbow method was used. For the visualization of the clustering and line chart results, the seaborn[5] Python library was used. The workflow used is shown in Fig. 1.

---

[3] https://github.com/carlostorrescubila/PyBiplots.
[4] https://scikit-learn.org/stable/.
[5] https://seaborn.pydata.org/.

## 4    Results

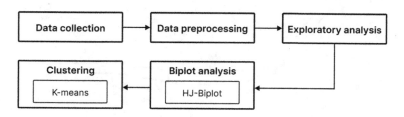

**Fig. 1.** Methodology followed in this work.

Figure 2 shows how the variables studied have evolved over the period studied. Since the variables were on a very different numerical scale, three graphs, 2a, 2b and 2c, were made. However, all three show a particularity, and that is that in February, the month in which Russia officially invaded Ukraine, is when the variables reach shallow values. Mainly in graphs 2a and 2c, it can be observed how in February, the values fall and then have a slow recovery in the following months.

### 4.1    December 2021

The HJ-Biplot depicted in Fig. 3a corresponds to the analysis for December 2021, explaining 99.21% of the variance, indicating an excellent representation. The variables "high," "low," "open," and "close" exhibit a strong positive correlation with each other, while "volume" and "market capitalization" show a comparatively weaker positive correlation with themselves and in relation to the other variables. The variable with the greatest variance is "volume." With respect to the quality of representation, both variables and individuals are well-represented and, thus, easily interpretable, as illustrated in Fig. 3b.

Using the elbow method, it was determined that the suitable number of clusters for classification is three. K-means was applied to this number using the Biplot coordinates, and the clustering results can be observed in Fig. 3a or Table 2. When projecting the individuals onto the vectors of the variables, BTC emerges with the highest values across all variables, with ETH following in second place. The remaining cryptocurrencies hover near the mean. In terms of dispersion, clusters 1 and 2 contain only one element, exhibiting no dispersion. Conversely, cluster 3 shows slight dispersion, with MATIC and SOL marginally apart from the other individuals in the cluster.

This observation can be further analyzed numerically in Fig. 4. Here, the mean of each cluster was calculated concerning all variables. Cluster 1 is distinguished by having higher values across all variables, particularly in market capitalization, almost doubling that of the other clusters. Meanwhile, Cluster 3 has the lowest values for all variables. Cluster 2 holds the second-highest market capitalization, following cluster 1, and in all other variables, it exhibits values close to cluster 1 and greater than cluster 3.

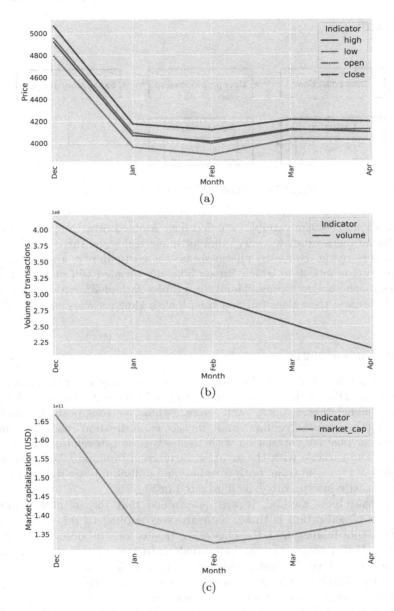

**Fig. 2.** Evolution of the indicators addressed between December 2021 and April 2022. (a) High, low, open and close prices. (b) Volume of transactions. (c) Market capitalization.

## 4.2   January 2022

The HJ-Biplot for January 2022 accounts for 99.59% of the variance, as depicted in Fig. 5a. The variables "high," "low," "open," and "closed" display a strong

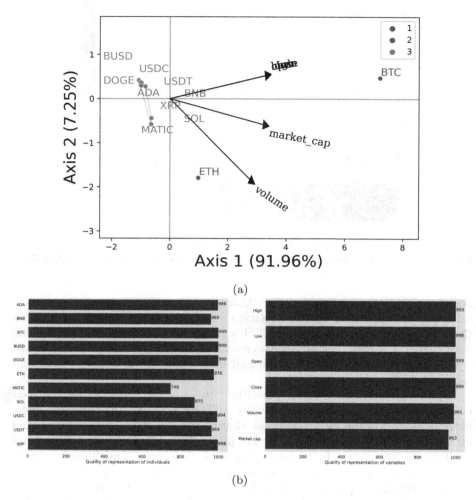

**Fig. 3.** (a) HJ biplot. (b) Quality of representation. Corresponding to December 2021.

**Table 2.** Cluster assignment for December 2021.

| Cluster | Elements |
| --- | --- |
| 1 | BTC |
| 2 | ETH |
| 3 | USDT, USDC, BNB, BUSD, XRP, ADA, SOL, DOGE, MATIC |

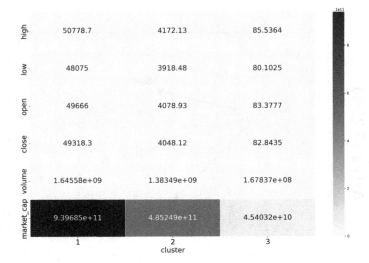

**Fig. 4.** Heatmap of the means of each cluster concerning each variable, December 2021.

positive correlation with each other. Conversely, "volume" and "market capitalization" manifest a positive correlation with each other, but less pronounced than the relationships among "high," "low," "open," and "closed." The variable with the most substantial variance seems to be "volume." In terms of the quality of representation, both variables and individuals are well represented and interpretable, as shown in Fig. 5b.

Upon applying the k-means algorithm, the clustering results can be seen either graphically in Fig. 5a or textually in Table 3. Projecting the individuals onto the vectors of the variables reveals that BTC holds the highest values across all variables, followed by ETH in second place. The rest of the cryptocurrencies cluster near the mean. In terms of dispersion, clusters 1 and 2 each contain only one element, and thus exhibit no dispersion. Cluster 3, however, demonstrates slight dispersion, with SOL being the most marginally separated individual within the cluster. This cluster displays less dispersion than was observed in December 2021.

Numerically, this behavior is also reflected in Fig. 6. Cluster 2 distinguishes itself by having a high market capitalization value. Cluster 3 records the lowest values in all variables in comparison to clusters 1 and 2. Cluster 1 exhibits intermediate values across all variables.

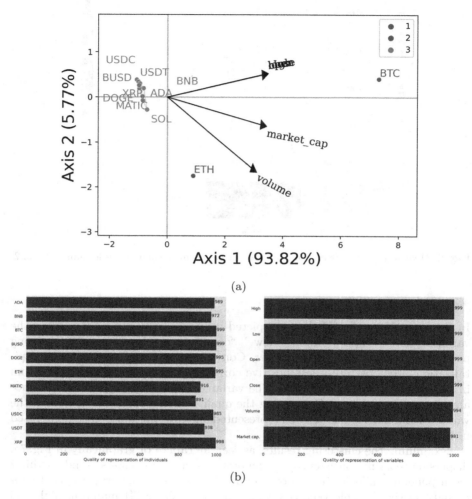

**Fig. 5.** (a) HJ biplot. (b) Quality of representation. Corresponding to January 2022.

**Table 3.** Cluster assignment for January 2022.

| Cluster | Elements |
|---------|----------|
| 1 | ETH |
| 2 | BTC |
| 3 | USDT, USDC, BNB, BUSD, XRP, ADA, SOL, DOGE, MATIC |

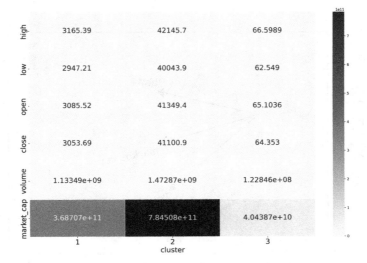

**Fig. 6.** Heatmap of the means of each cluster concerning each variable, January 2022.

### 4.3    February 2022

In February 2022, the HJ-Biplot depicted in Fig. 7a accounts for 99.66% of the variance. The variables "high," "low," "open," and "closed" exhibit a strong positive correlation with one another. Conversely, "volume" and "market capitalization" demonstrate a less positive correlation both among themselves and in relation to the other variables. The variable displaying the greatest variance appears to be "volume." Concerning the quality of the representation, both the variables and individuals are well represented and interpretable, as demonstrated in Fig. 7b.

Examining the clustering results, as seen in Table 4 or graphically in Fig. 7a, dispersion remains consistent with the previous month; Clusters 1 and 2 exhibit no dispersion, while cluster 3 shows minimal dispersion. The projections of individuals on the variable vectors reveal that BTC and ETH maintain high and medium-high values across all variables, respectively, while the remaining cryptocurrencies are proximal to the mean.

Figure 8 illustrates the means of the variables for each cluster. Cluster 1 presents moderately high values across all variables, while cluster 2 is notable for having elevated values in all aspects, particularly market capitalization. Cluster 3, in contrast, records low values across all variables.

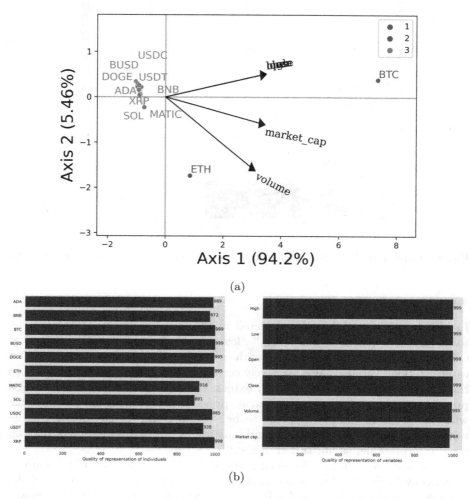

**Fig. 7.** (a) HJ biplot. (b) Quality of representation. Corresponding to February 2022.

**Table 4.** Cluster assignment for February 2022.

| Cluster | Elements |
|---|---|
| 1 | ETH |
| 2 | BTC |
| 3 | USDT, USDC, BNB, BUSD, XRP, ADA, SOL, DOGE, MATIC |

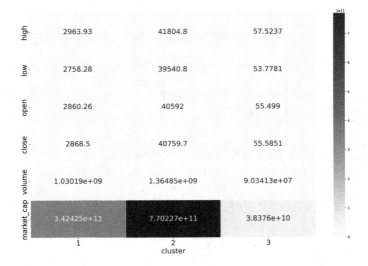

**Fig. 8.** Heatmap of the means of each cluster concerning each variable, February 2022.

### 4.4    March 2022

In March 2022, the HJ-Biplot depicted in Fig. 9a accounts for 99.65% of the total variance. The variables "high," "low," "open," and "closed" continue to exhibit a strong positive correlation with each other. The "volume" and "market capitalization" variables also positively correlate with each other and relative to the other variables, albeit to a lesser extent. Interestingly, this difference is less pronounced than what was observed in previous months. Again, the variable with the greatest variance appears to be "volume." As for the quality of the representation, both the variables and individuals are well represented, making them interpretable, as illustrated in Fig. 9b.

Upon applying k-means for clustering, the results are displayed in Table 5 or graphically in Fig. 9a. The projections of the individuals onto the vectors of the variables reveal that BTC and ETH are the cryptocurrencies with the highest values, with BTC significantly outperforming ETH and other cryptocurrencies. The dispersion remains consistent, with clusters 2 and 3 (corresponding to ETH and BTC) showing zero dispersion. Cluster 1, which encompasses the remaining cryptocurrencies, shows minimal dispersion.

Numerically, cluster 3 is highlighted by its high market capitalization value and is also the cluster with higher values across all variables when compared to others. Cluster 2, represented by ETH, exhibits higher market capitalization and other variable values than cluster 1. These observations are visually captured in Fig. 10.

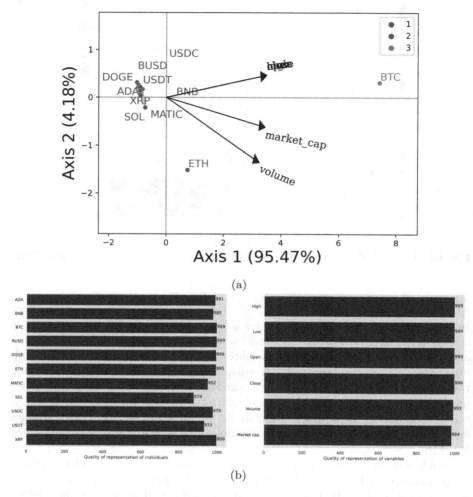

**Fig. 9.** (a) HJ biplot. (b) Quality of representation. Corresponding to March 2022.

**Table 5.** Cluster assignment for March 2022.

| Cluster | Elements |
|---------|----------|
| 1 | USDT, USDC, BNB, BUSD, XRP, ADA, SOL, DOGE, MATIC |
| 2 | ETH |
| 3 | BTC |

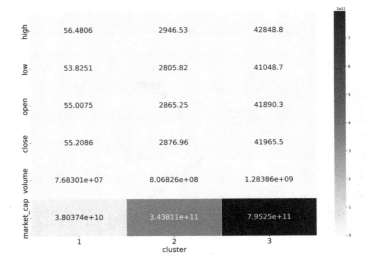

**Fig. 10.** Heatmap of the means of each cluster concerning each variable, March 2022.

### 4.5  April 2022

In April 2022, the HJ-Biplot illustrates a scenario where 99.58% of the variance is explained, as demonstrated in Fig. 11a. The variables "high," "low," "open," and "closed" continue to manifest a robust positive correlation. Similarly, "volume" and "market capitalization" also display a positive correlation, both among themselves and in relation to the other variables, although to a lesser degree. As has been a consistent trend, the variable with the highest variance remains "volume." The quality of representation in the biplot signifies that both variables and individuals are well represented, making them interpretable, as exhibited in Fig. 11b.

With respect to clustering, the K-means results can be found in Table 6 or graphically in Fig. 11a. The projections of the individuals on the variable vectors reaffirm that BTC and ETH are prominent, displaying higher values across all variables when compared to the other cryptocurrencies. Apart from BTC and ETH, the remaining cryptocurrencies are relatively average. Dispersion in clusters 1 and 2 is nonexistent, whereas it is minimal in cluster 3.

Shifting attention to the numerical insights, Fig. 12 provides a view of the means of the variables for each cluster. Notably, cluster 1 (consisting of BTC) boasts higher values than the others in all variables, with a particular emphasis on market capitalization. Additionally, cluster 2 (consisting of ETH) presents higher values across all variables compared to cluster 3, yet falls short of the values exhibited by cluster 1.

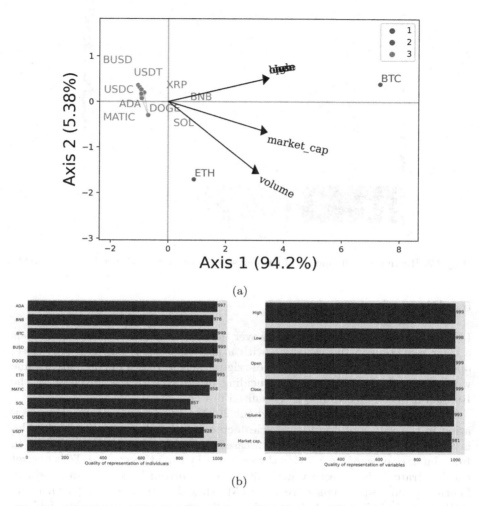

**Fig. 11.** (a) HJ biplot. (b) Quality of representation. Corresponding to April 2022.

**Table 6.** Cluster assignment for April 2022.

| Cluster | Elements |
| --- | --- |
| 1 | BTC |
| 2 | ETH |
| 3 | USDT, USDC, BNB, BUSD, XRP, ADA, SOL, DOGE, MATIC |

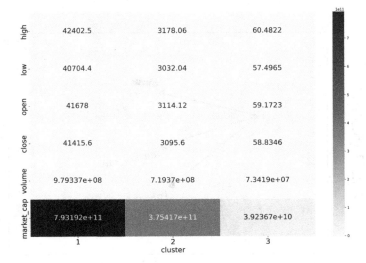

**Fig. 12.** Heatmap of the means of each cluster concerning each variable, April 2022.

## 5   Discussion

In evaluating the accumulated values over the months analyzed, the trend reveals a clear reduction in the variables, with a particular focus on high, low, close, open, and market capitalization. These significant decreases in cumulative value were most evident in February, coinciding precisely with the initiation of the Russian invasion of Ukraine, as visualized in Fig. 2.

Examining the heatmaps throughout 2022, a consistent pattern of depreciation in the values of cryptocurrencies across nearly all the analyzed variables is apparent. Although December showcased peak values, a steady decline set in from January onwards, persisting through April without recovery. BTC's market cap illustrates this trajectory well, hitting its zenith in December and nadir in February, and despite signs of revival in March and April, remaining far from its 2021 close. A similar trend characterizes other cryptocurrencies and variables.

An essential aspect of the analysis is the stability of the clusters across all months studied. BTC and ETH consistently occupied isolated clusters, with BTC invariably registering the highest values in all variables, especially market capitalization. ETH consistently ranked second, trailed by the remaining cryptocurrencies.

In terms of dispersion, the clusters comprising BTC and ETH exhibited none, while the cluster containing other cryptocurrencies typically displayed minimal dispersion. This group evidenced slightly more significant dispersion in December and April, with MATIC and SOL consistently demonstrating the most. Conversely, January, February, and March saw reduced dispersion within this cluster.

Turning to the HJ-Biplots, a persistent pattern emerges: the variables high, low, open, and close consistently manifested strong positive correlations. Volume and market capitalization likewise exhibited positive correlations, though marginally less robust. Interestingly, volume's correlation with other variables dipped in December, only to peak in March. Moreover, volume consistently appeared to present the most significant variance. The HJ-Biplots reliably described an extensive proportion of variance, consistently exceeding 90%. Additionally, both variables and individuals maintained a high quality of representation throughout the months studied, thereby enhancing interpretative clarity.

The findings herein not only provide a detailed understanding of the market behavior of various cryptocurrencies but also shed light on broader economic and geopolitical dynamics. The case of the significant declines during the Russian invasion of Ukraine serves as a poignant example, illuminating the intertwining of financial, political, and global events. Future research may wish to delve further into these complex relationships, offering more nuanced insights into the factors driving cryptocurrency values.

# 6   Conclusions

In this study, a statistical analysis was conducted on major cryptocurrencies from December 2021 to April 2022, focusing on the impact of the armed conflict between Russia and Ukraine. Cluster analysis and HJ-Biplot techniques were utilized to understand value changes.

February stood out as the month where the variables, particularly low, volume, and market capitalization, reached their lowest cumulative values. This drop was connected to the onset of the conflict, showing how geopolitical events can significantly affect the cryptocurrency market. BTC and ETH consistently presented the highest values in all variables, but they also seemed to have felt the most significant impact of the conflict. While the cryptocurrencies experienced their highest values in December, the lowest were observed in February, with a minor recovery in March and April.

Despite the slight improvements in the latter months, the values did not return to the highs of December 2021. The clusters of cryptocurrencies remained consistent over the analyzed period, with BTC and ETH always in isolated clusters and the others grouped together.

This research provides valuable insights for cryptocurrency users, traders, and market analysts. It highlights the susceptibility of cryptocurrencies to geopolitical events and the volatility of the market. It also offers a segmentation of cryptocurrencies according to variables studied, allowing a more nuanced understanding of the market landscape. Future studies could explore more detailed relationships between global events and cryptocurrency behavior for more refined trading strategies.

# References

1. Abbas, S.A., Aslam, A., Rehman, A.U., Abbasi, W.A., Arif, S., Kazmi, S.Z.H.: K-means and k-medoids: cluster analysis on birth data collected in city Muzaffarabad, Kashmir. IEEE Access **8**, 151847–151855 (2020). https://doi.org/10.1109/ACCESS.2020.3014021
2. Akyildirim, E., Goncu, A., Sensoy, A.: Prediction of cryptocurrency returns using machine learning. Ann. Oper. Res. **297**(1–2), 3–36 (2020). https://doi.org/10.1007/s10479-020-03575-y
3. Brauneis, A., Mestel, R., Theissen, E.: What drives the liquidity of cryptocurrencies? A long-term analysis. Financ. Res. Lett. **39**, 101537 (2021). https://doi.org/10.1016/j.frl.2020.101537
4. Carrasco, G., Molina, J.L., Patino-Alonso, M.C., Castillo, M.D.C., Vicente-Galindo, M.P., Galindo-Villardón, M.P.: Water quality evaluation through a multivariate statistical HJ-biplot approach. J. Hydrol. **577**, 123993 (2019). https://doi.org/10.1016/J.JHYDROL.2019.123993
5. Escobar, K.M., Vicente-Villardon, J.L., de la Hoz-M, J., Useche-Castro, L.M., Alarcón Cano, D.F., Siteneski, A.: Frequency of neuroendocrine tumor studies: using latent dirichlet allocation and HJ-biplot statistical methods. Mathematics **9**(18), 2281 (2021). https://doi.org/10.3390/math9182281
6. Fang, F., et al.: Cryptocurrency trading: a comprehensive survey. Financ. Innov. **8**, 1–59 (2022). https://doi.org/10.1186/S40854-021-00321-6/TABLES/11
7. Gabriel, K.R.: The biplot graphic display of matrices with application to principal component analysis. Biometrika **58**, 453–467 (1971). https://doi.org/10.1093/BIOMET/58.3.453
8. Giordani, P., Ferraro, M.B., Martella, F.: Introduction to clustering. In: Giordani, P., Ferraro, M.B., Martella, F. (eds.) An Introduction to Clustering with R. BQAHB, vol. 1, pp. 3–5. Springer, Singapore (2020). https://doi.org/10.1007/978-981-13-0553-5_1
9. Ikotun, A.M., Ezugwu, A.E., Abualigah, L., Abuhaija, B., Heming, J.: K-means clustering algorithms: a comprehensive review, variants analysis, and advances in the era of big data. Inf. Sci. **622**, 178–210 (2023). https://doi.org/10.1016/j.ins.2022.11.139
10. Kumar, A.S., Anandarao, S.: Volatility spillover in crypto-currency markets: some evidences from garch and wavelet analysis. Physica A Stat. Mech. Appl. **524**, 448–458 (2019). https://doi.org/10.1016/J.PHYSA.2019.04.154
11. Liadze, I., Macchiarelli, C., Mortimer-Lee, P., Juanino, P.S.: The economic costs of the Russia-Ukraine conflict - niesr. National Institute of Economic and Social Research (2022). https://www.niesr.ac.uk/publications/economic-costs-russia-ukraine-conflict?type=policy-papers
12. Maiti, M., Vyklyuk, Y., Vuković, D.: Cryptocurrencies chaotic co-movement forecasting with neural networks. Internet Technol. Lett. **3**(3) (2020). https://doi.org/10.1002/itl2.157
13. Mbah, R.E., Wasum, D.: Russian-Ukraine 2022 war: a review of the economic impact of Russian-Ukraine crisis on the USA, UK, Canada, and Europe. Adv. Soc. Sci. Res. J. **9**, 144–153 (2022). https://doi.org/10.14738/ASSRJ.93.12005
14. Nishisato, S., Beh, E.J., Lombardo, R., Clavel, J.G.: History of the biplot. In: Nishisato, S., Beh, E.J., Lombardo, R., Clavel, J.G. (eds.) Modern Quantification Theory. BQAHB, vol. 8, pp. 167–179. Springer, Singapore (2021). https://doi.org/10.1007/978-981-16-2470-4_9

15. Patel, E., Kushwaha, D.S.: Clustering cloud workloads: K-means vs gaussian mixture model. Procedia Comput. Sci. **171**, 158–167 (2020). https://doi.org/10.1016/j.procs.2020.04.017. Third International Conference on Computing and Network Communications (CoCoNet'19)
16. Umar, Z., Polat, O., Choi, S.Y., Teplova, T.: The impact of the Russia-Ukraine conflict on the connectedness of financial markets. Finance Res. Lett. **48**, 102976 (2022). https://doi.org/10.1016/J.FRL.2022.102976

# Human Trafficking in Social Networks: A Review of Machine Learning Techniques

Mike Bermeo(✉), Silvana Escobar, and Erick Cuenca

School of Mathematical and Computational Sciences, Yachay Tech University, Hda.
San José s/n y Proyecto Yachay, San Miguel de Urcuqui 100119, Ecuador
{mike.bermeo,sescobar,ecuenca}@yachaytech.edu.ec

**Abstract.** Human trafficking is a severe problem worldwide and social media platforms have emerged as a potential tool to detect and prevent this crime. Machine learning (ML) algorithms have shown promise in identifying human trafficking activity on these platforms. This paper comprehensively reviews ML techniques for human trafficking detection on social media, including supervised, unsupervised, and semi-supervised approaches. We identify each approach's advantages, limitations, and challenges for human trafficking detection. Finally, we provide future directions for research in this field, including the need for more standardized datasets and the development of explainable machine learning models to increase transparency and accountability. Our review provides a better understanding of the potential of machine learning in combating human trafficking and to guide future research efforts in this field.

**Keywords:** social media · human trafficking · machine learning · Twitter

## 1 Introduction

Human trafficking is a global problem affecting millions of people worldwide [29]. It is a form of modern slavery that involves the exploitation of individuals for various purposes, including forced labor, sexual exploitation, and organ removal, among others [43]. In recent years, social networks have emerged as a key platform for human traffickers to operate and reach potential victims [39]. Researchers and policymakers are interested in the role that social networks and other internet-based platforms play as facilitators of this type of crime that affects millions of people globally. Efforts are being made to employ various methodologies to identify and prevent these forms of exploitation.

The misuse of technology for human trafficking in all stages is increasing. For example, traffickers use deception techniques to hide their identities and avoid detection [25]. They can also use social networks to lure potential victims, often using emotional manipulation and other tactics to gain their trust [43].

J. Maldonado-Mahauad et al. (Eds.): TICEC 2023, CCIS 1885, pp. 22–36, 2023.
https://doi.org/10.1007/978-3-031-45438-7_2

In addition, the vast amount of data generated on social networks can make it difficult to identify and trace traffickers and their victims [4].

However, social media can also serve as a valuable tool for raising awareness of human trafficking and gathering support for victims and survivors [35]. Through social media campaigns and sharing of information and resources, individuals and organizations are able to take action in order to combat human trafficking. Additionally, social media provide a space for survivors to share their stories and connect with others, helping to break down isolation and stigma. While social media functionalities have the potential to play a significant role in anti-trafficking efforts, it is important to recognize its limitations and the need for broader actions to address the root causes of human trafficking and provide support to the victims [18].

In this context, technological advances present new opportunities for the detection and prevention of human trafficking. For instance, data generated on social networks can be utilized to identify patterns and trends in human trafficking activity [39]. Also, Machine Learning (ML) techniques and other data-driven approaches can be employed to create algorithms capable of automatically identifying and flagging suspicious activity on social networks, helping to address this social problem [17]. These technologies can also aid in the detection of human trafficking advertisements and the identification of relevant keywords used in social media to facilitate these crimes. [47].

In this paper, we present a comprehensive review of the current work that explores the application of Machine Learning techniques in social networks and other platforms to tackle the issue of human trafficking. Additionally, we delve into the challenges and opportunities associated with using ML approaches to detect and prevent human trafficking on social networks. The article is organized as follows: Sect. 2 presents the fundamental knowledge about ML techniques. In Sect. 3, we describe the methodology to follow to collect the related work. Section 4 reviews the existing research on ML techniques that address human trafficking on social media. Finally, in Sect. 5, we conclude the paper and discuss future directions for research in this area.

## 2   Background Study

This section provides definitions of human trafficking, discusses how this phenomenon behaves in social networks and outlines the concepts of Machine Learning, the various types of learning, and the techniques employed in each.

### 2.1   Human Trafficking on Social Media

Human trafficking is characterized by using force or coercion to recruit, transport, and exploit individuals for various purposes, including sexual exploitation, forced labor, and organ removal. It involves the abuse of power or vulnerability and the offering or receiving of payments or benefits in exchange for consent from those in positions of authority. Exploitation can include sexual exploitation, such as prostitution, and other forms of exploitation, including forced labor, slavery, servitude, and organ removal [43].

Social media platforms have become increasingly important in recruiting and grooming potential trafficking victims. For example, traffickers may use social media to lure individuals with false promises of employment or romantic relationships and then exploit them once they have been recruited [43]. In some cases, traffickers may use social media to advertise their victims for sexual exploitation or forced labor or to arrange transportation to different locations [3].

There are several ways in which social media can facilitate human trafficking [43]. First, it allows traffickers to reach a broad audience and target specific demographics, such as young people or those vulnerable due to economic or social circumstances. Second, social media can provide anonymity and secrecy, allowing traffickers to operate without detection. Third, it can be used to obscure the true nature of the exploitation, for example, by presenting it as legitimate work or a consensual relationship.

Combating human trafficking on social media requires a multifaceted approach involving governments, law enforcement agencies, stakeholders, and technology companies. They must work together to combat human trafficking and protect victims' rights. In addition, efforts to raise awareness and educate the public about the risks of human trafficking on social media can help prevent individuals from falling victim to these crimes [43]. Human trafficking is a severe global problem that the proliferation of social media has exacerbated.

### 2.2    Machine Learning Techniques

Machine Learning (ML) techniques involve using algorithms and statistical models to analyze and identify patterns of large amounts of data [15]. These techniques have been used in various fields, including image recognition [11], speech recognition [21], sentiment analysis [30,31], and predictive modeling [22]. They can be used as well in the battle against human trafficking. For instance, examining the content of social media posts and finding any that might be about trafficking [24], identifying patterns in the movements of individuals that may indicate trafficking activity [5,10,12], detecting anomalies in employment records that could indicate the presence of forced labor [34], predicting the likelihood of individuals becoming victims of trafficking [38,42], and identifying potential victims before they are exploited [27]. ML techniques are categorized into supervised, unsupervised, and semi-supervised learning.

- **Supervised Learning**: It is a subcategory of ML that uses labeled training data to predict outputs or classify data into predefined categories. The goal is to build a model to make accurate predictions or classifications based on input data. This is achieved by providing the model with a large set of labeled training examples consisting of input data and the corresponding correct outputs or classifications. The model is then trained to learn the relationship between the input data and the outputs or classifications, using this training data as a guide.

Considering human trafficking, several types of supervised learning algorithms have been used, including Linear regression, Logistic regression, K-Nearest Neighbors (KNN), Support Vector Machines (SVMs), Naive Bayes (NB), Random Forest (RF), Neural Networks (NN), Decision Tree (DT), AdaBoost, and so on.

- **Unsupervised Learning:** It is a type of ML in which a model is trained to discover patterns and relationships in a dataset without using labeled training examples [7]. In this learning, the goal is to find hidden patterns in the data rather than to make specific predictions or classifications [14]. This is achieved by providing the model with a large dataset and allowing it to learn the underlying structure of the data through techniques such as clustering [23] or dimensionality reduction [33].

  It is also important to evaluate the model's performance using appropriate evaluation metrics, such as silhouette scores (for clustering) or reconstruction errors (for dimensionality reduction) [36].

- **Semi-supervised Learning:** It is an ML type between supervised and unsupervised learning. It involves using labeled and unlabeled data to improve the accuracy of predictions or classifications where the goal is to leverage the available labeled data to make better predictions or classifications on the unlabeled data, using techniques such as self-training or co-training [44].

  There are several semi-supervised learning algorithms, including self-training algorithms, co-training algorithms, and multi-view learning algorithms [44]. Self-training algorithms use a single model trained on labeled and unlabeled data [26]. Co-training algorithms involve using two or more models trained on different views of the data and used to label the unlabeled data iteratively [28]. Multi-view learning algorithms use multiple models trained on different data views and combined to make a final prediction or classification [48].

## 3   Methodology

The scope of this work is to review and compile previous approaches that asses human trafficking detection on social networks using ML techniques and extract the main hints and trending paths used to address this problem. To fulfill this, we define the following steps:

1. Select the most relevant papers based on a selection criteria to obtain the most relevant works in this area.
2. Provide a deep insight of the main aspects used to analyze Human Trafficking in social media with ML.

### 3.1   Paper Selection

The selection criteria were based on the fact that the work should contain the following aspects:

- The focus of the work seeks to help the problem of human trafficking, such as sexual exploitation, forced labor, and modern slavery.

– One of the methods used to address the human trafficking problem must be a Machine Learning technique.
– The data used to work with must be a part of a social network or a website accessible to anyone.
– The work is at least from the year 2016.

The databases and repositories employed for this investigation included Scopus, ScienceDirect, ArXiv, IEEE XPLORE, and SpringerLink. This study aims to comprehensively review existing research on human trafficking by employing these resources and combining relevant variables. Specifically, the fixed variable *"human trafficking"* was identified and combined with three descriptive variables, namely *"social media"*, *"social networks"*, and *"machine learning"* to create multiple search queries. The utilization of these variables allowed for the identification of a diverse range of relevant papers. At the end of this search, 23 papers between 2016 and 2022 were selected.

### 3.2 Main Aspects

This work has considered six general aspects to analyze in each reviewed paper to identify the most relevant contributions. These aspects include the type of data used, the number of classes, the model or algorithm employed, the dataset utilized, the number of observations in the dataset, and the metrics that the paper considered to evaluate the performance of the ML algorithm.

## 4 Main Findings

This section analyzes the various sub-aspects based on the general aspects to be considered when addressing human trafficking in social networks through ML algorithms.

### 4.1 Supervised Approaches

Table 1 summarizes the works using supervised algorithms. Supervised ML algorithms are commonly used for detecting human trafficking. However, obtaining labeled data for human trafficking is challenging, as it involves sensitive information and can potentially put individuals at risk. Despite this challenge, several approaches have been taken to obtain labeled data, including using pre-existing data or manually labeling data pulled from social media platforms like Twitter.

The data extraction typically involves using web scraping techniques or social network APIs, followed by pre-processing steps such as removing links and non-relevant characters such as emoticons and emojis. The labeled data is then fed into the supervised ML algorithm for further analysis. Once the data is ready, it is commonly split into training and testing subsets, or in some cases, into three subsets: training, validation, and testing. The proportion of the split varies depending on the researcher, but a common split is 80% for training and 20% for testing.

**Table 1.** Supervised Machine Learning Approaches to Address Human Trafficking on Social Media.

| Authors | 9Input Feature | Classes | Model | Dataset |
|---|---|---|---|---|
| Vieira et al. [45] | 9Tweets: 13.6k Images: 11.1k | NA | OCR | TwitterPolice Data |
| Shishira et al. [38] | 9Tweets: 155.1k Images:89k | (suspicious, not suspicious), (man, woman), (under14, over14) | SVMVGG16 | TwitterIMDB-WikiOther DS |
| Hernández and Granizo [13] | 9Tweets: 55.1k Images: NA | (suspicious, not suspicious), (man, woman), (under14, over14) | SVM | Twitter |
| Wiriyakun et al. [47] | 9Ads: 10k | (trafficking, not trafficking) | LIMENBDT ANN | Trafficking-10k |
| Granizo et al. [10] | 9Tweets: 100k Images: 820 | (suspicious, not suspicious), (man, woman), (under14, over14) | SVMNBCNN | Twitter |
| Diaz et al. [8] | 9Reviews: 456k | (illegal activity, not illegal activity) | SVMNBRFANN | Yelp reviewsRubmaps DS |
| Hernandez [12] | 9Tweets: 55.1k | (suspicious, not suspicious) | SVMNB | Twitter |
| Goist et al. [9] | 9Text: 178 country reports | (sending relationship, receiving relationship) | LRSVMNBRF | TIP reports |
| Zhu et al. [49] | 9Ads: 10k | (high-risk, low-risk) | KenLMLRSVM | Trafficking-10k |
| Tong et al. [40] | 9Ads: 10k | (certainly no, likely no, weakly no, unsure, weakly yes, likely yes, certainly yes) | RFLRSVMHTDN | Trafficking-10k |

Supervised learning algorithms in human trafficking detection include Support Vector Machine (SVM) [1,5,8–10,12,13,38,40,49], Logistics Regression (LR) [1,5,9,40], Random Forest (RF) [1,5,8,9,40], Gaussian Naive Bayes (NB) [8–10,12,47], and Artificial Neural Networks [8,47]. These algorithms form the basis for supervised learning in classification, detection, and regression tasks.

To evaluate the performance of the classifiers, metrics such as Precision, Recall, F1-score, Accuracy, and AUC are commonly used. These metrics provide insights into the algorithm's effectiveness in detecting human trafficking and can guide future improvements in the methodology. Overall, supervised learning approaches have proven effective in detecting human trafficking. Despite the challenges of obtaining labeled data, various approaches have been taken to acquire it, such as using pre-existing datasets and manually labeling data extracted from social media platforms.

### 4.2   Unsupervised Approaches

Table 2 summarizes the works using unsupervised algorithms. These techniques have also been used to detect human trafficking, as they do not require labeled data to train the algorithms as in supervised learning. For instance, Clustering algorithms [19,20] are commonly used to similar group data together based on similarities in their features. One of the most used clustering algorithms in human trafficking detection is k-means clustering. Clustering [19,20] and anomaly detection [6,37] can also be effective tools in identifying instances of human trafficking since they can be used when labeled data is unavailable and can be used in conjunction with supervised learning algorithms to improve their accuracy.

Once the unsupervised techniques have been applied, the researcher can further refine the results by manually examining the data points flagged as potential instances of human trafficking. This manual approach can eliminate false positives and increase the accuracy of the results.

**Table 2.** Unsupervised Machine Learning Approaches to Address Human Trafficking on Social Media.

| Authors | Input Feature | Classes | Model | Dataset |
|---|---|---|---|---|
| Li et al. [20] | Ads: 10M | (positive, negative) | HDBSCAN | Backpage |
| Burbano and Hernández [6] | Tweets: 167k | NA | NLP | Twitter |
| Lee et al. [19] | Tweets: +18M | (certainly no, likely no, weakly no, unsure, weakly yes, likely yes, certainly yes) | InfoShield | Twitter |
| | Ads: 10k | | . | Trafficking-10k |
| Shelke et al. [37] | Images: +3M | NA | K-Means | FaceScrub[a] VGG[b] FPA[c] |

[a] http://vintage.winklerbros.net/facescrub.html
[b] https://www.robots.ox.ac.uk/~vgg/data/vgg_face/
[c] https://ibug.doc.ic.ac.uk/resources/facial-point-annotations/

## 4.3   Semi-supervised Approaches

Table 3 summarizes the works using semi-supervised techniques that combine unsupervised and supervised techniques. They have shown promising results in human trafficking detection. One such hybrid approach is to use unsupervised techniques for word embedding and supervised techniques for the detection task.

Word embedding is a technique used to represent words in a vector space, where words with similar meanings are closer to each other. Word embedding techniques such as a bag of words [41], word2vec, TF-IDF, FastText, and Skip-

**Table 3.** Semi-supervised Machine Learning Approaches to Address Human Trafficking on Social Media.

| Authors | Input Feature | Classes | Model | Dataset |
|---|---|---|---|---|
| Alvari et al. [1] | Ads: 20k | (positive, negative) | S3VM-R SVM KNN NB LR Adaboost RF | Backpage |
| Wang et al. [46] | Ads: 20kEmojis | (certainly no, likely no, weakly no, unsure, weakly yes, likely yes, certainly yes) | ORNN Skip-gram | Trafficking-10k |
| Alvari et al. [2] | Ads: 20k | NA | K-Means KNN RBF | Backpage |
| Kejriwal et al. [16] | Text | NA | Flexible and adaptive generation of indicators | Web Resources |
| Ramchandani et al. [32] | Posts: 13.5M | (suspicious, not suspicious) | CBOW | Deep Web |
| Burbano and Hernández [5] | News: 814 | (related to human trafficking, not related) | SVM LR RF DT Perceptron SGD KNN | News |
| Tudis et al. [41] | Tweets: 122k | (suspicious, not suspicious) | RF BoW | Twitter |

grams [46] are commonly used. In the context of human trafficking detection, word embedding can be used to represent words and phrases that are commonly associated with human trafficking, such as "sex trafficking" or "forced labor".

Once the word embedding is generated, it can be used as input to a supervised learning algorithm, such as an ANN or an SVM [1,5]. The supervised algorithm is trained on labeled data to learn the relationship between the word embedding and the presence of human trafficking activity. The labeled data can be obtained using earlier methods, such as manual labeling or web scraping.

The advantage of using a semi-supervised approach is that it leverages the strengths of both unsupervised and supervised techniques. Unsupervised techniques can generate high-quality word embedding, while supervised techniques can be used to learn the relationship between the embedding and human trafficking activity. This approach can also be effective when labeled data is limited, as it can augment the available labeled data with word embedding generated from a larger, unlabeled dataset.

Moreover, it is used for a small amount of labeled data to train a model and then used the trained model to label a larger amount of unlabeled data as in the work of [16]. The labeled and unlabeled data can be trained in a new model. This iterative process can be repeated until the model's accuracy is satisfactory.

### 4.4   Datasets

For data extraction, public web pages are used where there may be indications of human trafficking, such as pages of adult services and pornographic pages where sex work is offered [16]. Another common avenue for recruiters is social media. They can more easily contact potential victims by posing as friends, acquaintances, or job recruiters. Traffickers most widely use microblogging platforms because they allow for more meaningful interaction between strangers, and since they share everyday thoughts, they can more easily identify potential victims and form a relationship.

One of the most commonly used sites for data extraction using web scraping techniques is Backpage.com [1]. It was a classified ads website founded in 2004 which allowed users to post ads in categories such as personals, automotive, rentals, jobs, and adult services. The latter type was used by human trafficking rings to recruit potential victims for their network. For this same reason, it is widely used to extract advertisements related to human trafficking as used in [1].

Other sites used for data mining are news and advertisements [6,8]. These are known to contain job offers that are methods used by traffickers to recruit new victims. Likewise, YELP reviews are also used to detect places where sexual services are provided based on keywords such as massage, spa, and so on.

Finally, social media contain a wealth of data that can be used to detect this problem. One of the most widely used data extraction services is Twitter [5,6,10, 12,13,19,38,41,45], which has a freely available API that facilitates the retrieval of tweets using queries and keywords, without using web scraping techniques.

**Data Labeling.** Due to the complexity of the problem of human trafficking, it is very complicated to find publicly labeled data since it may contain sensitive information and data of persons who may or may not be involved, such as phone numbers, addresses, names, etc. Therefore, to request this data, it is usually necessary for the author to explain that it is for research and explain the area and what you plan to do with the data.

Manual data labeling relies on hand-checking and assigning a label to each piece of data, whether or not it is related to human trafficking. This process is highly dependent on the individual's judgment, and there may be bias in assigning the label. Therefore, this task typically requires a person with human trafficking experience to review and label the data. This process requires manual review where the amount of final data is limited. There aren't many people with experience in human trafficking willing to go through thousands or millions of pieces of data and label it. Furthermore, not all universities, research centers, or research groups have people with the ideal characteristics to carry out this task.

In human trafficking, there is a public dataset (upon request to authors) with labeled data that is used to train ML models to detect ads indicating human trafficking. This data is called Trafficking-10k and comprises 10 thousand ads and seven different labels: Certainly not, Probably not, Weakly no, Unsafe, Weakly yes, Probably yes, Certainly yes. Several papers have used this data set in their work [18, 40, 46, 47, 49].

## 4.5   Pre-processing

Several preprocessing steps are commonly followed by researchers when text is used in order to classificate it. These steps are aimed at cleaning and transforming the raw tweet data to a form suitable for further analysis. Some of the most commonly used preprocessing steps are:

- **Tokenization:** It is breaking a text into individual words or tokens. In tweets, tokenization can be challenging due to the presence of emoticons, hashtags, and mentions. Therefore, specialized tokenization techniques. The works of [5, 10, 13] tokenize the text from the tweets to better understand the model and gain performance.
- **Stopword Removal:** They are common words that do not carry much meaning, such as "the," "a," and "an." Removing stopwords can reduce the dimensionality of the data and improve the efficiency of subsequent analysis steps. However, the effectiveness of stopword removal in a text has been debated in the literature, with some studies suggesting that it may harm the performance of classification models. In the case of the works [8, 9, 38] extract the data from social media platforms, so they remove stopwords less dimensionality to the model, and gain meaningful data for the model.
- **Stemming/Lemmatization:** Stemming and lemmatization are techniques for reducing words to their root form. This can help reduce the data's sparsity and improve the accuracy of subsequent analysis steps. However, stemming

can also result in the loss of information, and lemmatization can be computationally expensive. Therefore, the choice of stemming/lemmatization technique may depend on the specific task and dataset.

- **Removing URLs, emojis, mentions, and hashtags:** Tweets often contain URLs, mentions, emojis, and hashtags, which can be irrelevant or misleading for classification tasks. Therefore, these elements are often removed before analysis. The works [12,41] extract the data from Twitter, so they come with too much poor information, such as URLs, emoticons, mentions, and hashtags, that are affecting the performance of the ML models.
- **Spell correction:** Text from social media often contains misspellings and abbreviations, making it challenging to analyze the data accurately. Therefore, spell correction techniques, such as spell-checker, can improve the accuracy of subsequent analysis steps.
- **Normalization:** Normalization refers to standardizing text data, which typically involves converting text to lowercase, removing punctuation, and replacing numbers with their word equivalents. The main goal of normalization is to reduce the variability in the text data and make it easier to process.

### 4.6   Machine Learning Tasks

The horrible crime of human trafficking, which affects millions of individuals globally, uses social media as a significant recruiting and victimization tool. Machine learning has become a potent weapon in the fight against human trafficking on social media, giving researchers the power to sift through massive volumes of data and spot possible instances of trafficking activity. Machine learning algorithms automate and streamline the detection and examination of probable human trafficking activity. In this context, ML can handle the following tasks:

- **Text Classification:** ML algorithms are trained to automatically classify social media posts, comments, and messages as potential cases of human trafficking. For example, a study by [49] used supervised machine learning to classify online escort ads as either indicative of sex trafficking or not.
- **Entity extraction:** ML is used to extract entities related to human trafficking, such as locations, names, and phone numbers, from social media posts. This can help to identify potential victims or perpetrators of trafficking. For example, a study by [47] used machine learning to extract entities related to human trafficking from ads.
- **Network analysis:** ML techniques analyze the connections and interactions between individuals and groups involved in human trafficking on social media. For example, a study by [9] used network analysis and machine learning to identify the most influential countries in the human trafficking network.
- **Image analysis:** ML is used to analyze images and identify potential instances of human trafficking. For example, a study by [10] used machine learning to analyze online images and identify potential victims of sex trafficking.

– **Topic modeling:** ML techniques are employed to identify and analyze the topics and themes on social media posts related to human trafficking. This can help to identify patterns and trends in trafficking activity, as well as to understand the experiences and perspectives of victims and survivors. For example, a study by [6,12] used topic modeling to analyze Twitter data related to human trafficking.

– **Sentiment analysis:** ML techniques are used to analyze the sentiment of social media posts related to human trafficking, such as whether they express positive or negative emotions. This can help to identify potential victims or perpetrators of trafficking, as well as to understand the public perception of human trafficking. For example, a study by [5] used sentiment analysis to identify behavioral patterns related to human trafficking from social media posts.

– **Predictive modeling:** ML techniques are employed to predict the likelihood of human trafficking activity based on social media data and identify potential victims and perpetrators. For example, a study by [19] used machine learning to predict Twitter bots and human trafficking activity with language-independent based on online escort ads.

## 5    Conclusions

Using machine learning techniques for assessing human trafficking in social media has shown promising results. Researchers have utilized supervised, unsupervised, and semi-supervised learning methods to analyze extensive data and datasets from social media platforms, intending to identify potential victims, traffickers, and understand the patterns and networks of trafficking activity. These methods have demonstrated high accuracy and efficiency in detecting potential cases of human trafficking and have the potential to assist law enforcement agencies in their efforts to combat this horrible crime. However, challenges remain in ensuring the ethical use of data, the sites where the data is extracted, how the corresponding label is assigned to the data, and developing models that can adapt to the dynamic and evolving nature of human trafficking networks. Nevertheless, the use of machine learning in this field has opened up new ways for understanding and combating human trafficking and holds great potential for further advancements in the future. Moving forward in this area, there is much work to do. One potential area is the development of hybrid models that combine multiple Machine Learning techniques to improve the accuracy and efficiency of trafficking assessments.

**Acknowledgment.** The authors express their gratitude to the Data Science and Analytics (DataScienceYT) group at Yachay Tech University for their assistance during the development of this work.

# References

1. Alvari, H., Shakarian, P., Snyder, J.: Semi-supervised learning for detecting human trafficking. Secur. Inform. **6**(1), 1–14 (2017)
2. Alvari, H., Shakarian, P., Snyder, J.K.: A non-parametric learning approach to identify online human trafficking. In: 2016 IEEE Conference on Intelligence and Security Informatics (ISI), pp. 133–138 (2016)
3. Andrews, S., Brewster, B., Day, T.: Organised crime and social media: detecting and corroborating weak signals of human trafficking online. In: Haemmerlé, O., Stapleton, G., Faron Zucker, C. (eds.) ICCS 2016. LNCS (LNAI), vol. 9717, pp. 137–150. Springer, Cham (2016). https://doi.org/10.1007/978-3-319-40985-6_11
4. Belcastro, L., Cantini, R., Marozzo, F.: Knowledge discovery from large amounts of social media data. Appl. Sci. **12**(3), 1209 (2022)
5. Burbano, D., Hernandez-Alvarez, M.: Identifying human trafficking patterns online, vol. 2017-January, pp. 1–6 (2018)
6. Burbano, D., Hernández-Alvarez, M.: Illicit, hidden advertisements on Twitter. In: International Conference on eDemocracy & eGovernment (ICEDEG), pp. 317–321. IEEE (2018)
7. Celebi, M.E., Aydin, K.: Unsupervised Learning Algorithms, vol. 9. Springer, Cham (2016). https://doi.org/10.1007/978-3-319-24211-8
8. Diaz, M., Panangadan, A.: Natural language-based integration of online review datasets for identification of sex trafficking businesses. In: 2020 IEEE 21st International Conference on Information Reuse and Integration for Data Science (IRI), pp. 259–264 (2020)
9. Goist, M., Chen, T.H.Y., Boylan, C.: Reconstructing and analyzing the transnational human trafficking network. In: Proceedings of the 2019 IEEE/ACM International Conference on Advances in Social Networks Analysis and Mining, ASONAM 2019, pp. 493–500 (2019)
10. Granizo, S., Caraguay, A., Lopez, L., Hernandez-Alvarez, M.: Detection of possible illicit messages using natural language processing and computer vision on twitter and linked websites. IEEE Access **8**, 44534–44546 (2020)
11. Hafiz, A.M., Hassaballah, M., Binbusayyis, A.: Formula-driven supervised learning in computer vision: a literature survey. Appl. Sci. **13**(2), 723 (2023)
12. Hernandez-Alvarez, M.: Detection of possible human trafficking in twitter, pp. 187–191 (2019)
13. Hernández-Álvarez, M., Granizo, S.: Detection of Human Trafficking Ads in Twitter Using Natural Language Processing and Image Processing, vol. 1213. AISC (2021)
14. James, G., Witten, D., Hastie, T., Tibshirani, R.: Unsupervised learning. In: James, G., Witten, D., Hastie, T., Tibshirani, R. (eds.) An Introduction to Statistical Learning. STS, pp. 497–552. Springer, New York (2021). https://doi.org/10.1007/978-1-0716-1418-1_12
15. Kamalov, F., Cherukuri, A.K., Sulieman, H., Thabtah, F., Hossain, A.: Machine learning applications for COVID-19: a state-of-the-art review. In: Tyagi, A.K., Abraham, A. (eds.) Data Science for Genomics, pp. 277–289. Academic Press (2023)
16. Kejriwal, M., Ding, J., Shao, R., Kumar, A., Szekely, P.: Flagit: a system for minimally supervised human trafficking indicator mining (2017)
17. Kleinberg, J., Ludwig, J., Mullainathan, S.: A guide to solving social problems with machine learning. Harv. Bus. Rev. **8**, 2 (2016)

18. Lee, M.: Human Trafficking. Routledge (2013)
19. Lee, M.C., et al.: Infoshield: generalizable information-theoretic human-trafficking detection. In: 2021 IEEE 37th International Conference on Data Engineering (ICDE), pp. 1116–1127 (2021)
20. Li, L., Simek, O., Lai, A., Daggett, M., Dagli, C.K., Jones, C.: Detection and characterization of human trafficking networks using unsupervised scalable text template matching. In: 2018 IEEE International Conference on Big Data (Big Data), pp. 3111–3120 (2018)
21. Liu, C., Shangguan, Y., Yang, H., Shi, Y., Krishnamoorthi, R., Kalinli, O.: Learning a dual-mode speech recognition model via self-pruning. In: 2022 IEEE Spoken Language Technology Workshop (SLT), pp. 273–279 (2023)
22. Liu, P., Yuan, W., Fu, J., Jiang, Z., Hayashi, H., Neubig, G.: Pre-train, prompt, and predict: a systematic survey of prompting methods in natural language processing. ACM Comput. Surv. **55**(9) (2023)
23. Madhulatha, T.S.: An overview on clustering methods (2012)
24. Mahesh, B.: Machine learning algorithms-a review. Int. J. Sci. Res. (IJSR) **9**, 381–386 (2020)
25. Mazza, M., Cola, G., Tesconi, M.: Ready-to-(ab)use: from fake account trafficking to coordinated inauthentic behavior on twitter. Online Soc. Netw. Media **31**, 100224 (2022)
26. McClosky, D., Charniak, E., Johnson, M.: Effective self-training for parsing. In: Proceedings of the Human Language Technology Conference of the NAACL, Main Conference, pp. 152–159 (2006)
27. Motseki, M., Mofokeng, J.: An analysis of the causes and contributing factors to human trafficking: a South African perspective. Cogent Soc. Sci. **8** (2022)
28. Ning, X., et al.: A review of research on co-training. Concurr. Comput. Pract. Exp. E6276 (2021)
29. Okech, D., Choi, Y.J., Elkins, J., Burns, A.C.: Seventeen years of human trafficking research in social work: a review of the literature. J. Evid.-Inf. Soc. Work **15**(2), 103–122 (2018). pMID: 29265959
30. Pijal, W., Armijos, A., Llumiquinga, J., Lalvay, S., Allauca, S., Cuenca, E.: Spanish pre-trained catrbeto model for sentiment classification in twitter. In: 2022 Third International Conference on Information Systems and Software Technologies (ICI2ST), pp. 93–98. IEEE (2022)
31. Quelal, A., Brito, J., Lomas, M.S., Camacho, J., Andrade, A., Cuenca, E.: Identifying the political tendency of social bots in twitter using sentiment analysis: a use case of the 2021 ecuadorian general elections. In: Abad, K., Berrezueta, S. (eds.) DSICT 2022. CCIS, vol. 1647, pp. 184–196. Springer, Cham (2022). https://doi.org/10.1007/978-3-031-18347-8_15
32. Ramchandani, P., Bastani, H., Wyatt, E.: Unmasking human trafficking risk in commercial sex supply chains with machine learning. SSRN Electron. J. (2021)
33. Reddy, G.T., et al.: Analysis of dimensionality reduction techniques on big data. IEEE Access **8**, 54776–54788 (2020)
34. Reynolds, M.: Teaching al to find forced labour camps. New Sci. (3132), 14 (2017)
35. Rodríguez-López, S.: (De)constructing stereotypes: media representations, social perceptions, and legal responses to human trafficking. J. Hum. Traffick. **4**(1), 61–72 (2018)
36. Shahapure, K.R., Nicholas, C.: Cluster quality analysis using silhouette score. In: 2020 IEEE 7th International Conference on Data Science and Advanced Analytics (DSAA), pp. 747–748. IEEE (2020)

37. Shelke, V., Mehta, G., Gomase, P., Bangera, T.: Searchious: locating missing people using an optimised face recognition algorithm, pp. 1550–1555 (2021)
38. Shishira, S.S., Patil, M.J.S.: Detection of illicit messages in twitter using support vector machine and VGG16. Inf. Technol. Ind. **9**(3), 794–804 (2021)
39. Sierra-Rodríguez, A., Arroyo-Machado, W., Barroso-Hurtado, D.: La trata de personas en twitter: finalidades, actores y temas en la escena hispanohablante. Grupo Comunicar **30**, 79–91 (2022)
40. Tong, E., Zadeh, A., Jones, C., Morency, L.P.: Combating human trafficking with deep multimodal models (2017)
41. Tundis, A., Jain, A., Bhatia, G., Muhlhauser, M.: Similarity analysis of criminals on social networks: an example on twitter, vol. 2019-July (2019)
42. Um, M., Rice, E., Palinkas, L., Kim, H.: Migration-related stressors and suicidal ideation in North Korean refugee women: the moderating effects of network composition. J. Trauma. Stress **33**, 939–949 (2020)
43. United Nations: Office on Drugs and Crime.: Human-Trafficking (2020)
44. Van Engelen, J.E., Hoos, H.H.: A survey on semi-supervised learning. Mach. Learn. **109**(2), 373–440 (2020)
45. Vieira, C.C., Alburez-Gutierrez, D., Nepomuceno, M., Theile, T.: Desaparecidxs: characterizing the population of missing children using Twitter, pp. 185–190 (2022)
46. Wang, L., Laber, E., Saanchi, Y., Caltagirone, S.: Sex trafficking detection with ordinal regression neural networks (2019)
47. Wiriyakun, C., Kurutach, W.: Feature selection for human trafficking detection models. In: Proceedings - 2021 IEEE/ACIS 21st International Fall Conference on Computer and Information Science, ICIS 2021-Fall, pp. 131–135 (2021)
48. Zhao, J., Xie, X., Xu, X., Sun, S.: Multi-view learning overview: recent progress and new challenges. Inf. Fusion **38**, 43–54 (2017)
49. Zhu, J., Li, L., Jones, C.: Identification and detection of human trafficking using language models. In: 2019 European Intelligence and Security Informatics Conference (EISIC), pp. 24–31 (2019)

# Exploring the Performance of Deep Learning in High-Energy Physics

Daniela Merizalde[1]([✉]) [ID], José Ochoa[1] [ID], Xavier Tintin[2] [ID], Edgar Carrera[1] [ID], Diana Martinez[2] [ID], and David Mena[2] [ID]

[1] Departamento de Física, Colegio de Ciencias e Ingeniería, Universidad San Francisco de Quito, Quito, Ecuador
{dmerizalde,jdochoa}@estud.usfq.edu.ec, ecarrera@usfq.edu.ec
[2] Facultad de Ingeniería de Sistemas, Escuela Politécnica Nacional, Quito, Ecuador
{xavier.tintin,diana.martinez,david.mena06}@epn.edu.ec

**Abstract.** This article presents a comprehensive investigation into the effectiveness of supervised deep learning techniques for classifying the outcome of high-energy particle collisions using CMS Open Data. The research primarily focuses on the conversion of particle and jet position and momentum information into images, followed by the application of convolutional neural networks (CNNs) to classify various particle processes. Two distinct scenarios are considered. The first scenario involves classifying images for processes that generate a known resonance with invariant masses at different energy ranges. The second scenario focuses on identifying signal and background processes with similar final states. Furthermore, alternative CNN architectures are evaluated based on their performance metrics within each scenario. The trained neural network models with the best performance metrics are subsequently employed for classifying real collision data.

**Keywords:** convolutional neural networks · high-energy physics · real collision data · hep · Cnns · machine learning · data analysis

## 1 Introduction

The Standard Model (SM) is a theoretical framework that describes matter in terms of its fundamental particles and their utmost interactions [1]. Its known limitations bring about many fundamental questions in modern physics.

Machine Learning (ML) techniques have been widely adopted in various scientific fields, including high-energy physics (HEP), in an attempt to evaluate and extract relevant information by analyzing and predicting outcomes based on extensive datasets recorded by different experiments [2].

The Compact Muon Solenoid (CMS) is a HEP experiment that explores physics at the TeV (teraelectronvolt) energy scale, exploiting the collisions delivered by the Large Hadron Collider (LHC) at the European Organization for Nuclear Research (CERN) in Geneva, Switzerland. This experiment uses different subdetectors with distinct technology and more than 75 million channels to

J. Maldonado-Mahauad et al. (Eds.): TICEC 2023, CCIS 1885, pp. 37–51, 2023.
https://doi.org/10.1007/978-3-031-45438-7_3

record petabytes (PB) of complex and high-dimensional data. Correctly analyzing this data is crucial when validating the SM or testing theoretical ideas that go beyond its scope.

Significant challenges arise in the analysis of HEP data due to the immense volume and complexity of the collected information. Manipulating and interpreting them is a demanding task. With approximately forty million proton-proton collisions occurring at the CMS detector each second, the data generated are vast and require advanced techniques for analyzing and extracting meaningful insights. Addressing these challenges is vital to unlock the full potential of the data and advance our understanding of new physics.

Traditional HEP analysis techniques can be time-consuming. However, ML algorithms offer a promising solution for classification analysis. In this paper, we test a novel approach by which we convert HEP collisions information into images [3]. Then, we use convolutional neural networks (CNNs) to apply deep learning techniques for the classification of various interaction processes that occur within these collisions. We leverage Monte Carlo simulations from the CERN Open Data Portal(CODP) [4] at 13 TeV to train and validate the procedure. By employing ML, specifically CNNs, we aim to improve the efficiency and accuracy of analyzing HEP data, ultimately enhancing our understanding of fundamental physics.

## 1.1 Fundamental Particles and Physics Objects

In our project, we are interested in quarks, leptons, neutrinos and bosons [5]. Not all of these fundamental particles are directly detected by the CMS. Consequently, the detected particles are referred to as physics objects.

From those physics objects the project focuses on muons, jets and Missing Transverse Energy (MET). Muons are fundamental particles that carry a negative electric charge and possess a mass of about 106MeV [6]. Jets are high sprays of particles (or antiparticles) [7] and MET is calculated as the sum of all negative momentum vectors of particles [8].

## 1.2 Physics Processes

In HEP collisions, various physical phenomena can occur due to complex interactions. In this study, we specifically investigate five processes within the SM framework.

**Drell-Yan**: this involves the production of Z bosons, which subsequently decay into a pair of muons with opposite charges [9].

**Higgs**: it decays into a pair of muons with opposite charges [10].

*J/ψ*: this process involves the production of a hadronic resonance called $J/\psi$, which is a meson formed by the bound state of a charm quark and an anti-charm quark. One of the common decay modes of $J/\psi$ is the generation of a muon-antimuon pair [11].

**W + jets**: this refers to the generation of a W boson in association with jets. The W boson can then decay into a muon and a neutrino [12].

$t\bar{t}$ **+ jets**: this process involves the generation of a top quark and an anti-top quark pair. Each top quark can subsequently decay into a b quark and a $W$ boson (and hence a muon) [13].

It is worth noting that all the processes investigated in this study lead to a final state containing a pair of muons.

### 1.3 Convolutional Neural Network Architecture

CNNs are specifically designed to process image data, distinguishing them from traditional neural networks. In this study, we utilize CNNs to analyze and classify image data derived from high-energy particle collisions obtained from the COPD. The input data consists of three-dimensional matrices that represent images characterized by its length, width, and depth. The term depth refers to the number of color channels present in the image, typically represented by the colors red, blue, and green. By isolating each color channel, we obtain a separate matrix where each entry represents the intensity of that color.

In a CNN, these matrices undergo convolution operations using kernels to extract key features from the images, resulting in multiple feature maps with reduced dimensionality. The number of feature maps is determined by the number of convolutions applied. Following the convolutional operation, a process called pooling is applied to reduce the dimensionality of the feature maps while retaining crucial information [14]. The combination of convolution and pooling operations allow the network to extract and preserve significant features from images, facilitating accurate image recognition.

The architecture of a CNN consists of three crucial components. The entry module handles the processing of input data, the characteristic extraction module involves the application of convolution and pooling operations, and finally, the classification module utilizes a neural network for the final classification task. Leveraging this comprehensive framework, CNNs are utilized to accurately classify high-energy particle outcomes based on labeled datasets, effectively distinguishing between various resonance processes and discerning events with similar final states.

## 2 Methodology

### 2.1 Study Strategy

This work studies two different scenarios that differ in the chosen physics processes. The first scenario involves processes that produce particle resonances with invariant masses that span different energy ranges. The second scenario aims to distinguish between signal and background processes that exhibit similar decay modes. In this paper, we refer to these scenarios as DHJW and DTW, respectively, providing a clear distinction between the two throughout our analysis.

**DHJW.** The physics processes chosen for the first scenario are the Drell-Yan, Higgs, $J/\psi$, and $W + jets$. The main characteristic of these processes is that the resonance involves decays into a very specific channel (or a very similar one in the case of the control process $W + jets$). It is, therefore, important to properly classify different resonances that may look similar, but in essence, are fairly different.

**DTW.** For our second scenario, we chose Drell-Yan, $t\bar{t}$, and $W + jets$. The Drell-Yan process, which produces a specific resonance (the $Z$ boson), is considered as the signal, whereas the $t\bar{t}$ and $W + jets$ are the background. In this scenario, we aim to classify events as signal or background that looks like our main signal but belongs to processes that do not generate a neutral resonance.

### 2.2   Data Collection

The CMS Collaboration provides open access to its data since 2014. The data accessible through the CODP, consist of both simulated and real collisions data. The simulated data are obtained using Monte Carlo generators, while the real collisions data are directly collected using the detectors at the CMS experiment. All the data used in our analysis involves decays in the muon channel. The trained neural network, derived from DTW, is subsequently tested using real collision data. The specific procedure for downloading and accessing these data is addressed in a recent CMS workshop [15]. The datasets in Table 1 correspond to the simulation and real data obtained in 2015 during CMS Run II at 13 TeV.

**Table 1.** Name of the Datasets.

| Decay | Dataset Name |
|-------|--------------|
| *Drell-Yan* | ZToMuMu-M-50-120-NNPDF30-13TeV-powheg-herwigpp [16] |
| W+jets | WJetsToLNu-TuneCUETP8M1-13TeV-amcatnloFXFX-pythia8 [17] |
| $t\bar{t}$ | TT TuneCUETP8M1-13TeV-powheg-pythia8 [18] |
| $J/\psi$ | JpsiToMuMu-JpsiPt8-TuneCUEP8M1-13TeV-pythia8 [19] |
| H | VBF-HToMuMu-M125-13TeV-powheg-pythia8 [20] |
| $\mu\,\mu$ | DoubleMuon/Run2015D-16Dec2015-v1/MINIAOD [21] |

### 2.3   Image Representation

All the physics objects in the events are represented as circumferences centered accordingly to their position in the detector. This is done by using the standard coordinates $\phi$ and the pseudo-rapidity $\eta$ defined in Eq. 1

$$\eta \equiv -\ln\left[\tan\left(\frac{\theta}{2}\right)\right].$$
(1)

The idea behind this approach is to take advantage of the CMS detector's cylindrical shape [3]. The radius of the circumferences is proportional to their transversal momentum $p_T$ as shown in Eq. 2.

$$R = \alpha \cdot \ln p_T \qquad (2)$$

Here $\alpha$ is a positive constant and $p_T = \sqrt{p_x^2 + p_y^2}$. Recall that $p_x$ and $p_y$ are the components of the particle's momentum in the transversal plane of the detector (perpendicular to the beam axis). We implement a color differentiation for each object being red for muons, black for MET, and blue for jets. The generated images have a size of 224 × 224 pixels, and the ranges for both $\eta$ and $\phi$ are $[-\pi, \pi]$. It is important to note that these value ranges correspond to the image window and not the ranges of the CMS coordinates. To ensure that each physics object circumference fits within the image, scale factors were applied along the $\eta$ axis and $\phi$ axis. For DTW datasets, a visual representation of the muons charge is taken into account. This is implemented as a thicker line in case of a positive muons, and a thinner one for negative muons. An example of a generated image composed with of all our physics objects is shown in Fig. 1.

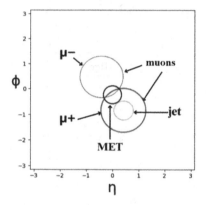

**Fig. 1.** Image representation of the collision.

## 2.4 DHJW Datasets Composition

A total of 3 datasets were generated. We refer to them as A, B, and C. All of them are made up with images that contain two muons that neither have visual charge representation or MET information. The main difference between these datasets are the number of jets represented in the images. Dataset A consists of images containing only the two muons. Dataset B expands upon this by including the most energetic jet in addition to the muons. Finally, dataset C goes even further by incorporating the two most energetic jets from each event. The exact number of images generated for each dataset can be found in Table 2.

**Table 2.** Number of jets and number of images presented on Datasets A, B and C.

| Dataset | Number of Jets | Number of Images |
|---------|----------------|------------------|
| A | 0 | 110796 |
| B | 1 | 110796 |
| C | 2 | 64028 |

It's important to note that on each given dataset, the number of jets is constant for all images. For say in dataset B, all 110796 images are guaranteed to contain only 1 jet, while in dataset C, all 64028 images will contain 2 jets. This can be better understood looking at Fig. 2 where the two jets are consistent through the images.

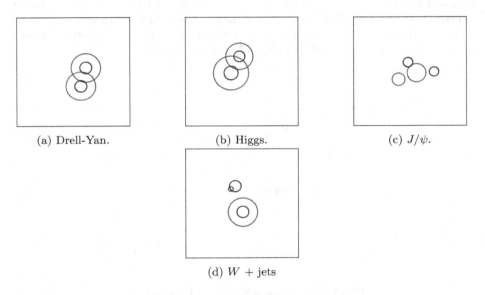

(a) Drell-Yan.           (b) Higgs.           (c) $J/\psi$.

(d) $W + $ jets

**Fig. 2.** Example of images belonging to dataset C.

## 2.5   DTW Datasets Composition

For the DTW case we generated a total of 4 datasets, which we call D, E, F, and G, respectively (Table 3). As mentioned earlier, the visual representation of the charge of the muons and the MET is drawn in all images. In a similar manner to DHJW datasets, what varies is the number of jets; however, in this scenario, the number of jets is not constant throughout the images due to the fact that the number of jets act as a maximum. This means that we are not asking for specific events that contain at least 2, 3, and 4 jets so that we can guarantee to have that number of jets in all the images, rather we ask for a minimum of two muons, MET, and 1 jet. Once the minimum conditions are satisfied, any extra existing jets are plotted.

**Table 3.** Number of jets and number of images presented on Datasets D, E, F, G.

| Dataset | Number of Jets | Number of Images |
|---------|----------------|------------------|
| D | 1 | 83097 |
| E | 2 | 83097 |
| F | 3 | 83097 |
| G | 4 | 83097 |

As a summary, all images on dataset D contain 2 muons, MET, and 1 jet. Dataset E contains 2 muons, MET and up to 2 jets if the events have that information. A similar pattern drives datasets F and G.

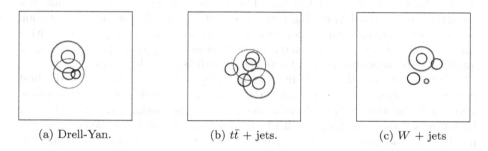

(a) Drell-Yan.          (b) $t\bar{t}$ + jets.          (c) $W$ + jets

**Fig. 3.** Example of images belonging to dataset G.

Notice in Fig. 3 that the number of jets is not consistent through the images despite all of them belonging to the same dataset.

## 2.6  Invariant Mass

The concept of invariant mass is needed in this research as it is an intrinsic characteristic for each particle. The difference among the invariant masses of different particles will generate distinct sized and positioned circumferences. We can express the invariant mass in terms of the variables that we are precisely using to generate the images using Eq. 3.

$$m^2 = 2p_{T1}p_{T2}\left(\cosh\left(\eta_1 - \eta_2\right) - \cos\left(\Phi_1 - \Phi_2\right)\right). \tag{3}$$

Here $m$ is the invariant mass of the particle that decays, $\eta_1$ and $\eta_2$ are the pseudo-rapidity of each particle according to the CMS reference system, $\Phi_1$ and $\Phi_2$ are related to each particle reference system at the CMS, and $p_{T1}$, $p_{T2}$ are the transverse momentum of each particle.

## 2.7    Types of Selected Neural Networks

The continuous research in supervised deep learning models within the field of computer science have propelled significant advancements in developing different techniques to tackle image-related tasks such as classification, object detection, and segmentation. A key aspect of this research was to evaluate various performance metrics on each dataset in order to rule out both invalid datasets and bad performing machine learning models. We conducted benchmarking experiments using four widely adopted supervised deep learning models: ResNet 50 [22], DenseNet [23], InceptionV3 [24], and MobileNet V2 [25]. These models were chosen as benchmarks due to their established performance and effectiveness in image classification.

The benchmark experiment focuses on distinguishing the most effective CNN model using high-energy particle collisions datasets obtained from both scenarios chosen in this study. The first scenario involves classifying images for processes that generate known resonances with invariant masses at different energy ranges, this aims to properly classify different resonances that may appear visually similar but have distinct characteristics. The physics processes chosen for this first scenario are the Drell-Yan, Higgs, $J/\psi$, and $W + jets$. Meanwhile, our second scenario attempts to distinguish between signal and background processes with a similar final states based on visual representations. The physics processes chosen for the second scenario are the Drell-Yan, $t\bar{t} + jets$, and $W + jets$.

All four benchmark models implement the specific requirements for the best performing dataset of each scenario. Although all four models utilize deep neural network architectures, they differ in their underlying design principles. ResNet 50 addresses the vanishing gradient problem and classify resonances and signal/background processes in both DHJW and DTW scenarios. Densenet also tackles the gradient problem similarly by densely interconnecting layers, seamlessly facilitating essential information flow through the entire network, thus substantially improving feature extraction in both scenarios. InceptionV3 improves computational efficiency while capturing distinctive patterns in particle decay events, and finally we explore the performance of state-of-the-art mobile models in physics object image classification.

When conducting benchmark experiments with deep learning models, we obtain performance and evaluation metrics in the two defined scenarios. Evaluating each model's accuracy, precision, recall and F1 score sets foreword the most suitable model(s) when classifying high-energy particle collision outcomes.

## 2.8    Training Process and Evaluation Metrics

The training process configuration for each dataset was set to 40 epochs, with the implementation of early stopping in order to prevent overfitting and improve generalization. The Adam optimization algorithm is the learning rule in every model's training. The image generation process was performed using Python on local machines, while the training and testing of the CNN models were conducted on Google Colaboratory using A100 GPU hardware accelerators.

# 3 Results

Deep learning was used to accomplish two distinct objectives in this study. The first application was based on discerning the best performing dataset for each scenario using the standard machine learning model Resnet 50. This was achieved when running ResNet 50 on all DHJW and DJW datasets in order to compare the results and identify the dataset that exhibits the highest accuracy and lowest loss value on the given model.

Subsequently, the second usage of CNNs involved conducting a benchmark experiment of the four different models over the resulting best dataset of each scenario. Based on performance and evaluation metrics of each CNN model, we were able to gain valuable insight on selecting optimal datasets and deep learning models for further analysis and classification.

## 3.1 DHJW

A split of $(60 - 20 - 20)$ % was used when training all DHJW datasets. These percentages correspond to the training, validation, and testing sets, respectively. The final performance metrics of each dataset are specified on Table 4.

**Table 4.** Accuracy and loss value of the DHJW datasets.

| Dataset | Test Acc [%] | Test Loss |
|---------|--------------|-----------|
| A | 0.7209 | 0.7463 |
| B | 0.7322 | 0.6944 |
| C | 0.7956 | 0.5148 |

Based on the results presented on Table 4, we can conclude that dataset C achieved the best performance metrics from the first scenario. Hence, dataset C was selected as the primary dataset for benchmarking purposes. The benchmark results depicted in Fig. 4 and in Fig. 5 provide a detailed analysis of the performance metrics of each CNN model. The performance metric F1 score served as a comprehensive metric that encapsulated both precision and recall for each class, providing a reliable assessment of the network's performance on dataset C in terms of their ability to accurately classify between different particle decay processes, namely Drell-Yan, Higgs, $J/\psi$, and $W + jets$ processes.

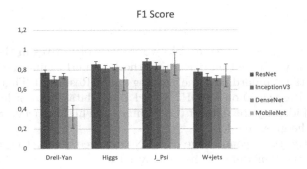

**Fig. 4.** F1 Score.

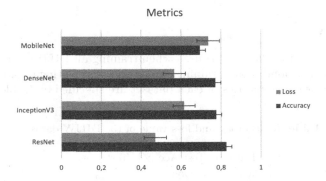

**Fig. 5.** Metrics.

Consequently, ResNet50 emerged as the top-performing model as it delivered the best results among all CNN models. The respective confusion matrices of the optimal outcome are shown in Fig. 6 and Fig. 7, indicating a noticeable confusion in image classification between Drell-Yan and Higgs processes. This confusion can be justified given the similar energy range in which the resonances occur for both processes.

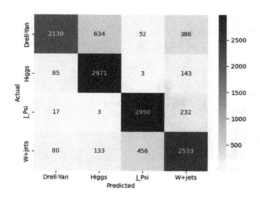 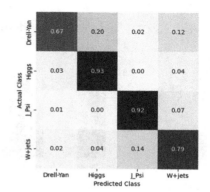

**Fig. 6.** Non-normalized matrix of the best model.

**Fig. 7.** Normalized matrix of the best model.

## 3.2 DTW

For the DTW datasets, a split of (70—20—10) % was employed. These percentages correspond to the training, validation, and testing sets, respectively. This partitioning allocated the accuracy and loss values achieved for each dataset can be found in Table 5, providing a comprehensive overview of the performance metrics.

**Table 5.** Accuracy and loss value of the DTW datasets.

| Dataset | Test Acc [%] | Test Loss |
|---------|--------------|-----------|
| D | 0.8012 | 0.4508 |
| E | 0.8208 | 0.4185 |
| F | 0.8355 | 0.3875 |
| G | 0.8416 | 0.3681 |

Upon the utilization of Table 5, it's evident that the model with the highest number of jets yields the best performance. This result is in accordance with the DJW scenario. Therefore, dataset G, having the highest number of jets, was selected as the primary dataset for benchmarking purposes. The benchmark results depicted in Fig. 8 and in Fig. 9 provide a detailed analysis of the performance metrics of each CNN model.

Consequently, ResNet 50 resulted once again, as the top-performing model. The confusion matrix produced by the best model are presented in Fig. 10 and Fig. 11.

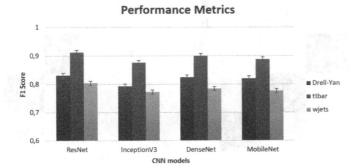

Fig. 8. F1 Score.

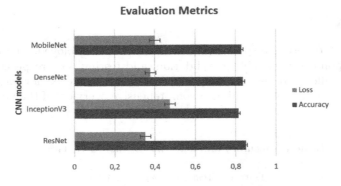

Fig. 9. Metrics.

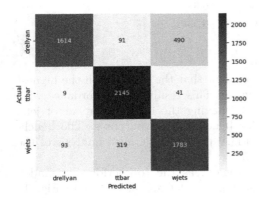

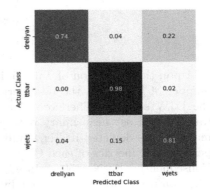

Fig. 10. Non-normalized matrix of the best model.

Fig. 11. Normalized matrix of the best model.

## 3.3   Results over Real Collision Data

We also evaluated the performance of our trained CNN using real collision data, we considered the Z boson resonance as the signal, while other processes were regarded as background. This means that each time an image was classified as $t\bar{t}$ or $W$ + jets, we would rename it as *fakes*. If the image was classified as Drell-Yan the same name was retained. To visually compare the differences between *fakes* and Drell-Yan, we utilized classification information to reconstruct the invariant mass of the dimuons for each respective category. A histogram of the invariant mass of all the data previous classification can be found in Fig. 12.

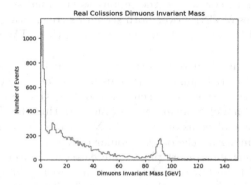

**Fig. 12.** Invariant mass real collision data.

Notice the characteristic peak at 91 GeV. As previously said, this peak correspond to the Z boson resonance.

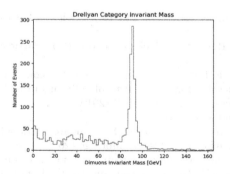

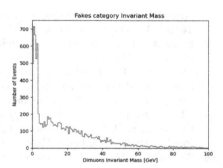

**Fig. 13.** Invariant mass from data classified as Drell-Yan.

**Fig. 14.** Invariant mass from data classified as *Fakes*.

We notice in Fig. 13 that the CNN was able to completely capture the resonance of the Drell-Yan process. Also in Fig. 14 is noticeable that the peak at 91 GeV got completely vanished.

## 4    Conclusions

This research tested the performance of CNNs for classifying the outcome of HEP particle collisions using CODP. The first step transformed the momentum and position of physics objects into images in order to use a CNN. The second step divided the data into two scenarios. The first scenario required classifying resonances with different invariant masses at different energy ranges. The selected data was related to Higgs, Drell-Yan, $W$ + jets and $J/\psi$, also referred as DHJW. The second scenario focused on identifying signal and background processes. The selected data was related to Drell-Yan, $t\bar{t}$ and $W$ + jets, also referred as DTW. All the data considered the muons as the final state. The third step tested different types of CNNs over both scenarios considering the best dataset. The final step used the best performance metric in the DTW scenario over real collision data.

The results presented in our work demonstrate the capabilities of CNNs as potential tools for HEP analysis. Promising results were obtained for both DHJW and DTW scenarios with accuracies greater than 80 % in both cases. Notably, the DTW model was capable of differentiating the Z boson resonance from a collection of real collision data. ResNet50 has demonstrated to be the best CNN model among all the other popular options.

Further extensions of this work plan to increase the dataset in order to achieve a better accuracy in the CNN model, as well as testing the best-trained CNN related to the DHWJ process with real data. Finally, in the HEP area, other physics processes can be considered using the methodology presented in this work.

## References

1. Griffiths, D.J.: Introduction to Elementary Particles; 2nd rev. version. Physics Textbook. Wiley, New York (2008)
2. Feickert, M., Nachman, B.: A Living Review of Machine Learning for Particle Physics (2021)
3. Madrazo, C.F., Heredia, I., Lloret, L., de Lucas, J.M.: Application of a convolutional neural network for image classification for the analysis of collisions in high energy physics. In: EPJ Web Conferences, vol. 214, p. 06017 (2019)
4. CERN Open Data Portal. https://opendata.cern.ch/
5. Cottingham, W.N., Greenwood, D.A.: An Introduction to the Standard Model of Particle Physics, 2nd edn. Cambridge University Press, Cambridge (2007)
6. Sirunyan, A.M., et al.: Performance of the CMS muon detector and muon reconstruction with proton-proton collisions at $\sqrt{s}$=13 TeV. J. Instrum. **13**(06), P06015–P06015 (2018)
7. Sirunyan, A.M., et al.: Identification of heavy-flavour jets with the CMS detector in pp collisions at 13 TeV. J. Instrum. **13**(05), P05011–P05011 (2018)
8. Sirunyan, A.M., et al.: Performance of missing transverse momentum reconstruction in proton-proton collisions at $\sqrt{s}$=13 TeV using the CMS detector. J. Instrum. **14**(07), P07004–P07004 (2019)

9. Chen, X., Gehrmann, T., Glover, N., Huss, A., Yang, T.-Z., Zhu, H.X.: Dilepton rapidity distribution in Drell-Yan production to third order in QCD. Phys. Rev. Lett. **128**(5), 052001 (2022)
10. Han, T., Li, S., Su, S., Su, W., Wu, Y.: BSM higgs production at a muon collider (2022)
11. Khachatryan, V., et al.: Measurement of prompt $j/\psi$ pair production in pp collisions at $\sqrt{s}$= 7 TeV. J. High Energy Phys. **2014**(9) (2014)
12. Larkoski, A.J.: Elementary Particle Physics: An Intuitive Introduction. Cambridge University Press, Cambridge (2019)
13. Berger, M.S.: The ttbar threshold at a muon collider (1995)
14. Aggarwal, C.C.: Neural networks and deep learning: a textbook (2018)
15. CERN. CMS Open Data Workshop 2022 (2022). https://cms-opendata-workshop. github.io/2022-08-01-cms-open-data-workshop/
16. CMS Collaboration: Simulated dataset ZToMuMu_M_50_120_NNPDF30_13TeV_ powheg_herwigpp in MINIAODSIM format for 2015 collision data. CERN Open Data Portal (2021). https://doi.org/10.7483/OPENDATA.CMS.X6BR.VOSN
17. CMS Collaboration: Simulated dataset WJetsToLNu_TuneCUETP8M1_13TeV-amcatnloFXFX-pythia8 in MINIAODSIM format for 2015 collision data. CERN Open Data Portal (2021). https://doi.org/10.7483/OPENDATA.CMS.FLGU. 07DD
18. CMS Collaboration: Simulated dataset TT_TuneCUETP8M1_13TeV-powheg-pythia8 in MINIAODSIM format for 2015 collision data. CERN Open Data Portal (2021). https://doi.org/10.7483/OPENDATA.CMS.JJEM.1DKC
19. CMS Collaboration: Simulated dataset JpsiToMuMu-JpsiPt8-TuneCUEP8M1-13TeV-pythia8 in MINIAODSIM format for 2015 collision data. CERN Open Data Portal (2021). https://doi.org/10.7483/OPENDATA.CMS.2TX8.NV9C
20. CMS Collaboration: Simulated dataset VBF-HToMuMu-M125-13Te-powheg-pythia8 in MINIAODSIM format for 2015 collision data. CERN Open Data Portal (2021). https://doi.org/10.7483/OPENDATA.CMS.QIQ9.ZH9W
21. CMS collaboration: DoubleMuon primary dataset /DoubleMuon/Run2015D-16Dec2015-v1/MINIAOD in MINIAOD format from Run of 2015 collision data. CERN Open Data Portal (2021). https://doi.org/10.7483/OPENDATA.CMS. H3TX.ZJZX
22. He, K., Zhang, X., Ren, S., Sun, J.: Deep Residual Learning for Image Recognition (2015)
23. Huang, G., Liu, Z., van der Maaten, L., Weinberger, K.Q.: Densely Connected Convolutional Networks (2018)
24. Szegedy, C., Vanhoucke, V., Ioffe, S., Shlens, J., Wojna, Z.: Rethinking the inception architecture for computer vision. arXiv 1512.00567 (2015). https://doi.org/ 10.48550/arXiv.1409.4842
25. Sandler, M., Howard, A., Zhu, M., Zhmoginov, A., Chen, L.-C.: Mobilenetv 2: inverted residuals and linear bottlenecks (2019)

# Human Actions Recognition System Based on Neural Networks

Juan Brito$^{(\boxtimes)}$ and Rigoberto Fonseca-Delgado$^{(\boxtimes)}$

Yachay Tech University, Urcuquí, Ecuador
{juan.brito,rfonseca}@yachaytech.edu.ec

**Abstract.** The recognition of human activities in videos is a relevant area of study due to its real-life applications, such as surveillance, security, healthcare, human-machine interaction, and monitoring. This research compares two recognition approaches, called simple and hybrid, using two specific data sets. The first set includes three classes: yoga, exercise, and dance; the second is a sample from the Kinetics-700 set, with five activities, four of which are violent. Both sets present low variability between classes and high variability within classes. To reduce computational costs, a pre-trained CNN model and simple techniques for reducing computational resources are used. The hybrid approach uses an additional model with three variants: GRU, LSTM, or BiLSTM. Even though all the models presented similar results, the simple approach, using a pre-trained architecture and a reconstructed top-head, proved to be the most effective, reaching an accuracy of 94%, while the hybrid approach using LSTM layers obtained 90%. The model demonstrated an adequate classification of violent activities, which could serve as a basis for developing a surveillance and security systems.

**Keywords:** Pretrained CNN · LSTM · GRU · BiLSTM

## 1 Introduction

The field of computer vision and machine learning has made significant strides in predicting and recognizing human actions, with applications in sectors like security and intelligent rehabilitation. The abundance of online video data has played a crucial role in refining video classification accuracy [14]. Action recognition, a complex process, involves two main tasks: action representation and action classification. The former converts video input into a machine-understandable representation, while the latter uses this representation to infer the performed action [23]. Artificial Neural Networks (ANNs) have been instrumental in recognizing complex patterns within data, contributing to the successful prediction and classification of human activities [7,12,15,16]. This study uses the TensorFlow library to develop ANN models for differentiating various human actions, considering factors like accuracy, computational cost, and classifiable activities. Addressing video classification challenges has led to the development of scalable

ⓒ The Author(s), under exclusive license to Springer Nature Switzerland AG 2023
J. Maldonado-Mahauad et al. (Eds.): TICEC 2023, CCIS 1885, pp. 52–67, 2023.
https://doi.org/10.1007/978-3-031-45438-7_4

models [1,2,5]. The research aims to evaluate two video classification approaches based on pre-trained 2D convolutional neural network and RNN architectures for identifying human actions in datasets with large inter-class and small intra-class variability.We work with Keras as a framework in the construction of the different models.

## 2    Related Work

Video classification, a branch of computer vision, involves devising algorithms for the automatic categorization of videos based on visual content [8]. It's a challenging task due to video data's high dimensionality and temporal nature, requiring advanced feature extraction methods and modelling of temporal dynamics. This field has gained interest owing to applications in video surveillance, sports analytics, and education, among others. The actions in videos for the machines are nothing more than a set of pixels so computers; therefore the first thing is to look for an adequate representation and then infer the action to be performed. These two problems constructing an adequate representation of the video as input and inferring from this representation what action it is performing [8]. The process of transforming video data into a feature-encapsulating vector or a sequence of vectors is termed action representation [9,10,13]. Subsequently, action classification deals with understanding the content of the video [11,18]. Multiple techniques, particularly in deep learning, successfully integrate these two components. Action recognition can be broadly categorized into Shallow Approaches, Deep Architectures as depicted in Fig. 1 [8].

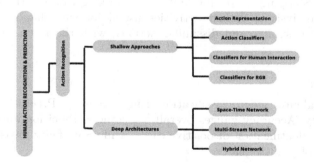

**Fig. 1.** General overview of the different human action recognition and prediction approaches.

## 3    Deep Learning Approaches

Deep learning methods address limitations of traditional features, modeling complex relationships and learning powerful features useful in video classification tasks [14]. 3D CNN models, despite training challenges, offer effective spatiotemporal feature learning and excel in action and object recognition [17,21]. Multistream networks use multiple CNNs to model appearance and motion information, integrating spatial fusion functions and residual connections to overcome interaction deficiencies [3,4,20]. Hybrid networks, merging CNNs and RNNs, capture spatial, temporal, and long-range dependencies, and apply enhancements like spatiotemporal graph convolution and attention models to further improve learning of structural and temporal information [6,19,22,24]. Nonetheless, they grapple with challenges like variations, cluttered background, camera motion, and uneven predictability.

## 4  Methodology

### 4.1  Movement Mix Dataset

Is a custom collection of high-definition TikTok and YouTube videos, with various resolutions, sizes, and a 30fps average frame rate. It features 172 training/validation and 29 test videos across three categories: dance, exercise, and yoga. The categories span multiple styles, environments, and exercises, leading to significant overlap and complexity in classification due to variations in body positions.

### 4.2  Danger Kinetics Dataset

A subsample of the large Kinetics-700 video collection, features 650,000 clips across 700 human action classes. It consists of YouTube videos of human-object and human-human interactions. Five classes - Punching Bag, Punching Person (boxing), Slapping, Throwing knife, and Walking through the snow - were selected for analysis of violent activities useful for surveillance. The classes encompass both similar and dissimilar actions, with the last one being non-violent.

### 4.3  Metrics

The study evaluates video classification using Accuracy, Precision, Specificity, and Sensitivity. Accuracy gauges overall correctness. Precision and Sensitivity assess correct identification of positive cases, while Specificity measures correct identification of negative cases.

### 4.4  Proposed Solution

This study aims to devise an efficient video classification model, focusing on neural network-based methods. Special emphasis is placed on minimizing computational demand.

1. Utilizing pre-trained 2D CNNs on individual frames.
2. Combining pre-trained 2D CNNs with GRUs.
3. Integrating pre-trained 2D CNNs with LSTMs.
4. Employing pre-trained 2D CNNs along with BiLSTMs.

## 4.5   Data Preprocessing

Both datasets utilized in the proposed models underwent identical preprocessing. A maximum of 220 frames per video was established, with each frame vectorized and labeled. To reduce noise, the first and last ten frames were removed, the frame rate was reduced to a third, and videos with potential mislabels or excessive noise were eliminated. All videos were resized to $224 \times 224$ without cropping and shuffled to ensure balanced distribution. The datasets were then partitioned into training (80%) and validation sets (20%).

1. For the first dataset: 172 videos for training, divided into exercise (68), dance (53), and yoga (52) classes, and 29 for testing, split into dance (8), exercise (10), and yoga (11) classes.
2. For the second dataset: 250 training videos, with 50 from each class, and approximately 65 for testing, with around 13 videos from each class.

## 4.6   Simple Approach

The simple approach used a two-part methodology: selection of a pre-trained convolutional neural network (CNN) model, and the reconfiguration of this model to suit video classification. The pre-trained model chosen was EfficientNetB0, selected for its excellent performance in various image classification tasks, and its efficiency owing to its optimized depth, width, and resolution. EfficientNetB0's architecture combines convolutional layers, depthwise separable convolutions, and squeeze-and-excitation blocks, enabling efficient feature extraction.

**Top Head of Model.** For the simple approach, EfficientNetB0 was used for feature extraction, and a custom classifier was built as the top head of the model. The top head consists of six layers: Global Average Pooling, Batch Normalization, two Dropout layers, and two Dense layers. The model was trained using both datasets with ReLU and softmax activation functions, Stochastic Gradient Descent optimization, and a batch size of 16 for a maximum of 50 epochs. Early stopping was implemented to prevent overfitting, and performance metrics including accuracy, recall, precision, and specificity were used for evaluation. In the training and validation process, the model was trained twice, once for each dataset, with the final dense layer's size varying. It is important to note some aspects of the training process, which are summarized in Table 1. The model comprises 4,219,304 total parameters. Out of these, 167,173 are trainable, and 4,052,131 are non-trainable. These parameters represent the model's complexity and the amount of data required for effective training. The model's evaluation process involves computing the mean of the probability vectors obtained from the trained model, owing to the use of a 2DCNN model and the aim of video classification. Figure 2 illustrates the process, showing the main steps in model building and the evaluation process.

**Table 1.** Summary of the Training and Validation Process.

| Aspect | Details |
| --- | --- |
| Activation functions | ReLU in the dense layer and softmax in the output layer |
| Dropout layers | Two dropout layers with a dropout rate of 0.4 |
| Epochs | 50 |
| Optimization algorithm | Stochastic Gradient Descent (SGD) with a learning rate of 1e-4 |
| Batch size | 16 |
| Early stopping | Monitors validation accuracy with a patience of 10 epochs |

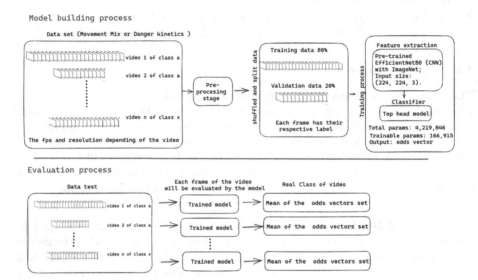

**Fig. 2.** Pipeline of the simple approach, encompassing both the model construction and the evaluation process.

### 4.7 Hybrid Approach

The hybrid approach consists of three stages. First, the pre-trained Efficient-NetB0 model is used for feature extraction, similar to the simple method. In the second stage, each video is converted into a set of feature vectors representing frames. Finally, in the third stage, various Recurrent Neural Network (RNN) models, including Gated Recurrent Units (GRUs), Long Short-Term Memory (LSTMs), and Bidirectional LSTMs (BiLSTMs), are applied for capturing temporal features. While this approach offers a richer understanding of time-dependent patterns, it comes with a higher computational cost due to the additional model. The preprocessing for RNN models in the hybrid approach encompasses two primary stages. In the first stage, dimensionality reduction is applied using a MaxPooling2D layer. The initial feature vector, extracted from the pre-trained EfficientNetB0 model, is reduced from $7 \times 7 \times 1280$ to $6 \times 6 \times 1280$, preserving essential features while decreasing data volume by approximately a factor of 13. The second stage of preprocessing involves preparing the videos as sequences of feature vectors. This procedure includes three primary components: (1) a feature vector array obtained by breaking down each video, (2) masks generated to manage sequences of varying lengths, and (3) encoded labels corresponding to each video. This preparation process is performed individually for each video and takes into account their varying lengths by defining a maximum frame limit and using masks to maintain uniform sequence lengths. The preprocessing stage results in the generation of feature vector arrays and mask vectors for each video, as well as the extraction of features from video frames using the EfficientNetB0 model. Ultimately, this process aims to ensure efficient computational processing and handle variable-length sequences in RNN models. Upon the completion of preprocessing, the extracted video features, masks, and encoded labels are used as inputs for RNN models such as GRU, LSTM, and BiLSTM, which are capable of analyzing temporal dependencies between frames for video classification. Figure 3 provides a schematic representation of the entire process. The Fig. 4 show it the architecture of the different RNN models, finally in the Fig. 5 it's possible observe the setting of the hyper parameters used during the training and validation process.

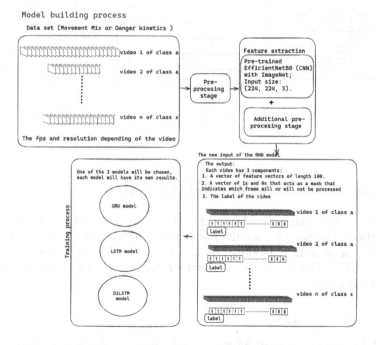

**Fig. 3.** Pipeline of the hybrid approach.

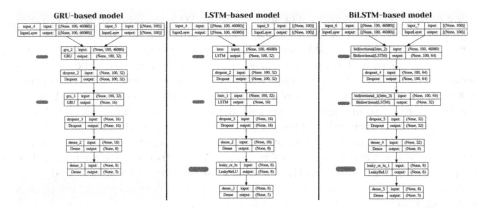

**Fig. 4.** Architecture of each of the RNN models.

|  | **GRU-based model** | **LSTM-based model** | **BiLSTM-based model** |
|---|---|---|---|
| Activation functions | ReLU in the dense layer and softmax in the output layer | Leaky ReLU in the dense layer with a value of 0.4 and softmax in the output layer | Leaky ReLU in the dense layer with a value of 0.2 and softmax in the output layer |
| Dropout layers | Two dropout layers with a dropout rate of 0.3 | First dropout layer with a rate of 0.5, Second dropout layer with a rate of 0.3 | First dropout layer with a rate of 0.5, Second dropout layer with a rate of 0.3 |
| Epochs | 100 | 100 | 100 |
| Optimization algorithm | Adam with a learning rate of 1e-4 | RMSprop with a learning rate of 1e-4 | RMSprop with a learning rate of 1e-4 |
| Batch size | 32 | 32 | 32 |
| Early stopping | Monitors validation accuracy with a patience of 20 epoch | Monitors validation accuracy with a patience of 20 epoch | Monitors validation accuracy with a patience of 20 epoch |
| Performance monitoring | Validation accuracy | Validation accuracy | Validation accuracy |

**Fig. 5.** Configuration for each of the RNN models during the training and validation process.

## 5    Summary of Experimental Analysis

The experimental analysis evaluates the effectiveness of various video classification methods on two distinct datasets. These include the simple frame approach and three hybrid models: 2D CNN+GRU, 2D CNN+LSTM, and 2D CNN+BiLSTM. The purpose is to identify the most suitable technique for video classification tasks.

### 5.1    Simple Approach

**First Dataset (Movement Mix).** This dataset is well-balanced, with a similar number of frames per class. The distribution is as follows (Table 2):

**Table 2.** Distribution of Frames in the Movement Mix Dataset.

| Data Type | Category | Number of Frames |
|-----------|----------|------------------|
| Training Data | Dance | 7,099 frames |
|  | Exercise | 6,798 frames |
|  | Yoga | 7,086 frames |
| Testing Data | Dance | 846 frames |
|  | Exercise | 915 frames |
|  | Yoga | 920 frames |

For the performance analysis, the following aspects are evaluated:

1. Examination of training metrics.
2. Evaluation of validation metrics.
3. Investigation of the relationship between accuracy and validation accuracy with the number of epochs.
4. Assessment of the loss function for both training and validation as a function of the number of epochs.

In the study, the model's efficacy was assessed over 50 epochs using training and validation datasets. Significant enhancements in accuracy, recall, precision, and specificity were observed across epochs. Training metrics improved as follows: accuracy (0.594 to 0.985), recall (0.362 to 0.981), precision (0.409 to 0.991), and specificity (0.725 to 0.999). Validation metrics also improved: accuracy (0.688 to 0.984), recall (0.591 to 0.998), precision (0.721 to 0.998), and specificity (0.971 to 0.996). The loss function consistently declined for both datasets, with training loss decreasing from 1.292 to 0.06, and validation loss from 0.368 to 0.02, indicating effective model performance. Refer to Fig. 6 for further details. See the Fig. 6 for more detail. In the study, the model's performance was evaluated using a confusion matrix and tested from two perspectives: frame-by-frame and considering the entire video, as illustrated in figure x. The frame-by-frame analysis revealed an accuracy of 79.38%, with significant misclassification issues in the yoga category, possibly due to similarities with exercise postures. When entire videos were evaluated, the overall accuracy further decreased to 69%, with 'Exercise' at 70%, 'Dance' at 100%, and 'Yoga' at 36%. This suggests potential overfitting, as the model performed well with training and validation data but struggled with testing data. The discrepancies may be due to the video classification process, which averages the sum of all probability vectors yielded by the model, potentially disregarding correctly labeled frames. The primary issue identified was the lack of diversity in the yoga category, as many videos were derived from a single long video, reducing source diversity. Additionally, many videos from a single YouTube channel performing yoga and exercise further decreased diversity, particularly for this class. These findings underscore the critical importance of dataset diversity in such problems for improving generalization and facilitating correct pattern recognition. The results are comprehensively represented in the confusion matrices depicted in the Figs. 7.

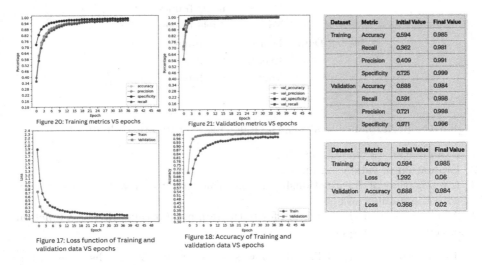

Figure 20: Training metrics VS epochs

Figure 21: Validation metrics VS epochs

| Dataset | Metric | Initial Value | Final Value |
|---|---|---|---|
| Training | Accuracy | 0.594 | 0.985 |
| | Recall | 0.362 | 0.981 |
| | Precision | 0.409 | 0.991 |
| | Specificity | 0.725 | 0.999 |
| Validation | Accuracy | 0.688 | 0.984 |
| | Recall | 0.591 | 0.998 |
| | Precision | 0.721 | 0.998 |
| | Specificity | 0.971 | 0.996 |

| Dataset | Metric | Initial Value | Final Value |
|---|---|---|---|
| Training | Accuracy | 0.594 | 0.985 |
| | Loss | 1.292 | 0.06 |
| Validation | Accuracy | 0.688 | 0.984 |
| | Loss | 0.368 | 0.02 |

Figure 17: Loss function of Training and validation data VS epochs

Figure 18: Accuracy of Training and validation data VS epochs

**Fig. 6.** General results for the first dataset.

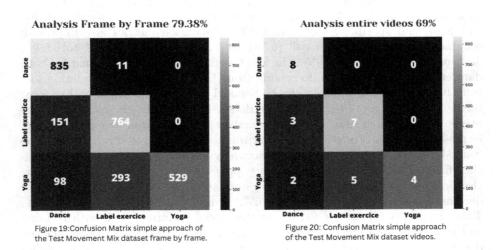

**Analysis Frame by Frame 79.38%**

**Analysis entire videos 69%**

Figure 19:Confusion Matrix simple approach of the Test Movement Mix dataset frame by frame.

Figure 20: Confusion Matrix simple approach of the Test Movement Mix dataset videos.

**Fig. 7.** Confusion matrix's for the first dataset.

**Second Dataset (Danger Kinetics).** The balanced dataset consists of training and testing frames for five categories: Punching Bag (6,658 training, 966 testing), Punching Person (7,717 training, 646 testing), Slapping (5,843 training, 894 testing), Throwing Knife (7,493 training, 1,079 testing), and Walking Through Snow (7,654 training, 865 testing). The analysis involves evaluating training and validation metrics, assessing the evolution of accuracy and loss function across epochs for both training and validation datasets. For the Danger Kinetics dataset, all training and validation metrics improved over 50 epochs. Training accuracy rose from 0.353 to 0.850, and validation accuracy from 0.642 to 0.939. Simultaneously, loss function values decreased, with training loss falling from 1.965 to 0.408, and validation loss from 0.9394 to 0.2010. Even though these results were slightly inferior to the ones obtained with the initial dataset, they were more consistent, indicating no overfitting. The problems experienced with the previous dataset seemed to stem from overfitting due to the inadequate diversity in the yoga class data. This suggests that the problem with the previous dataset was rooted in overfitting, caused by the inappropriate generalization of the yoga class data, which lacked diversity. In the Fig. 8 we can see the results in the training process and in Fig. 9 we can see the two confusion matrixs.

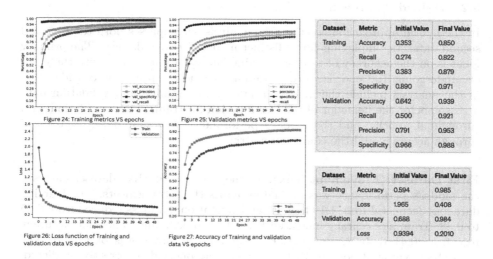

Figure 24: Training metrics VS epochs

Figure 25: Validation metrics VS epochs

Figure 26: Loss function of Training and validation data VS epochs

Figure 27: Accuracy of Training and validation data VS epochs

| Dataset | Metric | Initial Value | Final Value |
|---|---|---|---|
| Training | Accuracy | 0.353 | 0.850 |
| | Recall | 0.274 | 0.822 |
| | Precision | 0.383 | 0.879 |
| | Specificity | 0.890 | 0.971 |
| Validation | Accuracy | 0.642 | 0.939 |
| | Recall | 0.500 | 0.921 |
| | Precision | 0.791 | 0.953 |
| | Specificity | 0.966 | 0.988 |

| Dataset | Metric | Initial Value | Final Value |
|---|---|---|---|
| Training | Accuracy | 0.594 | 0.985 |
| | Loss | 1.965 | 0.408 |
| Validation | Accuracy | 0.688 | 0.984 |
| | Loss | 0.9394 | 0.2010 |

**Fig. 8.** Results for the second dataset.

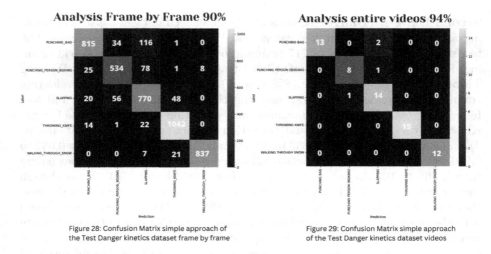

Figure 28: Confusion Matrix simple approach of the Test Danger kinetics dataset frame by frame

Figure 29: Confusion Matrix simple approach of the Test Danger kinetics dataset videos

**Fig. 9.** Confusion matrix's for the second dataset.

## 5.2    Hybrid Approach

In the hybrid approach subsection, the analysis encompasses both the first and second datasets, employing three distinct models for each dataset. The primary focus is on the accuracy of testing, training, and validation data, with the models undergoing 100 epochs during training. Critical aspects for consideration in the analysis include the model's accuracy for training and validation data across epochs, the behavior of the loss function for training and validation data throughout epochs, and the model's performance with test data, as assessed through accuracy and the confusion matrix.

**First Dataset (Movement Mix).** In the "Movement Mix" dataset analysis, the model's performance was evaluated across three key aspects. The training data loss decreased from 1.19 to 0.46, and validation data loss reduced from 0.95 to 0.38. Training accuracy increased from 0.32 to 0.95, and validation accuracy rose from 0.41 to 0.97. However, the test data accuracy was only 59%. The yoga class exhibited poor predictions, with only one video correctly predicted, attributed to the dataset itself. This bias towards the yoga and exercise classes prevented a fair comparison of the models. Consequently, the analysis was limited to the hybrid approach with GRUs, and focus was shifted to the second dataset.

**Second Dataset (Danger Kinetics).** The analysis of the second dataset, employing three different RNN models - GRU, LSTM, and BiLSTM, focused on three key aspects: the accuracy of the models for training and validation data across epochs, the behavior of the loss function for these data, and the performance of the models with test data. The GRU model demonstrated a consistent improvement in accuracy across 100 epochs, with the accuracy for training data increasing from 23.8% to 98.9%, and for validation data from 26.2% to 83.33%. However, the accuracy for test data was slightly lower at 87.9%. Class-specific performance varied, with 'Punching Bag' and 'Throwing Knife' classes achieving over 90% accuracy. The LSTM model outperformed the GRU model, with training data accuracy increasing from 29.5% to 99.4%, and validation data from 51.5% to 85%. The test data accuracy was higher at 90%. The LSTM model demonstrated superior performance, particularly for the 'Slapping' class. The BiLSTM model, despite being the most complex, yielded the least favorable results. The accuracy for training data increased from 30.1% to 99.8%, and for validation data from 44.3% to 88.43%. However, the test data accuracy was lower at 86.36%. Despite this, the BiLSTM model converged the fastest, stabilizing around epoch 15. The analysis also highlighted potential overfitting, as evidenced by the difference between training and validation results. However, the similar performance on test data suggested reasonable generalization. The computational cost was a significant factor, with hybrid models consuming up to 50GB of RAM and 20 GB of VRAM during the data preparation and training process. The size and diversity of the dataset were also crucial for improving model performance. In summary, all models performed well with minor differences in results. The LSTM model was the best performer, while the simple approach showed unexpected good results. Despite the lower accuracy, the BiLSTM model converged the fastest, offering potential advantages in scenarios where training time is a concern. In the Fig. 10 and 11 we can observe details about the training and validation process and about the testing. Finally, Fig. 12 presents a comparison of model sizes in terms of parameters and the accuracy achieved on the second dataset using test data. The largest difference is observed in the number of parameters, where RNN-based approaches possess significantly more parameters. Focusing on accuracy, though the simple approach scores highest, the difference is marginal. The figure illustrates the efficiency of the simple approach, concluding that despite its lack of complexity, this kind of model remains at the forefront. It suggests that this approach may be sufficient for many video classification problems, even when dealing with complex scenarios as demonstrated in this study.

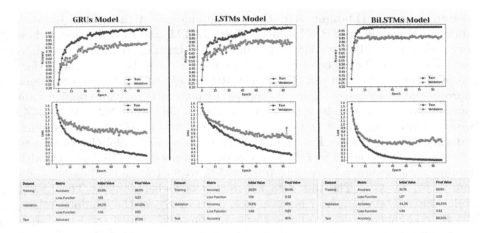

**Fig. 10.** Results of the training process for the second data set in a the RNN models.

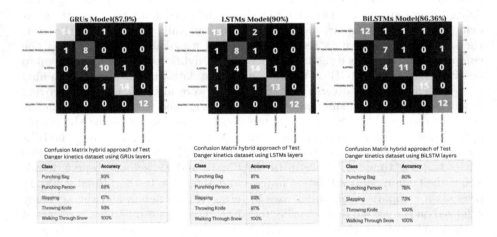

**Fig. 11.** Confusion matrix's for the second dataset in the RNN models.

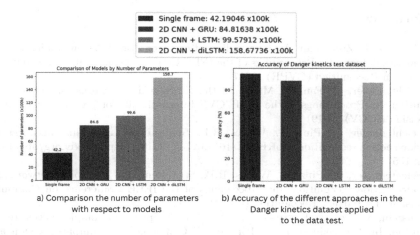

**Fig. 12.** Comparison of both the size and the accuracy of the different models based on neural networks.

# 6 Conclusions and Future Work

This study explored human activity video classification using both a simple approach (EfficientNetB0) and hybrid approaches (2D CNN + GRU, 2D CNN + LSTM, 2D CNN + BiLSTM) on two diverse datasets. Surprisingly, the simple approach, despite its simplicity, outperformed the more complex models, underscoring its effectiveness in video classification tasks. All models exhibited promising potential in classifying a variety of activities, even those characterized by high intra-class variation and low inter-class differences. However, the computational power required during the training phase posed a significant limitation, particularly for larger datasets. The study underscored the critical role of dataset variability, highlighting its profound impact when working with relatively small datasets in video classification tasks. Interestingly, the BiLSTM model, despite having the lowest accuracy, demonstrated superior convergence compared to the other models, including the simple approach. This factor is worth considering when training time is a crucial aspect. For future research, it would be beneficial to explore strategies to reduce computational resource requirements, experiment with larger and more diverse datasets, and investigate alternative lightweight pre-trained models or custom architectures. The findings of this study pave the way for further research in this direction, aiming to optimize the balance between model complexity, performance, and computational efficiency.

# References

1. Carreira, J., Zisserman, A.: Quo vadis, action recognition? A new model and the kinetics dataset. In: Proceedings of the IEEE Conference on Computer Vision and Pattern Recognition (CVPR) (2017)
2. Feichtenhofer, C., Fan, H., Malik, J., He, K.: Slowfast networks for video recognition. In: Proceedings of the IEEE/CVF International Conference on Computer Vision (ICCV) (2019)
3. Feichtenhofer, C., Pinz, A., Wildes, R.P.: Spatiotemporal residual networks for video action recognition. CoRR abs/1611.02155 (2016). http://arxiv.org/abs/1611. 02155
4. Feichtenhofer, C., Pinz, A., Wildes, R.P.: Spatiotemporal multiplier networks for video action recognition. In: Proceedings of the IEEE Conference on Computer Vision and Pattern Recognition (CVPR) (2017)
5. Hussein, N., Gavves, E., Smeulders, A.W.: Timeception for complex action recognition. In: Proceedings of the IEEE/CVF Conference on Computer Vision and Pattern Recognition (CVPR) (2019)
6. Ke, Q., Bennamoun, M., An, S., Sohel, F.A., Boussaïd, F.: A new representation of skeleton sequences for 3D action recognition. CoRR abs/1703.03492 (2017). http:// arxiv.org/abs/1703.03492
7. Kiranyaz, S., Avci, O., Abdeljaber, O., Ince, T., Gabbouj, M., Inman, D.J.: 1D convolutional neural networks and applications: a survey (2019)
8. Kong, Y., Fu, Y.: Human action recognition and prediction: a survey. Int. J. Comput. Vision **130**(5), 1366–1401 (2022). https://doi.org/10.1007/s11263-022-01594-9
9. Kong, Y., Tao, Z., Fu, Y.: Deep sequential context networks for action prediction. In: 2017 IEEE Conference on Computer Vision and Pattern Recognition (CVPR), pp. 3662–3670 (2017). https://doi.org/10.1109/CVPR.2017.390
10. Laptev, I.: On space time interest points. Int. J. Comput. Vision **64**(2), 107–123 (2005). https://doi.org/10.1007/s11263-005-1838-7
11. Liu, J., Kuipers, B., Savarese, S.: Recognizing human actions by attributes. In: CVPR 2011, pp. 3337–3344 (2011). https://doi.org/10.1109/CVPR.2011.5995353
12. Minallah, N., Tariq, M., Aziz, N., Khan, W., Rehman, A.U., Belhaouari, S.B.: On the performance of fusion based planet-scope and sentinel-2 data for crop classification using inception inspired deep convolutional neural network. PLoS ONE **15**(9), 1–16 (2020). https://doi.org/10.1371/journal.pone.0239746
13. Morency, L.P., Quattoni, A., Darrell, T.: Latent-dynamic discriminative models for continuous gesture recognition. Technical report, MIT-CSAIL-TR-2007-002, MIT Computer Science and Artificial Intelligence Laboratory (2007)
14. Rehman, A., Belhaouari, S.B.: Deep learning for video classification: a review. TechRxiv (2021). https://doi.org/10.36227/techrxiv.15172920.v1
15. Rehman, A.U., Bermak, A.: Averaging neural network ensembles model for quantification of volatile organic compound. In: 2019 15th International Wireless Communications & Mobile Computing Conference (IWCMC), pp. 848–852 (2019). https://doi.org/10.1109/IWCMC.2019.8766776
16. Samek, W., Montavon, G., Lapuschkin, S., Anders, C., Muller, K.R.: Explaining deep neural networks and beyond: a review of methods and applications. Proc. IEEE **109**, 247–278 (2021). https://doi.org/10.1109/JPROC.2021.3060483
17. Shen, J., Huang, Y., Wen, M., Zhang, C.: Toward an efficient deep pipelined template-based architecture for accelerating the entire 2-D and 3-D CNNs on

FPGA. IEEE Trans. Comput. Aided Des. Integr. Circuits Syst. **39**(7), 1442–1455 (2020). https://doi.org/10.1109/TCAD.2019.2912894

18. Shi, Q., Cheng, L., Wang, L., Smola, A.: Human action segmentation and recognition using discriminative semi-Markov models. Int. J. Comput. Vision **93**, 22–32 (2011). https://doi.org/10.1007/s11263-010-0384-0
19. Si, C., Chen, W., Wang, W., Wang, L., Tan, T.: An attention enhanced graph convolutional LSTM network for skeleton-based action recognition. CoRR abs/1902.09130 (2019). http://arxiv.org/abs/1902.09130
20. Simonyan, K., Zisserman, A.: Two-stream convolutional networks for action recognition in videos. In: Ghahramani, Z., Welling, M., Cortes, C., Lawrence, N., Weinberger, K. (eds.) Advances in Neural Information Processing Systems, vol. 27. Curran Associates, Inc. (2014). https://proceedings.neurips.cc/paper_files/paper/2014/file/00ec53c4682d36f5c4359f4ae7bd7ba1-Paper.pdf
21. Tran, D., Bourdev, L., Fergus, R., Torresani, L., Paluri, M.: Learning spatiotemporal features with 3D convolutional networks. In: 2015 IEEE International Conference on Computer Vision (ICCV), pp. 4489–4497 (2015). https://doi.org/10.1109/ICCV.2015.510
22. Yan, S., Xiong, Y., Lin, D.: Spatial temporal graph convolutional networks for skeleton-based action recognition. In: Proceedings of the AAAI Conference on Artificial Intelligence, vol. 32 (2018). https://doi.org/10.1609/aaai.v32i1.12328
23. Yu Kong, Y.F.: Human action recognition and prediction: a survey. Int. J. Forecast. **10**, 1–37 (2022)
24. Zhu, W., et al.: Co-occurrence feature learning for skeleton based action recognition using regularized deep LSTM networks. In: Proceedings of the AAAI Conference on Artificial Intelligence, vol. 30, no. 1 (2016). https://doi.org/10.1609/aaai.v30i1.10451. https://ojs.aaai.org/index.php/AAAI/article/view/10451

# Big Data Architecture for Air Pollution Spatial Visualization: Quito, Ecuador

Gabriela Mora-Villacís$^{(\boxtimes)}$ (ID) and Tania Calle-Jimenez (ID)

Escuela Politécnica Nacional, Quito, Ecuador
{maria.mora01,tania.calle}@epn.edu.ec

**Abstract.** The aim is to integrate the processing and visualization of geographic data related to air pollution within a massive data architecture, to optimize processing and response times. Air pollutant data and climatic variables from Quito, Ecuador, measured by the Atmospheric Monitoring Network of the city, were used. After cleaning, Quito Air Pollution Index was calculated. The proposed architecture is open-source and is made up of a cluster with a master node and two worker-nodes. This cluster consists of a unified analysis computational system in Spark, managed by Yarn, and linked to a graphical interface provided by Zeppelin. It processes data and displays it visually through geographic maps. To verify that this architecture improves response times, a comparison was made between using the system and not using it. The geographic interpolation results were 4.52 s with a Geographical Information System, while the proposed system showed an execution time of 2.0 s, indicating a reduction of 56%. This architecture showed an improvement in the traditional interpolation and map visualization processes, and generated a new open-source alternative with resources and time optimization. In addition, this research work could contribute to the making of strategic decisions through a new way of analyzing environmental problems.

**Keywords:** Parallel geo-computation · Big Data architecture · air pollution

## 1 Introduction

Air pollution is a problem that has had negative consequences for urban populations for centuries in that particles and gases present in the air have proved to be extremely harmful to human health [1]. According to the World Health Organization (WHO), 9 out of 10 people worldwide breathe air with high levels of pollutants and approximately 7 million people die each year as a result of ambient and domestic air pollution [2]. Particulate matter, especially particles less than or equal to 2.5 microns in diameter, is the most dangerous for human health, since they cause cardiovascular and respiratory diseases and cancer [3].

In Ecuador, a WHO study showed that in 2012, 1,771 people, 86 of whom were children, died from diseases directly related to air pollution, ischemic heart disease being the disease that stood out [4]. These statistics are worrying. In the Metropolitan District of Quito (DMQ), the situation follows the same trend. In 2018, there were

J. Maldonado-Mahauad et al. (Eds.): TICEC 2023, CCIS 1885, pp. 68–82, 2023.
https://doi.org/10.1007/978-3-031-45438-7_5

63 days when citizens breathed air that was harmful to their health, as pollutants found in the environment exceeded permissible limits; the main reason was the use of car or public transportation which meant the use of fossil fuel-using vehicles [5].

Related to this, the DMQ is responsible for preparing a Land Management Plan (PDOT, by its acronym in Spanish) which includes, among various topics, a diagnosis of the city environmental situation. In these analyses, indicators are represented through tables and statistical charts (lines, bars). This highlights the lack of knowledge with regard to geographic maps' importance as a complement to visualizing information. In addition, there is a lack of awareness of the support they in terms of strategic decision-making for developing public policies that promote a decrease in air pollution and which lead to population health improvement.

The volume of data that public and private organizations generate makes manual analysis impossible [6], so it is useful to use massive data architectures, based on parallel or distributed processing. These have become key elements with regard to supporting efficient information management and strategic decision-making [7], the last being an emerging research topic in recent decades and one which is considered a primary organizational activity. In this way, the public institution, the Quito Metropolitan Network for Atmospheric Monitoring (REMMAQ) has generated, since 2004, hundreds of items of data per hour about 13 different variables in approximately 11 stations distributed throughout the city, information that is increasingly complex to store, manage and analyze.

About distributed systems in Big Data, they are sets of computers connected by a network, generally called nodes, which coordinate activities and share resources in such a way that the user perceives an integrated computation, even though these machines are located in different places [8]. In the massive information age, distributed systems have gained strength and their use has become popular among organizations, since they allow a better handling of the large amount of data they generate, and help solve the growing applications performance that is needed [9]. This concept is important because the present form of processing is developed over this kind of systems, with Apache Spark being the principal piece. This is a unified analysis engine, based on open source distributed (or cluster) computing, used in the processing of massive data or Big Data [10]. Today, Spark has become a widely-used tool due to its offered advantages: (1) it is very fast and reliable when it comes to data analysis, program execution and data writing, (2) it provides application programming interfaces (APIs) in different languages such as Java, Scala, Python, and R, (3) it is designed for both in-memory processing and disk processing, (4) it is easy to install and (5) among other benefits it has the ability to gather datasets from multiple and diverse sources [11].

For building geographic maps, spatial interpolation plays an important role. It is a part of Geostatistics that allows estimating a variable linked to unknown points from known values with coordinates, obtaining, as a result, a continuous map or raster surface [12], which is a matrix of pixels with a z value. These maps can be used to represent contamination by using Air Contamination Index (ICA, by its acronym in Spanish). This is a dimensionless value that monitors air quality measured by monitoring stations allowing users to be aware of the evolution of the state of the air. In addition, it is the basis for issuing health recommendations to the population and especially to those who are sensitive to such pollution [13]. The DMQ has designed its own air quality index, adapted to its particular needs and environment - the Quito Air Pollution Index (IQCA, acronym in Spanish). It is on a numerical scale between 0 and 500; the higher the value the greater the air pollution level [14].

In the present work, the use of distributed systems is proposed by implementing an open-source Big Data architecture provided by Apache. This consists of an open cluster computational system with unified analysis in Spark, managed by Yarn and linked to a graphical interface provided by Zeppelin. This system stores air pollution data with regard to Quito (between 2005 and 2020) in the Hadoop Distributed File System (HDFS). It processes them and displays them visually using geographic maps. The pollutants considered for the analysis were carbon monoxide (CO), nitrogen dioxide ($NO_2$), ozone ($O_3$), sulfur dioxide ($SO_2$) and particulate matter ($PM_{2.5}$), extracted from monitoring stations located in the neighborhoods of Belisario, Carapungo, Centro and Cotocollao. Additionally, climatic variables were used to complement the study, including wind direction, humidity, precipitation and pressure, obtained from the Belisario, Carapungo, Cotocollao, El Camal, Los Chillos, and Tumbaco stations. This research allowed us to understand how spatial representation can support the decision-making process at the governmental level, and introduce new technologies to solve current problems such as those posed by Big Data architectures.

## 2   Materials and Methods

An efficient form of Big Data architecture dealing with geographic data is proposed in this paper. In summary, raw data requires cleaning to standardize it and for users to be able to work with it. Consequently, the architecture was designed by considering all the necessary technical aspects. It was launched in a cluster. The index that would allow air pollution to be represented was calculated, and finally maps were created, representing both contamination and climatic variables, to complement the investigation. All these steps are described in detail below.

**Download and Georeferencing Data.** Used data is released on Quito Environmental Municipal Secretary website in csv format, generated by the Atmospheric Monitoring Network of the city. This data was downloaded because they represent contaminants related to air pollution. In addition, climate variables were downloaded because they could complement the results.

These contaminates have, as source, natural dust containing biological matter, spores, pollen and bacteria; agricultural, insecticides and herbicides; and technological, industrial processes, industrial and domestic consumption of fossil fuels or motor vehicles [15].

These data did not have the spatial component (coordinates) necessary for spatial visualization. Consequently, they were georeferenced manually using base stations' addresses found on the Quito Environmental Municipal Secretary website. Figure 1 shows the geolocation of each station on a geographic map for a better understanding of the study area and the available data.

**Data Cleansing.** It was necessary to clean data due to the fact that the various files did not have the same format, were related to the same stations, or because there were

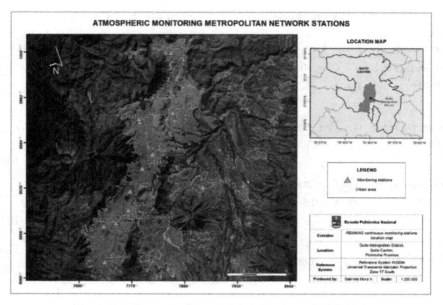

**Fig. 1.** Location map of the stations belonging to REMMAQ.

information gaps, among other problems. A quick data review was carried out and this process were carried out:

- Data type conversion: the column containing dates and times was transformed to 'timestamp', to allow later data aggrupation. The remaining columns were changed to 'float' to allow math operations.
- Data reduction: data were adapted to averages for every eight hours or daily depending on the pollutant (according to Table 1), for the subsequent IQCA calculation, given that the raw data was collected on an hourly basis.
- Time range choice: Data visualizations were used to analyze evolution and trends as a function of time, and availability by pollutant and climate variable (e.g., Fig. 2a). The existence of an overlap period was evaluated in those that are necessary for IQCA calculation (CO, $O_3$, $NO_2$, $SO_2$, $PM_{2.5}$, $PM_{10}$). Consequently, the chosen range was from 2005-01-01 to 2020-12-31 at Belisario, Carapungo, Centro and Cotocollao stations for contaminants; while Belisario, Carapungo, Cotocollao, El Camal, Los Chillos and Tumbaco were used for climatic analysis. The PM10 pollutant was eliminated because there is not a sufficient amount of data for the study.
- Data filling: Missing data was verified as not exceeding 25% of the total for each contaminant, the optimal filling percentage recommended in [16]. Interpolation method (interpolate in Python) was used to complete the time series.
- Data smoothing: Outliers were removed from each data group using the moving average method (rolling in Python). Figure 2b shows a comparison between interpolated data (blue color) and smoothed data (orange color).

**Table 1.** Mathematical expressions for calculating the IQCA [14].

| Contaminant | Range 1 | Range 2 | Range 3 | Range 4 |
|---|---|---|---|---|
| CO, average in 8 h, mg/m$^3$ | $0 < C_i \leq 10$ | $10 < C_i \leq 15$ | $15 < C_i \leq 30$ | $30 < C_i$ |
| | $IQCA = 10C_i$ | $IQCA = 20C_i - 100$ | $IQCA = 6.67C_i + 100$ | $IQCA = 10C_i$ |
| O$_3$, average in 8 h, $\mu$g/m$^3$ | $0 < C_i \leq 100$ | $100 < C_i \leq 200$ | $200 < C_i \leq 600$ | $600 < C_i$ |
| | $IQCA = C_i$ | $IQCA = C_i$ | $IQCA = 0.5C_i + 100$ | $IQCA = 0.5C_i + 100$ |
| NO$_2$, average in 1 h, $\mu$g/m$^3$ | $0 < C_i \leq 200$ | $200 < C_i \leq 1000$ | $1000 < C_i \leq 3000$ | $3000 < C_i$ |
| | $IQCA = 0.5C_i$ | $IQCA = 0.125C_i + 75$ | $IQCA = 0.1C_i + 100$ | $IQCA = 0.1C_i + 100$ |
| SO$_2$, average in 24 h, $\mu$g/m$^3$ | $0 < C_i \leq 62.5$ | $62.5 < C_i \leq 125$ | $125 < C_i \leq 200$ | $200 < C_i$ |
| | $IQCA = 0.8C_i$ | $IQCA = 1.333C_i + 66.67$ | $IQCA = 0.125C_i + 175$ | $IQCA = 0.125C_i + 175$ |
| PM$_{2.5}$, average in 24 h, $\mu$g/m$^3$ | $0 < C_i \leq 50$ | $50 < C_i \leq 250$ | $250 < C_i$ | – |
| | $IQCA = 2C_i$ | $IQCA = C_i + 50$ | $IQCA = C_i + 50$ | – |
| PM$_{10}$, average in 24 h, $\mu$g/m$^3$ | $0 < C_i \leq 100$ | $100 < C_i \leq 250$ | $250 < C_i \leq 400$ | $400 < C_i$ |
| | $IQCA = C_i$ | $IQCA = 0.667C_i + 33.33$ | $IQCA = 0.667C_i + 33.33$ | $IQCA = C_i + 100$ |

**Big Data Architecture Design.** Once data was cleaned and structured, the architecture that would allow the user to solve the problem was sketched out. The final version is illustrated in Fig. 3, where the principal difference with other architectures is in the visualization phase, by integrating a graphical interface.

- Data origin: Data comes from flat files (.csv), resulting from the previous cleaning phase.
- Batch processing: This allows the user to process large batches of jobs in smaller batches simultaneously, in sequential order, and without stopping. It consists of Hadoop HDFS to store the data source and results; Hadoop Yarn, which manages resources for each cluster node; and Apache Spark, which is the processing engine, using mainly PySpark and PyKrige.
- Visualization: Through a graphical interface provided by Apache Zeppelin, geographic maps with interpolated information from IQCA and climatic variables can be observed, using python libraries such as MatPlotLib and Contextily.

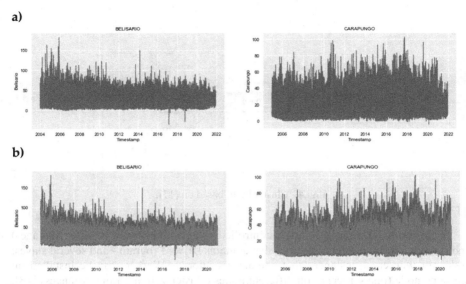

**Fig. 2.** NO2 measurement per Belisario and Carapungo stations since 2004: (a) Raw data; (b) Comparison between interpolated and smoothed data.

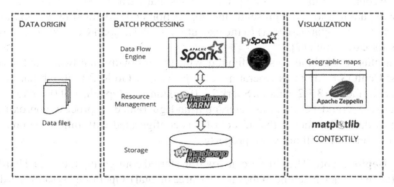

**Fig. 3.** Proposed architecture.

**Environment Preparation.** The proposed architecture was mounted on a cluster composed by virtual computers in Oracle VM VirtualBox. It has a master node and two workers or slave nodes, whose structure can be seen in Fig. 4.

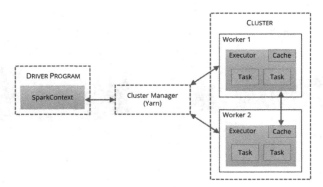

**Fig. 4.** Cluster built, based on [17].

In cluster mode, Apache Spark is controlled by an administrator (Cluster Manager) and is made up of a master, - instance that contains Driver Program - and several slaves, nodes, or workers, - instances that contain executors -. Workers can be installed on the same node (one server) or on different nodes (cluster with multiple instances) [18]. SparkContext, which acts as a Driver Program, connects to one of the cluster managers, whose role is to allocate resources to the applications to be run. Once connected, Spark obtains executors on the cluster nodes, processes that perform computations and store data for the application. It then sends the application code (defined by Python or JAR files passed to the SparkContext) to the executors. Finally, SparkContext sends tasks to workers for execution [17].

Each cluster machine was configured with the following hardware and software features: CentOS 8 Linux as Operating System (OS), 4 Gb RAM, 50 Gb hard disk, 1 CPU Cores, Hadoop 3.1.2 version, Spark 2.2.0 version and Zeppelin 0.9.0 version. These characteristics could be taken as referential and guarantee to process approximately 100 Mb of data. This means that if a cluster is configured with minor features other than those shown, it will not work properly.

**Cluster Deployment.** The cluster construction started configuring the virtual hardware and software for each machine of the cluster (three in total). Operating System was downloaded and installed, then IPs, SSH and hosts were configured for connection between machines and to guarantee parallel geo-computation in processing. Next, Hadoop was downloaded and installed, and environment variables were set. Subsequently, the master node was configured with its components: Java-Home, NameNode, HDFS, Yarn; and the same was done for slave nodes with their own components. HDFS and Yarn were then formatted and executed. It was then Spark's turn, and it was downloaded and installed. Spark and Yarn were then integrated, and finally a cluster mode was set up.

The next phase, and the most important one inside the proposed architecture, was web interface integration; this means that Apache Zeppelin was included, because installed virtual machines do not provide a graphical interface. It is a Jupyter-style web notebook focused on interactive data analytics through languages and technologies. To achieve this objective, Zeppelin was installed, environment variables were set up, and Yarn were integrated with Zeppelin. Spark interpreter needed additional configuration, and finally Zeppelin could be executed.

**Index Calculation.** Based on Table 1, UDFs (User Defined Functions were generated to calculate IQCA index depending on the contaminant, since it is not possible to apply a line-by-line calculation to a dataframe in Spark. The results obtained are observed in Fig. 5, where the table contains a column with date and time, another column describes the station, the next column is about pollutant measure and finally, a new column is created with index (*ica_co*).

```
+-------------------+----------+---------+---------+
|          Timestamp| estacion|       co|   ica_co|
+-------------------+----------+---------+---------+
|2005-01-06 00:00:00|  Belisario|  2.78125|  27.8125|
|2005-01-06 00:00:00| Carapungo|2.0719643|20.719643|
|2005-01-06 00:00:00|     Centro|2.6095917|26.095917|
|2005-01-06 00:00:00|Cotocollao|1.9767857|19.767857|
|2005-01-06 08:00:00|  Belisario|2.9064286|29.064285|
|2005-01-06 08:00:00| Carapungo|2.1205356|21.205357|
|2005-01-06 08:00:00|     Centro|2.6008418|26.008417|
|2005-01-06 08:00:00|Cotocollao|1.9709184|19.709185|
+-------------------+----------+---------+---------+
```

**Fig. 5.** Results of IQCA calculation for CO.

After calculating IQCA for all pollutants, an annual average was calculated (resample in Python), due to the amount of data that was handled. As a final step at this point, the overall index was established as a maximum value of analyzed contaminants. In addition, a new column was created to determine range that the index belongs to, as indicated in Table 2.

**Spatial Interpolation.** To obtain an interpolation map, it was necessary to generate a $100 \times 100$ latitude and longitude grid, where each matrix element will contain a z value of IQCA or climate variable. Then ordinary kriging method was applied because the mean is unknown [19]. This allowed that punctual z values could be transferred as a dispersion throughout the entire grid. Depending on the variable, the variogram models were alternated to find the best display. Therefore, maps were generated for each variogram, and were then compared to choose the most appropriate.

**Spatial Visualization.** It was possible to represent the variables under consideration with their geographic component with MatPlotLib and Contextily libraries.

**Table 2.** Numerical limits of each IQCA category ($\mu$g/m3) [14].

| Range | Category | CO | $O_3$ | $NO_2$ | $SO_2$ | $PM_{2.5}$ | $PM_{10}$ |
|-------|----------|-----|-------|--------|--------|-----------|-----------|
| 0–50 | Desirable or optimal level | 0–5000 | 0–50 | 0–100 | 0–62.5 | 0–25 | 0–50 |
| 51–100 | Acceptable or good level | 5001–10000 | 51–100 | 101–200 | 63.5–125 | 26–50 | 51–100 |
| 101–200 | Caution level | 10001–15000 | 101–200 | 201–1000 | 126–200 | 51–150 | 101–250 |
| 201–300 | Alert level | 15001–30000 | 201–400 | 1001–2000 | 201–1000 | 151–250 | 251–400 |
| 301–400 | Alarm level | 30001–40000 | 401–600 | 2001–3000 | 1001–1800 | 251–350 | 401–500 |
| 401–500 | Emergency level | >40000 | >600 | >3000 | >1800 | >350 | >500 |

## 3  Results

The extracted data from Quito Environmental Municipal Secretary website was refined, reviewed, and evaluated. It is important to mention that there were 13 archives in total, with approximately two million records since 2004. The maps obtained are made up of three parts:

- Header: includes a title that describes the map purpose, and subtitles with the year of the analyzed data.
- Map body: it is the fundamental part and is where IQCA or climatic variables evaluated spatially is represented, along with some lines that show value changes in a form resembling contour lines. It includes a basemap which contains some main roads and labels that allow speedy orientation; and the symbol ▲, referred to monitoring stations used in the study.
- Legend: it is located to the right of the map body and corresponds to a sequential color scale that explains value variations with regard to the index.

These maps were extracted by year (from 2005 to 2020) and by each climate variable (wind direction, humidity, precipitation, and barometric pressure). Next, due to the fact that these are extensive results, one of them are shown per variable in Fig. 6.

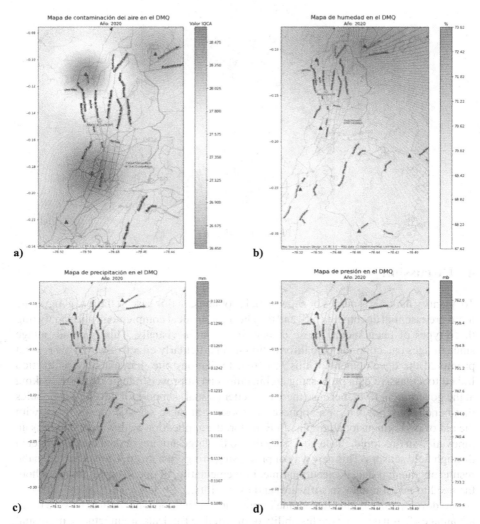

**Fig. 6.** Analyzed variables in DMQ in 2020: a) IQCA, b) humidity, c) precipitation, d) barometric pressure, e) wind direction.

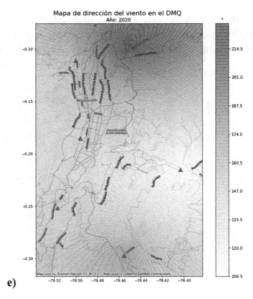

e)

**Fig. 6.** (*continued*)

## 4   Discussion

To quantify natural resources or show social problems, in this case pollution, geographic maps are essential documents [20] and they become an ideal complement when analyzing these types of phenomena. These display information visually. This is an advantage since images can communicate information in a particularly effective way. This is what prompted the development of this research: to demonstrate that spatial visualization linked to a massive data processing architecture can improve strategic decision-making at the government level, because there is a better (visual) support for developing policies that benefit city population as opposed to looking at these statistics textually or with the aid of two-dimensional graphs. In Ecuador, the application of this architecture is an innovation in this topic, made necessary due to the large amount of data that is collected through field sensors. This new way of processing brings benefits that are reflected in the results obtained: reduced execution time, implementation of open-source tools (without the need to invest money in software) and map utility.

To develop this architecture, some important contributions shown in [21] were taken advantage of, as it exposed the feasibility of integrating Big Data architecture with spatial interpolation to generate a predictive map of air pollution for the coming 24 h, implementing Apache Spark for improve processing speed. The same aspect was validated in our investigation. However, Pyspark was used as the programming language in processing and spatial visualization, due to its usefulness and the power of its tools, instead of using R, as proposed in the above-mentioned article. Furthermore, web platforms were found for use with regard to real-time, world-wide climate data processing, but the scale was too large to evaluate relatively small cities such as Quito, even though it is one of the largest cities in Ecuador.

On the other hand, results related the IQCA index were compared to the reality of the city. Air pollution levels were found to be desirable (optimal and good), so it could be inferred that the air quality of Quito is good. However, newspaper reports from 2018 stated: "On days with the highest contamination, the air in Quito exceeded 100 points, which is considered a 'caution' level" [5] as shown in Fig. 7.

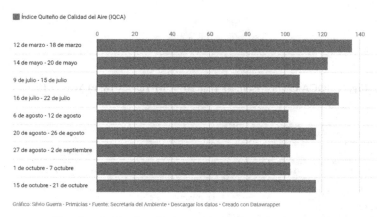

Índice Quiteño de Calidad del Aire (IQCA)

Gráfico: Silvio Guerra - Primicias • Fuente: Secretaría del Ambiente • Descargar los datos • Creado con Datawrapper

**Fig. 7.** Weekly air pollution evolution in Quito in 2018 [5].

Indeed, the index exceeded 100 points in a few weeks of the year (Fig. 7) and this could be deemed to be contrary to the results of the present investigation. However, it must be considered that all data had to be reduced to an annual average, due this data was large considerably; and since they were a few weeks with such a variation, the result was not affected. In Fig. 8, the index evolution can be appreciated one year before and one after the analyzed one, as evidence that there were no significant alterations, and almost the same pattern is perceived. In any case, at city level, analysis involving shorter time periods could be chosen. Another use that the system can be used for is monitoring increased values and searching for possible causes of change.

In relation to variables under consideration it is not possible to determinate the same pattern over the years, owing to various factors that affect them. For example, the air quality index is strongly affected by natural events such as volcanic eruptions [22], which cause value increments; or climate change effects that make it rain more or cause more droughts relative to previous years [23].

Finally, the efficiency of the proposed architecture was measured through a comparison of response times with and without using it. The spatial interpolation method (Kriging), in the Geographical Information System known as QGIS, took 4.52 s Fig. 9); while the developed system showed an execution time of 2.0 s (Fig. 10l), indicating a reduction of 56%.

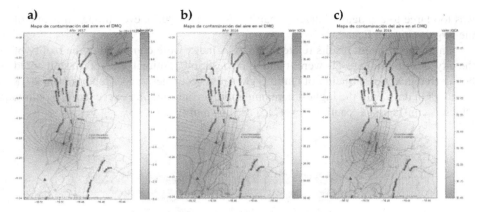

**Fig. 8.** IQCA Comparison: **a)** Year 2017; **b)** Year 2018; **c)** Year 2019.

```
C:\Users\Usuario\Documents>exit
Execution completed in 4.52 segundos
Resultados:
{'CV_RESIDUALS': 'C:/Users/Usuario/AppData/Local/Temp/processing_vdrkNK/
7c420152d52044e9ad0fe6f8be4ba33b/CV_RESIDUALS.shp',
'CV_SUMMARY': 'C:/Users/Usuario/AppData/Local/Temp/processing_vdrkNK/
a94c39217b234110abb95871c0fae328/CV_SUMMARY.shp',
'PREDICTION': 'C:/Users/Usuario/AppData/Local/Temp/processing_vdrkNK/
4365c5802cb04c0bbfbe489219916515/PREDICTION.sdat',
'VARIANCE': 'C:/Users/Usuario/AppData/Local/Temp/processing_vdrkNK/
ca81caf832334c85b5434869da2de556/VARIANCE.sdat'}
```

**Fig. 9.** Kriging runtime in QGIS.

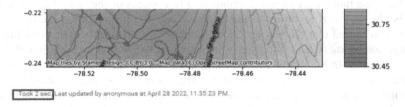

**Fig. 10.** Kriging runtime with proposed architecture.

Therefore, the research contribution of this work is an improvement in the traditional way of interpolation and map visualization, and offers a new open-source alternative providing an optimization of resources and time.

## 5  Conclusions and Further Work

According to the literature reviewed, research related to Big Data and geographic information has focused on evaluating prediction algorithm performance and time optimization. However, hardly any researchers have exposed the importance of visualizing this kind of data. The aim of this investigation was to concentrate on Big Data geographical management and visualization through maps, and corroborating that there is a time and resources saving in terms of this implementation.

In summary, the proposed architecture allows the processing of large volumes of data. In this case these include the geographical component based on a three-node cluster using the parallel data processing principle. It is open source and includes Apache Spark as the processing engine, managed by Yarn and linked to Zeppelin, to display spatially results through geographic maps.

In the case of Quito city, the IQCA index did not exceed an average of 100 points. This means that the air quality is within optimal and good levels. However, there are times of the year (days or weeks), when this index can increase due to excessive vehicular traffic, industrial discharges, or natural events. This was found in external sources and could not be validated by this study, since the data was added annually to present the maps. Data analysis with minor aggregation was proposed.

Based on this case study, the developed architecture can be used to model any environmental variable with large amounts of available data, which results in visualization in the form of maps, allowing data analytics to be linked with spatial representation in an innovative manner. In addition, this can contribute to making efficient decisions on public policy issues for example, because a continuous monitoring system could be implemented in conjunction with the city municipality in future.

In addition, subsequent studies could aim to improve air pollution prediction algorithms or any modeling of other environmental variables, whose results are presented by maps. Another idea is to implement data partitioning and spatio-temporal multi-perspective hierarchical organization as shown in [24], to effectively improve the storage and retrieval speed of trajectory Big Data.

**Acknowledgements.** We want to thank Francisco Gallegos and Brigitte Balón for their valuable ideas in the graphical interface integration into architecture. Since this article is derived from the postgraduate thesis of one of the authors, a special thanks to Lorena Recalde PhD. For her thesis writing review.

# References

1. Rodríguez, A., Cuvi, N.: Air pollution and environmental justice in Quito, Ecuador. Front. J. Soc. Technol. Environ. Sci. **8**(3), 13–46 (2019). https://doi.org/10.21664/2238-8869.2019v8i3.p13-46
2. World Health Organization (WHO), "Nine out of ten people around the world breathe polluted air." 2018
3. World Health Organization (WHO), "Ambient (outdoor) air quality and health." 2018
4. World Health Organization (WHO), "Ambient air pollution: A global assessment of exposure and burden of disease," 2016
5. Primicias Newspaper, "Quito air exceeds the permitted limits of contamination." 2019
6. Isabel, H., i Caralt, J.: Using analytics to support teacher decision-making. In: Actas de las XX JENUI, 2014, vol. 9, no. 11, pp. 83–90 (2014)
7. Barzaga, O., Vélez, H., Nevárez, J., Arroyo, M.: Information management and decision-making in educational organizations. Rev. Ciencias Soc. **XXV**(2), 120–130 (2019)

8. Rodríguez, Y., Pinto, M.: Information use model for strategic decision making in information organizations. Transinformacao **30**(1), 51–64 (2018). https://doi.org/10.1590/2318-088920 18000100005

9. Schmidt, D.C., Levine, D.L., Cleeland, C.: Architectures and patterns for developing high-performance, real-time ORB endsystems. Adv. Comput. **48**(C), 1–118 (1999). https://doi.org/10.1016/S0065-2458(08)60018-2

10. Apache Spark, "Spark Overview."

11. Ghaffar, A., Rahim, T.: Big data analysis: apache spark perspective. Glob. J. Comput. Sci. Technol. **XV**(1) (2015)

12. QGIS, "Spatial Analysis (Interpolation)," Documentation QGIS 2.18.

13. Ecological Transition and Demographic Challenge Ministry, "Air Quality Index."

14. MDMQ Environment Secretary, "Quito Air Quality Index." 2013

15. Romero, M., Diego, F., Álvarez, M.: Air pollution: its impact as a health problem. Rev. Cubana Hig. Epidemiol. **44**(2) (2006)

16. Campozano, L., Sanchez, E., Aviles, A., Samaniego, E.: Evaluation of infilling methods for time series of daily precipitation and temperature: the case of the Ecuadorian Andes. Maskana **5**(1) (2014)

17. Apache Spark, "Cluster Mode Overview."

18. Buitrago, B.: What's behind Apache Spark processing?, iWannaBeDataDriven (2020)

19. Dauphiné, A.: Models of basic structures: points and fields. Geogr. Model. Math. 163–197 (2017). https://doi.org/10.1016/B978-1-78548-225-0.50010-5

20. Delgado, E.: The map: an important means of support for the teaching of history. Rev. Mex. Investig. Educ. **7**(15), 331–356 (2002)

21. Asgari, M., Farnaghi, M., Ghaemi, Z.: Predictive mapping of urban air pollution using apache spark on a hadoop cluster. In: ACM International Conference Proceeding Series (ICPS), pp. 89–93 (2017). https://doi.org/10.1145/3141128.3141131

22. U.S. Environmental Protection Agency (EPA), "Volcanoes." 2021

23. National Geographic, "Climate change, droughts and floods." 2022

24. Yao, Z., Zhang, J., Li, T., Ding, Y.: A trajectory big data storage model incorporating partitioning and spatio-temporal multidimensional hierarchical organization. ISPRS Int. J. Geo-Inf. **11**(12) (2022). https://doi.org/10.3390/ijgi11120621

# The Role of Twitter in Media Coverage during Humanitarian Crises. Data mining from International News Agencies

Angel Torres-Toukoumidis[1,2]($\boxtimes$) (iD), Sofia E. Calle-Pesántez[1,2] (iD),
Santiago Castro[1,2] (iD), and Jorge Galán-Mena[1,2] (iD)

[1] Universidad Politécnica Salesiana, Cuenca 010105, Ecuador
atorrest@ups.edu.ec
[2] Universidad Nacional de Educación, Cañar 030154, Ecuador

**Abstract.** This study examines the use of Twitter during humanitarian crises and its impact on public opinion. The study analyzed over 3262 tweets related to crisis, war, tragedy, violence, riot, uprising, revolt, destruction, bombing, migration, and refugees from February 2021 to February 2023 from International News Agencies. The study found that Twitter, reveals the fragmentation of news consumption patterns on social media, which are influenced by the sources of information followed and strengthened by the platforms' algorithms. Furthermore, the study shows that news agencies' coverage of humanitarian crises is detectably fragmented, and governments and related organizations have an impact on them and use them for various purposes. The study concludes by recommending future research to expand the analysis to other social media and news agencies, as well as incorporate more advanced techniques for handling misinformation and analyzing the impact of social media on public opinion.

**Keywords:** Twitter · Humanitarian Crises · Data Mining · News Agencies · Tokenization · Python

## 1 Introduction

Social networks have revolutionised the way people communicate and exchange information worldwide. The progressive irruption of digital technologies affects the space where citizens inform themselves and debate issues of personal or collective interest, leading to normative and theoretical changes in the public sphere.

Social network users, being part of an open space together with an online community, influence and are influenced. The ongoing development of tools for advertising and propaganda within social platforms allows for mass or personalised targeting, based on people's online behaviour [1], with the potential for direct conscious or unconscious influence.

The role that social networks play in social capital and the determination of information acquisition through their use by users is relevant and allows us to understand the levels of retention and impact of the information that is disseminated, both positively and negatively [2].

Social networks play a fundamental role in the current life of society, with a direct impact on almost all aspects of its development. Therefore, platforms often have an impact on complex social processes, such as humanitarian crises, natural disasters, armed conflicts or other emergencies, where the rapid dissemination of information plays a crucial role, as well as misinformation and the spread of unverified data. Some empirically based studies have shown how fast, easy and widespread the dissemination of false, unverified or messy information is, and how its main means of dissemination is social media [3] and [4].

The negative effects and impact of this phenomenon are widely studied with the aim of mitigating or diminishing the collateral effects that harm social development; however, the strategies recognized by mass application by both the media and platform owners (identification, labelling, penalization, restriction, etc.) have not been effective, an argument supported by several research studies that demonstrate the permanence of disinformation even when false news has been restricted or discredited [5] and [6].

In the face of the various humanitarian crises that society is facing, social platforms have played a predominant role in the dissemination of information in real time, especially in relation to the aftermath of situations, the updating of information, the organization of efforts and the presentation of needs in order to request aid.

Understanding the needs of mitigating misinformation through social networks, it is essential to consider media literacy as a tool for this purpose. Several studies point to the need to incorporate this training into educational curricula so that users are equipped with the necessary knowledge to develop the ability to recognize and deal with fake news [7].

International news agencies play a key role in covering humanitarian crises, providing information globally. In the age of social media, these agencies have adapted their coverage strategies and used Twitter as a tool for gathering information, disseminating news and interacting with users.

Today, there are new elements that the digital environment has introduced into mass communication, which affect or socially influence this context. "New media question the role of professional journalists as the primary source of politically relevant information" [8].

This evokes a digital scenario with increased competition in news production and dissemination due to the proliferation of new, mainly digital media with unlimited access to audiences. This was not possible two decades ago because the media market was characterised by being restricted, more than anything else, in terms of the actors involved in it [9]. The present situation reveals unlimited possibilities for displaying information and informants, and therefore, the competition for attention and credibility is constantly growing.

With respect to Twitter, several authors, understanding the importance of the impact that the social network has on social phenomena and its users, have identified indicators to measure its influence on global political and social debates, with the challenge of finding measures to correctly calculate the impact and allow users to be classified according to relevance criteria that are very close to reality [10] and [11]. However, according to Casero-Ripollés [9] There is a lack of research on the use of Twitter indicators in the media system, so his study provides data on Spanish media and their impact on the political conversation on Twitter. He argues that these "come to play a key role in the digital context. They obtain the highest values in popularity and, above all, in authority on Twitter", for two reasons: (1) the agencies are primary producers of news for mass dissemination, so they have pre-eminence in information flows by volume of production; (2) a possible neutrality and their numerous users, which places them as privileged generators of connections with other relevant users on the network.

Meanwhile, studied the structure of news media networks in Indonesia, Malaysia and Singapore, where they found that the media in these countries have dispersed structures, so that "low density values indicate that the audience of each media outlet on Twitter does not massively overlap with each other", i.e. news consumption patterns on social networks are fragmented according to the sources of information that are followed [12]. Their results are consistent of news consumption patterns on Facebook. In closing, they indicate that social networks strengthen the fragmentation of news consumption patterns by encouraging users with similar preferences and overlapping opinions to establish contact.

Fragmentation at the news agency level is visible and detectable, much more so when humanitarian crises are unleashed, and just as official media accounts disperse information in line with the public agenda of the moment, governments and related organisations also have an impact on them and use them for various purposes. Boatwright & Pyle [13] in their study, indicate that "the official Twitter accounts of Ukraine and Kiev leveraged their online platforms to win the war of public opinion by broadcasting war atrocities in real time, engaging with other countries as a form of digital public diplomacy", with particular interests "related" to nationalism. Talabi, et al. [14] examined the use of storytelling for aid specifically for Nigerian refugees displaced as a result of the Russia-Ukraine war. The results showed a positive correlation between storytelling on social media and receiving aid.

## 1.1 The role of Twitter within complex social situations

Twitter, Facebook and Instagram are platforms that present the highest amount of interaction with respect to the issues addressed above, as well as being considerably more analyzed by academics due to their exposure of content in image and text, which facilitates the analysis and comparison of shared information. Likewise, these platforms are the ones that generate the most doubts when it comes to handling misinformation in complex social situations where their crowdsourcing methods and algorithms address the problem in a partial way and with almost unknown dynamics [15].

Twitter could be categorized as a convincing source for content analysis in social networks, mainly because its content is presented, for most users, in text, tagged by hashtags, with unique possibilities such as retweeting or sharing a tweet [2].

Twitter is one of the platforms that shows the most debate on global social phenomena. The public intellectual warfare from the Russia-Ukraine confrontation, which fights against physical, social and cyber systems, is an important example that needs to be addressed because of its current and future effects, not only on the current war landscape but also because of its effects on people's lives globally.

Wadhwani et al. [16] use the Twitter API and keywords to build a dataset that by applying TextBlog lexicon-based techniques searches for polarity and subjectivity of tweets related to the Russia-Ukraine conflict. Their results show the testing and development of models for understanding the phenomenon with engineering and machine learning techniques, with an important contribution to the current and future understanding of the exchange of information on the topic among users of the platform.

Mainych et al. [17] analyze the twitter discourse on the Russia-Ukraine war, considering the rhythms and changes that occur around the topic. They used a set of hashtags to study a cluster of popular tweets, where the majority of hashtags corresponded to #Ukraine, in second place #NATO and in third place #UkarinerussiaWar. The first week of the war was marked by a record 4 000 000 news formats on Twitter about the situation in Ukraine, but the second week the trend changes drastically and the number of mentions about the situation drops (during the 50 days since the beginning of the invasion the number decreases to 500 000). Finally, the study indicates that the cluster analysis shows a global focus on Ukraine as a victim of war and Russia as an aggressor.

Twitter has become a central platform for real-time information dissemination during humanitarian crises. Its unique features, such as the brevity of tweets, the ability to use hashtags to categorize content, and spread of messages through retweets, have made Twitter a popular channel for sharing news and reports related to emergency situations. It will examine how Twitter's immediacy and global reach allow critical information to reach a wide audience during humanitarian crises.

The profiles of users involved in the construction of public digital opinion debated on Twitter regarding the Ukraine-Russia conflict are a source of information that should be considered when analysing the issues within the network. Donofrio et al. [18] carried out a study of the audiences of the profiles of the Government of the Russian Federation (@GovernmentRF) and the Office of the President of Ukraine (@APUkraine). It is determined that followers show a recurrent use of the words "no war" or "reject" in their published tweets and the predominant hashtags are related to cities affected by the war:

Firstly, the predominance of the male gender among the followers of the Government of the Russian Federation and the Office of the President of Ukraine; secondly, a certain generational similarity also stands out, in the sense that the followers of both profiles have similar ages; and, thirdly, regarding the biographical descriptions, as demonstrated in the analysis, the audience of the two profiles share "interests", that is, taking into account the words most followed by the followers of both accounts, we can highlight the interest in values and areas such as love, peace and life. Turning to the differences, the most marked ones are in terms of the nationality and city of residence of the followers. In contrast to the considerable geographical dispersion of the social audience of the Russian government profile - which shows very high percentages in the USA and India among others - more than 80% of the followers of the profile of the Ukrainian President's Office are Ukrainian. Similar behaviour with respect to place of residence, data in which the territorial dispersion is maintained in the case of the followers of the Russian account and the preponderance of users from the largest cities in Ukrainian territory for the official Ukrainian account.

The above theoretical overview provides key parameters for identifying the impact of social media on public opinion, on the establishment of the media agenda and specifically, in humanitarian crises, its effects and possibilities. During humanitarian crises, social networks have proven to be a powerful tool for disseminating information and mobilising aid quickly and effectively. Previous studies have highlighted the capacity of social media to facilitate citizen participation, collaboration and response in emergency situations. In the context of this study, it will explore how Twitter, one of the main social networks, plays a crucial role in the dissemination of information during humanitarian crises. Therefore, the following research questions are established: How do different news sources cover humanitarian crises on Twitter, and what factors influence the fragmentation of news consumption patterns on social networks? What are the most effective strategies for managing misinformation on Twitter during humanitarian crises, and how can these strategies be applied to maximize citizen engagement and collaboration? How can social media platforms such as Twitter be leveraged to mobilize aid quickly and effectively during humanitarian crises, and what are the key challenges that need to be addressed to achieve this goal?

## 2  Methodology

The general objective of this research was to analyse the media coverage of international news agencies on Twitter. To do so, the specific objectives were to semantically categorise the news presented by the international news agencies and to review the discursive connection of the news presented in the agencies.

In order to achieve the aforementioned objectives, an exploratory study was conducted on lexical combinations to approach the metatextual properties and characteristics of the news [19 20], in which Twitter API and the Tweepy library were used to capture data presented in the following 31 international news agencies (Table 1):

Tweets from February 2022 to February 2023 referring to word families linked to crisis, war, tragedy, fight, violence, riot, uprising, revolt, destruction, bombing, migration and refugees were downloaded and stored in a PostgreSQL database, then Python programming language was applied for the selection process, in which data pre-processing was carried out to remove irrelevant mentions, links and hashtags. A text cleaning and tokenisation function was applied in which punctuation marks were removed, transforming all text to lowercase, suppressing web pages within tweets, multiple white spaces, numbers and special characters. Resulting in a total of 3262 tweets analysed on this research. The SQL query written in PostgreSQL language shows first the countries in humanitarian crises followed by the words linked to the crisis situations.

The programming code for the research was the following (Table 2):

It is worth mentioning that the Context library was used in the methodological process to carry out the analysis of word frequency in the tweets. The most common words in the tweets were identified and their distribution and variation over time were analysed. The most frequent and differentiating words for each agency were identified, i.e. those that are more common in certain groups of tweets and less common in others. The Context library to review the sentiments expressed in tweets. Tweets with positive, negative and neutral sentiment were identified. We analysed the distribution of sentiments expressed

**Table 1.** News Agency and country

| News agency | Country |
| --- | --- |
| 1. Ethiopia News Agency | Ethiopia |
| 2. Polish Press Agency | Poland |
| 3. Khaama Press | Afghanistan |
| 4. Armenpress News | Armenia |
| 5. 'Agência Lusa' | Portugal |
| 6. Catholic News Agency | United States |
| 7. Ukrainian News | Ukraine |
| 8. Sky News | United Kingdom |
| 9. Agencia Bolivariana de Información | Venezuela |
| 10. Philippine News Agency | Phillipines |
| 11. Qatar News Agency | Qatar |
| 12. Bloomberg | United States |
| 13. Agência Brasil' | Brazil |
| 14. FARS News Agency | Syria |
| 15. CTK_news | Czech Republic |
| 16. 'Press Trust of India' | India |
| 17. 'News Agency Nigeria | Nigeria |
| 18. 'South Sudan News Agency' | South Sudan |
| 19. 'Slovene Press Agency' | Slovenia |
| 20. 'BBC News Mundo' | United Kingdom |
| 21. 'EFE Noticias' | Spain |
| 22. 'Australian Associated Press | Australia |
| 23. Reuters | United Kingdom |
| 24. Agence France-Presse | France |
| 25. 'African News Agency' | South Africa |

in tweets over time and in relation to the main themes identified in the word frequency analysis. The correlation between bigrams and trigrams was analysed. Identifying the most common word combinations in the tweets and their relationship to the main themes in the word frequency analysis.

The results obtained in the different analyses are detailed below. The relationships between the main themes identified and the sentiments expressed in the tweets were analyzed. In addition, the main trends and patterns in the data were identified and their implications discussed. Using the Context library allowed the analyses of word clouds, word frequency, bigraphs, scatter plots, and concurrence plots.

**Table 2.** Programming code for SQL query

```
1.  SELECT * FROM public.tweets AS tn
2.  WHERE
3.  (LOWER(tn."Text") SIMILAR TO '%ukraine%|%afghanistan%|%sy
    ria%|%yemen%|%venezuela%|%ethiopia%|%myanmar%|%central
    african republic%|%iraq%|%south sudan%'
4.  AND (LOWER(tn."Text") SIMILAR TO '%displaced
    ukrain%|%displaced        afghanistan%|%displaced        sy-
    ria%|%displaced  yemen%|%displaced  venezuela%|%displaced
    ethiopia%|%displaced myanmar%|%displaced central african
    republic%|%displaced iraq%|%displaced south sudan%'
5.  OR LOWER(tn."Text") SIMILAR TO '%refugee%|%displaced peo-
    ple%|%displaced              person%|%refugee%|%asylum
    seek%|%exile%|%stateless people%'
6.  OR LOWER(tn."Text") SIMILAR TO '%crisis%|%war%|%conflict%
    |%tragedy%|%fight%|%violence%|%unrest%|%uprising%|%destru
    ction%|%bombing%|%migration%|%adlib%|%aleppo%')) OR
7.  (LOWER(tn."Text") SIMILAR TO '%ucrania%|%afghanistán%|%si
    ria%|%etiopía%|%etiopia%|%república          centroafrica-
    na%|%republica    centroafricana%|%irak%|%sudán      del
    sur%|%sudan del sur%'
8.  AND (LOWER(tn."Text") SIMILAR TO '%displaced
    ukrain%|%displaced        afghanistan%|%displaced        syr-
    ia%|%displaced  yemen%|%displaced  venezuela%|%displaced
    ethiopia%|%displaced myanmar%|%displaced central african
    republic%|%displaced iraq%|%displaced south sudan%'
9.  OR LOWER(tn."Text") SIMILAR TO '%refigiad%|%población
    desplazada%|%personas  desplazadas%|%solicitud  de  asi-
    lo%|%solicitante  de  asilo%|%solicitantes  de  asi-
    lo%|%exilio%|%personas sin estado%|%exilia%|%apátridas%'
10.    OR LOWER(tn."Text") SIMILAR TO '%guerra%|%tragedia%|%p
    elea%|%violencia%|%disturbios%|%sublevación%|%sublevacion
    %|%revuelta%|%destrucción%|%destruccion%|%bombardeo%|%bom
    bardeando%|%migración%|%migracion%'))
```

## 3   Results

The most frequent words found in the content from the analysis of the information from the tweets of the international agencies. In which we can see that the most frequent words are Ukraine, referring to the humanitarian crisis that the country is experiencing due to the Russian invasion, we can also observe the terms Sudan and Poland, which do not show that they have not been as frequently published as Ukraine. In short, from the data obtained, it was evident that the 5 most repeated monograms were: Ukraine with 1158 times, followed by war with 897 times, Russia which has been repeated 348 times, Sudan 206 times and conflict with 165 times (Fig. 1).

Figure 2 below on bigrams shows a word cloud on the most common bigrams. A bigram consists of two words that appear together frequently in the captured tweets. The most repeated have been war Ukraine (313 times), South Sudan (164 times), Ukraine

**Fig. 1.** Word cloud of most common monograms.

war (116 times), prime minister (82 times), Russia Ukraine (56 times), Ukraine Russia (54 times), Russia war (45 times).

**Fig. 2.** Word cloud of most common bigrams.

The trigram is a sequence of three words that appear together frequently in a specific text or corpus of data. In the trigram three words are re-presented on the horizontal axis, while the frequency of occurrence of the trigram is represented on the vertical axis, being mainly monopolized by terms related to the Russia-Ukraine war, among them are: "Ukraine Russia Attack", Russia War Ukraine" "Polish Prime Minister", "Prime Minister said", "President Vladimir Putin", "War torn Ukraine" (Table 3).

**Table 3.** Trigram Tweets in Humanitarian Crises

| Trigram | Frequency |
|---|---|
| "Ukraine Russia Attack" | 32 tweets |
| , Russia War Ukraine" | 29 tweets |
| "Polish Prime Minister", | 28 tweets |
| "Prime Minister said", | 24 tweets |
| "President Vladimir Putin", | 22 tweets |
| "War torn Ukraine | 19 tweets |
| Russia Ukraine war | 19 tweets |
| Morawiecki Polish Prime | 18 tweets |
| Russia invasion Ukraine | 16 tweets |
| Russia Ukraine Conflict | 13 tweets |

In the Fig. 3 on the dispersion of the frequency of Tweets, it can be observed that, although all international agencies address the issue of war, not all of them do so with the same frequency. A comparison of the terms "Ukraine" and "Sudan" clearly shows the different level of interest that international agencies have in each of these terms. This analysis demonstrates the dynamics and varied attention that international agencies pay to different global events, which can be of great relevance for understanding media coverage of these issues in international contexts.

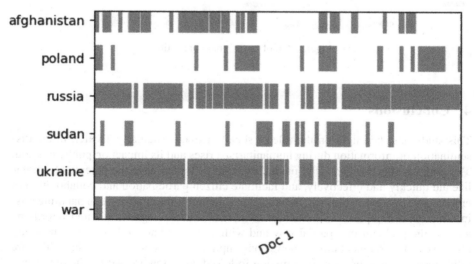

**Fig.3.** Graph of terms dispersion in news agencies.

Continuing with the presentation of results, a map shows the interconnection of the main keywords in a complex web (Fig. 4). In this map, it can be clearly seen that the words "Russia" and "Ukraine" are two of the main keywords at the center of the network, standing out as fundamental nodes in the represented connections. This visual approach allows to visualize in a striking way the relevance and prominence of these two keywords in the analyzed context, highlighting the importance they have in the identified connections. This graphical representation provides a deeper and more visual understanding of the relationship and interaction between the keywords.

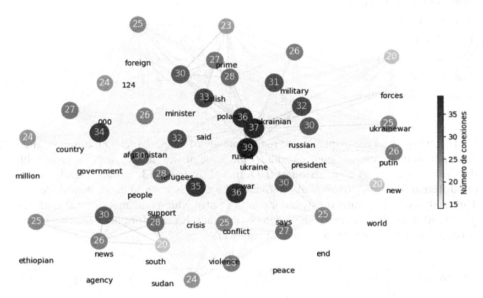

**Fig.4.** Map of terms' interconnection

## 4    Conclusions

This study has shed light on the role of social media, particularly Twitter, in the dissemination of information during humanitarian crises and its impact on public opinion. The findings suggest that social media, especially Twitter, have the potential to mobilize aid quickly and effectively, and facilitate citizen participation and collaboration in emergency situations. However, the study also highlights the challenges of handling misinformation in complex social situations, where crowdsourcing methods and algorithms address the problem in a partial way and with almost unknown dynamics. The study also reveals the fragmentation of news consumption patterns on social media, which are influenced by the sources of information followed and strengthened by the platforms' algorithms. Furthermore, the study shows that news agencies' coverage of humanitarian crises is detectably fragmented, and governments and related organizations have an impact on them and use them for various purposes. While 2 years of news coverage linked to humanitarian crises were covered on this research, Russia-Ukraine war has monopolized media coverage of humanitarian crises, overlapping other types of crises as it happened in Afghanistan, Syria, Yemen, Venezuela, Myanmar, Central African Republic and Iraq which are invisible to international news agencies. Irrespective of the underlying reasons for this trend, it is crucial to underscore that media products may be equally intertwined with the spectacle-driven setting, extensive media dissemination, polarization, and debates they evoke within the global public opinion sphere, thereby contributing to a more profound exploration of their content..

The limitations of this study include the focus on Twitter as the main social media and the limited number of international news agencies analyzed. Future research could expand the analysis to other social networks and news agencies, as well as incorporate more advanced techniques for handling misinformation and analyzing the impact of social media on public opinion. In conclusion, this study contributes to the understanding of the role of social media in humanitarian crises and its impact on public opinion. It highlights the potential of social networks to mobilize aid and facilitate citizen participation, but also the challenges of handling misinformation and the fragmentation of news consumption patterns. Future research could build on these findings to develop more effective strategies for handling misinformation and promoting a more accurate and diverse news coverage on social networks.

# References

1. Logan, A.P., LaCasse, P.M., Lunday, B.J.: Social network analysis of Twitter interactions: a directed multilayer network approach. Soc. Netw. Anal. Min. **13**(1), 89–124 (2023). https://doi.org/10.1007/s13278-023-01063-2
2. Bernardino, S., Santos, J.F., Silva, P.: Acquiring information for the social organization: the role of social media use and social capital. Soc. Netw. Anal. Min. **13**(1), 35–48 (2023). https://doi.org/10.1007/s13278-023-01039-2
3. Törnberg, P.: Echo chambers and viral misinformation: modeling fake news as com-plex contagion. PLOS ONE **13**(9) 234–456 (2018). e0203958. https://doi.org/10.1371/journal.pone.0203958
4. Vosoughi, S., Roy, D., Aral, S.: The spread of true and false news online. Science (2018). https://doi.org/10.1126/science.aap9559
5. Ecker, U.K.H., Hogan, J.L., Lewandowsky, S.: Reminders and repetition of misinformation: helping or hindering its retraction? J. Appl. Res. Mem. Cogn. **6**(2), 185–192 (2017). https://doi.org/10.1016/j.jarmac.2017.01.014
6. Pennycook, G., Rand, D.G.: Lazy, not biased: Susceptibility to partisan fake news is better explained by lack of reasoning than by motivated reasoning. Cognition **188**, 39–50 (2019). https://doi.org/10.1016/j.cognition.2018.06.011
7. Mihailidis, P., Viotty, S.: Spreadable spectacle in digital culture: civic expres-sion, fake news, and the role of media literacies in "post-fact" society. Am. Behav. Sci. **61**(4), 441–454 (2017). https://doi.org/10.1177/0002764217701217
8. Williams, B.A., Delli Carpini, M.X.: After Broadcast News | American Government, Politics and Policy. Cambridge University Press, UK (2011)
9. Casero-Ripollés, A.: Influencia de los medios de comunicación en la conversa-ción política en Twitter. Icono **14**, 18(1) (2020). https://doi.org/10.7195/ri14.v18i1.1527

10. Razis, G., Anagnostopoulos, I., Zeadally, S.: Modeling Influence with semantics in social networks: a survey. ACM Comput. Surv. **53**(1), 7–38 (2020). https://doi.org/10.1145/336 9780

11. Riquelme, F., González-Cantergiani, P.: Measuring user influence on Twitter: a survey. Inf. Process. Manage. **52**(5), 949–975 (2016). https://doi.org/10.1016/j.ipm.2016.04.003

12. Gaol, F.L., Maulana, A., Matsuo, T.: News consumption patterns on Twitter: fragmentation study on the online news media network. Heliyon **6**(10), e05169 (2020). https://doi.org/10.1016/j.heliyon.2020.e05169

13. Boatwright, B.C., Pyle, A.S.: "Don't mess with Ukrainian farmers": an examination of Ukraine and Kyiv's official Twitter accounts as crisis communication, public diplomacy, and nation building during Russian invasion. Public Relat. Rev. **49**(3), 102338 (2023). https://doi.org/10.1016/j.pubrev.2023.102338

14. Talabi, F.O., et al.: The use of social media storytelling for help-seeking and help-receiving among Nigerian refugees of the Ukraine-Russia war. Telematics Inform. **71**, 101836 (2022). https://doi.org/10.1016/j.tele.2022.101836

15. Andersen, J., Søe, S.O.: Communicative actions we live by: the problem with fact-checking, tagging or flagging fake news – the case of Facebook. Eur. J. Commun. **35**(2), 126–139 (2020). https://doi.org/10.1177/0267323119894489

16. Wadhwani, G.K., Varshney, P.K., Gupta, A., Kumar, S.: Sentiment analysis and comprehensive evaluation of supervised machine learning models using Twitter data on Russia-Ukraine war. SN Comput. Sci. **4**(4), 346 (2023). https://doi.org/10.1007/s42979-023-01790-5

17. Mainych, S., Bulhakova, A., Vysotska, V.: Cluster analysis of discussions change dynamics on Twitter about war in Ukraine, vol. 3396, pp. 490-530 (2023)

18. Donofrio, A., Rubio Moraga, Á.L., Abellán Guzmán, C.: Rusia-Ucrania, un aná-lisis comparativo de la audiencia en Twitter de los perfiles del Gobierno de la Federación Rusa y la Oficina del presidente de Ucrania. Revista Latina de Comunicación Social **81**, 2–14 (2023)

19. Torres-Toukoumidis, A., Lagares-Díez, N., Barredo-Ibáñez, D.: Accountability journalism during the emergence of COVID-19: evaluation of transparency in official fact-checking platforms. In: Rocha, Á., Reis, J.L., Peter, M.K., Cayolla, R., Loureiro, S., Bogdanović, Z. (eds.) Marketing and Smart Technologies. SIST, vol. 205, pp. 561–572. Springer, Singapore (2021). https://doi.org/10.1007/978-981-33-4183-8_44

20. Campos, M.M., Mujica, L.A.: El análisis de contenido: una forma de abordaje metodológico. Laurus **14**(27), 129–144 (2008)

# Applied Metaheuristics in International Trading: A Systematic Review

Esteban Crespo-Martínez[1]([✉])(iD), Luis Tonon-Ordóñez[1,2](iD),
Marcos Orellana[1](iD), and Juan Fernando Lima[1](iD)

[1] Computer Science Research & Development Laboratory (LIDI),
University of Azuay, Cuenca, Ecuador
{ecrespo,ltonon,marore,flima}@uazuay.edu.ec
[2] Economics School, University of Azuay, Cuenca, Ecuador

**Abstract.** In specific cases, computational techniques that support the operations of international trade can be a problem that must be evaluated to achieve the maximum benefit for companies. The application of metaheuristics as techniques to solve situations that may arise in operations, such as transportation, logistics, market forecasts, customs valuation, or trade agreements. This work aims to conduct a systematic review of the literature applying the PRISMA method for reviewing and quality assurance to determine the state of literature regarding the use of metaheuristic algorithms in commercial exchange. Four scientific databases were explored to collect and generate evidence to describe a qualitative analysis among the primary studies. In addition, textometric analysis was carried out using the Iramuteq software to identify groups of words enriching the analysis. It is concluded that the use of metaheuristics has been applied in several areas of commercial exchange such as shipping, fleet, and trajectory management; and these are part of a vast field in development.

**Keywords:** Metaheuristic approaches · PRISMA · Logistics · Commodities trading · Routing · Systematic Literature Review

## 1 Introduction

There are many essential challenges in goods trade, an important aspect in the second half of the twentieth century, where globalization is the principal phenomenon [7], followed by wars, instability, and markets [13]. Consequently, enterprises need to become more efficient in manufacturing, logistics and routing to create competitive advantages. People have used heuristics throughout history to solve numerous challenging optimization problems.

According to [45], the scientific study of Metaheuristics is a relatively new topic. In their work, they identify five stages in the time transition: (1) the pre-theoretical period, until 1940, where heuristics and metaheuristics were used but not formally studied; (2) the early period, between 1940 and 1980, where the first

© The Author(s), under exclusive license to Springer Nature Switzerland AG 2023
J. Maldonado-Mahauad et al. (Eds.): TICEC 2023, CCIS 1885, pp. 95–112, 2023.
https://doi.org/10.1007/978-3-031-45438-7_7

formal studies on heuristics appear; (3) the method-centric period, between 1980 and 2000, during which the field of metaheuristics truly takes off, and multiple methods are proposed; (4) the framework-centric period, between 2000 and now, during which the insight grows that metaheuristics are more usefully described as frameworks, and not as methods; and finally (5) the scientific period, the future, where the design of metaheuristics becomes science instead of an art.

According to [44] "A metaheuristic is a high-level problem-independent algorithmic framework that provides a set of guidelines or strategies to develop heuristic optimization algorithms". The term "metaheuristic" is used for two entirely different things: (1) the first consists of a high-level framework, a set of concepts and strategies that blend and offer a perspective on the development of optimization algorithms, and (2) the term "metaheuristic" denotes a specific implementation of an algorithm based on such a framework (or on a combination of concepts from different frameworks) designed to find a solution to a specific optimization problem [45]. There are many areas of metaheuristics application, for example, agricultural land use optimization [34], automated business process discovery [6], portfolio optimization and risk management [18–20], portfolio selection methods [22], supply chain management [37], among others. The literature review is essential to academic research [50]. In this way, the main goal of this paper is to provide both regular users and newcomers with a literature review of metaheuristics applied in international trade. Specifically, the research questions to solve are:

- Q1: What metaheuristics techniques can be used in international trading?
- Q2: What metaheuristic algorithms are the best for use in international trading?
- Q3: What are the main problems with metaheuristic algorithms application?
- Q4: How are metaheuristic algorithms addressed in exports and imports?

For those purposes, the methodology called PRISMA (Preferred Reporting Items for Systematic reviews and Meta-Analysis methodology) [47] was applied, an upgrade and ampliation from QUOROM (Quality of Reporting Of Meta-Analysis) [30]. The following scientific databases: ABI-ProQuest, Taylor and Francis, Emerald, and Scopus were consulted, considering papers, conference papers, and book chapters. This article is divided into the following sections: (1) the PRISMA method application, (2) the text analysis results and discussion, and (3) the conclusions.

## 2   Method

The relevance of metaheuristic algorithms inside enterprises is highlighted in problems such as Optimization problems, traveling salesman problem, job shop scheduling, multicast routing, among others. And metaheuristic algorithms as binary, chaotic, multiobjective, and hybrid are used to accomplish these tasks [26]. Therefore, a systematic method to collect data about algorithms in international trading is need. The PRISMA method was used for this literature review, as suggested by Bueno et al. [12]. This method is widely used in health, business management, education, and engineering. On the other hand, textometry analysis was performed. Textometry is a computational approach or methodology that involves the quantitative analysis of large collections of texts. It aims to extract meaningful information and patterns from texts using various statistical and linguistic techniques [40].

## 2.1  Information Sources

The scientific databases, which were described in the above section, were considered to perform the identification phase. Also, other literature was recompiled manually from Google Scholar. In Fig. 1, the application of the PRISMA method is exposed, considering their four phases: (1) identification; (2) screening; (3) eligibility; and (4) inclusion. At this stage, articles, book chapters and conference papers related to metaheuristics applied to commerce trading topics, specifically on goods importation and exportation activities.

## 2.2  Search

Different strategies were used to structure the search strings, highlighting: the logical connectors (OR, AND), Quotes, and parentheses operators were used for search string construction. Considering these operators and the keywords (1) metaheuristics, (2) importation; (3) exportation; (4) trade; and (5) commerce, the research strings were built. Then, these were applied to each database. Table 1 shows the search string used in each scientific repository.

## 2.3  Data Collection Process

Until 1940, heuristic and even metaheuristics are used bud not formally studied. But is between 1980 and 2000 where the field of metaheuristics truly takes off [45]. The intention of this work was to update the existing information in the last 5 years related with the application of metaheuristics in international trade. In this way, the time interval was from 2018 to 2022. Only works written in English and Spanish will be considered in this review based on the main objective. After completing these searches, 224 manuscripts were identified in total. Also, through a manual search, 5 manuscripts were added to the results. Three consecutive steps were used to filter the results obtained in the initial screening phase. First, defined search limiters, relevant subject areas, and duplications were filtered. Second, unrelated articles were excluded based on their titles and abstracts.

As a result, 0 duplicate and 4 scientific documents that did not meet the search criteria were excluded, and the remaining 90 were subsequently screened. In the third step, eligibility was evaluated, and 57 scientific documents were rejected, which left 27 eligible documents that were considered valid for systematic review purposes. The rejected documents did not address to solve the

**Table 1.** Search strings used per scientific repository.

| Repository | String | Total of articles | Selected articles after screening |
|---|---|---|---|
| ABI (Proquest) | ft((Metaheuristics OR metaheuristica)) AND ti((importation OR exportation OR trade OR international trading OR importacion OR exportacion OR intercambio OR international commerce OR comercio)) | 14 | 0 |
| Taylor | ((Metaheuristics OR metaheuristica)) AND ((importation OR exportation OR trade OR importacion OR international trading OR comercio internacional OR exportacion OR intercambio OR commerce OR comercio)) | 152 | 15 |
| Emerald | ((Metaheuristics OR metaheuristica)) AND ((importation OR exportation OR trade OR importacion OR exportacion OR intercambio OR commerce OR comercio OR international trading OR comercio internacional)) | 2 | 0 |
| Scopus | (TITLE-ABS-KEY ( international AND trading ) OR TITLE-ABS-KEY ( comercio AND exterior ) OR TITLE-ABS-KEY ( commerce ) OR TITLE-ABS-KEY ( exportation) OR TITLE-ABS-KEY ( importation ) OR TITLE-ABS-KEY ( importacion) OR TITLE-ABS-KEY ( exportacion ) AND TITLE-ABS-KEY ( metaheuristics) OR TITLE-ABS-KEY ( metaheuristica ) ) AND PUBYEAR ¿ 2017 AND PUBYEAR ¡ 2023 AND ( LIMIT-TO ( LANGUAGE , "English" ) OR LIMIT-TO ( LANGUAGE , "Spanish" ) ) | 51 | 4 |

research questions. Some of the obtained manuscripts were related to other topics, such as electrical energy, oil and gas, construction projects, manufacturing, and satellite systems. Finally, 17 studies were included in qualitative studies, and from those, 10 were quantitative for meta-analysis. Figure 1 exposes the application of the PRISMA method.

A spreadsheet was developed in Excel to classify the metadata of the collected articles. Seeking to answer the research question 1: "What metaheuristics techniques can be used in international trading?", the following variables were identified:

The following variables were considered to solve research question 2: "What metaheuristic algorithms are the best for use in international trading?"

To solve research question 3: "RQ3 What are the main problems that try to solve in international trading the metaheuristic algorithms application?"

Finally, to solve research question 4, the following variables were considered.

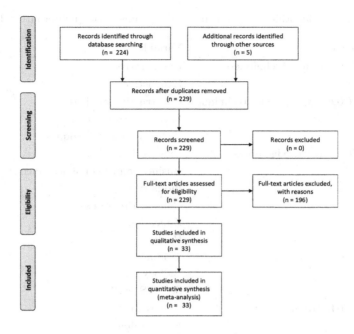

**Fig. 1.** Data collection using the PRISMA method.

## 3    Results

The following section shows the obtained results, set out in two sections. First, Sect. 3.1 exposes a general view of analyzed studies. Then, Sect. 3.2 sets out and discusses the results in detail.

### 3.1    Text Analysis

The text analysis was divided into three parts: (1) Lexicographic analysis, (2) Cluster analysis using Descending Hierarchical Classification (Reinert method), and (3) Similarity analysis. Iramuteq software, which helps to perform a clear and concise analysis of the information collected, was used for this purpose. Text analyses are exposed in this section. The steps for those aim, according to [42], was: (1) textual corpus unit reduction; (2) lemmatization or reducing words to their roots; (3) creating context units; (4) descending hierarchical classification; and (5) graph analysis. In this context, the meaning of the word "corpus" which comes from the Latin "body" is clarified, but in linguistics, corpus refers to a text collection stored in an electronic database (Table 2).

**Lexicographic Analysis.** Lexicographic analyses offer a fresh and comprehensive method for mapping literature. They employ content analyses to determine

**Table 2.** Variables identified in metaheuristics techniques used in international trading.

| Scope | Variable |
|---|---|
| EC01: Exact Techniques | Enumerative |
| | Exhaustive |
| EC02: Approximate Techniques | Constructive method |
| | Local search method |
| | Metaheuristic Techniques |
| EC03: Knowledge areas | Engineering Science |
| | Business and Economics Science |
| | Industry |
| | General Programs |
| | Education |
| | Health |
| | Trading |
| | Biology |
| | Social Science |
| EC04: Trading | Importation |
| | Exportation |

the extent of various journals and uncover the semantic and paradigmatic connections among the vocabulary (lexicon) employed within them [35]. The titles, keywords, and abstracts of 33 scientific papers were considered in this analysis, obtained from the PRISMA method application. The application of this lexicometry analysis provides the starting point for the systematic review, identifying the initial data for the rest of the analysis. To complement, a lemmatization process was applied to obtain these preliminary results, shown in Table 6.

## 3.2 Data Collection

**Cluster Analysis.** Five clusters were identified by applying the Reinert method [42] of cluster analyzed by applying the descending hierarchical classification of the active forms, as shown in Fig. 2.

Figure 3, on the other hand, presents another visualization of the cluster classification, grouping by the most repeatable words.

Factorial Correspondence Analysis (FCA) was performed to analyze categorical data and explore the relationships between multiple variables simultaneously. FCA is a multivariate statistical technique that allows for identifying latent factors that explain the associations between categorical variables [11]. Figure 5 exposes the FCA of frequently used words. This figure is the result of applying the descending hierarchical classification with the most frequent active words grouped together, potentially indicating common themes or topics within the

Table 3. Metaheuristics algorithms used in international trading.

| Scope | Variables |
|---|---|
| EC05: Metaheuristics algorithms | Simulated annealing (Kirkpatrick et al., 1983) |
| | Ant colony optimization (ACO) (Dorigo, 1992) |
| | Particle swarm optimization (PSO) (Kennedy & Eberhart, 1995) |
| | Harmony search (HS) (Geem, Kim & Loganathan, 2001) |
| | Artificial bee colony algorithm (Karaboga, 2005) |
| | Bees algorithm (Pham, 2005) |
| | Imperialist competitive algorithm (Atashpaz-Gargari & Lucas, 2007) |
| | River formation dynamics (Rabanal, Rodríguez & Rubio, 2007) |
| | Gravitational search algorithm (Rashedi, Nezamabadi-pour & Saryazdi,2009) |
| | Bat algorithm (Yang, 2010) |
| | Spiral optimisation (SPO) algorithm (Tamura & Yasuda 2011, 2016–2017) |
| | Artificial swarm intelligence (Rosenberg, 2014) |

dataset. This approach helps identify patterns and relationships between words, allowing a better understanding of the underlying data (Table 3).

**Cluster 1: Metaheuristics and Algorithms.** This is the most important cluster, representing the 28.9% of the total. According to [24], most real-world problems have high complexity, non-linear constraints, interdependencies amongst variables and ample solution space, where metaheuristic algorithms let to solve complex optimization problems in real time [3–19,21]. It is essential to know that multiple optimization methods allow for a reasonably good solution in a reasonable amount of time. The optimization methods refer to finding the best value of a set of variables to achieve the goal of minimizing or maximizing an objective function subject to a given set of constraints. Two techniques were identified by [46]: (1) the exact techniques that involve enumerative and exhaustive methods; and (2) approximate techniques, which consider the constructive method, the local search method and the metaheuristic technique. Figure 4 clearly shows in a bubble chart that metaheuristic techniques are used to solve business and economics science and trading situations, among others.

Metaheuristic methods are essential to global optimization algorithms, often inspired by nature with multiple interaction agents [24,44]. Here, Genetic Algorithms (GA) is a population-based algorithm [2], and it solves the problem of maintaining a population of candidate solutions and creating new solutions by combining existing ones with the usage of the crossover [43], mutation and selection operators and keeping the candidate solution with the currently best fit-

**Table 4.** Main problems that try to solve. Variables identified in metaheuristics techniques used in international trading.

| Scope | Variable |
|---|---|
| EC06: Transport | Maritime |
| | Aerial |
| | Terrestrial |
| EC7: Import and Export situations | Logistics |
| | Transport |
| | Market Prediction |
| | Tariff Classification |
| | Customs Valuation |
| | Free Trade Agreements / Trade Preferences |
| | Antidumping and Countervailing Duties |
| | Country of Origin Determinations and Country of Origin Marking |
| | Intellectual Property Rights |
| | Special Tariff Provisions |
| | Custom Penalties |
| | Drawback |
| | Customs compliance programs and Customs Audits |
| | Foreign Trade Zones |
| | Vessel Manifests and proprietary data |
| | Exports Subject to Control and the Agencies Involved |
| | Deemed Exports |
| | Encryption Items |
| | Export Control Reform |
| | Payment processing |
| | Language barriers |
| | Legal Systems |

ness [21]. GA is widely known as a probabilistic technique for solving optimization problems based on population genetics [1] (Table 4).

Multi genetic analysis is an essential tool in understanding the genetic makeup of organisms. It involves the analysis of multiple genes in an organism, allowing for a more comprehensive understanding of its traits and characteristics. In commercial exchange, multigenetic analysis can be used to identify the genetic makeup of crops and livestock, which is vital for ensuring the quality and safety of food products [39]. The application of genetic analysis techniques to assess and identify desirable traits in crops and livestock for commercial purposes. It involves the examination of multiple genes or genetic markers to understand the genetic composition of organisms and make informed decisions in breeding,

**Table 5.** Metaheuristic algorithms addressed in exports and imports by variables.

| Scope | Variables |
|---|---|
| EC08: Study evaluation method | Experimentation |
| | Proof of concept |
| | Case of study |
| EC09: Studio Continuity | New |
| | Extension |
| EC10: Research scope | Academy |
| | Industry |
| EC11: Analysis type | Descriptive |
| | Predictive |
| | Prescriptive |

**Table 6.** Preliminary analysis after lemmatization.

| Concept | Total number |
|---|---|
| Number of occurrence | 4752 |
| Number of lexical forms (words) | 1112 |
| Number of hapaxes legomenon (*) | 548 11,53% of occurrences |
| | 49,28% of forms |
| Mean of occurrences by text | 198 |
| (*) Words with frequency = 1 | |

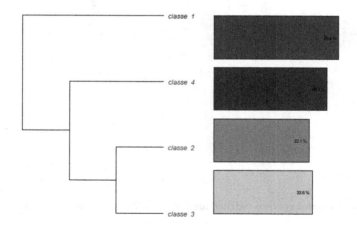

**Fig. 2.** Dendogram of cluster analysis.

selection, and trade. For example, analysis of multiple genes can be used to identify traits such as disease resistance, yield, and quality. This information can be
used to develop crops and livestock better suited for specific environments or

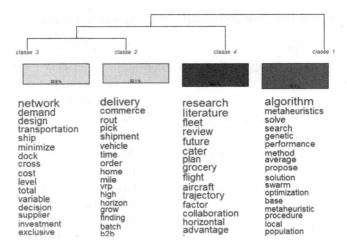

Fig. 3. Dendrogram of cluster classification, including cluster analysis and lexical clusters.

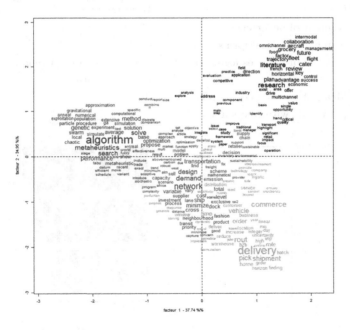

Fig. 4. Factorial correspondence analyses (FCA) of frequently used words.

markets, increasing productivity and profitability for farmers and producers [34] (Table 5).

Another relevant application of multigenetic analysis in commercial exchange is detecting genetic variability in crops and livestock. This information can be

ECO3 - ECO2

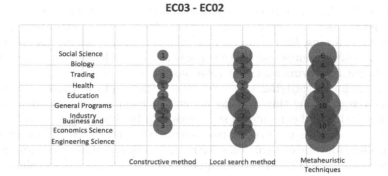

**Fig. 5.** Bubble chart of disciplines and used techniques to problem-solving.

used to develop breeding programs that improve specific traits, such as disease resistance or drought tolerance. By identifying genetic variability, developing new crops and livestock strains better suited for specific environments or markets is possible. As a synthesis of cluster 1, multigenetic analysis is an essential tool in commercial exchange for identifying desirable traits, detecting genetic variability, and ensuring the safety and quality of food products. As the demand for food continues to grow, a multigenetic analysis will become increasingly important for developing crops and livestock that are more productive, resilient, and safe for consumers.

**Cluster 2: Delivery, Commerce, and Shipment.**

This is the smallest cluster, representing the 22.1% of the total of clusters. The transportation of goods is a vital aspect of commercial exchange. Efficient vehicle routing can optimize transportation costs and ensure the timely delivery of goods. Proper vehicle routing can also reduce the carbon footprint associated with transportation. Various techniques, such as GPS, routing software, and predictive analytics, can improve vehicle routing efficiency [14]. This aspect also occurs in aviation, where operations generate large amounts of toxic gas emissions [27]. Optimizing vehicle routes can increase customer satisfaction and loyalty, ultimately contributing to the business's long-term success. Customer service is an integral part of international trading, including e-commerce. High-quality customer service can significantly impact a company's reputation, loyalty, and profitability [16]. Providing personalized customer services such as timely communication, tracking information, and handling customer complaints effectively can increase customer satisfaction and build trust. It can also lead to positive word-of-mouth marketing and repeat business. Proper training of customer service representatives, use of technology, and effective communication can enhance the quality of customer service.

Integrating vehicle routes and customer services can significantly improve commercial exchange. For example, real-time tracking of vehicles can provide customers with up-to-date delivery information. This can enhance customer satisfaction and reduce customer complaints. Moreover, companies can optimize vehicle routes based on customer preferences, delivery locations, gases emission and traffic conditions, leading to cost savings and timely delivery of goods [31]. Integrating vehicle routes and customer services can enhance transparency and accountability, improving customer relationships.

At this point, identifying sales routes and their optimization become relevant since the company thinks of the client, not itself, which is fundamental in current marketing and commercial strategies [32]. In this manner, vehicle routes and customer services are crucial components of commercial exchange. Optimizing vehicle routes can save costs, increase customer satisfaction, and reduce carbon footprint [41]. Providing high-quality customer services can enhance customer loyalty, reputation, and profitability. The integration of vehicle routes and customer services can lead to significant improvements in commercial exchange, ultimately contributing to the long-term success of businesses. Even more, maritime transport is the backbone of the international trade of goods, and seaports play a significant role in global transport, where the use of containers is significantly represented. Under this aspect, metaheuristics is considered as an alternative for solving optimization problems, considering metaheuristics based on problems of nature, such as bee, bat and firefly algorithms [25].

**Cluster 3: Network Design, Demand, Transportation, and Costs.**
According to [51], in the context of international trading networks, the problem faced by the decision-maker is how to realize the joint optimization of three types of investment schemes: (1) the construction of a scheme of the land transportation system; (2) the operation scheme of the shipping network, and (3) the expansion scheme of the port throughput capacity.

Here, aerial, maritime, and terrestrial transport becomes an exciting topic influencing trading. In the correlation matrix, Terrestrial (EC06: transport) is considered knowledge areas in Business and Economics science, industry and trading (EC03), and in logistics [4,16,17,25,29], transport [7,9,17,25] and market predictions [2,13,15–23] as the leading import and export situations. Give the best solution for a problem becomes a challenge. Here, optimization is the process of finding the best solution, and the global optimum is the maximum/minimum of a function [28]. Transport optimization is an important aspect of commercial exchange, as it enables the efficient movement of goods from one location to another. In today's globalized economy, businesses must transport goods over long distances, often across multiple borders and time zones. Optimizing the transport process can help businesses reduce costs, improve delivery times, and increase customer satisfaction [31].

Optimizing transport, including multimodal transport, involves finding the most efficient way to move goods from point A to point B, considering three phases: (1) pre-haul, (2) long-haul and (3) end-haul or last mile [5]. Therefore, this can be achieved through various methods, such as using the most direct route, selecting the best mode of transport, and minimizing the number of intermediaries involved. By optimizing transport, businesses can reduce the time and money spent on transportation, leading to cost savings [36] and increased profits [5]. Additionally, optimizing transport can improve delivery times, making it easier for businesses to meet customer demands and increase customer satisfaction [49].

While transport optimization offers many benefits, there are also challenges that businesses must overcome. For example, when enhancing transport, businesses must consider weather conditions, traffic congestion, and border crossings [5]. Additionally, businesses must work with multiple stakeholders, such as carriers, logistics providers, and customs officials, to ensure efficiency in goods transport. Overcoming these challenges requires careful planning and coordination and using advanced technology and data analysis tools [5].

The increasing demand for air transportation operations has further strained this already capacity-limited system, leading to significant flight delays that could directly impacts to importation and exportation activities, in addition to airport congestion [8]. International trade costs represent an important role in determining a nation's trade volume, encompassing those related to transportation, political barriers, contracts, legal and regulatory procedures, and finally those related to the use of different currencies. International trade costs are made up of three components, which are (1) the costs in the exporting country, (2) the costs incurred in the importing country, and (3) transportation with its respective insurance [48]. Transport optimization is critical for businesses engaged in international exchange. By improving transport, businesses can reduce costs, improve delivery times, and increase customer satisfaction [49]. However, optimizing transport also presents challenges that must be overcome through careful planning, coordination, advanced technology and data analysis tools [8]. Businesses must prioritize transport optimization to remain competitive in today's globalized economy.

**Cluster 4: Fleet and Trajectory Management.** This cluster represents the 22.8% of the total of clusters. Effective fleet and trajectory management is crucial in optimizing international trading operations by ensuring the efficient movement of goods across global supply chains. International trade, the backbone of the global economy, relies heavily on efficient logistics and transportation systems. Among the myriad factors influencing the success of international trading, fleet and trajectory management emerge as critical elements. Fleet management encompasses coordinating and optimization transportation assets, including ships, aircraft, trucks, and trains, while trajectory management involves strategic planning and route optimization [10]. Efficient fleet and trajectory management directly contribute to cost reduction in international trading. Transportation costs can be significantly lowered by minimizing empty runs, optimizing shipping routes, and enhancing cargo consolidation [27]. Leveraging advanced technologies, such as real-time data analytics, artificial intelligence, and optimization algorithms, enables precise fleet management decisions that maximize resource utilization and minimize fuel consumption [38]. Consequently, reduced costs enhance the competitiveness of trading entities, fostering sustainable economic growth, and expanding market access. Achieving optimal operational efficiency is paramount for successful international trading [29].

Fleet and trajectory management systems allow for streamlined logistics processes, ensuring timely delivery, reduced lead times, and improved order fulfillment. By integrating supply chain data, these systems facilitate seamless communication between stakeholders, enhancing coordination and minimizing disruptions. Real-time monitoring of fleet performance enables proactive decision-making, minimizing delays and enabling responsive adaptations to dynamic market conditions [10]. The environmental impact of international trading cannot be overlooked, and fleet and trajectory management play a pivotal role in promoting sustainability. Effective management practices help optimize transportation routes, reducing greenhouse gas emissions and energy consumption. Implementing eco-friendly technologies, such as alternative fuels, hybrid vehicles, and energy-efficient routing algorithms, further contributes to environmental preservation [52]. By prioritizing sustainability, fleet and trajectory management systems promote a greener and more resilient international trading landscape.

In an increasingly interconnected and competitive global market, efficient fleet and trajectory management provides a strategic advantage to trading entities. A well-managed fleet ensures timely deliveries, enhances customer satisfaction, and fosters long-term relationships with international partners. Optimal trajectory planning facilitates market access, enabling trading entities to reach geographically diverse regions efficiently. Furthermore, by leveraging data-driven insights and predictive analytics, fleet and trajectory management systems empower decision-makers to anticipate market trends, identify emerging opportunities, and mitigate potential risks, thus bolstering overall competitiveness. Finally, risk management is another critical aspect of international trading. Trading involves risk, and traders must have a risk management plan to mitigate losses. Effective risk management involves identifying potential risks, evaluating their likelihood and impact, and implementing measures to manage or mitigate them. This practice includes diversification of investments, using stop-loss orders, and setting limits on trading activities [33].

**Similarity Analysis.** This analysis was performed to identify close relationships between words by representing a graph according to the chi-square of association. In Fig. 6, these relationships are represented by lines. Two characteristics in the description are essential to consider: (1) line thickness, which indicates the strength of the relationship and potential semantic changes, and (2) font size, which is proportional to the term's frequency of occurrence. Figure 6 shows three nodes or communities of words: (1) algorithm, and (2) optimization, and the word "problem" that represents the central node (main word).

**Fig. 6.** Bubble chart of disciplines and used techniques to problem-solving.

## 4    Conclusions

Analyzing delivery, commerce, and shipping aspects in international trading is vital for optimizing operations, enhancing customer satisfaction, reducing costs, improving operational efficiency, and promoting sustainable practices. By leveraging data analytics and adopting informed decision-making processes, traders can optimize delivery processes, streamline commerce operations, and implement efficient shipping strategies. Embracing a comprehensive analysis of these critical components empowers stakeholders in international trade to navigate the complexities of global supply chains, foster customer loyalty, improve profitability, and contribute to a sustainable and resilient global trading landscape.

The significance of fleet and trajectory management in international trading cannot be overstated. By embracing innovative technologies, optimizing transportation routes, and promoting sustainable practices, trading entities can unlock substantial benefits such as cost reduction, operational efficiency, environmental sustainability, and enhanced competitiveness. As international trade continues to evolve, adopting and advancing fleet and trajectory management practices will be paramount for ensuring seamless global connectivity and driving economic growth in an increasingly interconnected world.

By other hand, metaheuristic analysis has emerged as a valuable tool in addressing the optimization challenges encountered in international trading. By leveraging computational intelligence and optimization algorithms, metaheuristic techniques enhance decision-making processes, optimize operational efficiency, and maximize profitability in international trade's dynamic and uncertain landscape. Through exploring large solution spaces and considering multiple trade-offs, metaheuristic analysis empowers traders to make informed choices, adapt to changing market conditions, and capitalize on emerging opportunities. As international trading continues to evolve, embracing and advancing metaheuristic analysis will be crucial for traders seeking to navigate the complexities of the global marketplace and achieve sustainable growth and profitability.

**Acknowledgements.** The authors wish to thank the Vice-Rector for Research of the University of Azuay for the financial and academic support, and all the staff of the Computer Science Research & Development Laboratory (LIDI).

# References

1. Abdi, H., Moradi, M., Lumbreras, S.: Metaheuristics and transmission expansion planning: a comparative case study. Energies **14**(12), 3618 (2021)
2. Agudelo Aguirre, A.A., Duque Méndez, N.D., Rojas Medina, R.A.: Artificial intelligence applied to investment in variable income through the MACD (moving average convergence/divergence) indicator. J. Econ. Finan. Adm. Sci. **26**(52), 268–281 (2021)
3. Ahrari, A., Atai, A.A., Deb, K.: A customized bilevel optimization approach for solving large-scale truss design problems. Eng. Optim. **52**(12), 2062–2079 (2020)
4. Akkerman, F., Lalla-Ruiz, E., Mes, M., Spitters, T.: Cross-docking: current research versus industry practice and industry 4.0 adoption. Smart Ind. Better Manage. **28**, 69–104 (2022)
5. Archetti, C., Peirano, L., Speranza, M.G.: Optimization in multimodal freight transportation problems: a survey. Eur. J. Oper. Res. **299**(1), 1–20 (2022)
6. Augusto, A., Dumas, M., La Rosa, M.: Metaheuristic optimization for automated business process discovery. In: Hildebrandt, T., van Dongen, B.F., Röglinger, M., Mendling, J. (eds.) BPM 2019. LNCS, vol. 11675, pp. 268–285. Springer, Cham (2019). https://doi.org/10.1007/978-3-030-26619-6_18
7. Ayuda, M.I., Belloc, I., Pinilla, V.: Latin American agri-food exports, 1994–2019: a gravity model approach. Mathematics **10**(3), 333 (2022)
8. Balakrishnan, H.: Control and optimization algorithms for air transportation systems. Annu. Rev. Control. **41**, 39–46 (2016)
9. Bălan, C.: The disruptive impact of future advanced ICTs on maritime transport: a systematic review. Supply Chain Manage. Int. J. **25**(2), 157–175 (2020)
10. Baykasoğlu, A., Subulan, K., Taşan, A.S., Dudaklı, N.: A review of fleet planning problems in single and multimodal transportation systems. Transportmetrica a: Transp. Sci. **15**(2), 631–697 (2019)
11. Benzécri, J.P.: Histoire et préhistoire de l'analyse des données. partie v l'analyse des correspondances. Cahiers de l'analyse des données **2**(1), 9–40 (1977)
12. Bueno, S., Banuls, V.A., Gallego, M.D.: Is urban resilience a phenomenon on the rise? A systematic literature review for the years 2019 and 2020 using textometry. Int. J. Disaster Risk Reduct. **66**, 102588 (2021)
13. Capoani, L., Barlese, A.: Markets, wars and instability: a theory of conflict in economics through the study of the gravitational field model in international trade. SSRN 3850912 (2021)

14. Cetin, S., et al.: A heuristic algorithm for vehicle routing problems with simultaneous pick-up and delivery and hard time windows. Open J. Soc. Sci. **3**(03), 35 (2015)
15. Chaney, T.: The gravity equation in international trade: an explanation. J. Polit. Econ. **126**(1), 150–177 (2018)
16. Colla, E., Lapoule, P.: E-commerce: exploring the critical success factors. Int. J. Retail Distrib. Manage. **40**(11), 842–864 (2012)
17. Delgoshaei, A., Norozi, H., Mirzazadeh, A., Farhadi, M., Pakdel, G.H., Aram, A.K.: A new model for logistics and transportation of fashion goods in the presence of stochastic market demands considering restricted retailers capacity. RAIRO-Oper. Res. **55**, S523–S547 (2021)
18. Doering, J., Kizys, R., Juan, A.A., Fito, A., Polat, O.: Metaheuristics for rich portfolio optimisation and risk management: current state and future trends. Oper. Res. Perspect. **6**, 100121 (2019)
19. Duro, J.A., et al.: Liger: a cross-platform open-source integrated optimization and decision-making environment. Appl. Soft Comput. **98**, 106851 (2021)
20. Faia, R., Lezama, F., Soares, J., Vale, Z., Pinto, T., Corchado, J.M.: Differential evolution application in portfolio optimization for electricity markets. In: 2018 International Joint Conference on Neural Networks (IJCNN), pp. 1–8. IEEE (2018)
21. Faia, R., Pinto, T., Vale, Z., Corchado, J.M., Soares, J., Lezama, F.: Genetic algorithms for portfolio optimization with weighted sum approach. In: 2018 IEEE Symposium Series on Computational Intelligence (SSCI), pp. 1823–1829. IEEE (2018)
22. Flechas Chaparro, X.A., de Vasconcelos Gomes, L.A., Tromboni de Souza Nascimento, P.: The evolution of project portfolio selection methods: from incremental to radical innovation. Revista de Gestão **26**(3), 212–236 (2019)
23. Garcia-Guarin, J., et al.: Smart microgrids operation considering a variable neighborhood search: the differential evolutionary particle swarm optimization algorithm. Energies **12**(16), 3149 (2019)
24. Gogna, A., Tayal, A.: Metaheuristics: review and application. J. Exp. Theor. Artif. Intell. **25**(4), 503–526 (2013)
25. Gulić, M., Maglić, L., Valčić, S.: Nature inspired metaheuristics for optimizing problems at a container terminal. Pomorstvo **32**(1), 10–20 (2018)
26. Guzman, E., Andres, B., Poler, R.: Metaheuristic algorithm for job-shop scheduling problem using a disjunctive mathematical model. Computers **11**(1), 1 (2022). https://doi.org/10.3390/computers11010001, https://www.mdpi.com/2073-431X/11/1/1
27. Hammad, A.W., Rey, D., Bu-Qammaz, A., Grzybowska, H., Akbarnezhad, A.: Mathematical optimization in enhancing the sustainability of aircraft trajectory: a review. Int. J. Sustain. Transp. **14**(6), 413–436 (2020)
28. Haupt, R.L., Haupt, S.E.: Practical Genetic Algorithms. Wiley, Hoboken (2004)
29. Huang, L., Murong, L., Wang, W.: Green closed-loop supply chain network design considering cost control and $CO2$ emission. Mod. Supply Chain Res. Appl. **2**(1), 42–59 (2020)
30. Hutton, B., Catalá-López, F., Moher, D.: La extensión de la declaración prisma para revisiones sistemáticas que incorporan metaanálisis en red: Prisma-nma. Med. Clin. **147**(6), 262–266 (2016)
31. Kunnapapdeelert, S., Johnson, J.V., Phalitnonkiat, P.: Green last-mile route planning for efficient e-commerce distribution. Eng. Manage. Prod. Serv. **14**(1), 1–12 (2022)
32. Kurz, A., Zäpfel, G.: Modeling cost-delivery trade-offs for distribution logistics by a generalized PVRP model. J. Bus. Econ. **83**, 705–726 (2013)

33. Lynn, T., Mooney, J.G., Rosati, P., Cummins, M.: Disrupting Finance: FinTech and Strategy in the 21st Century. Springer, Berlin (2019)
34. Memmah, M.M., Lescourret, F., Yao, X., Lavigne, C.: Metaheuristics for agricultural land use optimization, a review. Agron. Sustain. Dev. **35**, 975–998 (2015)
35. Mendes, A.M., Tonin, F.S., Buzzi, M.F., Pontarolo, R., Fernandez-Llimos, F.: Mapping pharmacy journals: a lexicographic analysis. Res. Social Adm. Pharm. **15**(12), 1464–1471 (2019)
36. Moons, S., Ramaekers, K., Caris, A., Arda, Y.: Integration of order picking and vehicle routing in a B2C e-commerce context. Flex. Serv. Manuf. J. **30**(4), 813–843 (2018)
37. Mosallanezhad, B., Hajiaghaei-Keshteli, M., Triki, C.: Shrimp closed-loop supply chain network design. Soft. Comput. **25**, 7399–7422 (2021)
38. Muñoz-Villamizar, A., Velázquez-Martínez, J.C., Mejía-Argueta, C., Gámez-Pérez, K.: The impact of shipment consolidation strategies for green home delivery: a case study in a Mexican retail company. Int. J. Prod. Res. **60**(8), 2443–2460 (2022)
39. Nisperuza, P.A., López, J.M., Hernández, H.E.: Una metaheurística basada en el algoritmo genético de ordenamiento no-dominado ii, aplicado al problema de ruteo de vehículos de productos perecederos. Inf. Tecnol. **30**(6), 223–232 (2019)
40. Pincemin, B., Heiden, S., Decorde, M.: Textometry on audiovisual corpora. In: 15th International Conference on Statistical Analysis of Textual Data JADT 2020. University of Toulouse (2020)
41. Prajapati, D., Kumar, M.M., Pratap, S., Chelladurai, H., Zuhair, M.: Sustainable logistics network design for delivery operations with time horizons in B2B e-commerce platform. Logistics **5**(3), 61 (2021)
42. del Río, C.M.: Uso de software lexical: una revisión comparativa. Repositorio de la Red Internacional de Investigadores en Competitividad **13**, 221–244 (2019)
43. Sajadi, S.J., Ahmadi, A.: An integrated optimization model and metaheuristics for assortment planning, shelf space allocation, and inventory management of perishable products: a real application. PLoS ONE **17**(3), e0264186 (2022)
44. Sörensen, K., Glover, F.: Metaheuristics. Encycl. Oper. Res. Manage. Sci. **62**, 960–970 (2013)
45. Sorensen, K., Sevaux, M., Glover, F.: A history of metaheuristics. arXiv preprint arXiv:1704.00853 (2017)
46. Talbi, E.G.: Machine learning into metaheuristics: a survey and taxonomy. ACM Comput. Surv. (CSUR) **54**(6), 1–32 (2021)
47. Urrútia, G., Bonfill, X.: Declaración prisma: una propuesta para mejorar la publicación de revisiones sistemáticas y metaanálisis. Med. Clin. **135**(11), 507–511 (2010)
48. Vásquez Bernal, J.V., Tonon Ordóñez, L.B.: Modelo de gravedad de las exportaciones de cacao en grano del ecuador. INNOVA Res. J. (2021)
49. Wang, C.N., Dang, T.T., Le, T.Q., Kewcharoenwong, P.: Transportation optimization models for intermodal networks with fuzzy node capacity, detour factor, and vehicle utilization constraints. Mathematics **8**(12), 2109 (2020)
50. Xiao, Y., Watson, M.: Guidance on conducting a systematic literature review. J. Plan. Educ. Res. **39**(1), 93–112 (2019)
51. Xin, X., Wang, X., Ma, L., Chen, K., Ye, M.: Shipping network design-infrastructure investment joint optimization model: a case study of west Africa. Marit. Policy Manage. **49**(5), 620–646 (2022)
52. Xue, N., Bai, R., Qu, R., Aickelin, U.: A hybrid pricing and cutting approach for the multi-shift full truckload vehicle routing problem. Eur. J. Oper. Res. **292**(2), 500–514 (2021)

# Finding an Integrated Ultraviolet Radiation Index Using Fuzzy Logic Techniques

Juan Pablo Huricocha Piedra[1], Marcos Orellana[1]([⊠]), Priscila Cedillo[2],
Jorge Luis Zambrano-Martinez[1]([⊠]), and Juan-Fernando Lima[1]

[1] Computer Science Research and Development Laboratory (LIDI),
Universidad del Azuay, Cuenca, Ecuador
`jhuiracochamsn@es.uazuay.edu.ec`,
`{marore,jorge.zambrano,flima}@uazuay.edu.ec`
[2] Universidad de Cuenca, Cuenca, Ecuador
`priscila.cedillo@ucuenca.edu.ec`

**Abstract.** The present study applies fuzzy logic techniques to find an integrated ultraviolet radiation index for Cuenca-Ecuador. This index integrates information on meteorological variables and ultraviolet rays, whose data were provided by the Research Department of the Institute for Sectional Regime Studies of Ecuador (IERSE), corresponding to 2018. Analysis techniques in data mining were used to process and segment this information. Subsequently, a fuzzy logic model with the Mamdani approach was generated to obtain an integrated ultraviolet radiation index. This model combines the values of the Ultraviolet radiation A and Ultraviolet radiation B components through 49 fuzzy inference rules. The results obtained were compared with the ultraviolet radiation indices of the tropospheric model. As a result, a slightly higher fuzzy index was obtained in terms of the index score concerning the tropospheric model.

**Keywords:** Ultraviolet Index · Fuzzy logic · Air quality · Data mining

## 1 Introduction

Nowadays, the monitoring and control of the radiation that comes from the sun has become fundamentally important in humanity because it can cause harmful effects on the skin and eyes of human beings [19]. The atmosphere of planet Earth, especially the ozone layer, is responsible for filtering the incidence of solar radiation [25]. According to Ipiña et al. [14], the ozone layer has been affected due to the increase in polluting gases from industries, vehicles, and others, negatively affecting radiation filtration.

The IERSE of the University of Azuay, together with the Municipal Company of Mobility, Transit and Transport of the city of Cuenca (EMOV EP), has implemented a plan for tracking and monitoring quality variables of the air in the city of Cuenca-Ecuador [24]. This plan allows for measurements of the

J. Maldonado-Mahauad et al. (Eds.): TICEC 2023, CCIS 1885, pp. 113–127, 2023.
https://doi.org/10.1007/978-3-031-45438-7_8

global incident radiation, raising the need to apply data mining and fuzzy logic techniques that give the possibility of generating knowledge for decision-making. As a fundamental aspect, there is data on atmospheric pollutants for the city of Cuenca-Ecuador for 2018.

Using as a base the data collected from the meteorological variables, solar radiation, ultraviolet radiation, and the definitions proposed by fuzzy logic, the present work focuses on the generation of an Ultraviolet (UV) radiation for the city of Cuenca-Ecuador through the application of data mining techniques and fuzzy logic in the atmospheric and meteorological variables that present a relationship with UV rays.

## 2    Related Work

This study aims to generate an integrated UV radiation index by applying fuzzy logic techniques to data related to solar radiation. The information provided by IERSE corresponds to the atmospheric variables and air pollutants of Cuenca-Ecuador in 2018, so it is essential to know what studies have been performed on these goals.

Therefore, it is necessary to know the importance and interference of UV radiation in human health. The study by Kyprianou et al. [18] declares an increase in the occurrence of skin cancer on a Mediterranean island with a high degree of solar radiation. Likewise, Umar et al. [23] mention that increased skin problems related to UV radiation have been observed worldwide since the fifties. Furthermore, the research by Bais et al. [3] highlight that the ozone layer is weakening due to air pollution, a product of the gases from industries, vehicles, paints, etc. This depletion of the ozone layer has caused the intensity of UV radiation to increase considerably over time.

The research by Ipiña et al. [14] relates the intensity of UV radiation to meteorological variables and air pollution. In the same way, the World Health Organization [26] comments on the importance of having a Ultraviolet Index (UVI) that allows the population to know the intensity of UV radiation and that it is an indicator to cause lesions in human skin.

On the other hand, various investigations and articles have applied fuzzy logic techniques because it is a methodology that solves complex problems in an elegant and simplified way and also admits the incorporation of expert knowledge in decision-making [9]. The study by Allana and Chua [2] propose using fuzzy logic through a fuzzy inference modelling system using MATLAB software to find an air quality index inside a bus.

Katushabe et al. [16] propose an air quality index, applying fuzzy logic to the data corresponding to the city of Kampala in East Africa. Similarly, Santigosa et al. [22] propose three models to obtain a daily global radiation index, the first model is based on linear regression, the second model on a non-linear regression and the third model on a fuzzy inference system. Likewise, Jaramillo et al. [15] suggest obtaining an integrated air quality index for Colombian cities by applying a fuzzy inference system. This study uses a similar model to get a UVI radiation, whose variables are related to air pollution. In addition, variables related to solar radiation are considered, such as Ultraviolet A (UVA), Ultraviolet B (UVB) and UVI radiation.

The research performed by Huillca et al. [12] concludes that it is possible to find a UV radiation index for the city of Puno-Peru using a linear regression model. Consequently, In our study, we propose to generate a fuzzy model that obtains an integrated UV radiation index using air quality data corresponding to 2018 and considering atmospheric and meteorological variables in Cuenca-Ecuador. These data are compiled and studied by the Municipality of Cuenca, EMOV EP, and the Research Department of IERSE [24]. For its quantification, fuzzy logic is used since the relationship between the variables is complex, admitting fuzzification techniques in the selected variables [10].

## 3     Materials and Methods

The method to develop this work is structured as follows: i) Data understanding that allows to tackle the used variables, ii) The international standards about UVI, iii) The fuzzification process allowed to translate the preprocessed variables into linguistic variables, and iv) The defuzzification process where the new UV index was obtained.

### 3.1    Data Understanding

To generate a document with the specification of the objectives that leads to the generation of a fuzzy UVI, it is necessary to execute the following sub-tasks: i) Understand the study area, ii) Describe the variables of pollutants and air quality, iii) Detail the UV radiation variables, and finally iv) Generate the objectives of the research that highlights the obtaining of the fuzzy UV radiation index.

During this stage, the experts met to obtain information on the UVI standards. This phase allowed us to understand the process of collecting information on air quality variables. The variables that are part of the data collection in the city of Cuenca-Ecuador are Nitrogen dioxide ($NO_2$), Sulfur dioxide ($SO_2$), Carbon monoxide (CO), Ozone $O_3$, UV global radiation (RADGLOBAL_AV). The information was captured by a real-time continuous monitoring station that uses specialized sensors to collect data every second.

This information is processed to generate a data set at an interval of ten minutes. The information collected helps to identify the importance of having an integrated ultraviolet radiation index that facilitates generating knowledge about the intensity of UV radiation in Cuenca-Ecuador. According to the Ecuadorian National Institute of Census and Statistics (INEC) [13], Cuenca is the third city with the most inhabitants in Ecuador, located in the center-south of the country, at an altitude of 2,550 m above sea level. It is located on the Equatorial line, two seasons are recognized, winter (rain) and summer (dry); with an annual Relative Humidity (RH) of 75%, and an average daily temperature of 15°C, its maximum

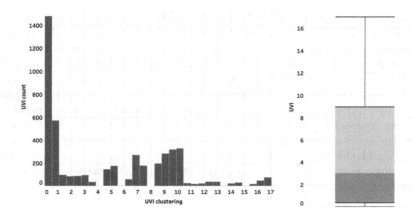

**Fig. 1.** Frequency and distribution of the UVI variable.

hourly temperature moves one or two hours after the maximum intensity of solar radiation, whose peak is around noon [11].

This study used the data on air pollutants and meteorological variables of the city of Cuenca-Ecuador for 2018. The data were provided by the Municipal of Cuenca, EMOV EP, and the Research Department of IERSE [24]. The information has been captured by a real-time continuous monitoring station belonging to the company EMOV EP. Each intake of air pollutants is performed at one-second intervals. However, the data provided for the study has a time interval of ten minutes [21]. The initial data set has 52,600 records, specifically the variables are: $O_3$, CO, $NO_2$, $SO_2$, Particulate Matter of 2.5 μm ($PM_{2.5}$), average temperature (TEMP), RH, Dew Point (DP), atmospheric pressure (PATM).

Figure 1 shows the data distribution corresponding to the UVI variable. As we can be observed, a bias or trend towards the zero value is identified due to the absence of radiation during certain hours of the day, especially between 6:00 pm and 6:00 am. Figures 2 and 3 show a similar situation with the variables UVA (315–400 nm) o *"UVA_315_400"* and UVB (280–315 nm) o *"UVB_280_315"*.

### 3.2 UVI Standards

During the targeting stage, it was essential to consider the scales that the World Health Organization (WHO) recommends for the measurement of UV radiation. These scales are used to inform about the possible damage that the intensity of UV radiation can cause in different areas of the planet. Although not strictly adopted by all countries, these scales are widely used as a reference. Solar radiation levels in regions of low and intermediate latitudes, where higher solar radiation intensity is observed, require more specific standardization or redefinition. Consequently, we decided to incorporate the scale proposed by Cañarte in the present research study [8].

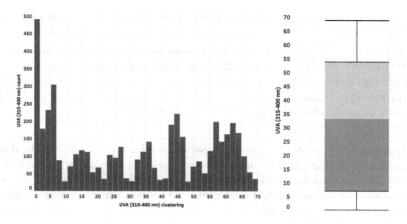

**Fig. 2.** Frequency and distribution of the variable UVA (315–400 nm).

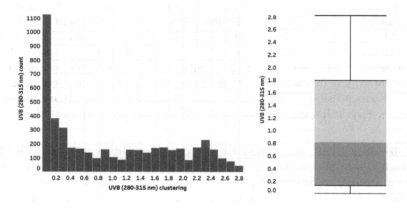

**Fig. 3.** Frequency and distribution of the variable UVB (280–315 nm).

**Data Preprocessing.** Once the objectives have been defined and the information on atmospheric variables and UV rays has been collected, the data preprocessing phase begins to assess its quality and apply data mining techniques that facilitate data collection. However, it is essential to consider that The data can present errors for various reasons, such as the lack of reliability of the sensor in the capture of information. Also, a small amount of data may need help capturing due to factors such as calibration or resetting of the sensors, creating a temporary gap in the information.

Likewise, it is essential to note that the sensors capture information on air pollutants every ten minutes, while meteorological variables are captured every minute. To solve this temporal dissonance between the variables, an average of ten one-minute records is used for each variable, thus achieving a ten-minute average record that avoids discordance between the atmospheric and meteorological variables [21].

The raw data is described at this stage, and pre-processing techniques are applied to improve the data quality. The raw data contain information on the atmospheric variables taken in ten minutes in Cuenca-Ecuador, 2018. Regarding data preprocessing, i) data cleaning, ii) data selection and iii) elimination of outliers, which are activities proposed in the methodology.

**Data Cleaning.** All records containing missing data for any variable in the data set were removed during the first data removal tests. As a result of the deletion process, 34,230 undeleted records were obtained, which represents 65% of the total data. However, to maintain the integrity of the data set, the missing values were filled in to recover the remaining 35% that was removed in this process. The methods proposed in [21] were used to impute missing data for atmospheric and pollutant variables, demonstrating that the most common imputation methods may be missing critical information for variable correlation analysis. In addition, using the mean or median to fill in the missing values would present disadvantages and biases in the covariance matrix. After several tests, it was determined that the prediction of missing data using Lasso regression is the process that fits the purpose of this investigation. In addition, it was necessary to eliminate outliers to obtain a regression model that fit the data distribution. As a result of this stage, it was possible to maintain a total of 52,560 records without missing values, and a correlation matrix concerning UV radiation was generated.

**Data Selection.** This stage used the Troposphere Ultraviolet and Visible (TUV) model [5] to obtain the UV radiation of a particular region. This model uses meteorological, surface and time of day parameters, such as ozone, cloudiness, aerosols present in the air, height and measurement time, among other parameters. Thus, Cañarte et al. [8] conclude that Ecuador receives a high intensity of erythematic radiation most of the year due to its location.

Once the UV radiation variables such as UVA, UVB and UVI were obtained, it was possible to analyze the relationship between the atmospheric and meteorological variables since one of the main objectives is generating a fuzzy UV radiation index. For this reason, it is necessary to determine the atmospheric variables and air pollutants related to the UV radiation index.

The variable correlation was determined using the r-square coefficient method [7]. This method obtains the relationship coefficients of two variables simultaneously, and the coefficient determines how related the two selected variables are. As a result, a correlation matrix was obtained where a positive correlation can be seen between the variables *TEMPAIRE_AV*, $O_3$, *UVA_315_400*, and *UVB_280_315*. Bi [7] states that the r-squared value ranges between 0 and 1, where 0 indicates that the model does not explain any variability in the dependent variable, 1 suggests that the model explains all the variability in the dependent variable. Therefore, the closer the r-squared value is to one, the better the model's ability to explain the variability in the dependent variable.

The variables that most influenced the UV radiation index were identified as part of this process. Then, the records in which the radiation index was zero were eliminated since they did not contribute to the final model due to their equivalence being null or non-existent. Also, the data collected from 6 pm to 6 am were included since there is no radiation, and these values are close to zero. Applying these criteria, a final data set of 4,745 records was obtained.

**Outlier Removal.** To eliminate outliers that have been found in the variables related to $RADGLOBAL\_AV$, the algorithm called Local Outlier Factor (LOF) was used. This algorithm determines which values are outside an established threshold. Such issues can affect and introduce biases in the search for a model that fits the distribution of the analyzed variable [1]. Therefore, this method was used to filter values within a threshold set to $UVA\_315\_400$, $UVB\_280\_315$, and $UVI$. By applying the LOF algorithm, 4,745 records were obtained, so it can be seen that there were no outliers in the range from 6 pm to 6 am, thus being 9% of the total records referring to the original data. The latest data facilitate the possibility of obtaining an index using fuzzy logic because each record in the data set provides relevant information on UV radiation.

### 3.3 Fuzzification Process

The modelling phase involved selecting, testing and using a fuzzy logic model based on Mamdanis' approach to meet the research expectations. We worked with previously prepared data in the data preprocessing phase. The first step was to define the discursive universe of each linguistic variable from the following variables obtained in the previous stage: $UVA\_315\_400$, $UVB\_280\_315$ and $UVI$.

To define the division of the data set, the criterion of using 70% of the records to train the fuzzy logic model was followed, and the remaining 30% to validate the model, as indicated by Kaur et al. [17]. The $UVB\_280\_315$ represents a wave of solar energy ranging between 280 and 315 nm. Decision trees generated by the RapidMiner Studio program were used to define the different ranges of UVB radiation intensity. The variable "CATEGORY_IUV" was defined as the variable to predict. This variable represents a categorisation of the numerical variable UVI. To form the rules defining the universe of discourse and linguistic variables, all columns except the numerical column UVB_280_315 were dropped. Using the rate of profit as a criterion and a depth of six levels, seven categories were formed on the same scale.

The universe of discourse was defined by applying decision trees to the categorical variable $CATEGORIA\_IUV$. This approach ensures an accurate classification of the samples into different radiation intensity categories, which was essential to generate the fuzzy logic model. Therefore, the values needed to create the trapezoids of the Mamdani approach, as shown in Fig. 4.

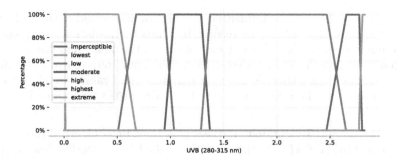

**Fig. 4.** Graphic trapezoidal definition of the variable UVB_280_315.

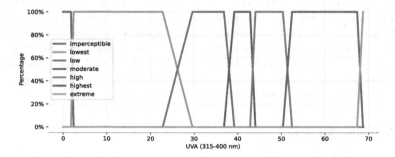

**Fig. 5.** Graphic trapezoidal definition of the variable UVA_315_400.

*UVA_315_400* contains information about UVA radiation, a wave of solar energy with wavelengths between 320 and 400 nm. To define the range of intensity of *UVA_315_400* radiation, the same method was applied to the variable *UVB_280_315*. The definition of the universe of discourse of the linguistic variable *UVA_315_400* with which the universe of speech can be generated using the Mamdani method, as illustrated in Fig. 5.

After defining the linguistic variables and the discursive universe of each variable, the rules that the fuzzy logic algorithm will use with the Mamdani approach are detailed. Consequently, a Fuzzy Associative Matrix (FAM) table was used to define two entries that conform to the fuzzy rule [4].

The FAM table shows that if one of the components of UV radiation is high, that category is established as a general rule. However, when the intensity scale in any of the components converges on the "high" categorization, the general rule is to classify with the following score on the region's normalized scale; for example, if *UVB_280_315* radiation is "high" and *UVA_315_400* radiation is "high", it is classified with the following score on the scale, which in this case is "very high". This decision is made based on the recommendations of the WHO, which indicates that a high rate means possible damage to human skin, so avoiding sun exposure and seeking shade is recommended.

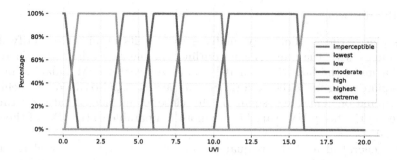

**Fig. 6.** Graphic trapezoidal definition of the UVI variable.

For the implementation of the linguistic variables and the definition of the fuzzy rules, the *fuzzy_expert* library of the Python programming language was used, where each variable is defined with its respective discursive universe through the *Fuzzy-Variable* module. Additionally, it has the *FuzzyRule* module where the rules defined in the FAM table are declared, whose implementations can be found in different programming languages such as Python.

### 3.4    Defuzzification Process

This stage evaluates each record of the data set obtained during the preprocessing phase to be used as input to the fuzzy model and, according to the decision rules, generates a unique output of a numerical value on a scale of 0 to 18, which corresponds to the intensity of the radiation in the UV radiation scale of the region. The process of converting inputs to unique outputs is called fuzzification. The *fuzzy_expert* library was used via the *DecompositionalInterface* module to implement a fuzzy model. The discourse universe of the UVI linguistic variable was defined by original data, reflecting the intensity of ultraviolet radiation in Ecuador on a scale from 1 to 16. This scale, proposed by Cañarte et al. [8], establishes that a value of one indicates a low level of radiation without health risk, while a value of 16 corresponds to an extreme level. Figure 6 illustrates how the trapezoids of Mamdanis' approach were constructed.

To obtain the UVI for each record in the dataset, a fuzzification process was applied to the input variables *UVA_315_400* and *UVB_280_315*. Next, a fuzzy model with the Mamdani approach was used to fuzzy and assigned a unique numerical value to each record.

This numerical value represents the corresponding ultraviolet radiation index. The fuzzy model was designed so that the fuzzification of the data was considered in the assignment of the UVI. The entire data set used iteration and index calculation to obtain the most accurate value possible.

## 3.5    Evaluation

In this phase, the methodology analyzes the results obtained to verify if the model aligns with the requirements outlined in the research study. Therefore, the behavior of the fuzzy logic model is analyzed with the Mamdani approach. The r-square determines the performance of the models, also called the coefficient of determination. Thus, an r-squared value close to one means that the estimates obtained in the fuzzy UVI variable are more comparable to the UVI of the TUV model [20].

The general idea of the r-squared value is to validate how well the fuzzy model fits the model used as the TUV reference. In addition, the Root Square Mean Error (RSME) is used to assess how well the predicted value of the fuzzy UVI fits against the UVI of the TUV model. The RSME value measures the error between the actual value against the expected value; consequently, the lower this value, the better the fuzzy model [6].

## 4    Results and Discussion

TThis section presents the results of the fuzzy model compared to the TUV model. To facilitate the understanding of the variability of the different indices, graphs have been used to reduce the visualization of the results. Due to the large data set size, displaying some of the predicted values is only feasible. Therefore, 20 records corresponding to noon have been randomly selected since, during this day, the UVI value reaches its maximum value [11]. In this way, it is possible to observe the differences between the actual and predicted values, as shown in Fig. 7.

Figure 8 reveals that the fuzzy index tends to assign higher values when one of the UV radiation variables is "high". The r-squared and RSME values were used to evaluate the performance of the generated model, and a more significant error was observed in the records where one of the components presented an "extreme" value. This behavior is attributed to the rules generated for the fuzzy model, where it is specified that any component of the UV radiation is "extreme". The TUV model index is based on an inferential mathematical formula. Therefore, it is essential to consider these differences when selecting a model to assess UV radiation exposure, with violet being extreme and red being very high.

Figure 9 presents the average of the results obtained by the fuzzy model, which are slightly higher than those of the TUV model. This effect is more noticeable when one of the components of UV radiation presents extreme values. These findings are consistent with the rules of the fuzzy model, which assigns higher values to the fuzzy index when the UV radiation components are extreme. Consequently, these results suggest that the fuzzy model may be more suitable for assessing exposure to excessive levels of UV radiation.

Thus, in Fig. 10, we can be observed that if any of the components of the fuzzy model is "extreme", it is very likely that the tendency is to locate the maximum value in the UV index. This finding is relevant since it suggests a

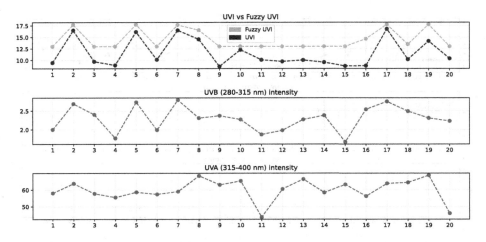

**Fig. 7.** Forecast values in the traditional method.

| EC_TIME_STAMP | UVB_280_3 | UVA_315_4 | IUV | IUV_DIFUS(-) | iuv_menos_iuv_difu | iuv_menos_iuv_difuso_cuadra | iuv_menos_iuv_promed | iuv_menos_iuv_promedio_cuadra |
|---|---|---|---|---|---|---|---|---|
| 2018-02-23 11:10:00 | | | 16,78 | 17,74 | -0,96 | 0,9216 | 12,09481981 | 146,2846662 |
| 2018-02-23 12:10:00 | 2,77 | 61,48 | 16,54 | 17,74 | -1,2 | 1,44 | 11,85481981 | 140,5367527 |
| 2018-02-25 12:10:00 | 2,78 | 57,81 | 16,34 | 17,74 | -1,4 | 1,96 | 11,65481981 | 135,8348248 |
| 2018-02-27 12:10:00 | 2,77 | 60,47 | 16,71 | 17,74 | -1,03 | 1,0609 | 12,02481981 | 144,5962915 |
| 2018-02-28 11:10:00 | 2,73 | 60,47 | 17 | 17,74 | -0,74 | 0,5476 | 12,31481981 | 151,654787 |
| 2018-03-01 11:10:00 | 2,82 | 67,5 | 16,65 | 17,74 | -1,09 | 1,1881 | 11,96481981 | 143,1569131 |
| 2018-03-01 12:10:00 | 2,81 | 64,56 | 16,63 | 17,74 | -1,11 | 1,2321 | 11,94481981 | 142,6787203 |
| 2018-03-02 11:10:00 | 2,25 | 68,67 | 12,71 | 17,74 | -5,03 | 25,3009 | 8,02481981 | 64,39773299 |
| 2018-03-03 11:10:00 | 2,31 | 68,7 | 14,14 | 17,74 | -3,6 | 12,96 | 9,45481981 | 89,39361765 |
| 2018-03-03 12:10:00 | 2,81 | 68,71 | 16,08 | 17,74 | -1,66 | 2,7556 | 11,39481981 | 129,8419185 |
| 2018-03-04 11:10:00 | 2,76 | 62,65 | 16,83 | 17,74 | -0,91 | 0,8281 | 12,14481981 | 147,4966482 |
| 2018-03-04 12:10:00 | 2,54 | 63,01 | 16,52 | 17,74 | -1,22 | 1,4884 | 11,83481981 | 140,0629599 |
| 2018-03-05 11:10:00 | 2,33 | 68,71 | 14,44 | 17,74 | -3,3 | 10,89 | 9,75481981 | 95,15650953 |
| 2018-03-06 11:10:00 | 2,34 | 68,71 | 14,26 | 17,74 | -3,48 | 12,1104 | 9,57481981 | 91,6771744 |
| 2018-03-07 11:10:00 | 2,8 | 68,71 | 16,65 | 17,74 | -1,09 | 1,1881 | 11,96481981 | 143,1569131 |
| 2018-03-08 11:10:00 | 2,4 | 68,71 | 12,95 | 17,74 | -4,79 | 22,9441 | 8,26481981 | 68,3072465 |
| 2018-03-09 11:10:00 | 2,25 | 68,69 | 11,41 | 17,74 | -6,33 | 40,0689 | 6,72481981 | 45,22320148 |
| 2018-03-09 12:10:00 | 1,76 | 69,15 | 16,35 | 17,74 | -1,39 | 1,9321 | 11,66481981 | 136,0680212 |
| 2018-03-10 11:10:00 | 2,77 | 69,15 | 16,92 | 17,74 | -0,82 | 0,6724 | 12,23481981 | 149,6908158 |
| 2018-03-11 11:10:00 | 2,23 | 68,66 | 11,61 | 17,74 | -6,13 | 37,5769 | 6,92481981 | 47,95312941 |
| 2018-03-12 11:10:00 | 2,42 | 68,66 | 12,99 | 17,74 | -4,75 | 22,5625 | 8,30481981 | 68,97003208 |

**Fig. 8.** Values obtained through the proposed index. (Color figure online)

significant relationship between the model components and their impact on the UV index results.

When analyzing Fig. 11, we observe the distribution of the fuzzy index throughout the day, which is slightly above the index obtained by the TUV model. In addition, a clear separation is identified at the points of maximum radiation, which occur between 11 am and 2 pm.

Therefore, we visualize that the intensity of UV radiation reaches its maximum at the highest point of the sun, between 12 and 13 h. The methodology used admits changes in the parameters to build a model that better fits the intensity of the UVA and UVB components. If one of the components had an "extreme" intensity, it was determined to be sufficient to classify the radiation intensity in a higher range on the UV radiation scale. In this way, an extreme component was prevented from being balanced by one of normal intensity.

In addition, the corresponding rules and values obtained through the fuzzy logic model are presented. To improve the accuracy of the fuzzy logic model,

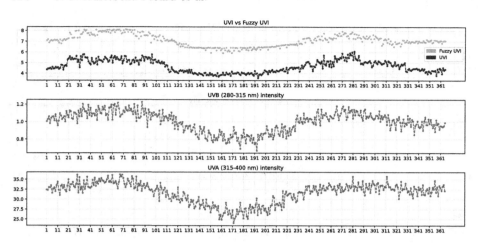

**Fig. 9.** Graph average value per day of the TUV model vs fuzzy UVI.

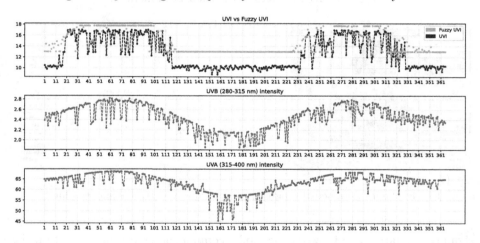

**Fig. 10.** Graph maximum value per day of the TUV model vs. fuzzy UVI.

the use of real data captured by UVA and UVB radiation sensors in the city of Cuenca-Ecuador is required. In this way, it will be possible to adapt the parameters of the fuzzy model to values obtained directly from a sensor, avoiding potential biases when using the TUV model.

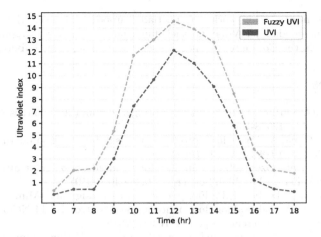

**Fig. 11.** Average graph year 2018 in the time range 6 am - 6 pm.

# 5    Conclusions

This research aims to demonstrate how to obtain a UV radiation index using a fuzzy logic model with a Mamdani approach. Therefore, it was shown that the fuzzy model is an effective alternative for getting a UV radiation index compared to the TUV mathematical model, and the integrated fuzzy index provides clear information when evaluating the components that make up the UV radiation index. The components are categorised on a scale from imperceptible to extreme, with seven levels between the scales, allowing understandable information transmission for decision-making. Furthermore, the model can be improved using accurate data from sensors corresponding to the study region to fit the fuzzy logic model precisely. In general, this approach is helpful for decision-making to report the harmful effects of UV radiation.

In this study, data mining techniques were applied to preprocess the information of the pollutant data corresponding to the city of Cuenca-Ecuador in 2018. Fuzzy logic was later used as a data model with the Mamdani approach to obtain data on UV radiation indices. For this, the values of the UVA and UVB components were combined using 49 rules, the results of which were compared with the UV radiation indices of the TUV model. As a result, we obtained a slightly higher fuzzy index in terms of the index score compared to the TUV model. The evaluation parameters used in the study were the coefficient of determination (r-square) with a value of 0.63 and the RSME with a value of 2.82. These parameters indicate that the fuzzy logic model with the Mamdani approach obtains an integrated UV index that resembles the TUV mathematical model. This model uses tropospheric ozone and other region parameters to calculate the UV radiation index.

**Acknowledgements.** This work was partially supported by the vice rectorate of Research at Universidad del Azuay for their financial and academic support, as well as the entire staff in the Computer Science Research & Development Laboratory (LIDI).

# References

1. Aggarwal, C.: Outlier Analysis, vol. 2. Springer, Cham (2017). https://doi.org/10. 1007/978-3-319-47578-3
2. Allana, A., Chua, A.: Fuzzy logic program for bus indoor environmental assessment. ASEAN Eng. J. **11**(4), 129–142 (2021)
3. Bais, A.F., et al.: Ozone-climate interactions and effects on solar ultraviolet radiation. Photochem. Photobiol. Sci. **18**(3), 602–640 (2019)
4. Baldovino, R.G., Dadios, E.P.: Fuzzy logic control: design of a 'Mini' fuzzy associative matrix (FAM) table algorithm in motor speed control. In: TENCON 2015-2015 IEEE Region 10 Conference, pp. 1–4. IEEE (2015)
5. Barnes, P.W., et al.: Ozone depletion, ultraviolet radiation, climate change and prospects for a sustainable future. Nat. Sustain. **2**(7), 569–579 (2019)
6. Barnston, A.G.: Correspondence among the correlation, RMSE, and Heidke forecast verification measures; refinement of the Heidke score. Weather Forecast. **7**(4), 699–709 (1992)
7. Bi, J.: A review of statistical methods for determination of relative importance of correlated predictors and identification of drivers of consumer liking. J. Sens. Stud. **27**(2), 87–101 (2012)
8. Cañarte, C., Salum, G., Ipiña, A., Piacentini, R.: Índice ultravioleta como indicador de riesgo en la piel. Dermatología Ibero-Americana on line (2011)
9. Dernoncourt, F.: Introduction to fuzzy logic, vol. 21, pp. 50–56. Massachusetts Institute of Technology (2013)
10. Dubois, D., Prade, H.: Fundamentals of Fuzzy Sets, vol. 7. Springer, New York (2012). https://doi.org/10.1007/978-1-4615-4429-6
11. Empresa Pública Municipal de Movilidad, Transito y Transporte de Cuenca: Calidad de aire (2017). https://www.emov.gob.ec/calidad-de-aire/. Accessed 29 June 2023
12. Huillca Arbieto, M., William Taipe, C., Saavedra, M.: Índice ultravioleta en la ciudad de puno para cielos claros. Revista de Investigaciones Altoandinas **19**(2), 211–218 (2017)
13. Instituto Nacional de Estadística y Censos: Población y Demografía (2010). https://www.ecuadorencifras.gob.ec/censo-de-poblacion-y-vivienda/. Accessed 29 June 2023
14. Ipiña, A., López-Padilla, G., Retama, A., Piacentini, R.D., Madronich, S.: Ultraviolet radiation environment of a tropical megacity in transition: Mexico city 2000–2019. Environ. Sci. Technol. **55**(16), 10946–10956 (2021)
15. Jaramillo, M., González, D.E., Núñez, M.E., Portilla, G.: Índice integrado de calidad del aire para ciudades colombianas. Revista Facultad de Ingeniería Universidad de Antioquia **1**(48), 97–106 (2009)
16. Katushabe, C., Kumaran, S., Masabo, E.: Fuzzy based prediction model for air quality monitoring for Kampala City in East Africa. Appl. Syst. Innov. **4**(3), 44 (2021)
17. Kaur, A., Kaur, A.: Comparison of mamdani-type and sugeno-type fuzzy inference systems for air conditioning system. Int. J. Soft Comput. Eng. (IJSCE) **2**(2), 323–325 (2012)

18. Kyprianou, D., Charalambidou, I., Famojuro, O., Wang, H., Su, D., Farazi, P.A.: Knowledge and attitudes of cypriots on melanoma prevention: is there a public health concern? BMC Public Health **22**(1), 53 (2022). https://doi.org/10.1186/s12889-021-12324-0
19. Lucas, R., et al.: Human health in relation to exposure to solar ultraviolet radiation under changing stratospheric ozone and climate. Photochem. Photobiol. Sci. **18**(3), 641–680 (2019)
20. Novales, A.: Análisis de regresión. Universidad Complutense de Madrid, Madrid (2010)
21. Peña, M., Ortega, P., Orellana, M.: A novel imputation method for missing values in air pollutant time series data. In: 2019 IEEE Latin American Conference on Computational Intelligence (LA-CCI), pp. 1–6. IEEE (2019)
22. Santigosa, L.R., Martinez, J.P., Lopez, L.M., de Cardona Ortin, M.S., Galvez, J.B.: Fuzzy inference systems applied to the daily ultraviolet radiation evaluation (295–385 nm) from daily global radiation. Sol. Energy **75**(6), 447–454 (2003)
23. Umar, S.A., Tasduq, S.A.: Ozone layer depletion and emerging public health concerns-an update on epidemiological perspective of the ambivalent effects of ultraviolet radiation exposure. Front. Oncol. **12**, 866733 (2022)
24. Walden, C.A.S.: Publicación de contaminantes atmosféricos de la estación de monitoreo de la ciudad de cuenca, utilizando servicios estándares OGC. ACI Avances en Ciencias e Ingenierías **9**(1) (2017)
25. Wilson, S.R., Madronich, S., Longstreth, J., Solomon, K.R.: Interactive effects of changing stratospheric ozone and climate on tropospheric composition and air quality, and the consequences for human and ecosystem health. Photochem. Photobiol. Sci. **18**(3), 775–803 (2019)
26. World Health Organization: International commission on non-ionizing radiation protection: global solar UV index: a practical guide. Technical report, World Health Organization (2002)

# Forecasting the Consumer Price Index of Ecuador Using Classical and Advanced Time Series Models

Juan Riofrio$^{(\boxtimes)}$ ⓘ, Saba Infante ⓘ, and Aracelis Hernández ⓘ

School of Mathematical and Computational Sciences, Yachay Tech University, Urcuqui, Ecuador
{jriofrio,sinfante,ahernandez}@yachaytech.edu.ec

**Abstract.** In this article, a set of tools are used to forecast and estimate time series models that characterize the patterns generated by Consumer Price Index (CPI) in Ecuador. Estimating this macroeconomic indicator is important because it allows designing public policies, issuing rules that govern the market, controlling inflation, investment risks, in addition to other relevant considerations. To achieve this goal, a variety of models were evaluated including: Support Vector Regression (SVR), Particle filter (PF), SARIMA, Fast Fourier Transform (FFT), Theta Method, among other models. The results obtained in this empirical study demonstrate two promising methods for the prediction of the Ecuadorian CPI. The technique implemented with FFT showed accuracy and forecast robustness, the model allows to identify and analyze the frequency components within a time series and provides valuable information on the dominant patterns, cycles and seasonality present in the data. FFT model obtained a Mean Absolute Error (MAE) of 0.7347 and 0.1340 in the testing and validation steps respectively. The 4Theta model also produced good results, this method allows capturing both the level and the trend of the components of a time series. The 4Theta method achieved a MAE of 0.3453 in the testing step and a validation MAE of 0.8678. This study is the first to employ PF for Ecuador's CPI forecast. Despite suboptimal results, it represents an important initial step in using this method for inflation prediction. To enhance accuracy, a refined movement equation and improved multi-step forecasting with PF are being developed for future work.

**Keywords:** Consumer Price Index · Time Series Forecasting · Forecasting Models · Darts Module · Inflation

## 1 Introduction

The consumer price index (CPI) is a measure of the average change over a time horizon in the prices paid by consumers for a common basket of assets and services. This index attempts to quantify and measure the average cost of life in the countries, estimating the purchasing power in terms of a monetary unit.

© The Author(s), under exclusive license to Springer Nature Switzerland AG 2023
J. Maldonado-Mahauad et al. (Eds.): TICEC 2023, CCIS 1885, pp. 128–144, 2023.
https://doi.org/10.1007/978-3-031-45438-7_9

It is also used to measure inflation or deflation and largely explain the behavior of market dynamics. Accurately estimating the next inflation rate is of great interest to the authorities in charge of designing state public policies and those in charge of dictating the rules that govern the market. For example, Central Banks predict future inflation trends in order to justify the setting of interest rates and control the variation of inflation within a confidence interval that includes the target set [4,12,18]. It is also important to predict future inflation for tax authorities because it allows them to adjust social security payments and tax revenues [4]. In the business sector, it is of interest to estimate future inflation, because it helps them to forecast price dynamics and mitigate investment risks. In the public and private debt sectors, interest payments are governed by the behavior of inflation [1,31].

To estimate the CPI in Ecuador we propose to use some classic time series models, Support Vector Regression, a sequential prediction algorithm, together with some machine learning methods implemented in the Darts Library. Support Vector Regression (SVR), first introduced in [7] in the field of statistical learning theory and structural risk minimization, has proven useful in a variety of prediction problems and classifications. SVR was developed as a regression variation of Support Vector Machine (SVM) method and has a reliable performance in predicting or forecasting time series data. The method tries to find the best hyperplane (dividing line) between classes, it also can address difficulties such as non-linearity, local minimum, and high dimension where the ARIMA model fails. In this cases, SVR overcome overfitting so it has a good performance and it has advantages in optimizing the pattern recognition system with good generalization and accuracy results [26].

Sequential Monte Carlo (SMC) algorithms are techniques used to simulate samples sequentially from distributions that evolve over time, are characterized by being highly flexible and widely applicable in many fields of science. In particular, in this paper we will discuss Particulate Filters (PF) that belongs to the SMC algorithms. The PFs were developed in the decade of the (1990) by [8,9,14,15,19,28], with the purpose of approximating arbitrary distributions, possibly multi-modal and in high-dimensional spaces. The method consists of generating a set of weighed samples called particles to approximate the posterior density of the unknown states. The prediction step involves a Markovian recursion that is updated iteratively based on the states predicted in past times.

The contribution of this work consists in predicting the consumer price index in Ecuador from macroeconomic and financial variables. To achieve the objective, a variety of classical time series models, a state-space model fitted by the particle filter, and machine learning models were estimated. The proposed models will be evaluated using some goodness-of-fit measures and the best forecasting models will be selected. Overall, this study contributes to the field of economic forecasting in Ecuador by providing empirical evidence on the performance of several methods in predicting the CPI. The findings suggest that these methods can serve as valuable tools for policymakers, economists, and businesses in making informed decisions, managing inflation risks, and formulating effective monetary and fiscal policies to ensure stability and economic growth in Ecuador.

The remaining of this paper is structured as follows: Sect. 2 extend the background of this work and explains similar works to the one proposed in this study. Section 3 describes the metrics, data set and overviews the proposed methods used in this study. Section 4 gathers the main results obtained from the experiments. Section 5 explores the significance of the work's results. Finally, the concluding remarks are drawn in Sect. 6.

## 2  Related Work

Inflation forecasting is a challenge of great importance and difficult to achieve. It has been for many decades an area of active research in academia, fiscal institutions, financial entities, central banks, and industry. The main lines of research include structural macroeconomic modeling, forecasting of macroeconomic variables, and the study of monetary policies. Some important works in this area include the work of [33] show that statistics such as average inflation rate, conditional volatility, and persistence levels are shifting in time. They concluded inflation is a non-stationary process, which further limits the amount of relevant historical data points. In [35], the authors compared traditional time series models with machine learning methods for inflation forecasts in the US between the years (1984) and (2014). In the study they concluded that the machine learning model prevails over time series models for forecasting core personal consumption expenditure inflation, and that time series models are better for forecasting core consumer price index inflation. The research developed in [23] compared inflation forecasting with several machine learning models such as lasso regression, random forests, and deep neural networks. The covariates considered were: availability of cash, availability of credit, online prices, housing prices, consumption data, exchange rates and interest rates, they focused on predicting the disaggregated indices that make up the CPI. [4] proposed a hierarchical architecture based on recurrent neural networks to predict the partial disaggregated CPI inflation components. They developed a hierarchical recurrent neural network model that uses information from the higher levels of the CPI hierarchy to improve the predictions at the more volatile lower levels, and concluded that the proposed methodology allows the use of additional forecasting measures to estimate sectoral price changes in some specific components.

In [27], the authors carried out a comparative study of predictive models that include Neural Networks based on a Long Short-Term Memory (LSTM) architecture, Support Vector Regression, SARIMA and Exponential Smoothing, to estimate the consumer price index in Ecuador in a horizon of (12) months. As a result, they obtain that the best model predictive is Support Vector Regression using a polynomial kernel. In [29], the researchers dealt with the CPI forecast problem in Ecuador by using different architectures of an LSTM network, and a convolutional network architecture (CNN). They conclude that combining the CNN network with an LSTM obtains the best forecast for the CPI time series of Ecuador. The method presented in [5] forecasted some time series of the macroeconomy of Ecuador using state-space models combined with Kalman and smoothed Kalman filters. The time series analyzed were Gross Domestic Product (GDP), GDP rate, CPI, industrial production index and active interest rate. In all the cases studied, the estimates obtained by the proposed models reflect the real behavior of the Ecuadorian economy.

## 3    Materials and Methods

### 3.1    Particle Filtering

The particle filter (PF) considers the estimation problem of sequentially generated observations, using a transition equation that describes the distribution of a hidden Markov process denoted by $\{x_t, \quad t \in \mathbb{N}\}$, called a vector of latent states (unobserved states), and an observation equation describing the plausibility of measured data at discrete times denoted by $\{y_t, \quad t \in \mathbb{N}\}$. The model is defined in terms of the probability densities:

$$\begin{aligned} x_t &= f(x_{t-1}) + u_t \quad u_t \sim N(0, \sigma_u^2) \quad \text{(state evolution density)} \\ y_t &= h(x_t) + v_t \quad v_t \sim N(0, \sigma_v^2) \quad \text{(observation density)} \end{aligned} \tag{1}$$

where $x_t \in \mathbb{R}^{n_x}$: represent the unobserved states of the system, $y_t \in \mathbb{R}^{n_y}$: represent observations over time $t$, $f(.), h(.)$: represent the nonlinear functions of the states and of the observations, $u_t \in \mathbb{R}^{n_u}, v_t \in \mathbb{R}^{n_v}$ :represents white noise processes. The interest lies in estimating the unknown states $\mathbf{x_{1:t}} = \{x_1, \dots x_t\}$ from the measurements $\mathbf{y_{1:t}} = \{y_1, \dots y_t\}$. The joint distribution of the states and observations can be obtained directly by the probability chain rule directly by the probability chain rule:

$$p(x_{1:t}, y_{1:t}) = f(x_1) \left( \prod_{k=2}^{t} f(x_k | x_{k-1}) \right) \left( \prod_{k=1}^{t} h(y_k | x_k) \right)$$

where $f(x_1)$ is the distribution of the initial state.

In order that this inference can be performed on high-dimensional models, and with nonlinear structures, many approximation techniques have been proposed; In particular, it is proposed to use the particle filtering methods, the filtering density is approximated with an empirical distribution formed from point masses, or particles. Suppose that we have at time $t-1$ weighted particles

$$\left\{ \mathbf{x}_{1:t-1}^{(i)}, \omega_{t-1}^{(i)}, i = 1, \dots, N \right\} \tag{2}$$

drawn from the smoothing density $p(x_{t-1} | \mathbf{y_{1:t-1}})$, We can consider this an empirical approximation for the density made up of point masses,

$$p_N(x_{t-1} | \mathbf{y_{1:t-1}}) \approx \sum_{i=1}^{N} \omega_t^{(i)} \delta_{x_{t-1}^{(i)}}(x_{t-1}), \quad \sum_{i=1}^{N} \omega_t^{(i)} = 1, \quad \omega_t^{(i)} \geq 0 \tag{3}$$

where $\delta_{x_{t-1}^{(i)}}(x_{t-1})$ denotes the Dirac-delta function.

To update the smoothing density from time $t-1$ to time $t$, factorize it as

$$p_N(x_t|\mathbf{y_{1:t}}) = p_N(x_{t-1}|\mathbf{y_{1:t-1}}) \frac{h(y_t|x_t) f(x_t|x_{t-1})}{p(y_t|\mathbf{y_{1:t-1}})} \qquad (4)$$

A new state is then generated randomly from an importance distribution, $q(x_t|x_{t-1}, y_t)$, and appended to the corresponding trajectory, $x_{t-1}$. The importance weight is updated to:

$$\omega_t^{(i)} = \frac{h(y_t|x_t^{(i)}) f(x_t^{(i)}|x_{t-1}^{(i)})}{q(x_t^{(i)}|x_{t-1}^{(i)}, y_t)} \omega_{t-1}^{(i)} \qquad (5)$$

where:

$$\omega_{t-1}^{(i)} = \frac{p(x_{t-1}^{(i)}|\mathbf{y_{1:t-1}})}{q(x_{t-1}^{(i)}|\mathbf{y_{1:t-1}})} \qquad (6)$$

then

$$p_N(x_t|\mathbf{y_{1:t}}) \approx \sum_{i=1}^{N} \omega_t^{(i)} \delta_{x_t^{(i)}}(x_t) \qquad (7)$$

Given at time $t-1$, $N \in \mathbb{N}$ random samples $\{\mathbf{x}_{1:t-1}^{(i)}\}$ distributed approximately according to $p(x_{t-1}|\mathbf{y_{1:t-1}})$, the Monte Carlo filter proceeds as follows at time $t$:

**Step 1:** Sequential Importance Sampling
- Generate $N$ i.i.d. samples $\{\tilde{x}_t^{(i)}, i = 1, \ldots, N\}$ from the proposal density $q(x)$:

$$\tilde{x}_t^{(i)} \sim q(x_t|\mathbf{x}_{1:t-1}^{(i)}, \mathbf{y_{1:t}}) = f(x_t|\tilde{x}_{t-1}^{(i)}) + u_t^{(i)}, \qquad u_t^{(i)} \sim N(0, \sigma_u^2)$$

and set $\tilde{\mathbf{x}}_{1:t}^{(i)} = \{\mathbf{x}_{1:t-1}^{(i)}, \tilde{x}_t^{(i)}\}$.
- For $i = 1, \ldots, N$, evaluate the importance weights up to a normalizing constant

$$\omega_t^{(i)} \propto \frac{h\left(y_t|\mathbf{y_{1:t-1}}, \tilde{\mathbf{x}}_{1:t}^{(i)}\right) f\left(\tilde{x}_t^{(i)}|\tilde{x}_{t-1}^{(i)}\right)}{q(x_t|\mathbf{x}_{1:t-1}^{(i)}, \mathbf{y_{1:t}})}$$

- For $i = 1, \ldots, N$, normalize the importance weights:

$$\tilde{\omega}_t^{(i)} = \frac{\omega_t^{(i)}}{\sum_{j=1}^{N} \omega_t^{(j)}}, \qquad \sum_{i=1}^{N} \tilde{\omega}_t^{(i)} = 1$$

- Evaluate $\hat{N}_{eff} = \frac{1}{\sum_{i=1}^{N} [\tilde{w}_t^{(i)}]^2}$

**Step 2:** Resampling
- If $\hat{N}_{eff} \geq N_{thres}$,

$$x_{1:t}^{(i)} = \tilde{x}_{1:t}^{(i)}, \quad for \quad i = 1, \ldots, N$$

otherwise
- For $i = 1, ..., N$, sample an index $j(i)$ distributed according to the discrete distribution with $N$ elements satisfying

$$p\left(j(i) = l\right) = \tilde{\omega}_t^{(l)}, \quad for \quad l = 1, \ldots, N$$

- For $i = 1, ..., N$, $\mathbf{x}_{1:t}^{(i)} = \tilde{\mathbf{x}}_{1:t}^{j(i)}$ and $\tilde{w}_t^{(i)} = \frac{1}{N}$.

### 3.2  Particle Filter Forecaster

PF uses the value of the last observation $y_t$ to predict the next value. Then, it has to be adapted to forecast several steps ahead from the last observation. We implemented a Particle Filter Forecaster (PFF) that uses the last observation to predict the next value. But as it does not have a new observation to update the particles weights, it uses the predicted value as an observation (it assumes $y_t = x_t$) to update the weights and proceed to predict the next value. This process repeats as many times as values needed for the forecast horizon. It is advisable to not forecast too long into the future. It is important to mention that normally PF uses sensors measurements or a movement equation to predict the next value. Equation (8) presents the movement equation used by our PFF to predict the CPI of Ecuador for the training step, and Eq. (9) shows the movement equation used by our PFF to forecast the CPI of Ecuador for the testing and validation steps, both of them represents the term $f(x_{t-1})$ from the state evolution density in Eq. 1.

$$f(x_{t-1}) = \sqrt{\mu}\eta x_{t-1} \tag{8}$$

$$f(x_{t-1]}) = \sqrt{\eta}\mu x_{t-1} \tag{9}$$

where $\mu$ is last month rate of change $\mu = y_{t-1}/y_{t-2}$ and $\eta$ is the rate of change in the same month but from last year, specifically $\eta = y_{t-12}/y_{t-13}$. The reason behind the use of this two different equations resides in the availability of true values. In both cases, $\eta$ in computed from actual values, but in Eq. (9), $\mu$ is calculated from predicted values. Then, it was decided to give less importance to $\mu$ in Eq. (9) by obtaining the square root of it.

### 3.3  Support Vector Regression

The Support Vector Regression (SVR) algorithm was formulated by [37] and is a machine-learning algorithm that is perhaps the most elegant of all kernel-learning methods. The SVR consist of a small subset of data points extracted by the learning algorithm from the training sample itself. Support Vector Machines (SVM) tackle binary classification problems by converting them into convex optimization problems [36]. The optimization task involves identifying the hyperplane that maximally separates classes while accurately classifying as many training points as possible. Support vectors are used to represent this optimal hyperplane. The SVM sparse solution and its ability to perform a good generalization make it suitable for regression problems. In the context of SVR, the concept of an $\epsilon$-insensitive region is introduced around the function, referred to as the $\epsilon$-tube. This tube reshapes the optimization problem to identify the best-fitting tube for the continuous-valued function while considering the trade-off between model complexity and prediction error. To formulate SVR as an optimization problem, a convex $\epsilon$-insensitive loss function is defined, and the flattest tube enclosing most training instances is sought. Consequently, a multiobjective function is constructed by combining the loss function and the geometric properties of the tube. The convex optimization problem, which has a unique solution, is then solved using appropriate numerical optimization algorithms. The hyperplane is expressed in terms of support vectors, which are training samples lying outside the tube boundary. Similar to SVM, the support vectors in SVR heavily influence the tube's shape [3]. SVR models have recently been used to handle problems such as nonlinear, local minimum, and high dimension. This model can even guarantee higher accuracy for long-term predictions compared to other computational approaches in many applications. We used the last 12 monthly records as input to predict the CPI value of the next month. Then, we encounter the same problem as PF, it can only predict one step ahead. To overcome this problem, we again use the model predictions as input values to predict the next step. This increase the prediction error as it uses predictions that already have an error to predict the next value, but it gives the model the ability to forecast several steps into the future.

### 3.4 Darts Module

Darts is a Python library developed by [16], which aims to forecast and detect anomalies in univariate and multivariate time series on large data sets. The methodology allows: curve fitting, regression, classification, forecasting, clustering, anomaly detection and reinforcement learning. The library contains a variety of classic time series models, Machine learning and global models, such as: ARIMA, AutoARIMA [32], Baseline Models, Block Recurrent Neural Networks [30], CatBoost model, Croston method, D-Linear, Exponential Smoothing (ES), Fast Fourier Transform (FFT), Kalman Filter Forecaster (KFF), LightGBM Model, Linear Regression model, Neural Basis Expansion Analysis for Interpretable Time Series forecasting (N-BEATS) [24,25], N-HiTS, N-Linear, Prophet [34], Random Forest, Regression ensemble model, Regression Model, Recurrent Neural Networks, Temporal Convolutional Network, Temporal Fusion Transformer (TFT) [20], Theta Method [2], Transformer Model, VARIMA and XGBoost Model. The library also allows to perform retrospective analysis of fitted models, to combine predictions and to simultaneously analyze many model structures at the same time.

FFT method [13] is a useful tool to decompose any deterministic or non-deterministic signal into its frequencies, from which information can be extracted. The FFT provides an excellent mechanism for calculating the Discrete Fourier Transform (DFT) of a time series, that is, discrete data samples [22]. It is widely used in applied mathematics, engineering, and computer science; in particular, in the theory of signal processing systems in high dimensions. The algorithm is fast and of low computational complexity and it allows finding the solution to complex spectral problems [21].

The Theta method was proposed in [2], with the objective of extracting more information from the data, which allows accurate, robust, and reliable univariate time series modeling and forecasting. The Theta model leading to the creation of a Theta line $z(\theta)$, is achieved as the solution of Eq. 10:

$$\nabla^2 z_t(\theta) = \theta \nabla^2 y_t = \theta(y_t - 2Y_{t-1} + y_{t+2}), \quad t = 3, 4, \ldots, n, \tag{10}$$

where $y_1, \ldots, y_n$ is the original time series, and $\nabla$ is the difference operator (i.e. $\nabla y_t = y_t - y_{t-1}$).

The methodology decomposes the original data into two or more lines, called Theta lines. Two first points of the Theta line, for $t = 1$ and $t = 2$, can be obtained by minimizing $\sum_{t=1}^{n} [y_t - z_t(\theta)]^2$. An analytical solution of Eq. 10 is Eq. 11 [17]:

$$z_t(\theta) = \theta y_t + (1 - \theta)(a + bt), \quad \theta \in (0,1), \quad t = 1, \ldots, n \tag{11}$$

where $a$ and $b$ are constants determined by minimization the sum of squared differences $\sum_{t=1}^{n} [y_t - z_t(\theta)]^2$. The resulting Theta line expressed by Eq. 11 is a linear regression model applied to the data directly [10].

The forecasting procedure when using Theta method is carried out in the following steps [11]:

- **Step [1].** Deseasonalization: Firstly, the time series is tested for statistical significant seasonal behaviour. If it expresses a seasonal component, it is deseasonalised using typically classical multiplicative decomposition.
- **Step [2].** Decomposition: The time series is decomposed into two Theta lines, $z(0)$ and $z(2)$.
- **Step [3].** Extrapolation: $z(0)$ is extrapolated as a normal linear regression line, while $z(2)$ is extrapolated using simple exponential smoothing.
- **Step [4].** Combination: The forecast is generated from the extrapolated $z(0)$ and $z(2)$ lines by their combination with equal weights.
- **Step [5].** Reseasonalisation: The forecast is reseasonalised if the original time series was identified as seasonal in step 1.

The method performed well, particularly for monthly series and for microeconomic data [2].

### 3.5   Data Set

The data set used during this research was the CPI of Ecuador. The CPI is a nationwide monthly measure that tracks fluctuations in the overall price level of goods and services (inflation) consumed by households in nine Ecuadorian cities. It represents the final consumption patterns of households across different income levels (high, medium, and low) residing in urban areas of the country. Each month, around 25350 price data points are gathered for the 359 items that constitute the CPI Basket of goods and services. As the Ecuadorian economy suffered a major crisis since 1998, the CPI values increased abnormally for a period. We decided to take only the CPI values since the Ecuadorian economy stabilized. Specifically, we only used the CPI values from January 2001 to May 2023. The data set contains 269 monthly records, the base (CPI = 100) was adjusted in 2014. The minimum and maximum values in the data set are 49.47 and 110.77 respectively. The mean of the data set is 87.78 and the standard deviation is 17.66. During experimentation, the data set was divided in 3: train, test and validation. The training data set consists of 252 records, from January 2001 to December 2021. The principal objective of this research is to predict the CPI 12 months into the future, then the testing data set has 12 records corresponding to the year 2022. Finally, the validation data set has only 5 records, from January to May 2023 as this are the values that have already been released. The data set can be found at https://github.com/ColdRiver93/CPI-Forecasting. Figure 1 shows the graph of the Ecuadorian CPI divided into the 3 data sets.

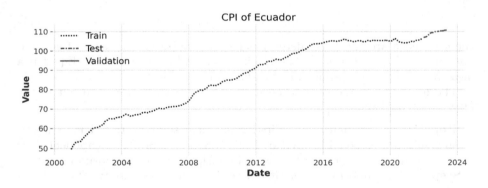

**Fig. 1.** CPI of Ecuador divided into train, test and validation data sets.

### 3.6    Metrics

In the literature there is a variety of metrics used to measure model performance, which are based on the difference between the true value and the estimated value $(y - \hat{y})$, or between the squared difference $(y - \hat{y})^2$. These metrics are related to the loss functions in the norms $L_1$ and $L_2$ that minimize the error when all differences are summed. These measures put emphasize errors; due to the use of an $L_2$ norm, predictions that are farther away from the actual values are penalized to a greater extent compared to closer predictions.

1. **The MSE (Mean Squared Error), and RMSE (Root Mean Squared Error)**, often referred to as quadratic loss or $L_2$ loss is a standard metrics used in model evaluation. For a sample of $n$ observations $(y_i)$ and $n$ corresponding model predictions $\hat{y}_i$, the MSE is given:

$$MSE = \frac{1}{n} \sum_{i=1}^{n} (y_i - \hat{y}_i)^2, \quad and \quad RMSE = \sqrt{\frac{1}{n} \sum_{i=1}^{n} (y_i - \hat{y}_i)^2} = \sqrt{MSE}$$

The square root does not affect the relative ranks of the models, but produces a metric with the same units of $y$, which is convenient for estimating the standard error under normally distributed errors. The RMSE has been used as a standard statistical metric to measure model performance in research studies, [6].

2. **The Mean Absolute Error (MAE)**, measures the average of the sum of absolute differences between observation values and predicted values. The MAE is another useful measure widely used in model evaluation. Then, MAE is defined as:

$$MAE = \frac{1}{n} \sum_{i=1}^{n} |y_i - \hat{y}_i|$$

Similarly to MSE and RMSE, this method can only have positive values. This is so that is can avoid the cancellation of positive and negative values. On the other hand, there is no error penalization, and therefore this method is not sensitive to outliers.

3. **The mean absolute percentage error (MAPE)**, is one of the most popular measures of the forecast accuracy due to its advantages of scale-independency and interpretability. MAPE is the average of absolute percentage errors (APE). Let $y_i$ At and $\hat{y}_i$ denote the actual and forecast values at data point $i$, respectively. Then, MAPE is defined as:

$$MAPE = \frac{1}{n} \sum_{i=1}^{n} \left| \frac{y_i - \hat{y}_i}{y_i} \right|$$

where $n$ is the number of data points.

## 4  Results

The main results of the experimentation phase are presented in this section. In Sect. 3 we explained the division of the data set into 3 smaller data sets for the training, testing and validation steps. We gathered the metrics of the testing and validation steps to compare the different models. We performed a grid search to get the best hyperparameters of each method explained in Sect. 3, and choose the model with the best MAE in the testing step. After selecting the best model, we forecasted the CPI for each month of 2023 and compared the first five months with the validation data set.

Normally, PF is used to estimate the value $x_t$ from $x_{t-1}$. Then, this method is good if we want to predict 1 step into the future. During this research, the task was to forecast the next 12 values from the last actual value obtained. Therefore, we performed some adjustments to the method so it can forecast the next 12 values. We present the results of both implementations to compare their performance. As expected, the performance of the PF is better than the PFF as it uses the actual recent values to update the weights. PFF trades accuracy for the ability to forecast several months into the future. PF obtained a MAE of 0.2906 in the testing step, compared to the MAE of 1.9181 obtained by the PFF. During the validation step, PF and PFF obtained a MAE of 0.1019 and 0.3599, respectively. This results proved that PF is a good method to predict one step into the future, but some work should be done to apply PF to the forecasting problem (PFF).

SVR method also has 2 different implementations. The first implementation uses the actual CPI values as input to the model, but it only predicts one step into the future. The other implementation, uses its own predictions as input to predict several steps into the future (i.e. 12 months into the future). We named this second implementation as SVR Forecaster (SVRF). Here it is also expected that SVR has better error scores than SVRF, but SVRF is able to forecast the CPI for the complete year. SVR scored a testing and validation MAE of 0.3537 and 0.0889 respectively, showing a great performance when the task is to predict one step into the future. On the other hand, SVRF scored a higher testing MAE of 2.0972 and an a slightly higher validation MAE of 0.1054. It is important to mention that both models were the same (same hyperparameters), the difference in both implementations were the input given to the model in the forecasting step. The best model found had a polynomial second degree kernel with a kernel coefficient equal to 15 and an independent term equal to 15. The model used an epsilon value of 0.001 and a regularization parameter of 0.01.

In macroeconomic indicators' forecasting, usually KFF is used instead of PFF. Darts module has an implementation of KFF that we used to forecast the next 12 months. After the grid search, we found that the best size of the Kalman filter state vector is 1 for this particular problem. We can compare the KFF with the PFF as they performed the same task. The KFF outperformed the PFF in the testing step obtaining a MAE of 1.1821, but during validation the proposed PFF had better results than KFF that scored a MAE of 0.8831. We used other methods implemented in the Darts module, not only the KFF.

We also used the ES method presented by Holt and Winters from Darts module to forecast the next 12 months. The hyperparameters of the best model found were a multiplicative type of trend component that is damped, an additive type of seasonal component and three periods in a complete seasonal cycle. This model obtained a MAE of 0.7212 in the testing step and a MAE of 3.4545 in the validation step. This values indicates that the model was overfitted to the test data set during the grid search, and had a poor performance during validation.

ARIMA method, is broadly used for time series forecasting. Darts module also presents an implementation of SARIMA, as well as an AutoARIMA implementation. AutoARIMA automatically search for the best ARIMA model that looses the less information about the time series. AutoARIMA produced bad results scoring a MAE of 2.1585 and 3.1185 in the testing and validation steps respectively. The best SARIMA model found had the parameters (1, 2, 1) and for the seasonal component (4, 2, 4) with 3 periods per season. This model got a MAE of 0.2618 in the testing step and during validation it obtained a MAE of 1.6064. SARIMA obtained the best score in the testing step, but during validation this model did not behave like expected. This model was overfitted to the testing data and did not forecasted correctly for the validation data set.

The 4Theta method included in Darts module obtained one of the best results in the testing step. Even though, SARIMA was the model with the best testing score, as explained before, it was overfitted. The best 4Theta model was the model with a value of the theta parameter equal to 24, a seasonality period of 24, an additive type of model combining the Theta lines, a multiplicative type of seasonality, and an exponential type of trend to fit. The best model of this method obtained a testing MAE of 0.3453 and a validation MAE of 0.8678.

We considered FFT model to be the best model to predict the CPI of Ecuador for 2023 together with the 4Theta model. This model got a testing MAE of 0.7347, and a validation MAE of 0.1340, the best validation score of all the models. Although, this model did not obtained the best testing score, according to the validation score it was the best model to predict the Ecuadorian CPI for the next months of 2023. The best model used one frequency for forecasting, and a polynomial kind of detrending was applied before performing DFT, with a second degree polynomial used for detrending.

We also used an Artificial Neural Network (ANN) method called Neural Basis Expansion Analysis Time Series Forecasting (N-BEATS). This method implemented in the Darts module, provide us with a powerful forecasting tool. In this method we tuned several hyperparameters to create the ANN architecture. The best ANN architecture found using grid search had six stacks that make up the whole model with 12 blocks making up every stack. It was formed of six fully connected layers preceding the final forking layers in each block of every stack, made up of 12 neurons each. The expansion coefficients was set to six. We used the Softplus as the activation function of the encoder/decoder intermediate layer. The length of the input sequence fed to the model was 12 records, representing an entire year of monthly records. The length of the output forecast of the model was one, meaning we use the 12 previous months to forecast the next month. The testing and validation MAE obtained by the model were 1.3110 and 1.2793 respectively.

The complete results of all the methods are presented in Table 1, the t-MAE, t-MAPE and t-RMSE columns show the testing errors, while the t-MAE, t-MAPE and t-RMSE columns present the validation errors. It is important to remember that PF and SVR had better results because they used actual values to predict only one step into the future.

**Table 1.** Testing and validation MAE, MAPE, RMSE for each method.

| Method | t-MAE | t-MAPE | t-RMSE | v-MAE | v-MAPE | v-RMSE |
|---|---|---|---|---|---|---|
| PF | 0.2906 | 0.002676 | 0.3832 | 0.1019 | 0.000922 | 0.1161 |
| PFF | 1.9181 | 0.017537 | 2.0747 | 0.3599 | 0.003254 | 0.4178 |
| SVR | 0.3537 | 0.003252 | 0.4479 | 0.0889 | 0.000805 | 0.0971 |
| SVRF | 2.0972 | 0.019172 | 2.2754 | 0.1054 | 0.000954 | 0.1145 |
| KFF | 1.1821 | 0.010815 | 1.2676 | 0.8831 | 0.007992 | 0.8994 |
| ES | 0.7212 | 0.006574 | 1.0032 | 3.4545 | 0.031248 | 3.5001 |
| AutoARIMA | 2.1585 | 0.019734 | 2.3369 | 3.1185 | 0.028215 | 3.1193 |
| SARIMA | 0.2618 | 0.002395 | 0.3541 | 1.6064 | 0.014526 | 1.7247 |
| 4Theta | 0.3453 | 0.003176 | 0.4228 | 0.8678 | 0.007845 | 1.0098 |
| FFT | 0.7347 | 0.006817 | 1.0391 | 0.1340 | 0.001213 | 0.1432 |
| N-BEATS | 1.3110 | 0.011989 | 1.4175 | 1.2793 | 0.011576 | 1.2852 |

## 5    Discussion

In this section the results presented in Sect. 4 are analyzed. Also, the limitations encountered during this work are discussed and the ground for future work is determined. First, lets start by defining the best methods according to the results. The best methods in the testing step were SARIMA, 4Theta and ES and FFT in that order. While, the best methods in the validation step were SVRF, FFT, PFF and 4Theta in that order. Then, we consider FFT and 4Theta methods to be the best methods to forecast the CPI of Ecuador one year into the future because of their good performance during both, testing and validation. Table 2 shows the forecasted CPI values for the remaining months of 2023 performed by FFT and 4Theta methods. While, Fig. 2 visually presents the forecasted CPI values for 2023.

**Table 2.** Forecasted CPI values for the remaining months of 2023 using FFT and 4Theta methods.

| Method | Jun | Jul | Aug | Sep | Oct | Nov | Dec |
|---|---|---|---|---|---|---|---|
| FFT | 110.97 | 111.07 | 111.17 | 111.26 | 111.34 | 111.43 | 111.51 |
| 4Theta | 112.26 | 112.4 | 112.53 | 113.22 | 113.59 | 113.96 | 114.33 |

In Fig. 2, it can be seen that FFT forecast is more conservative, predicting little inflation for the rest of the year. While, 4Theta forecast predicts a high inflation during the last months of 2023. The best case scenario for Ecuadorians is the predictions made by the FFT model, as it predicts prices are slightly increasing, but not too much.

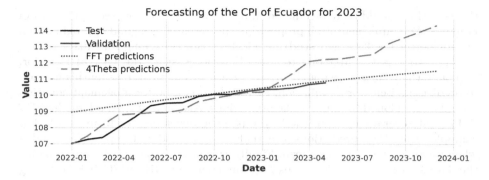

**Fig. 2.** Forecasted CPI of Ecuador for 2023 using FFT and 4Theta methods.

The CPI is a macroeconomic indicator that reflects the inflation of a country. Inflation in Ecuador greatly increased since the first months of 2022. This brings complications during the forecasting task performed in this study. The problem is that the testing data set contains the values of 2022 when Ecuador faced the greater inflation increase since 2015. Then, some models could not predict this high inflation as the last months of the training data set present little or no inflation. Also, as we tested the models with the values showing a great inflation increase, some models predicted the same high inflation increase for the next year. This problem makes the models prone to overfitting, thus a different train-test-validation data set split should be considered.

We believe the N-BEATS model can generate better results. Due to the high number of hyperparameters to tune and the computational cost of the algorithm, we did not tested enough models until we find an optimal result. A wider grid search should be performed to find a model that better forecast the CPI of Ecuador. Even better, an optimization algorithm can be used to find the optimal ANN architecture for the used data set. The Darts module implementation of the N-BEATS method is a powerful tool that should be better exploited.

It has been seen that PF works well for this kind of problem. The proposed PF moves the particles according to the inflation variation of the last month and last year, so it predicts better when we have a constant inflation increase or decrease over the months. On the other hand, the proposed PF does not behave well when the values are continuously increasing and decreasing over time (e.g. FOREX data). On other words, the proposed method works better with smooth time series with trend. As we can see in Fig. 1, this data set mostly complies with this characteristics. Also PF adjust the particle weights according to the last actual observation, giving this method the ability to correct the measurements once a new value is received. PF showed to be a good method when we need to predict only one step ahead.

The accuracy of the PF method depends on the movement equation to predict the movement of the particles from time $t - 1$ to $t$. We used Eq. 8 and Eq. 9 to predict the movement of the particles trying to predict the actual value, but this equation should be reformulated in future work to better predict the CPI of Ecuador. The implementation proposed in this research is a good approximation, but for better results a new study should be done concerning that matter.

This work is the first one to use PF in forecasting the CPI of Ecuador. Although the results were not the best, it was a good first step using this method to predict the Ecuadorian inflation. As said before, a better movement equation should be developed to improve the predictions. Also, a best method for the PFF to forecast several steps into the future is being developed for future work. For example, using FFT predictions as actual values to update the particles weights when we forecast 12 months ahead. Finally, this work is completely reproducible, the data set can be found at https://github.com/ColdRiver93/CPI-Forecasting along with the Python implementation used during this research.

## 6    Conclusions

This work proposed a methodology to forecast the CPI of Ecuador for the remaining months of 2023. Several methods were used to complete this task, ranging from classical models like SARIMA to more recent methods as N-BEATS. We also used other methods during this research, in specific we used PF, SVR, KFF, ES, 4Theta, and FFT methods. We searched for the best method to forecast the CPI of Ecuador one year into the future. The study aimed to provide insights into the accuracy and effectiveness of these forecasting techniques in capturing the complex dynamics of CPI fluctuations in the Ecuadorian economy.

The findings of this research indicate that two methods have demonstrated promising results in predicting the CPI. FFT showed strong forecasting accuracy and robustness, with its capability to identify and analyze the frequency components within a time series and to provide valuable information about the dominant patterns, cycles, and seasonality present in the data. The 4Theta method, which combines exponential smoothing and linear regression to capture both the level and trend components of a time series, also produced accurate predictions.

However, it is worth noting that forecasting accuracy can be influenced by various factors, such as the length and quality of the available historical data, the choice of model parameters, and the specific characteristics of the CPI series. Therefore, future research should explore additional approaches, such as ensemble models or hybrid methodologies, to further enhance forecasting accuracy and robustness.

**Acknowledgements.** This work was carried out under the project Statistical methods for modeling data generated by complex systems with registration MATH23-04, Yachay Tech University. The authors would like to acknowledge the help received from "Laboratorio de la Facultad de Ingeniería de Sistemas" from Escuela Politécnica Nacional. Without the computational resources provided by the laboratory, this research would not have been possible.

# References

1. Almosova, A., Andresen, N.: Nonlinear inflation forecasting with recurrent neural networks. J. Forecast. **42**(2), 240–259 (2023)
2. Assimakopoulos, V., Nikolopoulos, K.: The theta model: a decomposition approach to forecasting. Int. J. Forecast. **16**(4), 521–530 (2000)
3. Awad, M., Khanna, R.: Support vector regression. In: Awad, M., Khanna, R. (eds.) Efficient Learning Machines, pp. 67–80. Apress, Berkeley, CA (2015). https://doi.org/10.1007/978-1-4302-5990-9_4
4. Barkan, O., Benchimol, J., Caspi, I., Cohen, E., Hammer, A., Koenigstein, N.: Forecasting CPI inflation components with hierarchical recurrent neural networks. Int. J. Forecast. **39**(3), 1145–1162 (2023)
5. Bautista Vega, H., Infante, S., Amaro, I.R.: Estimation of the state space models: an application in macroeconomic series of Ecuador. In: Salgado Guerrero, J.P., Chicaiza Espinosa, J., Cerrada Lozada, M., Berrezueta-Guzman, S. (eds.) TICEC 2021. CCIS, vol. 1456, pp. 31–45. Springer, Cham (2021). https://doi.org/10.1007/978-3-030-89941-7_3
6. Chai, T., Draxler, R.R.: Root mean square error (RMSE) or mean absolute error (MAE)?-Arguments against avoiding RMSE in the literature. Geosci. Model Dev. **7**(3), 1247–1250 (2014)
7. Cortes, C., Vapnik, V.: Support-vector networks. Mach. Learn. **20**, 273–297 (1995). https://doi.org/10.1007/BF00994018
8. Doucet, A., De Freitas, N., Gordon, N.: An introduction to sequential Monte Carlo methods. In: Doucet, A., de Freitas, N., Gordon, N. (eds.) Sequential Monte Carlo Methods in Practice. ISS, pp. 3–14. Springer, New York (2001). https://doi.org/10.1007/978-1-4757-3437-9_1
9. Doucet, A., Godsill, S., Andrieu, C.: On sequential Monte Carlo sampling methods for Bayesian filtering. Stat. Comput. **10**, 197–208 (2000)
10. Dudek, G.: Short-term load forecasting using theta method. In: E3S Web of Conferences, vol. 84, p. 01004. EDP Sciences (2019)
11. Fiorucci, J.A., Pellegrini, T.R., Louzada, F., Petropoulos, F., Koehler, A.B.: Models for optimising the theta method and their relationship to state space models. Int. J. Forecast. **32**(4), 1151–1161 (2016)
12. Friedman, M.: The lag in effect of monetary policy. J. Polit. Econ. **69**(5), 447–466 (1961)
13. Ghaderpour, E., Pagiatakis, S.D., Hassan, Q.K.: A survey on change detection and time series analysis with applications. Appl. Sci. **11**(13), 6141 (2021)
14. Godsill, S.J., Doucet, A., West, M.: Monte Carlo smoothing for nonlinear time series. J. Am. Stat. Assoc. **99**(465), 156–168 (2004)
15. Gordon, N.J., Salmond, D.J., Smith, A.F.: Novel approach to nonlinear/non-Gaussian Bayesian state estimation. IEE Proc. F (Radar Sig. Process.) **140**(2), 107–113 (1993)
16. Herzen, J., et al.: Darts: user-friendly modern machine learning for time series. J. Mach. Learn. Res. **23**(1), 5442–5447 (2022)
17. Hyndman, R.J., Billah, B.: Unmasking the Theta method. Int. J. Forecast. **19**(2), 287–290 (2003)
18. Ida, D.: Sectoral inflation persistence and optimal monetary policy. J. Macroecon. **65**, 103215 (2020)
19. Kitagawa, G.: Monte Carlo filter and smoother for non-Gaussian nonlinear state space models. J. Comput. Graph. Stat. **5**(1), 1–25 (1996)

20. Lim, B., Arık, S.Ö., Loeff, N., Pfister, T.: Temporal fusion transformers for inter-pretable multi-horizon time series forecasting. Int. J. Forecast. **37**(4), 1748–1764 (2021)
21. Liu, C., Chen, K., Zhang, J., Wang, Y., Wang, H.: Using FFT to reduce the com-putational complexity of sub-Nyquist sampling based wideband spectrum sensing. In: Journal of Physics: Conference Series, vol. 1237, p. 022004. IOP Publishing (2019)
22. Liu, W., Liao, Q., Qiao, F., Xia, W., Wang, C., Lombardi, F.: Approximate designs for fast Fourier transform (FFT) with application to speech recognition. IEEE Trans. Circ. Syst. I Regul. Pap. **66**(12), 4727–4739 (2019)
23. Medeiros, M.C., Vasconcelos, G.F., Veiga, Á., Zilberman, E.: Forecasting inflation in a data-rich environment: the benefits of machine learning methods. J. Bus. Econ. Stat. **39**(1), 98–119 (2021)
24. Oreshkin, B.N., Carpov, D., Chapados, N., Bengio, Y.: N-BEATS: neural basis expansion analysis for interpretable time series forecasting. arXiv preprint arXiv:1905.10437 (2019)
25. Oreshkin, B.N., Carpov, D., Chapados, N., Bengio, Y.: Meta-learning framework with applications to zero-shot time-series forecasting. In: Proceedings of the AAAI Conference on Artificial Intelligence, vol. 35, no. 10, pp. 9242–9250 (2021)
26. Ramageri, B.M., et al.: Data mining techniques and applications. Indian J. Com-put. Sci. Eng. **1**(4), 301–305 (2010)
27. Riofrío, J., Chang, O., Revelo-Fuelagán, E., Peluffo-Ordóñez, D.H.: Forecasting the consumer price index (CPI) of Ecuador: a comparative study of predictive models. Int. J. Adv. Sci. Eng. Inf. Technol. **10**(3), 1078–1084 (2020)
28. Ristic, B., Arulampalam, S., Gordon, N.: Beyond the Kalman Filter: Particle Fil-ters for Tracking Applications. Artech House (2003)
29. Rosado, R., Abreu, A.J., Arencibia, J.C., Gonzalez, H., Hernandez, Y.: Consumer price index forecasting based on univariate time series and a deep neural network. In: Hernández Heredia, Y., Milián Núñez, V., Ruiz Shulcloper, J. (eds.) IWAIPR 2021. LNCS, vol. 13055, pp. 33–42. Springer, Cham (2021). https://doi.org/10.1007/978-3-030-89691-1_4
30. Salinas, D., Flunkert, V., Gasthaus, J., Januschowski, T.: DeepAR: probabilistic forecasting with autoregressive recurrent networks. Int. J. Forecast. **36**(3), 1181–1191 (2020)
31. Shibitov, D., Mamedli, M.: Forecasting Russian CPI with data vintages and machine learning techniques. Technical report, Bank of Russia (2021)
32. Smith, T.G., et al.: pmdarima: ARIMA estimators for Python (2017). Retrieved from 309
33. Stock, J.H., Watson, M.W.: Why has US inflation become harder to forecast? J. Money, Credit, Bank. **39**, 3–33 (2007)
34. Taylor, S.J., Letham, B.: Forecasting at scale. Am. Stat. **72**(1), 37–45 (2018)
35. Ülke, V., Sahin, A., Subasi, A.: A comparison of time series and machine learning models for inflation forecasting: empirical evidence from the USA. Neural Comput. Appl. **30**, 1519–1527 (2018). https://doi.org/10.1007/s00521-016-2766-x
36. Vapnik, V.: The support vector method of function estimation. In: Suykens, J.A.K., Vandewalle, J. (eds.) Nonlinear Modeling, pp. 55–85. Springer, Boston (1998). https://doi.org/10.1007/978-1-4615-5703-6_3
37. Vapnik, V.N.: A note on one class of perceptrons. Automat. Rem. Control **25**, 821–837 (1964)

# Forecasting PM$_{2.5}$ Concentrations in Ambient Air Using a Transformer Based Neural Network

Jorge L. Charco[1]([envelope])[iD], César Espín-Riofrio[1][iD], Angela Yanza-Montalvan[1], Angélica Cruz-Chóez[1], and Andrés Quevedo-Sacoto[2][iD]

[1] Universidad de Guayaquil, Delta and Kennedy Avenue, Guayaquil, Ecuador
{jorge.charcoa,cesar.espinr,angela.yanzam,angelica.cruzc}@ug.edu.ec
[2] XR-LAB, Universidad Católica de Cuenca, De las Américas and Tarqui Avenue, Cuenca, Ecuador
asquevedos@ucacue.edu.ec

**Abstract.** This paper presents a comparative of the performance of Multi-Layer Perceptron, Long-Short Term Memory and Transformer models in predicting PM$_{2.5}$ concentrations. As first step, a pre-processing is applied to dataset collected between 2019 and 2021, which was provided by Metropolitan Network of Atmospheric Monitoring of Quito. For this, a variance inflation factor is used to detect multicollinearity among the independent variables to reduce the input parameters considering their statistical significance. The proposed models were trained to predict PM$_{2.5}$ concentrations up to 24 h in advance. The experimental results of the proposed models using time windows of 6, 12 and 24 h show that the transformer model obtains better performance, mainly, if the model is trained using a time windows of 24 h.

**Keywords:** PM$_{2.5}$ concentrations · Multi-Layer Perceptron · Long-Short Term Memory · Transformer · Urban air pollution · Attention modules

## 1 Introduction

Urban air pollution is a problem that is affecting to big cities due to the increasing of industrial area near to the city, dust, agricultural waste, gasoline powered vehicles, among other. Although the problem affects everyone, it has a greater impact on children and elderly. According to mentioned in the report State Global Air [22], polluted air has been the fourth leading risk factor for early death worldwide in 2019, surpassed only by high blood pressure, tobacco use, and poor diet. It is therefore necessary to understand the serious health consequences of being exposed to air pollution and the impacts of different pollutants. Short-term exposures to air pollution can increase the risk for cardiovascular diseases and asthma symptoms, even cause death from ischemic heart disease, lung cancer, chronic obstructive pulmonary disease [3,10,18]. The World Health

J. Maldonado-Mahauad et al. (Eds.): TICEC 2023, CCIS 1885, pp. 145–159, 2023.
https://doi.org/10.1007/978-3-031-45438-7_10

Organization [26], estimates that 99% of the world's population live in places where air pollution levels exceed its guideline limits. Likewise, they mention that exposure to ambient air pollution has caused 6.7 million deaths each year.

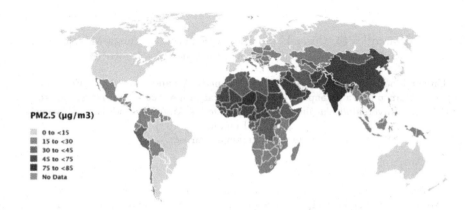

**Fig. 1.** State of Global Air [22]: Average annual population-weighted PM$_{2.5}$ concentrations.

There are three types of air pollution known to impact human health: ambient (outdoor) fine particle pollution, ambient tropospheric ozone, and household air pollution. The air quality is related to these pollutants, mainly, ambient fine particle air pollution, which is referred to PM$_{2.5}$. This type of pollutant is emitted from vehicles, industrial activities, agricultural waste burning, among other. They can be harmful when the exposure to concentrations of PM$_{2.5}$ is high by several years. Figure 1 shows a global map of population-weighted annual average PM$_{2.5}$ concentrations. According to mentioned by World Health Organization, the air quality guideline is $10\,\mu g/m^3$. However, over 90% of the world's population have an average PM$_{2.5}$ concentrations that exceed this value, mainly in regions from Asia, Africa, and the Middle East.

Over time, extensive networks around of 10408 ground monitors from 116 countries have been used to obtain information about the health effects of air pollution and changes in air quality, and which have helped to development different sophisticated techniques that combined available ground measurements with observations from satellites. During last decades, different statistical models such as regression, ARIMA method, projection pursuit model and principal component analysis, have been applied for pollution estimation problem. The authors in [21] have proposed to use an univariate linear stochastic model, referred to as ARIMA. It consists of extracting trends and serial corrections from all observed data. The model is used to predict short-term real-time of air pollution considering only the past records of pollutants. A similar work is proposed in [2], where the authors have developed an analytical model to predict next day's maximum ozone concentration. The relationship between ozone values and meteorological variables is examined, including near surface air (temperature and relative humidity) with air pollution variables. Multiple linear regression is developed to establish the relationship between the above mentioned parameters and peak ozone (O$_3$) concentration. A novel technique SPA (Single Point Areal Estimation) is proposed in [25]. This proposal takes advantage of relationship between PM$_{10}$ and PM$_{2.5}$. It is used to estimate PM$_{2.5}$ concentrations. In details, PM$_{10}$ observations is used as key secondary information that help to improve the estimation of PM$_{2.5}$ concentrations.

Other methods based on artificial intelligence (AI) techniques have been proposed to tackle this problem. In [7], the authors have developed an artificial neural network to predict NO$_2$ concentrations using eight predictor variables, which have been extracted from routinely-available meteorological parameters and the emission pattern of sources present in traffic emissions. A back propagation neural network based on wavelet decomposition has been proposed in [1]. The model considers local meteorological data like additional information to predict daily air pollutants (PM$_{10}$, SO$_2$ and NO$_2$) concentrations. The authors in [24] have proposed a hybrid forecasting method to predict pollutant concentrations. The hybrid model is developed using a back propagation neural network combined with a probabilistic parameter model, and thus, take in account the uncertainties involved in future air quality prediction. Likewise, other neural network has been also proposed in [15]. This model considers a multitask learning, i.e., explore different subtasks such as PM$_{2.5}$, SO$_2$ and NO$_2$ concentrations to find correlations between them, and thus, improve learning for one task by using the information contained from other related tasks. Solutions based on Recurrent Neural Network (RNN) architectures using the long short-term memory (LSTM), have been also developed during the last years to solve the pollutant concentrations estimation problem. In [14], the authors have proposed an architecture with a LSTM approach to predict O$_3$, PM$_{2.5}$, NO$_2$ and CO concentrations using parameters such as vehicular emissions, meteorological conditions, traffic data, and pollutant levels.

Recent studies have leveraged the attention mechanisms to improve the analysis of relationship between meteorological data and pollutant concentrations, and thus, capture the spatial and temporal dependencies for solutions more precise [8,16,28]. Based on these attention mechanisms, different architectures have been proposed, among them, the transformer model. The authors in [4] have proposed a hybrid model, i.e., CNN and a Transformer model, which have the abilities to focus on the global features of time series data, to predict O$_3$ concentration. A similar work has presented in [17]. The model is based on deep transformer networks to tackle the pollutant concentrations estimation (O$_3$ concentration levels) as classification problem. Likewise, the authors in [27] have proposed a multi-head attention-based deep learning architecture, considering useful contextual information across spatial, temporal, and variable-wise dimensions, to improve predictions of PM$_{2.5}$ concentrations.

In the current work, a Transformer model based architecture is implemented for PM$_{2.5}$ concentration estimation in ambient air. The proposed architecture learns the spatio-temporal trends of air pollutant, including meteorological data and traffic conditions to improve the results. This research has the following contributions:

- Analyze the correlation between the input variable of model by variance inflation factor (VIF).
- Develop a Transformer model based architecture for $PM_{2.5}$ concentration estimation
- Compare the experimental results of proposed model with obtained results of Multi-Layer Perceptron (MLP) and Long-Short Term Memory (LSTM) to show that the approaches based on transformer models offer better performance.

The remainder of the paper is organized as follows. In Sect. 2, the material and methods used in this article are presented, including dataset, proposed models and metrics used in this study. Experimental results are reported in Sect. 3, the discuss of obtained results are presented in Sect. 4. Finally, conclusions are given in Sect. 5

## 2   Material and Methods

### 2.1   Study Area

Quito city is located in the province of Pichincha, being the capital and largest city of Ecuador, with coordinates 0° 10′ 50.3508″ S and 78° 28′ 4.2168″ W. The city is surrounded by many mountains like Guagua Pichincha, Cotopaxi, Cayambe volcanoes, and a few others, and it has an estimated population of 2.8 million in its urban area. The major governmental and cultural institutions are located within the city, including the majority of transnational companies with a presence in Ecuador. The climate is a fairly constant cool and has two seasons: dry and wet. Annual precipitation, depending on location, is over 1000 mm mm. Due to its altitude (2850 mt/9350 ft ft above sea level), the population receives some of the greatest solar radiation in the world, sometimes reaching a UV Index of 24 by solar noon [19]. Some factors have negatively impacted on the quality air such as population growth, local industry, gasoline powered vehicles increase, including mining, illegal logging as well as the topography and the climatic characteristics. Currently, Quito is one of the most polluted cities in Ecuador [13]. In this study, the selected area is situated near to the Independence Square, where an air pollution monitoring station is available.

### 2.2   Dataset

The dataset used in this study is obtained from Metropolitan Network of Atmospheric Monitoring of Quito (REMMAQ), which was installed in 2002; it includes nine stations. These stations are located on important zones of the city such as Carapungo, Cotocolloa, Jipijapa, Belisario, Camal, Centro, Guamaní, Tumbaco and Chillos. Each station is able to measure the concentration of pollutants as well as the meteorological variables. The measured meteorological variables are: atmospheric pressure (AP, $hPa$), relative humidity (RHavg, %), temperature (Tavg, °C), solar radiation (SR, $W/m^2$), wind direction (WD, °), wind speed (WS, $m/s$) and ultraviolet radiation (UV, $IUV$), rainfall (RF, mm), including month and day for each measurement. Likewise, the available pollutant concentrations are: carbon monoxide (CO, $\mu g/m^3$), sulfur dioxide (SO$_2$, $\mu g/m^3$), nitrogen oxides (NO$_2$, $\mu g/m^3$), ozone (O$_3$, $\mu g/m^3$) and particulate matter (PM$_{2.5}$, $\mu g/m^3$). For this paper, the used information corresponds from an air polluting monitoring station located in Center of Quito City.

The data covers the years 2019–2021. The highest carbon monoxide register in this period is 3.26 $\mu$g/m$^3$, the nitrogen oxides reaches a maximum of 92.72 $\mu$g/m$^3$, and the maximum sulfur dioxide is 51.46 $\mu$g/m$^3$. With respect to the title of months, there is a continuous and 12-month periodic component.

**Table 1.** List of meteorological variables considered in this study and their descriptive statistics.

| Input Variable | Minimum | Maximum | Average | Standard Deviation |
|---|---|---|---|---|
| Day (number) | 1 | 31 | 15.72 | 8.79 |
| Month (number) | 1 | 12 | 6.36 | 3.36 |
| Year (number) | 2019 | 2021 | 2019.97 | 0.8 |
| Hour (number) | 5 | 21 | 13 | 4.89 |
| CO ($\mu/m^3$) | −0.69 | 3.26 | 0.68 | 0.36 |
| NO$_2$ ($\mu g/m^3$) | −0.29 | 92.72 | 26.32 | 13.84 |
| O$_3$ ($\mu g/m^3$) | 0.39 | 123.15 | 27.7 | 21.4 |
| SO$_2$ ($\mu g/m^3$) | −4.7 | 51.46 | 3 | 2.1 |
| Atmospheric pressure ($hPa$) | 721.11 | 1056.91 | 727.35 | 8.42 |
| Solar radiation ($W/m^2$) | 0 | 1209.57 | 285.01 | 315.72 |
| UV radiation ($IUV$) | 0 | 20.6 | 2.51 | 2.75 |
| Relative humidity (%) | 9.62 | 98.94 | 62.07 | 18.58 |
| Wind direction (°) | 0.23 | 359.93 | 126.32 | 72.53 |
| Wind speed ($m/s$) | 0.02 | 5.63 | 1.65 | 0.82 |
| Rainfall (mm) | 0 | 36.3 | 0.16 | 1.05 |
| Temperature (°C) | 7.91 | 23.2 | 15.6 | 2.94 |
| Traffic (number) | 1 | 4 | 2.73 | 0.82 |
| PM$_{2.5}$ ($\mu g/m^3$) | 0 | 221 | 14,7 | 9,49 |

The Table 1 shows a detail of the meteorological variables obtained from a monitoring station located in Center of Quito City, and their descriptive statistics. This dataset consists of 18105 records, which are randomly divided into two parts: 80% is used for the training process and the remaining 20% is used in the testing phase. The meteorological variables are normalized between 0 and 1. This process is applied to avoid numerical complexities, which could affect to the learning process of the proposed models.

**VIF for Variable Selection.** The meteorological variables are analysed using model's variance inflation factors (VIFs). They allow to detect multicollinearity among the independent variables to reduce the input parameters considering their statistical significance. VIFs are computed in two steps, which are shown in the Table 2. Considering the results obtained in the Table 2, the meteorological variables whose VIF is more greater than 5.0, are highlighted with boldface and lightgray color, since they have a strong correlation with others independent variables. As second step, according to the mentioned in [5], the variables that have a value of VIF greater than 5.0 should be excluded as input parameters in the proposed model. However, although the variables of temperature, solar radiation and relative humidity have a value major than 5.0, only the first two variables mentioned, i.e., temperature and solar radiation, are no longer included as input parameters in the proposed models, since they have a strong correlation with the relative humidity. As final process, the VIF is recalculated without considering these two variables mentioned previously, where 16 meteorological variables are selected as a consequence of this analysis.

**Table 2.** Results of the VIF analysis. The variables with VIF greater than 5.0 are highlighted with boldface and lightgray color.

| Step 1 | | Step 2 | |
|---|---|---|---|
| Variable | VIF | Variable | VIF |
| **Temperature** | **8.86** | $O_3$ | 3.18 |
| **Solar radiation** | **5.76** | Relative humidity | 2.94 |
| **Relative humidity** | **5.45** | CO | 2.71 |
| UV radiation | 3.70 | $NO_2$ | 2.45 |
| $O_3$ | 3.45 | UV radiation | 2.05 |
| CO | 2.75 | Traffic | 1.82 |
| $NO_2$ | 2.56 | $SO_2$ | 1.76 |
| Traffic | 2.03 | Wind speed | 1.63 |
| Hour | 1.83 | Hour | 1.52 |
| $SO_2$ | 1.77 | $PM_{2.5}$ | 1.47 |
| Wind speed | 1.64 | Year | 1.22 |
| $PM_{2.5}$ | 1.51 | Wind direction | 1.18 |
| Wind direction | 1.30 | Month | 1.14 |
| Year | 1.27 | Rainfall | 1.08 |
| Month | 1.21 | Atmospheric pressure | 1.02 |
| Rainfall | 1.08 | Day | 1.01 |
| Atmospheric pressure | 1.02 | | |
| Day | 1.01 | | |

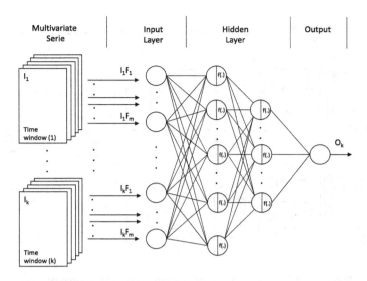

**Fig. 2.** General scheme of MLP network for multivariate time series forecasting.

## 2.3 Methods

A set of machine learning algorithms are considered to predict PM$_{2.5}$ concentrations in ambient air. The dataset used by these algorithms for solving this task contains more than one time-dependent variable; hence, it is necessary to take into account that each variable depends on its pasts and also on other variables.

**Multi-layer Perceptron (MLP) Network.** It is a class of feed-forward neural network, which consists of three layers: an input layer for each feature of problem to solve, one or more hidden layers of neurons and an output layer [11,12]. As mentioned in [6], MLP has two important characteristic. The first, it is able to solve nonlinear problems since each neuron uses a nonlinear activation function; and second, the features pass through of all neurons of each layer since they are massive interconnected. Depending of problem and its complexity, the parameters such as activation function, number of hidden layers and neurons in each layer) could be set with different values. The back-propagation algorithm is used for learning process of this network. The errors obtained from training of model are propagated through the network to adapt the weights of the hidden layers, and thus, improve the results.

In the case of multivariate time series data, the general scheme of MLP network is showed in Fig. 2, where $k$ corresponds to the number of time windows considered for PM$_{2.5}$ concentrations estimation. $I_k F_m$ corresponds to $m$-$th$ meteorological variable of $k$-$th$ time windows. $f(.)$ is activation function used for each node of each hidden layer of proposed architecture. $O_k$ corresponds to the output of $k$-$th$ time windows.

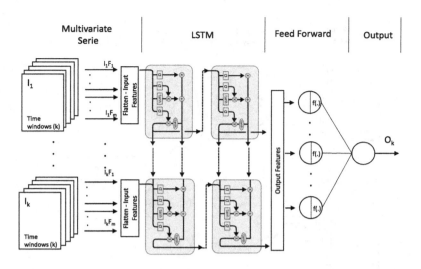

**Fig. 3.** LSTM model for multivariate time series forecasting.

**LSTM.** It is kind of recurrent neural network, which is able to learn long-term dependencies in sequential data, being appropriate for tasks such as language translation, speech recognition, and time series forecasting. In [9], the authors have proposed a LSTM based on recurrent neural network to solve vanishing and exploding gradient difficulties, taking in account the dependencies of data over large periods of time. In order to stores memory important information of input data, which is processed throughout of network, *cell states* are considered. Each cell state known as block contains a set of one or more self-recurrent cells, including three units (input, forget and output gates), which are used for different operations in the cell such as read, write and reset. Each block is used to store information, which has been processed by gate controls previously, and sent to the next block, doing more precise to examine data. LSTM model is able to handle the sequence nature of time series data, being useful to tackle meteorological problems. Figure 3 shows the general scheme of LSTM model used in this study.

**Transformers.** The authors in [23] have proposed this architecture to capture the spatio-temporal relationship using attention modules. These attention modules allow to identify important features of input data instead of take attention to non-useful information, doing that the problem is effectively tackled. The attention modules are known as Multi-Head attention, which are run several time in parallel to capture important information from input data. The obtained output are concatenated and linearly transformed (see Fig. 4). According to [23], a vector of dimension $d_k$ is used for a set of *"queries"* and *"keys"*. Likewise, other vector of dimension $d_v$ is considered for a set of *"values"*. The scaled dot-product attention of Multi-head attention is computed for each *"query"* with all *"keys"*.

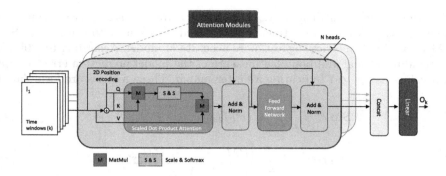

**Fig. 4.** Encoder of transformer model using attention modules [23] for multivariate time series forecasting.

Each result is divided by $\sqrt{d_k}$, and then, a softmax is applied to get the weights on the *"values"*. According to [23], the matrix of outputs is computed as:

$$Attention(Q, K, V) = softmax\left(\frac{QK^T}{\sqrt{d_k}}\right) \times V. \tag{1}$$

The attention modules are run $h$ times, i.e., linearly project $h$ times the *"queries"*, *"keys"* and *"values"* in parallel, generating $h$ outputs, which are concatenated and projected again to produce a final result. The multi-head attention is formulated as:

$$MultiHead(Q, K, V) = Concat(head_1, ..., head_h)W^o,$$
$$where \quad head_i = Attention(QW_i^Q, KW_i^K, VW_i^V). \tag{2}$$

where $h$ corresponds to the number of attention mechanisms to execute in parallel and $W_i^Q \in \mathbb{R}^{d_{model} \times d_k}$, $W_i^K \in \mathbb{R}^{d_{model} \times d_k}$, $W_i^V \in \mathbb{R}^{d_{model} \times d_v}$ and $W^o \in \mathbb{R}^{hd_v \times d_{model}}$ are parameter matrices.

The attentions modules are composed of several Multi-head attention, allowing to capture how much dependency has each sequence by query-key-value attention. According to [23], the position and order of input data are important for the attention modules, since they contains information about relative or absolute position of input data. The positional encoding is formulated as:

$$PE_{(pos,2m)} = sin(pos/10000^{2m/d_{model}}). \tag{3}$$

where $pos$ and $m$ correspond to the position information of input data, including its index respectively, and $d_{model}$ represents the dimension of feature vector.

## 2.4   Metrics

A set of metrics such as Root Mean Square Error (RMSE), Mean Absolute Percentage Error (MAPE), Mean Absolute Error (MAE) and Index of Agreement

(IA) are considered in this study. These metrics are commonly used evaluation metrics in time series forecasting. The obtained values near to 0 using RMSE, MAPE and MAE metrics suggest more accurate of model. According to [20], IA is a nondimensional and bounded measure of the model prediction error degree with values closer to 1 indicating a better match. These metrics are formulated as:

$$RSME = \frac{1}{n} \sum_{i=1}^{n} \sqrt{(PM_{2.5_{pred(i)}} - PM_{2.5_{gt(i)}})^2} \tag{4}$$

$$MAPE = \frac{1}{n} \sum_{i=1}^{n} \frac{\left| PM_{2.5_{pred(i)}} - PM_{2.5_{gt(i)}} \right|}{PM_{2.5_{gt(i)}}} \tag{5}$$

$$MAE = \frac{1}{n} \sum_{i=1}^{n} \left| PM_{2.5_{pred(i)}} - PM_{2.5_{gt(i)}} \right| \tag{6}$$

$$IA = 1 - \frac{\sum_{i=1}^{n}(PM_{2.5_{pred(i)}} - PM_{2.5_{gt(i)}})^2}{\sum_{i=1}^{n}(\left| PM_{2.5_{pred(i)}} - \overline{PM_{2.5_{gt}}} \right| + \left| PM_{2.5_{gt(i)}} - \overline{PM_{2.5_{gt}}} \right|)^2} \tag{7}$$

where $n$ is number of data sample, $PM_{2.5_{pred(i)}}$ corresponds to $i\text{-}th$ prediction of proposed models and $PM_{2.5_{gt(i)}}$ is $i\text{-}th$ ground-truth of data sample.

## 3　Experimental Results

As mentioned above, a transformer based neural network is used to predict $PM_{2.5}$ concentrations in ambient air. Additionally, two different architectures have been also considered such as Multi-Layer Perceptron and Long-Sort Term Memory. Keras library in python is used to implement these models. The details on the experimental results using the proposed models mentioned above are presented in this section. The selection of meteorological variables were performed using model's variance inflation factors, which was mentioned in Sect. 2.2. For the pre-processing of data, MinMaxScaler estimator is used to transform features by scaling each feature to a given range (e.g. between zero and one). Since that the inputs data of $PM_{2.5}$ concentrations in ambient air corresponded to a multivariate time series, they were re-framed as supervised learning problem. For this, windows time of 24 h have been used to build a new dataset with 400 transformed features for each data sample. For the training process of all the proposed models, a set of 14k data of sample were used to feed to the proposed networks, which was trained until 100 epochs. In the evaluation a set of 4k data of sample were considered. The Multi-Layer Perceptron used in this study was set using three hidden layers (64, 32 and 16 neurons) with ReLU as activation function for each hidden layer. RMSprop optimizer is used to train the network with a learning rate of 0.001, and batch size of 4. For a fair comparison, LSTM model used the same configuration of hidden layers of MLP, i.e., three hidden layers. However, unlike of MLP, the first two hidden layers used LSTM layer and last one used Dense layer. Activation function, optimizer, learning rate and batch size were same that MLP model. The last proposed model, transformer,

**Table 3.** Comparison of proposed models for forecasting $PM_{2.5}$ concentrations in ambient air using RMSE, MAPE, MAE and IA as metrics.

| Models | Metrics | Time windows | | |
|--------|---------|------|------|------|
| | | 6 h | 12 h | 24 h |
| MLP | RMSE ($\mu g/m^3$) | 5.67 | 5.38 | 5.69 |
| | MAPE ($\mu g/m^3$) | 0.52 | 0.58 | 0.66 |
| | MAE ($\mu g/m^3$) | 4.33 | 4.13 | 4.38 |
| | IA [0–1] | 0.82 | 0.83 | 0.80 |
| LSTM | RMSE ($\mu g/m^3$) | 5.66 | 5.63 | 5.63 |
| | MAPE ($\mu g/m^3$) | 0.54 | 0.56 | 0.50 |
| | MAE ($\mu g/m^3$) | 4.33 | 4.30 | 4.33 |
| | IA [0–1] | 0.82 | 0.82 | 0.83 |
| Transformer | RMSE ($\mu g/m^3$) | 5.19 | 5.01 | **4.98** |
| | MAPE ($\mu g/m^3$) | 0.49 | 0.52 | **0.48** |
| | MAE ($\mu g/m^3$) | 4.02 | 3.90 | **3.86** |
| | IA [0–1] | 0.85 | 0.86 | **0.85** |

the parameters corresponding to the number of attention head and size of each one of those of Multi-Head Attention module used in transformer models, are 8 and 10 respectively. Likewise, Feed Forward Part corresponding to the encoder of transformer model was set to 10.

Experimental results obtained with the proposed models are presented in Table 3, which were trained using different time windows of 6, 12 and 24 h, and compared between them by using metrics mentioned in Sect. 2.4. The obtained results by transformer model outperforms the obtained results by MLP and LSTM models. The predictions of MLP, LSTM and Transformers models using each time windows mentioned above are showed in Fig. 5. The blue line is the ground-truth $PM_{2.5}$ concentrations from station of Center of Quito City, the brown, green and red lines correspond the predicted $PM_{2.5}$ concentrations by MLP, LSTM and Transformer models respectively. Additionally, a comparative between the obtained results obtained of trained transformer model by each time windows of 6, 12 and 24 h are showed in Fig. 6.

## 4   Discussion

Different time windows of 6, 12 and 24 h were used to train MLP, LSTM and Transformer models. The obtained results for each proposed models are showed in Table 3. The results of prediction using MLP model trained with time windows of 12 h show a low error of RMSE and MAE metrics (5.38 and 4.13, respectively) if they are compared with other time windows used to train the model (i.e.,6 and 24 h). Likewise, the IA metric, which is a standardized measure of the degree of model prediction error which varies between 0 and 1, the obtained result was

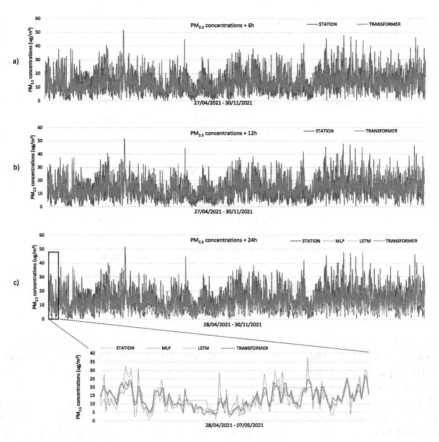

Fig. 5. Results of PM$_{2.5}$ concentrations obtained from transformer model for: a) 6 h, b) 12 h. For c), MLP, LSTM and Transformer models are compared using time windows of 24 h.

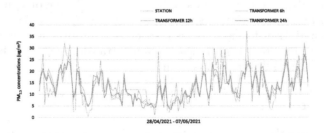

Fig. 6. Comparative of results obtained between Transformer model using time windows of 6, 12 and 24 h, and observations from station located in Center of Quito City.

of 0.83 (IA value of 1 indicates a perfect match). Since the MLP model are not able of learning large order dependence in sequence prediction problems, the time windows of 24 h obtained the most high error. However, for the time windows of

6 h, these results are not better than the time windows of 12 h. This may be due to low variability of PM$_{2.5}$ concentrations found in the time windows used to trained the model, being necessary more information to find patterns that allow to get more accuracy. The obtained results using LSTM model show a low error of RMSE, MAPE, MAE and IA metrics (5.63, 0.50, 4.33 and 0.83, respectively) when the model is trained using time windows of 24 h. Unlike of MLP model, the LSTM model is able to process entire sequence of data, being useful to learn large order dependence in sequence prediction problems. Hence, the obtained results using time windows of 24 h have better accuracy if they are compared with the model trained using time windows of 6 and 12 h, including the obtained results of MLP model. Likewise to the LSTM model, the transformer models are also able to learn large order dependence in data sequence, however, the used architecture for the transformer models use attention modules, which allow to focus on important features of input data instead of take attention to non-useful information. Considering the mentioned above, the transformer model trained using time windows of 24 h obtained better results for RMSE, MAPE, MAE and IA metrics (4.98, 0.48, 3.86 and 0.85), being more accurate than the results obtained using MLP and LSTM models (see Fig. 5c), including the transformer model trained with time windows of 6 and 12 h (see Fig. 6).

## 5   Conclusions

This paper addresses the challenging problem of forecasting PM$_{2.5}$ concentrations in ambient air due to variability of air pollutants as well as atmospheric variables. Monitoring air quality has become important, mainly in big cities, where there are a increase of air pollution due to the use of fossil fuels, cars, etc., and where monitoring stations is limited. During last years, the use of artificial intelligence tools have allowed to develop early warning systems to solve some problems of real-world such as, prediction of temperature, solar radiation, rain among other.

In this study, the analysis of correlation using VIF shows the importance of reducing those meteorological variables that are not useful for training process of the proposed models, doing these models (MLP, LSTM and Transformer) more accurate to estimate PM$_{2.5}$ concentrations up to 24 h in advance. The three models are compared to determine the accuracy of trained models using different time windows of 6, 12 and 24 h. Experimental results and comparisons between them are provided, showing improvements on the obtained results when transformer model is used, mainly, using a time windows of 24 h. The manuscript shows how the attention modules of transformer models can help to find relevant features in the data and estimate PM$_{2.5}$ concentrations more accurately. The obtained precision of PM$_{2.5}$ concentrations using transformer models could be used like a base to develop new proposals that allow take advantage of attention modules. Future works will be focused on extending the usage of other variables that allow to leverage the features of all vehicles that move within the urban areas such as type of vehicle (bus or car), vehicle year, type of fuel, number of vehicle by hour among other.

# References

1. Bai, Y., Li, Y., Wang, X., Xie, J., Li, C.: Air pollutants concentrations forecasting using back propagation neural network based on wavelet decomposition with meteorological conditions. Atmos. Pollut. Res. **7**(3), 557–566 (2016). https://doi.org/10.1016/j.apr.2016.01.004
2. Banja, M., Papanastasiou, D.K., Poupkou, A., Melas, D.: Development of a short-term ozone prediction tool in Tirana area based on meteorological variables. Atmos. Pollut. Res. **3**(1), 32–38 (2012). https://doi.org/10.5094/APR.2012.002
3. Beelen, R., et al.: Effects of long-term exposure to air pollution on natural-cause mortality: an analysis of 22 European cohorts within the multicenter escape project. Lancet **383**(9919), 785–795 (2014)
4. Chen, Y., Chen, X., Xu, A., Sun, Q., Peng, X.: A hybrid CNN-transformer model for ozone concentration prediction. Air Qual. Atmosphere Health 1533–1546 (2022). https://doi.org/10.1007/s11869-022-01197-w
5. Demir, V., Citakoglu, H.: Forecasting of solar radiation using different machine learning approaches. Neural Comput. Appl. **35**(1), 887–906 (2023). https://doi.org/10.1007/s00521-022-07841-x
6. Deshpande, R.R.: On the rainfall time series prediction using multilayer perceptron artificial neural network. Int. J. Emerg. Technol. Adv. Eng. **2**(1), 2250–2459 (2012)
7. Elangasinghe, M.A., Singhal, N., Dirks, K.N., Salmond, J.A.: Development of an ANN-based air pollution forecasting system with explicit knowledge through sensitivity analysis. Atmos. Pollut. Res. **5**(4), 696–708 (2014). https://doi.org/10.5094/APR.2014.079
8. Grigsby, J., Wang, Z., Qi, Y.: Long-range transformers for dynamic spatiotemporal forecasting. arXiv (2021)
9. Hochreiter, S., Schmidhuber, J.: Long short-term memory. Neural Comput. **9**(8), 1735–1780 (1997). https://doi.org/10.1162/neco.1997.9.8.1735
10. Hoek, G., et al.: Long-term air pollution exposure and cardio-respiratory mortality: a review. Environ. Health **12**(1), 1–16 (2013)
11. Hornik, K.: Approximation capabilities of multilayer feedforward networks. Neural Netw. **4**(2), 251–257 (1991)
12. Hornik, K., Stinchcombe, M., White, H.: Multilayer feedforward networks are universal approximators. Neural Netw. **2**(5), 359–366 (1989)
13. IQAir: Quality air in Ecuador. https://www.iqair.com/es/ecuador (2022). Accessed 27 Dec 2022
14. Krishan, M., Jha, S., Das, J., Singh, A., Goyal, M.K., Sekar, C.: Air quality modelling using long short-term memory (LSTM) over NCT-Delhi, India. Air Qual. Atmos. Health 899–908 (2019). https://doi.org/10.1007/s11869-019-00696-7
15. Li, J., Shao, X., Sun, R., Visioli, A.: A DBN-based deep neural network model with multitask learning for online air quality prediction. J. Control Sci. Eng. **2019**, 1–9 (2019). https://doi.org/10.1155/2019/5304535
16. Li, Y., Moura, J.M.F.: Forecaster: a graph transformer for forecasting spatial and time-dependent data. In: European Conference on Artificial Intelligence, pp. 1293–1300 (2019). https://doi.org/10.3233/FAIA200231
17. Méndez, M., Montero, C., Núñez, M.: Using deep transformer based models to predict ozone levels. In: Nguyen, N.T., Tran, T.K., Tukayev, U., Hong, T.P., Trawiński, B., Szczerbicki, E. (eds.) ACIIDS 2022. LNCS, vol. 13757, pp. 169–182. Springer, Cham (2022). https://doi.org/10.1007/978-3-031-21743-2_14

18. Newby, D.E., et al.: Expert position paper on air pollution and cardiovascular disease. Eur. Heart J. **36**(2), 83–93 (2015)
19. Parra, R., Cadena, E., Flores, C.: Maximum UV index records (2010–2014) in Quito (Ecuador) and its trend inferred from remote sensing data (1979–2018). Atmosphere **10**(12), 787 (2019). https://doi.org/10.3390/atmos10120787
20. Qi, Y., Li, Q., Karimian, H., Liu, D.: A hybrid model for spatiotemporal forecasting of pm2.5 based on graph convolutional neural network and long short-term memory. Sci. Total Environ. **664**, 1–10 (2019). https://doi.org/10.1016/j.scitotenv.2019.01.333
21. Sharma, P., Chandra, A., Kaushik, S.C.: Forecasts using Box-Jenkins models for the ambient air quality data of Delhi city. Environ. Monit. Assess. **157**, 105–112 (2009). https://doi.org/10.1007/s10661-008-0520-2
22. State Global Air: A special report on global exposure to air pollution and its heath impacts (2022). https://www.stateofglobalair.org/health. Accessed 07 Dec 2022
23. Vaswani, A., et al.: Attention is all you need. In: Advances in Neural Information Processing Systems, vol. 30 (2017)
24. Wang, J., Zhang, X., Guo, Z., Lu, H.: Developing an early-warning system for air quality prediction and assessment of cities in China. Expert Syst. Appl. **84**, 102–116 (2017). https://doi.org/10.1016/j.eswa.2017.04.059
25. Wang, J.F., Hu, M.G., Xu, C.D., Christakos, G., Zhao, Y.: Estimation of citywide air pollution in Beijing. PLoS ONE **8**(1), e53400 (2013)
26. World Health Organization. https://www.who.int/data/gho. Accessed Nov 2022 (2022)
27. Yu, M., Masrur, A., Blaszczak-Boxe, C.: Predicting hourly pm2.5 concentrations in wildfire-prone areas using a spatiotemporal transformer model. Sci. Total Environ. 160446 (2022). https://doi.org/10.1016/j.scitotenv.2022.160446
28. Zhou, H., et al.: Informer: beyond efficient transformer for long sequence time-series forecasting. In: The AAAI Conference on Artificial Intelligence, vol. 35, pp. 11106–11115 (2021)

# Machine Learning Applied to the Analysis of Glacier Masses

Harvey Marin-Calispa$^{(\boxtimes)}$ ⓘ, Erick Cuenca ⓘ, Diego Morales-Navarrete ⓘ, and Ruben Basantes ⓘ

Yachay Tech University, Hacienda San José, Urcuquí 100119, Ecuador
{harvey.marin,ecuenca,dmorales,rbasantes}@yachaytech.edu.ec

**Abstract.** Glaciers play a vital role as climate change indicators, offering valuable insights into global climate evolution and the wide-ranging impacts of glacier melting on nearby cities, including water supply and ecosystems. The hydrology of Antisana glacier, which provides high-quality drinking water to Quito and its surrounding region, is of critical research importance. In this context, this work aims to explore the potential of machine learning in predicting the mass balance of glaciers in Ecuador, specifically in Antisana Glacier 12 $\alpha$. To achieve this, a comprehensive dataset of climatic variables from a region of Antisana was collected and processed using TerraClimate and ERA5 datasets. Many ARIMA models, were developed and compared. The ARIMA(0,0,1) configuration provided reliable predictions. Precipitation and surface pressure were identified as significant variables, with precipitation having a substantial effect on glacier mass balance, as confirmed by the forecast results. This study emphasizes the importance of machine learning to improve our understanding of glacier dynamics and support informed decision-making in the face of climate change. Collecting additional specific data to enhance accuracy and comprehensive experience of volcano dynamics is recommended. Incorporating these additional data into the analysis will allow for model refinement and more accurate forecasts. Furthermore, considering alternative machine learning techniques alongside traditional statistical approaches can capture complex interactions, reveal non-linear relationships, and further improve prediction accuracy.

**Keywords:** Glaciers · Climate change · Machine Learning · ARIMA · Glacier Mass Balance · Time Series · Forecasting · Climate Variables

## 1 Introduction

Understanding the transitions of glaciers and their impact on hydrological and climate configurations is crucial for societies to adapt to changing environments. Accurate and long-time series of glacier mass balances measured on reference glaciers play a vital role in comprehending the evolution of glaciers at regional and sub-regional scales. These data are essential for the monitoring strategy of the Global Terrestrial Network for Glaciers, which aims to improve process understanding and modeling calibration in major climatic zones [2].

Gaining a comprehensive understanding of polar ice sheet evolution holds significant societal importance [19]. Predicting potential outcomes of different climate scenarios relies on glacier and hydro-glaciological models, but determining the appropriate level of complexity for these models can be challenging [4]. It is essential to consider the complexities of glacier evolution and their impacts on the environment and society while relying on accurate data. Such information guides strategies for mitigating and adapting to climate change effectively.

Studying the evolution of glaciers under different climatic scenarios presents numerous challenges, including a lack of continuous observations, the abundance of recent satellite data, and the complexity of climatic variables along the Andes. Conventional physical approaches have proven insufficient in tackling these obstacles. However, the application of machine learning models has emerged as a promising and powerful alternative for modeling glacier mass changes with minimal data. Machine learning models have the potential to revolutionize glacier research by addressing complex challenges more efficiently and effectively, providing researchers with valuable tools.

## 2  Materials and Methods

Figure 1 displays the phases proposed for this study. It comprises the four following phases: data collection, dataset preparation, model training and tuning, and model evaluation. The sections that follow go into great detail about each step.

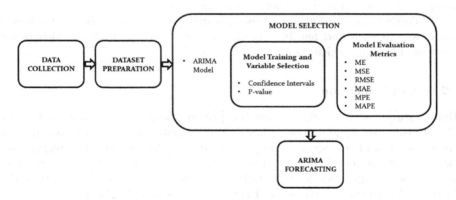

**Fig. 1.** Proposed Methodology flowchart.

### 2.1  Available Data

Antisana has 17 glaciers, one of which being Glacier 15. The glacier faces northwest and has two parallel tongues known as $15\alpha$ (south) and $15\beta$ (north) [14].

The zone to analyze in this study is the glacier $15\alpha$, which extends from 4850 m m a.s.l. up to 5720 m m a.s.l.

To analyze the mass balance of Antisana glacier 15 $\alpha$, collecting data that could provide insight into the long-term trends, variability, and change in climate conditions in the region was a crucial part of this study. However, we faced significant challenges when attempting to collect data from the glaciological stations in the area. These challenges included bureaucratic hurdles involved in obtaining data from responsible institutions, such as the National Institute of Meteorology and Hydrology (INAMHI), as well as limited access to traditional observations in the region.

To overcome these challenges, we opted to use reanalysis data obtained from satellites, specifically the Terraclimate[1] and ERA5[2] databases. Reanalysis data is a type of climate dataset that combines historical observations and numerical models to create a consistent and accurate record of weather and climate conditions over a long period of time. While reanalysis data may not be as precise as in situ data for certain variables, it provided a more practical and feasible alternative for our study.

ERA5 is a comprehensive reanalysis dataset produced by the European Centre for Medium-Range Weather Forecasts (ECMWF) that covers the period from 1979 to the present. It contains hourly data on various climate variables, including temperature, precipitation, wind, and humidity, among others, with a spatial resolution of approximately 31 km. Terraclimate, produced by the University of Idaho, covers the period from 1958 to the present and provides monthly data on various climate variables, including temperature, precipitation, and potential evapotranspiration, among others. Terraclimate incorporates satellite data and other sources of information to improve the accuracy of the dataset, particularly in regions where traditional observations are limited.

While there are limitations to using reanalysis data, we believe that it was the most practical and feasible option for our study, given the challenges we faced in obtaining in situ data.

## 2.2 Data Collection

Temperature and precipitation are the primary factors that influence Glacier 15's melting and annual mass balance. Furthermore, the lack of seasonality in precipitation and temperature suggests that local fluctuations are responsible for variations in mass balance [14]. Thus, data including precipitation and temperature were considered for this study, as well as other variables taken from the TERRACLIMATE as well as the ERA5 data sets [1,17]. This data was taken from the years 1995 to 2017. At the same time, the annual mass balance calculations made by Basantes et al. [2] were taken as a CSV file. It is in annual timestamp because monthly data is difficult to obtain due to errors and gaps in

---

[1] https://www.climatologylab.org/terraclimate.html.
[2] https://cds.climate.copernicus.eu/cdsapp#!/dataset/reanalysis-era5-land-monthly-means.

the equipment that make us not have reliable monthly data, so the mass balance provided by Basantes was an interpolation of the existing and validated mass balance using the Liboutry approach. The mass balance time series representation are shown in Fig. 2.

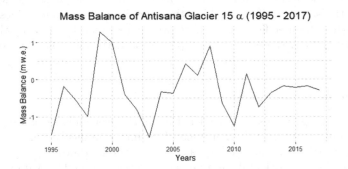

Fig. 2. Time series of Mass Balance of the Antisana Glacier 15 $\alpha$ from 1995 to 2017.

## 2.3   Region of Interest

In order to extract the relevant data for subsequent analysis, the first crucial step was to define a Region of Interest (ROI). To accomplish this, the Google Maps application was utilized. A trace was created around the specific region of interest associated with the Antisana volcano, which holds significance for this study. This trace delineated the region starting from an altitude of 5000 m above sea level, as depicted in Fig. 3. The coordinates captured, form a polygon with 54 vertices.

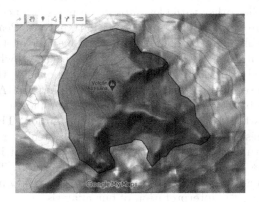

Fig. 3. Antisana ROI in Google Maps.

## 2.4   Data Extraction

A software tool known as *Origins Lab Pro 2023*[3] [18] was utilized. This software facilitated the processing and extraction of information from the Terraclimate and ERA5 files, which were originally in NetCDF format.

To extract the desired data, the coordinates obtained from Google Maps were input into the software. This enabled the extraction of average values for each variable within the specified region of interest. Subsequently, monthly time series were extracted from these files and exported as CSV files, allowing for further analysis.

## 2.5   Dataset Preparation

The data cleaning process involved a three-step procedure to consolidate the raw data from the previously mentioned files into a unified dataset, which was subsequently utilized in the subsequent steps of the methodology.

To begin with, the original variable data was transformed into annual data, as the mass balance records available were in an annual temporal format. Hence, all the data used in the analysis needed to have an annual periodicity. To accomplish this, a Python script was employed to calculate the average annual values for each variable by computing the annual means. In the next step, the mass balance information was converted into a CSV file format. Finally, the newly obtained annual variable values were merged with the mass balances, resulting in a single file that incorporated all the aforementioned variables, along with the annual mass balance, in a CSV format. This procedure was performed separately for both Terraclimate and ERA5 variables.

## 2.6   Correlation Analysis

Before continuing, the correlation analysis was an important part of this study to determine whether other variables impact the mass balance data. Three distinct methods were employed in our correlation analysis: Pearson, Spearman, and Kendall. Notably, Pearson demonstrated the highest level of result reliability among them. In Fig. 4 we can see The initial heatmap which encompasses 13 variables sourced from the Terraclimate dataset, alongside the year and mass balance, while the second set comprises 17 variables from ERA5, also including the year and mass balance variables. The heatmaps employ a color scheme that intuitively conveys the degree and direction of correlation. The color key is as follows: Red signifies a strong positive correlation, denoted by a value of 1; White indicates no discernible correlation, with values near 0; and Blue represents a significant negative correlation, designated by a value of -1. This visual representation provides a clear and concise portrayal of the relationships among the variables, facilitating the interpretation of our analysis.

In general, correlation analysis showed a low correlation between the variables from both datasets. As we can see in the Pearson correlation matrix for

---

[3] https://www.originlab.com/.

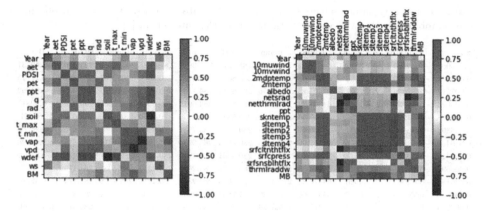

**Fig. 4.** Pearson Correlation matrix for Terraclimate (Right) and ERA5 (Left) extracted variables.

Terraclimate, the correlation was very low for this dataset variables. On the other hand, some ERA5 variables had better correlation results (see Fig. 4).

Errors in reanalysis datasets can contribute to a low correlation between variables. This is particularly relevant in Ecuador, which experiences frequent cloud cover. Cloud cover can introduce uncertainties and inaccuracies in satellite data used for reanalysis. As a result, the data may not fully capture the true relationship between variables, leading to a lower correlation.

Furthermore, when average values are derived from a region rather than specific stations in the Antisana, there is a risk of generalization. Averaging values over a larger area can overlook local variations and specific regional characteristics. This generalization may result in a loss of detailed information and potentially impact the accuracy and relevance of the findings.

Using Pearson correlation, we can identify the most significant variables from ERA5. Table 1 shows a selection of 10 climatic variables along with the mass balance variable. These variables were chosen because they had the highest correlations, as identified through the correlation heatmaps. The selected climatic variables included: Total precipitation ("ppt"), Surface latent heat flux ("srfcltntht-flx"), 2m dewpoint temperature ("2mdptemp"), Surface pressure ("srfcpress"), 2m temperature ("2mtemp"), Skin temperature ("skntemp"), Soil temperature level 1 ("sltemp1"), Soil temperature level 2 ("sltemp2"), Soil temperature level 3 ("sltemp3"), and Soil temperature level 4 ("sltemp4"). Each of these variables comprises 23 data points, each representing the annual average of the respective variable spanning the years from 1995 to 2017.

## 2.7  Model Selection

In this section, we are going to present an ARIMA model that aims to predict the mass balance values for the data-set we have. Furthermore, the error metrics to

**Table 1.** Final variables selected from the ERA5 dataset based on a correlation analysis, combined with SMB values obtained from Basantes et al. [2].

| ppt | srfcltnthtflx | 2mdptemp | srfcpress | 2mtemp | sltemp4 | sltemp1 | skntemp | sltemp3 | sltemp2 | MB |
|---|---|---|---|---|---|---|---|---|---|---|
| 0.006068 | −7002736 | 277.4332 | 64474.91 | 279.5704 | 281.107 | 284.3991 | 280.5885 | 282.5316 | 284.2996 | −1.49737 |
| 0.006634 | −6828209 | 277.3568 | 64446.67 | 279.3139 | 280.809 | 284.0732 | 280.2382 | 282.2191 | 283.9814 | −0.17725 |
| 0.007212 | −6647874 | 277.7721 | 64477.23 | 279.5375 | 280.8244 | 284.1165 | 280.2894 | 282.2101 | 284.0298 | −0.54962 |
| 0.006626 | −6828720 | 278.1991 | 64523.79 | 280.0382 | 281.3697 | 284.6911 | 280.8668 | 282.7589 | 284.6005 | −0.99811 |
| 0.007206 | −6611292 | 277.2287 | 64435.64 | 279.0128 | 280.532 | 283.7196 | 279.845 | 281.8589 | 283.6064 | 1.288051 |
| 0.006803 | −6783087 | 277.1574 | 64428.21 | 279.0434 | 280.4414 | 283.7917 | 279.8963 | 281.8502 | 283.6508 | 0.998324 |
| 0.006436 | −6931791 | 277.2353 | 64451.95 | 279.1148 | 280.5674 | 283.9956 | 280.1173 | 282.0413 | 283.8894 | −0.40008 |
| 0.006415 | −6853066 | 277.5671 | 64475.89 | 279.3684 | 280.8991 | 284.1275 | 280.287 | 282.289 | 284.0711 | −0.81029 |
| 0.006695 | −6756433 | 277.7779 | 64484.38 | 279.4983 | 280.9676 | 284.2079 | 280.4312 | 282.4034 | 284.1794 | −1.56175 |
| 0.006187 | −6972975 | 277.4526 | 64476.83 | 279.3955 | 280.9646 | 284.2362 | 280.4311 | 282.4029 | 284.174 | −0.32781 |
| 0.006859 | −6936224 | 277.6767 | 64480.68 | 279.6029 | 281.1833 | 284.424 | 280.5822 | 282.5719 | 284.3424 | −0.37475 |
| 0.006993 | −6832003 | 277.5299 | 64473.57 | 279.3924 | 280.8907 | 284.1566 | 280.3207 | 282.301 | 284.1005 | 0.417214 |
| 0.006476 | −6919211 | 277.4659 | 64467.99 | 279.3737 | 280.922 | 284.2298 | 280.3266 | 282.3083 | 284.1005 | 0.106932 |
| 0.008092 | −6720154 | 277.4268 | 64441.47 | 279.2653 | 280.6467 | 284.0287 | 280.0719 | 282.0458 | 283.8474 | 0.902848 |
| 0.006887 | −6854879 | 277.8052 | 64463.63 | 279.6489 | 280.9724 | 284.3715 | 280.5794 | 282.4747 | 284.3067 | −0.62759 |
| 0.006659 | −6961449 | 277.7418 | 64493.98 | 279.784 | 281.3973 | 284.5813 | 280.6665 | 282.6819 | 284.4482 | −1.26494 |
| 0.007812 | −6710856 | 277.4483 | 64444.09 | 279.4252 | 280.7893 | 284.0745 | 280.2845 | 282.1615 | 283.9351 | 0.14635 |
| 0.007383 | −6751297 | 277.3538 | 64469.4 | 279.2046 | 280.6166 | 283.9013 | 280.0347 | 282.015 | 283.8167 | −0.74621 |
| 0.00745 | −6776609 | 277.681 | 64489.84 | 279.4735 | 280.8931 | 284.1503 | 280.3403 | 282.281 | 284.1053 | −0.36074 |
| 0.007645 | −6669033 | 277.7833 | 64496.8 | 279.5106 | 280.8646 | 284.1409 | 280.3196 | 282.2749 | 284.0844 | −0.17774 |
| 0.007409 | −6732414 | 277.9804 | 64517.87 | 279.6804 | 280.9779 | 284.2478 | 280.4808 | 282.3926 | 284.2358 | −0.21574 |
| 0.00722 | −6985172 | 278.228 | 64555.55 | 280.0385 | 281.4656 | 284.7355 | 280.9792 | 282.9242 | 284.7325 | −0.17574 |
| 0.00759 | −6799733 | 277.6899 | 64517.45 | 279.6621 | 281.1249 | 284.3428 | 280.5308 | 282.4529 | 284.2505 | −0.28974 |

evaluate how well these models are adjusted to the data are the $R^2$, the adjusted $R^2$, MSE, RMSE and MAE.

## 2.8  Tools

The experiments used R and its integrated development environment (IDE) called R Studios. The libraries implemented were the following:

- tidyverse
- GGally
- broom
- readr
- forecast
- tseries
- car

You can see the used code for this work in the following GitHub repository: https://github.com/HarveyM98/ML_applied_GlacierMB_prediction

## 2.9  ARIMA

Several esteemed authors in the field of glacier mass balance interpretations, including Basantes et al. [2], Gruell [12], Braithwaite and Zhang [6,7], Marzeion et al. [15], Box [5], Guillete [13], and Caro et al. [9], have frequently employed linear approaches in their research, becoming a prevaling choice within this field. Moreover, In recent years, various novel approaches have emerged, such as the Geodetic spatial sampling design (SSD) [3] and the utilization of ASTERIX [11]. However, there is a substantial gap in the existing literature regarding applying ARIMA models for similar purposes, particularly in the context of glacier mass balance research in Ecuador. As a result, this study utilizes the ARIMA model to address this underexplored aspect and contribute valuable insights to the field.

The ARIMA model is a statistical method used for time series analysis, which extends the ARMA model to handle non-stationary data by incorporating a differencing step. Differencing refers to subtracting the current value from the previous value of a time series, thereby converting it into a stationary series. The ARIMA model has three parameters, namely $p$, $d$, and $q$, which denote the order of the autoregressive component, the number of differencing steps required to achieve stationarity, and the order of the moving average component, respectively. The autoregressive component models the relationship between the current observation and its previous values, while the moving average component models the relationship between the current observation and the previous error terms. The model equation can be expressed as follows:

$$(1 - \phi_1 B - \cdots - \phi_p B^p)(1 - B)^d X_t = (1 + \theta_1 B + \cdots + \theta_q B^q) e_t$$

where $X_t$ is the value of the time series at time $t$, $\phi_1, \ldots, \phi_p$ are the autoregressive parameters, $\theta_1, \ldots, \theta_q$ are the moving average parameters, $B$ is the backward shift operator, $d$ is the number of times the time series is differenced, and $e_t$ is a white noise error term [8, 10, 16].

The inputs utilized in our ARIMA model for predicting glacier mass balance consist of the variables' time series that goes from 1995 to 2017 presented in Table 1. Among these variables, the first ten, collectively referred to as climatic variables, serve as the features used to forecast the final variable denoted as where the first 10 climatic variables are taken as features to predict the last variable called "MB", which represents the Mass Balance of the glacier.

**Augmented Dickey-Fuller Test Analysis.** The Dickey-Fuller test was used to assess the stationarity of the mass balance time series data set, which is an important assumption before using ARIMA. The test was implemented with the R function `adf.test()`.

**ACF and PACF Analysis.** The examination of the Autocorrelation Function (ACF) and Partial Autocorrelation Function (PACF) was employed in the investigation of the correlation structure of Mass balance time series data. The analysis of ACF and PACF graphs was carried out to determine the appropriate order of autoregressive and moving average terms in an $ARIMA$ model being constructed. These two analysis were implemented in R by using the `acf()` and `pacf()` functions.

**Parameters Selection.** The `forecast` library in R was leveraged to construct the model.

The `auto.arima()` function from the "forecast" library of R to determine was employed to have the optimal combination of $ARIMA$ Parameters that would yield the most accurate predictions for our model.

To further enhance the precision of our results, we incorporated confidence interval analysis to eliminate certain variables deemed statistically insignificant. This process had nine-step iterations. The model that resulted using the `auto.arima()` function in R is one with the configuration of a Regressive component only, which is an ARIMA(1,0,0)

Moreover, two additional ARIMA models were used with the selected variables. The configurations were the following, considering the MA and AR parts:

- ARIMA(0,0,1)
- ARIMA(1,0,1)

**Evaluation.** The evaluation metrics to evaluate how well these models are adjusted to the data are the MSE, RMSE and MAE.

**Forecasting.** Finally, considering the advantages of this method, forecasting was made for the following 5 years of the annual timestamp present in the time series.

## 3    Results and Discussion

**Durbin-Watson Test.** The Durbin-Watson test was conducted on a regression model, yielding a D-W statistic of 1.349459, an autocorrelation value of 0.311, and a p-value of 0.008.

These results indicate the presence of positive autocorrelation in the residuals. The Durbin-Watson test statistic being less than 2 suggests moderate positive autocorrelation. Additionally, the autocorrelation value of 0.311 further supports this finding.

The statistically significant p-value of 0.008 provides strong evidence against the null hypothesis of no autocorrelation. Consequently, we can reject the null hypothesis and conclude that the residuals have moderate positive autocorrelation.

### 3.1    ARIMA Results

**Augmented Dickey-Fuller Test.** The Mass Balance time series underwent the Augmented Dickey-Fuller test to assess its stationarity. The Augmented Dickey-Fuller test evaluates two hypotheses: the null hypothesis ($H_0$), which suggests that the time series is non-stationary with time-dependent structure and varying variance, and the alternative hypothesis ($H_A$), proposing that the time series is stationary. To accept the alternative hypothesis, the p-value must be below the significance level.

In this study, the Augmented Dickey-Fuller test yielded a p-value of 0.1532, which is greater than the significance level of 0.05. Consequently, we cannot reject the null hypothesis, indicating that the time series is non-stationary. However, it is important to acknowledge that this result may be influenced by the limited number of data points available in the time series, potentially introducing bias into the analysis.

The ACF and PACF resulting plots can be seen in Fig. 5. The ACF and PACF plots provide valuable insights into the autocorrelation structure of a time series. In these plots, there is a dot-limited area that represents the 95% confidence interval, serving as a significance threshold. Points within this area indicate that the corresponding autocorrelation values are statistically close to zero. Conversely, points outside this area suggest statistically significant non-zero autocorrelations. In the present analysis, the ACF and PACF plots exhibit some auto-correlations i.e. outside the limited area, indicating that these correlations are statistically significant and non-zero. This implies that the time series is non-random and exhibits some underlying patterns or dependencies.

Furthermore, in the ACF plot, a strong correlation can be observed between the variable and itself at the same time point, resulting in an autocorrelation of 1 at lag 0. This is a natural outcome since a series always perfectly correlates with itself at the same point. Additionally, these plots reveal a high degree of autocorrelation at lag=4. This suggests a significant correlation between the current value and the values at a lag of four time periods in the past. The presence of this autocorrelation indicates that past values at that specific lag have an influence on the current value.

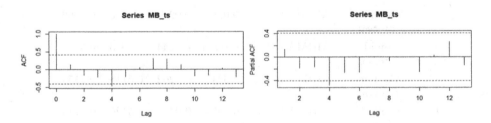

**Fig. 5.** ACF(right) and PACF(left) plots of the Mass Balance time series used in this study.

**Variables Selection.** The analysis conducted involved the use of nine ARIMA models with different numbers of variables. The variables were systematically discarded one by one based on a confidence interval of 97.5% and utilizing the `auto.arima()` function, which identifies the optimal parameter configuration for each ARIMA model. Variables with confidence intervals encompassing zero were considered statistically insignificant predictors and thus excluded from the model. In the initial seven steps, the proposed configuration by the R function was ARIMA(0,0,0). However, the final two models resulted in an ARIMA configuration of ARIMA(1,0,0), indicating an autoregressive (AR) model. Table 2 presents the evaluation metrics of the models. Notably, the model with nine variables exhibited better performance in terms of MSE, RMSE, and MAE than the other models. However, it is important to consider that some of the variables used in this model were not statistically significant. Consequently, the results may be biased. Ultimately, the model that demonstrated the best configuration and included the most statistically significant variables was the one with only two variables: precipitation and surface pressure. To further investigate the significance of these two variables, two additional ARIMA models with different configurations were tested. The results and evaluation metrics are in Table 3.

**Table 2.** Values of different statistical metrics obtained from an iterative process using the ARIMA method. The climatic variables used in the regression model were selected based on their statistical significance in a confidence interval of 97.5%. The table displays the general p-value, values of mean squared error (MSE), root mean squared error (RMSE), and mean absolute error (MAE) obtained from each set of variables.

| Var # | Variables selection method | ARIMA structure | P-value | MSE | RMSE | MAE |
|---|---|---|---|---|---|---|
| 10 | None | ARIMA(0,0,0) | 0.0230 | 0.0262 | 0.5120 | 0.3783 |
| 9 | Confidence Interval | ARIMA(0,0,0) | 0.0134 | **0.0185** | **0.4303** | **0.3492** |
| 8 | Confidence Interval | ARIMA(0,0,0) | 0.0408 | 0.0213 | 0.4620 | 0.3732 |
| 7 | Confidence Interval | ARIMA(0,0,0) | 0.0039 | 0.0244 | 0.4943 | 0.3969 |
| 6 | Confidence Interval | ARIMA(0,0,0) | **0.0031** | 0.0244 | 0.4943 | 0.3967 |
| 5 | Confidence Interval | ARIMA(0,0,0) | 0.0045 | 0.0262 | 0.5118 | 0.4154 |
| 4 | Confidence Interval | ARIMA(0,0,0) | 0.0053 | 0.0262 | 0.5120 | 0.4145 |
| 3 | Confidence Interval | ARIMA(1,0,0) | 0.1004 | 0.0252 | 0.5023 | 0.4392 |
| 2 | Confidence Interval | ARIMA(1,0,0) | 0.1025 | 0.0268 | 0.5178 | 0.4390 |

The results obtained from the various ARIMA configurations exhibit a remarkable level of similarity in terms of their evaluation metrics. This suggests that the choice of these configurations has minimal influence on the model's

**Table 3.** Summary of statistical metrics derived from four different models, including ARIMA(1,0,1), ARIMA(0,0,1), and ARIMA(1,0,0). The models were built using surface pressure and precipitation variables from the ERA5 dataset.

| Model | ME | MSE | RMSE | MAE | MPE | MAPE |
|-------|-----|------|------|------|------|-------|
| ARIMA(1,0,1) | 0.0139 | 0.2425 | 0.4924 | 0.4191 | −9.3601 | 107.7088 |
| ARIMA(0,0,1) | 0.0080 | 0.2506 | 0.5006 | 0.4134 | −0.8408 | 105.8390 |
| ARIMA(1,0,0) | 0.0146 | 0.2430 | 0.4930 | 0.4207 | −9.6305 | 108.3419 |

performance. Considering the substantial quantity of data utilized in the analysis, the predictions generated by the selected model can be deemed acceptable in their accuracy and reliability. To visualize these predictions, refer to Fig. 6, which effectively demonstrates the model's ability to provide meaningful insights.

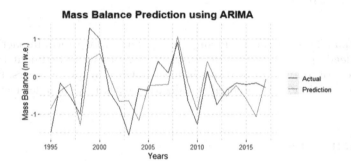

**Fig. 6.** Prediction of Mass Balance from the year 1995 to 2017 made by ARIMA(1,0,0) model.

**Forecasting.** Figure 7 showcases the forecasting results for precipitation and surface pressure derived from the ERA5 dataset. These visual representations offer a comprehensive depiction of the predicted values spanning 5 years into the future. By analyzing these figures, valuable insights can be gleaned regarding the anticipated trends and patterns associated with precipitation and surface pressure. These predictions serve as valuable tools for understanding the future behavior of these variables.

The three forecasts of glacier mass balance, conducted over five years using ARIMA(1,0,0), ARIMA(1,0,1), and ARIMA(0,0,1), exhibit striking similarities. These forecasts reveal highly consistent trends, suggesting that this glacier may experience a decline in the coming years, followed by an upturn towards the end of the projection period. However, given the remarkable resemblance in the graphical representations of these forecasts in Fig. 7 we opted for the one with slightly less uncertainty in its confidence intervals.

In general, the illustrations in Fig. 5 consistently reveal a decline in the uppermost segments of the mass balance data, indicating a reduction in mass balance

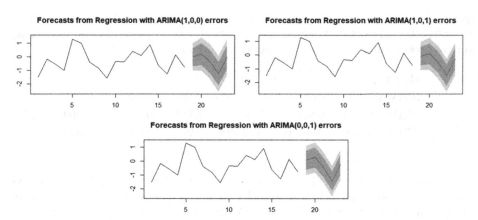

**Fig. 7.** Forecasting of the next five years made by ARIMA(1,0,0) ARIMA(1,0,1) ARIMA(0,0,1) models.

accumulation. This decline might suggest a potential long-term impact of global warming, leading to mass loss. However, it's important to highlight that there are instances of temporary increases in mass balance in specific years, hinting at a degree of variability or potential stabilization within the broader trend in this glacier.

## 4    Conclusions

This research study utilized an unconventional methodology, combining reanalysis data from ERA5 and Terraclimate datasets with the Origins software and a machine learning technique called ARIMA. The primary goal was to predict the mass balance of the Antisana volcano's Glacier 15α in Ecuador using a machine learning algorithm. The study followed a structured approach, covering data collection, pre-processing, model development, and performance evaluation. Existing glaciology techniques were reviewed and opportunities to integrate machine learning algorithms were found, particularly when data is limited.

The time series analysis of the mass balance data revealed non-random behavior and time-dependent structures, highlighting the importance of using appropriate statistical tests to handle non-stationarity. A machine learning algorithm was developed and fine-tuned to predict the glacier's mass balance effectively. The ARIMA(0,0,1) configuration was the most effective in forecasting the Antisana glacier's mass balance. Precipitation and surface pressure were identified as significant variables affecting the glacier's mass balance. Furthermore, this marks the inaugural application of ARIMA for these objectives, thereby ushering in a new opportunity for heightened focus on the utilization of such machine-learning techniques within our region. However, the study faced limitations due to the lack of direct measurements at the Antisana stations, leading to the use of reanalysis data from a broader region. This substitution introduced potential uncertainties and limitations, particularly in a cloud-prone region like Ecuador.

In terms of future research directions, we recommend a concerted effort to gather precise data pertaining to glacier geometry, coupled with a heightened emphasis on the incorporation of machine learning techniques, particularly ARIMA models, into glacier monitoring protocols. Additionally, we advocate for the exploration of alternative methodologies such as neural networks and ensemble methods using more data to further enhance prediction accuracy. Addressing the study's limitations can contribute to a better comprehension of the complex interactions between glaciers, their environment, and climate change. This knowledge is crucial for developing effective adaptation and mitigation strategies globally and preserving natural resources like glaciers.

**Acknowledgment.** The authors express their gratitude to the Data Science and Analytics (DataScienceYT) group at Yachay Tech University for their assistance during the development of this work.

# References

1. Abatzoglou, J.T., Dobrowski, S.Z.: Terraclimate, a high-resolution global dataset of monthly climate and climatic water balance from 1958–2015. Sci. Data **5**(1), 180160 (2018)
2. Basantes-Serrano, R., et al.: Slight mass loss revealed by reanalyzing glacier mass-balance observations on Glaciar Antisana 15α (inner tropics) during the 1995–2012 period. J. Glaciol. **62**(231), 124–136 (2016). https://doi.org/10.1017/jog.2016.17
3. Basantes-Serrano, R., Rabatel, A., Vincent, C., Sirguey, P.: An optimized method to calculate the geodetic mass balance of mountain glaciers. J. Glaciol. **64**(248), 917–931 (2018)
4. Bolibar, J., Rabatel, A., Gouttevin, I., Galiez, C., Condom, T., Sauquet, E.: Deep learning applied to glacier evolution modelling. Cryosphere **14**(2), 565–584 (2020). https://doi.org/10.5194/tc-14-565-2020. https://tc.copernicus.org/articles/14/565/2020/
5. Box, J.E.: Greenland ice sheet mass balance reconstruction. PART II: Surface mass balance (1840–2010). J. Clim. **26**(18), 6974–6989 (2013)
6. Braithwaite, R.J., Zhang, Y.: Modelling changes in glacier mass balance that may occur as a result of climate changes. Geogr. Ann. Ser. B **81**(4), 489–496 (1999)
7. Braithwaite, R.J., Zhang, Y.: Sensitivity of mass balance of five swiss glaciers to temperature changes assessed by tuning a degree-day model. J. Glaciol. **46**(152), 7–14 (2000)
8. Brockwell, P.J., Davis, R.A.: Introduction to Time Series and Forecasting. Springer Texts in Statistics, Springer, Heidelberg (2016). https://doi.org/10.1007/978-3-319-29854-2
9. Caro, A., Condom, T., Rabatel, A.: Climatic and morphometric explanatory variables of glacier changes in the Andes (8-55°s): new insights from machine learning approaches. Front. Earth Sci. **9** (2021). https://doi.org/10.3389/feart.2021.713011. https://www.frontiersin.org/articles/10.3389/feart.2021.713011
10. Cryer, J.D., Chan, K.S.: Time Series Analysis. Springer, New York (2008). https://doi.org/10.1007/978-0-387-75959-3

11. Dussaillant, I., et al.: Two decades of glacier mass loss along the Andes. Nat. Geosci. **12**(10), 802–808 (2019)
12. Greuell, W.: Hintereisferner, Austria: mass-balance reconstruction and numerical modelling of the historical length variations. J. Glaciol. **38**(129), 233–244 (1992)
13. Guillete, R.: Dynamics of climate change: explaining glacier retreat mathematically. Undergradute Rev. **11**, 73–80 (2014). http://vc.bridgew.edu/honors_proj/55
14. Manciati, C., Villacís, M., Taupin, J.D., Cadier, E., Galárraga-Sánchez, R., Cáceres, B.: Empirical mass balance modelling of South American tropical glaciers: case study of Antisana volcano, Ecuador. Hydrol. Sci. J. **59**(8), 1519–1535 (2014). https://doi.org/10.1080/02626667.2014.888490
15. Marzeion, B., Hofer, M., Jarosch, A., Kaser, G., Mölg, T.: A minimal model for reconstructing interannual mass balance variability of glaciers in the European alps. Cryosphere **6** (2012). https://doi.org/10.5194/tc-6-71-2012
16. Mills, T.: Applied Time Series Analysis: A Practical Guide to Modeling and Forecasting. Elsevier Science (2019). https://books.google.com.ec/books?id=ntoxvQEACAAJ
17. Muñoz Sabater, J.: ERA5-Land monthly averaged data from 1950 to present. Copernicus Climate Change Service (C3S) Climate Data Store (CDS) (2019). https://doi.org/10.24381/cds.68d2bb30. Accessed 24 Apr 2023
18. OriginLab Corporation: OriginPro
19. Rignot, E., Thomas, R.H.: Mass balance of polar ice sheets. Science **297**(5586), 1502–1506 (2002)

# Profit vs Accuracy: Balancing the Impact on Users Introduced by Profit-Aware Recommender Systems

Juan Riofrío[1,2]([✉]) [ID], Lorena Recalde[1] [ID], and Rosa Navarrete[1] [ID]

[1] Department of Informatics and Computer Sciences, Escuela Politécnica Nacional, Ladrón de Guevara E11-253, Quito, Ecuador
{juan.riofrio,lorena.recalde,rosa.navarrete}@epn.edu.ec
[2] School of Mathematical and Computational Sciences, Yachay Tech University, Urcuquí, Ecuador

**Abstract.** This work proposes the design of a profit-aware recommender system named Multi-Aware Recommender System (MARS), where the impact on the user is subject to adjustment. The item re-ranking process is based on the profit generated for the business and other important attributes (i.e. price of the item), and it is performed using a weighted rank aggregation method. The weights are optimized iteratively using a variant of the Gradient Descent algorithm, in order train the model and control the desired impact on the user. In this way, the model controls the impact on the user so as not to compromise the customer loyalty, while increasing the profit for the company. The weights can be unique for every user, making this approach personalized. The MARS method also controls the impact on the user by adjusting the ranking threshold $T_R$, which determines the minimum rating that items must have to be re-ranked. Experiments showed that MARS models have the ability to control the impact on the user while increasing the profit by varying the weights associated to the considered attributes. It is important to notice that the training of the model can be parallelized; thus, the weights and results may be obtained for each user separately. By implementing MARS on the MovieLens-1M data set and various configurations, we increased the profit generated in all the experiments and got an acceptable or desired impact on the user.

**Keywords:** Recommender System · Profit-Aware · Re-ranking · Profit · Impact on the user

## 1 Introduction

Recommender systems are widely used by a large number of companies worldwide to recommend products to their customers. Generally, what is sought with the recommendations made to the client is to benefit the company, suppliers or even the client, and it is commonly intended to satisfy several of these at the

© The Author(s), under exclusive license to Springer Nature Switzerland AG 2023
J. Maldonado-Mahauad et al. (Eds.): TICEC 2023, CCIS 1885, pp. 175–192, 2023.
https://doi.org/10.1007/978-3-031-45438-7_12

same time [16]. Recommender systems serve several purposes depending on who they want to generate value for and in what way. For example, from the user's point of view, the objective is to find products that meet their preferences in the short or long term, or to support the user in the decision-making process; while from provider's point of view, it may create additional demand or increase the engagement of users [9]. It is important to take into account that the benefit for the user is indirectly transformed into a benefit for the company [11], since the user loyalty is built. This increases the users' satisfaction and loyalty [17], making the users want to buy more products and stay in a specific company generating profit for the business. The main benefit of recommender systems for the customers is that they help them find products that the users like and that they might not find on their own, while the main benefit for the business is to sell more products due to the correct recommendations [13]. Given these benefits, the field of recommender systems research has been greatly exploited seeking to improve these tools and produce greater and better benefits for both the client and the company.

Initially, recommender systems sought to make suggestions based on what the user was believed to like or need, but this approach does not always produce the greatest economic benefits for the company. Although, it is true that user satisfaction produces benefits for the business, other techniques have been applied to take into account the economic profit generated by each product sold and thus recommend products not only based on the items relevance, but also based on the profit generated by the products. The recommender systems that use this approach are PARS, since they take into account the probability that a user buys the product and also the profitability for the sellers [6]. This approach is not the best from the user perspective, but [3] have shown that a company can greatly benefit from providing users with recommendations that meet business needs. When taking into account the items profitability for the recommendations, we have to be careful thus the trust of the client in the company or in the recommendations is not compromised [1]. If customers stop buying from a certain company because they realize that the recommendations they are given are for expensive and unnecessary products, the PARS would be producing less profit and losing customers. When the trust of the user in the recommender system or the company is low, it is better to restore confidence with optimal recommendations for the user, even if this means reducing profits for a while [8]. As long as the seller makes recommendations that are similar to the customer's tastes, the customer maintains a high level of trust [1]. The novelty of this work lies in the attempt to establish a way to balance the benefits for both the user and the company using machine learning techniques in the in- and post-processing stages. Therefore, this work aims to control and balance the impact on customers and generate more profits for companies with the proposed recommender system. In other words, the objective is to produce recommendations to the users that are relevant for them, but also increase the profitability of the company by recommending products based on the profit they generate.

This work proposes the design of a PARS, where the impact on the user is subject of adjustment. The proposed recommender system considers different attributes like the preferences of the user, the price and the profit generated by each item. For each user, the items are ranked based on the highest predicted ratings. Then, the items with predicted ratings above a defined threshold are re-ranked. The re-ranking process is based on the profit generated for the business and other important attributes (i.e. price of the item), and it is performed using a weighted rank aggregation method. The weights used in the weighted rank aggregation method determine the importance given to each attribute (e.g. profit, user preference). The weights are optimized iteratively using a variant of the Gradient Descent algorithm, in order to train the model and control the desired impact on the user. The weights can be unique for every user, making this approach personalized. We performed the experiments over the MovieLens-1M data set (described in Sect. 3.1), and measured the impact on the user for the new recommendations. The results show that the proposed method balances the impact on the user while generating higher profit for the business, and allows the service provider to customize this variable depending on the business needs.

The remaining of this paper is structured as follows: Sect. 2 extend the background of this work and explains similar works to the one proposed in this study. Section 3 defines and describes the approach proposed in this study. Section 4 describes the metrics, data set and gathers the main results obtained from the experiments. Section 5 explores the significance of the work's results. Finally, the concluding remarks are drawn in Sect. 6.

## 2   Related Work

In this section, the related studies conducted in the field of PARS and rank aggregation recommender systems are presented. It is important to mention that the limitations in the model presented by [10] motivated this study. In [10], the authors designed a PARS to balance the accuracy and the profit of the items. The authors modified the re-ranking method presented by [2]. The designed PARS takes the recommendations made by a matrix factorization algorithm and re-ranks the items based on the profit generated to the company. The re-ranking step is performed for each user, and only the items surpassing a predicted rating threshold $T_R$ are re-ranked to avoid accuracy reduction. Items with predicted ratings above $T_R$ are ranked according to the profit, while items that are below $T_R$ are ranked according to the predicted rating. Notice that all items that are below $T_R$ get ranked behind of all items that are above $T_R$. This work showed that including the threshold $T_R$ can control and balance the impact on the user while increasing the profitability, as only the items considered relevant (above $T_R$) are re-ranked. Although the impact on the user is considered, there is still a considerable impact on the user when recommending the topN items with this method. The final list presented to the user may have many new items introduced to it depending on the value of $T_R$. For example, we have $X$ items with predicted rating over $T_R$, now all this $X$ items are re-ranked based in the profit, and only the TopN items are presented to the user. In this method it does not matter if the item was in the $X^{th}$ position according to the user preference, now can be presented $1^{st}$ if it has the best profit out of the $X$ items.

The researchers proposed a multi-criteria collaborative filtering recommender system using learning to rank and rank aggregation in [14]. The approach is a three-step hybrid ranking order system that finds the topN list based on multiple criteria (attributes) of the items (i.e. overall rating, story, acting, direction and visuals of movies). The first step of the method decomposes the multi-criteria tensor of rank 3 into single-criteria user-item matrices. Each channel of the multi-criteria tensor of size $(Users \times Items \times NumberOfCriteria)$ represents a matrix of size $(Users \times Items)$ for a single criteria. The second step applies the list-wise FM learning-to-rank method [15] to each individual matrix to find the partial-ranked lists. The single-criteria matrices are rating matrices with missing values. By using learning-to-rank, the method finds the ranking of all the items for every user on every criteria. The third step uses rank aggregation to obtain a global-ranked list from the parital-ranked lists. The researchers used a rank-based method, specifically, the Borda Count method. The experiments over the Yahoo! Movie data set showed that the proposed approach is better for capturing the user preferences than traditional methods. The method also performs better in terms of recommendation accuracy.

The study [5] has developed a recommender system based on swarm intelligence named MOABC (multi-objective artificial bee colony) that takes into account both profit and liking probability in a multi-objective environment. Unlike existing algorithms that rely solely on randomness, the system incorporates a specialized mutation operator with intelligent capabilities that aim to improve both objectives simultaneously in each iteration. This approach significantly enhances the quality of recommendations compared to current state-of-the-art methods. To evaluate their proposal, the authors conducted experiments using different sizes of the MovieLens datasets. The results demonstrate that MOABC outperforms collaborative filtering (CF) and Non-dominated Sorting Genetic Algorithm II (NSGA-II), in terms of accuracy and overall profit. Additionally, statistical analysis confirms that the proposed approach generates superior and more consistent outcomes, highlighting the importance of leveraging the multi-objective nature of the problem.

## 3   Proposed Approach

The proposed re-ranking method is independent from the algorithm used to predict the ratings. It is assumed that the predicted rating matrix $R^*$ is the optimal on a user perspective. The method considers a ranking threshold $T_R$, which determines the items to re-rank for each user. $T_R$ is a number between the minimum and maximum possible ratings. The re-ranking is only performed over items that were predicted above $T_R$ to ensure an acceptable level of accuracy, and to reduce the impact on the users. $T_R$ prevents items with low ratings from being presented to a certain user after re-ranking. The re-ranking is performed based on the ranking obtained by each item when considering other attributes, these attributes can be user-dependent or user-independent. If it is user-independent, only a vector of size $I$ is considered. For example, the rating based on the profit generated by each item is a user-independent attribute. Normally, the price and profit of items do not vary among users, all the users perceive the items equally according to this attribute. If the attribute is user-dependent, a matrix of size $U \times I$ is considered, meaning that every user rates each item differently. For example, the rating of every item based on the price preference of each user is a user-dependent attribute. This matrix can also be a predicted rating matrix from a different approach. For example, the predicted rating matrix resulting from applying a profit aware recommender system, or any other type of recommender system. When the attribute is user-independent a matrix can also be defined, but all the $U$ rows are the same. It is important to mention that the higher ratings must be given to the best items while the lower values to the worst items for this method to work properly. As mentioned before, the values for the attributes can be considered as the rating, if and only if higher values are associated with the best items (i.e. profit), otherwise a conversion should be done. To control the extent to which an attribute is given importance, this method works with a weight matrix $\lambda$ of size $U \times (1 + M + V)$. Each user have their own weights for every attribute, making this re-ranking method personalized for every user. The weight matrix can be updated according to the future users' interactions with the recommendations. As this re-ranking method is able to consider several attributes to base the recommendations on, it is named MARS, which stands for Multi-Aware Recommender System.

The re-ranking method takes as inputs $R^*$, $T_R$, $R_M$, $R_V$, and $\lambda$. First, scaling is executed over $R_M$ and $R_V$ by following Eq. 1.

$$R_K^* = \frac{R_K - \min R_K}{\max R_K - \min R_K} * (\max R^* - \min R^*) + \min R^* \tag{1}$$

where $K \in (M \cup V)$, are all the attribute matrices and vectors. This scaling ensures that all the rating attribute matrices and vectors are on the same scale $[\min R^*, \max R^*]$, avoiding very high, very low, or even negative values. Normally, values in $R^*$ can be in range $(0, 5]$, but other positive values are also accepted. The next step is ranking the items based on the ratings obtained in the previous step. Ranking is performed by following Eq. 2 over all the matrices and vectors, including $R^*$.

$$rank_J = (R_J^* + 1)^{-1} \tag{2}$$

where $J \in (K \cup std)$ are all the matrices and vectors$(R^*, R_M, R_V)$ passed as inputs for the ranking method. The operation $+1$ in Eq. 2, ensures that the values obtained in the ranking step are in range $(0, 1]$, specifically in range $[1/(\max R^* + 1), 1/(\min R^* + 1)]$. Once all the ranking matrices and vectors are obtained, the re-ranking is performed. The re-ranking method only re-ranks items that have a rating $R^*(u, i)$ higher or equal to $T_R$, according to Eq. 3. Otherwise, if the rating $R^*(u, i)$ is less than $T_R$, Eq. 4 is used. Equation 5 describes the proposed method.

$$\lambda(u, std) * rank_{std}(u, i) + \sum_{m \in M} \lambda(u, m) * rank_m(u, i) + \sum_{v \in V} \lambda(u, v) * rank_v(i) \quad (3)$$

$$\lambda(u, std) * rank_{std}(u, i) + \alpha_u, \quad \text{where } \alpha_u = \sum_{j \in J} \max rank_j \quad (4)$$

$$rank_x(u, i, T_R) = \begin{cases} (3), & \text{if } R^*(u, i) \geq T_R \\ (4), & \text{else} \end{cases} \quad (5)$$

the constant $\alpha_u$ is calculated from the maximum rankings (worst rating) of each method. This constant ensures that items rated lower than $T_R$ are not ranked ahead of items rated higher than $T_R$. Items with rating below $T_R$ preserve their positions after re-ranking, while items with rating above $T_R$ may change their position after re-ranking according to the attributes and their corresponding weights.

The accuracy of the re-ranking method depends on the variables $T_R$ and $\lambda$. Increasing the $T_R$ threshold towards $\max R^*$ results in higher accuracy, as fewer items are re-ranked based on the considered attributes, thus becoming more similar to $rank_{std}$. On the other hand, when decreasing $T_R$ towards $\min R^*$, the method re-ranks more items (if $T_R = \min R^*$, all the items are re-ranked). At this point, the accuracy of $rank_x$ is completely controlled by $\lambda$. In both cases, if the weight given to the standard method is much greater than the weights of the attribute matrices and vectors ($\lambda(u, std) \gg \lambda(u, K)$), then, the re-ranked list is more similar to $rank_{std}$, resulting in high accuracy. On the other hand, decreasing $\lambda(u, std)$ or increasing $\lambda(u, K)$, results in a loss of accuracy because more importance is given to the attributes than to $rank_{std}$.

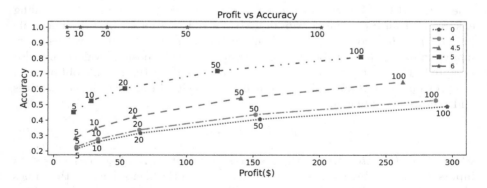

**Fig. 1.** Accuracy vs Profit of MARS models for different $T_R$ values

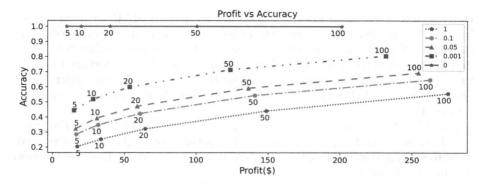

**Fig. 2.** Accuracy vs Profit of MARS models for different weights of the profit attribute

Therefore, choosing different values of $T_R$ and different weights ($\lambda$) allows establishing the desired balance between accuracy and the objectives sought given the attributes. In particular, in the example of Profit-Awareness re-ranking illustrated in Fig. 1, the accuracy in TopN recommendations of MARS could be improved by increasing $T_R$. At the same time, as shown in Fig. 2, the accuracy in TopN recommendations could also be improved by decreasing the weight given to the *profit* attribute.

**Table 1.** General overview of standard method ranking, profit ranking and MARS method ranking for user u

| Rating | Standard | Profit | MARS | Rating | Standard | Profit | MARS |
|---|---|---|---|---|---|---|---|
| 5.00 | 1 | 1657 | 3 | 4.60 | 11 | 2887 | 16 |
| 5.00 | 2 | 2369 | 5 | 4.59 | 12 | 1922 | 12 |
| 4.94 | 3 | 1439 | 4 | 4.57 | 13 | 604 | 9 |
| 4.93 | 4 | 989 | 2 | 4.56 | 14 | 1872 | 13 |
| 4.85 | 5 | 535 | 1 | 4.53 | 15 | 245 | 7 |
| 4.82 | 6 | 1704 | 6 | 4.53 | 16 | 1226 | 10 |
| 4.77 | 7 | 3464 | 17 | 4.51 | 17 | 1732 | 14 |
| 4.75 | 8 | 2449 | 11 | 4.49 | 18 | 3004 | 18 |
| 4.65 | 9 | 934 | 8 | 4.48 | 19 | 1339 | 19 |
| 4.63 | 10 | 2499 | 15 | 4.48 | 20 | 1468 | 20 · |

Table 1 shows the difference in the Top20 list for the standard method ranking, the profit ranking, and the MARS ranking. The rating column indicates the rating obtained for a certain item, the other columns show the position or ranking of a certain item in the corresponding method. The profit column is the item's position according to its profit. That is, the higher the profit an item generates, the lower (better) the position of the item on the ranking. For example, the item that was ranked $1^{st}$ in the standard method, in MARS it is ranked $3^{rd}$ because it is ranked $1657^{th}$ according to its profit, while the item ranked $5^{th}$ in the standard method, in MARS is ranked $1^{st}$ because it is ranked $535^{th}$ (the item has much better ranking) according to its profit. It is important to notice that $T_R = 4.5$, and that is the reason why the items with rating under 4.5 do not move in the MARS method ranking, even though they have a better profit ranking than other items.

As it has been shown in Fig. 2, choosing different values of the weights leads to obtain the desired impact on the user. It is a variation of gradient descent. We want to find the optimal weights to obtain the desired impact. The cost function is computed using Eq. 6:

$$cost@N = \frac{|Y - \hat{Y}|}{N} \tag{6}$$

where $Y$ is the desired impact on the user and $\hat{Y}$ is the obtained impact on the user. The objective of the optimization step is to minimize this cost function. This means that the users should have an impact close to the desired one for the algorithm to converge. To solve this optimization process, we divided the update process of the weights in two parts. If the error $Y - \hat{Y}$ is positive, then, there is not enough impact on the user and we can increase the impact. In this case, the weights related to the increase in impact are updated (e.g. $\lambda(profit)$). On the other hand, if the error $Y - \hat{Y}$ is negative, it means that the impact on the user is higher than the desired and we should decrease the impact. In this case, the weights related to the decrease in the impact are updated (e.g. $\lambda(std)$). This update process follows Eq. 7.

$$update(\lambda) = \begin{cases} \lambda(att) + \gamma(Y - \hat{Y}), & \text{if } Y - \hat{Y} > 0 \\ \lambda(std) - \gamma(Y - \hat{Y}), & \text{else} \end{cases} \tag{7}$$

where $\lambda(att)$ are the weights related to the attributes that increase the impact on the user, and $\lambda(std)$ are the weights related to the standard method and attributes that reduce the impact on the user. The learning rate $\gamma$ indicates the size of the next step and controls the convergence process of the algorithm. The value of $\gamma$ decays across iterations. The algorithm stops when some criteria are met, in this case, it stops if the cost function increases instead of decreasing after an iteration. It also stops if the cost functions difference is small, or if it reaches the specified number of iterations. This optimization problem finds a good solution, but may not find the optimal solution. Not all the users will have the desired impact. Some users will have greater impact and others less impact. In this case, we want to update the users' weights that have a greater impact than desired. An aggressive update process is performed for this users by following Eq. 8:

$$aggresiveUpdate(\lambda(std)) = \lambda(std) * \tau \tag{8}$$

in this case, the optimization algorithm only updates the weights of the attributes that decrease the impact on the user. The weights increase by a factor of $\tau$, which increases with each iteration. This leads to the reduction of the impact on the user until the impact on all the users is lower or equal to the desired impact.

### 3.1   Data Set

The data set used for the experiments is MovieLens-1M [7]. For the MovieLens-1M data set, we created a random variable for the profit of each item. The values were chosen randomly using a Gaussian distribution with a mean value of $2 and defined minimum and maximum profit ($0 and $4, respectively), like proposed by [10]. The data set contains 1000209 ratings of 3706 different items performed by 6040 users. The sparsity of the data set is 0.0447. The final data set used in this paper can be found in https://www.kaggle.com/datasets/juanriofrio/mars-method.

### 3.2   Metrics

**Accuracy.** In this paper, the accuracy of the proposed approach is measured by the comparison between the list of TopN recommended items in the standard method ($rank_{std}$) and the list of TopN recommended items in the proposed method. The accuracy at TopN items for user $u$ is defined in Eq. 9:

$$accuracy@N = \frac{|std_N(u) \cap L_N(u)|}{N} \qquad (9)$$

where N is the number of items being recommended (the length of the lists), $std_N(u)$ is the TopN recommendation list for user $u$ based on the standard method ($R^*$), $L_N(u)$ is the TopN recommendation list for user $u$ in the proposed approach ($rank_x$), $|std_N(u) \cap L_N(u)|$ is the number of items present in both lists (number of correct items recommended in the new ranking). Consequently, the number of new items introduced to the list is defined by $N - |std_N(u) \cap L_N(u)|$.

**Impact.** In this study, we are aiming to reduce or control the impact on the user arising from the re-ranking task. Then, it is important to mention that the impact is directly related to the accuracy and it is defined in Eq. 10:

$$impact@N = 1 - accuracy@N \qquad (10)$$

**Normalized Discounted Cumulative Gain (NDCG).** The NDCG is an evaluation metric proposed by [12] and commonly used when a ranking task is performed in the information retrieval field. As stated by the authors, the benefit of this metric is that NDCG combines document rank (position) and degree of relevance (rating); which makes this metric perfect for this study. We can calculate the NDCG for any permutation of a set of items with known relevance, by comparing the Discounted Cumulative Gain (DCG) of the proposed approach with the DCG of the standard approach. The parameter N determines how many items to consider in the ranked lists [4]. We can express the $DCG@N$ for user $u$ by Eq. 11.

$$DCG@N = \sum_{i \in L_N(u)} \frac{2^{R^*(u,i)} - 1}{\log_2(1 + \hat{p}(i))} \qquad (11)$$

where $L_N(u)$ is the TopN recommendation list for user $u$ in the proposed approach ($rank_x$), item $i$ is an element of $L_N(u)$, $R^*(u,i)$ is the predicted rating (relevance) of item $i$, and $\hat{p}(i)$ is the position of item $i$ in the list $L_N(u)$. To calculate the $NDCG@N$, we need to calculate the $DCG@N$ of the proposed approach and the $DCG@N$ of the ideal ranking (standard method). We call this value $iDCG@N$ for user $u$ and it is calculated by following Eq. 12, while the $NDCG@N$ is calculated by using Eq. 13.

$$iDCG@N = \sum_{i \in std_N(u)} \frac{2^{R^*(u,i)} - 1}{\log_2(1 + p(i))} \qquad (12)$$

$$NDCG@N = \frac{DCG@N}{iDCG@N} \qquad (13)$$

where $std_N(u)$ is the TopN recommendation list for user $u$ in the standard method or the ideal TopN list, item $i$ is an element of $std_N(u)$, $R^*(u,i)$ is the predicted rating of item $i$, and $p(i)$ is the position of item $i$ in the list $std_N(u)$.

**Precision.** This metric compares the amount of truly highly ranked items to the amount of truly ranked items. The amount of truly ranked items is equal to the number of items in $L_N(u)$ that has been actually rated by the user $u$ ($R(u,i) > 0$). The amount of truly highly ranked items is equal to the number of items in $L_N(u)$ that has been actually rated above $T_H$ by the user $u$ ($R(u,i) \geq T_H$)

$$trulyRated@N = \sum_{i \in L_N(u)} \begin{cases} 1, & \text{if } R(u,i) > 0 \\ 0, & \text{else} \end{cases} \qquad (14)$$

$$trulyHighlyRated@N = \sum_{i \in L_N(u)} \begin{cases} 1, & \text{if } R(u,i) \geq T_H \\ 0, & \text{else} \end{cases} \qquad (15)$$

$$precision@N = \frac{trulyHighlyRated@N}{trulyRated@N} \qquad (16)$$

**Mean Absolute Error (MAE).** This metric calculates the average positions that one item in list $L_N(u)$ is moved, compared to the optimal list $std_N$. This is a positional metric, which means that it calculates the value using only the new position and the optimal position, and not the scores.

$$MAE@N = \frac{1}{N} \sum_{i \in L_N(u)} |p(i) - \hat{p}(i)| \qquad (17)$$

where $p(i)$ is the position of the item $i$ in the standard method or the optimal position, and $\hat{p}(i)$ is the position of the item $i$ in the list $L_N(u)$ or the position predicted by the proposed approach.

**Root Mean Squared Error (RMSE).** Since the errors are squared before they are averaged, the RMSE gives a relatively high weight to large errors. This means that the RMSE should be more useful when large errors are particularly undesirable. This is a positional metric, which means that it calculates the value using only the new position and the optimal position, and not the scores.

$$RMSE@N = \sqrt{\frac{1}{N} \sum_{i \in L_N(u)} (p(i) - \hat{p}(i))^2} \tag{18}$$

where $p(i)$ is the position of the item $i$ in the standard method or the optimal position, and $\hat{p}(i)$ is the position of the item $i$ in the list $L_N(u)$ or the position predicted by the proposed approach.

## 4 Results

In this section we present the data set and define the evaluation metrics used during the experiments, also the main results derived from the experiments performed over data set are presented. The Python implementation of the proposed approach used to obtain the results presented in this section can be found in https://github.com/ColdRiver93/MARS.

### 4.1 Experimental Design

The results obtained from matrix $R^*$ are considered the standard method. We assume that the ranking obtained by using this matrix is optimal on terms user tastes or the items relevance. Therefore, all the new TopN lists obtained from different models are compared to the TopN list obtained from ranking items by their rating in $R^*$. We considered the method proposed by [10] to be the baseline method. We differentiate the MARS models by their attributes weights ratio. "MARS($ratio_\lambda$)" means a MARS model with a ratio of attributes weights equal to $ratio_\lambda$. The attributes weights ratio is calculated by following Eq. 19:

$$ratio_\lambda = \frac{\sum \lambda(std)}{\sum \lambda(profit)} \tag{19}$$

where $\lambda(profit)$ are the weights related to the attributes that increase the impact on the user, and $\lambda(std)$ are the weights related to the attributes that decrease the impact on the user. From Eq. 19 we can interpret that higher values of $ratio_\lambda$ means higher accuracy and lower values of $ratio_\lambda$ means higher impact on the user. In all the experiments we used $N = 20$ to obtain the TopN lists.

$$att_\lambda = \frac{\sum \lambda(att)}{U} \tag{20}$$

where $att_\lambda$ is the average of the weights of the considered attribute, $\lambda(att)$ are the weights associated to the attribute, and $U$ is the total number of users. Specifically in this experiment, $att \in [std, profit, price]$.

## 4.2   MovieLens-1M Results

For the experiments performed on the MovieLens-1M data set, first we used matrix factorization to calculate $R^*$. The values in the predicted matrix are in the range $R^*(u, i) \in [0, 5]$. We performed four different experiments with MovieLens-1M data set by modifying the value of $T_R$. The chosen values for the experiments were $T_R = 0$, $T_R = 4.5$, $T_R = 5$, and $T_R = 6$. In each experiment, we calculate the metrics for the standard method, the baseline method and various MARS models with different weight distributions. The attributes considered for the experiments with this data set are the relevance of the items and the profit generated by each item. The weight associated to the relevance of the items is $\lambda_{std}$. Higher values of $\lambda_{std}$ contribute to reduce the impact on the user. On the other hand, the weight associated to the profit generated is $\lambda_{profit}$. Higher values of $\lambda_{profit}$ leads to higher profit.

**Table 2.** Scores obtained by the standard method, the baseline method and various MARS models, using $T_R = 0$ on MovieLens-1M data set

| Model | Accuracy | Impact | NDCG | RMSE | MAE | Precision | Profit | Items |
|---|---|---|---|---|---|---|---|---|
| Standard | 1.0000 | 0.0000 | 1.0000 | 0.0000 | 0.0000 | 0.9040 | 40.31 | 2189 |
| MARS(749.60) | 1.0000 | 0.0000 | 0.9999 | 0.9775 | 0.6875 | 0.9040 | 40.31 | 2189 |
| MARS(159.12) | 0.9462 | 0.0538 | 0.9982 | 2.2354 | 1.7007 | 0.9050 | 42.56 | 2210 |
| MARS(58.3852) | 0.8528 | 0.1472 | 0.9921 | 4.7666 | 3.6049 | 0.9036 | 46.25 | 2195 |
| MARS(17.0681) | 0.6791 | 0.3209 | 0.9729 | 15.2338 | 11.0732 | 0.8944 | 52.70 | 2062 |
| MARS(4.2983) | 0.4281 | 0.5719 | 0.9292 | 65.3827 | 47.9337 | 0.8743 | 61.68 | 1655 |
| MARS(0.0) | 0.0068 | 0.9932 | 0.4781 | 2004.4725 | 1705.5477 | 0.5093 | 78.93 | 20 |
| Baseline | 0.0068 | 0.9932 | 0.4781 | 2004.4725 | 1705.5477 | 0.5093 | 78.93 | 20 |

The results obtained from the experiment using $T_R = 0$ are presented in Table 2. When $T_R \leq \min R^*$, all the items are re-ranked based on the selected attributes and their corresponding weights. A greater impact is obtained since all the items are re-ranked and more items have the chance of being introduced to the new Top20 list. At the same time, when $T_R \leq \min R^*$ and $\lambda_{std} \approx 0$, we achieved the same results as if we recommended only based on the profit generated by the items. This is the case of the baseline model and the MARS(0.0) model in Table 2, which obtained the same results. This two models recommend the 20 most profitable items to all the users, decreasing the diversity, increasing the impact on the user and increasing the profit. Actually, these models have the greatest impact on the user among all the experiments, but they also achieved the highest profit of all the experiments performed with this data set.

The maximum possible profit is achieved with these models. They increased the maximum obtainable profit by 95.81%. This models greatly increased the MAE, obtaining a value of 1705.5477. This means that in average an item moved 1705 positions when re-ranked, affecting the accuracy of the models considerably. When $\lambda_{profit} \approx 0$, MARS model behaves like the standard model. The standard model and the MARS(749.6017) model got the same results in terms of accuracy, impact, profit, and number of items being recommended. The standard method had the best accuracy, while the baseline method had the worst accuracy of all the models. The results proved that higher values of $ratio_\lambda$ lead to higher accuracy and lower profit, while lower values of $ratio_\lambda$ produce lower accuracy and higher profit. MARS models have the ability to control the impact on the user by varying $ratio_\lambda$. When $T_R = 0$, MARS models can introduce an impact on the user in the range from 0 to 0.9932 and can generate profit in the range from $40.31 to $78.93. In other words, MARS models can reproduce the results of the standard model and the baseline model, plus any result in the middle in terms of impact on the user and profit. This experiment clearly shows that impact and profit are directly correlated, while accuracy and profit are inversely correlated.

**Table 3.** Scores obtained by the standard method, the baseline method and various MARS models, using $T_R = 4.5$ on MovieLens-1M data set

| Model | Accuracy | Impact | NDCG | RMSE | MAE | Precision | Profit | Items |
|---|---|---|---|---|---|---|---|---|
| Standard | 1.0000 | 0.0000 | 1.0000 | 0.0000 | 0.0000 | 0.9040 | 40.31 | 2189 |
| MARS(6.6967) | 1.0000 | 0.0000 | 0.9985 | 1.0637 | 0.7511 | 0.9040 | 40.31 | 2189 |
| MARS(4.074) | 0.9661 | 0.0339 | 0.9969 | 1.9095 | 1.4571 | 0.9052 | 41.70 | 2206 |
| MARS(3.5671) | 0.9086 | 0.0914 | 0.9925 | 3.4505 | 2.6577 | 0.9059 | 43.91 | 2231 |
| MARS(2.5901) | 0.7733 | 0.2267 | 0.9803 | 10.1749 | 7.5398 | 0.9057 | 48.45 | 2273 |
| MARS(1.4969) | 0.5909 | 0.4091 | 0.9578 | 29.6759 | 23.0266 | 0.8999 | 54.27 | 2230 |
| MARS(0.0) | 0.3058 | 0.6942 | 0.8847 | 224.5113 | 188.3836 | 0.8871 | 64.98 | 1839 |
| Baseline | 0.3058 | 0.6942 | 0.8847 | 224.5113 | 188.3836 | 0.8871 | 64.98 | 1839 |

Table 3 shows the results from the experiment using $T_R = 4.5$. When $\min R^* < T_R < \max R^*$, some of the items are re-ranked. If $T_R$ gets closer to $\max R^*$, less items are available for re-ranking, while if $T_R$ gets closer to $\min R^*$ more items are available. A lower impact on the user is achieved when $T_R$ gets closer to $\max R^*$. The baseline and MARS(0.0) models again got the same results and they both have the greatest impact on the user in this experiment, however they also got the highest profit of all the models in this experiment. The maximum possible profit in this experiment is achieved with these two models. This models increased the MAE, obtaining a value of 188.3836. This means that in average an item moved 188 positions when reranked, affecting the accuracy of the models but not as much as the previous experiment. When $\lambda_{profit} \approx 0$, MARS model behaves like the standard model. The standard model and the MARS(6.6967) model attained the same results in terms of accuracy, impact, profit, and number of items being recommended. The standard method had the best accuracy, while the baseline method had the worst accuracy of all the models similarly to the previous experiment. This experiment also proved that higher values of $ratio_\lambda$ lead to higher accuracy and lower profit, while lower values of $ratio_\lambda$ produce lower accuracy and higher profit. When $T_R = 4.5$, MARS models can introduce an impact on the user in the range from 0 to 0.6942 and can generate profit in the range from \$40.31 to \$64.98. Increasing $T_R$ from 0 to 4.5 decreased the impact on the user by a maximum of 30.10% when we compared the MARS(0.0) models of the two experiments. This experiment also proved that the impact and profit are directly correlated, while accuracy and profit are inversely correlated.

**Table 4.** Scores obtained by the standard method, the baseline method and various MARS models, using $T_R = 5$ on MovieLens-1M data set

| Model | Accuracy | Impact | NDCG | RMSE | MAE | Precision | Profit | Items |
|---|---|---|---|---|---|---|---|---|
| Standard | 1.0000 | 0.0000 | 1.0 | 0.0000 | 0.0000 | 0.9040 | 40.31 | 2189 |
| MARS(2.4217) | 1.0000 | 0.0000 | 1.0 | 0.5396 | 0.3535 | 0.9040 | 40.31 | 2189 |
| MARS(1.8134) | 0.9896 | 0.0104 | 1.0 | 0.8167 | 0.5653 | 0.9036 | 40.68 | 2196 |
| MARS(1.4044) | 0.9655 | 0.0345 | 1.0 | 1.3814 | 1.0241 | 0.9031 | 41.49 | 2219 |
| MARS(1.0856) | 0.9075 | 0.0925 | 1.0 | 3.1615 | 2.4595 | 0.9023 | 43.24 | 2277 |
| MARS(0.7841) | 0.8239 | 0.1761 | 1.0 | 9.3877 | 7.2642 | 0.9015 | 45.88 | 2362 |
| MARS(0.0) | 0.6053 | 0.3947 | 1.0 | 63.0612 | 52.6788 | 0.9001 | 53.57 | 2149 |
| Baseline | 0.6053 | 0.3947 | 1.0 | 63.0612 | 52.6788 | 0.9001 | 53.57 | 2149 |

Table 4 shows the results from the experiment using $T_R = 5$. When $T_R = \max R^*$, only the items with the highest possible rank ($\max R^*$) are re-ranked. As mentioned before, if $T_R$ gets closer to $\max R^*$, less items are available for re-ranking. In this case, only the items with predicted rating of 5 were re-ranked. Similar to the previous experiments, the baseline and MARS(0.0) models got the same results and they both have the highest impact on the user and profit in this experiment. When $ratio_\lambda$ is high enough, MARS model behaves like the standard model. In this experiment, MARS(2.4217) was the model that got the same results as the standard model in terms of accuracy, impact, profit, and number of items being recommended. This experiment reaffirms the idea that higher values of $ratio_\lambda$ lead to higher accuracy and lower profit, while lower values of $ratio_\lambda$ produce lower accuracy and higher profit. We found a correlation between the variables $T_R$ and $ratio_\lambda$ when we compared the result of all the experiments. When $T_R$ was closer to $\min R^*$, $ratio_\lambda$ needed higher values to obtain the same results as the standard model (i.e. when $T_R = 0$, $ratio_\lambda = 749.6017$). On the other hand, when $T_R$ was closer to $\max R^*$, $ratio_\lambda$ needed lower values to obtain the same results as the standard model (i.e. when $T_R = 5$, $ratio_\lambda = 2.4217$). If we use $T_R = 5$, MARS models can introduce an impact on the user in the range from 0 to 0.3947, and the models can generate profit in the range from

$40.31 to $53.57. Increasing $T_R$ from 0 to 5, decreased the impact on the user by a maximum of 60.26% when we compared the highest impact of the two experiments. It also decreased the maximum obtainable profit by 32.98% when we compared the maximum obtainable profit of the two experiments. In this experiment it is important to notice that the NDCG did not changed and it stayed at 1. This was due to the fact that even though items were reranked, all of them have the rating equal to 5. The NDCG was not affected because all the items had the same relevance, and in terms of NDCG all the results of the models were equally valid.

## 5   Discussion

The results of this research have provided a solid foundation on how to control the impact on the user when profit is taken into account for products recommendation. All the experiments have shown that MARS models have the ability to control the impact on the user while increasing the profit by varying the weights associated to the considered attributes. Normally, if a lower impact is desired, we need to give higher weights to the attributes that favor the accuracy. Depending on the parameters given to the model, MARS can achieve several different results in terms of impact and profit. MARS method results may vary between only taking into account the preferences of the users (standard) to only taking into account the most profitable items. The results proved that higher values of $ratio_\lambda$ lead to higher accuracy and lower profit, while lower values of $ratio_\lambda$ produce lower accuracy and higher profit. MARS can control the impact on the user not only by the weights given to the system, but also by adjusting the threshold $T_R$. The number of items being re-ranked depends on the value of $T_R$. If $T_R \leq \min R^*$, then all the items are re-ranked. On the other hand, if $T_R > \max R^*$ none of the items are re-ranked. When $\min R^* < T_R \leq \max R^*$, some items are going to be re-ranked. The diversity may be affected by the proposed method, but this depends on the data set being used and the parameters given to the model. In some experiments the diversity increases, and in other experiments the diversity decreases when the model is trained. If diversity is an important factor to take into account, an attribute that favors diversity can be added to the MARS model, like proposed by [2]. It is important to notice that the training of the model can be parallelized. In other words, the weights and results can be obtained for each user separately. The model is not needed to be trained with all the users, or the complete matrix. During the experiments we noticed that we could not introduce impact on certain users. This depends on the value of $T_R$ and the predicted ratings of the items for that user ($R^*(u)$). In specific, if $T_R > \max R^*(u)$, then no items are re-ranked and no impact can be introduced to user $u$.

MARS method depends on the accuracy of the predicted rating matrix $R^*$. If $R^*$ does not adequately reflect the user preferences, MARS model will not either. In this work, we assume that the matrix $R^*$ perfectly reflects the user preferences and the accuracy is calculated based on this assumption. Then, in future work, it is important to find a suitable method to predict $R^*$. Also, a better weights optimization method is needed when having multiple attributes. The optimization method proposed in this work divides all the considered attributes into two groups, those that favor the accuracy and those that favor the objective sought by the model (profit in this case). It would be a better approach to optimize each attribute independently. An important part of the MARS method is that the weights can be updated based on the user interaction with the products to obtain more personalized recommendations as the user makes use of the system.

For future work, MARS models can be trained with more and different attributes. Other data sets may be considered in new experiments to obtain insights on how the properties of the data sets affect on the MARS models. Also, other optimization algorithms can be designed to train the model in a better way or to optimize using a multi-objective algorithm. Finally, MARS is not only designed to work with an impact vs. profit trade-off, since other objectives may be defined. For example, we can use the MARS method to increase diversity, to promote certain items, or to give an advantage to a certain item provider by using the corresponding attributes that favor the sought objective.

## 6    Conclusion

Nowadays, recommender systems are being used widely by companies to recommend relevant products to each user and help the user in the decision-making process. These advantages for the user build customer loyalty in a company only if the recommendations are relevant to the user. Some recommeder systems make their recommendations based on the profit generated by each item. This type of recommender systems (PARS) introduce an impact on the user with the recommendations being made. If we are not careful about the impact, customer loyalty can be affected.

This work proposed a recommender system named MARS that re-ranks items based on different attributes selected by the service provider. Specifically, in this work we used the profit of the items in all the experiments, and the price of the items in some experiments. To avoid compromising the relevance of the items being presented, MARS uses a threshold $T_R$ that determines which items are re-ranked. If the item has a low predicted rating (lower than $T_R$), it is not going to be re-ranked and it is not climbing up in the ranking. MARS uses a score-based weighted rank aggregation method to obtain the final recommendation list. The weights can be personalized for each user, and are updated by an optimization algorithm. MARS is trained by a modified gradient descent algorithm that update the weights to obtain the desired impact on the user. In this way, the model controls the impact on the user so as not to compromise the customer loyalty, while increasing the profit for the company. We got promising results in terms of impact on the user and profit when we implemented MARS on the MovieLens-1M data set under different configurations.

# References

1. Abdollahpouri, H., et al.: Multistakeholder recommendation: survey and research directions. User Model. User-Adap. Inter. **30**, 127–158 (2020). https://doi.org/10.1007/s11257-019-09256-1
2. Adomavicius, G., Kwon, Y.: Improving aggregate recommendation diversity using ranking-based techniques. IEEE Trans. Knowl. Data Eng. **24**(5), 896–911 (2011). https://doi.org/10.1109/TKDE.2011.15
3. Azaria, A., Hassidim, A., Kraus, S., Eshkol, A., Weintraub, O., Netanely, I.: Movie recommender system for profit maximization. In: Proceedings of the 7th ACM Conference on Recommender Systems, pp. 121–128 (2013). https://doi.org/10.1145/2507157.2507162
4. Balakrishnan, S., Chopra, S.: Collaborative ranking. In: Proceedings of the Fifth ACM International Conference on Web Search and Data Mining, pp. 143–152 (2012). https://doi.org/10.1145/2124295.2124314
5. Concha-Carrasco, J.A., Vega-Rodríguez, M.A., Pérez, C.J.: A multi-objective artificial bee colony approach for profit-aware recommender systems. Inf. Sci. **625**, 476–488 (2023). https://doi.org/10.1016/j.ins.2023.01.050
6. Ghanem, N., Leitner, S., Jannach, D.: Balancing consumer and business value of recommender systems: a simulation-based analysis. Electron. Commer. Res. Appl. **55**, 101195 (2022). https://doi.org/10.1016/j.elerap.2022.101195
7. Harper, F.M., Konstan, J.A.: The movielens datasets: history and context. ACM Trans. Interact. Intell. Syst. (TiiS) **5**(4), 1–19 (2015). https://doi.org/10.1145/2827872
8. Hosanagar, K., Krishnan, R., Ma, L.: Recommended for you: the impact of profit incentives on the relevance of online recommendations, pp. 31–47 (2008)
9. Jannach, D., Adomavicius, G.: Recommendations with a purpose. In: Proceedings of the 10th ACM Conference on Recommender Systems, pp. 7–10 (2016). https://doi.org/10.1145/2959100.2959186
10. Jannach, D., Adomavicius, G.: Price and profit awareness in recommender systems. In: Workshop on Value-Aware and Multi-Stakeholder Recommendation (2017). https://doi.org/10.48550/arXiv.1707.08029
11. Jannach, D., Jugovac, M.: Measuring the business value of recommender systems. ACM Trans. Manag. Inf. Syst. (TMIS) **10**(4), 1–23 (2019). https://doi.org/10.1145/3370082
12. Järvelin, K., Kekäläinen, J.: Cumulated gain-based evaluation of IR techniques. ACM Trans. Inf. Syst. (TOIS) **20**(4), 422–446 (2002). https://doi.org/10.1145/582415.582418
13. Ko, H., Lee, S., Park, Y., Choi, A.: A survey of recommendation systems: recommendation models, techniques, and application fields. Electronics **11**(1), 141 (2022). https://doi.org/10.3390/electronics11010141
14. Kouadria, A., Nouali, O., Al-Shamri, M.Y.H.: A multi-criteria collaborative filtering recommender system using learning-to-rank and rank aggregation. Arab. J. Sci. Eng. **45**(4), 2835–2845 (2020). https://doi.org/10.1007/s13369-019-04180-3
15. Shi, Y., Larson, M., Hanjalic, A.: List-wise learning to rank with matrix factorization for collaborative filtering. In: Proceedings of the Fourth ACM Conference on Recommender Systems, pp. 269–272 (2010). https://doi.org/10.1145/1864708.1864764

16. Wang, Y.Y., Luse, A., Townsend, A.M., Mennecke, B.E.: Understanding the moderating roles of types of recommender systems and products on customer behavioral intention to use recommender systems. IseB **13**, 769–799 (2015). https://doi.org/10.1007/s10257-014-0269-9
17. Zhong, J., Negre, E.: Towards improving user-recommender systems interactions. In: 2022 IEEE/SICE International Symposium on System Integration (SII), pp. 816–820. IEEE (2022). https://doi.org/10.1109/SII52469.2022.9708869

# Augmenting Data with DCGANs
# to Improve Skin Lesions Classification

Claudia Moncada[1]([🖂])[ID], Fabricio Crespo[2][ID], Anthony Crespo[1][ID],
and Rigoberto Fonseca-Delgado[1][ID]

[1] School of Mathematical and Computational Sciences, Yachay Tech University,
100119 Urcuquí, Ecuador
{claudia.moncada,brian.crespo,rfonseca}@yachaytech.edu.ec
[2] Deep Learning for Autonomous Vehicles, Robotics, and Computer Vision
(DeepARC Research), Imbabura, Ecuador
jonnathan.crespo@yachaytech.edu.ec

**Abstract.** One of the main problems in computer vision applied to medical field is the limited amount of data. This represents a limitation in making an early diagnosis of diseases. Therefore, synthetic data has proven significantly crucial in minimizing the problems of acquiring medical images. This paper proposes using Generative Adversarial Networks (GANs) to generate synthetic skin lesion data. These data are helpful in the process of classifying benign and malignant skin lesions such as melanoma. Hence, the Deep Convolutional Generative Adversarial Network (DCGAN) was used to produce malignant synthetic images. An Inception V3 classification network was used to evaluate the impact of adding this synthesized data to a binary classification task. With the increase of synthetic data to the malignant class, an accuracy score of 0.88 was obtained. These synthetic images were used in the training set to improve the final performance of the classification network for skin lesions. The achieved results were compared with the classification of the original data. They showed that the augmentation of images generated by the DCGAN improves the network's performance for the classification task.

**Keywords:** GAN · DCGAN · Melanoma · Image classification · Data augmentation

## 1 Introduction

Detection of medical pathologies is one of the significant challenges in Artificial Intelligence for healthcare. One of the topics with a meaningful presence in research is the early detection of cancer. In 2020, the World Health Organization (WHO) [1] reported more than 10 million deaths in 2020 related to different types of cancer. In particular, they report around 1.20 million cases of skin cancer. Additionally, in 2023 the American Cancer Society [2] estimates that only

J. Maldonado-Mahauad et al. (Eds.): TICEC 2023, CCIS 1885, pp. 193–206, 2023.
https://doi.org/10.1007/978-3-031-45438-7_13

in the United States about 97,610 new melanomas will be diagnosed, and about 7,990 people may die because of this disease.

Melanoma is one of the most common skin cancer pathologies, with a death rate of 75% incidence [3]. In medical terms, melanoma is a malignant neoplasm originating from melanocyte cells. Those are skin cells responsible for the production of melanin. Melanin is the pigment responsible for skin, hair and eye color. Melanoma occurs when melanocytes begin to grow and multiply abnormally and become malignant [4].

The challenge with this pathology is classifying benign and malignant skin lesions because there are different clinical subtypes, and it isn't easy to differentiate between them. In addition, if the pathology is detected early, it should be treaty only with rapid resection, making fast diagnosis extremely important. To look for a quick and automatic melanoma classification tool, the International Skin Imaging Collaboration (ISIC) has released a large-scale publicly accessible dataset of dermoscopic images [5]. The main objective of ISIC is to promote collaboration and knowledge sharing among experts in dermatology, research and technology to advance the detection and diagnosis of skin diseases. They even provide competencies in skin lesion analysis, including segmentation, feature extraction and lesion classification [6].

Although some organizations continue to release datasets, the amount of images for specific malignant pathologies is still limited [7]. Because of this, synthetic images seem to be an alternative to increase the number of samples for datasets. However, generating synthetic images related to medicine is difficult for some reasons: the anatomical structure features a large amount of detail, individual patient characteristics, accuracy, realism, and the protection of patient privacy. Some Deep Learning and Computer Vision techniques currently focus on generating synthetic images through different approaches [8,9]. One of them are the Generative Adversarial Networks (GANs) [10]. GANs can be helpful in medicine where limited data is available and make the task hard to identify pathologies. This tool has proven to help generate realistic images that contribute to creating relevant data for various medical studies. Therefore, synthetic images help improve performance in tasks like classification and segmentation of pathologies.

In this work, a study about the use of GANs to generate synthetic images for skin cancer classification is presented. The ISIC dataset is used, and the number of images in the training phase is increased through synthetic images generated by GANs. To evaluate the impact of the GANs in the performance of skin cancer classification, an Inception V3 architecture is used. The evaluation consists of two main stages: The first one is related to training the Inception model only with the original and unbalanced data retrieved from the ISIC dataset. The second stage is training the Inception model using the dataset augmented with synthetic images generated using GANs. This work's core objective is to generate images of skin lesions in the most realistic way possible.

## 2    Related Works

### 2.1    Image Classification on Skin Lesions

Image classification is a Computer Vision (CV) task that assigns a specific label or category to an image according to the information retrieved from an input image. In the medical field, recognizing and distinguishing different pathologies can be crucial.

Li *et al.* [11] proposed a FCRN-50 and FCRN-101 architectures for classifying melanoma, seborrheic keratosis and nevus images. Also, they constructed a Lesion Indexing Network (LIN) for skin lesion image analysis. Similarly, Yilmaz *et al.* [12] took data from ISIC 2017 challenge and applied MobileNet, MobileNetV2, and NASNetMobile with transfer learning to perform the classification task. They obtained the best performance with the NASNetMobile with a batch size of 16 and got an accuracy of 82%.

The authors in [13] presented an experiment with different neural networks for classifying benign and malignant skin lesions. They implement a PNASNet-5-Large, InceptionResNetV2, SENet154, and InceptionV4. Data pre-processing and data augmentation was performed. The pre-processing consists of normalization to convert the pixel values into 0 and 1. For data augmentation, transformations were applied to reduce possible performance loss due to the dataset imbalance. The transformations applied to the images were rotation, random crop, brightness and contrast adjustment, pixel jitter, aspect ratio, random shear, zoom, and vertical and horizontal shift and flip. Better results were obtained by the PNASNet-5-Large model, which has a 0.76 in validation score. Furthermore, Devries *et al.* [14] used a multi-scale convolutional network to classify data retrieved from ISIC 2017 skin lesion classification challenge. They performed a fine-tuning using a pre-trained Inception-v3 model trained in the ImageNet dataset to get better results. Also, it was important to add images from the ISIC_MSK2_1 dataset to improve the results of melanoma prediction. As a result of the training, they obtained an accuracy of 0.893 for melanoma, 0.913 for seborrheic keratosis, and an average of 0.903 for the general classification task.

### 2.2    ISIC Data Augmentation with GANs

In recent years, Deep Learning techniques have proven to help offer efficient alternatives for data augmentation. Mainly, the use of Generative Adversarial Networks (GANs) helps generate synthetic images similar to the real data. Pollastri *et al.* [15] proposed using GANs to augment data in the skin lesion segmentation task. They use the 2017 ISIC dataset in this implementation. For this purpose, the authors implemented a Deep Convolutional Generative Adversarial Network (DCGAN) and Laplacian GAN (LAPGAN) to generate the synthetic data. Ultimately, they used a Convolutional-Deconvolutional Neural Network (CDNN) to measure the accuracy improvement by adding the synthetic data into the training process. The DCGAN was better for one experiment, while the

LAPGAN performed best in four experiments. Both achieve an improvement near 1%. In addition, using a U-Net with original and synthetic data showed better results (a gain of about 1% of accuracy with the DCGAN).

Additionally, Baur *et al.* [16] proposed generating realistic and high-resolution images of skin lesions with GANs. They use the 2017 ISIC dataset with three classes: benign lesions, seborrheic keratosis samples and melanoma. They implemented a DCGAN and LAPGAN to generate the synthetic data. Those images were used to train a variety of classifiers for skin lesions. For the classification task, a ResNet-50 was used with different variations of the original data and adding the synthetic images generated by GANs. Finally, they achieved a near 1% more accuracy score with the images from LAPGAN in training (99.29%) and validation (74.00%) sets.

Another work was presented by Rashid *et al.* [7]. They proposed using GANs to solve the problem of the limited amount of data in medical imaging. They use a Vanilla GAN to generate realistic images using the 2018 ISIC dataset for this task. Also, an interesting feature of this GAN is that it can also be used for classification. Therefore, for the classification task, they used fine-tuned DenseNet and ResNet architectures together with the Vanilla GAN as baseline models. The metric used to compare the experiments' performance is the balance accuracy score due to the unbalance data presented. Consequently, they achieve a balance accuracy score of 0.815 with DenseNet, 0.792 with ResNet, and 0.861 with GANs.

There are also more modern applications of GANs that offer more significant opportunities for generating images with great detail and style. Limeros *et al.* [17] implemented a StyleGAN2-ADA using an original implementation from the NVIDIA Research group. This was performed using ISIC 2020 and ISIC 2019 datasets. The classification task was performed using the EfficientNet-B2 model pre-trained on ImageNet. They balance the malignant class by adding 22.000 synthetic images. After this, they performed different classification scenarios to compare the results with baseline and augmented data. In all cases, they tested on the same real image validation set. As a result, the authors achieved better performance, with the augmented data getting 0.979 accuracy.

## 3     System Model and Methodology

### 3.1     Dataset

The dataset is provided by the International Skin Imagin Collaboration (ISIC) [18]. It was designed to release digital skin images to produce tools that help to reduce skin cancer mortality. They provide an extensive image gallery and filters to search through the dataset, letting us browse inside a lot of public images. For the purpose of this work, we only focused on the first filter of the gallery, which is diagnostic attributes. With this filter, we retrieved 8833 benign and 7361 malignant images. Each image has a size of $1769 \times 1769$. Figure 1 shows some examples of this dataset.

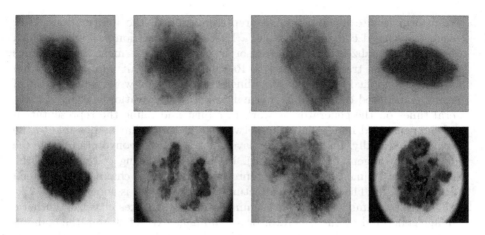

**Fig. 1.** Examples of ISIC dataset. First row: benign images. Second row: malignant images.

### 3.2 Proposed Model

**Deep Convolutional Generative Adversarial Network (DCGAN).** Deep Convolutional Generative Adversarial Networks (DCGANs) are based on the operation of traditional GANs but by adding convolution layers to replace the multilayer perceptron. The convolution layer part discriminates between the images received by the discriminative network. Meanwhile, the deconvolution layer part generates the images in the generative network [19]. DCGANs use various techniques to improve the training phase. These techniques are the following: convert max-pooling layers to strides convolution layers for the discriminator and convert fractional-strides convolutions for the generator; convert fully connected layers to global average pooling layers in the discriminator; using batch normalization layers either in the generator and in the discriminator (except the output layer for generator and input layer for discriminator); the using of rectified linear unit (ReLu) in the generator (except for the output which uses hyperbolic tangent function (Tanh); and the using of leaky ReLU activation functions in the discriminator.

This generative model derives from the original Generative Adversarial Network (GAN) proposed by [10], which has a generative and discriminative network. The details of the implementation of botch networks are described below:

1. DCGAN Generator: The generator network takes a 100-dimensional uniform distribution Z random noise input to feed a fully connected layer that resizes it and converts it to a suitable size for the next layer in the network. Next, transposed convolution layers (unsampling layers) are used to increase the dimension of the input tensor up to the desired size. This increase occurs for the height and width, whereas there is a reduction in channel dimensions. These transposed convolution layers help to decompress the noise and

transform it into a more detailed representation of the information. After each transposed convolution stage, a Batch Normalization is applied, which helps to normalize the output tensor by adjusting the mean and variance to stabilize the training process. A Rectified Linear Unit (ReLu) activation function is applied to introduce nonlinearity into the network. This process of using transposed convolutions, normalization and activation is repeated several times on the generator network to adjust and refine the representation of the generated images into the network to be as similar as possible to the real data. Finally, for the output layer, a transposed convolution with the hyperbolic tangent function (Tanh). In the case of using color images, the output is a 3-dimensional tensor representing the color channels (red, green and blue) [19]. The general architecture of this network is shown in Fig. 2.

2. DCGAN Discriminator: The discriminative network takes either a synthetic image generated by the generator or a real image extracted from the training dataset as input. This image goes through several convolution layers that aim to extract relevant features from the image. These features can be edges, textures or shapes that are specific image patterns. After each convolution layer, a Batch Normalization layer is applied to join to a LeakyReLy activation function. Then, the Sigmoid activation function generates a final probability as output. For this step, fully connected layers are used to classify the features and produce the final output, which is the probability that an image be real or fake using a binary classification (0 indicates that the image is fake, 1 indicates that the image is real) [19].

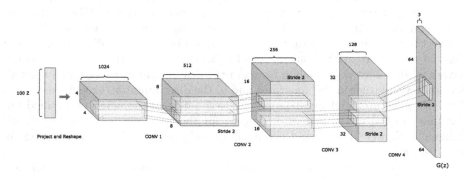

**Fig. 2.** DCGAN Generator Architecture. A 100-dimensional uniform distribution (Z) is projected to a small spatial convolutional representation with some feature maps. This is followed by four fractionally-strided convolutions. Finally, this converts to a representation of 64 × 64 pixel image [19].

### 3.3 Evaluation Metrics

This section describes metrics to evaluate the synthetically generated images' quality and the classification task performance. First, we mentioned the metrics for the evaluation of the quality of the synthetic generated images from the DCGAN:

1. Fréchet inception distance (FID): Several metrics are used to evaluate generative models, including the FID. It is used to calculate the distance between feature vectors calculated for real and synthetic generated images [20] i.e., and it compares the features extracted from the generated synthetic images with the features of the real image set. A pre-trained InceptionV3 neural network is used to perform the calculation of the FID [21]. With the extracted feature vectors given by the InceptionV3, the distribution of generated feature vectors versus the distribution of the feature vectors from the original images is calculated and compared using the Fréchet distance [22]. A low FID value represents a better quality of the generated images since the characteristics are similar to those of the original images.

2. Inception Score (IS): Another metric used to measure the quality of generative model images is the Inception Score. The IS works with an InceptionV3 pre-trained on ImageNet to calculate some statistics of the network's outputs [23]. After generating a set of synthesized images, each of them is sent to the InceptionV3 network. This evaluates the probability of each generated image belonging to the set of real images. Additionally, the entropy of the probability distributions is calculated to measure the diversity of the generated images [24]. Hence, a high value of IS indicates a higher quality and diversity of images.

Second, we mentioned the metrics used for the evaluation of the performance of the InceptionV3 network for the classification task. This network is used because it has proven to be useful in medical image classification tasks due to the detection of features at different scales [25]. Therefore, it allows both fine features and larger structures to be detected [26]. This is relevant because these features may be subtle and dispersed in the images. The metrics are as follows:

1. Accuracy: It represents the proportion of correct predictions out of the total number of samples evaluated.

$$accuracy = \frac{TP + TN}{TP + FN + FP + TN} \tag{1}$$

2. Precision: It represents the number of positive predictions out of the total number of true positive samples.

$$precision = \frac{TP}{TP + FP} \tag{2}$$

3. Recall: It represents the proportion of positive samples correctly identified.

$$recall = \frac{TP}{TP + FN} \tag{3}$$

4. F1-Score: It is a measure that takes into account precision and recall. It helps to evaluate the correct prediction of true positive samples. This is useful to identify classification errors by class, especially when there is an imbalance between classes.

$$F1\ Score = 2 \cdot \frac{Precision \cdot Recall}{Precision + Recall} \qquad (4)$$

### 3.4  Hardware Acceleration

The training process of the DCGAN was performed using an NVIDIA GeForce RTX 4090 graphical processing unit (GPU) with 24 GB of VRAM and 21 Gbps, together with a 5.40GHz Intel ®Core i7-13700K CPU and 32 GB of RAM DDR5.

## 4    Results and Discussion

### 4.1    First Approach: Classification Without DCGAN Augmentation

This section describes the characteristics of the training phase for the classification model with the original data obtained from the ISIC dataset. This step is essential first to know how the classification task performs without any increase in data and then to have a point of comparison for the training performance with the augmented dataset with synthetic images. For the classification task, we get an InceptionV3 model, trained during 20 epochs, with a batch size of 128, a learning rate of 0.001, Adagrad as optimizer, and Cross-Entropy as loss function. Data augmentation techniques include random horizontal and vertical flips and random rotation. All the input data was normalized before entering the network. With these parameters, we obtained the results shown in Table 1, computed from the confusion matrix values presented in Fig. 3.

**Table 1.** Precision, recall and f1-score values for the classification of ISIC dataset.

| Classes   | precision | recall | f1-score |
|-----------|-----------|--------|----------|
| Benign    | 0.89      | 0.89   | 0.89     |
| Malignant | 0.87      | 0.86   | 0.86     |

### 4.2    Second Approach: Classification with DCGAN Augmentation

In this part, we present the results obtained by balancing the dataset by adding synthesized images generated by DCGAN. First, 1176 images were added to the malignant class of the original dataset. This balances both classes to 8833 images each. Second, the same parameters as in Sect. 4.1 were used for the classification task with the InceptionV3 network. It is important to highlight this point to

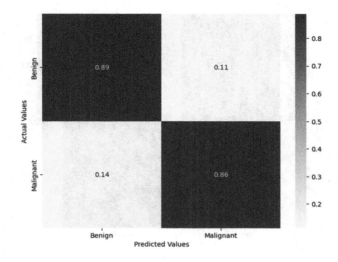

**Fig. 3.** Confusion matrix for the ISIC dataset classification.

demonstrate that the improvement was obtained following the same hyperparameters. The results by class obtained for the classification with synthetic data augmentation are shown in Table 2. In addition, the confusion matrix is displayed to determine the amount of correctly classified new augmented dataset in Fig. 4.

**Table 2.** Precision, recall and f1-score values for the classification of ISIC dataset augmented with DCGAN synthetic images.

| Classes | precision | recall | f1-score |
|---|---|---|---|
| Benign | 0.90 | 0.89 | 0.90 |
| Malignant | 0.87 | 0.88 | 0.88 |

With the values obtained for each dataset class, the accuracy score for each approach can be obtained. This metric allows us to measure the overall performance of the network. The results are shown in Table 3.

### 4.3   DCGAN Training and Synthetic Image Quality Evaluation

The DCGAN network was trained during 300 epochs, with an image size and a batch size of 64. The evolution of the loss function both for the discriminator and generator networks is shown in Fig. 5. On the one hand, the value of the loss function began to increase until approximately 2500 iterations. After that, this value begins to decrease. This indicates that the network began to produce better synthetic images and that the discriminator began to classify synthetic generated images as real. On the other hand, the values of the discriminator

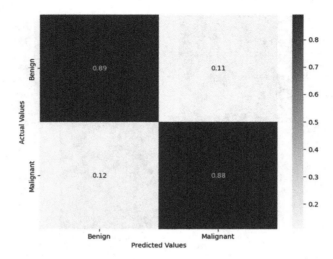

**Fig. 4.** Confusion matrix for the ISIC dataset classification augmented with DCGAN synthetic images.

**Table 3.** Performance comparison using InceptionV3 for the original ISIC dataset and DCGANs augmented dataset.

| Approach | Accuracy Score |
|---|---|
| Original Dataset | 0.8770 |
| DCGANs Augmented Dataset | **0.8875** |

loss function began to have a minimal increase due to the incorrect classification images performed by the discriminator.

Finally, the quantitative and objective evaluation of image quality using FID and IS is presented in Fig. 6. The FID value until the 50th epoch is high. After this epoch, this value begins to decrease. On the contrary, the IS value before the 50th epoch begins small. After this epoch, this value begins to increase. The evolution of both values indicates that the synthetic images produced by the generator are good enough, as we can see in Fig. 7 where a comparison between real and synthetic images generated with the DCGAN is shown.

## 4.4 Discussion

It is shown how the imbalance in a dataset can hurt performance in a classification model. In the same way, it is shown how we can fix this problem using GANs to generate synthetic images to balance the dataset. In particular, if we use the original unbalanced data from the ISIC dataset for the skin lesion classification, we got an accuracy score of 0.8770. Then, if we add 1176 images generated by DCGAN to the malignant class, an accuracy score of 0.8875 was obtained, which

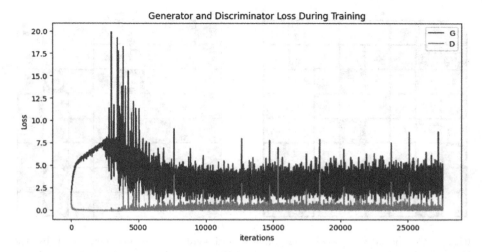

**Fig. 5.** Evolution of the loss function for the generator and discriminator during training phase of the DCGAN for the ISIC dataset into malignant class.

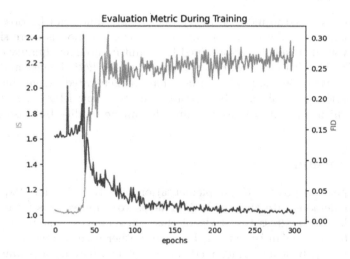

**Fig. 6.** Evolution of FID and IS metrics during the DCGAN training phase.

is higher. In addition, other metrics show a better performance of the model. For the benign class, there was an increase in precision (0.89 vs. 0.90) and f1-score (0.89 vs. 0.90). For the malignant class, there was an increase in recall (0.86 vs. 0.88) and f1-score (0.86 vs. 0.88). These improvements, however small they seem, help make correct diagnoses, reduce false positives and negatives, and improve disease management with early diagnosis.

In addition, the confusion matrices can be observed the reduction of false positives and the increase in true positives values. Similarly, the reduction of

Real Images

Fake Images

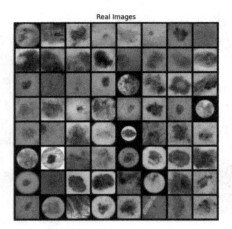 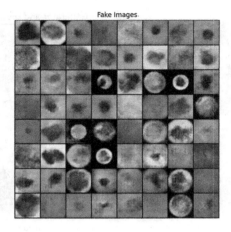

**Fig. 7.** Comparison between real images and synthetic images generated by the DCGAN. Left batch: real images from the ISIC dataset in the malignant class. Right batch: synthetic images for the malignant class.

false negatives and the increase in true negatives values can be observed. For the malignant class, the improvement in value classification is more significant. Finally, favorable results were obtained for quantifying image quality employing FID and IS. The distance between the generated synthetic images and the original images was close enough to deduce that the generated images have similar qualities as the original ones. It is represented by a low FID score and a high IS score, which not only represent values for image quality but also for image diversity.

## 5 Conclusion

In this paper, we present the implementation of a DCGAN for data augmentation and demonstrate that such data helps to improve classification tasks. In particular, we address the study of classifying images of skin lesions. However, this technique can be extended to many other case studies in the medical industry. This is beneficial since medicine is a field where data is limited. Data augmentation using GANs has been shown to increase the accuracy rate for the skin lesion classification task. This is demonstrated by comparing the results obtained in the skin lesion classification model training with the original images from the ISIC dataset and the dataset with the synthesized data enhancement produced by GAN for the malignant class. In the same way, the quality of the generated images was proved by evaluating them using the FID and IS metrics.

## 6 Future Works

Future work could include using skin lesion synthetic images with other existing GAN models. A comparison between the presented model and other existing models for generating synthetic images would be interesting to differentiate the characteristics of the generated images. In addition, an important task is to work with a larger number of images. This could be used to evaluate whether there is a better performance for classifying skin lesions.

# References

1. Cancer (2022). https://www.who.int/news-room/fact-sheets/detail/cancer. Accessed 21 June 2023
2. American Cancer Society. Key statistics for melanoma skin cancer (2023). Accessed 21 June 2023
3. Saginala, K., et al.: Epidemiology of melanoma. Med. Sci. **9**(4), 63 (2021)
4. Adegun, A.A., Viriri, S.: Deep learning-based system for automatic melanoma detection. IEEE Access **8**, 7160–7172 (2019)
5. Combalia, M., et al.: Validation of artificial intelligence prediction models for skin cancer diagnosis using dermoscopy images: the 2019 International Skin Imaging Collaboration Grand Challenge. Lancet Digit. Health **4**(5), e330–e339 (2022)
6. Wen, D., et al.: Characteristics of publicly available skin cancer image datasets: a systematic review. Lancet Digit. Health **4**(1), e64–e74 (2022)
7. Rashid, H., Tanveer, M.A., Khan, H.A.: Skin lesion classification using GAN based data augmentation. In: 2019 41st Annual International Conference of the IEEE Engineering in Medicine and Biology Society (EMBC) (2019)
8. Mahmood, F., Chen, R., Durr, N.J.: Unsupervised reverse domain adaptation for synthetic medical images via adversarial training. IEEE Trans. Med. Imaging **37**(12), 2572–2581 (2018)
9. Crespo, F., et al.: A computer vision model to identify the incorrect use of face masks for COVID-19 awareness. Appl. Sci. **12**(14), 6924 (2022)
10. Goodfellow, I., et al.: Generative adversarial nets. In: Advances in Neural Information Processing Systems, pp. 2672–2680 (2014)
11. Li, Y., Shen, L.: Skin lesion analysis towards melanoma detection using deep learning network. Sensors **18**(2), 556 (2018)
12. Yilmaz, A., et al.: Benchmarking of lightweight deep learning architectures for skin cancer classification using ISIC 2017 dataset. arXiv preprint arXiv:2110.12270 (2021)
13. Milton, Md.A.A.: Automated skin lesion classification using ensemble of deep neural networks in ISIC 2018: skin lesion analysis towards melanoma detection challenge. arXiv preprint arXiv:1901.10802 (2019)
14. DeVries, T., Ramachandram, D.: Skin lesion classification using deep multi-scale convolutional neural networks. arXiv preprint arXiv:1703.01402 (2017)
15. Pollastri, F., et al.: Augmenting data with GANs to segment melanoma skin lesions. Multimed. Tools Appl. **79**, 15575–15592 (2020)
16. Baur, C., Albarqouni, S., Navab, N.: MelanoGANs: high resolution skin lesion synthesis with GANs. arXiv preprint arXiv:1804.04338 (2018)
17. Limeros, S.C., et al.: GAN-based generative modelling for dermatological applications-comparative study. arXiv preprint arXiv:2208.11702 (2022)
18. The International Skin Imaging Collaboration, ISIC. https://gallery.isic-archive.com/#!/topWithHeader/onlyHeaderTop/gallery?filter=%5B%5D. Accessed 1 June 2023

19. Radford, A., Metz, L., Chintala, S.: Unsupervised representation learning with deep convolutional generative adversarial networks. arXiv preprint arXiv:1511.06434 (2015)

20. Heusel, M., et al.: GANs trained by a two time-scale update rule converge to a local Nash equilibrium. In: Advances in Neural Information Processing Systems, vol. 30 (2017)

21. Jung, S., Keuper, M.: Internalized biases in Fréchet inception distance. In: NeurIPS 2021 Workshop on Distribution Shifts: Connecting Methods and Applications (2021)

22. Mathiasen, A., Hvilshøj, F.: Backpropagating through Fréchet inception distance. arXiv preprint arXiv:2009.14075 (2020)

23. Barratt, S., Sharma, R.: A note on the inception score. arXiv preprint arXiv:1801.01973 (2018)

24. Song, Y., Ermon, S.: Improved techniques for training score-based generative models. In: Advances in Neural Information Processing Systems, vol. 33, pp. 12438–12448 (2020)

25. Wang, C., et al.: Pulmonary image classification based on inception-v3 transfer learning model. IEEE Access **7**, 146533–146541 (2019)

26. Guan, Q., et al.: Deep convolutional neural network Inception-v3 model for differential diagnosing of lymph node in cytological images: a pilot study. Ann. Transl. Med. **7** (2019)

# Unraveling the Power of 4D Residual Blocks and Transfer Learning in Violence Detection

Mike Bermeo$^{(\boxtimes)}$ (iD), Manuel Eugenio Morocho-Cayamcela(iD),
and Erick Cuenca(iD)

School of Mathematical and Computational Sciences, Yachay Tech University,
Hda. San José s/n y Proyecto Yachay, San Miguel de Urcuqui 100119, Ecuador
{mike.bermeo,mmorocho,ecuenca}@yachaytech.edu.ec

**Abstract.** In recent years, action recognition has seen significant
advancements in using Convolutions Neural Networks (CNNs) models for
video analysis. One of the essential fields in this area is violence detection, which determines whether or not violent scenes use videos from
surveillance cameras. One popular approach to handle this is the Flow
Gated Network, two separate networks that extract the features from
the frames and the optical flow of the videos using convolutions. However, it cannot capture the spatio-temporal characteristics of the video,
which are crucial for accurate action recognition. To address this limitation, researchers have proposed using 4D convolutions at the video level
(V4D) and stream buffer in the case of MoViNets. These networks are
designed to preserve the 3D spatio-temporal representation of the video
while also incorporating residual connections, which allow for better feature propagation and improved performance. In this work, we propose
using 4D residual blocks and MoViNets for violence detection on the
data set RWF-2000 to achieve state-of-the-art results in action recognition. Furthermore, this approach compares the strengths of MoViNet
and V4D, resulting in more robust and used models for violence detection getting 0.885 for 4D residual block and 0.895 for MoViNet A1 in
terms of accuracy, beating the benchmark architecture.

**Keywords:** Video Classification · Violence Detection · MoViNet · 4D
Residual Blocks · RWF-2000 · CNNs

## 1 Introduction

Action recognition refers to the task of identifying and classifying human activities in videos or sequences of images [6]. Determining the action performed,
such as walking, running, and fighting entails analyzing human movements and
gestures. Typically, computer vision and machine learning techniques are used
to accomplish this task, enabling the system to see patterns in the data and
make predictions based on them [10]. Action recognition aims to deliver a high-
level interpretation of human behavior, making it possible to automate various

© The Author(s), under exclusive license to Springer Nature Switzerland AG 2023
J. Maldonado-Mahauad et al. (Eds.): TICEC 2023, CCIS 1885, pp. 207–219, 2023.
https://doi.org/10.1007/978-3-031-45438-7_14

procedures that call for knowledge of human activities. Action recognition is crucial because it enables machines to analyze and comprehend human actions in real-time, which has a variety of uses in robotics, daily human actions detection [7], sports analysis [17], and video surveillance [8]. Surveillance video footage is increasingly being used to detect and prevent violence in public spaces and other areas of concern [14]. Violence detection is identifying instances of violence in videos. This approach can be used in various fields, such as law enforcement, media monitoring, or security [11]. The classical techniques for violence detection are machine learning algorithms such as Support Vector Machines, or clustering [12]. The goal of violence detection is to provide a means of detecting and mitigating violence for the safety and well-being of individuals. With the development of advanced computer vision, it is now possible to automate identifying violent incidents faster and more accurately. One such technology that has emerged as a powerful tool for violence detection is deep learning algorithms, specifically Convolutional Neural Networks (CNNs).

In this paper, we propose adding 4D residual blocks into 3D CNNs, namely using two-stream architecture and ResNet-18. Moreover, the use of MoViNet architecture using transfer learning for violence detection outperforms the state-of-the-art in terms of accuracy.

## 2  Related Work

### 2.1  Action Recognition

Researchers have recently sought ways to use computer vision techniques for action recognition such us the two-stream architecture [16]. The two-stream architecture was first introduced by Simonyan et al. [16], where one stream focuses on learning from color images, and the other stream is designed to capture optical flow information. Various video identification tasks have yielded outstanding results for two-stream CNNs [21]. However, the fundamental drawback is the high cost of computing optical flow, which makes parallel optimization challenging to implement and requires extensive resource exploration.

Other authors try to enhance the models using depth features. The use of in-depth features for video classification has been encouraged by the outstanding performance of CNN features on image analysis tasks [4,13]. The central concept is to interpret a video clip as a collection of frames, from which a feature representation might be created for each frame by using a feed-forward pass until a particular fully-connected layer using deep models already trained in image classification data sets such as ImageNet. It is possible by extending 2D image networks on the temporal dimension to construct video recognition models to examine the material information of video data. This approach is used in [2,19,20]. The problem is the increased computational cost and parameters of 3D CNNs. Other authors research how to improve the efficiency of 3D convolutions. Several efficient architectures of 3D CNNs leverage the idea of efficient 3D CNNs with Neural Architecture Search (NAS) [23] as we can see in MoViNets [9]. The introduction of the Stream Buffer approach allows 3D CNNs to include arbitrary-length streaming video sequences for both training and inference with a minimal constant memory footprint. This technique decouples memory from video clip time. The problem with the existing 3D CNNs often takes a short-term snippet as input without considering the evolution of 3D spatio-temporal features for video-level representation. That is why the work of [22] proposes the usage of 4D convolutions to not only catch the short-term spatio-temporal features but also take into account a complete long-term perspective of what is happening in the video.

In the violence detection subfield, some authors used previous works, such as the two-stream architecture, to detect violence using videos from surveillance cameras [3]. However, this approach has a problem, and it is the computational cost that it takes because of the optical flow. Another author [5] uses two-stream architecture but uses Long-Short Term Memory (LSTM).

## 3   System Model and Methodology

In this section, we will detail the data sets to be used, the proposed architecture and finally the pipeline to be followed to address the problem.

### 3.1   Data Set

There are video data sets for violence identification. However, they have drawbacks, including small scale, little variety, and low imaging resolution, according to RWF2000 [3]. Furthermore, some high-quality violence statistics come from fictionalized situations that do not accurately reflect actual events. RWF2000 is a collection of 2000 YouTube videos taken from real-world security cameras and cut into 5-second segments at a frame rate of 30 fps to solve the problem of the lack of high-quality data from actual incidents of violence. The data set is split into the training set (80%), and the test set (20%). Half of the videos include violent behaviors, while others belong to nonviolent activities. We can see an example of the data set in Fig. 1.

### 3.2   Proposed Model/Architecture

**Flow Gated Network:** The Flow Gated Network [3] is composed of the RGB channel, the Optical Flow channel, the Merging Block, and the Fully Connected Layer. RGB and Optical Flow channels consist of cascaded 3D CNNs, and they have consistent structures so that their output can be fused. Merging Block comprises basic 3D CNNs, which process information after self-learned temporal pooling. Finally, the fully-connected layers generate output, as we can see in Fig. 2.

**Fig. 1.** Example frames of a violent video from RWF200.

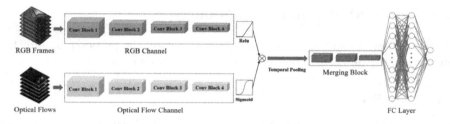

**Fig. 2.** Benchmark Architecture [3].

**V4D ResNet-18:** V4D is being used to learn spatio-temporal interactions of 3D convolution kernels that are particularly excellent at modelling short-term spatio-temporal features. Utilising operations that can model both short-term and long-term spatio-temporal representations at the same time. As a result, four-dimensional convolutions have been employed to better describe long-range spatio-temporal interactions. Four-dimensional convolutions are fed a tensor composed by $(U, C, T, W, H)$ where $W$, $H$ is the width and height of the frame, $T$ is the temporal size, $C$ is the number of channels, $U$ is the number of action units (the fourth dimension). Basically, each action unit $U_i$ is a group of tensors $(T, W, H)$ for each channel $C$.

$$Y_{3D} = X_{3D} + \phi_{(U,C)}(F_{4D}(\phi_{(U,C)}(X_{3D}; W_{4D})))$$

where $F_{4D}(X_{3D}; W_{4D})$ is the introduced 4D convolution. $X_{3D}$, $Y_{3D} \in R^{U \times C \times T \times H \times W}$ is merged into batch dimension so that X3D, Y3D can be directly processed by standard 3D CNNs. Dimensions can be permuted using a permutation function $\phi$. $\phi$ is used to permute the dimensions of $U \times C \times T \times H \times W$ of $X_{3D}$ to $C \times U \times T \times H \times W$ so that 4D convolutions can handle it. The output dimensions of the 4D convolution are then permuted back to 3D form to match $X_{3D}$. See Fig. 3.

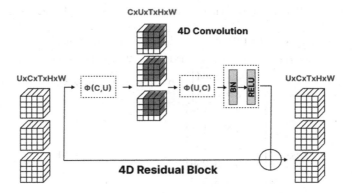

**Fig. 3.** 4D Residual Block [22].

For action recognition, four dimensional convolutions may be incorporated into current 3D CNN architecture. 3DResNet-18 has been used, detailed structure of 3D backbone is shown in Table 1.

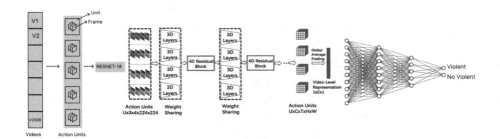

**Fig. 4.** 3DResNet-18 + 4D residual block architecture.

The network's convolutional layers are made up of 3D convolution layers with Residual 4D Blocks in the fourth training. Each action unit is trained independently and parallel in the 3D convolution layers, which have similar parameters. The 3D feature action units are then sent into the Residual 4D Block, which may simulate the succeeding action unit's long-term temporal evolution. Finally, global average pooling is a collection of all action units from video representation that is supplied to fully connected layers and softmax for violence detection, as seen in Fig. 4.

**Table 1.** 3DResNet-18, where the input has a size of $4 \times 224 \times 224$.

| Layer | Operation | | Output size |
|---|---|---|---|
| $conv_1$ | $1 \times 7 \times 7$, 64, stride 1, 2, 2 | | $4 \times 112 \times 112$ |
| $res_2$ | $\begin{bmatrix} 1 \times 3 \times 3, 64 \\ 1 \times 3 \times 3, 64 \end{bmatrix}$ | $\times 2$ | $4 \times 56 \times 56$ |
| $res_3$ | $\begin{bmatrix} 1 \times 3 \times 3, 128 \\ 1 \times 3 \times 3, 128 \end{bmatrix}$ | $\times 2$ | $4 \times 28 \times 28$ |
| $res_4$ | $\begin{bmatrix} 3 \times 3 \times 3, 256 \\ 3 \times 3 \times 3, 256 \end{bmatrix}$ | $\times 2$ | $4 \times 14 \times 14$ |
| $res_5$ | $\begin{bmatrix} 3 \times 3 \times 3, 512 \\ 3 \times 3 \times 3, 512 \end{bmatrix}$ | $\times 2$ | $4 \times 7 \times 7$ |
| global average pool, fc | | | $1 \times 1 \times 1$ |

**Table 2.** MoViNet-A0, where the input has a size of $4 \times 172 \times 172$.

| Layer | Operation | Output size |
|---|---|---|
| $data$ | stride 5, RGB | $4 \times 172 \times 172$ |
| $conv_1$ | $1 \times 3 \times 3$, 8 | $4 \times 86 \times 86$ |
| $block_2$ | $\begin{bmatrix} 1 \times 5 \times 5, 8, 40 \end{bmatrix}$ | $4 \times 43 \times 43$ |
| $block_3$ | $\begin{bmatrix} 5 \times 3 \times 3, 32, 80 \\ 3 \times 3 \times 3, 32, 80 \\ 3 \times 3 \times 3, 32, 80 \end{bmatrix}$ | $4 \times 21 \times 21$ |
| $block_4$ | $\begin{bmatrix} 5 \times 3 \times 3, 56, 184 \\ 3 \times 3 \times 3, 56, 112 \\ 3 \times 3 \times 3, 56, 184 \end{bmatrix}$ | $4 \times 10 \times 10$ |
| $block_5$ | $\begin{bmatrix} 5 \times 3 \times 3, 56, 184 \\ 3 \times 3 \times 3, 56, 184 \\ 3 \times 3 \times 3, 56, 184 \\ 3 \times 3 \times 3, 56, 184 \end{bmatrix}$ | $4 \times 10 \times 10$ |
| $block_6$ | $\begin{bmatrix} 5 \times 3 \times 3, 104, 344 \\ 1 \times 5 \times 5, 104, 280 \\ 1 \times 5 \times 5, 104, 280 \\ 1 \times 5 \times 5, 104, 344 \end{bmatrix}$ | $4 \times 5 \times 5$ |
| $conv_7$ | $1 \times 1 \times 1$, 480 | $4 \times 5 \times 5$ |
| $pool_8$ | $4 \times 5 \times 5$, 480 | $1 \times 1 \times 1$ |
| $dense_9$ | $1 \times 1 \times 1$, 2048 | $1 \times 1 \times 1$ |
| $dense_{10}$ | $1 \times 1 \times 1$, 2 | $1 \times 1 \times 1$ |

**MoViNet.** MoViNet [9] is a deep neural network architecture designed for video understanding tasks. It is optimized for efficient computation on mobile and embedded devices while achieving high accuracy in action recognition tasks. It incorporates a temporal stream, which captures the motion information across frames, and a spatial stream, which analyzes the content of individual frames. These two streams are fused to provide a comprehensive understanding of the video. MoViNet has pre-trained models on Kinetics-600. It is helpful for us to use transfer learning to train with the RWF-2000 data set and spend only a little time in the training phase. Its efficiency and accuracy make it well-suited for real-time video analysis on mobile and embedded devices. We can see in Table 2 the MoViNet A0 architecture.

### 3.3   Methodology

In order to compare the performance of 3D and 4D convolutions for violence detection, we will use two different architectures with 4d residual blocks and MoViNet architecture [9] using transfer learning.

The first model is composed of the Flow Gated Network (see Fig. 2) architecture with 4D residual blocks, as we can see in Fig. 3. The second one is 3D ResNet-18 architecture with 4D residual blocks, as shown in Fig. 4. Finally, the third one is three different models of MoViNet, in this case, A0, A1, and A2.

For the pipeline to follow, we first need to divide into 80% for training 1600 videos, 800 violent and 800 non-violent, and 20% for validation of 400 videos, 200 for violent and 200 for non-violent. Then, resize the data set frames to be used. RWF-2000 has different sizes of the video frame scale so we will crop them all to $224 \times 224$ in the case of V4D ResNet-18, and for MoViNet models, we will resize to $172 \times 172$.

For the V4D ResNet-18 model, we need to define the convolutional kernels. The authors recommend three typical forms of kernels: $k \times 1 \times 1 \times 1$, $k \times k \times 1 \times 1$, and $k \times k \times k \times k$. Because of the computational cost that requires the kernels with more $k$, we will use the first two options with $k = 3$. The number of actions units does not have a significant impact on performance [22], we will set $U = 4$.

For MoViNet (A0, A1), we must crop the frames into $172 \times 172$. Then we will use transfer learning. We will load the pre-trained weights of the MoViNet-A0 model trained with Kinetics-600, freeze all the layers, and replace the last layers with two classes (violent, Non-violent). Finally, we train the last layer with the RWF-2000 data set. In the case of MoViNet-A2, the input size of the frames is $224 \times 224$.

## 4   Results

In this case, nine different experiments were conducted. The first three were adding 4D residual blocks to the benchmark architecture. They were trained for 30 epochs with a frame size of 64 with a batch size of 8. The optimizer was Stochastic Gradient Descent (SGD) with a learning rate decay of 30% per 10 epochs.

For the model using 3DResNet-18, we removed the entire network that received the RGB images and replaced it with 3DResNet-18. In this case, we used Adam as an optimizer with a learning rate of 0.001 for 30 epochs. Also, in the case of the model with the 4D residual block, we added it later between the third and fourth residual blocks. For MoViNet models, we use transfer learning to take advantage of the pre-trained models the author provided us. In addition, we use ADAM as an optimizer for the three models (A0, A1, A2) with a learning rate of 0.001. Also, we use the hard-sigmoid activation function as the authors' recommendation. Finally, we train during five epochs with a batch size of 8 and a frame size of 64.

**Table 3.** Results of the propose model comparing with Flow Gated Network (FGN).

| Method | Train Accuracy | Validation Accuracy | Parameters |
|---|---|---|---|
| FGN [3] | 0.884 | 0.873 | 272,690 |
| **FGN + one RGB 4D residual block** | 0.842 | **0.885** | 272,902 |
| **FGN + one OPT 4D residual block** | 0.854 | 0.870 | 272,902 |
| **FGN + two 4D residual blocks** | 0.834 | 0.860 | 273,114 |
| **FGN + eight 4D residual blocks** | **0.924** | **0.875** | 274,386 |

**Table 4.** Results of 3D ResNet models comparing with Flow Gated Network (FGN).

| Method | Train Accuracy | Validation Accuracy | Parameters |
|---|---|---|---|
| FGN [3] | 0.884 | 0.873 | 272,690 |
| 3DResNet-18 + opt | 0.796 | 0.765 | 34,984,610 |
| **3DResNet-18 + 4D Residual Block + opt** | **0.896** | 0.770 | 34,985,782 |

**Table 5.** Results of the MoViNet models comparing with Flow Gated Network (FGN).

| Method | Train Accuracy | Validation Accuracy | Parameters |
|---|---|---|---|
| FGN [3] | 0.884 | 0.873 | 272,690 |
| **MoViNet A0 base** | 0.876 | **0.875** | 1,900,765 |
| **MoViNet A1 base** | **0.922** | **0.895** | 3,492,610 |
| **MoViNet A2 base** | 0.881 | 0.865 | 4,055,620 |

## 5   Discussion

As shown in Fig. 5, the benchmark model attempts to be overfitted if we pass the 15 epochs. Moreover, the training phase is chaotic because the data set is not too big to train along more epochs, and the benchmark architecture is not

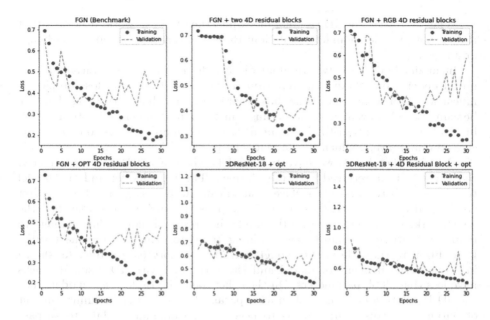

**Fig. 5.** Loss of the FGN and 3D ResNet-18 models.

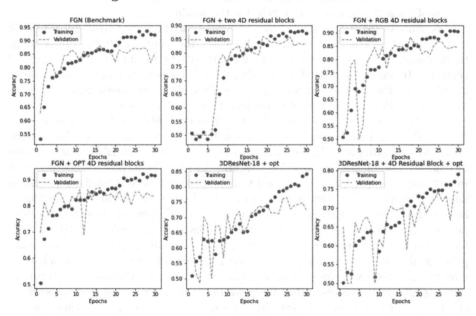

**Fig. 6.** Accuracy of the the FGN and 3D ResNet-18 models.

following a pattern design. As we add 4D residual blocks, it is seen to give more stability for the training phase. In this case, the best model is when we only add the 4d residual block into the RGB network (Fig. 6).

When we insert the 4D residual block into the OPT Network, it notices that it does not provide enough information; therefore, the network does not change dramatically.

In model FGN with two residual blocks, the loss remains invariant in the initial epochs, but there is a step around epoch 10, where the loss drops significantly. As a result, the model has greater stability during training than the benchmark. This event may be because, in the initial epochs, the 4D residual blocks have to be fitted to the input data to feed more information to the 3D convolutional layers, which take about ten epochs.

On the other hand, we have two models where a 3D ResNet-18 replaced the network that received the RGB frames. The base model and the model that uses a 4D residual block have a significant drop in the loss after the first epoch, and it is observed that the training phase is much more stable than the benchmark. It happens because the model has residual blocks that manage to reduce overfitting but need more training times to achieve the same results. In addition to that, these two models have many more parameters. As shown in Table 3, the benchmark model and the variations with 4D residual blocks have less than 300k parameters. On the other hand, in Table 4, the models that use 3D ResNet-18 have more than 34M parameters; this overwhelming amount of parameters causes the models to need a huge amount of data to surpass the benchmark model. Moreover, since the RWF-2000 data set barely has 2000 videos of 5 s each, this is a limitation for the models.

We can compare the 3D ResNet-18 models without the residual 4D block and with the residual 4D block. In this case, the model with the 4D residual block manages to outperform the model without the residual block in terms of accuracy. It occurs because the 4D residual block gives more context to the data; in this case, it gives more information about the spatio-temporal information of the frames, allowing the model to achieve more performance.

Finally, we can see in Table 5 that the MoViNet A0 and A1 models outperformed the benchmark paper in accuracy. Even though the models have more than 1M+ parameters, they could learn from the little available data because of transfer learning. The MoViNet A0 and A1 models outperformed the more robust ones since the latter has many more parameters and needs much more data to perform better. On the other hand, the best model is the A1 since this is balanced in terms of parameters and performance. Likewise, these models outperform models that use Flow Gated Networks with and without 4D residual blocks since they do not have to be retrained from scratch. Many hours and computational power are not required to adjust the already pre-trained models with massive data to new tasks such as violence detection. In addition, the advantage of using MoViNet models is that they can be used in embedded systems such as cell phones or microchips, where they can make inferences in real-time and be faster when detecting violence (see Table 5).

# 6    Conclusions

This work explores the effectiveness of 4D residual blocks using Flow Gated Network and 3D ResNet-18. Moreover, MoViNet models assess violence detection using transfer learning. We test all the architectures using the RWF-2000 data set. As a result, the two-stream architecture model with one residual block in the RGB Network, and the two-stream architecture model with eight 4D residual blocks outperform the benchmark model (Flow Gated Network) in terms of accuracy, respectively. Additionally, MoViNet A0 and A1 outperform the benchmark model using transfer learning.

The results show that the 4D residual block handles RGB data better than OPT. Furthermore, it is shown that transfer learning is a good approach when we lack data and only want to spend a small amount of time in the training phase if we want to outperform models in accuracy.

Finally, we saw that the fact that a model has many more parameters does not mean that it performs better on any data set. In this case, models with few parameters performed better than ResNet-18 3D models with millions of parameters due to different problems, such as the small amount of data, the way the network weights are initialized, and the number of parameters.

# 7    Future Work

In this work, we experiment with 4D residual blocks for assessing violence detection. However, we do not experiment with what happens if we use that 4D residual block in a MoViNet architecture. In addition, to improve the performance of the 3D ResNet-18, we can use pre-trained weights from ImageNet to pass some knowledge to the architecture and then train with the data set used in this work. Another approach we can work on is fine-tuning the hyper-parameters of the models used in this work. Furthermore, test the models presented here with other data sets for assessing violence detection such us Movie Fights [15], Crowd violence [18], or Hockey Fights [1]. The code, the dataset and all the material is available at: https://github.com/mikebermeo99/Unraveling-the-power-of-4D-residual-blocks-in-violence-detection.

**Acknowledgment.** The authors express their gratitude to CEDIA for allowing us to use the CEDIA HPC cluster for this work.

# References

1. Bermejo Nievas, E., Deniz Suarez, O., Bueno García, G., Sukthankar, R.: Violence detection in video using computer vision techniques. In: Real, P., Diaz-Pernil, D., Molina-Abril, H., Berciano, A., Kropatsch, W. (eds.) CAIP 2011. LNCS, vol. 6855, pp. 332–339. Springer, Heidelberg (2011). https://doi.org/10.1007/978-3-642-23678-5_39
2. Carreira, J., Zisserman, A.: Quo Vadis, action recognition? A new model and the kinetics dataset (2017). https://arxiv.org/abs/1705.07750

3. Cheng, M., Cai, K., Li, M.: RWF-2000: an open large scale video database for violence detection (2019). https://arxiv.org/abs/1911.05913
4. Girshick, R., Donahue, J., Darrell, T., Malik, J.: Rich feature hierarchies for accurate object detection and semantic segmentation (2013). https://arxiv.org/abs/1311.2524
5. Islam, Z., Rukonuzzaman, M., Ahmed, R., Kabir, M.H., Farazi, M.: Efficient two-stream network for violence detection using separable convolutional LSTM. In: 2021 International Joint Conference on Neural Networks (IJCNN). IEEE (2021). https://doi.org/10.1109/ijcnn52387.2021.9534280
6. Jhuang, H., Gall, J., Zuffi, S., Schmid, C., Black, M.J.: Towards understanding action recognition. In: Proceedings of the IEEE International Conference on Computer Vision, pp. 3192–3199 (2013)
7. Kay, W., et al.: The kinetics human action video dataset (2017). https://arxiv.org/abs/1705.06950
8. Khan, M.A., et al.: Human action recognition using fusion of multiview and deep features: an application to video surveillance. Multimed. Tools Applications 1–27 (2020)
9. Kondratyuk, D., et al.: MoviNets: mobile video networks for efficient video recognition (2021). https://arxiv.org/abs/2103.11511
10. Kong, Y., Fu, Y.: Human action recognition and prediction: a survey (2018). https://arxiv.org/abs/1806.11230
11. Lejmi, W., Khalifa, A.B., Mahjoub, M.A.: Challenges and methods of violence detection in surveillance video: a survey. In: Vento, M., Percannella, G. (eds.) CAIP 2019. LNCS, vol. 11679, pp. 62–73. Springer, Cham (2019). https://doi.org/10.1007/978-3-030-29891-3_6
12. Omarov, B., Narynov, S., Zhumanov, Z., Gumar, A., Khassanova, M.: State-of-the-art violence detection techniques in video surveillance security systems: a systematic review. PeerJ Comput. Sci. **8**, e920 (2022)
13. Razavian, A.S., Azizpour, H., Sullivan, J., Carlsson, S.: CNN features off-the-shelf: an astounding baseline for recognition (2014). https://arxiv.org/abs/1403.6382
14. Roshan, S., Srivathsan, G., Deepak, K., Chandrakala, S.: Chapter 11 - Violence detection in automated video surveillance: recent trends and comparative studies. In: Peter, D., Alavi, A.H., Javadi, B., Fernandes, S.L. (eds.) The Cognitive Approach in Cloud Computing and Internet of Things Technologies for Surveillance Tracking Systems, pp. 157–171. Intelligent Data-Centric Systems. Academic Press (2020). https://doi.org/10.1016/B978-0-12-816385-6.00011-8
15. Serrano Gracia, I., Deniz Suarez, O., Bueno Garcia, G., Kim, T.K.: Fast fight detection, vol. 10, pp. 1–19. Public Library of Science (2015). https://doi.org/10.1371/journal.pone.0120448
16. Simonyan, K., Zisserman, A.: Two-stream convolutional networks for action recognition in videos. In: Proceedings of the 27th International Conference on Neural Information Processing Systems, NIPS 2014, vol. 1, pp. 568–576. MIT Press, Cambridge (2014)
17. Soomro, K., Zamir, A.R.: Action recognition in realistic sports videos. In: Moeslund, T.B., Thomas, G., Hilton, A. (eds.) Computer Vision in Sports. ACVPR, pp. 181–208. Springer, Cham (2014). https://doi.org/10.1007/978-3-319-09396-3_9
18. Hassner, T., Itcher, Y., Kliper-Gross, O.: Violent flows: real-time detection of violent crowd behavior. In: 3rd IEEE International Workshop on Socially Intelligent Surveillance and Monitoring (SISM) at the IEEE Conference on Computer Vision and Pattern Recognition (CVPR) (2012). www.openu.ac.il/home/hassner/data/violentflows/

19. Tran, D., Bourdev, L., Fergus, R., Torresani, L., Paluri, M.: Learning spatiotemporal features with 3D convolutional networks. In: 2015 IEEE International Conference on Computer Vision (ICCV), pp. 4489–4497 (2015). https://doi.org/10.1109/ICCV.2015.510
20. Tran, D., Wang, H., Torresani, L., Ray, J., LeCun, Y., Paluri, M.: A closer look at spatiotemporal convolutions for action recognition (2017). https://arxiv.org/abs/1711.11248
21. Wang, L., Xiong, Y., Wang, Z., Qiao, Y.: Towards good practices for very deep two-stream convnets (2015). https://arxiv.org/abs/1507.02159
22. Zhang, S., Guo, S., Huang, W., Scott, M.R., Wang, L.: V4D:4D convolutional neural networks for video-level representation learning (2020). https://arxiv.org/abs/2002.07442
23. Zoph, B., Vasudevan, V., Shlens, J., Le, Q.V.: Learning transferable architectures for scalable image recognition (2017). https://arxiv.org/abs/1707.07012

# ICTs and their Applications

# Brainwaves Communication System for People with Reduced Mobility and Verbal Impairment

Eduardo Carabalí Farinango and Javier Rojas Urbano[✉]

Salesian Polytechnic University, Quito, Ecuador
jrojasu@ups.edu.ec

**Abstract.** The development of capture brain activity sensors has made it possible to develop applications that allow interaction with people and objects only by using the level of concentration on a given action; this represents an opportunity for people with total or partial reduction of mobility in their limbs as well as the ability to speak, since they have difficulty communicating with others and require specialized assistance to identify and meet their basic needs. Brain activity signals constitute a communication tool, improving independence and quality of life not only for people with this condition but also opens up a wide variety of applications for people in general. In this research, a communication system based on brain waves is developed with the use of the Emotiv Insight sensor, in combination with the Emotiv Xavier Controlpanel and Emotiv Xavier EmoKey programs, to translate and send the brain waves via Bluetooth to a graphic interface in Matlab, where the need is visually identified. The system has remote communication through a mobile application that favors the prompt attention of needs and emergency situations. The evaluation of the system has 93.6% effectiveness in recognizing the patient's need, with an average response time of 4[s] to activate the HMI indicator, the message in the mobile device arrives immediately when it is in the same wifi network, and takes approximately 2[s] in a different network, demonstrating that it is possible to establish basic communication between patient and caregiver, through brain waves.

**Keywords:** Brainwaves · Biomedical signals · Bluetooth · Remote communication · Emotiv Xavier Control Panel · Emotiv Xavier Emokey

## 1 Introduction

The electrical nature of the brain to generate signals that determine and control the functions of organs and muscles of the human body has always been of special interest in applications related to bionics, especially for people who due to an accident, chronic disease or advanced age have total or partial reduction of mobility in their limbs as well as the ability to speak, as it hinders the process of

J. Maldonado-Mahauad et al. (Eds.): TICEC 2023, CCIS 1885, pp. 223–233, 2023.
https://doi.org/10.1007/978-3-031-45438-7_15

communication with other people and thus meet their needs [1,2]. These people require constant assistance from trained medical personnel to identify and meet their basic needs of daily living, one of the methods of assistance used is to perform body scans every certain time interval, usually 30 min. This is a functional method but creates problems when needs arise between check-up intervals, as they will not be attended, it generates anxiety or complications in the patient. In addition, if there is no strict time control there is the possibility of needs or emergency situations that are treated too late and may cause a deterioration in the patient's health [3,4]. Although patients have reduced mobility and speech difficulties, their cognitive functions are fully intact, so the patient has brain activity and is aware of their needs, making the idea of using these brain functions to communicate their needs at the time they need to be addressed by the assistant appealing and reducing the risk of complications, improving the patient's quality of life [5,10].

The use of brain activity signals has been extensively investigated for the management of robotic prostheses to provide independence in movement, however, it requires the combination of sophisticated and expensive technology and invasive cranial implants [7,11,12]. Case Western and Chicago University developed an arm and hand prosthesis that transmits the sensation of touch and determine the pressure that needs to be applied to a given object, also worth mentioning is the work of the U.S. Defense Advanced Research Projects Agency (Darpa), where by means of chips implanted in the brain, a person is able to move a prosthetic arm and hand [10].

Regarding the acquisition of non-invasive brain activity signals, sensors such as the INVOS5100, by Covidien, allows monitoring and measurement the cerebral oxygen saturation through sensors placed on the patient's head. There is also the Emotiv Insight, from Emotiv Inc. [18] it is a headband with 5 electrodes that detect brain wave patterns generated by sensory stimuli. Some research has been conducted on the use of this device such as the project from the Faculty of Electronic Engineering of the University of Chimborazo, who used the Emotiv Insight sensor to obtain data in a computer to manage a terrestrial explorer robot [8]. Other project was developed by the students of the Polytechnic University Salesiana to manipulate the Mitsubishi RV-2AJ robot, by means of brain waves collected in by the Emotiv Insight brain sensor [9]. Several works have been developed in which the control of a computer by means of brain waves has been used to enable people with impaired movement of their limbs or reduced mobility to take advantage of the benefits of computing [15,16] and adapt in a better way to the working world as well as to technological advances. This work has demonstrated a high degree of user satisfaction even though the computer control options are limited, so they have motivated the development of a non-invasive communication system using brain waves [13,14].

This paper focuses on the use of the Emotiv Insight for the acquisition of brain waves that allow the communication of people with total or partial reduction of mobility through a graphical interface developed in Matlab, it also provides remote communication with the patient's assistant through the use of a mobile application that receives information from a database hosted in the cloud, in which the information of the Emotiv Insight already proceeded is stored, so that the assistant can be informed and attend the patient's need no matter where he is. The paper is divided into 4 sections, Sect. 2 describes the methodology and the design implemented, Sect. 3 presents the results obtained and finally in Sect. 4 the conclusions are mentioned.

## 2   Methodology

The development of the system is based on the scheme showed in Fig. 1, where the hardware and software components that are part of the communication system for people with reduced mobility and verbal difficulties can be identified. The system consists of the use of the Emotiv Insight brain headband by the user, which will acquire the user's brainwaves in response to a specific need, these waves are conditioned and sent wirelessly to a computer via Bluetooth 4.0.

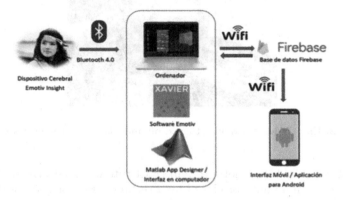

**Fig. 1.** Block diagram of the implemented system.

In the computer Emotiv Xavier Controlpanel and Emotiv Xavier Emokey programs are executed. In the first one the training of the user is done so that the acquired signals are associated with a certain action, in this case to move a virtual cube, and in the second program, characters are assigns to an identifier character for each trained action. Using Emotiv Xavier Emokey, the identifiers are sent to Matlab, where they are linked to the programming of the graphic interface, so that the caregiver can identify the patient's need. In the programming of the Matlab screens, there is a link that connects with a Firebase database, the data is sent via wifi in real time to the database, for this it is necessary that the computer has internet access, immediately the data is sent via wifi from Firebase to an application installed on a mobile device with Android operating system as shown in Fig. 1, allowing the patient need's data to be viewed remotely. The mobile device can be connected either on the same wifi network as the computer, as well as on a different network.

## 2.1  Brainwave Acquisition

The acquisition of brain waves is performed with the Emotiv Insight sensor, the headband is placed on the patient's head, its shape ensures that the electrodes are located in the right position to detect brain waves to different stimuli, the electrodes are placed in the right position to detect the brain waves to different stimuli. The electrodes must be moistened with a saline solution and ensure contact with the scalp, not with the hair. The sensor sends the electrode's information to a computer using Bluetooth 4.0 interface, this form of wireless transmission gives freedom of movement and comfort to the patient. In the computer, the data of the brainwave's voltage levels are received, the voltage levels are collected with the Emotiv Xavier Control Panel software [17,18]. These connections can be seen in Fig. 2.

**Fig. 2.** Emotiv Insight device turned on and placed on the user's head.

The data acquired by Emotiv Insight constitute wave patterns that are associated to the brain activity produced by a certain action or need of the patient using the Emotiv Xavier Controlpanel. The association consists in a training process where the patient moves a cube by focusing on a specific need until a percentage around 50% is achieved in the indicator of degree of association, which ensures the identification of the need each time the respective wave pattern is acquired.

Then using Emotiv Xavier Emokey program an alphanumeric indicator is assigned to each of the trained actions, and thus link the waves acquired by the headband with other computer programs; in this case values from 1 to 6 are assigned for the needs that the patient is going to communicate to his caregiver, and an f for the action of neutral state or relaxation. Trough Emotiv Xavier Emokey the indicator is transmitted to the Matlab workspace. Figure 3 shows the interface of Emotiv Xavier Controlpanel and Emotiv Xavier Emokey.

## 2.2  Graphical Interface

For the correct identification of the patient's needs by the physician or caregiver, a graphical interface is developed using a Matlab GUI. The interface has an initial

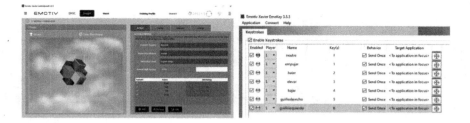

**Fig. 3.** Emotiv Xavier Controlpanel and Emotiv Xavier Emokey interfaces.

screen where the user chooses to continue to the identification screen or to go to the tutorial screen.

The tutorial screen has 5 interactive buttons as, the first one presents on the screen a guide for the training of a new patient with the Emotiv Xavier Controlpanel program, the second button shows the character assignment in Emotiv Xavier Emokey, the third one presents a guide to load the data of a new patient and also allows the assignment of needs to each indicator of the interface, taking into account the indicators of the Emotiv Xavier Emokey, the program has the capacity to store the data of up to 7 patients. The fourth button can be used to load patient data while the fifth button can be used to return to the main screen, as shows Fig. 4.

**Fig. 4.** Matlab interface, initial and tutorial screens.

The Home button on the main screen leads to the main control page, which can be seen in Fig. 5. This screen displays the patient data and needs indicators, which are updated in real time according to the signals which are updated in real time according to the signals acquired by the headset. These indicators will be gray when the patient does not have any of the needs that have been trained, otherwise, the respective indicator will turn light blue.

**Fig. 5.** Main control screen. (Color figure online)

### 2.3 Remote Communication

It is developed from a mobile application that displays the information stored in a database that can be accessed through an internet connection. For this, the graphic interface allows sending the indicator processed by the Emotiv Xavier Emokey program to a Firebase database through an https link in the programming developed in Matlab. The Firebase data are sent via Wifi connection to a mobile device on which an application developed to present on the screen of the mobile device a message indicating the name of the patient, as well as the need that the patient has, the message will remain active until the caregiver discards the message or until the patient sends a new need signal; when the patient has no need, no message will be sent. The application has been developed in Android Studio and its main screen can be seen in Fig. 6, it works on most mobile devices with Android operating system, as long as it has Internet connection [19, 20].

**Fig. 6.** Movil application screen.

## 3 Results

To evaluate the developed communication system, some functional tests are performed with 2 patients, a 32 years old male and a 57 years old female as shown in Fig. 7. The test subjects do not have mobility conditions or reduced speech ability, however, considering that the performance of the system depends on the success in the training process, the condition does not become an impediment to evaluate the system.

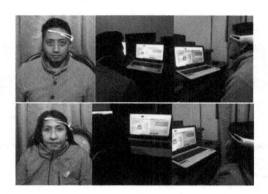

**Fig. 7.** System test subjects.

As for the training process, it took an average of 30 min for each need to reach a percentage of at least 50%, and according to the patients' comments, it is complex at the beginning and requires a lot of concentration to make the brain wave pattern similar in each training of a given need and to make the software perceive it as the desired movement. After training and assigning the respective indicators for each need, the identification of needs is evaluated by means of the graphic interface through tests in a room that reduces the sources of distraction and thus provides better results. For the test, each patient is asked to concentrate on the action of pushing the bucket and the time it takes for the respective indicator on the graphic interface to change color is recorded, it is also recorded if a different indicator is activated, immediately the patient relaxes the indicator is turned off and the same function is tested again. This test is repeated 40 times for the same need, and the whole process again for each of the 6 previously trained actions. The results obtained are shown in Table 1, and the graphs showing the curves of the results obtained are shown in Table 1, and the graphs showing the curves of the 40 data are shown in Fig. 8.

According to the data it can be seen that for test subject 1 there is a 93.3% average success rate in the indicator and an average time of 4. 1[s], which in comparison to the response time to the ringing of a hospitalized patient in a third level institution, which should be from 0 to 2 min and the number of answered rings around 85%, is a low time and has a high percentage of successes, which shows that the system is effective for a patient to express the need and the caregiver can identify it [6].

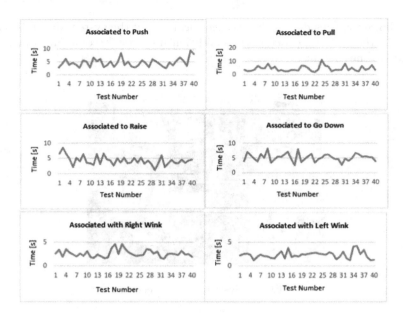

**Fig. 8.** Response times for each associated action.

For the subject 2, there is an average 93.8% success rate in the indicator and an average time of 3.9 93.8% average success rate in the indicator and an average time of 3.9[s], which in comparison to the response time to the ringing of a response time to the ringing of a hospitalized patient in a third level institution, which should be from 0 to 2 min and the number of answered rings around 85%, is a low time and has a high hit rate, that the system is effective for a patient to express the need and for the caregiver to identify it.

**Table 1.** Signal sending test for a need.

| Subject 1 | Push time [s] | Pull time [s] | Rise Time [s] | lower time [s] | right wink [s] | left wink [s] |
|---|---|---|---|---|---|---|
| average | 4.3 | 5.6 | 5.4 | 4.5 | 2.2 | 2.6 |
| training [%] | 57 | 50 | 51 | 53 | NA | NA |
| Fails | 1 | 1 | 0 | 1 | 6 | 7 |
| effectiveness [%] | 97.5 | 97.5 | 100 | 97.5 | 85 | 82.5 |
| Subject 2 | Push time [s] | Pull time [s] | Rise Time [s] | lower time [s] | right wink [s] | left wink [s] |
| average | 4.7 | 4.4 | 4.3 | 5.2 | 2.6 | 2.3 |
| training [%] | 51 | 57 | 64 | 42 | NA | NA |
| Fails | 1 | 0 | 0 | 2 | 5 | 7 |
| effectiveness [%] | 97.5 | 100 | 100 | 95 | 8 | 82.5 |

In both test subjects, the needs associated with winks with the right and left eye are the ones that have the most problems to be detected, because during facial expression training the software sent ambiguous signals in several cases, besides the software does not show a percentage of training for facial expressions, however the values obtained are still useful and in turn the facial expressions allow to communicate the need more quickly, if necessary the data could be improved with an adjustment in the training process.

In Fig. 9, the control screen of patient 1 can be observed for activated need 1, in which the action of pushing the bucket is related to the need to urinate, while for test subject 2 need 1 is associated with the need for pain. Similar results are obtained for each of the needs, validating the operation of the screen as a means of communication for the patient.

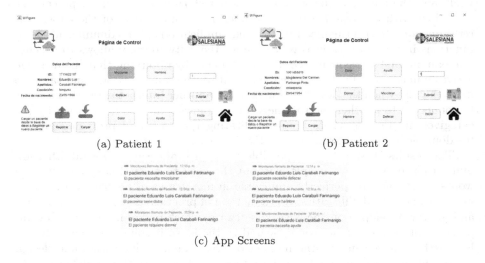

(a) Patient 1                                  (b) Patient 2

(c) App Screens

**Fig. 9.** HMI screen for patients during need detection.

To evaluate remote communication, a test was performed to determine the time it takes for the indicator on the Matlab screen to light up and the time it takes for the message to be displayed on the mobile device. This test is performed for the situation where the mobile device is connected to the same wifi network as the GUI computer, as well as when it is in a different network, for the first case the message reception was practically at the same time that the GUI indicator was turned on. For the second case the message reception time is approximately 2 s, this time is low compared to the response time of the medical staff. Compared to the response time of the medical and nursing staff to the help buzzer. (Navarrete and Gonzalez, 2022). The test was performed 60 times under similar network operating conditions and the same result was obtained 100% of the repetitions. These results demonstrate that the system allows remote communication with the caregiver. Figure 9c, shows the message that arrives on the screen of the mobile device during the tests for the test subject.

## 4   Conclusions

The success of the communication system has a direct relationship with the training process, for a high effectiveness percentage, the communication is faster between the patient and the graphic interface and error is reduced. Therefore, it is therefore recommended to train until reaching a percentage as high as possible, without overwhelming the patient. The patient, although the results show that with a training percentage of at least 50% very acceptable times are obtained. The results show that with a training percentage of at least 50% very acceptable times are obtained, 4 s on average and 93.6% efficiency. In view of the number of errors detected in the training with facial expressions of right wink and left wink, and the fact that the software does not show me the training percentage as it does with the training of three-dimensional movements of the cube, it is recommended to use this headset to make applications of maximum 4 needs or functions instead of 6 as in this case, since the software only allows to execute a maximum of 4 movements. On the other hand, by observing that the message arrives immediately to the mobile device within the same network, and takes no more than 2 s when the device is connected to another Internet network, it allows to connected to another Internet network, it allows real-time monitoring by the caregiver, no matter where he is, facilitating his work and providing greater freedom for him to perform other activities at the same time.

The results show that it is possible through brain waves to establish communication between two people, without the need to move limbs or pronounce words, so it could be perfectly applicable in most cases of people with reduced mobility and verbal difficulties. It is a method of practical use, safe, non-invasive, and mainly developed on the basis of software, which makes it economical compared to other much more sophisticated methods, so it could be used at home. For further improvements, the number of users could be increased, and design improvements could be made to the interfaces of both Matlab and Matlab. In the interfaces of both Matlab and the mobile application in order to have more user options and improve its versatility, user options to improve its versatility.

## References

1. Ochoa, C., Gonzales, N., Vera, A., Franco, O.: Impacto de diferentes medidas de mitigación en el curso de la pandemia de COVID-19 en Chile: proyección preliminar para el periodo del 14de abril al 14 de mayo. In: Rev. Salud Pública, p. 2 (2020)
2. Cuartas, D., et al.: Análisis espacio temporal del SARS-COV-2 en Cali, Colombia. In: Rev. Salud Pública, p. 2 (2020)
3. Martínez, F., Farré, G., Andreu, E.: Rehabilitación domiciliaria, principios, indicadores y programas terapéuticos. In: Rev. Salud Pública España, p. 200 (2015)
4. García, A., Méndez, M.: Atención de enfermería en el paciente politraumático. España, p. 38 (2011)
5. Lacida, M.: Deterioro de la Movilidad física y continuidad de cuidados, p. 5, 7 (2016)
6. Navarrete, N., Gonzalez, l.: Tiempo de respuesta al timbre del paciente hospitalizado en una institución de tercer nivel. Enfermería, Colombia, vol. 9 (2022)

7. Alfonso, I., Papazian, O., Dunomoyer, C., Yaylali, I.: Nuevas técnicas de monitorización cerebral en el recién nacido. Reb Neurol, pp. 27–30 (2012)

8. Lozano, D., Aguirre, R..: Diseño e implementación de un sistema de teleprecencia basado en la lectura de bioseñales e interacción háptica para el control de un robot explorador terrestre

9. Gómez, F., Yaguana, S.: Implementación de un sistema de control para el manipulador Mitsubishi RV-2AJ mediante ondas cerebrales emplenado el sensor Emotive Insight (2018)

10. Rodriguez, C.: Protesis robóticas e implantes cerebrales frente a la discapacidad. EFE News Service, Madrid-España (2016)

11. Bento, V., et al.: Advances in EEG-based Brain-Computer Interfaces for Control and Biometry. IEETA, University of Aveiro, Aveiro (2016)

12. Palaniappan, R.: Electroencephalogram-based brain–computer interface: an introduction. In: Miranda, E.R., Castet, J. (eds.) Guide to Brain-Computer Music Interfacing, pp. 29–41. Springer, London (2014). https://doi.org/10.1007/978-1-4471-6584-2_2

13. Ramadan, R.A., Vasilakos, A.V.: Brain computer interface: control signals. Neurocomputing **223**, 31–34 (2016)

14. Pérez, I.: Desarrollo de una plataforma para experimentación con interface cerebro ordenador (BCI), Cartagena (2017)

15. Abdulkader, S.N., Atia, A., Mostafa, M.-S.M.: Brain computer interfacing: applications and challenges. Egypt. Inform. J. **16**, 219–222 (2015)

16. Schalk, G., Mellinger, J.: A Practical Guide to Brain-Computer Interfacing with BCI2000. Springer, London (2010). https://doi.org/10.1007/978-1-84996-092-2

17. EMOTIV Inc.: Emotiv Software Development Kit, User Manual for Emotiv Xavier ControlPanel, p. 20 (2017)

18. EMOTIV Inc.: Insight User Manual, p. 2 (2020). https://emotiv.gitbook.io/insight-manual

19. Firebase. Fire Base Real Time Data Base (2016). https://firebase.google.com/products/realtimedatabase?hl=es

20. Android Studio, Developers, Introducción al Android Studio (2021). https://developer.android.com/studio/intro?hl=es-419

21. PR. Newswire en Español (South America). El primer brazo robótico exitoso de la historia controlado por la mente sin implantes cerebrales, New York (2019)

# Advanced Metrics to Evaluate Autistic Children's Attention and Emotions from Facial Characteristics Using a Human-Robot-Game Interface

Dennys Paillacho Chiluiza[1,3](✉) (iD), Nayeth Solórzano Alcívar[2] (iD),
Michael Arce Sierra[3], Edwin Eras[3], and María Fernanda Plúas[4]

[1] Escuela Superior Politécnica del Litoral, ESPOL – CIDIS, Guayaquil, Ecuador
`dpaillac@espol.edu.ec`
[2] Escuela Superior Politécnica del Litoral, ESPOL – FADCOM, Guayaquil, Ecuador
`nsolorza@espol.edu.ec`
[3] Escuela Superior Politécnica del Litoral, ESPOL – FIEC, Guayaquil, Ecuador
`{micxarce,edaneras}@espol.edu.ec`
[4] Escuela Superior Politécnica del Litoral, ESPOL – FCSH, Guayaquil, Ecuador
`ajpincay@espol.edu.ec`

**Abstract.** Several studies have discussed how to support children with autism spectrum disorder (ASD) using technological resources and the difficulties in their social interaction and non-verbal communication. In recent years, some authors have explained that a way to treat ASD syndrome has been through robot-assisted therapy, expecting to capture their attention. This study analyses aspects of the results obtained using the social robot 'LOLY,' which allows the children's interaction with games, recorded for therapeutic and behavioral analysis. Aiming to refine the metrics used to automatically assess the degree of attention and emotions of children with ASD when interacting with a social robot, several human-robot interaction sessions were analyzed in the laboratory and the field. The results of the automatic processing of the video signals corresponding to the interactions were compared with classical observational techniques. Part of the analysis will also consist of comparing the results of the videos taken from different reference points of the robot, such as from the head and bust. As a result of the trial-error follow-up, the comparative analysis between automatic and observational techniques proves the effectiveness of these adjustments.

**Keywords:** Human-Robot Interaction · Social Robot · ASD · Socially Assistive Robot · Videogames · Serious Games

## 1 Introduction

Children with Autism Spectrum Disorder (ASD) have difficulties in social interaction and non-verbal communication [1], which represents an issue in interacting with others, disconnecting them from their environment and affecting their development and comprehension. This disorder is a neurobiological condition that affects people from an early

J. Maldonado-Mahauad et al. (Eds.): TICEC 2023, CCIS 1885, pp. 234–247, 2023.
https://doi.org/10.1007/978-3-031-45438-7_16

age, where behavior patterns that affect the children's, daily activities remain throughout the patients' lives [2]. This condition also directly impacts children's education; overwhelming stimuli such as their classmates, ringing bells, or bright lights that may cause anxiety or aggressive behavior [3].

In recent years, a way to treat ASD has been through robot-assisted therapy since robots seem attractive to children [4]. Research shows that computers, phones, tablets, and robotic games help children with ASD to improve their communication [5]; this is because the most challenging part for them is eliminated since it is not necessary to have to look into the eyes or understand the facial expression of robots [6]. Within this area, social robots have been developed to interact with children with ASD. For example, some studies introduce the RUBI robot, which is presented as an excellent tool to obtain and maintain children's attention [8]. Another robot is Kaspar, which acts as an intermediary between children with ASD and other people to improve communication [9]. In some cases, these social robots can recognize the facial emotions of the person in front of them throughout the interaction to act on the mood variations observed, thus helping to improve the communication of children with ASD [10].

Complementary, serious games or educational videogames linked to robot interaction have proven effective in the communicative, emotional, and symbolic development of children with ASD [7]. This is the case of the LOLY-MIDI platform [11] project, which includes a social robot named 'LOLY' that performs movements, sounds, and gestures to interact with serious videogames in real time, following a human-robot-game (HRG) approach. This robot also allows the video recording of the child with ASD once the game session on the tablet has started through a fisheye camera embedded in LOLY's forehead or on the LOLY's bust [12]. It was possible to implement a dashboard linked to the robot to obtain results of facial metrics from the videos recorded by the robot's camera, allowing the evaluation of a child's attention, head position, and emotions during the game session recording [13]. The analysis of the videos evaluated is based on supervised classification learning, receiving as input variables the images taken by the robot's camera [10].

Following this same context, the present work focuses on analyzing the results of the established metrics: head position, attention to the tablet, and the child's emotions, through the LOLY-MIDI control board and the LOLY social robot to further correct and update them until reaching the desired level of metrics' precision.

## 2  Theoretical Framework

Three main characteristics have been attributed to ASD among them are: (1) Difficulties of the person in terms of social skills, including aspects such as intercommunication with peers, eye contact, facial expressions, and shared attention. (2) Limitation in the ability to speak and communicate implies saying words incorrectly, inability to follow orders, and lack of language, among others. (3) Frequent repetitive and restricted activities and interests [14].

Thus, children with this syndrome may face several obstacles in their learning development, which can overwhelm them and cause their isolation. These issues do not mean that children with ASD cannot acquire knowledge correctly; instead, they learn facts, details, routines, or complex content; however, inconveniences arise when attempting to transfer this knowledge to a different context [1].

Concerning the exposed problem, the LOLY-MIDI research and development project was undertaken [11], which consists of a Human-Robot-Game (HRG) platform that implements the social robot named LOLY [12] and educational digital games of the MIDI-AM series (Spanish acronym of "Children's Educational Interactive Multimedia - Mobile Applications.") [15]. These games are oriented to capture the attention and stimulate the learning of children with ASD. LOLY robot has a fisheye camera on the forehead or a camera on the bust that records gaming sessions and sends them to the MIDI-AM server, where facial metrics related to emotions, head posture, and attention are analyzed and extracted, to be later able to observe the results on a web platform or dashboard and be helpful for learning and treatment by psychologists [16].

In the project, particular emphasis is placed on the recognition of characteristics such as attention, emotions, and head posture in children with ASD by processing the videos of the recorded sessions using the OpenFace 2.0 tool, a computer vision and machine learning that helps analyze the facial behavior of a person to extract information (as shown in Fig. 1), representing it as a data set with several variables, of which those used in LOLY-MIDI stand out, which are: Head Pose Estimation, Gaze Estimation, 3D Facial Landmark and Facial Action units [17].

In the LOLY-MIDI project, six emotions are based (neutral, surprise, happiness, anger, disinterest, and sadness). In addition, there are levels of attention: attention to the robot's bust, attention to the robot's face, attention to the tablet, or no attention in the case of inability to identify a face. Finally, the position of the head is also evaluated: inclined downwards, perpendicular, or without information (in the case that no face is identified).

**Fig. 1.** Openface 2.0 image example.

In later versions of the LOLY-MIDI project, metrics were defined based on the set of facial points of the face detected by OpenFace 2.0 when recording play sessions with the child. However, in the emotion detection, mainly neutral and anger, they presented a very high number of false positives, so in this analysis, it was decided to change the parameters of emotions recognition metrics from facial points to action units, which are based on identifying facial expressions or action units [17] and, through combinations, to determine any emotion more precisely.

Therefore, in the LOLY-MIDI project, it is sought that the results of the metrics of attention, emotions, and head posture adjust to the parameters previously indicated in the programming of the LOLY's social robot to proceed for making the appropriate inferences about the social and cognitive abilities of both children with ASD and neurotypical children.

# 3  Materials and Methods

The present study used the robotic platform LOLY-MIDI [13], which consists of a LOLY robot (with two cameras positioned both on the forehead and on the bust) together with a tablet containing educational game applications downloaded, as well as a control board with information related to the position of the head, the degree of attention and the emotions detected in the form of graphs. The procedure carried out consists of three phases:

Phase 1: Setting parameters. In this first phase, videos of previous human-robot interactions were analyzed from the fisheye camera on the robot's forehead and the camera on the robot's bust. This analysis consisted of extracting the graphs of the different metrics from the dashboard. The graphs are of the pie and radial type, which reflect the data sectioned by time in the video. Once the metrics graphs were extracted, they were compared with the information observed in the videos, respecting the division of time the graphs handle. The main objective of this comparison was to detect possible differences between the two recording forms to look for improvements or adjustments in the metrics that can be corrected before carrying out new tests with children. In addition, we sought to verify the hypothesis that: the results observed from the dashboard are more favorable and closer to reality from the camera on the bust than with the fisheye since the latter is in the robot's forehead, which is in motion during the sessions, producing distortions in the recordings that are represented as blurred images due to this movement.

Phase 2: Parameter validation. To validate the metric accuracy, several human-robot interaction tests were carried out with people using the LOLY robot and recreating the procedure described in Phase 1. In the same way, the generated videos were analyzed in detail; however, to facilitate the analysis process, these were divided into 10-s time slots to facilitate the analysis process. Thus, they began to be examined for each block, again considering the metrics of head position, attention, and emotions that the subjects reflected.

Phase 3: Field tests. After testing with test subjects and correcting the metrics, field tests were undertaken with children, considering the authorization of their representatives, and following the same procedure, except for the analysis by time segments.

# 4  Results

## Phase 1: Setting Parameters

The analysis of the videos began by analyzing the videos of previous tests to improve the established metrics. The graphs of the metrics of these videos were compared between the recording with the fisheye camera on Loly's forehead and the camera on the robot's

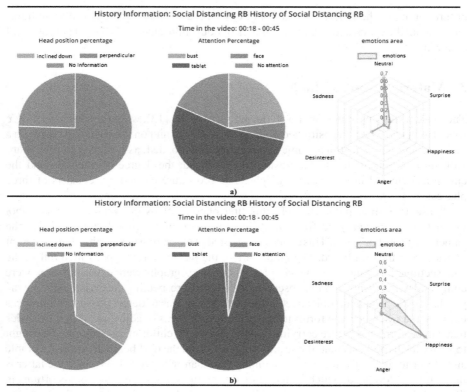

**Fig. 2.** Comparison with test subject for parameter adjustment, with the camera: **a)** on the bust and **b)** on the robot's head.

bust. In addition, the videos were observed more carefully to find differences in the graphs' results (Fig. 2).

It was found that particularities differed from reality for the two cameras, but the differences occurred more frequently with the fisheye camera. In the case of emotions, the most critical metric of inconsistency came in surprise and anger. It was noted that reviewing the action units for both emotions (units 10 and 23) are facial expressions that can be associated more with anger than surprise, and this information may be incorrectly interpreted as a surprise at the time of analysis. Therefore, action units 10 and 23 of the surprise emotion were removed, leaving only action units 01, 02, 05, 25, and 26; while the emotion of anger was characterized by action units 04, 05, 07, 09, 10, and 23 (as shown in Fig. 3):

Surprise: (au01_c | au02_c | au05_c) & (au25_c | au26_c)

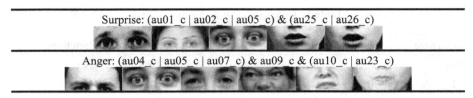

Anger: (au04_c | au05_c | au07_c) & au09_c & (au10_c | au23_c)

**Fig. 3.** Action units added to surprise and anger.

As for the other emotions, these were not modified because they were followed by what was observed in the videos. On the other hand, in the head position metrics, there was inconsistency in the inclined posture. It was found that the lower mean posture was not being used to determine head tilt and that the same range of in-axis tilt remained, so the metrics were modified to include these parameters.

**Phase 2: Parameter Validation**
New human-robot-game interaction sessions were recorded to check the effectiveness of the adjustments made in Phase 2. During these sessions, the inclination of the face, the gaze toward the camera placed on the robot's chest, and different changes in facial expressions were intentionally tested to capture the existence of other novelties (as shown in Fig. 4).

**Fig. 4.** Test Subjects for Phase 2.

With the results obtained, a comparative analysis was carried out between what was observed in the videos and the graphics generated in the dashboard of the LOLY-MIDI platform. In addition, to arrive at more objective evidence about the improvements already made, the videos were watched again but divided into 10-s sections. The results of this observation are shown in Table 1.

**Table 1.** Comparison by segments of 10 s.

| Initial time | Final time | Head position | Attention | Emotions |
|---|---|---|---|---|
| 0:00 | 0:10 | P-IA | BRT-SA | NA |
| 0:11 | 0:20 | P | RT-SA | NSD |
| 0:21 | 0:30 | P | BT-SA | NA |
| 0:31 | 0:40 | P | RT-SA | NFD |
| 0:41 | 0:50 | P | T-SA | DE |
| 0:51 | 1:00 | P | RT | NF |
| 1:01 | 1:10 | PSI | RT-SA | NA |

In Table 1, the position of the head is classified as inclined downwards (IA), perpendicular (P), without information (SI); the subject's attention during the sessions is represented as a bust (B), face (R), tablet (T) and without attention (SA); and finally, the emotions were represented as neutral (N), sadness (T), disinterest (D), anger (E), happiness (F) and surprise (S). Therefore, based on the time presented on the left side of the table, the subject performed a series of actions registered through the camera. For example, in the first 10 s, the subject maintained a certain percentage of the time, the head perpendicular and inclined downwards, while the attention from both cameras was kept on the bust, on the face, on the tablet, and there were moments when it was without attention. Finally, his emotions were neutral and disinterested.

In the subsequent tests, better results were obtained in the detection of attention and emotions since, when performing a comparative analysis between the measurements of the past and adjusted metrics, it was possible to show improvements in the prediction of emotion recognition and levels of attention, together with a good fit about the position of the face.

**Phase 3: Field Test**

With the corrections made to the metrics, we carried out tests with children from Three to eight years old with the LOLY robot. In total, 14 tests were carried out, and each session was recorded with the camera on the forehead and the bust, resulting in 28 videos.

For the analysis, these videos were observed together with the results during children's interaction with the robot. For study purposes, the videos recorded for a child were randomly chosen and analyzed; that is, two videos of the total were evaluated in detail frame by frame since it was considered that this number was necessary to corroborate the metrics' effectiveness.

Below are comparative tables where contrast is made between the results obtained with the camera on the bust and the camera on the forehead and observations of differences between the graphs and what is viewed in the videos, as performed with the test subjects (as shown in Fig. 5).

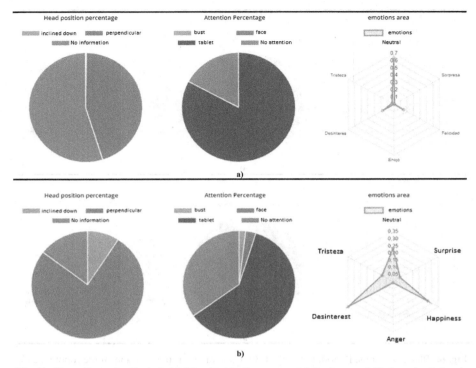

**Fig. 5.**  Phase 3 graphs. Period: 00:00 – 01:17. Camera on: **a)** the bust and **b)** the robot's head.

In the first period selected (Fig. 5), by carefully observing the video made with the camera on the robot's bust, it was possible to show that the child maintains the position of his head entirely perpendicularly in a much higher percentage than revealed in the graphs. Additionally, it can be noted that the proportion of what is classified as "without information" is less to the same extent and even tends to be zero. Likewise, it was observed that the child not only paid attention to the tablet but that there was a level of attention to the bust and face of the robot, although the time that this happens is slightly short. The emotions in the data collected in the graphs coincide with what was examined in the videos. On the other hand, when analyzing the video recorded with the fisheye camera, it is shown that the percentage of inclination below the head is smaller since it keeps it perpendicular for a longer time. Likewise, it was possible to show that the percentage of "without attention" is somewhat lower, and at the same time, it was observed that the percentage of attention to the tablet is more significant than what is presented. Finally, the child shows fewer emotions, such as disinterest and happiness; instead, he/she chooses to remain neutral during the time studied.

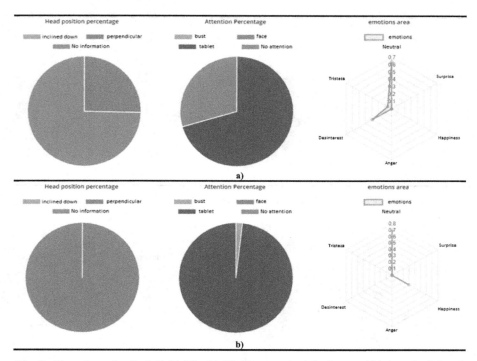

**Fig. 6.** Phase 3 graphs. Period: 01:28 – 01:39. Camera on: **a)** the bust and **b)** the robot's head.

For the second period selected (see Fig. 6), in the video captured by the camera in the bust, no percentage of "no information" is recorded regarding the position of the head. The child keeps his head perpendicular during the entire analysis time without tilting it at any time. In addition, it was observed that most of the time being analyzed paid attention to the tablet, dedicating only a minimum percentage of attention to the bust, thus decreasing the proportion dedicated to the "without attention" section. Regarding emotions, the child did not show disinterest but remained utterly neutral. Regarding the video captured with the fisheye camera, the only difference found, compared to the graphs, is the absence of happiness emotion on the part of the child, and as previously stated, he/she was neutral throughout the process.

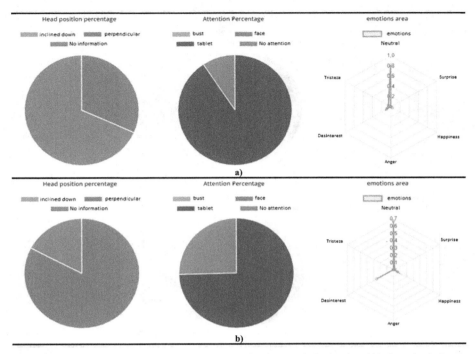

**Fig. 7.** Phase 3 graphs. Period: 01:44 – 02:01. Camera on: **a)** the bust and **b)** the robot's head.

In the following period (as shown in Fig. 7), the camera on the bust captures that the child constantly maintained the position of the head perpendicularly most of the time, without indicating any action that implies tilting down the head. Head or "no information." Regarding the percentage of attention, what the graph reflects coincides with what was observed during the video analysis; that is, it is evident that the child paid attention to the tablet a large proportion of the time. Additionally, it cannot be verified that the infant shows disinterest or happiness in his facial expressions; somewhat, he remains neutral. On the other hand, in the fisheye camera, it was not observed that there is what is classified as "without information" but that the child maintains the position of his head perpendicular throughout the period analyzed. In addition, the percentage of "no attention" and attention to the tablet is equivalent to what was studied in the respective video, maintaining the same way the lack of attention to the bust and face of the LOLY robot. Likewise, it is evident that the child expressed neutrality, but it does not reflect disinterest.

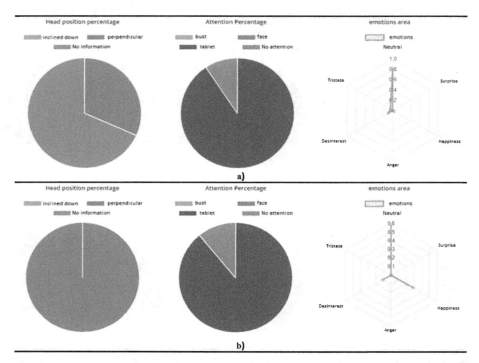

**Fig. 8.** Phase 3 graphs. Period: 02:05 – 02:52. Camera on: **a)** the bust and **b)** the robot's head.

For the last period analyzed (see Fig. 8), the bust camera details that the child has the position of the head perpendicular most of the time. Concerning the percentage of attention, this does not vary if the data shown in the graphs are compared with what was observed in the video since it was evidenced that the infant paid more attention to the tablet than to the bust or face of the robot. Other than that, the child showed a neutral expression and no emotions of disinterest or happiness. About the fisheye camera, both the graphs corresponding to the position of the head and those referring to the percentage of attention do not show changes with what was examined in the respective video, but there are differences in emotions since there is no evidence of disinterest or happiness.

## 5 Discussion

The findings within the last analysis indicate that although there were still differences between what was observed in the videos and the information in the graphs, these were smaller than those that had been previously identified, and many discrepancies were minor. Even these differences can be caused more by failures in the observer and not by the consequence of errors in the metrics. Likewise, it can be noted in these same tables that the detection is not very accurate, mainly for the emotions of happiness and disinterest; in most of the graphs, these emotions are identified when they should not be that way.

Even though the metrics were significantly improved thanks to the tests carried out and the subsequent corrections, the research had some limitations and difficulties that could be areas for improvement and points to consider in future research within the project. For example, the video file provided by the camera on the robot's head had frozen parts. Therefore, there may be distortions when watching the video, resulting in incomplete results, since at those moments, the child performing the test may have changed the position of his head or another vital action in the study that could not be detected.

In addition, given the movement of the robot's head and consequently the movement of the camera in it, it was impossible to observe with greater precision the emotions and the degree of attention, even in one of the cases where the position was analyzed. The child's head was difficult to detect; this was also due to the camera's focus.

In general, the research and analysis of the videos during the gaming sessions have shown their potential to decrease the error rate regarding the practical interpretation of the metrics and subsequent representation of the graphs on the dashboard, helping in this way to reinforce the concentration skills and social skills that are desired in the project. Removing action units from the surprise emotion has decreased the chances of it being confused with the anger emotion. Likewise, by correcting the head position metrics, especially its inclination, it was possible to include the lower average posture of the person for the detection of this action to be more accurate. Finally, using the bust Camera yields more precise results, corroborating the hypothesis raised in Sect. 3.

# 6   Conclusions and Future Work

The analysis developed throughout this document has yielded satisfactory results that allow us to fulfill the objective for which this investigation was given. In this way, during the present study, a couple of techniques have been explored that start from observing several videos made by test subjects interacting with the robot LOLY and playing on the tablet, and the effectiveness of the metrics when making a detection was evaluated. More precise about the position of the head, the percentage of attention, and the person's emotions, to later correct the exposed errors and finally carry out the tests with children.

As future work, we will continue with the evaluation and iterative improvement of the facial metrics of attention, posture, and emotions, using data collected through the interactions of the LOLY robot with the children; develop new techniques to improve recognition of children's emotions during interactions, since each person may have different features and facial expressions. Also, avoid carrying objects that serve as a distraction for the child when carrying out the tests, and look for tools that allow the video files recorded with the camera on the robot's head not to remain frozen; thus, in this way, it can be recognized facial changes during the analysis of said videos. It should also be mentioned that the personnel in charge of the investigation ensure the sessions are correctly recorded. Therefore, the videos can be used for the respective analysis and thus not incur delays due to poorly recorded material. Furthermore, finally, the tests must be carried out under the supervision of the personnel in charge of the LOLY robot in case any problem arises and so that the latter gives the proper instructions for the game session.

# References

1. Gil, V., Quintero, C., Velez, J., Gómez, N.: Analysis of learning abilities in children with autism. ESPACIOS **41**(48), 341–349 (2020). https://doi.org/10.48082/spaces-a20v41n48p25
2. Cardona, V.: Social Robots and Autism. Proposal for intervention in the educational context
3. Delgado, P.: Autism Spectrum Disorder (ASD) in education. Observatory/Institute for the Future of Education, 18 June 2021. https://observatorio.tec.mx/edu-news/autism-spectrum-disorder-tea-education/. Accessed 5 June 2023
4. Pinel, V., Rendón, L., Adrover-Roig, D.: Social robots as promoters of communication in Autism Spectrum Disorders (ASD). Letras de Hoje **53**(1), 39–47 (2018). https://doi.org/10.15448/1984-7726.2018.1.28920
5. Bennington, J.: Robots will soon become our children's tutors. Here is why that's a good thing. NBC News, 19 April 2017. https://www.nbcnews.com/mach/technology/robots-will-soon-become-our-children-s-tutors-here-s-n748196. Accessed 5 June 2023
6. Ferrer, S.: Siri, why do they call me autistic at school?. elconfidencial.com, 23 October 2014. https://www.elconfidencial.com/tecnologia/2014-10-23/siri-why-at-school-they-call-me-autistic_403728/. Accessed 5 June 2023
7. González, C.: Intervention in a child with autism through play. Rev. Fac. Med. **66**(3), 365–374
8. Tanaka, F., Kimura, T.: The use of robots in early education: a scenario based on ethical consideration. In: RO-MAN 2009 - The 18th IEEE International Symposium on Robot and Human Interactive Communication, Sep. 2009, pp. 558–560 (2009). https://doi.org/10.1109/ROMAN.2009.5326227
9. Dautenhahn, K., Nehaniv, C., Walters, M.: KASPAR – a minimally expressive humanoid robot for human-robot interaction research. Appl. Bionics Biomech. **6**, 369–397 (2009). https://doi.org/10.1155/2009/708594
10. Baños, G.: Recognition of human emotions and its application to Social Robotics
11. Solorzano, N., Herrera, L., Lima, L., Paillacho, J., and Paillacho, D.: Metrics design of usability and behavior analysis of a Human-Robot-Game platform. In: Botto-Tobar, M., Montes León, S., Camacho, O., Chávez, D., Torres-Carrión, P., Zambrano Vizuete, M. (eds.) Applied Technologies. ICAT 2020. CCIS, vol. 1388, pp. 164–178. Springer, Cham (2021). https://doi.org/10.1007/978-3-030-71503-8_13
12. Paillacho, D., Solorzano, N., Paillacho, J.: LOLY 1.0: a proposed Human-Robot-Game platform architecture for the engagement of children with autism in the learning process. In: Botto-Tobar, M., Zamora, W., Larrea Plúa, J., Bazurto Roldan, J., Santamaría Philco, A. (eds.) Systems and Information Sciences. ICCIS 2020. AISC, vol. 1273, pp. 225–238. Springer, Cham (2021). https://doi.org/10.1007/978-3-030-59194-6_19
13. Solorzano, N., Paillacho, D., Arce, M., Tomala, J.: Metrics for a Human-Robot-Game platform to evaluate attention and emotion in children with ASD. In: 2022 International Conference on Electrical, Computer, Communications and Mechatronics Engineering (ICECCME), Nov. 2022, pp. 01–06 (2022). https://doi.org/10.1109/ICECCME55909.2022.9988747
14. Castro, P.: Validation in a Real Environment of the CASTOR Social Robot for Use in Therapies with Children with Autism. Universidad del Rosario, Bogotá (2020). https://repository.urosario.edu.co/server/api/core/bitstreams/7ff66895-692f-4c51-9796-39725e16b3cb/content
15. Solórzano, N., Elizalde, E., Carrera, D., Park, D., Sornoza, L.: MIDI-AM model to identify a methodology for the creation of innovative educational digital games: a proposed serious game methodology based on university research experiences. In: Improving University Reputation Through Academic Digital Branding, IGI Global, 2021, pp. 133–167 (2021). https://doi.org/10.4018/978-1-7998-4930-8.ch009
16. Solorzano, N., Herrera, L., Lima, L., Paillacho, D., Paillacho, J.: Visual metrics for educational videogames linked to socially assistive robots in an inclusive education framework.

In: Mesquita, A., Abreu, A., Carvalho, J.V. (eds.) Perspectives and Trends in Education and Technology. SIST, vol. 256, pp. 119–132. Springer, Singapore (2022). https://doi.org/10.1007/978-981-16-5063-5_10

17. Baltrusaitis, T., Zadeh, A., Lim, Y., Morency, L.: OpenFace 2.0: facial behavior analysis Toolkit. In: 2018 13th IEEE International Conference on Automatic Face & Gesture Recognition (FG 2018), Xi'an: IEEE, May 2018, pp. 59–66 (2018). https://doi.org/10.1109/FG.2018.00019

# Performance Analysis of You Only Look Once, RetinaNet, and Single Shot Detector Applied to Vehicle Detection and Counting

Iván Andrés Buitrón[1] ⓘ and Sang Guun Yoo[1,2](✉) ⓘ

[1] Departamento de Informática y Ciencias de la Computación, Escuela Politécnica Nacional, Quito, Ecuador
sang.yoo@epn.edu.ec
[2] Smart Lab, Escuela Politécnica Nacional, Quito, Ecuador

**Abstract.** Artificial intelligence has experienced significant growth in recent decades. As a result, several architectures have been developed for object detection, classification, and recognition. Currently, there are several alternatives that fulfill these purposes; however, there is no rigid framework defining how these architectures are formed. This work presents an updated performance analysis of real-time vehicle detection and counting using You Only Look Once (YOLOv8) version 8, RetinaNet (RN), and Single Shot Detector (SSD). For such analysis, the Google Colaboratory was used as the main retraining environment. The Research-Action methodology was employed to develop the practical case, and a systematic literature review was also conducted to determine the state of the art in this problem domain. For feature extraction, RESNET-50 and MobileNet were used in RN and SSD, respectively. The results indicated that YOLOv8 (which has undergone the most adjustments since its inception) exhibits the best performance in terms of detection time, precision considering the frames that need to be analyzed to enable real-time usage, and ease of implementation.

**Keywords:** Vehicle Detection · Vehicle Counting · YOLOv8 · SSD · RetinaNet · Computer Vision · Artificial Intelligence

## 1 Introduction

The article highlights the evolution of computer vision over the past sixty years, starting with early publications such as Larry Roberts' PhD thesis on machine perception of three-dimensional solids [1] and in the experiment developed by Papert Seymou on image description by computers [2]. As processing power increased and more digital data became available, computer vision advanced rapidly [3]. The creation of the "Neocognitron" [4] in the 1980s marked a significant milestone, representing one of the first convolutional neural network models.

The survey article titled "Object Detection in 20 Years" [5] summarizes the advancements in the field, focusing on two-stage detectors like R-CNN, SPPNet, Fast R-CNN, and Faster R-CNN, which improved speed and accuracy through spatial features and

J. Maldonado-Mahauad et al. (Eds.): TICEC 2023, CCIS 1885, pp. 248–262, 2023.
https://doi.org/10.1007/978-3-031-45438-7_17

region proposals. However, the need for real-time applications led to the emergence of parallel proposals like YOLOv8, RetinaNet (RN), and Single Shot Detector (SSD), which perform detection in a single pass, making them more efficient for high frame rates [6].

The present research work aims to compare the performance of the latest versions of YOLO, RN, and SSD algorithms by conducting fine-tuning [7] or custom training with a specific dataset for real-time vehicle detection and counting. The document is structured into sections, starting with a review of the state-of-the-art architectures, followed by an explanation of the methodology, including the tools used for the experiment and implementation details of each architecture. The discussion section presents a brief analysis, and the study concludes in the final section.

## 2    State of the Art

Before conducting the analysis of the different computer vision tools, a literature review of existing works was carried out to understand their state of the art [8]. For this part of the study, a rigorous and structured process was conducted with the aim of collecting, evaluating, and comprehensively analyzing digital libraries and/or repositories of scientists in search of available scientific evidence on YOLO, SSD, and RN. We followed a three-stage approach to perform this task (see Fig. 1). Each stage consists of subtasks that allow for an organized and objective process, eliminating any potential biases that may exist.

**Fig. 1.** Stages of the adopted strategy based on the systematic review.

During the analysis and planning stage of a systematic literature review, the research question was clearly defined, and the objectives, inclusion criteria, and exclusion criteria for the studies were established. Furthermore, relevant keywords were identified, and a list of terms to be used in the literature search was developed. Additionally, the repositories or electronic databases where the search was conducted were determined.

The initial phase of the research involved formulating research questions related to comparing YOLO, SSD, and RN, as well as determining the most used neural network architectures for real-time detection and vehicle counting. Keywords such as You Only Look Once, Single Shot Detector, RetinaNet, computer vision, deep learning, detection and classification, neural networks, and real-time were identified to address these questions. The selected databases for the literature search included ACM Digital Library, IEEE Xplore, Arxiv, Google Scholar, and Scopus.

A systematic literature review was conducted, utilizing the identified keywords, and applying filters and search criteria to obtain relevant results. The obtained articles were then reviewed based on their titles and abstracts, excluding those that did not meet the inclusion criteria. A detailed analysis of the selected articles' abstracts was performed to evaluate their relevance and pertinence to the research questions. The selected articles underwent a comprehensive analysis, including a thorough reading and extraction of relevant data using data extraction matrices. Finally, a final selection of articles was made based on their relevance, methodological quality, and contribution to the research questions.

Once the articles were filtered, they were systematically classified and tabulated. Table 1 summarizes the findings of the identified articles, considering the title and publication date, references to the source code implementations, official websites of the architecture creators, as well as the abstract and content of each article.

**Table 1.** Results table of the systematic review.

| | ACM Digital | IEEE Xplore | Arxiv | Google Scholar | Scopus | Partial | Title filter | Abstract filter | Content filter | Final |
|---|---|---|---|---|---|---|---|---|---|---|
| SSD | 86 | 24 | 11 | 6 | 29 | 156 | 100 | 32 | 14 | 10 |
| YOLO | 101 | 14 | 32 | 19 | 15 | 181 | 87 | 39 | 43 | 12 |
| RN | 57 | 19 | 4 | 8 | 2 | 90 | 45 | 17 | 20 | 8 |
| Deep Learning Y SSD, YOLO, RN | 14 | 8 | 4 | 2 | 0 | 28 | 11 | 1 | 10 | 6 |
| Car Detection Y SSD, YOLO, RN | 16 | 6 | 4 | 2 | 1 | 29 | 19 | 1 | 6 | 3 |
| Car Counting Y SSD, YOLO, RN | 11 | 6 | 66 | 2 | 14 | 99 | 90 | 5 | 2 | 2 |
| Others | 8 | 3 | 6 | 11 | 4 | 32 | 12 | 10 | 6 | 4 |

In conclusion, this provides a comprehensive and up-to-date overview of the state of knowledge in the field of single-stage architectures for object detection. This allows for the identification of YOLO as a method that has been extensively studied over time, highlighting trends, and obtaining solid evidence to support future projects or research in this area.

Next, we present the analysis of some of the selected previous works to understand their functionalities and, if applicable, their limitations.

Bilel Benjdira et al. in their article "Car Detection using Unmanned Aerial Vehicles: Comparison between Faster R-CNN and YOLOv3" [9] focus on comparing the architectures of Faster R-CNN and YOLOv3 for car detection. The limitations involved are related to YOLO since it has been updated to version 8, which presents significant changes from version 3 that directly impact performance.

On the other hand, the article "A Real-Time Vehicle Counting, Speed Estimation, and Classification System Based on Virtual Detection Zone and YOLO" [10] describes a real-time system for vehicle counting, speed estimation, and classification using a Virtual Detection Zone and the YOLOv3 neural network. The weakness of this work is that, as far as we could review, customized datasets based on different daytime and nighttime scenarios were not considered.

The article "The improvement in obstacle detection in autonomous vehicles using YOLO non-maximum suppression fuzzy algorithm" [11] focuses on improving obstacle detection in autonomous vehicles using the fuzzy non-maximum suppression algorithm. This work is specifically applied to autonomous vehicles, constituting a different field.

The article "Deep Learning for Computer Vision: A Brief Review" written by Athanasios Voulodimos [12] provides a concise review of deep learning applied to computer vision. This work serves as a knowledge foundation to establish the know-how for the development of our own study, as it addresses concepts about deep learning that should be considered in our practical case.

The article by Lu Tan et al. [13] is based on the comparison of the same selected models by our team, but with the difference that, as far as we know, this article does not refer to the second major feature of these models, which is recognition. This work focuses on classification that can be achieved with these models, and additionally, the versions used in the experiments are different. In this work, SSD with VGG16 is used as a feature extractor, unlike our approach where we use the backbone layers with MobileNet, which is a newer and updated model with its advantages.

In the experiment by Almeida et al. [14], the problem of vehicle detection and counting using OpenCV as a framework is addressed. It involves an iterative development approach, incorporating algorithms such as Mixture of Gaussian (MOG), k-Nearest Neighbor (KNN), and Geometric Multigrid.

Due to modifications in the structure of each neural network in their subsequent versions, as well as the exploration of model combinations such as RetinaNet with ResNet50 and Single Shot Detector with MobileNet, there is a new range of possibilities in real-time vehicle detection and counting. Therefore, a new and improved interpretation of the performance of these techniques is desirable.

## 3 Methodology

According to Altrichter et al. [15], the purpose of action research is to create societies of people committed to learning in direct relation to the circumstances of the environment in which they live; thus, the social problems that arise in the communities should serve as an impulse to carry out public research that provides solutions for the collective.

Lewis' model recognizes these needs that had been previously presented in Kemmis' work and shows as an alternative the cyclical model that presents a constant flow of continuous improvement (see Fig. 2).

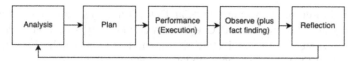

**Fig. 2.** Stages of the Research-Action methodology.

The application of the action research model oriented in this case study involves a collaborative and practical approach to address specific challenges. We begin by identifying the specific problem of having the YOLOv8, SSD, and RN architectures, and then a series of actions are planned and carried out to address the comparative analysis. This includes data collection, implementation, and adaptation of YOLOv8, SSD, and RN models, training and fine-tuning of these models with custom datasets, and deployment of solutions in real-world environments. As the process unfolds, data is collected and reflection on the results obtained takes place, leading to continuous adjustments and improvements. Action research applied to computer vision aims to achieve practical and tangible impact by solving specific problems and enhancing detection and image analysis systems.

### 3.1 Development Tools and Work Environment Configuration

The selection of experiment tools was based on the nature of the study. A fundamental part of the experiment was the real-time analysis of vehicle detection and counting. This led us to choose single-stage architectures primarily due to their combination of speed and efficiency, such as:

- Efficiency: Single-stage detectors are generally faster in terms of detection speed since they perform detection directly in a single pass of the neural network.
- Simplicity: They tend to be simpler in terms of architecture and detection process, as they do not require additional stages of region proposals or refinement.
- Direct detection: They detect objects and their locations directly in the image without the need for intermediate stages. This can result in a higher ability to detect small and densely packed objects.

Following the chronological order and the evolution of each architecture, we considered those with a greater bibliographic and documentary foundation i.e., YOLO, SSD, and RN.

During this action stage, the practical case was implemented based on different approaches and techniques to improve the accuracy of the detection system. Notebook environments were created for each architecture, alternatives were explored to include other architectures in the feature extraction stage, and the official documentation of each one was thoroughly examined to ensure the experiment's accuracy.

Next, a brief explanation of the selected technology and tools for this study is provided to allow readers to have a clearer understanding of the following sections.

**Convolutional Neural Networks.** Convolutional neural networks (CNNs) are a specialized type of artificial neural network (ANN) used for image analysis. To capture the spatial relationship between pixels, convolutional neural networks employ stacked layers of mathematical operations known as convolutions [16]. Convolutions are mathematical operations that, within image processing, aggregate pixels within the image, resulting in enhanced feature detection [17]. The backbone of these computer vision models relies on the concept of convolutional neural networks (CNNs), which play a fundamental role as they are specifically designed to analyze images and extract relevant features from them.

**SSD: Single Shot MultiBox Detector.** The article "SSD: Single Shot MultiBox Detector" by Wei Liu et al. [18], introduces the first version of SSD, a method for object detection, in 2015/2016. The authors highlight the need for fast and accurate object detection in images, which SSD aims to address. SSD proposes an architecture that offers an efficient and effective solution. Unlike other approaches that rely on exhaustive region proposal searches, SSD predicts multiple bounding boxes and their corresponding object classes simultaneously at different scales and resolutions. In the original experiment, a VGG-16 [19] type feature extraction network is used, but the article mentions that any network can perform well. To make a significant contribution, this work utilizes the MobileNet network.

**MobileNet.** The focus of MobileNet is to achieve computational efficiency and reduced model size without compromising too much on the accuracy of image classification task. The operation of MobileNet is based on the use of separable convolutions instead of standard convolutions. Separable convolution consists of two stages: depth wise convolution and pointwise convolution. In the depth wise convolution, $1 \times 1$ convolutions are performed to reduce the dimension of the feature space [20] (see Fig. 3).

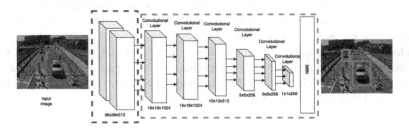

**Fig. 3.** Single Shot Detector Neural Network Architecture

**Feature Pyramid.** The article "Feature Pyramid Networks for Object Detection" [21] introduces a convolutional neural network architecture called Feature Pyramid Network (FPN) to address the challenge of detecting objects in images at different scales. FPN tackles the limitation of standard convolutional networks that struggle to detect small objects due to pooling layers [22] that reduce spatial resolution. The FPN architecture proposes a feature pyramid, where feature maps at different scales are constructed, capturing both fine-grained features and contextual features of the image.

**YOLO: You Only Look Once.** YOLO has 16 versions since its inception in 2016 [23], the first versions of YOLO worked with PASCAL VOC and from YOLOv3 onwards it uses COCO [24], and its fundamental premise is to be a real-time object detection method that uses a single pass through a convolutional neural network. Instead of dividing the image into regions of interest, YOLO divides the image into a grid and assigns each cell the responsibility of detecting objects. It uses multiple convolution layers to predict bounding boxes and object class probabilities in each cell. Although the original version had limitations in detecting small objects, later versions such as YOLOv2 and YOLOv3 improved accuracy and solved some problems [25].

In general, the differences between YOLO variants focus on aspects such as the size and depth of the convolutional neural network used, the number of layers and filters, and the accuracy and speed of detection (See Table 2).

**Table 2.** YOLOv8 Processing Features.

| Model | Size (pixels) | mAP | Speed CPU ONNX | Speed A100 TensorRT | Params (M) | FLOPs (B) |
|---|---|---|---|---|---|---|
| YOLOv8n | 640 | 37.3 | 80.4 | 0.99 | 3.2 | 8.7 |
| YOLOv8s | 640 | 44.9 | 128.4 | 1.20 | 11.2 | 28.6 |
| YOLOv8m | 640 | 50.2 | 234.7 | 1.83 | 25.9 | 78.9 |
| YOLOv8l | 640 | 52.9 | 375.2 | 2.39 | 43.7 | 165.2 |
| YOLOv8x | 640 | 53.9 | 479.1 | 3.53 | 68.2 | 257.8 |

The YOLOv8 architecture features a feature extraction stage, utilizing multiple convolutional layers to process the input image and extract high-level features. These convolutional layers are responsible for detecting patterns and relevant characteristics in the image, such as edges, textures, and shapes.

Subsequently, dimensionality reduction is achieved through pooling layers, which decrease the size of the features while preserving their most pertinent information. This reduction in dimensionality enables the attainment of a more concise representation of the image and facilitates object detection, as illustrated (See Fig. 4).

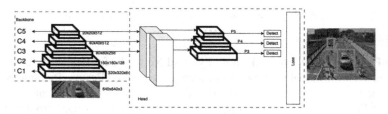

**Fig. 4.** YOLO Neural Network Architecture.

**RN: RetinaNet.** Is a convolutional neural network (CNN) architecture proposed by Tsung-Yi Lin, Priya Goyal, Ross Girshick, and Kaiming [26] in 2017 for the task of object detection in images. The main feature of RetinaNet is the combination of two key components: the Detection Head and the Retina Anchors. The Detection Head is a subnetwork that takes the input features and produces predictions for both object classification and bounding box regression. It utilizes a combination of convolutional layers and cascaded convolution layers (3x3 convolution and 1x1 convolution) to extract relevant features and make predictions [27]. RetinaNet incorporates focal loss as a training loss function to address challenging classification regions and improve class balance.

**ResNet-50** is a deep CNN architecture introduced by Kaiming He et al. in 2015 [28], known for its residual connections. ResNet-50's key feature is the ability to skip layers, mitigating the issue of gradient vanishing and enabling successful training of deep networks.

The solution of the ResNet-50+ RetinaNet architecture would be as follows (See Fig. 5).

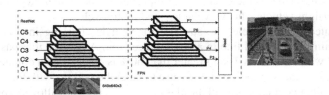

**Fig. 5.** Solution Architecture based on ResNet-50 and RetinaNet.

The article by Vivienne Sze [3] discusses the challenges and opportunities related to hardware requirements in machine learning. It provides an overview of the demands in this field and highlights specialized solutions being developed to enhance performance and efficiency of machine learning models. Cloud computing has revolutionized access to computational resources, storage, and software, allowing users to utilize cloud service providers instead of managing physical infrastructures. Google Colaboratory was chosen as a flexible solution for the project due to its cloud-based nature and interactive Python coding capabilities. Colab offers a collaborative notebook environment and the ability to run code in the cloud, providing free access to computational resources like CPU, GPU, and TPU [29] for intensive computations and model training. For this study, an additional 100 on-demand processing units were contracted on the platform to supplement the resources offered in the free tier.

## 4   Implementation of You Only Look Once, RetinaNet, and Single Shot Detector Applied to Vehicle Detection and Counting

For this experiment, a dataset of 300 images was constructed from videos that are not copyrighted, captured from different security cameras on bridges and highways, with various angles, perspectives, and weather conditions. Additionally, the platform's ecosystem was leveraged, allowing for interconnection with its storage services to store training checkpoints, metrics, and resource availability for read/write operations.

Labeling refers to the process of annotating training data to indicate the class or category to which they belong. Within the work "Types for Information Flow Control:

Labeling Granularity and Semantic Models" [30], regarding semantic models, the article examines how information labels are represented and managed in relation to the semantic meaning of the data.

For the emulation of real-time detection and counting process of video fragments captured by drones of 30 s, 60 s, and 120 s, the results of the experiments were collected.

The annotations described in the article "Fine-Tuning Pretrained Language Models: Weight Initializations, Data Orders, and Early Stopping" [7] were considered. The article focuses on the fine-tuning technique of pretrained language models. The authors explore different aspects of the fine-tuning process and how they affect the model's performance. They investigate the impact of weight initializations on fine-tuning, analyzing different initialization methods and how they affect the model's ability to capture relevant information during fine-tuning.

Since these three models are pretrained networks that were retrained to adjust their weights and focus on the "vehicle" class, it is important to note that the keyword "vehicle" encompasses (light vehicles, heavy vehicles, and motorcycles).

As presented in the article, the strategy for vehicle counting in this experiment involves defining a threshold line in a certain direction. Any class that passes through this threshold with a certainty level greater than 60% is considered a counted vehicle.

The makesense.ai web tool, which we use to label the regions with the class that we are going to train, in our case we call the class "vehicle", this tool allows exporting these annotations in XML and CSV format (See Fig. 6).

**Fig. 6.** MakeSense.ai XML and CSV annotation tool.

Once the image labeling task is completed, it is exported in both formats. We create a new notebook using our Google account in Google Colaboratory, which provides a cloud-based development environment. We connect the notebook with our Google Drive to serve as the storage provider.

For all three architectures, we have chosen pre-trained models that we will retrain with our custom dataset. This allows us to expedite the training time as the models already have initialized weights. In the case of YOLOv8, its official documentation provides updated parameters necessary for training. We will work with each model for a total of fifty epochs. As a conceptual project, our aim is to achieve the best possible results with the limited training available, even though training for 50 epochs, considering we have almost 300 images, will take a considerable amount of time.

In all experiments, we have set the batch size to 8 to ensure a fair comparison between the models. During training, we have set the image size to 1280 x 768 because the objects of interest can be relatively small in some images. By increasing the image resolution from the default 640, we have anticipated improved results, although this would require more time for training. After that, the goal of Multiple Object Tracking (MOT) was to estimate the boundaries and identities of objects in videos. A simple approach to achieve this involves several steps.

Firstly, the boundaries of objects (in this case, people) are detected in every frame using an object detection algorithm. In the example image, the detected boundaries of people in each frame are highlighted in yellow, along with an associated confidence threshold. This process is repeated for every frame of the video (see Fig. 7).

**Fig. 7.** YOLOv8 Tracking and Counting Inference.

In the case of SSD, it follows essentially the same approach. We have retrained a pretrained model, specifically SSD300, using our own dataset. For this purpose, we have utilized the custom repository from weiliu89/caffe. Additionally, with this architecture, it was necessary to use TensorFlow. The annotations need to be in a specific format called TFRecord, which is an efficient and optimized way to store data in TensorFlow, especially when working with large datasets.

Since the objective is to expose the architectures to the same training conditions, we have also chosen to train SSD for 50 epochs with a batch size of 8, like YOLO. This will result in a model with the following inference capabilities and for the counting part, the same strategy was adopted. A bounding line was created, and when the inference percentage for the "vehicle" class exceeds 60%, the counter is incremented by one (see Fig. 8).

Within the RetinaNet case study, we utilized the original repository from the first article "fizyr/keras-retinanet," as mentioned. We used the same hyperparameters for training and a pre-trained model to fine-tune it for detecting our new classes. This architecture also relies on TensorFlow as its convolution library. After training for 50 epochs with a batch size of 8, the resulting inference is displayed in the illustration. The difference is that it is necessary to reduce the number of frames for improved accuracy.

For the counting phase, we employed the same approach. We established a reference line and checked whether the detected objects intersected or crossed that line. This was achieved by comparing the object coordinates with the position of the lines (see Fig. 9).

**Fig. 8.** Inference Single Shot Detector Detection.

**Fig. 9.** Inference RetinaNet Detection.

After the implementation, the observation and reflection stage were carried out, where we tabulate the obtained results and analyze the collected data, reflecting on the outcomes.

Likewise, in order to provide an unbiased overview of the performances of the 3 models, we adopted a quantitative approach based on metrics that are commonly used to evaluate these models, in this case, precision, recall, and F1 score (see Fig. 10).

The precision of predictions is determined by the ratio of true positives to negatives. Recovery is the relationship between the number of true positives and the total number of classes, and a weighted average of precision and recall is used for the F1 score, as discussed by Padilla [31] in their article.

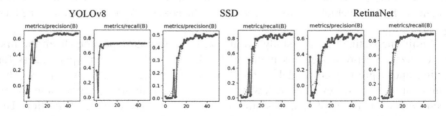

**Fig. 10.** YOLOv8, SSD, RetinaNet metrics of precision and recall.

In the following tables, we can observe the results obtained for 3 videos with durations of 30 s, 60 s, and 90 s, respectively. The columns display the absolute error, which represents the number of vehicles that were not detected, followed by the relative error, which is the percentage of the absolute error compared to the total number of vehicles circulating in the videos. We also have false positives, which occur when the detection algorithm or model incorrectly identifies an object that is not actually present in the analyzed image or video. Conversely, the last column represents false negatives, which occur when the detection algorithm or model fails to correctly identify an object that is present in the analyzed image or video (Tables 3, 4, 5 and 6).

**Table 3.** SSD, YOLO, RN inference results chart in a 30 s video

| Algorithm | % Absolute Error | % Relative Error | False Positive | False Negative |
|---|---|---|---|---|
| YOLO v8 | 5 | 11.46% | 0 | 2 |
| SSD + Mobilnet | 9 | 16.55% | 1 | 8 |
| RetinaNet + ResNet50 | 3 | 9% | 0 | 2 |

**Table 4.** SSD, YOLO, RN inference results chart in a 60 s video

| Algorithm | % Absolute Error | % Relative Error | False Positive | False Negative |
|---|---|---|---|---|
| YOLO v8 | 5 | 8.86% | 0 | 6 |
| SSD + Mobilnet | 13 | 19.23% | 3 | 14 |
| RetinaNet + ResNet50 | 6 | 12.01% | 1 | 4 |

**Table 5.** SSD, YOLO, RN inference results chart in a 90 s video

| Algorithm | % Absolute Error | % Relative Error | False Positive | False Negative |
|---|---|---|---|---|
| YOLO v8 | 8 | 9.11% | 1 | 6 |
| SSD + Mobilnet | 12 | 17.29% | 2 | 19 |
| RetinaNet + ResNet50 | 12 | 17.29% | 2 | 6 |

**Table 6.** SSD, YOLO, RN metrics

| Algorithm | % Precision | % Recall | % F1 | % MAP |
|---|---|---|---|---|
| YOLO v8 | 66.31% | 75.19% | 70.47% | 79.01% |
| SSD + Mobilnet | 59.98% | 84.83% | 70.27% | 83.32% |
| RetinaNet + ResNet50 | 61.69% | 88.03% | 72.54% | 87.54% |

## 5 Discussion

The experiment involved two challenges: real-time vehicle detection and vehicle counting within the frame. It was divided into three stages: Data Collection and Model Retraining, Vehicle Detection, and Vehicle Counting. Initial data collection involved extracting images from security cameras on bridges and avenues, which were then labeled using makesense.ai. The YOLOv8, SSD + MobileNet, and RetinaNet + ResNet50 models were retrained using this custom dataset with the help of Google Colaboratory.

Among the models evaluated, YOLOv8 demonstrated a significant advantage due to its periodic updates. In terms of accuracy, YOLO outperformed MobileNet SSD, but the latter had faster detection speed. MobileNet SSD, a single-shot detector, offered improved speed compared to YOLO and achieved comparable accuracy to slower techniques like faster R-CNN.

MobileNet SSD performed better for small objects (see Fig. 11), while YOLO was recommended for its accuracy. RetinaNet exhibited high accuracy but limited processing speed, making it less suitable for real-time applications. For the vehicle counting challenge, YOLOv8 with ByteTrack and Supervision showed superior performance compared to SSD with tensorflow_object_counting_api.

**Fig. 11.** Comparison of small objects inference.

Future work could involve exploring complementary model iterations, such as combining RetinaNet with other models like MobileNet or EfficientNet for enhanced feature extraction and improved performance.

# 6 Conclusion

We subjected the one-stage object detection architectures YOLOv8, SSD, and RN to fine-tuning with our own vehicle dataset to analyze their performance in vehicle detection and counting. We used makesense.ai for image labeling and Google Colab for architecture retraining. SSD300 was complemented with MobileNet, achieving a mAP of around 83% but at 45 frames per second and presenting a higher relative error. RetinaNet was used with ResNet-50, obtaining a mAP of approximately 87% at 22 frames per second. However, since this problem is directly proportional to frame rate for real-time detection, YOLOv8 can sacrifice some mAP (around 79%) for its detection speed of 60 frames per second. Additionally, YOLOv8 benefits from a large support community and significantly easier implementation, making it the best alternative for this purpose.

In conclusion, we consider that the question transforms from simply selecting a categorical architecture to finding the best combination of algorithms and models that enhance the performance of this task. Furthermore, this work did not delve into the hardware aspect of the solution, which could be considered in future research.

# References

1. Roberts, L.G.: Machine perception of three-dimensional solids. In: Outstanding Dissertations in the Computer Sciences (1963). http://hdl.handle.net/1721.1/11589. Accessed 04 June 2023
2. Papert, S.A.: The Summer Vision Project, Massachusetts, July 1966. http://hdl.handle.net/1721.1/6125. Accessed 04 June 2023
3. Sze, V., Chen, Y.-H., Emer, J., Suleiman, A., Zhang, Z.: Hardware for Machine Learning: Challenges and Opportunities (2017)
4. Fukushima, K.: Neocognitron: a self-organizing neural network model for a mechanism of pattern recognition unaffected by shift in position. Biol. Cybern. **36**(4), 193–202 (1980). https://doi.org/10.1007/BF00344251
5. Zou, Z., Shi, Z., Guo, Y., Ye, J.: Object Detection in 20 Years: A Survey. CoRR, vol. abs/1905.05055 (2019): http://arxiv.org/abs/1905.05055
6. Zhang, H., Cloutier, R.: Review on one-stage object detection based on deep learning. EAI Endorsed Trans. e-Learn. **7**, 174181 (2022). https://doi.org/10.4108/eai.9-6-2022.174181
7. Dodge, J., Ilharco, G., Schwartz, R., Farhadi, A., Hajishirzi, H., Smith, N.: Fine-Tuning Pretrained Language Models: Weight Initializations, Data Orders, and Early Stopping (2020). https://github.com/huggingface/. Accessed 04 June 2023
8. Williams, R.I., Clark, L.A., Clark, W.R., Raffo, D.M.: Re-examining systematic literature review in management research: additional benefits and execution protocols. Eur. Manag. J. **39**(4), 521–533 (2021). https://doi.org/10.1016/J.EMJ.2020.09.007
9. Benjdira, B., Khursheed, T., Koubaa, A., Ammar, A., Ouni, K.: Car Detection using Unmanned Aerial Vehicles: Comparison between Faster R-CNN and YOLOv3 (2018)
10. Lin, C.-J., Jeng, S.-Y., Lioa, H.-W.: A Real-Time Vehicle Counting, Speed Estimation, and Classification System Based on Virtual Detection Zone and YOLO (2021). https://doi.org/10.1155/2021/1577614
11. Zaghari, N., Fathy, M., Jameii, S.M., Shahverdy, M.: The improvement in obstacle detection in autonomous vehicles using YOLO non-maximum suppression fuzzy algorithm. J. Supercomput. **77**(11), 13421–13446 (2021). https://doi.org/10.1007/s11227-021-03813-5
12. Voulodimos, A., Doulamis, N., Doulamis, A., Protopapadakis, E.:: Deep Learning for Computer Vision: A Brief Review (2018). https://doi.org/10.1155/2018/7068349

13. Tan, L., Huangfu, T., Wu, L., Chen, W.: Comparison of RetinaNet, SSD, and YOLO v3 for real-time pill identification. BMC Med. Inform. Decis. Mak. **21**(1), 324 (2021). https://doi.org/10.1186/s12911-021-01691-8
14. Almeida, J., Guamán, S., Yoo, S.G.: Vechicle counting system in urban areas: a practical case. In: 2022 IEEE 7th International conference for Convergence in Technology (I2CT), 2022, pp. 1–6 (2022). https://doi.org/10.1109/I2CT54291.2022.9823982
15. Altrichter, H., Kemmis, S., McTaggart, R., Zuber-Skerritt, O.: The concept of action research. Learn. Organ. **9**(3), 125–131 (2002). https://doi.org/10.1108/09696470210428840
16. Zhao, Z.-Q., Zheng, P., Xu, S.-T., Wu, X.: Object detection with deep learning: a review. IEEE Trans. Neural Netw. Learn. Syst. **30**(11), 3212–3232 (2019). https://doi.org/10.1109/TNNLS.2018.2876865
17. Bhatt, D., et al.: Electronics CNN Variants for Computer Vision: History, Architecture, Application, Challenges and Future Scope (2021). https://doi.org/10.3390/electronics1020 2470
18. Liu, W., et al.: SSD: Single Shot MultiBox Detector, CoRR, vol. abs/1512.02325 (2015). http://arxiv.org/abs/1512.02325
19. Cheng, C.: Real-time mask detection based on SSD-MobileNetV2. In: 2022 IEEE 5th International Conference on Automation, Electronics and Electrical Engineering (AUTEEE), 2022, pp. 761–767 (2022). https://doi.org/10.1109/AUTEEE56487.2022.9994442
20. Howard, A.G., et al.: MobileNets: Efficient Convolutional Neural Networks for Mobile Vision Applications, CoRR, vol. abs/1704.04861 (2017). http://arxiv.org/abs/1704.04861
21. Lin, T.-Y., Dollár, P., Girshick, R.B., He, K., Hariharan, B., Belongie, S.J.: Feature Pyramid Networks for Object Detection, CoRR, vol. abs/1612.03144 (2016). http://arxiv.org/abs/1612.03144
22. He, K., Zhang, X., Ren, S., Sun, J.: Spatial Pyramid Pooling in Deep Convolutional Networks for Visual Recognition, CoRR, vol. abs/1406.4729 (2014). http://arxiv.org/abs/1406.4729
23. Terven, J.R., Cordova-Esparaza, D.M.: A comprehensive review of yolo: from YOLOV1 and beyond under review in ACM computing surveys (2023)
24. Redmon, J., Farhadi, A.: YOLO9000: better, faster, stronger (2016). http://pjreddie.com/yolo9000/. Accessed 04 June 2023
25. Redmon, J., Farhadi, A.: YOLOv3: An Incremental Improvement (2018). https://pjreddie.com/yolo/. Accessed 04 June 2023
26. Lin, T.-Y., Goyal, P., Girshick, R., He, K., Dollár, P.: Focal Loss for Dense Object Detection (2018)
27. Zhang, L., et al.: Vehicle object detection based on improved RetinaNet. J. Phys. Conf. Ser. **1757**(1), 12070 (2021). https://doi.org/10.1088/1742-6596/1757/1/012070
28. Wightman, R., Touvron, H., Jégou, H.: ResNet strikes back: an improved training procedure in timm (2021)
29. Chhabra, S., Singh, A.K.: A comprehensive vision on cloud computing environment: emerging challenges and future research directions a preprint (2022)
30. Rajani, V., Garg, D.: Types for Information Flow Control: Labeling Granularity and Semantic Models (2018)
31. Padilla, R., Netto, S.L., da Silva, E.A.B.: A survey on performance metrics for object-detection algorithms. In: 2020 International Conference on Systems, Signals and Image Processing (IWSSIP), 2020, pp. 237–242 (2020). https://doi.org/10.1109/IWSSIP48289.2020.9145130

# Tumor Kidney Segmentation from CT Images Using Residual U-Net Architecture

Alejandro Delgado[1] , Carlos Quinteros[2] , Fernando Villalba Meneses[1] ,
Andrés Tirado-Espín[2] , Carolina Cadena-Morejón[2] , Jonathan Cruz-Varela[1] ,
and Diego Almeida-Galárraga[1(✉)]

[1] School of Biological Sciences and Engineering, Yachay Tech University, Hacienda San José
s/n, San Miguel de Urcuquí 100119, Ecuador
dalmeida@yachaytech.edu.ec
[2] School of Mathematical and Computational Sciences, Yachay Tech University, Hacienda San
José s/n, San Miguel de Urcuquí 100119, Ecuador

**Abstract.** Kidney cancer is a highly heterogeneous disease, with renal cell carcinoma being the most prevalent and severe form. Diagnosis typically involves analyzing computerized tomography (CT) scans, and Deep Learning technology has shown great potential for automating medical imaging classification and segmentation. This technology can greatly assist physicians in early tumor detection and localization, as well as determining its size and type, allowing for more timely treatment planning. In this study, we present a segmentation-trained model that was developed using a dataset of 300 patients. The dataset underwent preprocessing, normalization, and data augmentation techniques to increase variance. The proposed method utilized a convolutional neural network with a residual U-Net model, incorporating 3D convolutional blocks architecture for four-class segmentation. We achieved an average Dice coefficient of 68% through cross-validation of the trained model, we achieved significant efficiency using less epochs by getting better results than other models, that translate in reduction of computational cost of approximately 55% compared to similar model. Our findings suggest that the proposed method may improve the accuracy and efficiency of kidney cancer diagnosis, providing physicians with a valuable tool for early detection and treatment planning. This study highlights the potential of Deep Learning technology in medical imaging applications and contributes to the growing body of research in this field.

**Keywords:** Kidney Segmentation · Convolutional Neural Networks · Kidney cancer · Computer Tomography

## 1 Introduction

Advances in medical imaging and artificial intelligence have enabled the creation of technology that enhances the accuracy and efficiency of tumor segmentation. The precise segmentation of kidney tumors from medical images, such as computed tomography (CT) scans, plays a pivotal role in early detection, diagnosis, and treatment planning.

J. Maldonado-Mahauad et al. (Eds.): TICEC 2023, CCIS 1885, pp. 263–276, 2023.
https://doi.org/10.1007/978-3-031-45438-7_18

In this context, the significance of kidney tumor segmentation becomes evident when considering its impact on global and regional health, particularly in developing countries like Ecuador. This research aligns with the broader goal of improving patient outcomes by enabling healthcare providers to intervene at the right time with tailored treatments. By addressing the challenges associated with kidney tumor segmentation, including issues of anatomical complexity, image quality, and data variability, this research contributes directly to both global and regional healthcare objectives.

In the subsequent sections, our study presents the risk associated with not detecting the cancer at time; moreover, prognosis for patient depending on the stage of the tumor which are determinant factors for planning treatment. Furthermore, the methodology employed for kidney tumor segmentation, showcasing how cutting-edge techniques such as data augmentation and deep learning are harnessed to enhance the accuracy and reliability of segmentation outcomes. Through this exploration, we aim to underscore the critical role of advanced image analysis techniques. This research aligns with the broader goal of improving patient outcomes by enabling healthcare providers to intervene at the right time with tailored treatments.

## 1.1 Renal Tumor

Kidney cancer is a common urologic malignancy which depending on the stage of the cancer can be approached with partial or radical nephrectomy, as seen in Table 1, as therapeutic options for localized tumors. In 2022 there were an estimation of 79,000 new cases of kidney cancer attributed to renal cell carcinoma (RCC) in the US [1]. Moreover, following surgical intervention for localized renal cell carcinoma (RCC), it has been observed that around 20 to 30% of patients may experience a recurrence of the disease. Various contemporary studies have reported a range of 5-year disease-free survival rates, spanning from 91% to 51% [2]. In other words, it is crucial to detect malignancy in early stages where the cancer has not spread out from the kidney or to distant part of the body [2, 3], because the probability of 5 years survival increases.

These vital organs serve the crucial purpose of eliminating surplus water, salt, and waste from the bloodstream by converting these substances into urine [4]. Similar to other bodily organs, the kidneys consist of cellular tissue, rendering them susceptible to the development of renal tumors, commonly known as kidney cancer. Renal tumors rank among the top ten most prevalent types of cancer afflicting both men and women [5]. The origin of renal tumors can be traced to uncontrolled growth of body cells, specifically within the kidneys. The predominant form of kidney cancer is RCC [6]. Epidemiologically, it is noteworthy that renal cell carcinoma is the most frequently occurring solid tumor in the kidneys, accounting for approximately 90% of cases, with a male-to-female frequency ratio of 2:1 [7].

## 1.2 Risk Factors, Symptoms Stages and Prognosis

The likelihood of developing kidney cancer can be influenced by various risk factors. Among these factors, smoking and individuals that presents obesity have a heightened risk in increasing the developing of RCC, which stands as the most prevalent form of kidney cancer [8, 9]. Furthermore, the presence of high blood pressure has been associated with an increased risk of kidney cancer. Hereditary types might influence the cancer with von Hippel-Lindau disease being the most common which helps to proliferate RCC elevating the chance of developing this type of cancer [8–10].

Certain workplace exposures, such as contact with substances like trichloroethylene, have been linked to an increased risk of RCC [8, 11]. Those with advanced kidney disease, particularly those who require dialysis, are also at a higher risk of developing RCC [8]. Furthermore, specific rare inherited conditions can further raise an individual's risk of kidney cancer [1]. It is important to note that the presence of one or more risk factors does not guarantee the development of kidney cancer, and it is possible for individuals with few or no known risk factors to still develop the disease. In the initial phases of renal cancer, symptoms and indications may not manifest, but larger tumors can sometimes give rise to noticeable signs RCC commonly spreads include the lungs, lymph nodes, bones, liver, adrenal gland, and brain [9]. Potential indications and symptoms of kidney cancer encompass the presence of blood in the urine, persistent pain in the back or sides of the body, diminished appetite, unexplained weight loss, persistent fatigue, fever, and night sweat [12].

The staging system for kidney cancer is crucial in assessing the extent and progression of the disease. Table 1 outlines the various stages based on tumor size and invasion characteristics. In Stage I, tumors are classified as pT1a if their size is equal to or less than 4 cm, or as pT1b if they measure between 4 to 7 cm [13, 14]. Stage II encompasses pT2a tumors ranging from 7 cm to 10 cm, limited to the kidney, and pT2b tumors larger than 10 cm but confined to the kidney. Moving to Stage III, pT3a signifies cancer invasion into the renal vein, its branches, perirenal fat, and renal sinus. On the other hand, pT3b denotes an extension of the cancer to the vena cava, both below and above the diaphragm [13]. Finally, Stage IV is characterized by pT4 tumors that have surpassed the Gerota fascia, including an extension to the adrenal gland [12–14]. This classification system offers valuable insights into tumor growth and spread, aiding in the comprehensive evaluation and management of kidney cancer.

**Table 1.** Kidney Cancer Staging Based on Tumor Size and Extent of Invasion. This table shows the different stages of kidney cancer based on the size and extent of invasion of the tumor (pT: primary tumor).

| Stage | Group stage | Description | References |
|-------|-------------|-------------|------------|
| I | pT1a | Tumor size is less than or equal to 4 cm | [12–14] |
| | pT1b | Tumor size is between 4 to 7 cm | [12–14] |
| II | pT2a | Tumor size is between 7 cm and 10 cm limited to the kidney | [12–14] |
| | pT2b | Tumor size is larger than 10 cm limited to the kidney | [12–14] |
| III | pT3a | Cancer invades renal vein and branches; perirenal fat, renal sinus | [12–14] |
| | pT3b | Extend to vena cava below and above the diaphram | [12–14] |
| IV | pT4 | Invades beyond Gerota fascia, including extension to adrenal gland | [12–14] |

The presented Table 2 outlines the different stages of kidney cancer, along with their corresponding group stage, prognosis, and primary treatment option. In Stage I, which includes pT1a and pT1b, the cancer is localized without lymph node or distant metastasis (N0 M0). The primary treatment options in this stage involve either partial or radical nephrectomy, which may also include ablative techniques for certain cases. Moving to Stage II, encompassing pT2a and pT2b, the cancer remains localized without lymph node or distant metastasis (N0 M0). The recommended primary treatment options at this stage involve either radical or partial nephrectomy [13, 14].

Furthermore, has been describe by Motzer et al. (2017) Stage III comprises pT3a and pT3b, where the cancer has extended further within the kidney and potentially involved nearby lymph nodes (N1 M0). The primary treatment options for Stage III kidney cancer are radical or partial nephrectomy, aimed at removing the cancerous tissue and addressing any affected lymph nodes. Finally, Stage IV, represented by pT4, indicates advanced kidney cancer with local invasion beyond the kidney and potential lymph node or distant metastasis (N M1). The primary treatment for Stage IV kidney cancer is more complex, as it may involve potentially surgical options if the tumor is resectable or unresectable if it cannot be completely removed [13, 14].

**Table 2.** Staging, Prognosis, and Primary Treatment Options for Kidney Cancer where N0: No regional lymph node involvement; M0: No distant metastasis; N1: Regional lymph node involvement; M1: Distant metastasis.

| Stage | Group stage | Prognosis | Primary Treatment | References |
|-------|-------------|-----------|-------------------|------------|
| I | pT1a | N0 M0 | Partial or radical nephrectomy or ablative techniques | [2, 13] |
| | pT1b | N0 M0 | Partial or radical nephrectomy | [2, 13] |
| II | pT2a | N0 M0 | Radical or partial nephrectomy | [2, 13] |
| | pT2b | N0 M0 | Radical or partial nephrectomy | [2, 13] |
| III | pT3a | N1 M0 | Radical or partial nephrectomy | [2, 13] |
| | pT3b | N1 M0 | Radical or partial nephrectomy | [2, 13] |
| IV | pT4 | N M1 | Potentially surgically or unresectable | [2, 13] |

## 1.3 Residual U-Net Convolutional Neural Network for Segmentation

CT scans are used between the steps of diagnosis and staging. Accurate Computed Tomography (CT) image segmentation of kidney and renal mass will help provide quantitative information for the diagnosis, treatment, and surgical planning [15, 16]. But, manually identifying tumors from CT scans is a tedious and time-consuming process. In some cases, the boundaries of lesions can also be unclear in CT scan images and the images can also have poor contrast and structure definition. For these problems, machine vision-based deep learning methods have been developed, with which lesions can be segmented or classified. Among the methods developed is U-Net which can be modified for 3D convolutions and with residual units, as proposed in [17, 18].

This study uses residual U-Net, an innovative neural network architecture, combines the strengths of residual learning and U-Net, demonstrating exceptional efficacy in image segmentation tasks. Its successful application extends to various domains, particularly in the realm of medical image segmentation [19]. By harnessing the potential of U-Net, residual networks, and recurrent convolutional neural networks, Residual U-Net offers several notable advantages for segmentation tasks. Firstly, the integration of a residual unit proves invaluable in effectively training deep architectures. This facilitates the optimization of complex models, ensuring efficient learning and improved performance. Secondly, the incorporation of feature accumulation through recurrent residual convolutional layers enhances the representation of critical features, enabling more accurate and precise segmentation. This aspect is particularly vital for the challenging intricacies of medical image segmentation. Lastly, Residual U-Net empowers the creation of enhanced U-Net architectures without increasing the number of network parameters, resulting in superior performance in medical image segmentation while maintaining computational efficiency [19–21].

In this study, we proposed a method of kidney tumor segmentation in CT images, where we use architecture which residual U-net architecture. The following sections describe in detail the data methods and some parameter variations for a learning residual U-Net model used in our research. The development and refinement of these systems also benefit from the increasing number of people using them in other to prevent the pathology [22–24].

## 2   Materials and Methods

This section presents the proposed method of kidney tumor segmentation in CT images. The first section introduces the obtaining of data from the KiTS19 database to carry out the segmentation [25]. For this purpose, different methodologies are used to obtain, process and train the datasets. Techniques for feature extraction were considered, the methodologies will focus on the combination of these techniques and the number of features that are extracted [26, 27]. The second section presents the steps of kidney tumor segmentation, namely, the data preprocessing to underline the texture aspects present in the images, data augmentations, and finally, the segmentations obtained from CNN, residual U-Net. Figure 1 illustrates the steps of the proposed method. We will explain each piece in detail next.

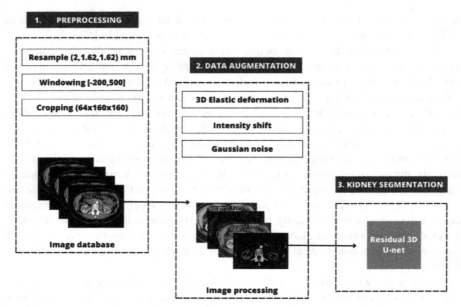

**Fig. 1.** Overview of the Methodology which consists of three key steps. **Preprocessing:** The initial step involves resampling, windowing, and cropping of the input data to enhance and facilitate subsequent processing. **Data Augmentation:** In the second step, data augmentation techniques are employed to enhance the diversity of the dataset. This aids in training a robust and accurate segmentation model. **Segmentation:** The final step focuses on training a residual U-Net architecture. This deep learning model is specifically designed for segmentation tasks, enabling precise identification and delineation of kidney tumors in medical images.

## 2.1   Image Acquisition

This research uses the CT images from the official challenge called KiTS21. Which main goal is to accelerate the process of research and development of new methods for prognosis and treatment planning for kidney tumors [25]. The database was collected by the University of Minnesota Medical Center between 2010 and 2018, and a collaboration of other institutions such as Charleton college, and the University of North Dakota. Mainly consist of CT images of 300 patients who went to partial or radical nephrectomy for one or more kidney tumors. Moreover, semantic segmentation masks (annotations) were provided we have used the "aggregated\_AND" base final mask to train our model. Further, manual segmentations were provided by medical students under the supervision of a surgical pathological expert to characterize the precise location of the tumors and the exclusion of cysts.

The CT scans images and masks are provided in NIfTI (Neuroimaging Informatics Technology Initiative) format which is commonly used to store CT scans as 3D volume slices with voxel size information and other metadata. The images are grayscale images with a Hounsfield Unit (HU) with a resolution of $512 \times 512$ and the number of slices per image range between 29 to 1059. The data were split in a 70:20:10 ratio for training, validation, and testing respectively. The proposed method will segment the images to obtain four classes that represent the background, kidney, tumor, and cyst.

As depicted in Fig. 2, we are presented with a compelling example of a CT scan slice obtained from a kidney cancer patient. The image provides a clear representation of the raw grayscale data, enabling a comprehensive examination of the affected region. Furthermore, the segmentation process, conducted manually by expert professionals, plays a crucial role in both validating and training our model. This meticulous and necessary step ensures the accuracy and reliability of the segmentation results, forming the foundation for the development and refinement of our advanced computational approach.

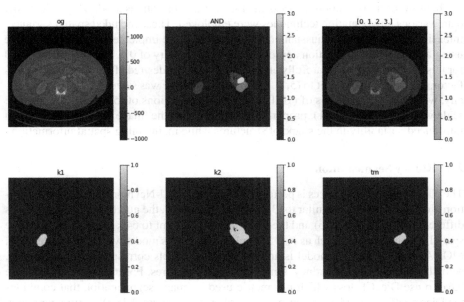

**Fig. 2.** Image taken from the dataset of one slice CT scan of a patient that presents tumor. (og: grayscale CT scans; AND: base final mask for training; k1: right kidney manual segmentate; k2: left kidney manual segmentate; tm: tumor manual segmentate)

## 2.2 Pre-processing

The CT images extracted from the database undergo an initial pre-processing stage that comprises three distinct steps. The first step, given the varying number of slices in each volume, some of which can be high and consume too many resources, involves resampling the data to a uniform voxel spacing of $2 \times 1.62 \times 1.62 \times 1.62$ mm. This ensures consistency in the z-axis, which is crucial for improving the generalization of the model by increasing the number of trained slices per patient [28, 29].

In the second step, to extract the most relevant spatial information and retain only essential anatomical structures, the images underwent a frame cropping process. Specifically, the foreground of each image was divided into contiguous chunks with dimensions of $64 \times 160 \times 160$. In the second step, we truncated the volume intensity values to remove irrelevant details such as air, bone, and fat for the range of $[-200,500]$ HU followed by a rescaling between 0 and 1 for all images. In order to optimize training performance and mitigate the risk of memory bottlenecks, we implemented an innovative approach by employing the Nvidia Clara SmartCache Dataset Loader. Specifically, we set the cache rate to 0.4 and the replace rate to 0.5, which optimizes the caching of training data and minimizes CPU memory usage. By following this approach, we can ensure that sufficient training data is available in the cached memory during training while maintaining an efficient replacement of 50% of the cached data at each epoch. This methodology effectively enhances the training process, promoting stable and consistent performance.

In the third step of our pre-processing, further transformations to add variability of the data, various augmentation techniques were employed. These included spatial variance, intensity variations, and Gaussian noise. Specifically, we implemented spatial variance using a 3D elastic deformation approach with a probability of 0.5. The parameters used for this deformation were carefully chosen to achieve the desired effect. The smoothness factor, denoted by $\sigma$, was set to $(5,8)$, while the magnitude was set to $(50,150)$. Additionally, we applied translations of $(10,10,5)$ pixels and rotations of $(5,5,180)$ degrees. The scale was set to $(0.1,0.1,0.1)$, proportional to the size of the image. This transformation introduced variability in the shape of structures while maintaining spatial information.

## 2.3  Kidney Segmentation

The classification of the slices is performed by a residual U-Net model with 3D Convolution blocks, the model is similar to [30], on the other hand, the number of feature maps is different $(16,32,64,125,256)$ and the patch size is different to $64 \times 160 \times 160$ to increase spatial information per patch as in [31] implemented. This model was implemented with MONAI framework, the model is an output of 4 channels corresponding to 4 classes, actually the background, kidney, tumor, and cyst structures. For training the model we have to use DiceCE loss which is a metric used in image segmentation that combines the Dice coefficient and cross-entropy loss. Moreover, we use AdamW optimizer which is a variant of Adam that improves weight decay regularization with a learning rate of $10e-5$.

This model was trained for 120 epochs on Google Colab servers with GPU 15 GB of RAM, leveraging the processing power of a GPU. To ensure the quality of the model, a mean dice score was employed as a validation metric at the end of each epoch. For the inference procedure, the model was trained on a $64 \times 160 \times 160$-sized chunk of the input volume and sliding window inference with an overlap of 0.8 was utilized to enhance the segmentation results. Although this technique incurred additional inference time, it led to a superior segmentation performance. The resulting 4-channeled output was then collapsed into a single channel using the maximum probability of segmented classes. Lastly, to maintain the original voxel spacing of the input volume, an inverse transform was employed.

## 3   Results and Discussion

This section shows the main results obtained from the experiments performed to validate our approach. First of all, we presented the results and discuss the segmentation from the testing dataset, later we show the metrics used for the performance validation. To illustrate the performance of our model, in Fig. 2 is shown a case of study from slice 115 the segmentation performed for each 4-output channel which show the predicted image and the true label, this visualization allows to see how well the model performed. Moreover, a visual comparison can be observed between the segmentation obtained by the proposed model and the actual segmentation. There is similarity between each graph, but there is always a notable difference, which is expected given the values shown in Table 4 with the approximation measures obtained by the proposed model. It should be noted that channel 1 is for background, channel 2 is for kidney segmentation, channel 3 is for kidney tumor segmentation, and finally, Cys, in the last channel, is where the most difference can be observed, which is corroborated by the values in Table 3, (Fig. 3).

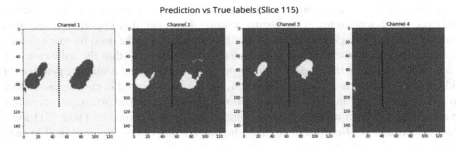

**Fig. 3.** Segmented images from a testing dataset show the predicted (left) and the true label (right) segmentation for each of four classes, background, kidney, tumor, cyst segmentations.

Moreover, we can have an idea about the performance in computational cost, when comparing our model with the one proposed in [31] on the testing data, we find that our average Dice coefficient (0.674) is not significantly distant from the result (0.757) obtained by [31]. Now, assuming that the relationship between the number of epochs and the average F1-score is linear, and we calculate the epochs (267) needed to achieve our result for comparison with the 120 epochs we conducted, it becomes clear that the computational cost is lower. This results in a reduction in computational cost of approximately 55%.

Furthermore, the following tables are shown that compare the results obtained with our model based on residual U-Net for training and validation. Our model was trained for 120 epochs, while the model used for comparison was trained for 300 epochs. Furthermore, results in Table 3 show the mean average sample Dice coefficient for all classes on the validation and testing dataset, with our approach, and with residual U-Net as [31] it should be noted that the testing value for the Residual U-Net model is not available. As can be seen in Table 3, it is clear that better results are obtained with the proposed model.

**Table 3.** Comparative results of Dice coefficient from the final kidney segmentation for validation and testing dataset.

| Dataset | Our approach | Residual U-net |
|---------|--------------|----------------|
| Validation | 0.683 | 0.543 |
| Testing | 0.674 | – |

Additionally, Table 3 summarizes the results for each class segmentation on the testing dataset with our approach compare with the residual U-net from [31], and when comparing the segmentation of each individual element in Table 4, the only value where the proposed model is inferior is Cys. Therefore, it can be inferred that the proposed model does not work properly for the segmentation of that class, probably due to a lack of Cyst images because this structure is tiny with respect to a tumor.

As we can observe from Table 4, the final Kidney segmentation yields a remarkable Dice coefficient with a precision level of 0.93. This outcome is expected, possibly due to the fact that the structures analyzed in this case are larger in comparison to the tumor and cyst, which tend to lower the accuracy value. However, it is important to mention that there could be various factors contributing to this, such as the need for more epochs or improvements in the network parameters, among others, within the dataset of CT scans analyzed during the model's training process. The obtained results are positive for kidney segmentation and tumors, while deficiencies are observed in cyst segmentation. At this point, we will analyze the computational cost and achieved precision percentage in comparison to other models. We will compare the computational cost with [31] and a classical Residual U-Net model, emphasizing the number of epochs performed in each model and on the validation dataset, rather than the training dataset.

Furthermore, as illustrated in Table 4 we obtained a Dice coefficient value of 0.69, as observed in the table (table with obtained values), which is lower than other results achieved by models solely focused on renal tumor segmentation. In this particular subsection, tumor size classification was not performed, hence the anticipated outcome obtained. The obtained value for the Dice coefficient is not as expected when compared to previously obtained results. With a value of 0.39, it is evident that our model encounters difficulties in performing the segmentation. Upon observing the Table 4, it is evident that our model encounters challenges in cyst segmentation, but demonstrates higher precision in tumor cases, even with fewer than half the epochs used by other models. If we disregard the cyst situation, the average obtained by our model surpasses that of the other models. Therefore, appropriate treatment of the dataset and proper parameter variation in the models yield better results with lower computational cost.

Now, we will solely focus on the Dice coefficient precision of segmentation when comparing with other models. As seen in the table, some models solely focus on kidney and tumor segmentation and do not perform cyst segmentation. It should be noted that, in the case of tumors, the majority of models perform size classification to enhance precision, which is clearly observable in the table. The Enhanced UNET model, trained for 300 epochs, obtains promising results with a Dice coefficient of 0.952 for kidney segmentation, 0.665 for tumor segmentation, and 0.656 for cyst segmentation, yielding a mean Dice coefficient of 0.757. This model is referenced as [31].

Another model, 2D_PSPNET, demonstrates a Dice coefficient of 0.902 for kidney segmentation, 0.638 for tumor segmentation, and a mean Dice coefficient of 0.770. However, no information is available for cyst segmentation [33]. The 3D_NET model achieves a Dice coefficient of 0.927 for kidney segmentation, 0.751 for tumor segmentation, and a mean Dice coefficient of 0.839. Similarly, the 3D_FCN_PPM model records a Dice coefficient of 0.931 for kidney segmentation, 0.802 for tumor segmentation, and a mean Dice coefficient of 0.866 [32, 34]. Lastly, the Residual UNET model, trained for 300 epochs, exhibits a Dice coefficient of 0.900 for kidney segmentation, 0.456 for tumor segmentation, and 0.273 for cyst segmentation. The mean Dice coefficient for this model is 0.543 [31]. In summary, Table 4 showcases the performance of various models in kidney, tumor, and cyst segmentation, providing valuable insights for future research and development in the field.

**Table 4.** Comparative results of Dice coefficient from final Kidney segmentation for each class and mean for the testing data set.

| Model | Epochs | Kidney | Tumor | Cys | Mean | Reference |
|-------|--------|--------|-------|-----|------|-----------|
| Our approach | 120 | 0.935 | 0.696 | 0.392 | 0.674 | – |
| Enhanced UNET | 300 | 0.952 | 0.665 | 0.656 | 0.757 | [31] |
| 2D_PSPNET | – | 0.902 | 0.638 | – | 0.770 | [33] |
| 3D_NET | – | 0.927 | 0.751 | – | 0.839 | [34] |
| 3D_FCN_PPM | – | 0.931 | 0.802 | – | 0.866 | [32] |
| Residual Unet | 300 | 0.900 | 0.456 | 0.273 | 0.543 | [31] |

## 4   Conclusion

In this article, we proposed a model for kidney tumor segmentation through the implementation of a pre-processing stage which includes normalization and data augmentation techniques, and a Residual 3D U-net for the segmentation procedure. Our model achieved a high accuracy dice coefficient of 93.5% in identifying kidney-related features, reflecting its robust learning capabilities. Moreover, with an accuracy dice coefficient of 69.6% in detecting tumors. While accuracy dice coefficient for cysts is 39.2%, indicating some potential for refinement in capturing all instances, the overall mean performance of 67.4%.

Further, we were able to enhance the model's efficiency by training the network with 120 epochs, as opposed to others that have reported using up to 300 epochs, in other words we improve computational cost by a reduction of approximately 55%. Our findings demonstrate that proper pre-processing of the dataset and thorough parameter tuning is critical in achieving more accurate segmentation results.

Our approach has demonstrated promising results, but there is still room for improvement. Certainly, the obtained result is not very favorable in segmenting all elements, but this is due to the limitations faced during the development of this work, in terms of computational resources. This is because there were constraints when training our models as the demand for GPU memory exceeded the available capacity. For instance, if we were to acquire more GPU memory, we could increase the number of epochs in the training of the neural network and increase the batch size, which could potentially enhance the results presented in this article.

# References

1. Kidney tumor - malignant tumors - staging. https://www.pathologyoutlines.com/topic/kidney tumormalignantstaging.html
2. Renal cancer (2022). https://www.mayoclinic.org/es-es/diseases-conditions/kidney-cancer/symptoms-causes/syc-20352664
3. Aguiar Salazar, E.D., Alcivar Carmigniani, A.S., Aldaz Luna, B.P., Clavijo Calderón, D.F., Echeverría Ortíz, P.P., Madrid Pérez, M.A., Villalba-Meneses, G.F., Almeida-Galárraga, D.: Design of a glove controlled by electromyographic signals for the rehabilitation of patients with rheumatoid arthritis. In: Rodriguez Morales, G., Fonseca C., E.R., Salgado, J.P., Pérez-Gosende, P., Orellana Cordero, M., Berrezueta, S. (eds.) TICEC 2020. CCIS, vol. 1307, pp. 3–11. Springer, Cham (2020). https://doi.org/10.1007/978-3-030-62833-8_1
4. Lhotska, L., Sukupova, L., Lacković, I., Ibbott, G.S. (eds.): World Congress on Medical Physics and Biomedical Engineering 2018. IP, vol. 68/3. Springer, Singapore (2019). https://doi.org/10.1007/978-981-10-9023-3
5. Almeida-Galárraga, D., et al.: Glaucoma detection through digital processing from fundus images using matlab. In: 2021 Second International Conference on Information Systems and Software Technologies (ICI2ST), pp. 39–45 (2021). https://doi.org/10.1109/ICI2ST51859.2021.00014
6. Alom, M.Z., Hasan, M., Yakopcic, C., Taha, T.M., Asari, V.K.: Recurrent residual convolutional neural network based on U-Net (R2U-Net) for medical image segmentation. arXiv preprint arXiv:1802.06955 (2018)
7. Alom, M.Z., Yakopcic, C., Hasan, M., Taha, T.M., Asari, V.K.: Recurrent residual u-net for medical image segmentation. J. Med. Imaging 6(1), 014006 (2019). https://doi.org/10.1117/1.JMI.6.1.014006
8. Alvarado-Cando, O., Torres-Salamea, H., Almeida, D.A.: Uda-$\mu$biolab: Teaching microcontrollers with bioinstrumentation. In: Lhotska, L., Sukupova, L., Lacković, I., Ibbott, G.S. (eds.) World Congress on Medical Physics and Biomedical Engineering 2018. IP, vol. 68/1, pp. 877–880. Springer, Singapore (2019). https://doi.org/10.1007/978-981-10-9035-6_163
9. American Cancer Society: ¿Qué es el cáncer de riñón? [What is kidney cancer?] (nd)
10. Chow, W.H., Shuch, B., Linehan, W.M., Devesa, S.S.: Epidemiology and risk factors for kidney cancer. Nat. Rev. Urol. 15(9), 517–531 (2018). https://www.ncbi.nlm.nih.gov/pmc/articles/PMC6299342/
11. Choyke, P.L., Glenn, G.M., Walther, M.M., et al.: Hereditary renal cancers. Radiology 226(1), 33–46 (2003)
12. DeVita, V.T., Jr., Lawrence, T.S., Rosenberg, S.A.: Cancer: Principles & Practice of Oncology, 8th edn. Lippincott Williams & Wilkins, Philadelphia, PA (2008)
13. Eggener, S., et al.: Renal tumors in young adults. J. Urol. 171(1), 106–110 (2004)

14. Gohil, S., Lad, A.: Kidney and kidney tumor segmentation using spatial and channel attention enhanced U-Net. In: Heller, N., Isensee, F., Trofimova, D., Tejpaul, R., Papanikolopoulos, N., Weight, C. (eds.) KiTS 2021. LNCS, vol. 13168, pp. 151–157. Springer, Cham (2022). https://doi.org/10.1007/978-3-030-98385-7_20

15. Gonzalez, R.C.: Digital image processing. Pearson education India (2009)

16. Havaei, M., et al.: Brain tumor segmentation with deep neural networks. Med. Image Anal. **35**, 18–31 (2017)

17. Heller, N., et al.: The kits19 challenge data: 300 kidney tumor cases with clinical context, CT semantic segmentations, and surgical outcomes (2019). https://doi.org/10.48550/ARXIV. 1904.00445, https://arxiv.org/abs/1904.00445

18. Isensee, F., Maier-Hein, K.H.: An attempt at beating the 3d U-Net (2019). https://doi.org/10. 48550/ARXIV.1908.02182, https://arxiv.org/abs/1908.02182

19. Kerfoot, E., Clough, J., Oksuz, I., Lee, J., King, A.P., Schnabel, J.A.: Left-ventricle quantification using residual U-Net. In: Pop, M., Sermesant, M., Zhao, J., Li, S., McLeod, K., Young, A., Rhode, K., Mansi, T. (eds.) STACOM 2018. LNCS, vol. 11395, pp. 371–380. Springer, Cham (2019). https://doi.org/10.1007/978-3-030-12029-0_40

20. Kutikov, A., Uzzo, R.G.: The renal nephrometry score: a comprehensive standardized system for quantitating renal tumor size, location and depth. J. Urol. **182**(3), 844–853 (2009)

21. Lin, Z., et al.: Automated segmentation of kidney and renal mass and automated detection of renal mass in ct urography using 3D U-Net-based deep convolutional neural network. Eur. Radiol. **31**, 5021–5031 (2021)

22. Mattila, K.E., et al.: A three-feature prediction model for metastasis-free survival after surgery of localized clear cell renal cell carcinoma. Sci. Rep. **11**(1), 8650 (2021)

23. Motzer, R.J., et al.: Kidney cancer, version 2.2017, NCCN clinical practice guidelines in oncology. J. Nat. Compr. Cancer Netw. **15**(6), 804–834 (2017). https://doi.org/10.6004/jnccn. 2017.0100

24. Pereira-Carrillo, J., Suntaxi-Dominguez, D., Guarnizo-Cabezas, O., Villalba-Meneses, Gandhi, Tirado-Espín, A., Almeida-Galárraga, D.: Comparison between two novel approaches in automatic breast cancer detection and diagnosis and its contribution in military defense. In: Rocha, Á., Fajardo-Toro, C.H., Rodríguez, J.M.R. (eds.) Developments and Advances in Defense and Security. SIST, vol. 255, pp. 189–201. Springer, Singapore (2022). https://doi.org/10.1007/978-981-16-4884-7_15

25. Ranjan, M., Shukla, A., Soni, K., Varma, S., Kuliha, M., Singh, U.: Cancer prediction using random forest and deep learning techniques, pp. 227–231 (2022)

26. Siegel, R.L., Miller, K.D., Fuchs, H.E., Jemal, A.: Cancer statistics, 2022. CA: Cancer J. Clin. **72**(1), 7–33 (2022)

27. Society, A.C.: Risk factors for kidney cancer (2022). https://www.cancer.org/cancer/types/kidney-cancer/causes-risks-prevention/risk-factors.html

28. Society, A.C.: Survival rates for kidney cancer (2022). https://www.cancer.org/cancer/types/kidney-cancer/detection-diagnosis-staging/survival-rates.html

29. Suquilanda-Pesantez, J., Aguiar Salazar, E., Almeida-Galarraga, D., Salum, G., Villalba-Meneses, F., Gomezjurado, M.G.: NIFtHool: an informatics program for identification of NifH proteins using deep neural networks [version 1; peer review: 2 approved]. F1000Research **11**(164) (2022). https://doi.org/10.12688/f1000research.107925.1

30. Vásquez-Ucho, P.A., Villalba-Meneses, G.F., Pila-Varela, K.O., Villalba-Meneses, C.P., Iglesias, I., Almeida-Galárraga, D.A.: Analysis and evaluation of the systems used for the assessment of the cervical spine function: a systematic review. J. Med. Eng. Technol. **45**(5), 380–393 (2021). https://doi.org/10.1080/03091902.2021.1907467

31. Yanchatuña, O.P., et al.: Skin lesion detection and classification using convolutional neural network for deep feature extraction and support vector machine. Int. J. Adv.

Sci. Eng. Inf. Technol. **11**(3), 1260–1267 (2021). https://doi.org/10.18517/ijaseit.11.3.13679, http://ijaseit.insightsociety.org/index.php?option=com_content&view=article&id=9&Itemid=1&article_id=13679

32. Yang, G., et al.: Automatic segmentation of kidney and renal tumor in CT images based on 3D fully convolutional neural network with pyramid pooling module. In: 2018 24th International Conference on Pattern Recognition (ICPR), pp. 3790–3795. IEEE (2018)
33. Zhang, Z., Liu, Q., Wang, Y.: Road extraction by deep residual U-Net. arXiv preprint arXiv:1711.10684 (2018)
34. Abdulkadir, A.Ö., Lienkamp, S., Brox, T., Ronneberger, O.: 3D U-Net: learning dense volumetric segmentation from sparse annotation. In: MICCAI, pp. 424–432 (2016)

# Classification of Alzheimer Disease's Severity Using Support Vector Machine and Deep Feature Extraction of Convolutional Neural Networks: A Contrasting of Methodologies

Israel Reyes Vázquez[1] , Francisco J. Cedeño[1] , Juana E. Loza[1] ,
Fernando Villalba Meneses[1] , Andrés Tirado-Espín[2] ,
Carolina Cadena-Morejón[2] , Omar Alvarado-Cando[3] ,
and Diego Almeida-Galárraga[1(✉)]

[1] School of Biological Sciences and Engineering, Yachay Tech University, Hacienda San José S/N, San Miguel de Urcuquí 100119, Ecuador
dalmeida@yachaytech.edu.ec
[2] School of Mathematical and Computational Sciences, Yachay Tech University, Hacienda San José S/N, San Miguel de Urcuquí 100119, Ecuador
[3] Universidad del Azuay, Cuenca 010107, Ecuador

**Abstract.** Alzheimer disease (AD) is a widely spread cell degenerative condition that induces cognitive abnormalities ranging from confusion and memory loss to inability to conduct daily activities at severe stages. The current landscape for treatment has been increasingly changing towards the application of novel and more accurate imaging processing techniques based on machine learning for AD detection at different stages, and mainly for preventive diagnosis at the verge of ambiguous interpretation of early progression. Hence, the purpose of this work is to compare the efficacy of a pre-trained Convolutional Neural Network (VGG-16) in the classification of AD severity based on a Feature Extraction approach for implementation to a machine learning system. The results may upscale the range of CNN applications as classification systems for recognition of the AD progression stages that could serve as a tool for automated-early diagnosis with increased accessibility and precision.

**Keywords:** Convolutional Neural Network · Alzheimer Disease · Feature Extraction · Transfer learning · Support Vector Machine

## 1 Introduction

### 1.1 Alzheimer's Disease

Alzheimer Disease (AD) is a neurodegenerative disorder that affects cognitive functions and is the most common cause of dementia worldwide, impacting over 50 million people, particularly the elderly [1, 2]. The disease's history dates back several centuries, but it

J. Maldonado-Mahauad et al. (Eds.): TICEC 2023, CCIS 1885, pp. 277–293, 2023.
https://doi.org/10.1007/978-3-031-45438-7_19

was in 1906 that Alois Alzheimer presented the case of Auguste Deter, a 51-year-old woman exhibiting symptoms such as memory loss, disorientation, hallucinations, and delusions. The discovery of neurofibrillary tangles and senile plaques distinguished Alzheimer's disease as a unique condition [3–5]. As of 2018, there were approximately 50 million cases of Alzheimer's globally, with 60% concentrated in low- and middle-income countries.

Mortality rates for the disease are high among individuals in their late 50s to early 70s, with an average life expectancy of 7–10 years [6, 7]. Extensive research has been conducted over the past century to find a cure for Alzheimer's, but to date, there is no definitive known cure. However, pharmacological treatments based on cognitive enhancers have been developed, offering temporary symptom improvement and control. Similarly as other neurodegenerative disorders, the early diagnosis of AD plays a crucial role in providing appropriate treatment and prolonging the patient's cerebral function, increasing life expectancy [8, 9].

### 1.2 Relevance of Alzheimer's Study in Low-Income Countries

Alzheimer's disease is a leading cause of disability and dependency among the elderly worldwide. Access to appropriate treatment is challenging, particularly in low-income countries where 60–65% of global Alzheimer's cases are found, mainly due to the high cost of treatments [10]. Over the past few decades, significant advancements have been made in Alzheimer's diagnostic methods, including neuropsychological testing, laboratory tests, neuroimaging techniques, and genetic markers [11]. Convolutional Neural Networks (CNNs) have been tested and shown to improve the detection of Alzheimer's, leading to reduced costs and increased diagnostic accuracy.

### 1.3 Application of Convolutional Neural Networks in Medicine

**Historical Context.** A Convolutional Neural Network (CNN) is a type of neural network used for image processing, based on the properties of Artificial Neural Networks (ANNs) [12]. ANN research has been ongoing since the mid-20th century, with pioneers such as McLouch, Pitts, and Rosenblatt introducing key concepts and models [12–14]. Despite initial discrediting and a decline in interest during the 1970s, research on ANNs continued and led to advancements such as perceptrons, back-propagation algorithms, and multilayered neural networks [15, 16].

The introduction of the term "convolution" in LeNet CNN marked a significant milestone in neural network applications [12]. Further developments, including layerwise pretraining and multi-hidden layer ANNs proposed by Krizhevsky et al., have improved deep neural network training [16] and served as references for both classic and new-generation neural networks [12–14, 18].

**Current Landscape of Applications.** Deep learning, particularly Convolutional Neural Networks (CNNs), has been successfully applied to various problem domains. In the medical field, CNNs have proven to be efficient in analyzing biomedical signals, improving detection accuracy, reducing costs, and increasing diagnosis availability in low-income countries. Examples include arrhythmia and atrial fibrillation detection using 1-D CNNs, medical imaging classification and feature extraction, solving inverse problems in MRI and CT using convolutional networks, and identification of several biomarkers such as relevant proteins [13, 19–24].

Specifically in MRI classification, numerous publications have applied original and pretrained hybrid CNNs for Alzheimer's disease (AD) detection, such as AlzNet and Siamese convolutional neural network (SCNN), often utilizing transfer learning methods [25, 26]. The use of pertained CNNs is presented in Table 1, adapted from bibliographic revisions such as [25] regarding the application of CNNs for AD detection along with other publications.

**Table 1.** Summary of transfer learning-based and original work prediction models for AD detection. Adapted from [25]

| Prediction Model | Baseline | Accuracy% | Ref |
|---|---|---|---|
| VGG | AlexNet, GoogLeNet, VGG16/19, ResNet-18/50/101, MobileNetV2, InceptionV3, Inception-ResNet-V2 and DenseNet201 | 99.3 | [27] |
| VGG16 | Inception V4 | 99 | [28] |
| VGG-19 | VGG-19, VGG-16, Resnet-50 and Xception | 97 (-,-, 96) | [29] |
| SegNet and ResNet-101 | VGG-16, VGG-19 | 96.3 (96.1, 96.7,98.1) | [30] |
| ResNet-18 | LeNet-5, AlexNet, VGG-16, SqueezeNet, GooLeNet | 91.8 (92, 91.6) | [31] |
| ResNet18 and DenseNet201 | Resnet18 and SVM, 3D CNN, Resnet 18 | 98.9 (-,-, 98.9, 98.9) | [32] |
| LeNet-5 | 3D CNN | 99 (-,-, 94.8, 89.4, 80.2) | [33] |
| Depthwise Separable Convolution | AlexNet, GoogleNet | 77.79 | [34] |
| DenseNet | AlexNet, GoogLeNet, VGG-16, Inception-ResNet-v2, ResNet18/50/101, MobileNetV2, InceptionV3, Inception-ResNet-V2 and DenseNet201 | 99.05 | [35] |
| AlzNet | RELU and five convolution layers | 99.30 | [36] |
| SCNN | VGG16 | 99.05 | [26] |

## 2 Methodology

### 2.1 Proposed Convolutional Neural Network

Nowadays, several Convolutional Neural Networks have been developed to overcome some of the common problems in different fields such as literacy, measuring people behavior, and overcome pathology classification problems in the medical field. In this context, a pre-trained Convolutional Neural Network (VGG-16) will be used for the classification of the degree of severity of subjects with Alzheimer's disease. Simultaneously, an analysis of the performance of the classification task using two different environments, Python and Matlab, will be considered.

**VGG-16 Convolutional Neural Network.** At 2014, the Visual Geometry Group (VGG) from Oxford University developed a Convolutional Neural Network with 16 deep layers (being, therefore, called "VGG-16") which resulted in the second place of the ILSVRC. The CNN is composed of 13 Convolutional Layers with 3 Fully Connected layers both with ReLU activation, 5 MaxPool layers, and one SoftMax Layer. The RGB input of this Convolutional Neural Network has an image dimension of 224×224 [37]. Figure 2 Shows the architecture of the VGG-16 (Fig. 1).

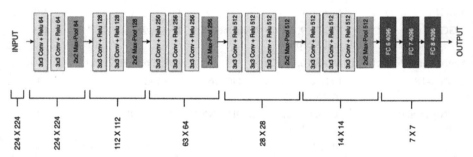

**Fig. 1.** Vgg16 Architecture. It consists of a 224×224 input layer, 13 convoluted hidden layers and a dense network layer connected to an output layer. Common deep feature extraction occurs in the last convolutional layer or in "Fc 7" dense layer.

### 2.2 Database Used for Transfer Learning

The database used for this work was obtained from Kaggle, an online community platform for data scientists and machine learning study. The creation of this database is motivated by the necessity of making a very highly accurate model to predict the stages of Alzheimer [38]. Kaggle provides an open database consisting of MRI images, divided in four classes of images for both training and validation sets. This dataset represents the progression from normal to moderate, mild and very mild stages of the disease (Fig. 2). These stages can be distinguished by their clinical dementia rating (CDR). Kaggle's dataset provides a total of 6400 MRI images divided into training and validation sets (Table 2).

**Table 2.** Image counts for the training and validation set provided in the Kaggle's Alzheimer database [38]

| Stage | Training | Validation |
|---|---|---|
| Mild Demented | 717 | 179 |
| Moderate Demented | 52 | 12 |
| Non Demented | 2560 | 640 |
| Very Mild Demented | 1792 | 448 |

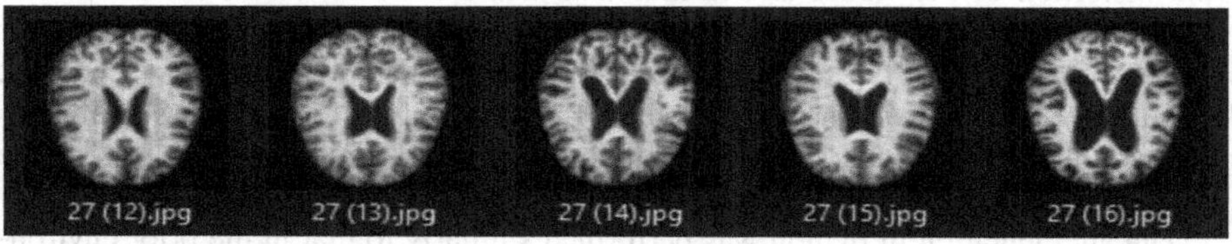

**Fig. 2.** Visualization of cross-sectional samples of AD patients in a very mild demented stage. [38]

## 2.3 Pre-processing

The MRI inputs that will be used in the CNNs must be converted from a 2D to a 3D Dimension image. The VGG-16 architecture has been pre-trained on Imagenet [39], one of the largest image databases. For this matter, most of the training inputs are colored images, which in turn, consider three dimensional arrays of values in the RGB range. In order to avoid common problems of formatting and input recognition, the MRI data has been pre-processed to RGB format, by overlapping the data in three image layers. Moreover, data augmentation will be considered in this process as well as class balancing. Resizing logarithms will be also applied since proper functions of the VGG-16, may require an image dimension of $224 \times 224 \times 3$.

**Matlab Pre-processing.** The preprocessing in this environment will be done by calling the function '*augmentedImageDatastore*'. Matlab will automatically detect the input size of the CNN by using the '*net.Layers(1).InputSize*' command, then by using this parameter within the '*augmentedImageDatastore*' function the image will be resized.

Data augmentation is used in image pre-processing for increasing the number of the dataset by using the original inputs and transforming them into new images. In this case, data augmentation will be done by applying the 'augmentedImageDatastore' function and using the 'imageDataAugmenter' function as input of the aforesaid function. In this case, 90° degrees rotation, random scaling image from 0.98× and 1.02×, and random left-right rotation with a 50% probability will be used as parameters in the data augmentation.

Oversampling is another useful technique when training and validation sub-dataset samples are not equal between them. This variation may lead to wrong assumptions since overfitting of one class may be represented, hence, wrong accuracy values may be obtained from this procedure. The functionality of this technique is based on the reduction-increasing parameters. As an example, in the database, 'ModerateDemented' class has 64 items whereas the 'MildDemented' class has 896. As the reader may notice, there exists a tremendous variation between these classes and some corrections may be taken into account. In this case, top values of 1247 and 500 were settled in for training and validation, respectively.

**Python Pre-processing.** The Kaggle's Dataset considers $208 \times 176$ image sizes. To avoid distortion of the values and to maintain the aspect ratio of the MRI inputs, a 16-point edge trimming was performed over the image to obtain a $176 \times 176$ size for posterior rescaling. For this a python script was used for this preprocessing step. First, the data was obtained from the online source, following a transformation of the images to arrays, and a later reconversion after removing the top and bottom 16 rows to generate a square image.

Data augmentation in python was performed similarly to that in the prior environment. Zoom, shift and brightness range and horizontal flip were parameters considered to understand the effects of artificial data values on the final prediction profile of the CNN-SVM model. However, for this process to produce enough training and validation images for each class, a significant batch size value was used. Moreover, as the batch size approximates the total number of training and validation original images, the oversampling processing yields better results.

Oversampling has become one of the many techniques to overcome imbalance in information in the input data. The Kaggle's Dataset contained low image counts mainly for Moderate Dementia class, which in turn, reduced the sensibility of the model and the overall accuracy of the SVM classifier. To solve this problem, a batch size approximate to the total image count was used for image generation, which was followed by an oversampling of the data based major class count value. A random seed was used for the fitting process, and the final sample count was divided between training, validation and test sets. The same splitting parameters as in the Matlab environment were considered.

**General pre-processing approaches.** Based on the considerations of each environment regarding the limitations of data generation, data augmentation, computational viability and the outcomes of the prediction model, the training process followed three different routes based on the application of data augmentation. Figure 3 shows the different approaches used in preprocessing to be contrasted based on the prediction results. Group 1 considered oversampling and data augmentation techniques in the preprocessing of the data; for Group 2, instead, data augmentation was not considered and a rescaling of the generated data was performed to normalize the outcome features; lastly, neither oversampling or data augmentation was applied to Group 3, although a high batch size was maintained for the generation process to keep the same image counts in each set.

## 2.4 Transfer learning

Transfer learning is a powerful tool given the possibility of using pre-trained Convolutional Neural Networks as arbitrary feature extractors and then, applying their outcomes

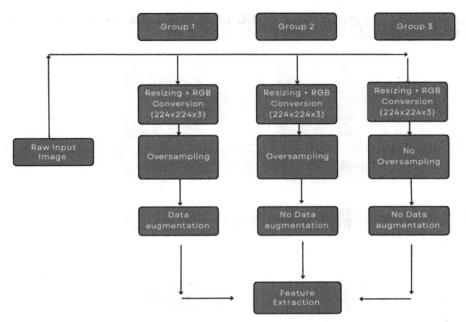

**Fig. 3.** Overall preprocessing for both Python & Matlab environments of the Kaggle's Alzheimer Dataset.

as inputs in several learning models. Feature extraction has an advantage over other similar deep learning techniques in that it can be configured at a desired level of the convolutional architecture (usually at the Pooling and Activation layer) and extract that information to use as an input for supervised learning models. The latter, commonly tend to be linear models which do not commit high computational resources. Hence, algorithms such as Support Vector Machine, Linear regression, and Naive Bayes are widely used in Supervised learning models. [40].

This work will use VGG-16 as a feature extractor and a Support Vector Machine multiclass-classifier (SVM) as the main Supervised Learning Model for both Matlab & Python environments. To comply with what has been described, Keras Library, an open source machine learning library built in Python language, will be used, whereas 'activations' functions will be used in matlab. The training and validation datasets will be split in 80% and 20% from a general data pool, respectively, in environments. For the case of Matlab, the feature extraction will be done by using the features in the layer "c7" which stands for 'Fully Connected Layer 7', whereas in python 'Fc1' will be used. As compared in Fig. 4, for the pre-trained architecture in Keras and Matlab repositories Fc7 and Fc1 are considered as the same stop layer.

### 2.5 Support Vector Machine

In order to convey two different approaches, CNNs for feature extraction and classic machine learning algorithms, the classification process was based on the deep extraction of predictions at a specific layer of VGG-16 which were fed afterwards to a SVM classifier for multiclass-classification.

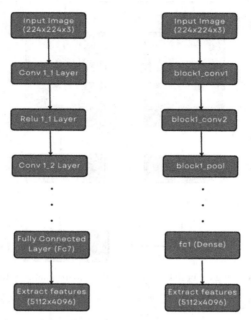

**Fig. 4.** Feature extraction workflow for both Matlab (left) and Python (right) environments with pre-trained VGG-16 CNN.

The workflow for the prediction model is presented in Fig. 5. The reliability of classic machine learning problems with the feasibility of CNNs for quick feature recognition based on pretrained weights allows for the application of straightforward approaches at different user levels. As such, the capacity of different environments to be able to apply this methodology is a quality of relevance of this work, as the latter may elucidate different trends that may conduct researches on the field to adapt to one of the analyzed environments based on their research necessities and exposition to programming paradigms.

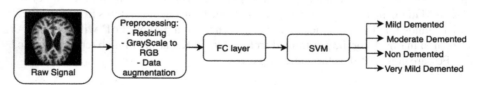

**Fig. 5.** Workflow of the proposed prediction model based on VGG-16 deep feature extraction and SVM multiclass-classification.

# 3   Results

## 3.1   VGG16-SVM results in Matlab Environment

**Group 1.** This group is based on the application of both data augmentation and over-sampling techniques. Figure 6 shows the confusion matrix of the classification model for this group. Accuracy and F1 scores are 69% and 69.08%, respectively. Note that F1 score was calculated with the traditional method where values were taken from the confusion matrix.

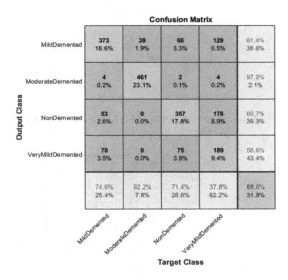

**Fig. 6.** Confusion matrix of Group 1 for Matlab-VGG16-SVM model.

**Group 2.** For this subsection, group 2 is based on the application of oversampling without data augmentation techniques. Figure 7 shows the confusion matrix of the model. For this case, accuracy and F1 score are 79.3% and 79.58%, respectively.

**Group 3.** Finally, Group 3 is based on the application of neither oversampling nor Data augmentation techniques. Figure 8 shows the confusion matrix for the training process with this group. Accuracy and F1 score are 85.5% and 87.6% respectively. The absence of both pre-processing techniques has the best result in this environment within the groups.

Confusion Matrix
MildDemented
ModerateDemented
NonDemented
VeryMildDemented
Output Class
Target Class
375 18.8%
0 0.0%
17 0.9%
51 2.5%
84.7% 15.3%
0 0.0%
500 25.0%
0 0.0%
1 0.1%
99.8% 0.2%
55 2.8%
0 0.0%
371 18.6%
107 5.3%
69.6% 30.4%
70 3.5%
0 0.0%
112 5.6%
341 17.1%
65.2% 34.8%
75.0% 25.0%
100% 0.0%
74.2% 25.8%
68.2% 31.8%
79.3% 20.7%

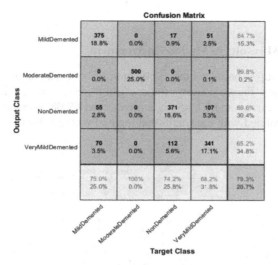

**Fig. 7.** Confusion matrix of Group 2 for Matlab-VGG16-SVM model.

Confusion Matrix
MildDemented
ModerateDemented
NonDemented
VeryMildDemented
Output Class
Target Class
147 11.5%
0 0.0%
11 0.9%
14 1.1%
85.5% 14.5%
0 0.0%
12 0.9%
0 0.0%
0 0.0%
100% 0.0%
14 1.1%
0 0.0%
553 43.2%
52 4.1%
89.3% 10.7%
18 1.4%
1 0.1%
76 5.9%
382 29.8%
80.1% 19.9%
82.1% 17.9%
92.3% 7.7%
86.4% 13.6%
85.3% 14.7%
85.5% 14.5%

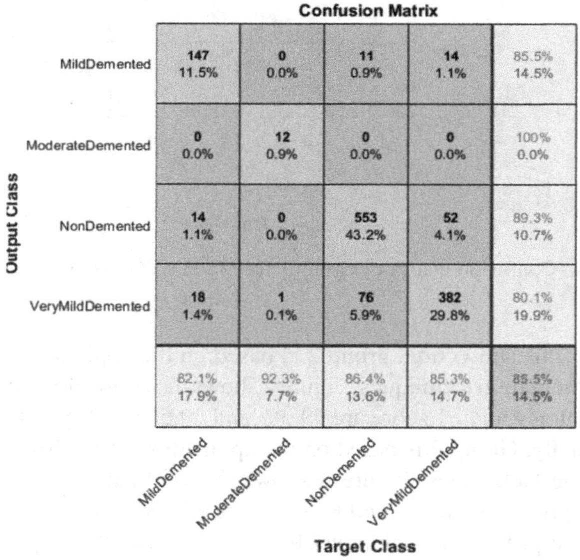

**Fig. 8.** Confusion matrix of Group 3 for Matlab-VGG16-SVM model.

### 3.2 VGG16-SVM results in Python Environment

In Python, the prediction model was based on the experimentation of different kernels supported by SVM. As Scikit-learn states in their documentation, the application of different kernels changes de hyperplane fitting to the different clusters of data [41]. In the case of multiclass-classification, this procedure can be done by using polynomials of radial kernels in order to correct the classification of intricate data disposition of parameters. Thus, a third degree polynomial kernel and a RBF (radial basis function) kernel were used to predict the Alzheimer severity employing normal SVM classifiers. Despite this, all the study groups demonstrated better performance and precision rates at the basis of a Radial Function Kernel. Other parameters of the SVM classifier were tuned according to the data behavior. For example, the gamma value of the RBF kernel was set to significantly low values so that its relation with high C values were best suited for the classification problem.

**Group 1.** The prediction model using the python environment yielded high contrastable results in terms of accuracy and metrics score in comparison to the Matlab environment. The confusion matrix for this group is presented in Fig. 9. And the sensibility and recall values of each class are shown in Table 3.

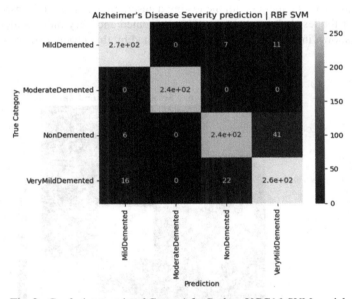

**Fig. 9.** Confusion matrix of Group 1 for Python-VGG16-SVM model.

The confusion matrix shows a high specificity in each class during prediction, attaining overall score metrics of 91,55% of accuracy and a F1 factor of 91.65%. Nevertheless, by analyzing the sensibility of each class to predict true classes, it is noticed that a high sensibility is mostly obtained for the Mild Demented class, and a complete effectivity in prediction for the Moderate Demented class, which was previously balanced by oversampling and data augmentation. However, lower prediction profiles are observed for Non-demented and Very Mild Demented classes, with misleading classification of negative cases between both classes, as seen by the increment of wrong values in the confusion matrix in the sub $2\times2$ disposition for those classes.

**Group 2.** For the second group, the lack of extra parameters in the data augmentation process produced different results in the accuracy profile. As seen in Fig. 10.

**Table 3.** Sensibility for each class of Group 1 using the Python environment.

| Class | Sensibility |
|---|---|
| Mild Demented | 0.93684 |
| Moderate Demented | 1.00000 |
| Non Demented | 0.83566 |
| Very Mild Demented | 0.87417 |

The confusion matrix of the SVM classifier shows a more consistent classification of true values in the correct categories when no data augmentation is conceived more than bit normalization. The accuracy of this approach approximates the 93.19% during the sensibility assay of the model with the testing dataset; higher values of sensibility were observed for the less balanced classes (Non demented and Very mild Demented). The results are shown in Table 4. The F1 score obtained by this group also corresponds to 93.19%

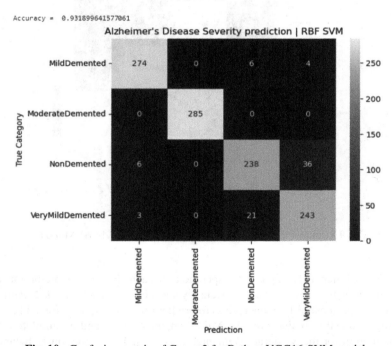

**Fig. 10.** Confusion matrix of Group 2 for Python-VGG16-SVM model.

**Group 3.** The last group considers the generated data without the application of oversampling for the imbalanced class nor the augmentation of data more than the normalization procedure. By considering this limitation of the preprocessing the results obtained by the same SVM classifier model showed a drop in the accuracy profile and

**Table 4.** Sensibility for each class of Group 2 using the Python environment.

| Class | Sensibility |
|---|---|
| Mild Demented | 0.96479 |
| Moderate Demented | 1.00000 |
| Non Demented | 0.85 |
| Very Mild Demented | 0.91011 |

in the overall metrics of the model. The confusion matrix of Fig. 11. Demonstrates a reduction in the multiclass-classification of the model, obtaining an overall accuracy of 46.25% and an F1 score of 46.23%. No sensibility was observed for the Mild and moderate dementia classes, being that most of the prediction results are shifted towards higher severity classes. The confusion between Non demented and Very Mild Demented subjects without the application of oversampling and data augmentation increased in comparison to previous groups to significant levels of low prediction resolution.

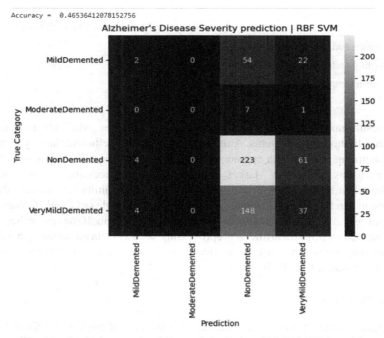

**Fig. 11.** Confusion matrix of Group 3 for Python-VGG16-SVM model.

## 4  Discussion

### 4.1  Matlab and Python Environments

The performance tests conducted show that different environments imply different results. Group 1 shows a higher accuracy level and high F-Score in the python environment, with an accuracy difference of 21.59% above the model in Matlab. This can be explained by the fact that Python has an open-built-in-environment where several advantages such as manipulation of the support vector machine intrinsic settings and more complex configurations in oversampling and data augmentation when compared with Matlab are taken into account. Since Matlab has a closed-build-in-environment, restrictions in core-programming parameters which does not happen in Python may occur. The same outcome happens with Group 2 where there is a difference between both environments of 13.93% where Python has higher accuracy values. When there is no oversampling and no data augmentation (Group 3), Matlab has higher values with an advantage of 39.5% in accuracy. Table 4 shows a brief summary of accuracy values between Matlab and Python environments (Table 5).

**Table 5.**  Summary of the Accuracy values of Matlab and Python environments.

| Group | Matlab model (%) | Python model (%) |
|---|---|---|
| Oversampling and data augmentation | 69.2 | 90.8 |
| Oversampling and without data augmentation | 79.2 | 93.1 |
| Without Oversampling and without data augmentation | 86 | 46.5 |

The results uncovered in this work highlight the advantages and disadvantages of both Matlab and Python environments. Although Matlab is more efficient than Python where no oversampling and no data augmentation is required, when the opposite is needed, Python performs better than Matlab. Based on this, the necessities of the researcher should be taken into account given that if computational limits are present, Python's environment can be applied to online resources such as Kaggle or Google Collab, which offers a more complex and tuneable configuration than Matlab. If the researcher's needs are represented by no extra artificial preprocessing such as Data augmentation and oversampling, and limitations on computational costs are barely low, Matlab may show greater performance than Python.

## 5  Conclusions

The Kaggle database proved to be adequate for the aim of the FE and SVM training, owing to its size and the correct division of the four stages of Alzheimer's disease with MRI images. The pathology could be successfully classified and organized in folders according to the severity, from normal to mild, moderate and very mild demented stage, which facilitated the further segmentation. The possible limitations of the dataset were overcome with a preprocessing of the signals in which the resizing, conversion of the images and data augmentation helped with the scope of the data needed.

The VGG16 CNN used, followed by the FE and SVM algorithm, allowed the implementation of high-accuracy and fast classification models of the different stages of the disease in both Matlab and Python environments. The mean accuracies registered ranged from 69.2% to 86% in Matlab whereas accuracy values in Python go from 46.5% up to 93.13%. The researcher's necessities may be a crucial factor when determining one environment or another. This work shows a complete comparison between Matlab and Python environments using similar configurations in the programming setup of each environment and elucidate significant changes in performance, usability, adaptability, among others.

To sum up, the results obtained in both environments demonstrate a clear advantage in Python over Matlab; in addition, the supplementary work showed another advantage in this study, the accuracy presented in the SVM algorithm resulted to be the highest (93.13%), and therefore permits a higher quality classification of the Alzheimer's disease severity.

# References

1. Cummings, J.L.: Alzheimer disease. JAMA **287**, 2335 (2002). https://doi.org/10.1001/jama.287.18.2335
2. Scheltens, P., De Strooper, B., Kivipelto, M., et al.: Alzheimer's disease. Lancet **397**, 1577–1590 (2021). https://doi.org/10.1016/s0140-6736(20)32205-4
3. Castellani, R.J., Rolston, R.K., Smith, M.A.: Alzheimer disease. Dis. Mon. **56**, 484–546 (2010). https://doi.org/10.1016/j.disamonth.2010.06.001
4. Vatanabe, I.P., Manzine, P.R., Cominetti, M.R.: Historic concepts of dementia and Alzheimer's disease: from ancient times to the present. Revue Neurologique **176**, 140–147 (2020). https://doi.org/10.1016/j.neurol.2019.03.004
5. Cipriani, G., Dolciotti, C., Picchi, L., Bonuccelli, U.: Alzheimer and his disease: a brief history. Neurol. Sci. **32**, 275–279 (2010). https://doi.org/10.1007/s10072-010-0454-7
6. Liang, C-S., et al.: Mortality rates in Alzheimer's disease and non-Alzheimer's dementias: a systematic review and meta-analysis. SSRN Electr. J. (2021). https://doi.org/10.2139/ssrn.3791432
7. LW; C Alzheimer's disease: Early diagnosis and treatment. In: Hong Kong medical journal = Xianggang yi xue za zhi (2023)
8. Rasmussen, J., Langerman, H.: Alzheimer's disease – why we need early diagnosis. Degenerative Neurol. Neuromuscul. Dis. **9**, 123–130 (2019). https://doi.org/10.2147/dnnd.s228939
9. Suquilanda-Pesántez, J.D., Zambonino-Soria, M.C., López-Ramos, D.E., Pineda-Molina, M.G., Milán, N.S., Muñoz, M.C., Villalba-Meneses, G.F., Almeida-Galárraga, D.: Prediction of Parkinson's disease severity based on gait signals using a neural network and the fast Fourier transform. In: Botto-Tobar, M., Cruz, H., Díaz Cadena, A. (eds.) CIT 2020. AISC, vol. 1326, pp. 3–18. Springer, Cham (2021). https://doi.org/10.1007/978-3-030-68080-0_1
10. WHO Dementia. In: World Health Organization. https://www.who.int/news-room/fact-sheets/detail/dementia. Accessed 25 June 2023
11. Leifer, B.P.: Early diagnosis of Alzheimer's disease: clinical and economic benefits. J. Am. Geriatr. Soc. (2003). https://doi.org/10.1046/j.1532-5415.5153.x
12. Macukow, B.: Neural networks – state of art, brief history, basic models and architecture. In: Saeed, K., Homenda, W. (eds.) CISIM 2016. LNCS, vol. 9842, pp. 3–14. Springer, Cham (2016). https://doi.org/10.1007/978-3-319-45378-1_1

13. Li, Z,. Liu, F., Yang, W., Peng, S., Zhou, J.: A survey of convolutional neural networks: analysis, applications, and prospects. In: IEEE Transactions on Neural Networks and Learning Systems. PUBMED (2023). https://pubmed.ncbi.nlm.nih.gov/34111009/
14. Alom, MZ., et al.: The history began from AlexNet: a comprehensive survey on deep learning approaches. ArXiv.org (2018). https://arxiv.org/abs/1803.01164
15. Fukushima, K.: Neocognitron: a hierarchical neural network capable of visual pattern recognition. Neural Netw. **1**, 119–130 (1988). https://doi.org/10.1016/0893-6080(88)90014-7
16. Fukushima, K.: Cognitron: a self-organizing multilayered neural network. Biol. Cybern. **20**, 121–136 (1975). https://doi.org/10.1007/bf00342633
17. Krizhevsky, A., Sutskever, I., Hinton, G.: ImageNet classification with deep convolutional neural networks. Commun. ACM **60**, 84–90 (2017). https://doi.org/10.1145/3065386
18. Zhang, X., et al.: Survey of convolutional neural network. In: Proceedings of the 2018 International Conference on Network, Communication, Computer Engineering (NCCE 2018) (2018). https://doi.org/10.2991/ncce-18.2018.16
19. Li, Q., et al.: Medical image classification with convolutional neural network. In: 2014 13th International Conference on Control Automation Robotics & Vision (ICARCV) (2014). https://doi.org/10.1109/icarcv.2014.7064414
20. McCann, M.T., Jin, K., Unser, M.: Convolutional neural networks for inverse problems in imaging: a review. IEEE Signal Process. Mag. **34**, 85–95 (2017). https://doi.org/10.1109/msp.2017.2739299
21. Almeida-Galarraga, D., et al.: Glaucoma detection through digital processing from fundus images using MATLAB. In: 2021 Second International Conference on Information Systems and Software Technologies (ICI2ST) (2021). https://doi.org/10.1109/ici2st51859.2021.00014
22. Yanchatuña, O., et al.: Skin lesion detection and classification using convolutional neural network for deep feature extraction and support vector machine. Int. J. Adv. Sci. Eng. Inf. Technol. **11**, 1260 (2021). https://doi.org/10.18517/ijaseit.11.3.13679
23. Pereira-Carrillo, J., Suntaxi-Dominguez, D., Guarnizo-Cabezas, O., Villalba-Meneses, G., Tirado-Espín, A., Almeida-Galárraga, D.: Comparison between two novel approaches in Automatic Breast Cancer Detection and diagnosis and its contribution in military defense. In: Rocha, Á., Fajardo-Toro, C.H., Rodríguez, J.M.R. (eds.) Developments and Advances in Defense and Security. SIST, vol. 255, pp. 189–201. Springer, Singapore (2022). https://doi.org/10.1007/978-981-16-4884-7_15
24. Suquilanda-Pesántez, J.D., et al.: NIFtHool: an informatics program for identification of NifH proteins using deep neural networks. F1000Research **11**, 164 (2022). https://doi.org/10.12688/f1000research.107925.1
25. Singh, S., Sambyal, N., Aggarwal, A.: Automated glaucoma detection using deep convolutional neural networks (2023). https://doi.org/10.21203/rs.3.rs-2788554/v1
26. Mehmood, A., Maqsood, M., Bashir, M., Shuyuan, Y.: A deep Siamese convolution neural network for multi-class classification of Alzheimer disease. Brain Sci. **10**, 84 (2020). https://doi.org/10.3390/brainsci10020084
27. Naz, S., Ashraf, A., Zaib, A.: Transfer learning using freeze features for Alzheimer neurological disorder detection using ADNI dataset. Multimed. Syst. **28**, 85–94 (2021). https://doi.org/10.1007/s00530-021-00797-3
28. Raju, M., Thirupalani, M., Vidhyabharathi, S., Thilagavathi, S.: Deep learning based multilevel classification of Alzheimer's disease using MRI scans. In: IOP Conference Series: Materials Science and Engineering, vol. 1084, p. 012017 (2021). https://doi.org/10.1088/1757-899x/1084/1/012017
29. Rajeswari, S., Nair, M.: A transfer learning approach for predicting Alzheimer's disease. In: 2021 4th Biennial International Conference on Nascent Technologies in Engineering (ICNTE) (2021). https://doi.org/10.1109/icnte51185.2021.9487746

30. Buvaneswari, P.R., Gayathri, R.: Deep learning-based segmentation in classification of Alzheimer's disease. Arabian J. Sci. Eng. **46**(6), 5373–5383 (2021). https://doi.org/10.1007/s13369-020-05193-z

31. Ebrahimi, A., Luo, S., Chiong, R.: Deep sequence modelling for Alzheimer's disease detection using MRI. Comput. Biol. Med. **134**, 104537 (2021). https://doi.org/10.1016/j.compbiomed.2021.104537

32. Odusami, M., Maskeliūnas, R., Damaševičius, R.: An intelligent system for early recognition of Alzheimer's disease using neuroimaging. Sensors **22**, 740 (2022). https://doi.org/10.3390/s22030740

33. Heising, L., Angelopoulos, S.: Operationalizing fairness in medical AI adoption: detection of early Alzheimer's disease with 2D CNN. BMJ Health Care Inform. **29**, e100485 (2022). https://doi.org/10.1136/bmjhci-2021-100485

34. Liu, J., Li, M., Luo, Y., et al.: Alzheimer's disease detection using depthwise separable convolutional neural networks. Comput. Meth. Programs Biomed. **203**, 106032 (2021). https://doi.org/10.1016/j.cmpb.2021.106032

35. Ashraf, A., Naz, S., Shirazi, S.H., Razzak, I., Parsad, M.: Deep transfer learning for Alzheimer's neurological disorder detection. Multimed. Tools Appl. **80**(20), 30117–30142 (2021). Accessed 25 May 2023

36. Al-Khuzaie, F. E., Bayat, O., Duru, A.D: Diagnosis of Alzheimer disease using 2D MRI slices by convolutional neural network. Appl. Bionics Biomech. (2021)

37. Simonyan, K., Zisserman, A.: Very deep convolutional networks for large-scale image recognition. In: arXiv.org (2015). https://arxiv.org/abs/1409.1556

38. Dubey, S.: Alzheimer's dataset (4 class of images). In: Kaggle. (2019). https://www.kaggle.com/datasets/tourist55/alzheimers-dataset-4-class-of-images. Accessed 25 May 2023

39. Keras Team Keras: Documentation: VGG16 and VGG19. In: Keras. https://keras.io/api/applications/vgg/. Accessed 25 May 2023

40. Rosebrock, A.: Transfer learning with keras and deep learning. In: PyImageSearch. (2021). https://pyimagesearch.com/2019/05/20/transfer-learning-with-keras-and-deep-learning/

41. Scikit-learn 1.4. Support Vector Machines. In: Scikit-learn. https://scikit-learn.org/stable/modules/svm.html#svm-classification. Accessed 25 May 2023

# Creation of an Alert Device for Early Detection of Epilepsy Using an EEG Signal Power Threshold

Karen Cáceres-Benítez[1] , Ana Marcillo[2] , Denisse Enríquez-Ortega[1] ,
Bryan Chulde-Fernández[1] , Fernando Villalba Meneses[1] ,
Omar Alvarado-Cando[1] , and Diego Almeida-Galárraga[1(✉)]

[1] School of Biological Sciences and Engineering, Yachay Tech University,
Hacienda San José s/n, San Miguel de Urcuquí 100119, Ecuador
dalmeida@yachaytech.edu.ec
[2] School of Mathematical and Computational Sciences, Yachay Tech University,
Hacienda San José s/n, San Miguel de Urcuquí 100119, Ecuador

**Abstract.** In this study, signal processing techniques such as baseband filters and the wavelet transform method are used to analyze specific patterns in EEG signals from patients with epilepsy, collected from the Siena Scalp database. The goal is to identify predictive indicators of epileptic seizures by analyzing three key points in the fast delta wave: 1) Normal brain activity, 2) Sudden increase in amplitude, and 3) A dead stop. The results obtained will be used for the implementation of an alert device based on the power threshold of the EEG signal, and the comparison of the measured values with the pre-established power threshold. If brain activity exceeds the threshold, the device could issue an alert or signal to indicate that a desired state has been reached or to signal an abnormal or worrisome condition. This text discusses the efficacy of visual analysis of preictal phases and electronic devices for detecting and predicting seizures. Although the study shows evidence for these methods, there were limitations, including a small sample size and the use of a single electronic device.

**Keywords:** Detection · EEG · Epilepsy · Physionet · Power threshold

## 1 Introduction

One of the most common neurological diseases present in people of all ages, races, and geographic locations is epilepsy [1]. Epilepsy is a central nervous system (neurological) disorder in which the normal activity of the brain is disturbed, resulting in abnormal neuronal discharges or hyperexcitability of neurons or periods of unusual behavior and sensations, and sometimes loss of consciousness. Epilepsy involves not only studying nervous system cells in seizure behavior, but also in associated neuropsychological comorbidities. The most recent definition of epilepsy requires at least one epileptic seizure to be present [2, 3].

© The Author(s), under exclusive license to Springer Nature Switzerland AG 2023
J. Maldonado-Mahauad et al. (Eds.): TICEC 2023, CCIS 1885, pp. 294–308, 2023.
https://doi.org/10.1007/978-3-031-45438-7_20

Seizures associated with encephalopathies can present in different forms and degrees. For example, a partial-onset impaired-awareness (IAS) seizure affects consciousness and originates in a specific part of the brain. On the other hand, partial onset seizure without disturbance of consciousness (WIAS) does not affect consciousness and starts in a specific region of the brain. In addition, there is the phenomenon of bilateral generalized tonic-clonic seizure (FBTC), which spreads to both cerebral hemispheres and causes a generalized seizure throughout the body [4]. These different forms of seizures may be characteristic of different types of encephalopathies and provide important information for the diagnosis and management of these neurological conditions.

In addition, during the epileptic seizure cycle, four main transition periods can be identified. The first is the pre-ictal, which occurs before the crisis. The second is the ictal, which represents the moment in which the crisis develops. Next, there is the post-ictal, which corresponds to the period after the crisis. Finally, there is the inter-ictal, which is the time between two successive crises. These transitional stages are identified using the EEG signal, and the ictal stage can be easily distinguished by intracranial EEG recording [5].

Epilepsy occurs in approximately 56 cases per 100,000 adults annually. Furthermore, the prevalence and incidence rates of epilepsy are slightly higher in males compared to females. The severity of the disease is linked to the frequency, intensity and control of the seizures, which can be treated through medication adjustments and surgical procedures [1, 4]. The diagnosis of epilepsy by electroencephalogram is non-invasive, useful and allows the EEG signals to be analyzed and to identify the different stages of the seizures. Treatment with antiepileptic drugs or surgery can control epilepsy in most people. Some need permanent treatment, while others experience spontaneous remission. Carbamazepine CBZ (Tegretol) is an antiepileptic indicated for partial seizures [6].

However, antiepileptic drugs have limitations and side effects and often fail to control seizures in one third of patients [1]. In addition, surgery is not always an option, and diagnosis of nonconvulsive status epilepticus requires EEG analysis, which is expensive, time consuming, and inefficient. Therefore, seizure prediction methods can be an accurate tool for these cases [7]. In fact, early prediction could allow patients or caregivers to take appropriate measures, such as alerting with an alarm, applying short-acting drugs and activating stimulating devices.

Therefore, algorithmic methods of early seizure prediction can be a crucial application in the prevention of damage and loss of life, by allowing early detection of seizures. This enables the implementation of preventive measures to avoid accidents and deaths. Furthermore, an accurate prediction provides the opportunity for patients and caregivers to take appropriate actions to minimize the severity of seizures. Therefore, algorithmic seizure prediction is emerging as a significant tool to preserve lives and improve the quality of life of people with epilepsy [8].

To develop a detection algorithm, several concepts are used, such as the wavelet transform and the delta wave. The Wavelet transform is a useful tool for detecting subtle changes in the EEG signal that are difficult to detect with the naked eye. Wavelet can extract important features and be used in time frequency localization. Discrete wavelet transforms the input signals of the process with a finite moment. Similarly, complex Morlet wavelets can be used to examine unstable data for time-frequency analysis.

Furthermore, when these wavelets are convolved with a specific signal, a simpler signal is obtained to extract instantaneous power and phase at each chosen time point [9–11].

In previous research, the delta band (0.5–4 Hz) has been shown to be highly effective in detecting seizures in patients with epilepsy, achieving markedly superior accuracy compared to other frequency bands. This choice is based on the proven efficacy of the delta band and its ability to provide satisfactory accuracy, sensitivity and specificity with less complexity, thus improving seizure diagnosis on EEG. In addition, the study of brain electrical activity in the delta band has advanced the understanding of physiological processes related to epilepsy [12]. Although the use of the fast delta wave as an indicator of seizures and prediction of convulsion has been proposed, further research is needed to develop a robust and reliable approach to seizure prediction prior to seizure onset.

Table 1 shows different epilepsy detection methods, their data sets, scalp location, EEG frequency, performance measures and references. Of note are the RNN method with 70.00% accuracy and 87.00% sensitivity [7], and the SDCN method with 98.82% accuracy, 98.90% sensitivity and 98.75% specificity [13]. The CNN method achieves an accuracy of 99.90–100%, sensitivity of 100.00% and specificity of 99.80–100% [14], while the BNLSTM-CASA achieves an accuracy of 91.40%, sensitivity of 96.20%, specificity of 96.80% and AUC of 0.961 [15]. The GCNNN shows an AUC of 0.991 [16], and the SVM presents ranges of accuracy (99.87–98.14%), sensitivity (99.91–98.16%) and specificity (99.82–98.12%) [17]. The Deep Learning method obtains accuracy of 99.60%, sensitivity of 99.72%, specificity of 99.70% and AUC of 0.95–0.98 [18]. Finally, Linear SVM shows an accuracy of 23.07%, sensitivity of 3.50% and specificity of 99.05% [8].

In the field of early disease detection, various techniques and computational models have been developed to improve the accuracy and accessibility of diagnoses. For example, in the case of glaucoma, a computational technique for early diagnosis has been implemented using image processing in MATLAB. Similarly, in the field of skin cancer detection, models capable of detecting different types of skin lesions have been developed. In the case of Parkinson's disease, analysis that can predict the severity of the disease has been used [19–22]. In the field of military medicine, the use of convolutional neural networks for the identification of breast cancer has been investigated. In addition, in other areas such as the identification of diazotrophic bacteria, a high-precision system that uses neural networks has been proposed. In summary, the development of computational techniques and machine learning models have significantly improved the early detection of various diseases [23–25].

This study will focus on the usefulness of the EEG for the study of epilepsy, allowing the identification of focal or generalized alterations to guide or establish the diagnosis of epilepsy and specific epileptic syndromes. Using concepts such as the wavelet transform and the delta wave, an algorithm will be developed to predict the preictal phase in patients with epilepsy from EEG signals, analyzing patterns and specific characteristics in the signals. This approach will improve the understanding and management of epilepsy, as well as provide tools for the prediction and early treatment of epileptic seizures.

**Table 1.** Epilepsy seizures detection and classification studies found in literature

| Method | Dataset (size) | Scalp localization | EEG Frequency | Performance Measure | | | | Ref |
|---|---|---|---|---|---|---|---|---|
| | | | | Accuracy (%) | Sensitivity (%) | Specificity (%) | AUC | |
| RNN | CHB-MIT Scalp EEG (23) | 10–20 system | – | 70.00 | 87.00 | – | 0.875 | [7] |
| SDCN | Training set (3503) and testing set (3283) | – | – | 98.82 | 98.90 | 98.75 | – | [13] |
| CNN | Bonn EEG (5) and New Delhi (10) | 10–20 system | 0 ~ 80 Hz | 99.90–100 | 100.00 | 99.80–100 | – | [14] |
| BNLSTM–CASA | Training set (154) and testing set (50) | 10–20 system | – | 91.40 | 96.20 | 96.80 | 0.961 | [15] |
| GCNN | Neonatal EEG (342) | Longitudinal bipolar | 0.5–30 Hz | – | – | – | 0.991 | [16] |
| SVM | CHB-MIT (22) and Private EEG (27) | 10–20 system | 0.5–30 Hz | 99.87–98.14 | 99.91–98.16 | 99.82–98.12 | – | [17] |
| Deep learning | CHB-MIT (22) | 10–20 system | – | 99.60 | 99.72 | 99.70 | 0.95–0.98 | [18] |
| Linear SVM | Siena Scalp Database (14) | 10–20 system | 0–100 Hz | 23.07 | 3.50 | 99.05 | – | [8] |

## 2   Materials and Methods

The methodology employed in this study involves collecting electroencephalographic signals from individuals with epilepsy, followed by analyzing specific patterns and characteristics to identify potential seizure indicators (see Fig. 1). This approach introduces a new technique for early detection of epileptic seizures by examining EEG signal power during the preictal phase. Rather than relying on artificial intelligence, we have identified a power threshold that effectively detects the onset of the preictal phase. Additionally, we have designed a custom electronic circuit capable of receiving the EEG signal in real-time and triggering an audible alert when the power threshold is reached. This innovative approach has the potential to enhance seizure prevention in individuals with epilepsy and minimize the risk of severe complications.

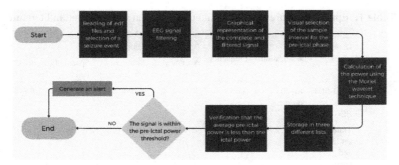

**Fig. 1.** Summarized methodology of the data pre-processing.

## 2.1 Data Collection

As per this analysis, the Siena Scalp EEG Database from the Physionet website was utilized. The database consisted of EEG recordings from 14 patients monitored with a Video-EEG at a sampling rate of 512 Hz. Electrode placement followed the International 10–20 System (see Fig. 2A). Patients used EB Neuro and Natus Quantum LTM amplifiers with silver/gold electrodes. Ethical approval from the University of Siena's Ethical Committee was obtained in accordance with the Declaration of Helsinki. Patients provided written informed consent for video recording and use of the data for scientific purposes [4].

The database consists of 14 folders containing EEG recordings in EDF format. Each folder corresponds to a specific subject and contains 1 to 5 data files with a maximum size of 2.11 GB each. Additionally, in each folder, there is a text file providing information about the data and epileptic seizures (see Fig. 2B). It's important to note that patient identifiers range from PN00 to PN17, totaling 14 patients. However, to avoid confusion, it's relevant to mention that patients with the following identifiers are not included: PN02, PN04, PN08, and PN15.

Overall, the database includes 47 epileptic seizures recorded over approximately 128 h. This dataset, named Siena-scalp-eeg, was downloaded from the PhysioNet platform and subsequently extracted into the specific directory for analysis. The complete reference to access this database is available in reference article [4]. When describing the results obtained from this database, it is crucial to clarify that two distinct and relevant aspects are being considered. On one hand, a total of 30,720 samples corresponding to the pre-ictal phase in both male and female patients have been acquired. Each of these samples reflects the 60-s period preceding an epileptic seizure. Each sample, in turn, represents a data point captured during that specific time interval.

On the other hand, it's essential to emphasize that within this same database, a total of 47 epileptic seizures have been recorded. Each of these seizures constitutes a singular event occurring at specific moments during the recording of each patient. Understanding that these seizures are unique and independent events in time is of utmost importance. This distinction is essential for a precise interpretation of the results and to avoid any potential misunderstanding.

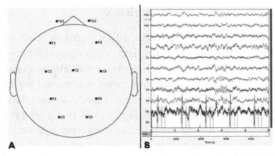

**Fig. 2.** A are the electrodes place according to the International 10–20 System. B is the visual representation of the EEG signal of patient PN00-3 without processing.

Each EEG was individually placed in a folder named 'EEGDatabase" for later use in the code. The files follow a pattern "PN00-1.edf" through "PN17-2.edf", where the patient number and the number of EEG files acquired are identified. The three types of seizures classificated by sex are in Table 2 and Table 3 where we observe the level of criticality based on the number of seizures, with the least critical at the top and the most critical at the bottom. The least critical row is highlighted in green and the most critical in red.

**Table 2.** Classification of representative Male Patients by Criticality Level

| Patient ID | Age (years) | Seizure | Locali-zation | Laterali-zation | EEG channel | Number of sei-zures | Recording Time (minutes) |
|---|---|---|---|---|---|---|---|
| PN14 | 49 | WIAS | T | L | 29 | 4 | 1408 |
| PN00 | 55 | IAS | T | R | 29 | 5 | 198 |
| PN10 | 25 | FBTC | F | Bilateral | 20 | 10 | 1002 |

**Table 3.** Classification of representative Female Patients by Criticality Level

| Patient ID | Age (years) | Seizure | Locali-zation | Laterali-zation | EEG channel | Number of sei-zures | Recording Time (minutes) |
|---|---|---|---|---|---|---|---|
| PN11 | 58 | IAS | T | R | 29 | 1 | 145 |
| PN07 | 20 | IAS | T | L | 29 | 1 | 523 |
| PN13 | 34 | IAS | T | L | 29 | 3 | 519 |

## 2.2 Data Preprocessing and Transformation

The complete code for the project is stored in 'EEGproject.py' and was developed using Python in Spider IDE. The code includes data cleaning and filtering using functions such as butter, filter, and convolve in the 'Data pre-processing' section. Libraries such as 'pyedflib', 'numpy', 'pywt', 'scipy', and 'datetime' were used for this task. 'pyedflib' handles EDF files, 'numpy' provides mathematical functions and data structures, 'pywt' implements the Wavelet Transform, 'scipy.signal' offers signal processing functions, and 'datetime' handles dates and times. The code involves opening EDF files, reading each channel, and storing the channels in a list for filtering.

**First Signal Processing Using Wavelet Transform.** EEG signals were processed using the wavelet transform (Eq. 1). This technique allowed us to identify different frequency bands, including the delta band (0.5–4 Hz), offering a deeper insight into the underlying brain activity. The choice to focus on the 0.5–4 Hz frequency range is based on previous research, specifically [12] that has demonstrated its efficacy in detecting seizures in epilepsy. In addition, a Butterworth band-pass filter (Eq. 2) was applied to isolate the specific time window corresponding to the fast delta wave, which is associated with epileptic pathology. Finally, a smoothing filter with a kernel size of 10k (Eq. 3) was applied to reduce noise and ensure a smoother representation of the signal.

$$W(a, b) = \frac{1}{\sqrt{a}} \int_{-\infty}^{\infty} f(t) \psi(\frac{t - b}{a}) dt \qquad (1)$$

where $f(t)$ is the signal to be analyzed, $\psi(t)$ is the wavelet function, a is the scale factor, b is the translation factor.

$$H(s) = \frac{1}{\sqrt{(s/\omega_c)^2 + 1}^2} \qquad (2)$$

where $H(s)$ is the transfer function of the filter, it is the amplification factor of the different frequencies of the input signal, $\omega$ is the cutoff frequency, it is the value that determines which frequencies are a lowed through the filter.

$$y[n] = \frac{1}{N} \sum_{k=0}^{N-1} x[n - k] \qquad (3)$$

where, $y[n]$ is the output of the filter at time n, $x[n]$ is the input signal at time instant n, N is the window size of the filter, k is the time instant inside the window. The filtered signal was plotted alongside the complete signal and seizure events in a 1x4 graph array. The most distinct seizure event was selected for further analysis. The pre-ictal phase was extracted by visually choosing a time interval before the seizure onset, which was then transformed into time domain data for further analysis.

**Second Signal Processing Using Morlet Wavelet Technique.** The EEG signal was processed using the Morlet wavelet transform technique to obtain its time-frequency representation (Eq. 4). The power of the pre-ictal, ictal, and post-ictal phases was then calculated numerically for all channels of the convulsive event using the same technique (Eq. 5).

$$\psi(t) = \pi^{-1/4} e^{-i\omega_0 t} e^{-t^2/2} \tag{4}$$

$$P_f = \frac{1}{N} \sum_{i=1}^{N} |W_f(s_i)|^2 \tag{5}$$

where $P_f$ is the power at frequency f, N is the total number of data points,

$s_i$ is the ith scale factor, and $W_f(s_i)$ is the wavelet coefficient at scale $s_i$ and frequency f. Power values were stored in separate lists. The average power of the pre-ictal phase (PW1) was lower than the ictal phase (PW2). The power threshold based on PW1 accurately detected the pre-ictal phase, crucial for early seizure detection.

**Parameters of Preventive Detection of an Epilepsy Seizure.** Pre-seizure manifestations in epilepsy reflect the variability of brain activity. Auras, premonitory symptoms, arise from abnormal activity in specific brain regions, signaling the origin of the epileptic discharge [26]. To understand this, the average powers of fast delta waves before, during and after seizures were evaluated in relation to an established threshold.

This threshold was calculated from the maximum and minimum power values at each phase for the different brain waves. Similarly, the average powers of fast delta waves were determined by recording channel, patient and seizure type, establishing thresholds to account for variability in each case. The selection criteria of these thresholds were based on peaks and notable variations in the EEG signal graphs (see Fig. 4), discarding peaks far from the seizure. Finally, the average power after the seizure was also evaluated.

The real-time EEG signal is continuously checked against the pre-ictal power threshold at interval T. If the signal falls within the threshold, a logical "1" is triggered, activating an alert. The accuracy of the epileptic seizure prediction model was evaluated using the following formula:

$$accuracy = \frac{TP + TN}{TP + FP + TN + FN} \tag{6}$$

where TP represents true positives, TN represents true negatives, FP represents false positives, and FN represents false negatives. For the evaluation of the epileptic seizure prediction model, two important metrics are considered: specificity and sensitivity. Specificity measures the ability of the model to correctly identify non-seizure instances.

$$Specificity = \frac{TN}{TN + FP} * 100 \tag{7}$$

On the other hand, sensitivity (also known as recall or true positive rate) quantifies the model's ability to correctly detect seizure events.

$$Sensitivity = \frac{TP}{TP + FN} * 100 \tag{8}$$

The model's prediction was deemed correct if it detected a seizure within the specified pre-ictal phase. Accuracy serves as a measure of the model's performance in seizure prediction. To determine accuracy, the number of true positives, true negatives, false positives, and false negatives were identified. The accuracy was calculated using the formula mentioned earlier.

**Implementation of a Real-Time Electronic Warming Circuit for the Early Detection of Epileptic Seizures.** To create the epileptic seizure alarm device, the following materials are needed: an Arduino Uno board, a 16x2 LCD, a 10 kΩ potentiometer, two 220 Ω resistors, and a buzzer. The circuit is assembled by connecting the LCD pins to the digital pins of the Arduino. The potentiometer is used to adjust the LCD contrast, and the resistors are connected in series with the buzzer to protect it from excessive current. The Arduino code is programmed to read the signal from an EEG sensor and detect values indicating a possible seizure. If a seizure is detected, the code activates the buzzer and displays a message on the LCD indicating the occurrence of a seizure (see Fig. 3).

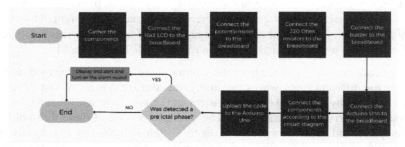

**Fig. 3.** Summarized process of the implementation of a real-time electronic warning circuit.

Finally, an EEG signal is processed using the Morlet wavelet transform to analyze its power in the pre-ictal phase. If the power reaches the threshold, an alert is triggered on the Arduino. The Python-Arduino communication is established through the pyserial library. The Arduino code activates the LCD and buzzer, displaying the text "Alert! Inject X gr Carbamazep" while emitting an alert tone.

## 3  Results

The proposed warning device for early detection of epilepsy using an EEG signal power threshold was tested on four different types of epilepsy: WIAS, IAS in males, IAS in females, and FBTC. Calculations were performed for each type of epilepsy, including pre-ictal time, maximum and minimum threshold values, accuracy, sensitivity, specificity, and response time. All these data are summarized in Table 4, providing a comprehensive view of the results obtained. It should be noted that the values obtained represent the averages obtained from the results of all channels for each seizure, according to the number of seizures each patient had in their respective classification.

Preictal visual analysis is crucial in seizure prediction. We obtained 30,720 samples of the preictal phase in male and female patients. The average duration of this phase

**Table 4.** Threshold values, accuracy, sensitivity characteristics, specificity and response time for each type of epilepsy.

| Type of epilepsy | Pre-ictal time ±1 [s] | Threshold maximum ±0.01 [uV²/Hz] | Threshold minimum ±0.01 [uV²/Hz] | Accuracy (%) ±0.1 | Sensitivity (%) ±0.1 | Specificity (%) ±0.1 | Response time (s) ±0.001 |
|---|---|---|---|---|---|---|---|
| WIAS | 60 | 4.27E-05 | 2.40E-09 | 86.60 | 85.71 | 87.50 | 0.042 |
| IAS (males) | 60 | 1.50E-07 | 3.91E-09 | 70.00 | 80.00 | 60.00 | 0.204 |
| IAS (females) | 60 | 5.50E-05 | 3.98E-09 | 72.72 | 80.00 | 66,70 | 0.105 |
| FBTC | 60 | 3.50E-07 | 8.38E-10 | 66.66 | 66.67 | 66.67 | 0.405 |

was 60 s (see Fig. 4). EEG signal power thresholds varied for different seizure types and genders. For example, for IAS seizures, the maximum and minimum thresholds were 1.5e-7 and 3.91e-9 respectively for males, and 5.50e-5 and 3.98e-9 for females. In addition, the system had a mean response time of 0.189 s to detect IAS, WIAS, and FBTC seizures in both male and female patients.

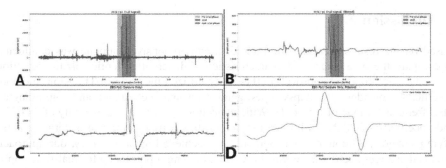

**Fig. 4.** IAS Seizures in Males - EEG Signal Representation

In addition, the data obtained for the accuracy of detection of epileptic activity for each type of epilepsy is indicated, with a margin of error of ± 0.1%. The values range from 66.66% to 86.60%, indicating the efficiency of the detection method in each case. Likewise, the sensitivity, represented in the table, shows the ability to correctly detect epileptic activity in each type of epilepsy. Sensitivity values range from 66.67% to 85.71%, indicating how well the presence of epileptic activity is identified in relation to the total number of positive cases. On the other hand, specificity indicates the ability to correctly rule out epileptic activity in negative cases. The specificity values range from 60.00% to 87.50%, indicating the ability of the detection method to correctly identify negative cases. On average for the model, an accuracy of 73.99%, sensitivity of 78.09% and specificity of 70.21% with their respective range of error were obtained.

Furthermore, the prototype was assembled with all its electronic components, showcasing a prompt on the screen upon loading the processed data. The prototype can be observed in Fig. 5.

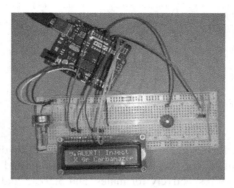

**Fig. 5.** Assembled real-time electronic warning circuit.

## 4 Discussion

Based on the results presented in Table 5, a comprehensive dialogue was conducted to compare the parameters and characteristics of different epileptic seizure detection methods. The proposed approach in this study utilized the Umbral Threshold method, specifically considering epilepsy types, gender during development, and employing an EEG frequency range of 0.5–4 Hz. With an accuracy of 73.99%, sensitivity of 78.09%, and specificity of 70.21%, the method demonstrated its potential in accurately identifying seizures. Although other methods may achieve higher accuracy, our approach offers advantages such as faster response time, making it promising for real-time applications and emergency situations. However, further research is needed to validate its effectiveness in diverse populations and different epilepsy pathologies.

In this section, it is relevant to address the difference in frequency range between our approach and the approaches of other authors, as noted in the literature. Our research focused on an EEG frequency range of 0.5–4 Hz, in contrast to the broader approaches spanning frequencies up to 30 Hz or even 100 Hz used by other investigators in similar studies. The deliberate choice of this narrower frequency range is based on the proven efficacy of the delta band (0.5–4 Hz) in detecting seizures in patients with epilepsy, as mentioned in the introduction [12]. Numerous studies have highlighted the usefulness of this band in achieving outstanding accuracy in the identification of epileptic events. In addition, our methodology included a smoothing filter that helped to maintain a more coherent representation of the signal in this frequency range.

When we compared it to other detection methods, an approach based on Recurrent Neural Networks (RNN) achieved an accuracy of 70.00% and a sensitivity of 87.00%, although it did not consider specific types of epilepsy. Another approach using Convolutional Neural Networks (CNN) achieved an accuracy of 99.90–100%, a sensitivity of

**Table 5.** Comparison between related studies

| Ref | Method | Device development | Gender consideration | Consideration of epilepsy types | EEG Frequency | Performance Measure | | |
|---|---|---|---|---|---|---|---|---|
| | | | | | | Accuracy (%) | Sensitivity (%) | Specificity (%) |
| – | Umbral Threshold | YES | YES | YES | 0.5–4 Hz | 73.99 | 78.09 | 70.21 |
| [7] | RNN | YES | YES | NO | – | 70.00 | 87.00 | – |
| [13] | SDCN | NO | NO | NO | – | 98.82 | 98.90 | 98.75 |
| [14] | CNN | NO | NO | NO | 0–80 Hz | 99.90–100 | 100.00 | 99.80–100 |
| [15] | BNLSTM–CASA | NO | YES | NO | – | 91.40 | 96.20 | 96.80 |
| [16] | GCNN | NO | NO | NO | 0.5–30 Hz | – | – | – |
| [17] | SVM | YES | YES | NO | 0.5–30 Hz | 99.87–98.14 | 99.91–98.16 | 99.82–98.12 |
| [18] | Deep learning | YES | YES | NO | – | 99.60 | 99.72 | 99.70 |
| [8] | Linear SVM | NO | NO | NO | 0 –100 Hz | 23.07 | 3.50 | 99.05 |

100.00% and a specificity of 99.80–100% for an EEG frequency of 0–80 Hz. Likewise, the BNLSTM-CASA method does not consider specific types of epilepsy, obtaining an accuracy of 91.40%, sensitivity of 96.20% and specificity of 96.80%. On the other hand, a GCNN-based method did not provide specific accuracy, sensitivity or specificity data.

Additionally, an approach using Support Vector Machine (SVM) considering an EEG frequency of 0.5–30 Hz obtained an accuracy of 99.87–98.14%, sensitivity of 99.91–98.16% and specificity of 99.82–98.12%. In addition, a method based on Deep Learning achieved 99.60% accuracy, 99.72% sensitivity and 99.70% specificity, without considering specific types of epilepsy. Another approach using Linear SVM using the same "Siena Scalp Database" as the present work obtained an accuracy of 23.07%, a sensitivity of 3.50% and a specificity of 99.05% for an EEG frequency of 0–100 Hz.

The histogram presents a comparison of results of eight methods for the detection of epilepsy (see Fig. 6). It stands out that the "Umbral Threshold" method shows a high sensitivity and specificity in relation to other methods evaluated. However, its low precision raises questions about its general classification ability. On the other hand, the "Deep learning" method stands out by achieving high values in all metrics, indicating its potential to obtain accurate and reliable results. The "SDCN", "CNN" and "GCNN" methods perform poorly on all metrics, highlighting the need to improve their effectiveness. It is important to consider the specifics of each method, such as development considerations and input features.

Furthermore, in Fig. 5, the fully assembled warning prototype can be observed, with all its electronic components in place and loaded with processed data. In the framework of this research, the prototype was not tested with real patients, but was solely evaluated using the previously selected database to validate its functionality. On the LCD screen, a preemptive alert can be displayed, indicating the approach of a seizure and recommending the administration of a specific dose of Carbamazepine. It is important to emphasize that the recommended injection dosage must be determined by a medical professional, as it will vary for each patient.

This approach provides an analytical and exploratory understanding of how brain signals vary around epileptic seizures and how these patterns can be identified by visual and numerical criteria. These thresholds were selected exploratorily because of abnormalities

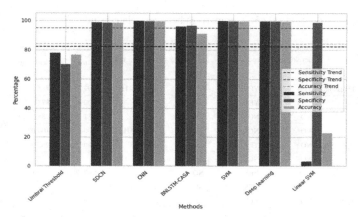

**Fig. 6.** Histogram of sensitivity, specificity and accuracy of methods.

in pre-seizure EEG traces. By comparing average powers during and around seizures with these thresholds, patterns of change in brain activity were identified, providing insight into variations before and after seizures. Although this analysis revealed valuable insights into the temporal complexities of brain signaling during seizures, variations between individuals, genders, and seizure types pose challenges that require a careful implementation strategy. A more personalized approach could improve its effectiveness in a variety of cases.

## 5 Conclusion

In conclusion, while our study provides evidence for the effectiveness of visual analysis of the pre-ictal phase and the use of electronic devices for seizure detection and prediction, it is important to acknowledge that there were some limitations to our study, including the small sample size and the use of a single electronic device. Additionally, there were some instances of false positives and false negatives in our results, which may be attributed to the complexity of the EEG signal and the presence of noise.

Therefore, further research is needed to address these issues and to develop more sophisticated algorithms for seizure detection and prediction. One potential avenue for future research is the development of software that can process EEG signals in a more optimal manner, including the use of machine learning techniques to improve accuracy and reduce the risk of false positives and false negatives. Another important direction for future studies is the exploration of non-invasive methods for seizure detection, which may reduce the discomfort and inconvenience associated with current invasive techniques.

Our study highlights the importance of considering gender differences in seizure detection and prediction, as we found differences in accuracy and response time be-tween male and female patients for certain types of seizures. These findings can guide future research in the field of epilepsy management, such as the development of mathematical models that incorporate the coordinates of the electrodes and the signal emitted at each point, along with signal processing techniques, to generate heat maps of potential seizures over time.

This approach may lead to even more accurate predictions and personalized treatment plans for patients with epilepsy. Another potential avenue for further research is the development of mobile prediction applications that incorporate additional analysis parameters such as temperature, blood saturation, blood pressure, and other relevant health metrics. Such applications could provide patients with real-time alerts and guidance for managing their condition, improving their overall quality of life. Overall, the insights gained from this study have the potential to drive innovation in the field of epilepsy management and improve the lives of millions of people living with this condition.

# References

1. Beghi, E.: The epidemiology of epilepsy. Neuroepidemiology **54**(2), 185–191 (2020). https://doi.org/10.1159/000503831
2. Anwar, H., Khan, Q.U., Nadeem, N., Pervaiz, I., Ali, M., Cheema, F.F.: Epileptic seizures. Discoveries **8**(2), e128 (2020). https://doi.org/10.15190/D.2020.7
3. Milligan, T.A.: Epilepsy: a clinical overview. Am. J. Med. **134**(7), 840–847 (2021). https://doi.org/10.1016/J.AMJMED.2021.01.038
4. Detti, P., Vatti, G., de Lara, G.Z.M.: EEG synchronization analysis for seizure prediction: a study on data of noninvasive recordings. Processes **8**(7), 846 (2020). https://doi.org/10.3390/PR8070846
5. Abbasi, M.U., Rashad, A., Basalamah, A., Tariq, M.: Detection of epilepsy seizures in neonatal EEG using LSTM architecture. IEEE Access **7**, 179074–179085 (2019). https://doi.org/10.1109/ACCESS.2019.2959234
6. Beydoun, A., DuPont, S., Zhou, D., Matta, M., Nagire, V., Lagae, L.: Current role of carbamazepine and oxcarbazepine in the management of epilepsy. Seizure **83**, 251–263 (2020). https://doi.org/10.1016/J.SEIZURE.2020.10.018
7. Espinoza, J.I.V.: Clasificación automatizada de actividad cerebral anormal en pacientes neurocríticos para mejorar capacidad diagnóstica (2022). Accessed 23 June 2023. https://reposi torio.uchile.cl/handle/2250/187117
8. Jairo, J., Saiz, M.: Predicción de la fase pre-ictal de convulsiones en pacientes con epilepsia a partir de señales electroencefalográficas y electrocardiográficas. instname:Universidad Antonio Nariño (2021_. Accessed 23 June 2023. http://repositorio.uan.edu.co/handle/123456789/5015
9. Yumatov, E.A., et al.: Possibility for recognition of psychic brain activity with continuous wavelet analysis of EEG. J. Behav. Brain Sci. **9**(3), 67–77 (2019). https://doi.org/10.4236/JBBS.2019.93006
10. Cohen, M.X.: A better way to define and describe Morlet wavelets for time-frequency analysis. Neuroimage **199**, 81–86 (2019). https://doi.org/10.1016/J.NEUROIMAGE.2019.05.048
11. Pawar, S.S., Chougule, S.R.: Diagnosis of epileptic seizure a neurological disorder by implementation of discrete wavelet transform using electroencephalography. Lect. Notes Electr. Eng. **656**, 687–699 (2020). https://doi.org/10.1007/978-981-15-3992-3_59/COVER
12. Sameer, M., Gupta, B.: Time–frequency statistical features of delta band for detection of epileptic seizures. Wirel. Pers. Commun. **122**(1), 489–499 (2022). https://doi.org/10.1007/S11277-021-08909-Y/METRICS
13. Hussein, R., Lee, S., Ward, R., McKeown, M.J.: Semi-dilated convolutional neural networks for epileptic seizure prediction. Neural Netw. **139**, 212–222 (2021). https://doi.org/10.1016/J.NEUNET.2021.03.008

14. Chen, W., et al.: An automated detection of epileptic seizures EEG using CNN classifier based on feature fusion with high accuracy. BMC Med. Inf. Decis. Mak. **23**(1), 96 (2023). https://doi.org/10.1186/S12911-023-02180-W

15. Ma, M., et al.: Early prediction of epileptic seizure based on the BNLSTM-CASA model. IEEE Access **9**, 79600–79610 (2021). https://doi.org/10.1109/ACCESS.2021.3084635

16. Raeisi, K., Khazaei, M., Croce, P., Tamburro, G., Comani, S., Zappasodi, F.: A graph convolutional neural network for the automated detection of seizures in the neonatal EEG. Comput. Methods Progr. Biomed. **222**, 106950 (2022). https://doi.org/10.1016/j.cmpb.2022.106950

17. Shariat, A., Zarei, A., Karvigh, S.A., Asl, B.M.: Automatic detection of epileptic seizures using Riemannian geometry from scalp EEG recordings. Med. Biol. Eng. Comput. **59**(7–8), 1431–1445 (2021). https://doi.org/10.1007/S11517-021-02385-Z

18. Daoud, H., Bayoumi, M.A.: Efficient epileptic seizure prediction based on deep learning. IEEE Trans. Biomed. Circuits Syst. **13**(5), 804–813 (2019). https://doi.org/10.1109/TBCAS.2019.2929053

19. Almeida-Galarraga, D., et al.: Glaucoma detection through digital processing from fundus images using MATLAB. In: Proceedings - 2021 2nd International Conference on Information Systems and Software Technologies, ICI2ST 2021, pp. 39–45 (2021). https://doi.org/10.1109/ICI2ST51859.2021.00014

20. J. D. Suquilanda-Pesántez *et al.*, "Prediction of Parkinson's Disease Severity Based on Gait Signals Using a Neural Network and the Fast Fourier Transform," *Advances in Intelligent Systems and Computing*, vol. 1326 AISC, pp. 3–18, 2021, doi: https://doi.org/10.1007/978-3-030-68080-0_1/COVER

21. Pereira-Carrillo, J., Suntaxi-Dominguez, D., Guarnizo-Cabezas, O., Villalba-Meneses, G., Tirado-Espín, A., Almeida-Galárraga, D.: Comparison between two novel approaches in automatic breast cancer detection and diagnosis and its contribution in military defense. In: Rocha, Á., Fajardo-Toro, C.H., Rodríguez, J.M.R. (eds.) Developments and Advances in Defense and Security: Proceedings of MICRADS 2021, pp. 189–201. Springer, Singapore (2022). https://doi.org/10.1007/978-981-16-4884-7_15

22. Yanchatuña, O.P., et al.: Skin lesion detection and classification using convolutional neural network for deep feature extraction and support vector machine. Int. J. Adv. Sci. Eng. Inf. Technol. **11**(3), 1260–1267 (2021). https://doi.org/10.18517/IJASEIT.11.3.13679

23. Suquilanda-Pesántez, J.D., Salazar, E.D.A., Almeida-Galárraga, D., Salum, G., Villalba-Meneses, F., Gomezjurado, M.E.G.: NIFtHool: an informatics program for identification of NifH proteins using deep neural networks. F1000Research **11**, 164 (2022). https://doi.org/10.12688/f1000research.107925.1

24. Salazar, E.D.A., et al.: Design of a glove controlled by electromyographic signals for the rehabilitation of patients with rheumatoid arthritis. Commun. Comput. Inf. Sci. **1307**, 3–11 (2020). https://doi.org/10.1007/978-3-030-62833-8_1/COVER

25. Almeida-Galárraga, D.A., Felip, A.S., Martínez, F.M., Serrano-Mateo, L.: Photoelastic analysis of shoulder arthroplasty: current descriptive analysis of research in scientific journals. IFMBE Proc. **68**(2), 713–717 (2018). https://doi.org/10.1007/978-981-10-9038-7_132/COVER

26. De Rivera, J.L.G.: Psicopatología de la epilepsia (1981)

# Optimal Location of the Electric Vehicle Charging Stands Using Multi-objective Evolutionary Algorithms: Cuenca City as a Case Study

Hector Utreras and Rolando Armas[✉]

Yachay Tech University, Urcuqui Ibarra, Ecuador
{hector.utreras,tarmas}@yachaytech.edu.ec
http://www.yachaytech.edu.ec

**Abstract.** Optimizing infrastructure is crucial for increasing the adoption of electric vehicles due to the current lack of support. This paper focuses on optimizing the placement of electric vehicle (EV) charging stations in Cuenca City (Ecuador). The study employs multi-objective evolutionary algorithms (MOEA) and a custom interface integrating a transportation simulator and MOEA framework. The mobility simulator configures Cuenca's transportation scenario, including mobility plans and agent movement around charging stations. MOEA sets up the genetic algorithm by defining individuals, populations, parameters, evaluation functions and operators. Location optimization involves minimizing travel time and the number of stations and maximizing Quality of Service (QoS) simultaneously. The algorithm optimizes the placement of 20 potential charging station locations. The Pareto Optimal Set obtained from the evolutionary process highlights the optimal solutions regarding travel time, number of stations and QoS. These configurations are then mapped onto Cuenca's road network. Analyses include hypervolume and objective correlation. These evaluations assess solution quality and quantify objective relationships. The study demonstrates the successful integration of traffic and mobility simulator and MOEA framework, enabling optimal solutions. The results provide valuable insights for decision-makers in designing and optimizing EV charging infrastructure. Overall, this research contributes to optimizing EV charging station placement in Cuenca, addressing environmental concerns and infrastructure limitations.

**Keywords:** Electric vehicle charging stations · multi-objective evolutionary algorithms · Optimization · Simulation

## 1 Introduction

Mobility has always been a primary concern for city planners around the world. With the increasing population and urbanization, sustainable and efficient transportation systems are becoming crucial. The emergence of electric shared and

J. Maldonado-Mahauad et al. (Eds.): TICEC 2023, CCIS 1885, pp. 309–323, 2023.
https://doi.org/10.1007/978-3-031-45438-7_21

intelligent mobility is seen as a general trend in the industry and is expected to play a significant role in addressing this challenge [7]. Electric shared mobility, which includes electric buses, cars, bikes, and scooters, has the potential to reduce the carbon footprint and improve air quality. These vehicles are also cost-effective and easy to maintain, making them an attractive option for individuals and businesses. On the other hand, intelligent mobility, which involves using data and technology to optimize transportation systems, can improve traffic flow, reduce congestion, and enhance safety. By combining these two trends, cities can create a more sustainable and efficient transportation network that benefits citizens. The rising need for eco-friendly transportation has led to the creation of electric vehicles (EVs) as a sustainable alternative to gasoline-powered cars. The automotive industry is introducing more clean energy options to the market [12,13], while cities worldwide are constructing infrastructure to support the shift towards eco-friendly mobility. However, implementing this change requires careful consideration of location, infrastructure, costs, and demand. Electric vehicles have become popular due to the increasing demand for sustainable transportation. The primary challenge for these vehicles is the need for charging infrastructure, which hinders their widespread adoption. To tackle this problem, we conducted a study to find the optimal network of charging stations for EVs.

In recent years, researchers have dedicated significant attention to the problem of locating optimal electric vehicle (EV) charging stations. Several methods and algorithms have been proposed to address this challenge. Genetic and heuristic algorithms have been successfully applied to determine the best charging station locations [11]. For instance, Wang et al. [14] focused on optimizing the location and dimensions of charging stations along highway networks, considering budget constraints. They developed a model based on Genetic Algorithms and a heuristic algorithm specifically tailored to this problem. Zhou et al. [15] developed a model that considered the total social cost and the cost of operating charging stations under different distribution conditions. Genetic Algorithms determined optimal charging station locations while considering various objectives such as building, charging, and environmental costs.

Our approach involved a multi-objective optimization strategy that aimed to minimize travel time, optimize the number and capacity of stations, and enhance the quality of service for drivers. We chose Cuenca, Ecuador, as our scenario because of its initiatives in implementing electric transportation. Our interdisciplinary research involves transportation, optimization, data science, and computer science areas. The optimal charging infrastructure solution can significantly impact EV adoption, reduce greenhouse gas emissions, and mitigate climate change. To solve this complex problem, we used a traffic simulator, multi-objective evolutionary algorithms framework, and data exploration methods to determine the best location and capacity for charging stations. Our approach is designed to provide city planners with an instrument that facilitates making informed decisions based on multiple criteria.

The paper is structured as follows. Section 2 presents the method and its components. Section 3 presents and analyzes the results. Finally, our conclusions and possible future research directions are given in Sect. 4.

# 2  Method and Components

## 2.1  Overview

The EV charging station allocation problem refers to the challenge of efficiently distributing and allocating charging stations for electric vehicles in a given area or region. The goal is to find the optimal location and number of charging stations to ensure electric vehicle owners can access reliable and convenient charging options. This section discusses the phases involved in solving this problem.

The problem definition phase determines the scenario simulation design, configuration, experimental setup and integration with a multi-objective evolutionary algorithms (MOEA) framework. Figure 1 shows the model components integration. The simulation phase utilizes the Multi-Agent Transportation Simulator (MATSim) framework [6] to model charging infrastructure, EV configuration, and agent movements given by mobility plans. The road network is obtained from OpenStreetMap [8]. The MOEA phase concerns the definition of solution representation, objective optimization functions and algorithm settings.

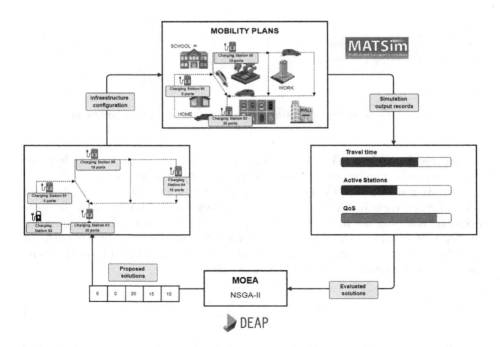

**Fig. 1.** Integration of the model components

We define the candidate or potential locations for charging stations based on places that concentrate several activities, such as malls, universities, schools, etc. The genetic representation phase translates the location into a genetic configuration, using a chromosome with genes representing a specific location and capacity. The simulator takes that genetic configuration to create the scenario, run and output records that are used as fitness functions for each solution. MOEA evaluates each solution based on the output simulation and proposes new solutions or configurations the simulator will test for the next generation.

## 2.2 The MOEA Configuration

**Representation:** The algorithm represents solutions as individuals, which are chromosomes composed of 20 genes representing charging stations. Each gene has an integer value ranging from 0 to 4, indicating the absence of a charging station or the presence of stations with different numbers of ports for charge. The values 1, 2, 3 and 4 are codes for 5, 10, 15 and 20 ports respectively. The genetic configuration of individuals allows for exploring various combinations of charging stations and evaluating their performance based on the three objectives (Fig. 2).

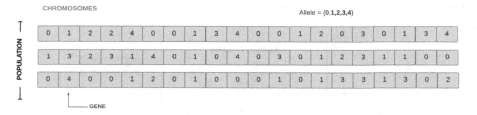

**Fig. 2.** Genetic representation of a population of possible solutions

**Objective Functions:** The algorithm aims to find an optimal balance between travel time, the number of stations, and the quality of service for EVs.

The **travel time (tt)** objective calculates the average time required for EVs to reach their destination. It only considers the commuting time between activities and does not include charging or waiting time. Travel time is computed by Eq. 1. It considers the travel time on each link of the route, represented by $t_{il}$, where $l$ is the link, and $i$ is the vehicle. $L$ means the total links in the route and $n_{EV}$ is the total number of electric vehicles.

$$f_1 = tt = \frac{1}{n_{EV}} \sum_{i=1}^{n_{EV}} \sum_{l=1}^{L} t_{il} \tag{1}$$

The **number of stations** $(n_{st})$ objective counts the active stations and determines the optimal number required for efficient mobility and accessibility.

A solution is represented by an array of integers $C_1, C_2 \cdots, C_j, \cdots C_P$. Each value $C_j$ codes the capacity for each possible location, where $C_j = \{0, 1, 2, 3, 4\}$ $(j = 1, \cdots, P)$. This objective counts the active stations, expressed as $(C_j \neq 0)$ in the representation and can be calculated using Eq. 2, where P represents the total number of stations.

$$f_2 = n_{St} = \sum_{j=1}^{P} D_j, \text{ where } D_j = \begin{cases} 1, & \text{if } C_j \neq 0 \\ 0, & \text{otherwise} \end{cases} \tag{2}$$

The **quality of service (QoS)** objective measures the ratio of vehicles charging $(Ev_{charg})$ to vehicles in the queue $(Ev_{waiting})$. It is expressed by Eq. 3. The variable $t$ represents a time interval of 5 min, while $T$ refers to the entire duration of the 24 h of simulation.

$$QoS = \frac{\sum_t^T Ev_{charg}(t)}{\sum_t^T Ev_{\text{waiting}}(t)} \tag{3}$$

**Algorithm and Operators:** The NSGA-II algorithm [3] is employed to generate a diverse set of individuals representing different combinations of charging stations. Each individual's fitness is evaluated based on the multi-objective optimization function, which considers all three objectives simultaneously. The algorithm aims to find a set of individuals representing the Pareto Optimal Set, where no individual can be improved in one objective without sacrificing performance in the other. This set provides decision-makers with a range of solutions to choose from. The Distributed Evolutionary Algorithms in Python (DEAP) framework [4] is used to adapt the NSGA-II algorithm. DEAP provides genetic operators such as selection, crossover, and mutation, which are essential for evolution. The selection operator applies the NSGA-II selection algorithm to a group of individuals. The crossover operator performs a one-point crossover on the individuals. Additionally, a mutation operator is designed to increment or decrease each gene's value within the chromosome.

The algorithm is tested and deployed to determine the best set of charging stations that can serve the population of EVs with minimal travel time, a reduced number of stations, and high quality of service. Integrating DEAP and MATSim enables evaluating the algorithm's performance and its impact on the overall transportation system.

### 2.3   Cuenca's Mobility Scenario

The research was conducted in Cuenca City (Ecuador), using MATSim to model agent movement. The scenario setup involved mobility plans, network infrastructure, and charging stands. The city of Cuenca was studied to identify 20 potential locations for charging stations based on proximity to areas with high activity or space availability. Open Street Map was used to extract road network information, which was converted into the required XML format for MATSim. The

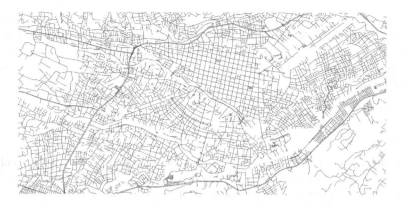

**Fig. 3.** Cuenca's network infrastructure obtained from Open Street Map

resulting network consisted of 26.361 links covering an area of 56 km$^2$. Figure 3 displays Cuenca's street network.

A synthetic scenario was created to ensure the simulator's optimal functioning, although it only used partly real data about Cuenca's transportation. The number of circulating vehicles was set to 500 EVs, and only one type of vehicle was considered. Real trend as peak-hour traffic, mobility plans based on places with high activity, and space availability were incorporated into the scenario. Mobility patterns were defined to determine the distribution of trips executed by agents, representing their behaviour. Mobility plans specified the details of individual agent trips, including starting and ending locations, activity type and duration, and vehicle types. Agents have two main trips: home-activity and activity-home. There are four types of activities: Home (H), Personal(P), Shop(S) and Work(W). Figure 4 shows a mobility plan configuration example for a specific agent.

Agents' travel origins were assigned based on the proportion of the current population, with the home location as the starting point. Agents travel through the network until reaching destinations associated with shopping, work or personal activities.

When choosing locations for charging stations, we focused on areas with a lot of activity, including schools, parking lots, stadiums, markets, shopping centres, transportation stations, and airports. Places that provided the necessary space for electric charging stations were considered. A total of 20 locations meeting the requirements were identified. Figure 5 depicts the street network of Cuenca, the selected geographical area, and the potential locations of the 20 electric charging stations. Finally, we set 500 EVs with a total capacity of the battery of 40 KW and a low initial state of charge to force each EV to go to the charge station to complete their trip.

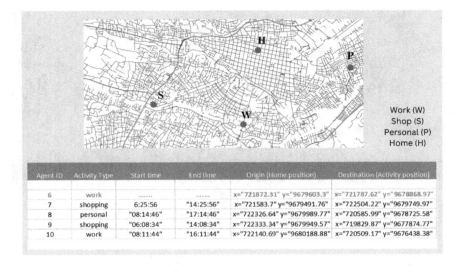

| Agent ID | Activity Type | Start time | End time | Origin (Home position) | Destination (Activity position) |
|---|---|---|---|---|---|
| 6 | work | ........ | ........ | x="721872.31" y="9679603.3" | x="721787.62" y="9678868.97" |
| 7 | shopping | 6:25:56 | "14:25:56" | x="721583.7" y="9679491.76" | x="722504.22" y="9679749.97" |
| 8 | personal | "08:14:46" | "17:14:46" | x="722326.64" y="9679989.77" | x="720585.99" y="9678725.58" |
| 9 | shopping | "06:08:34" | "14:08:34" | x="722333.34" y="9679949.57" | x="719829.87" y="9677874.77" |
| 10 | work | "08:11:44" | "16:11:44" | x="722140.69" y="9680188.88" | x="720509.17" y="9676438.38" |

**Fig. 4.** Mobility plan of agents trips

## 3 Results

### 3.1 Experimental Settings

The process of parameter selection for the multi-objective evolutionary algorithm (MOEA) involved choosing appropriate values for population size, mutation probability, number of generations, and the number of experiments. These parameters play a crucial role in the performance and convergence of the algorithm. The population size determines the number of individuals in each generation, while the mutation probability determines the likelihood of genes being changed during the evolution process. The number of generations represents the number of iterations the algorithm will go through to find optimal solutions. Lastly, the number of experiments refers to running the algorithm multiple times with different random seeds to ensure reliable results [1]. Research suggests that a low mutation probability can lead to premature convergence, while a high probability can result in chaotic behavior. The recommended range for mutation probabilities in evolutionary algorithms is between 1% and 5% [2,9,10].

After conducting experiments and evaluating different parameter values, we have identified optimal values for our MOEA. These values were determined through empirical studies and are expected to balance exploration and exploitation of the search space, leading to better convergence and more accurate results. Our experimental study aligns with the research efforts of several scholars who have also conducted empirical studies to find optimal parameter values for genetic algorithms [5]. It is important to note that there is no one-size-fits-all solution to parameter selection, as different problems may require different values to achieve optimal results. Table 1 shows the selected parameter and operator values during experimentation.

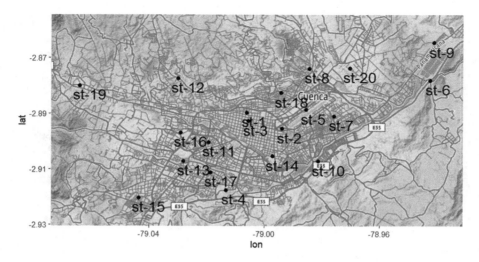

**Fig. 5.** Geographical potential location of the 20 charging stations

**Table 1.** Selected evolutionary parameters during experimentation

| Parameter | Value |
|---|---|
| Population size | 20 |
| Crossover probability (CXPB) | 0.95 |
| Mutation probability (MUTPB) | $\frac{1}{20} = 0.05$ |
| Number of generations (NGEN) | 50 |
| Number of experiments | 12 (with different random seeds) |

## 3.2    Algorithm Convergence

Calculating the hypervolume is a useful method to assess the quality of the Pareto front approximation generated by a multi-objective optimization algorithm. The hypervolume results show the quality of the solutions obtained from the optimization process. The hypervolume was calculated for each generation in 12 experiments, each consisting of 50 generations. The hypervolumes were combined and plotted using boxplots (Fig. 6), with the x-axis representing generations and the y-axis representing hypervolumes. The plot reveals initial variability in hypervolumes, which gradually increases over generations. Some boxplots have longer upper whiskers, indicating outliers with higher hypervolumes, suggesting significant performance differences among solutions. The key observation is that the hypervolume steadily increases until generation 40, after which it begins to flatten out. This indicates that the set of solutions improves across all objectives. The flattening curve suggests convergence, with improvements becoming less significant beyond that generation.

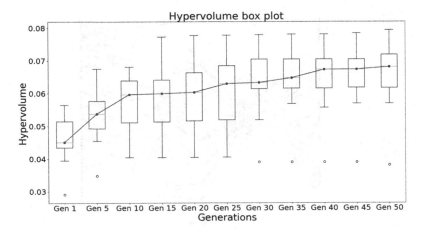

**Fig. 6.** Hypervolume calculation by generations

### 3.3   Trade-off

When optimizing multiple objectives in a problem, it is often evidence of trade-offs between them. Improving one objective may come at the expense of another, making understanding the intricate relationships between different objectives crucial. This section explores the trade-off between three objectives: travel time, number of stations, and quality of service. Two analytical techniques, namely the parallel coordinate plot and correlation analysis, are employed to gain insights into these trade-offs.

**Analysis Using Parallel Coordinate Plot.** To analyze the trade-off between the objectives, we employed a parallel coordinate plot, which facilitates the visualization of multiple variables on a single plot. We plotted the fitness values of the three objectives: travel time, number of stations, and quality of service. The fitness values were obtained from the Pareto Optimal Set (POS) and normalized for comparison. The parallel coordinate plot (Fig. 7) revealed a trade-off between travel time and the number of stations, indicating that reducing the number of stations results in increased travel time. However, the relationship between the number of stations and service quality appeared less straightforward, with no apparent pattern observed.

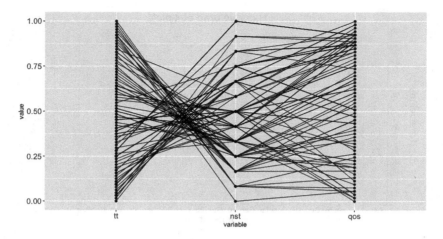

**Fig. 7.** Parallel coordinate plot between objectives

**Correlation Analysis.** We conducted a correlation analysis to gain a more precise understanding of the relationships between the objectives. The analysis (Fig. 8) revealed a negative correlation coefficient of −0.81 between travel time and the number of stations, confirming the trade-off between these objectives. Furthermore, we found a positive correlation coefficient of 0.58 between the number of stations and the quality of service, suggesting a potentially positive relationship. Additionally, there was a negative correlation coefficient of −0.16 between travel time and the quality of service. Overall, the correlation analysis provided a quantitative perspective on the relationships between the objectives.

## 3.4   Solutions

The study conducted a simulation and evolutionary process using the NSGA-II algorithm to obtain a Pareto Optimal Set (POS) of solutions for optimizing the number of stations ($n_{st}$), quality of service ($QoS$), and travel time ($tt$). The analysis focused on solutions prioritizing a lower number of stations to reduce construction costs while maintaining an acceptable quality of service and travel time. The results showed limited solutions with both a low number of stations and high quality of service. However, solutions with a low number of stations and acceptable quality of service were identified. It was observed that a higher quality of service correlated with a greater number of available stations and chargers. Two-dimensional and a 3D plot were presented to visualize the Pareto Optimal Set and the trade-offs between the objectives.

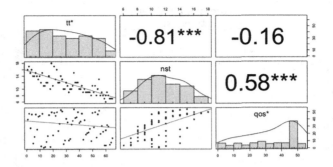

**Fig. 8.** Quantitative analysis of objectives correlation

Figure 9 shows the 3D representation of Pareto Optimal Set based on the three objectives.

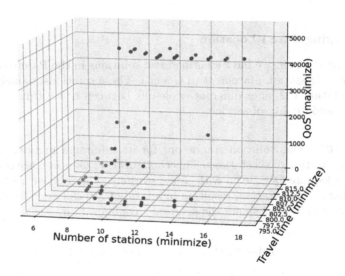

**Fig. 9.** 3D plot of Pareto Optimal Set

Figure 10 shows a 2D plot of the Pareto Optimal set with the following configurations: travel time vs. the number of stations, and colored according to the QoS.

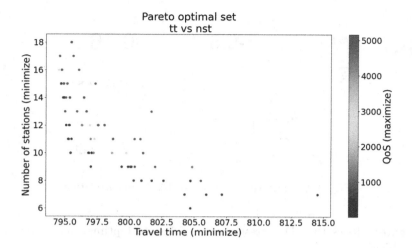

**Fig. 10.** 2D plot of Pareto Optimal Set (tt vs Nst coloured by QoS)

## 3.5 Charging Stand Location

Based on the analysis, we have identified two solutions in the Pareto optimal set for the charging station placement in Cuenca. These solutions, namely Solution 107 and Solution 112, offer different trade-offs between travel time, the number of stations, and quality of service.

**Solution 107.** This solution stands out for its minimum number of stations, with a configuration of six stations. This configuration reduces construction costs and offers adequate QoS, even with a few stations. The solution requires either 15 or 20 chargers per station, resulting in a total of 110 chargers. Figure 11 plots the solution and Table 2 shows the solution's configuration.

**Table 2.** Configuration of solution 107

| Genetic configuration (solution 107) | | | |
|---|---|---|---|
| 0 0 0 0 3 0 4 0 0 3 4 0 4 4 0 0 0 0 0 0 | | | |
| **tt** | **nst** | **QoS** | **Chargers** |
| 804.7112334 | 6 | 150.2686567 | 110 |

**Solution 112.** It offers a configuration with seven stations, slightly increasing the number of stations compared to Solution 107. This configuration maintains a reasonable travel time but provides a restrictive QoS compared with the previous

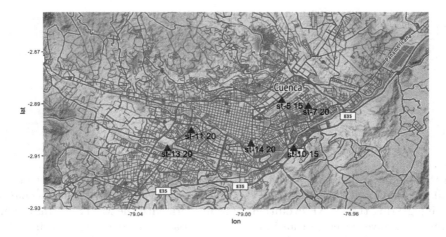

**Fig. 11.** Solution 107 spatial location of the stations

solution. The number of chargers ports in this solution is mostly 15 or 20 per station, resulting in 110 chargers. Figure 12 plots the solution and Table 3 shows the solution's configuration. Note that the total capacity of the solution is similar to solution 107. However, the station's distribution in the area reduces the QoS even with one more station, compared with solution 107. By choosing those solutions, we exhibit that city planners can discriminate different configurations to support their decisions in a better way.

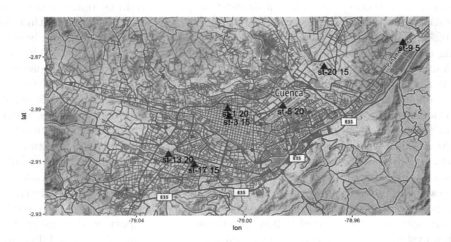

**Fig. 12.** Spatial location of the stations on the Cuenca's map (solution 112)

**Table 3.** Configuration of solution 112

| Genetic configuration (solution 112) | | | |
|---|---|---|---|
| 4 0 3 0 4 0 0 0 1 0 0 0 4 0 0 0 3 0 0 3 | | | |
| **tt** | **nst** | **QoS** | **Chargers** |
| 814.5467789 | 7 | 46.96330275 | 110 |

## 4   Conclusions and Future Work

In this study, we have addressed the complex challenge of determining the optimal locations and capacities of EVs charging stations in the Cuenca scenario. By integrating the DEAP evolutionary framework with the MATSim traffic simulator, we have developed an innovative approach that considers the interdisciplinary nature of the problem and effectively balances conflicting objectives. Through analyzing various mobility scenarios and collecting relevant data from simulations, we have achieved a comprehensive analysis of the charging infrastructure. The integration of evolutionary algorithms and traffic simulation has allowed us to evaluate different solution options and provide recommendations for the design of EV charging infrastructure. Our research contributes to the advancement of transportation engineering, electrical engineering, computer science, and data analytics, while also promoting the adoption of electric cars and fostering the development of sustainable transportation systems.

We can summarize our findings in the following: - Integrating DEAP and MATSim through a Python-based interface has enabled comprehensive analysis and data collection, providing a foundation for determining optimal charging station locations and capacities. - Utilizing the NSGA-II algorithm within the DEAP framework has achieved multi-objective optimization, effectively balancing travel time, the number of charging stations, and service quality. - Through simulations in the MATSim environment, we have evaluated the performance of the EV charging infrastructure, gaining valuable insights into its effectiveness.

There are several areas for extension and improvement in future work. Incorporating real-world transportation data, including the number of cars, different types of transport, and actual traffic flows, would enhance the accuracy of our simulations and better reflect traveller behaviour in the area. Additionally, adding objectives such as building costs, energy efficiency, and environmental sustainability would provide a more comprehensive evaluation of the trade-offs between different transportation options, informing policy decisions. Furthermore, exploring scenarios that consider the use of electric buses as a public transportation option would allow us to assess their impact on the transportation system and analyze their potential benefits in terms of sustainability and energy efficiency. By pursuing these future directions, we can advance the field of transportation and mobility research and contribute to the development of efficient and sustainable transportation systems that promote the adoption of EVs and benefit society as a whole.

# References

1. Alaya, M.B., Louati, W., Hammami, M., Alimi, A.M.: Comparison of some meta-heuristic algorithms for the flexible job-shop scheduling problem. J. Intell. Manuf. **30**(5), 2145–2161 (2019)
2. De, S., Saha, S., Chakraborty, U.: Multimodal optimization using adaptive binary differential evolution with mutation probability-based adaptation. Swarm Evol. Comput. **65**, 100902 (2021)
3. Deb, K., Agrawal, S., Pratap, A., Meyarivan, T.: A fast elitist non-dominated sorting genetic algorithm for multi-objective optimization: NSGA-II. IEEE Trans. Evol. Comput. **6**(2), 182–197 (2002)
4. Fortin, F.A., Rainville, F.M.D., Gardner, M.A., Parizeau, M., Gagné, C.: DEAP framework documentation (2012). https://deap.readthedocs.io/en/master/
5. Goldberg, D.E., Wang, L., Yao, X., Liu, S.: The effects of parameter tuning on genetic algorithm performance. Front. Comput. Sci. **13**(2), 330–341 (2019)
6. Horni, A., Nagel, K., Axhausen, K.W.: The Multi-Agent Transport Simulation MATSim. Ubiquity Press, London (2016)
7. Kamiya, G., Teter, J.: Shared, automated... and electric? (2019). https://www.iea.org/commentaries/shared-automated-and-electric
8. OpenStreetMap contributors: Planet dump (2017). https://planet.osm.org. https://www.openstreetmap.org
9. Qin, A., Huang, V., Suganthan, P.: Analysis and optimization of mutation probabilities in differential evolution. IEEE Trans. Cybern. **50**(6), 2387–2399 (2019)
10. Rostami, M., Bahreininejad, A.: Mutation operators in evolutionary algorithms: a review. Neural Comput. Appl. **32**(21), 15989–16021 (2020)
11. Shaikh, P.W., El-Abd, M., Khanafer, M., Gao, K.: A review on swarm intelligence and evolutionary algorithms for solving the traffic signal control problem. IEEE Trans. Intell. Transp. Syst. **23**(1), 48–63 (2020)
12. Techxplore: Opel to be 100% electric in Europe by 2028: Ceo (2021). https://techxplore.com/news/2021-07-opel-electric-europe-ceo.html
13. Techxplore: Stellantis keeps UK plant to produce electric vehicles (2021). https://techxplore.com/news/2021-07-stellantis-uk-electric-vehicles.html
14. Wang, Y., Shi, J., Wang, R., Liu, Z., Wang, L.: Siting and sizing of fast charging stations in highway network with budget constraint. Appl. Energy **228**, 1255–1271 (2018)
15. Zhou, G., Zhu, Z., Luo, S.: Location optimization of electric vehicle charging stations: based on cost model and genetic algorithm. Energy **247**, 123437 (2022)

# Detecting Parkinson's Disease with Convolutional Neural Networks: Voice Analysis and Deep Learning

Kevin Saltos[1] , Luis Zhinin-Vera[2,3,4]([✉]) , Cristina Godoy[1] ,
Roberth Chachalo[3] , Diego Almeida-Galárraga[1] ,
Carolina Cadena-Morejón[3] , Andrés Tirado-Espín[1] ,
Jonathan Cruz-Varela[1] , and Fernando Villalba Meneses[1]

[1] School of Biological Sciences and Engineering, Yachay Tech University,
100119 Urcuquí, Ecuador
[2] LoUISE Research Group, University of Castilla-La Mancha, 02071 Albacete, Spain
luis.zhinin@uclm.es
[3] School of Mathematical and Computational Sciences, Yachay Tech University,
100650 Urcuquí, Ecuador
[4] MIND Research Group - Model Intelligent Networks Development, Ibarra, Ecuador

**Abstract.** Parkinson's disease, the second most prevalent neurodegenerative disorder among individuals over the age of 65, poses challenges in early-stage detection, often requiring multiple tests to confirm diagnosis. However, advancements in neural network technology have facilitated the analysis, simplification, and prediction of complex problems that surpass human capacity in terms of speed and efficiency. With its diverse array of physical symptoms, we have specifically focused on vocal pitch changes and alterations, as they manifest in approximately 90% of Parkinson's patients. Furthermore, the acquisition of vocal data is non-invasive and easily accessible. In this study, we employ a convolutional neural network (CNN) to assess the predictive accuracy of Parkinson's disease using voice data from affected individuals. Our results demonstrate promising accuracy, achieving a classification accuracy of 95%. By training our CNN model, we aim to provide an affordable and convenient solution for detecting this neurodegenerative condition.

**Keywords:** parkinson's disease · voice analysis · convolutional neural network

## 1 Introduction

Parkinson's disease (PD) is a neurodegenerative disorder that affects a global population exceeding 10 million individuals. Epidemiological studies indicate that around 1% of individuals aged 65 and older worldwide are affected by PD [1]. However, there is a notable lack of comprehensive research regarding the epidemiological landscape of PD in Ecuador. Consequently, the prevalence of this

J. Maldonado-Mahauad et al. (Eds.): TICEC 2023, CCIS 1885, pp. 324–336, 2023.
https://doi.org/10.1007/978-3-031-45438-7_22

condition in Ecuador can only be assumed to be consistent with global statistics. Despite its high frequency, PD is not considered a catastrophic disease within the Ecuadorian context [6], resulting in a perception of limited significance.

PD is primarily characterized by the progressive deterioration of motor and cognitive functions. The notable attention of medical practitioners and researchers towards PD stems from its enigmatic etiology and the absence of curative interventions, leaving treatment options as the primary approach. Diagnosis of PD does not rely on a single definitive test [7].

Alternatively, the current diagnostic approach for Parkinson's disease (PD) relies on a comprehensive examination of patients' medical records, which unfortunately exhibits significant limitations. Research conducted by the National Institute of Neurological Disorders and Stroke reveals a meager 53% accuracy rate in early detection using this method, only marginally surpassing random guessing [10]. This emphasizes the pressing need for improved early detection strategies to optimize treatment outcomes. While levodopa-based pharmacotherapy remains the cornerstone of PD intervention, it is accompanied by challenges such as non-adherence, dyskinesia, and limited effectiveness in addressing speech and cognitive impairments. Moreover, the financial burden and associated discomfort associated with this treatment approach further compound the difficulties faced by patients [4].

In recent years, Artificial Intelligence (AI) and Machine Learning (ML) techniques have revolutionized the field of medical diagnosis and prognostication. Specifically, CNNs have demonstrated remarkable capabilities in extracting complex features from various data modalities, including images, audio, and time-series data. Its name is associated with a complex processing called convolution as a shown in Fig. 1. The inherent ability of CNNs to learn hierarchical representations and capture intricate patterns makes them an ideal candidate for analyzing voice signals and detecting subtle vocal changes associated with PD.

In this paper, we propose a novel approach that harnesses the capabilities of CNNs to predict PD based on voice analysis. By utilizing a dataset of voice recordings from both PD patients and healthy individuals, we train a CNN model to classify and differentiate between the two groups accurately. Our study aims to investigate the efficacy of this approach in early PD prediction and its potential as a non-invasive, cost-effective, and accessible tool for screening and monitoring individuals at risk of developing PD.

The paper is organized as follows. Section 2 provides a comprehensive review of related work in the field of PD diagnosis and the utilization of AI techniques. Section 3 describes the methodology employed in our study, including dataset collection, preprocessing techniques, and the architecture of the CNN model. Section 4, we present and discuss the results obtained from our experiments, evaluating the accuracy, sensitivity, and specificity of the proposed model. Section 5 concludes the paper, summarizing the key contributions, and suggests avenues for future research in this domain.

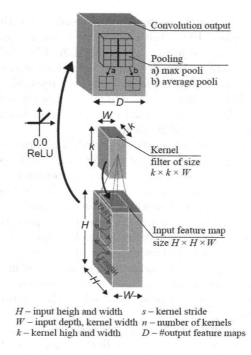

$H$ – input heigh and width        $s$ – kernel stride
$W$ – input depth, kernel width   $n$ – number of kernels
$k$ – kernel high and width         $D$ – #output feature maps

**Fig. 1.** Convolution process [11]

## 2    Related Works

### 2.1    Parkinson's Disease

PD is characterized by impairments in the control, coordination, and regulation of movement, including muscle tone and body posture. However, it is crucial to recognize the significant impact that PD has on speech production, leading to notable alterations in this domain. Voice alterations have been reported in approximately 90% of individuals diagnosed with PD [19]. Involuntary motor manifestations can affect the musculature of the larynx, resulting in modifications in laryngeal function and subsequent phonatory alterations [12].

Furthermore, a noticeable decrease in the kinematic activities of the respiratory, phonatory, and articulatory musculature has been observed and affected in individuals with PD. Commonly observed symptoms in Parkinson's patients include difficulty initiating oral aperture, resting tremor of the tongue, impaired mobility of the lips and base of the tongue, and incomplete elevation of the velum, resulting in rhinolalia [3]. These alterations occur due to the rigidity exhibited by the laryngeal musculature and structures involved in phonation. This concurrent rigidity impacts the respiratory system, which is responsible for facilitating the necessary airflow and air pressure essential for vocal production.

As a result, a decrease in subglottic pressure is observed, leading to insufficiently low pitch, posterior guttural resonance, reduced intensity, monotonous vocal quality, and hypo nasality [25]. These alterations are often misinterpreted as age-related modifications associated with presbyopia in older individuals [12] or symptoms indicative of depressive conditions [2]. Patients diagnosed with PD experience a significant decline in the ability of the laryngeal musculature to maintain a stable position during prolonged enunciation of vowel sounds [17].

In recent times, numerous computerized systems have emerged as potential solutions for early detection of Parkinson's disease through the analysis and monitoring of voice patterns [18]. At the University of Oxford [27], a comprehensive set of dysphonia measures was established and subjected to comparison through the utilization of four feature selection and binary classification algorithms. Meanwhile, researchers from the Computer Science Applied to Signal Processing research group at the Universidad Politécnica de Madrid (UPM), in collaboration with the Biomedical Technology Center, have developed a biomechanical simulator capable of emulating the distinctive characteristics of the phonatory system. Moreover, they have assessed various parameter extraction approaches to detect the presence of pathologies through the analysis of patients' vocal signals [25]. By conducting an articulatory analysis involving the rapid repetition of syllables such as /pa-ta-ka/ and calculating temporal and spectral features extracted from the voice onset time segments [7], a proposition is made to develop an expert system aimed at early Parkinson's disease detection. As speech impairment frequently manifests as an initial symptom of the disease, it holds potential as a valuable biomarker for aiding diagnosis and monitoring the progression of Parkinson's disease, considering the aforementioned characteristics [7].

## 2.2  Computational Models

Many studies have focused on the imaging treatment of PD patients. However, ANNs currently use speech problems and vocal impairment data to detect this neurological disease as shown in Table 1. Rahman et al. [21] used deep learning and machine learning to analyze a dataset including voice measurements from 31 individuals, 23 with PD. This dataset is from the ML ICU. The authors developed different models such as Extreme Gradient Boosting (XGBoost), Ada Boost, Light Gradient Boosting Machine, Naive Bayes, and deep neural networks (DNN1, DNN2, DNN3). 92% (XGBoost) and 95% (DNN2) accuracy were obtained depending on the classifier.

Yusra et al. [23] also analyzed a speech dataset from Oxford University to diagnose the disease. A Multi-layer ANN Perceptron with a backpropagation algorithm was used to effectively identify diseased patients from healthy ones by comparing two ANN architectures. The accuracy results of this work were 100% (training dataset) and 93% (test dataset). Manideep et al. [16] analyzed the vocal parameters of healthy and PD patients. The dataset for this study was collected from Kaggle. The authors used CNN and ANN (Artificial Neural Networks) and determined Gradient Boosting and Random Forest as the best classifiers. The proposed model obtained 99.53% accuracy on the test dataset, 100% specificity, and 99.76% sensitivity. Khan et al. [13] proposed a method using CNN from spectrograms generated from an IEMOCAP dataset. The data was collected by the Speech Analysis and Interpretation Laboratory (SAIL) of the University of Southern California (USC). This work obtained an accuracy of 82% (raw spectrogram) and 99% (clean spectrogram).

Shivangi et al. [22] used two neural network-based models: VGFR Spectrogram Detector and Voice Impairment Classifier. Using CNN and ANN and the database from the UCI ML Repository, they obtained outstanding results compared to other established models. Accuracy of 88.1% (VGFR) and 89.15% (Voice Impairment Classifier). Also, Maa et al. [15] used a double-sided deep learning ensemble model, and their results were very promising: 98.4% and 99.6%. This work is novel not only for its structure but also for its highly relevant results. Two data sets were used for this work.

Likewise, another work [26] using a CNN and ResNet with spectrograms, obtained 90% validation. The database produced audio recordings of 50 healthy people and 50 people with PD. Almaloglou et al. [5], and collaborators using a 2D CNN developed considerable structure and precision (98%). Two voice sources were collected: mPower and Saarbruecken. An interesting work [24] using a CNN he was able to identify ataxic and hypokinetic speech. The detection accuracy in this work was 89.75%. Finally, Khaskhoussy et al. [14] combined SVM and CNN with very positive results. This model obtained an accuracy of approximately 100%, a precision of 0.99.

## 3   Methodology

In this section, we delve into the methodology employed for our study, which encompasses two key components: Dataset Description and Data Preprocessing. These integral stages lay the foundation for our analysis and insights.

### 3.1   Dataset Description

The development of this paper encompassed several stages, as illustrated in Fig. 2. The dataset[1] employed for training the convolutional neural network was sourced from the Synapse platform [9], an open software platform that facilitates scientific research by providing accessible data. Importantly, obtaining this audio dataset did not require any specific request as it was readily available through the aforementioned link.

The dataset comprises a total of 779 voice recordings obtained from 620 patients diagnosed with Parkinson's disease, including 377 women and 326 men. In addition to this primary dataset, another supplementary database was utilized to test, consisting of 50 audio recordings from both individuals with Parkinson's disease and healthy individuals, sourced from free software. All audio recordings in the dataset are in .wav format and have durations ranging from 5 to 10 s.

---

[1] Dataset access: https://www.synapse.org/#!Synapse:syn2321748.

**Table 1.** Literature Review

| Ref. | Model | Database | Performance metrics |
|------|-------|----------|---------------------|
| [26] | CNN, ResNet | The PC-GITA database | 90% accuracy |
| [22] | CNN, ANN | UCI ML Repository | 88.17% and 89.15% of accuracy respectively |
| [5] | Two-dimensional (2D) CNN | mPower database and Saarbruecken Voice Database | 98% accuracy |
| [15] | Deep dual-side learning ensemble model | Data set 1-LSVT_voice _rehabilitation data set: Data set 2-Sakar data set | 98.4% and 99.6% accuracy |
| [24] | CNN with a AI system for audio classification (PWSI-AI-AC) | Neurology Department of Samsung Medical Center (parkinsonian disorders) | 89.75% accuracy |
| [13] | CNN | Speech Analysis and Interpretation Laboratory (SAIL) | 82% and 99% of accuracy on the raw and clean spectrogram, respectively |
| [23] | ANN (two models) | University of Oxford Repository by M.A. Little | 100% accuracy on training set and 93% on the test set |
| [21] | Extreme Gradient Boosting (XGBoost), DNN | UCI ML Parkinson dataset | 92% acc. (XGBoost); 95% acc. (DNN2) |
| [14] | SVM, CNN | Data obtained from speech tasks | 100% accuracy |
| [16] | CNN, ANN | Kaggle | 99.53% accuracy |

The inclusion of a diverse range of patients, both in terms of gender and disease status, ensures a comprehensive representation of the Parkinson's population within the dataset. This diversity enhances the generalizability of the trained model and strengthens its ability to accurately classify and differentiate voice patterns associated with Parkinson's disease. The availability of both primary and supplementary datasets further enriches the training process, facilitating a more robust and comprehensive analysis of the voice characteristics linked to the disease.

## 3.2 Data Preprocessing

Data preprocessing plays a crucial role in preparing the audio dataset for training the convolutional neural network. In this section, we describe the various steps involved in this process, starting with the visualization of the sound waves.

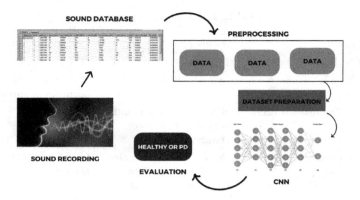

**Fig. 2.** The general methodology used in this approach.

To gain insights into the frequency characteristics of the audio data, a code was implemented to trace the sound waves of each audio file in the dataset. This visualization technique allows us to observe the temporal aspects of the audio signals, providing an initial understanding of their patterns and variations. Figure 3 shows an example of a sound wave from one of the audios in the dataset.

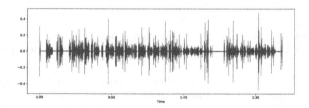

**Fig. 3.** Sound waveform extracted from the audio in *.wav* format

From the sound wave visualization, we proceed to generate *spectrograms*, which offer a more detailed representation of the audio signals. Spectrograms are obtained using the Fourier Transform, allowing us to pass the vocal signals to the frequency domain and calculate the spectrogram. This technique provides a visual representation of the intensity of sound as a function of frequency over time. By examining spectrograms, we can discern color variations that indicate the intensity of the sound at different frequencies over time. In Fig. 4 (left), it can visualize the intensity of the sound through color variations, over time as a function of frequency [8].

In addition to spectrograms, we extract Mel Frequency Cepstral Coefficients (MFCCs) from the audio signals. MFCCs are widely used for representing speech based on human auditory perception. They capture the characteristics of the audio components and describe the general shape of the spectral envelope. The

MFCCs are computed by segmenting the audio signal, applying the discrete Fourier Transform to each segment, and obtaining the spectral power. The resulting MFCCs vectors provide concise information about the audio signals, suitable for identifying relevant content. Figure 4 (right) shows an example of the extraction of the MFCCs vectors.

**Fig. 4.** Spectrogram of sample audio of the dataset (left) and Mel frequency cepstral coefficients (right).

With the preprocessed audio data, we proceed to develop the model architecture for the convolutional neural network. For this study, we selected the widely used AlexNet architecture (Fig. 5), originally designed for image processing tasks. We adapted the architecture to accommodate the MFCCs dataset, enabling the recognition and classification of audio from individuals with and without Parkinson's disease. The AlexNet architecture consists of eight layers, including five convolutional layers and three fully-connected layers, providing a robust framework for training the network.

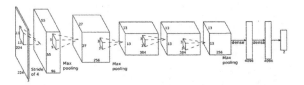

**Fig. 5.** AlexNet Architecture [20].

In terms of network characteristics, AlexNet incorporates various features that optimize the training process. One notable feature is the use of the Rectified Linear Unit (ReLU) activation function, known for its computational efficiency. ReLU enhances the speed of training, resulting in faster convergence compared to other activation functions. The choice of AlexNet, coupled with its features, provides a solid foundation for effectively processing the MFCC images and classifying the audio signals. Thus, neural networks like AlexNet are highly scalable to large datasets and very useful in audio-based tasks such as Parkinson's disease detection using MFCCs. However, it requires careful consideration of data representation, architecture adjustments, and evaluation strategies.

By employing these data preprocessing techniques, we transform the raw audio data into meaningful representations suitable for training the convolutional neural network. This comprehensive approach allows us to capture important frequency characteristics and extract relevant features from the audio signals. The subsequent sections delve into the experimental results and analysis derived from this preprocessing methodology, shedding light on the accuracy and performance of our proposed approach.

## 4    Results and Discussion

Various researchers have explored the use of CNN's for Parkinson's disease detection, employing different methodologies based on the available databases. In this study, CNNs were employed for Parkinson's detection, specifically utilizing the AlexNet architecture. The database used in this research consisted of audio recordings, from which spectrograms were generated and MFCC vectors were extracted.

To evaluate the performance of the proposed model, the training and validation curves were plotted, showcasing the neural network's performance over the training epochs (see Fig. 6). The use of diverse databases contributed to a significant enhancement in the accuracy of the CNN's performance. By leveraging the frequency characteristics extracted from the audio recordings, the neural network was trained to effectively classify individuals into two groups: a healthy control group and a group of individuals diagnosed with Parkinson's disease.

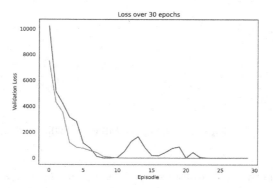

**Fig. 6.** Training curves and validation.

The proposed model was further examined by training the network with different numbers of epochs (10 and 30) and employing two different activation functions: Sigmoid and Softmax. The approximate accuracies obtained for the sigmoid function were around 80% and 95%, while for the softmax function, they were approximately 56% and 65% (see Table 2). The resulting confusion matrix is shown in Fig. 7. It is worth noting that training the network for 50 epochs resulted in overfitting, and the network took longer than expected. To mitigate these issues, future work should explore and implement techniques that prevent overfitting and enhance the efficiency of the network.

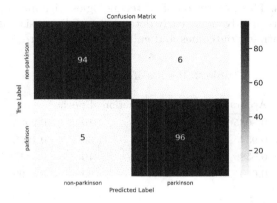

**Fig. 7.** Confusion Matrix of sample dataset.

The conversion of voice recordings into image-based representations, specifically spectrograms, enabled the neural network to effectively learn and perform the classification task. The dataset consisted of two distinct groups, including a healthy control group and a group of individuals diagnosed with Parkinson's disease. By training the network on this dataset, we were able to achieve encouraging results in distinguishing between the two groups based on the frequency characteristics extracted from the audio signals.

In a thorough comparison with prior research, this study stands out for its distinct emphasis on utilizing convolutional neural networks (CNNs) for Parkinson's disease detection, particularly highlighting the application of the AlexNet architecture. This distinguishes it from investigations employing various neural network architectures such as Multi-layer ANN Perceptron, VGFR Spectrogram Detector, Voice Impairment Classifier, and double-sided deep learning ensemble models. Despite the commendable accuracies achieved by these alternative models, the deliberate choice of the AlexNet architecture empowers the exploitation of its unique feature extraction capabilities, potentially revealing salient patterns inherent in spectrogram-based representations. Unlike previous efforts that often amalgamate classifier algorithms with neural networks, this study's principal concentration on the CNN architecture affords a focused elucidation of its role in accurately discriminating between healthy individuals and those with Parkinson's disease. Notably, the integration of insights from diverse methodologies, as showcased in related works, holds promise for future investigations, poised to enhance the precision and robustness of disease detection systems in upcoming research endeavors.

The obtained results highlight the potential of utilizing CNNs and spectrogram-based representations for Parkinson's disease detection. However, it is important to acknowledge that there are additional factors that may contribute to the accuracy and performance of the model. Therefore, the findings demonstrate the feasibility of using CNNs for Parkinson's disease detection based on voice analysis. The integration of AI technologies with medical research holds significant promise in advancing early detection and diagnosis, ultimately leading to improved treatment outcomes and enhanced patient care.

**Table 2.** Results of training AlexNet

| Accuracy | Activation Function | Epochs | Loss |
|----------|---------------------|--------|--------|
| 0.8035   | Sigmoid             | 10     | 0.2965 |
| 0.9545   |                     | 30     | 0.1055 |
| 0.5586   | Softmax             | 10     | 0.4414 |
| 0.6501   |                     | 30     | 0.3499 |

## 5  Conclusion

The results obtained in this investigation hold great significance, as they provide valuable insights into the classification of Parkinson's disease based solely on frequency characteristics. This ability to accurately distinguish between classes forms the foundation of our work. In this research, we employed an optimized version of the AlexNet architecture in our neural network, yielding exceptional results. The accuracy achieved for the validation set exceeded 90%, which is comparable to the performance of Resnet, a well-known architecture that achieved 89% accuracy in similar studies. Furthermore, considering the limited availability of direct statistical data on Parkinson's disease, our software holds the potential to contribute to the establishment of a comprehensive database of Parkinson's patients in Ecuador. This database can be utilized for rigorous statistical analysis, facilitating future investigations into the prevalence of the disease in the region. Moreover, integrating this database into the system can significantly enhance the early prediction of Parkinson's disease in Ecuador, providing valuable insights for improved patient care.

These findings contribute to the growing body of knowledge in the field of Parkinson's disease detection and prediction using advanced AI techniques. Our research underscores the potential of neural networks, specifically the optimized AlexNet architecture, as a powerful tool in improving early diagnosis and intervention strategies. By leveraging the capabilities of AI and continuously refining our methodologies, we can strive towards enhanced patient outcomes, better quality of life, and more efficient healthcare practices for individuals affected by Parkinson's disease.

Future research could focus on ensemble learning, longitudinal data analysis, multi-modal data integration, explainability, real-time monitoring, bias mitigation, clinical validation, user-centered design, and long-term outcomes analysis. By exploring these directions, researchers aim to create more accurate, interpretable, and effective AI-driven solutions for enhancing the lives of individuals affected by Parkinson's disease.

# References

1. Enfermedad de párkinson no es considerada como catastrófica en el sistema de salud ecuatoriano (2019). https://www.edicionmedica.ec/secciones/salud-publica/
2. Focus on Parkinson's disease research — national institute of neurological disorders and stroke (nd). https://www.ninds.nih.gov/current-research/focus-disorders/focus-parkinsons-disease-research
3. Parkinson's disease (nd). https://medlineplus.gov/parkinsonsdisease.html
4. Ahmad, M.A., et al.: Interpretable machine learning in healthcare, pp. 559–560 (2018)
5. Almaloglou, E.E., et al.: Design and validation of a new diagnostic tool for the differentiation of pathological voices in parkinsonian patients. Adv. Exp. Med. Biol. **1339**, 77–83 (2021)
6. Barnish, M.S., et al.: Speech and communication in Parkinson's disease: a cross-sectional exploratory study in the UK. BMJ Open **7**(5), e014642 (2017)
7. Eskofier, B.M., et al.: Recent machine learning advancements in sensor-based mobility analysis: deep learning for Parkinson's disease assessment (2016)
8. Gualsaquí, M.G., et al.: Convolutional neural network for imagine movement classification for neurorehabilitation of upper extremities using low-frequency EEG signals for spinal cord injury. In: Narváez, F.R., Proaño, J., Morillo, P., Vallejo, D., González Montoya, D., Díaz, G.M. (eds.) SmartTech-IC 2021. CCIS, vol. 1532, pp. 272–287. Springer, Cham (2022). https://doi.org/10.1007/978-3-030-99170-8_20
9. Herrera-Romero, B., et al.: GUSignal: an informatics tool to analyze glucuronidase gene expression in arabidopsis thaliana roots. IEEE/ACM Trans. Comput. Biol. Bioinf. **20**, 1073–1080 (2023)
10. Hertrich, I., Ackermann, H.: Gender-specific vocal dysfunctions in Parkinson's disease: electroglottographic and acoustic analyses. Ann. Otol. Rhinol. Laryngol. **104**(3), 197–202 (1995)
11. Ivars, N.: Deep convolutional neural networks: structure, feature extraction and training. Inf. Technol. Manage. Sci. **20**(1), 40–47 (2017)
12. Jiménez-Jiménez, F.J.: Acoustic voice analysis in untreated patients with Parkinson's disease. Parkinsonism Relat. Disord. **3**(2), 111–116 (1997)
13. Khan, H., et al.: Deep learning based speech emotion recognition for Parkinson patient. Electron. Imaging **35**, 298 (2023)
14. Khaskhoussy, R., Ayed, Y.B.: Improving Parkinson's disease recognition through voice analysis using deep learning. Pattern Recogn. Lett. **168**, 64–70 (2023)
15. Ma, J., et al.: Deep dual-side learning ensemble model for Parkinson speech recognition. Biomed. Signal Process. Control **69**, 102849 (2021)
16. Manikya, N., et al.: Parkinson's disease prediction using vocal parameters (2023)
17. Montaña, D., et al.: A diadochokinesis-based expert system considering articulatory features of plosive consonants for early detection of Parkinson's disease. Comput. Methods Programs Biomed. **154**, 89–97 (2018)

18. National Institute of Neurological Disorders and Stroke: Parkinson's disease: Hope through research (2022)

19. Orozco, J.R., et al.: New Spanish speech corpus database for the analysis of people suffering from Parkinson's disease. Synthetic structure of industrial plastics. In: Peters, J., (eds.) Plastics, 2nd ed, vol. 3, pp. 15–64. McGraw-Hill, New York 1964 (2014)

20. Pedraza, A., et al.: Glomerulus classification with convolutional neural networks, pp. 839–849 (2017)

21. Rahman, S., et al.: Classification of Parkinson's disease using speech signal with machine learning and deep learning approaches. Eur. J. Electr. Eng. Comput. Sci. **7**, 20–27 (2023)

22. Shivangi, et al.: Parkinson disease detection using deep neural networks. In: 2019 12th International Conference on Contemporary Computing, IC3 2019 (2019)

23. Snwr, S., et al.: Parkinson's disease detection by processing different ANN architecture using vocal dataset. Eurasian J. Sci. Eng. **9**, 161–172 (2023)

24. Song, J., et al.: Detection and differentiation of ataxic and hypokinetic dysarthria in cerebellar ataxia and parkinsonian disorders via wave splitting and integrating neural networks. PLoS ONE **17**, e0268337 (2022)

25. Tsanas, A., et al.: Novel speech signal processing algorithms for high-accuracy classification of Parkinson's disease. IEEE Trans. Biomed. Eng. **59**(5), 1264–1271 (2012)

26. Wodzinski, M., et al.: Deep learning approach to Parkinson's disease detection using voice recordings and convolutional neural network dedicated to image classification. In: Proceedings of the Annual International Conference of the IEEE Engineering in Medicine and Biology Society, EMBS, pp. 717–720 (2019)

27. Yuan, I., et al.: Virtual reality therapy and machine learning techniques in drug addiction treatment, pp. 241–245 (2019)

# Hyperparameter Tuning in a Dual Channel U-Net for Medical Image Segmentation

Krishna Román[1]([envelope]) [iD], José Llumiquinga[1] [iD], Stalyn Chancay[1,3] [iD], and Manuel Eugenio Morocho-Cayamcela[1,2,3] [iD]

[1] Yachay Tech University, Hacienda San José, San Miguel de Urcuquí 100650, Imbabura, Ecuador
{krishna.roman,jose.llumiquinga,stalyn.chancay,
mmorocho}@yachaytech.edu.ec
[2] Deep Learning for Autonomous Driving, Robotics, and Computer Vision (DeepARC Research), Urcuqui, Ecuador
[3] Yachay Scientific Computing Group (SCG), Urcuqui, Ecuador
https://www.yachay-scg.com, https://www.deeparcresearch.com

**Abstract.** Deep learning has been receiving a lot of attention lately, specially in the computer vision research community. In particular, the image segmentation task has revolutionized the treatment of medical imagery for diagnose and illness prediction. U-Net is one of the most extensively employed convolutional neural network (CNN) architectures for medical image segmentation. Moreover, U-Net is recognized to excel in segmenting multimodal medical images in general and complicated circumstances. However, the traditional U-Net architecture still has significant limitations with medical images segmentation. To tackle this limitations, a novel CNN architecture called dual channel-UNet (DC-UNet) has emerged as a possible replacement for the U-Net model. However, the performance and accuracy of the model are not the greatest when inferring on endoscopy images. This paper contributes to the research field by proposing a hyperparameter tuning of DC-UNet on the CVC-ClinicDB endoscopy dataset. Among several factors, we determine the optimum hyperparameter setup for this dataset, considering different values of: (i) batch sizes, (ii) learning rates, (iii) gradient-based optimizers, and (iv) dropout layers. We have also included a contrast limited adaptive histogram equalization, as a preprocessing technique to analyze the effect of the different experiments on the model's performance.

**Keywords:** DC-UNet · Medical Image Segmentation · Convolutional Neural Network · Hyperparameter Tuning

© The Author(s), under exclusive license to Springer Nature Switzerland AG 2023
J. Maldonado-Mahauad et al. (Eds.): TICEC 2023, CCIS 1885, pp. 337–352, 2023.
https://doi.org/10.1007/978-3-031-45438-7_23

# 1  Introduction

Medical imaging is crucial in today's medicine research and innovation since it may disclose a patient's anatomy, help in the prediction of diseases, and helping doctors to make a better diagnosis. However, to use all the potential of medical images, a preprocessing stage must be considered for evaluation. Among all the image preprocessing tasks, *image segmentation* is one of the essential clinical techniques used today. An efficient medical image analysis aims to give radiologists and clinicians an efficient diagnosis and treatment [12]. Additionally, the process of automatically or semi-automatically detecting boundaries is a highly-desired computer vision tool in medical analysis [23]. The great diversity of medical images is a crucial challenge in image segmentation. For instance, images acquired from X-ray, computed tomography, magnetic resonance imaging, microscopy, positron emission tomography, single-photon emission computerized tomography, endoscopy, optical coherence tomography, etc., should be treated differently, and the results of the segmentation can be used in different ways to get additional diagnostic information (i.e., automatic organ measuring, cell counting, simulations based on the retrieved boundary information, etc.).

Today, there are a variety of classic algorithms for segmenting tissues or bodily organs. These methods can be region-based as the *Canny detector* [10], edge-based detector [8], or threshold and feature-based clustering as $k$-means [18]. The most recent literature on deep-learning-based image segmentation includes over 100 different approaches proposed to date [21]. Some of these techniques are fully convolutional networks, convolutional models with graphical models, encoder-decoder-based models, multi-scale and pyramid network-based models, Recurrent CNN based models, dilated convolutional models, etc.

One of the characteristics of classical image processing techniques is to extract features in a hand-crafted way. The data must be processed, and the most suitable features must be used for the respective model, which needs an appropriate input dataset. At the same time, dimensionality reduction techniques can be used as a preprocessing block in classical methods [27]. The latter process has some difficulty and can be tedious, especially if one wants to use another model to accomplish the same task. An improvement to the classical machine learning techniques for image segmentation has been using deep learning (DP), which has become more critical since the hardware improvement in the 2000 ss [9]. Currently, DP is one of the main options for medical image segmentation, whose models have brought several advantages when segmenting medical images. For instance, automatic feature extraction using various neural network structures. However, some challenges are still being addressed with different classical techniques [14]. One of the challenges is the limited existence of datasets with labeled data, since collecting annotated data from medical images is a complex and time-consuming task. Overfitting, which is mainly caused by a short dataset size, is also a problem to be addresses in medical applications.

An extra challenge in medical image processing is that of unbalanced classes because, in medical images, it is typical for the area of interest to occupy only a tiny portion of the picture. Finally, one of the most critical issues is the heterogeneous appearance of medical imaging structures. There are many variations in size and the shape of different individuals' areas of interest. In addition, these medical image structures have areas of interest with ambiguous boundaries that are difficult to detect, especially for classical segmentation techniques.

In this paper, we propose a hyperparameter tuning of the DC-UNet model on the CVC-ClinicDB dataset. We find the best configuration for this dataset among some parameters. The parameters under study are: (i) batch size, (ii) learning rate, (iii) gradient-based optimizers (i.e., Adam [17], SGD with momentum, Adagrad [11], Nadam, Amsgrad [24], Adamax, and RMSprop). Additionally, we have included early stopping to avoid the model taking too long during training when it has already converged to a solution. Furthermore, we have used the Contrast Limited Adaptive Histogram Equalization (CLAHE) as a preprocessing technique to improve the contrast of the images and analyze if it helps the model to perform better.

## 2    Related Works

From the literature, a few models are based on fully-connected networks (FCNs) [19], and encoder-decoder networks [22]. One of them is the U-Net, which was proposed by [26] for effectively segmenting biological microscope images. U-Net was designed with a contracting path to record context and a symmetric expanding approach to enable exact localization. The U-Net training highly depends on data augmentation to learn from a small number of annotated images. Moreover, the U-Net design uses a skip connection to carry the output from the encoder to the decoder. The output of the up-sampling procedure is concatenated with these feature maps, and the concatenated feature map is propagated to the subsequent layers. The skip connections allow the network to recover spatial details lost due to pooling processes.

According to the state-of-the-art literature in medical image segmentation, most of the techniques correspond to variations of the U-Net architecture, which was one of the most widely used in medical image segmentation years ago. Some of those variations are MultiResUNet [15] which demonstrated some improvements such as quicker convergence, more immunity to perturbations, and reliability against outliers. Also, recurrent residual U-Net [2] allowed a better feature representation of the segmentation, AdaResU-Net [3] helped to reduce the number of trainable parameters around 30% when compared with U-Net in order to avoid unnecessary computations in hyperparameter fine-tuning, and UNet++ [29] ensembled several U-Net architectures of varying depths to improve performance in size varying objects.

There are several approaches to segment single structures of an elliptical shape using DL. For instance, [16], proposed an architecture called ColonSegNet, specialized for real-time polyp segmentation [28]. ColonSegNet is considered an encoder-decoder architecture, with two encoder blocks and two decoder blocks. This segmentation network has far fewer trainable parameters than U-Net, making it a very lightweight architecture that leads to real-time performance. [13]

proposed a context encoder network called CE-Net to capture high-level and spatially preserved information.

Preprocessing methods can be used to improve the accuracy of the studied segmentation neural networks. There are several preprocessing methods such as data augmentation [5], or image enhancement techniques such as the histogram equalization technique [1], which can improve image contrast. In addition to these techniques, image transformations such as those presented in [6], can also be employed. The authors have proposed the use of polar image transformations to improve the segmentation network performance and data efficiency. The image transformation from cartesian coordinates to a new coordinate system reduces dimensionality and as a result, it allows convergence in fewer epochs, enhancing the performance even in architectures with few parameters.

## 3   System Model and Design

DC-UNet is based on: i) the MultiResUNet [15], and ii) in the U-Net architecture; where the use of convolutional layers is of paramount importance. The U-Net architecture is an asymmetric network and can be understood by studying it in two parts: encoder and decoder [7]. The encoder part functions as a convolutional neural network and serves for feature extraction. The encoder has four convolutional blocks, each of which contains the following sequence of operations: two $3 \times 3$ convolution operations, max-pooling with a pooling size of $2 \times 2$, and stride of 2. The decoder part is used to construct the segmentation map of the features extracted by the encoder. The decoder stage performs the following sequence of operations 4 times: a $2 \times 2$ transposed convolution, and two $3 \times 3$ convolutions. Then, the encoder part is connected with the decoder with a progression of two $3 \times 3$ convolution operations. At the end of the decoder a $1 \times 1$ convolution operation is performed to generate the final segmentation map. Also, in the U-Net network there are skip connections from encoder to decoder in order to obtain the spatial features lost by the previous pooling operations.

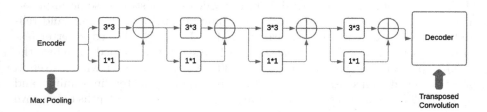

**Fig. 1.** Skipped connections (Res-Path) between the encoder and the decoder.

DC-UNet introduces dual channel blocks (see Fig. 2), that replace the convolutional layers of a U-Net and are also based on MultiRes blocks [15]. DC-UNet takes a sequence of three $3 \times 3$ convolutional layers to replace the residual connection in MultiRes block [20]. In addition, the same Res-Path connection between the encoder and decoder is applied in MultiResUNet [20]. The Res-Path system model is illustrated in Fig. 1.

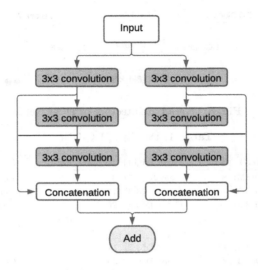

**Fig. 2.** Dual-Channel block based on a MultiRes convolutional block.

Finally, all convolutional layers of the DC-UNet are triggered by the Rectifier Linear Unit avtivation function and use batch normalization to avoid overfitting. Moreover, the final output layer is activated by the Sigmoid activation function. In this way, and following the proposal of [20], we have constructed our model following the illustration in Fig. 3. For detail information on the filters and convolutions used, see Table 1.

## 4    Experimental Setup and Methodology

In this section, we address the experimental setup and methodology used for our study. We detail the hardware, software, dataset, performance metric, preprocessing block, and training stage.

### 4.1    Hardware and Software

To build and train our model, we have used TensorFlow as the main DL framework, and Python 3 as the programming language. The training process was conducted in an instance workstation created in Azure with Intel Xeon E5-2690 v3 (2.6 GHz), 56.0 GB RAM, with NVIDIA Tesla M60 GPUs.

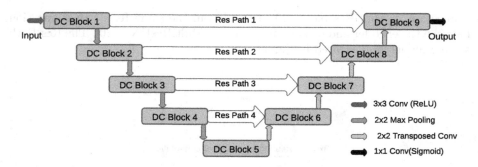

**Fig. 3.** Overall architecture of DC-UNet.

**Table 1.** Details of DC-UNet.

| Block | Layer (left) | #Filters | Layer (right) | #Filters | Path | Layer | #Filters |
|---|---|---|---|---|---|---|---|
| DC Block 1 | Conv2D(3,3) | 8 | Conv2D(3,3) | 8 | | Conv2D(3,3) | 32 |
| DC Block 9 | Conv2D(3,3) | 17 | Conv2D(3,3) | 17 | | Conv2D(1,1) | 32 |
| | Conv2D(3,3) | 26 | Conv2D(3,3) | 26 | | Conv2D(3,3) | 32 |
| | | | | | Res Path 1 | Conv2D(1,1) | 32 |
| | | | | | | Conv2D(3,3) | 32 |
| DC Block 2 | Conv2D(3,3) | 17 | Conv2D(3,3) | 17 | | Conv2D(1,1) | 32 |
| DC Block 8 | Conv2D(3,3) | 35 | Conv2D(3,3) | 35 | | Conv2D(3,3) | 32 |
| | Conv2D(3,3) | 53 | Conv2D(3,3) | 53 | | Conv2D(1,1) | 32 |
| | | | | | | Conv2D(3,3) | 64 |
| DC Block 3 | Conv2D(3,3) | 35 | Conv2D(3,3) | 35 | | Conv2D(1,1) | 64 |
| DC Block 7 | Conv2D(3,3) | 71 | Conv2D(3,3) | 71 | Res Path 2 | Conv2D(3,3) | 64 |
| | Conv2D(3,3) | 106 | Conv2D(3,3) | 106 | | Conv2D(1,1) | 64 |
| | | | | | | Conv2D(3,3) | 64 |
| | | | | | | Conv2D(1,1) | 64 |
| DC Block 4 | Conv2D(3,3) | 71 | Conv2D(3,3) | 71 | | | |
| DC Block 6 | Conv2D(3,3) | 142 | Conv2D(3,3) | 142 | | Conv2D(3,3) | 128 |
| | Conv2D(3,3) | 213 | Conv2D(3,3) | 213 | Res Path 3 | Conv2D(1,1) | 128 |
| | | | | | | Conv2D(3,3) | 128 |
| | | | | | | Conv2D(1,1) | 128 |
| DC Block 5 | Conv2D(3,3) | 142 | Conv2D(3,3) | 142 | | | |
| | Conv2D(3,3) | 284 | Conv2D(3,3) | 284 | Res Path 4 | Conv2D(3,3) | 256 |
| | Conv2D(3,3) | 427 | Conv2D(3,3) | 427 | | Conv2D(1,1) | 256 |

## 4.2 Dataset

We have selected the public CVC-ClinicDB dataset, containing 612 images with a resolution of 384 × 288. The images correspond to frames from 29 colonoscopy video sequences that contain polyps. The ground truth is a mask that shows the zone of the polyp in the original image.

## 4.3    Performance Metric

There are several methods to evaluate the performance of image segmentation. In this case, a Tanimoto similarity metric is used with two images: $A$ and $B$, with the same size considered as sets. Also, this metric performs a pixel-wise comparison of $a_i \in A$, and $b_i \in B$, where $a_i$ represents a pixel from the set $A$, and $b_i$ represents a pixel from the set $B$. The cardinality calculation of the intersection, and the union sets are in equations (1), and (2), respectively. Then, the Tanimoto performance metric (see Eq. (3)) is used to compare the segmented image with the ground truth regions [25]. The authors [20], have determined that the Tanimoto similarity is better than Jaccard similarity(JS) and mean absolute error (MAE). The Tanimoto similarity avoids binarization of the results, preventing a loss of information, and it is stable to images of different sizes and object radius. Tanimoto similarity is also known as extended JS, because the JS is used for binary-to-binary comparison, whereas Tanimoto similarity can handle grayscale images.

$$|A \cap B| = \sum a_i b_i \tag{1}$$

$$|A \cup B| = |A| + |B| - |A \cap B|$$
$$= \sum \left( a_i{}^2 + b_i{}^2 - a_i b_i \right) \tag{2}$$

$$T(A, B) = \frac{\sum a_i b_i}{\sum \left( a_i{}^2 + b_i{}^2 - a_i b_i \right)} \tag{3}$$

## 4.4    Image Preprocessing

Before training the DC-UNet model, a preprocessing technique was built to improve the image segmentation results. The preprocessing method selected is CLAHE, which enhances the image's contrast. CLAHE calculates histograms from different regions to redistribute the number of pixels for each grayscale value of the image, obtaining a uniform distribution. After this initial preprocessing, the images are resized from $384 \times 288$ pixels to $128 \times 96$ pixels due to hardware limitations.

## 4.5    Training

In this section, we explain the sub-processes of the training stage of our proposal.

**Dropout.** Dropout is an additional layer that can be added to a neural network and it is used to help prevent overfitting. The dropout layer randomly ignores or sets neurons to zero during the training phase [4]. In our experiment, we have added dropout layers in the DC-UNet encoding stage, specifically between the DC blocks and the Res-Paths, after the Max-Pooling layer.

**Early Stopping.** Early stopping is a regularization technique, and its objective is to avoid over-adjustment. This technique is used to stop training when a monitored metric stops improving. In this case, the Tanimoto similarity was the monitored value during training.

**Data Augmentation.** We applied data augmentation techniques to increase the model's accuracy and reduce overfitting by generalizing the input data. Those methods were flipping, rotation, brightness, and ZCA whitening. However, we do not use those techniques to increase the size of the dataset as we apply them randomly when images are read during the training process.

**Hyperparameter Tuning.** The hyperparameters of a network are set before the network training and are not modified during the training process. Therefore, a correct choice of hyperparameters allows accurate results and good model performance. One of the most used techniques to conduct hyperparameter tuning is grid search. Grid search is one of the simplest algorithms since the parameter domain is divided into a discrete grid, then different combinations of the grid values are tested, and performance metrics are calculated to find the hyperparameters that maximize the performance metric, in this specific case, the Tanimoto similarity.

Adam, SGD with momentum, Adagrad, Nadam, Amsgrad, Adamax and RMSprop were used as gradient-based optimizer to train our model. Table 2 lists the learning rate and batch size parameters, as well as the dropout used to train the model.

**Table 2.** Hyperparameters setup for training our model.

| Hyperparameter | Values |
|---|---|
| Batch Size | 2 |
| | 4 |
| | 8 |
| Dropout | 0 |
| | 0.1 |
| | 0.2 |
| | 0.3 |
| Optimizer | Adam |
| | SGD with momentum |
| | Nadam |
| | Adamax |
| | Adagrad |
| | RMSprop |
| | Amsgrad |

# 5   Results and Discussion

According to the results, the best optimizer in the hyperparameter tuning was Amsgrad with 78.76% of accuracy, followed by Nadam, RMSprop, and Adam, whit 78.35%, 77.24%, and 77.14%, respectively. The best accuracy is highlighted for each optimizer, and the combinations are sorted by their dropout values. We have attempt to use a layer of data augmentation to apply flip, rotation, and zoom randomly to the inputs; however, this approach did not output good results. The reason might be because in the CVC-ClinicDB dataset the images corresponds to video frames. Therefore, both training and testing images are very similar. Using those preprocessing techniques only to the training dataset might have caused the images to leave the dataset's domain.

In the case of the Adam optimizer, we have noticed that increasing the default learning rate $1e^{-3}$ helps the model to converge to a solution very fast. Although it does not increase the accuracy, the early stop functionality makes it to run approximately from 20 to 50 less epochs. Also, the default configuration appears to be the best in this case as seen in Table 3. Another fact we have noticed about the SGD optimizer is that with batch size of 2, our model does not work as well as with batch size of 4 (see Table 4). In the case of Adagrad, there was not a noticeable difference between the performance metric (Table 5).

Furthermore, adding Nesterov momentum to Nadam seems to be a good choice to this dataset, since it overcomes the results from Adam. We have noticed a similar behaviour with (see Table 6, and Table 7).

The infinite norm that the Adamax optimizer uses seems not to be useful for this dataset as Table 8 shows. In the other hand, the RMSprop optimizer with a

**Table 3.** Performance of Adam optimizer.

| Dropout | Learning Rate | Batch Size | Accuracy |
|---|---|---|---|
| 0 | 0.0001 | 2 | 0.6889 |
| **0** | **0.001** | **4** | **0.7714** |
| 0 | 0.00025 | 2 | 0.7228 |
| 0 | 0.0025 | 4 | 0.7270 |
| 0 | 0.0005 | 2 | 0.7673 |
| 0 | 0.005 | 4 | 0.7090 |
| 0.2 | 0.0001 | 2 | 0.6947 |
| 0.2 | 0.0001 | 4 | 0.7189 |
| 0.2 | 0.001 | 4 | 0.7496 |
| 0.2 | 0.00025 | 2 | 0.7337 |
| 0.2 | 0.00025 | 4 | 0.7445 |
| 0.2 | 0.0025 | 4 | 0.7566 |
| 0.2 | 0.0005 | 2 | 0.6895 |
| 0.2 | 0.0005 | 4 | 0.7619 |
| 0.2 | 0.005 | 4 | 0.7686 |
| 0.3 | 0.0001 | 2 | 0.7040 |
| 0.3 | 0.0001 | 4 | 0.7201 |
| 0.3 | 0.001 | 4 | 0.7447 |
| 0.3 | 0.00025 | 2 | 0.7646 |
| 0.3 | 0.00025 | 4 | 0.7401 |
| 0.3 | 0.0025 | 4 | 0.7416 |
| 0.3 | 0.0005 | 2 | 0.7502 |
| 0.3 | 0.0005 | 4 | 0.7644 |
| 0.3 | 0.005 | 4 | 0.7529 |

**Table 4.** Performance of SGD with momentum.

| Dropout | Learning Rate | Batch Size | Accuracy |
|---|---|---|---|
| 0 | 0.001 | 2 | 0.4116 |
| 0 | 0.01 | 4 | 0.5852 |
| 0 | 0.0025 | 2 | 0.5572 |
| 0 | 0.025 | 4 | 0.6849 |
| 0 | 0.005 | 2 | 0.5989 |
| 0 | 0.05 | 4 | 0.6954 |
| 0.2 | 0.001 | 2 | 0.5311 |
| 0.2 | 0.01 | 4 | 0.6829 |
| 0.2 | 0.0025 | 2 | 0.6677 |
| 0.2 | 0.025 | 4 | 0.7249 |
| 0.2 | 0.005 | 2 | 0.6732 |
| 0.2 | 0.05 | 4 | 0.7029 |
| 0.3 | 0.001 | 2 | 0.5196 |
| 0.3 | 0.01 | 4 | 0.7107 |
| 0.3 | 0.0025 | 2 | 0.6472 |
| **0.3** | **0.025** | **4** | **0.7322** |
| 0.3 | 0.005 | 2 | 0.6665 |
| 0.3 | 0.05 | 4 | 0.7274 |

**Table 5.** Performance of Adagrad.

| Dropout | Learning Rate | Batch Size | Accuracy |
|---|---|---|---|
| 0 | 0.5 | 2 | 0.7283 |
| 0 | 0.5 | 4 | 0.7288 |
| 0 | 0.5 | 8 | 0.6592 |
| 0 | 1 | 2 | 0.7653 |
| 0 | 1 | 4 | 0.7453 |
| 0 | 1 | 8 | 0.5784 |
| 0.1 | 0.5 | 2 | 0.7450 |
| 0.1 | 0.5 | 4 | 0.7328 |
| 0.1 | 0.5 | 8 | 0.6208 |
| 0.1 | 1 | 2 | 0.7585 |
| **0.1** | **1** | **4** | **0.7669** |
| 0.1 | 1 | 8 | 0.7466 |
| 0.2 | 0.5 | 2 | 0.7447 |
| 0.2 | 0.5 | 4 | 0.7454 |
| 0.2 | 0.5 | 8 | 0.7130 |
| 0.2 | 1 | 2 | 0.7485 |
| 0.2 | 1 | 4 | 0.7286 |
| 0.2 | 1 | 8 | 0.7561 |
| 0.3 | 0.5 | 2 | 0.7588 |
| 0.3 | 0.5 | 4 | 0.7387 |
| 0.3 | 0.5 | 8 | 0.5242 |
| 0.3 | 1 | 2 | 0.7633 |
| 0.3 | 1 | 4 | 0.7350 |
| 0.3 | 1 | 8 | 0.7470 |

discounting factor for history gradient of 0.9 slightly overcame Adam (Table 9). This effect can mean that in all Adam variants, the RMSprop contribution takes a significant role and more important than the momentum hyperparameter. These gradient-based optimizers where the only ones where a batch size of 2

**Table 6.** Performance of Nadam.

| Dropout | Learning Rate | Batch Size | Accuracy |
|---------|---------------|------------|----------|
| 0 | 0.0005 | 2 | 0.7616 |
| 0 | 0.0005 | 4 | 0.7569 |
| 0 | 0.0005 | 8 | 0.7271 |
| 0 | 0.001 | 2 | 0.7468 |
| 0 | 0.001 | 4 | 0.7286 |
| 0 | 0.001 | 8 | 0.5078 |
| 0 | 0.0015 | 2 | 0.7419 |
| 0 | 0.0015 | 4 | 0.7707 |
| 0 | 0.0015 | 8 | 0.7636 |
| 0.1 | 0.0005 | 2 | 0.7424 |
| 0.1 | 0.0005 | 4 | 0.7481 |
| 0.1 | 0.0005 | 8 | 0.7477 |
| 0.1 | 0.001 | 2 | 0.7427 |
| **0.1** | **0.001** | **4** | **0.7835** |
| 0.1 | 0.001 | 8 | 0.7499 |
| 0.1 | 0.0015 | 2 | 0.7711 |
| 0.1 | 0.0015 | 4 | 0.7735 |
| 0.1 | 0.0015 | 8 | 0.7419 |
| 0.2 | 0.0005 | 2 | 0.7599 |
| 0.2 | 0.0005 | 4 | 0.7164 |
| 0.2 | 0.0005 | 8 | 0.7480 |
| 0.2 | 0.001 | 2 | 0.7687 |
| 0.2 | 0.001 | 4 | 0.7738 |
| 0.2 | 0.001 | 8 | 0.7707 |
| 0.2 | 0.0015 | 2 | 0.7510 |
| 0.2 | 0.0015 | 4 | 0.7775 |
| 0.2 | 0.0015 | 8 | 0.7688 |

**Table 7.** Performance of Amsgrad.

| Dropout | Learning Rate | Batch Size | Accuracy |
|---------|---------------|------------|----------|
| 0 | 0.001 | 2 | 0.7598 |
| 0 | 0.001 | 4 | 0.7676 |
| 0 | 0.001 | 8 | 0.7738 |
| 0 | 0.0025 | 2 | 0.7469 |
| 0 | 0.0025 | 4 | 0.7711 |
| 0 | 0.0025 | 8 | 0.7600 |
| 0.1 | 0.001 | 2 | 0.7426 |
| 0.1 | 0.001 | 4 | 0.7670 |
| 0.1 | 0.001 | 8 | 0.7679 |
| 0.1 | 0.0015 | 2 | 0.7455 |
| 0.1 | 0.0015 | 4 | 0.7542 |
| 0.1 | 0.0015 | 8 | 0.6836 |
| 0.1 | 0.002 | 2 | 0.7632 |
| 0.1 | 0.002 | 4 | 0.7679 |
| 0.1 | 0.002 | 8 | 0.7645 |
| 0.1 | 0.0025 | 2 | 0.7653 |
| 0.1 | 0.0025 | 4 | 0.7579 |
| 0.1 | 0.0025 | 8 | 0.7321 |
| 0.2 | 0.001 | 2 | 0.7442 |
| 0.2 | 0.001 | 4 | 0.7753 |
| 0.2 | 0.001 | 8 | 0.7577 |
| 0.2 | 0.0015 | 2 | 0.7289 |
| 0.2 | 0.0015 | 4 | 0.7815 |
| 0.2 | 0.0015 | 8 | 0.7624 |
| 0.2 | 0.002 | 2 | 0.7479 |
| 0.2 | 0.002 | 4 | 0.7762 |
| 0.2 | 0.002 | 8 | 0.6758 |
| 0.2 | 0.0025 | 2 | 0.7402 |
| **0.2** | **0.0025** | **4** | **0.7876** |
| 0.2 | 0.0025 | 8 | 0.7507 |

overcome a batch size of 4. Additionally, the batch size of 4 seems to be a good default configuration among all optimizers. Finally, a value of 8 for the batch size gave us poor results, probably due to the reduced size of the dataset (612 images). The replicated results with the default hyperparameter values and Adam optimizer reached an accuracy of 77.14%. Our hyperparameter tuning with Amsgrad reached an accuracy of 78.76%, overcoming the previous configuration by 1.62%.

Figure 4 and 5 show the images result taken from the test dataset (image 5 and image 0, respectively). Both figures have an input image (Fig. 4a and 5a), the segmentation ground truth (Fig. 4b and 5b), the benchmark paper prediction according to [20] (Fig. 4c and 5c), and the result of our prediction (Fig. 4d and 5d). The best prediction in Fig. 4d and 5d refers to our results with hyperparameter tuning. For the segmentation of Fig. 5a with tuning is obtained a Jaccard of 0.8953. On the other hand, in Fig. 5c, without tuning, we got a Jac-

**Table 8.** Performance of Adamax.      **Table 9.** Performance of RMSprop.

| Dropout | Learning Rate | Batch Size | Accuracy |
|---------|---------------|------------|----------|
| 0 | 0.0005 | 2 | 0.6468 |
| 0 | 0.0005 | 4 | 0.6277 |
| 0 | 0.0005 | 8 | 0.6062 |
| 0 | 0.001 | 2 | 0.6873 |
| 0 | 0.001 | 4 | 0.6714 |
| 0 | 0.001 | 8 | 0.6813 |
| 0 | 0.0015 | 2 | 0.7221 |
| 0 | 0.0015 | 4 | 0.7456 |
| 0 | 0.0015 | 8 | 0.7347 |
| 0.1 | 0.0005 | 2 | 0.6834 |
| 0.1 | 0.0005 | 4 | 0.6788 |
| 0.1 | 0.0005 | 8 | 0.6853 |
| 0.1 | 0.001 | 2 | 0.7329 |
| 0.1 | 0.001 | 4 | 0.7150 |
| 0.1 | 0.001 | 8 | 0.7185 |
| **0.1** | **0.0015** | **2** | **0.7496** |
| 0.1 | 0.0015 | 4 | 0.7437 |
| 0.1 | 0.0015 | 8 | 0.7128 |
| 0.2 | 0.0005 | 2 | 0.6606 |
| 0.2 | 0.0005 | 4 | 0.7033 |
| 0.2 | 0.0005 | 8 | 0.6983 |
| 0.2 | 0.001 | 2 | 0.6930 |
| 0.2 | 0.001 | 4 | 0.7215 |
| 0.2 | 0.001 | 8 | 0.7412 |
| 0.2 | 0.0015 | 2 | 0.7377 |
| 0.2 | 0.0015 | 4 | 0.7197 |
| 0.2 | 0.0015 | 8 | 0.7356 |

| Dropout | Learning Rate | Batch Size | Accuracy |
|---------|---------------|------------|----------|
| 0 | 0.001 | 2 | 0.7204 |
| 0 | 0.001 | 4 | 0.7211 |
| 0 | 0.001 | 8 | 0.7331 |
| 0 | 0.0015 | 2 | 0.7084 |
| 0 | 0.0015 | 4 | 0.7471 |
| 0 | 0.0015 | 8 | 0.6938 |
| 0 | 0.002 | 2 | 0.7313 |
| 0 | 0.002 | 4 | 0.7168 |
| 0 | 0.002 | 8 | 0.7612 |
| 0 | 0.0025 | 2 | 0.7234 |
| 0 | 0.0025 | 4 | 0.6946 |
| 0 | 0.0025 | 8 | 0.6419 |
| 0.1 | 0.001 | 2 | 0.7380 |
| 0.1 | 0.001 | 4 | 0.6935 |
| 0.1 | 0.001 | 8 | 0.7633 |
| 0.1 | 0.0015 | 2 | 0.7483 |
| 0.1 | 0.0015 | 4 | 0.7333 |
| 0.1 | 0.0015 | 8 | 0.7536 |
| 0.1 | 0.002 | 2 | 0.7317 |
| 0.1 | 0.002 | 4 | 0.7186 |
| 0.1 | 0.002 | 8 | 0.7033 |
| **0.1** | **0.0025** | **2** | **0.7724** |
| 0.1 | 0.0025 | 4 | 0.7250 |
| 0.1 | 0.0025 | 8 | 0.7269 |
| 0.2 | 0.001 | 2 | 0.7563 |
| 0.2 | 0.001 | 4 | 0.7560 |
| 0.2 | 0.001 | 8 | 0.7360 |
| 0.2 | 0.0015 | 2 | 0.7374 |
| 0.2 | 0.0015 | 4 | 0.7479 |
| 0.2 | 0.0015 | 8 | 0.7483 |
| 0.2 | 0.002 | 2 | 0.7577 |
| 0.2 | 0.002 | 4 | 0.7595 |
| 0.2 | 0.002 | 8 | 0.7607 |
| 0.2 | 0.0025 | 2 | 0.7197 |
| 0.2 | 0.0025 | 4 | 0.7667 |
| 0.2 | 0.0025 | 8 | 0.6658 |

card of 0.8697, indicating an improvement in segmentation. Unfortunately, the segmentation of objects with a minimal area does not have good results both with and without tuning, as shown in Fig. 4c and 4d.

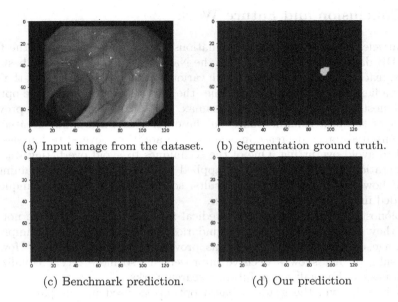

(a) Input image from the dataset.    (b) Segmentation ground truth.

(c) Benchmark prediction.    (d) Our prediction

**Fig. 4.** Results from an image taken from the dataset (image 5) showing: (a) the input image from the dataset, (b) the segmentation ground truth, (c) the benchmark paper prediction [20], and (d) the result of our prediction.

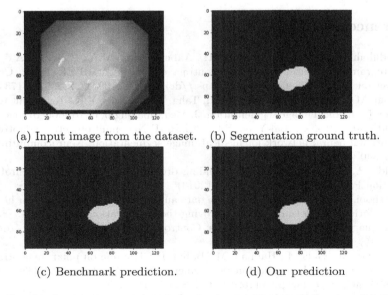

(a) Input image from the dataset.    (b) Segmentation ground truth.

(c) Benchmark prediction.    (d) Our prediction

**Fig. 5.** Results from an image taken from the dataset (image 0) showing: (a) the input image from the dataset, (b) the segmentation ground truth, (c) the benchmark paper prediction [20], and (d) the result of our prediction.

## 6    Conclusion and Future Work

This article discloses the best combinations of hyperparameters for the CVC-ClinicDB dataset. The Amsgrad and the Nadam are found to be the best optimizers, reaching the best accuracy with various combinations. However, the Amsgrad gradient-based optimizer ourcomes the best results among all the optimizers. In most optimizers, except for Adamax, the batch size of 4 always prevailed as part of the best combinations. On the other hand, a dropout greater than 2 is translated into a decrease in accuracy. In addition, several techniques were tested to avoid overfitting. One of the techniques to avoid overfitting was data augmentation. This technique was applied to the dataset before training the model; however, it worsened the results, so this preprocessing technique was discarded in the final experimentation.

Colonoscopy images and other medical field images generally are not very clear, they have noise or blurred boundaries. Therefore, the idea of improving the image contrast with CLAHE was proved to work in our case. However, the results do not show a decisive improvement, so more recent equalization techniques can be analyzed in future research works.

As it is known, the gradient-based optimizers used in this paper are not deterministic, so a future work that studies hyperparameter tuning with cross-validation taking an average accuracy among all folds is strongly recommended. We expect that the guidelines given for future researcher will increase the significance of the final results, and the ease of replicating them.

## References

1. Abdullah-Al-Wadud, M., Kabir, M.H., Akber Dewan, M.A., Chae, O.: A dynamic histogram equalization for image contrast enhancement. IEEE Trans. Consum. Electron. **53**(2), 593–600 (2007). https://doi.org/10.1109/TCE.2007.381734
2. Alom, M.Z., Yakopcic, C., Hasan, M., Taha, T.M., Asari, V.K.: Recurrent residual u-net for medical image segmentation. J. Med. Imaging **6**(1), 014006–014006 (2019)
3. Baldeon-Calisto, M., Lai-Yuen, S.K.: AdaResU-Net: multiobjective adaptive convolutional neural network for medical image segmentation. Neurocomputing **392**, 325–340 (2020)
4. Baldi, P., Sadowski, P.J.: Understanding dropout. In: Advances in Neural Information Processing Systems, vol. 26 (2013)
5. Barshooi, A., Amirkhani, A.: A novel data augmentation based on Gabor filter and convolutional deep learning for improving the classification of COVID-19 chest X-Ray images. Biomed. Signal Process. Control **72**, 103326 (2021). https://doi.org/10.1016/j.bspc.2021.103326
6. Benčević, M., Galić, I., Habijan, M., Babin, D.: Training on polar image transformations improves biomedical image segmentation. IEEE Access **9**, 133365–133375 (2021). https://doi.org/10.1109/ACCESS.2021.3116265
7. Blanc-Durand, P., Gucht, A., Schaefer, N., Itti, E., Prior, J.: Automatic lesion detection and segmentation of 18F-FET PET in gliomas: a full 3D U-Net convolutional neural network study. PLoS ONE **13**, e0195798 (2018). https://doi.org/10.1371/journal.pone.0195798

8. Canny, J.: A computational approach to edge detection. IEEE Trans. Pattern Anal. Mach. Intell. **6**, 679–698 (1986)

9. Dean, J.: 1.1 the deep learning revolution and its implications for computer architecture and chip design. In: 2020 IEEE International Solid- State Circuits Conference - (ISSCC), pp. 8–14 (2020). https://doi.org/10.1109/ISSCC19947.2020.9063049

10. Ding, L., Goshtasby, A.: On the canny edge detector. Pattern Recognit. **34**(3), 721–725 (2001)

11. Duchi, J., Hazan, E., Singer, Y.: Adaptive subgradient methods for online learning and stochastic optimization. J. Mach. Learn. Res. **12**(7) (2011)

12. Gao, J., Jiang, Q., Zhou, B., Chen, D.: Convolutional neural networks for computer-aided detection or diagnosis in medical image analysis: an overview. Math. Biosci. Eng. **16**(6), 6536–6561 (2019)

13. Gu, Z., et al.: Ce-net: context encoder network for 2d medical image segmentation. IEEE Trans. Med. Imaging **38**(10), 2281–2292 (2019). https://doi.org/10.1109/TMI.2019.2903562

14. Hesamian, M.H., Jia, W., He, X., Kennedy, P.: Deep learning techniques for medical image segmentation: achievements and challenges. J. Digital Imaging **32**, 582–596 (2019). https://doi.org/10.1007/s10278-019-00227-x

15. Ibtehaz, N., Rahman, M.S.: Multiresunet: rethinking the u-net architecture for multimodal biomedical image segmentation. Neural Netw. **121**, 74–87 (2020)

16. Jha, D., et al.: Real-time polyp detection, localization and segmentation in colonoscopy using deep learning. IEEE Access **9**, 40496–40510 (2021). https://doi.org/10.1109/ACCESS.2021.3063716

17. Kingma, D.P., Ba, J.: Adam: A method for stochastic optimization. arXiv preprint arXiv:1412.6980 (2014)

18. Likas, A., Vlassis, N., Verbeek, J.J.: The global k-means clustering algorithm. Pattern Recognit. **36**(2), 451–461 (2003)

19. Long, J., Shelhamer, E., Darrell, T.: Fully convolutional networks for semantic segmentation. In: Proceedings of the IEEE Conference on Computer Vision and Pattern Recognition, pp. 3431–3440 (2015)

20. Lou, A., Guan, S., Loew, M.: DC-Unet: rethinking the U-Net architecture with dual channel efficient CNN for medical image segmentation. In: Medical Imaging 2021: Image Processing, vol. 11596, pp. 758–768. SPIE (2021)

21. Minaee, S., Boykov, Y., Porikli, F., Plaza, A., Kehtarnavaz, N., Terzopoulos, D.: Image segmentation using deep learning: a survey. IEEE Trans. Pattern Anal. Mach. Intell. **44**(7), 3523–3542 (2021)

22. Noh, H., Hong, S., Han, B.: Learning deconvolution network for semantic segmentation. In: Proceedings of the IEEE International Conference on Computer Vision, pp. 1520–1528 (2015)

23. Norouzi, A., et al.: Medical image segmentation methods, algorithms, and applications. IETE Tech. Rev. **31**(3), 199–213 (2014)

24. Reddi, S.J., Kale, S., Kumar, S.: On the convergence of Adam and beyond. arXiv preprint arXiv:1904.09237 (2019)

25. Rogers, D.J., Tanimoto, T.T.: A computer program for classifying plants. Science **132**(3434), 1115–8 (1960)

26. Ronneberger, O., Fischer, P., Brox, T.: U-Net: convolutional networks for biomedical image segmentation. In: Navab, N., Hornegger, J., Wells, W.M., Frangi, A.F. (eds.) MICCAI 2015. LNCS, vol. 9351, pp. 234–241. Springer, Cham (2015). https://doi.org/10.1007/978-3-319-24574-4_28

27. von Landesberger, T., Bremm, S., Kirschner, M., Wesarg, S., Kuijper, A.: Visual analytics for model-based medical image segmentation: opportunities and challenges. Expert Syst. with Appl. **40**(12), 4934–4943 (2013). https://doi.org/10.1016/j.eswa.2013.03.006https://www.sciencedirect.com/science/article/pii/S0957417413001565

28. Wang, S., Yin, Y., Wang, D., Lv, Z., Wang, Y., Jin, Y.: An interpretable deep neural network for colorectal polyp diagnosis under colonoscopy. Knowl.-Based Syst. **234**, 107568 (2021). https://doi.org/10.1016/j.knosys.2021.107568,https://www.sciencedirect.com/science/article/pii/S0950705121008303

29. Zhou, Z., Siddiquee, M.M.R., Tajbakhsh, N., Liang, J.: Unet++: redesigning skip connections to exploit multiscale features in image segmentation. IEEE Trans. Med. Imaging **39**(6), 1856–1867 (2019)

# Vitreous Hemorrhage Segmentation in Fundus Images by Using an Efficient-UNet Network

Byron Ricardo Zapata[✉][iD], Jaime Heredia[iD], Silvana Zapata[iD], and Fabián R. Narváez[iD]

GIB&B Research Group, Department of Biomedicine,
Universidad Politécnica Salesiana, Quito, Ecuador
{bzapata,fnarvaeze}@ups.edu.ec

**Abstract.** Eye exams based on fundus image are used to detect abnormalities in the retina and optic nerve. These exams are able to detect issues such as diabetic retinopathy, retinal detachment, glaucoma, ocular melanoma, thrombosis, hemorrhages, among others. Fundus image examinations are also used to detect diseases such as macular degeneration, diabetes, hypertension, and coagulation disorders associated with vitreous hemorrhage, which is a common issue in individuals over the age of 50. Usually, Computer vision and artificial intelligence techniques have been used to support some diagnosis process associated to vitreous hemorrhage. However, there are still challenges during the fundus image analysis and lesions detection, these are due to the position, shape, and image color obtained from fundus examination. In this work, an automatic vitreous hemorrhages segmentation strategy is presented, which improve the well know segmentation techniques based on image thresholding. For doing that, fundus images are binarized by applied an segmentation image thresholding technique, which produces a subset of images. These binarized images are used as inputs to train an fully convolutional neural network. Our CCN architecture is based on Efficient-UNet network. The performance was evaluated by using a set of 200 images extracted from the IDRID dataset, an open access set of fundus images examination. The obtained results reports a rate of precision of 85.93%, compared to the 56% achieved by using a classic segmentation image thresholding strategy.

**Keywords:** Fundus · Vitreous hemorrhages · Otsu · Efficient-UNet · accuracy

## 1 Introduction

Eye fundus exams (EFE) are important and non-invasive tests, which are used to early diagnosis of ocular health conditions and vascular diseases. The EFE reveal retinal vascular images, such as the condition of the retina, intraocular

J. Maldonado-Mahauad et al. (Eds.): TICEC 2023, CCIS 1885, pp. 353–364, 2023.
https://doi.org/10.1007/978-3-031-45438-7_24

pressure, ocular tumors, arteriovenous crossings, glaucoma, vascular occlusion, hemorrhages, among others [5]. Figure 1 depicts an EFE displaying the key components of a healthy fundus captured through an angiography examination [3].

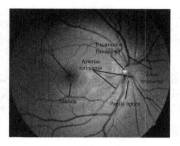

**Fig. 1.** Normal fundus of the eye [3].

In Fig. 1, the fundus of the eye can be observed, which is mainly composed of the macula, responsible for detailed vision and movement; the optic disc, the area where optic fibers from retinal cells exit the eye towards the brain; and the blood vessels, responsible for supplying blood and nutrients to the retina [4].

The main problems that can be found in fundus exams are: cataracts, retinal detachment, macular edema, inflammation, hemorrhages, etc.

Vitreous hemorrhage is the result of bleeding in the macular area, as shown in Fig. 2. This bleeding creates a cavity that is filled with a transparent and gelatinous substance composed mainly of water [1].

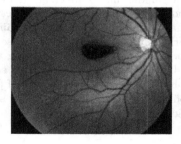

**Fig. 2.** Vitreous hemorrhage in the fundus of the eye [1].

The main causes of vitreous hemorrhage are primarily ocular trauma, eye surgeries, and rupture of blood vessels in the retina, among others.

The most common symptoms of vitreous hemorrhage include:

– Partial or total blindness in the affected eye in severe and acute cases.
– Blurry vision with spots resembling the silhouette of a fly.

Nowadays, the application of artificial intelligence techniques has enabled the automatic detection and classification of ocular diseases, which has contributed to early diagnosis and improved ocular health. Some applications developed using artificial intelligence have allowed for the detection of diabetic retinopathy, macular degeneration, identification of signs of glaucoma, detection of hemorrhages, among others.

With the advancement of artificial intelligence techniques, tools are continuously being developed to improve precision and accuracy in disease detection. Since health is crucial for the social and economic well-being of a community, providing doctors with a non-invasive imaging diagnostic tool facilitates the timely detection and control of diseases. In this study, two segmentation techniques based on Otsu and Efficient-Unet are employed to enhance the accuracy in detecting vitreous hemorrhages. The work includes a review of the state of the art, the methodology used, the results obtained, and the conclusions reached.

### 1.1    Related Works

In the field of image processing and artificial intelligence-based segmentation, various techniques have been proposed to enhance image quality and highlight relevant details. Among these works, [13] stands out, where a method for diabetic retinopathy detection is presented. This work employs a modified convolutional neural network to segment vitreous hemorrhages in fundus images, achieving specificity and precision values of 80.49%, 99.68%, and 98.68%, demonstrating the effectiveness of the predictions.

Another relevant article in this area is [10] which utilizes a CNN-based convolutional neural network to extract features from fundus images. These images are classified into three groups (glaucoma, macular degeneration, and hemorrhages) using a fast regional convolutional neural network (FRCNN) architecture. Subsequently, the images undergo a segmentation phase to extract relevant factors depending on their respective groups. This article demonstrates the efficacy of combining deep learning clustering techniques and segmentation.

In [12], the authors delve into automated advancements for diabetic eye disease detection through a survey. This survey analyzes available datasets, image processing techniques, deep learning models, and evaluation metrics used for diagnosing diabetes using fundus images. The majority of the selected articles in this survey employ deep learning techniques based on convolutional neural networks, with a notable mention of the use of generative adversarial networks (GAN), which provide increased robustness in training compared to other techniques.

An article focused on the subject of this research is [15], which centers around the diagnosis of retinal hemorrhages in neonatal patients through the utilization of a convolutional neural network (DCNN). Prior to training the neural network, preprocessing procedures were conducted on the images to rectify lighting issues, thereby achieving enhanced images for the DCNN's training. The DCNN was trained using a dataset of 48,996 images of the neonatal retinal background, which were assessed by experts to differentiate between normal ocular backgrounds and the various grades of hemorrhages: normal background, grade 1 (minor hemorrhage), grade 2 (mild hemorrhage), and grade 3 (hemorrhage exceeding the diameter of the optic disc). Through this methodology, the authors were able to attain an overall accuracy of 97.44%, providing a high level of reliability in the obtained results.

## 2   Methodology

For the segmentation of vitreous hemorrhage in the fundus of the eye, the methodology outlined in Fig. 3 was proposed. This methodology includes image acquisition, application of image preprocessing techniques, Otsu-based segmentation, application of Efficient-UNet, and validation using Ground Truth. It's worth noting that in this study, the Otsu method has been chosen, as it's one of the most commonly used segmentation techniques, owing to its simplicity and effectiveness when dealing with images containing well-defined pixels. Furthermore, the Efficient UNet has been employed, given its capability to produce efficient segmentation with low computational cost [2].

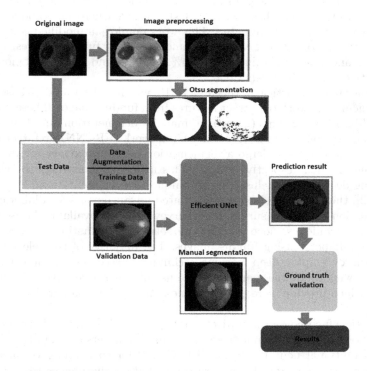

**Fig. 3.** Methodology for vitreous hemorrhage segmentation

## 2.1   Preprocessing of the Images

For image preprocessing, a high-pass spatial filter is used to enhance the areas of higher viability and preserve fine details of the image, correcting the blur from the acquisition process. Additionally, median subtraction can be applied to enhance details after passing through a low-pass filter, using Eq. 1 [6].

$$\frac{\partial g}{\partial n} = g[n+1] - g[n] \tag{1}$$

Eq. 2 displays the filter applied to the fundus of the eye.

$$f(i,j) = \begin{bmatrix} -1 & -1 & -1 \\ -1 & 10.7 & -1 \\ -1 & -1 & -1 \end{bmatrix} \otimes g(m,n) \tag{2}$$

where:

- $g(m,n)$ = be the input image.
- The $3 \times 3$ matrix is the kernel used to enhance the colors of the image, which is obtained heuristically.

Figure 4 shows the application of the spatial filter to the original input image.

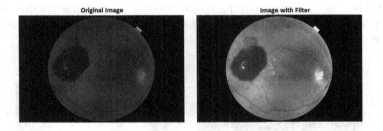

**Fig. 4.** Original image vs Image with high-pass filter

## 2.2   Image Segmentation

Segmentation aims to separate objects or areas of interest in an image, which allows for solving classification problems [4]. Among the various segmentation techniques, Otsu segmentation, also known as thresholding, is one of them. This method calculates the threshold value in such a way that the dispersion within each group is as small as possible, while the dispersion between different groups is as high as possible [14].

The Otsu segmentation algorithm is based on the following steps:

- Calculate the normalized histogram of the image.
- Compute the cumulative sum of pixels belonging to a class.

– Calculate cumulative measures and global measures.
– Calculate and maximize the inter-class variance.

To determine the optimal threshold $t$ for Otsu segmentation, Eq. 3 is used,

$$\sigma^2_{inter-class} = w_1(t).w_2(t).(\mu_1(t) - \mu_2(t))^2 \tag{3}$$

where:

– $w_1(t)$ = Is the probability of belonging to class 1 for intensity values less than or equal to $t$.
– $w_2(t)$ = Probability of belonging to class 2 for intensity values greater than $t$.
– $\mu_1(t)$ = Intensity measure of class 1.
– $\mu_2(t)$ = Intensity measure of class 2.

To determine the value of optimal of $t$, Eq. 4 is used, aiming to find the value of t that maximizes the variance between the classes.

$$t_{opt} = max_t(\sigma^2_{inter}(t)) \tag{4}$$

Fig. 5 presents the original image and the image obtained after applying Otsu segmentation and dilation. Dilation allows increasing or expanding the size of objects in the binary image, which allows the pixels detected by Otsu to expand and fill the entire segmentation. By importing the accuracy_score from the Sklearn library in Python, an average accuracy of 56% is obtained for Otsu-based segmentation.

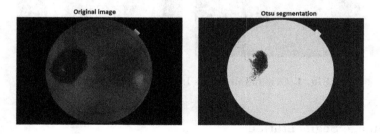

**Fig. 5.** Original image vs Otsu segmentation

In Fig. 5, it can be observed at a glance that the vitreous hemorrhage is not completely segmented. Therefore, the application of Efficient-UNet is sought to improve the segmentation.

## 2.3   Data Augmentation

Data augmentation is a technique that allows generating a new set of images based on the originals. It involves applying transformations to the original images through image processing, including displacement, rotation, flipping, random cropping, noise augmentation, scale variation, and among others. The main objective of data augmentation is to increase the amount of training data to reduce the risk of overfitting, thus improving the model's performance and its ability to generalize patterns in new test data [8]. In the Fig. 6, an example of horizontal and vertical flipping applied to the original Otsu images to feed the Efficient-UNet model is shown.

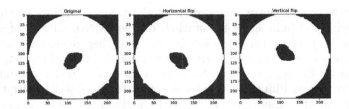

**Fig. 6.** Image horizontal and vertical flip.

The image in Fig. 7 demonstrates a ±45° rotation of the image, enabling the simulation of an angle change in the exploration of vitreous hemorrhage.

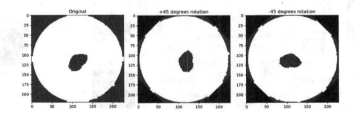

**Fig. 7.** ±45° image rotation

Figure 8 displays the application of blurring and the addition of Gaussian noise to simulate capturing low-light retinal background images with noise caused by the quality and limitations of the equipment used.

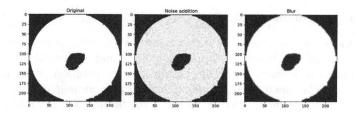

**Fig. 8.** Image with blur and noise

## 2.4   Efficient-UNet

Efficient UNet is an optimized variant of the UNet convolutional neural network, widely used in image segmentation. Efficient UNet consists of an encoder and a decoder that capture relevant features and then reconstruct and expand important features of the image for segmentation [7]. One of the improvements introduced by Efficient UNet is the "skip connection," which establishes links between layers with different spatial scales, facilitating object localization in segmentation. Another important feature of this neural network is the incorporation of an expansion layer at the end of the UNet model, which enhances the quality of predictions [9].

Figure 9 depicts the architecture of Efficient-UNet using a simplified block diagram.

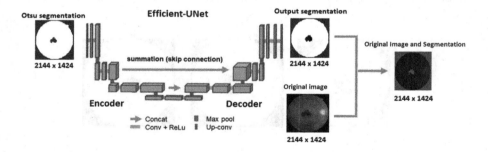

**Fig. 9.** Architecture of Efficient-UNet

To extract the features from the convolutional layers, ReLU is employed in the Encoder. This reduces the size of the input and enables the neural network to extract relevant characteristics from the input image.

For the reconstruction of the feature map in segmentation, transposed convolutional layers are used in the decoder through Max pool, which allows obtaining the same dimensions as the input image at the output.

# 3 Results

In this section, we present the results of the segmentation performed by Efficient-Unet, which are compared using the Ground Truth technique to assess and contrast the outcomes with Otsu's segmentation.

## 3.1 Experimental Protocol

For the realization of this work, the freely available IDRID dataset [11] was used, which contains a set of fundus images with different pathologies. Additionally, the assistance of a medical intern was enlisted for manual classification and the generation of images for the Ground Truth test.

## 3.2 Efficient-UNet Training and Validation

For the training of the neural network, data augmentation was applied to the Otsu-segmented images to increase the number of samples and improve the prediction of Efficient-UNet. The neural network was trained using 200 images for 600 iterations, resulting in an accuracy of 95.97%, as shown in Fig. 10.

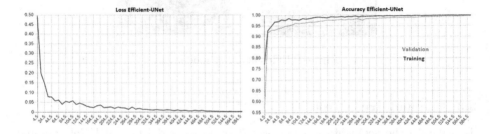

**Fig. 10.** Training loss and accuracy of Efficient-UNet

The results of model training present an accuracy of 95.97% and an average Jaccard index (IoU) between the segmentation predicted by Efficient-UNet and the segmentation performed by Otsu (Macro Avg IoU) of 95.93%. These values demonstrate the high accuracy of the model in both the training and validation data.

For the validation of the model, images that were not used in the Efficient-Unet training were used, an example of the result obtained from the segmentation is shown in Fig. 11.

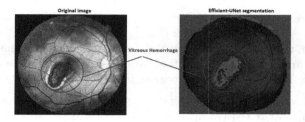

**Fig. 11.** Efficient-UNet segmentation

To evaluate the accuracy of the model, images that were not used during training were employed. The results obtained are presented in Fig. 12, with a prediction accuracy of 85.93%.

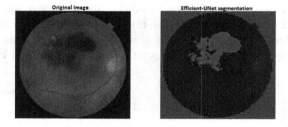

**Fig. 12.** Efficient-UNet model test

### 3.3  Ground Truth Test

To validate the segmentation performed by Otsu and Efficient-UNet, manual segmentation was carried out with the assistance of a medical intern and a digital tablet. Figure 13 shows the fundus images obtained from the three segmentation results.

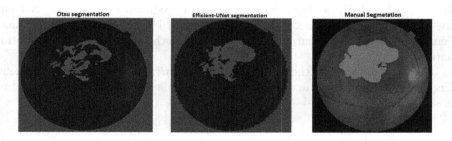

**Fig. 13.** Segmentations applied to fundus exams

To evaluate the differences between the different segmentations, the Ground Truth is used. This method allows for a pixel-by-pixel comparison and counting of the differing pixels between the two images [11]. This comparison is done by taking the manually segmented image as the reference and comparing it with the segmentations generated by the Efficient-Unet and Otsu algorithms. The averages obtained from the segmentation comparison of the 200 fundus images are presented in Table 1.

**Table 1.** Ground Truth Test

| Segmentation | Number of different pixels |
|---|---|
| Otsu | 1089 |
| Efficient-UNet | 387 |

From Table 1 it can be seen that the segmentations performed by Efficient-UNet are closer to the manually segmented images compared to the traditional Otsu segmentation.

## 4 Conclusions

– Through the research of related articles and the bibliography used in this study, it is confirmed that the application of artificial intelligence techniques in the field of ophthalmology has shown promise in improving accuracy in predicting various eye conditions. The advancements in artificial intelligence combined with medicine have led to the development of innovative tools that have the potential to reduce the workload of physicians, thus improving the timelines for the detection and diagnosis of eye diseases.
– The Otsu-based segmentation exhibits an average precision percentage below 57% in the detection of vitreous hemorrhage. This is due to its static nature and lack of learning and adaptation capabilities. On the other hand, Efficient U-Net, based on a convolutional neural network, has demonstrated a precision of 95.97% in vitreous hemorrhage detection, showcasing a significant improvement in accuracy. This is attributed to its ability to learn specific image features, thereby achieving better segmentation outcomes.
– Using images that were not included in the training and validation datasets, it has been confirmed that the Efficient U-Net segmentation model achieves an accuracy of 85.93%. This outcome has been supported by validation conducted through Ground Truth, demonstrating the similarity between the results of Efficient U-Net and manual segmentation, as depicted in Table 1.
– Using image processing and artificial intelligence, this study puts forth an alternative to assist medical personnel in the automated detection and monitoring of vitreous hemorrhage. Furthermore, a future perspective focused on treating this condition is taken into account.

# References

1. Atlas de angiografía del fondo de ojo. https://amolca.com.ec/libro/atlas-de-angiografia-del-fondo-de-ojo
2. Agarwal, D., Tripathi, K., Krishen, K.: Concepts of Artificial Intelligence and its Application in Modern Healthcare Systems (2023). https://doi.org/10.1201/9781003333081
3. Besenczi, R., Tóth, J., Hajdu, A.: A review on automatic analysis techniques for color fundus photographs (2016). https://doi.org/10.1016/j.csbj.2016.10.001
4. Bueno, G., Dorado, J.: Gestión, procesado y análisis de imágines biomédicas (2007). https://www.casadellibro.com/libro-gestion-procesado-y-analisis-de-imagenes-bio medicas/9788484274988/1138103
5. Flores-González, I., Calonje, D.H.: Telemedicina para detección de enfermedades oculares con potencial de ceguera en méxico. Revista Mexicana de Oftalmología **91**, 297–305 (2017). https://doi.org/10.1016/j.mexoft.2016.12.002
6. Gonzales, R.C., Woods, R.E.: Digital Image Processing Fourth Edition, vol. 1 (2018)
7. Jahanifar, M., et al.: Stain-robust mitotic figure detection for the mitosis domain generalization challenge. In: Aubreville, M., Zimmerer, D., Heinrich, M. (eds.) MICCAI 2021. LNCS, vol. 13166, pp. 48–52. Springer, Cham (2022). https://doi.org/10.1007/978-3-030-97281-3_6
8. Kneusel, R.T.: Practical Deep Learning, vol. 53 (2021)
9. Liu, W., Luo, J., Yang, Y., Wang, W., Deng, J., Yu, L.: Automatic lung segmentation in chest X-ray images using improved U-net. Sci. Rep. **12**(1), 1–10 (2022). https://doi.org/10.1038/s41598-022-12743-y. https://www.nature.com/articles/s41598-022-12743-y
10. Nazir, T., Irtaza, A., Javed, A., Malik, H., Hussain, D., Naqvi, R.A.: Retinal image analysis for diabetes-based eye disease detection using deep learning. Appl. Sci. **10**, 6185 (2020). https://doi.org/10.3390/APP10186185
11. Nisar, H., Tan, Y.R., Yeap, K.H.: Eczema skin lesions segmentation using deep neural network (U-net) (2023). https://doi.org/10.1007/978-3-031-23239-8_10
12. Sarki, R., Ahmed, K., Wang, H., Zhang, Y.: Automatic detection of diabetic eye disease through deep learning using fundus images: a survey (2020). https://doi.org/10.1109/ACCESS.2020.3015258
13. Skouta, A., Elmoufidi, A., Jai-Andaloussi, S., Ouchetto, O.: Hemorrhage semantic segmentation in fundus images for the diagnosis of diabetic retinopathy by using a convolutional neural network. J. Big Data **9**, 1–24 (2022). https://doi.org/10.1186/s40537-022-00632-0
14. Vala, M.H.J., Baxi, A.: A review on Otsu image segmentation algorithm. Int. J. Adv. Res. Comput. Eng. Technol. **2** (2013)
15. Wang, B., et al.: Application of a deep convolutional neural network in the diagnosis of neonatal ocular fundus hemorrhage. Biosci. Rep. **38** (2018). https://doi.org/10.1042/BSR20180497

# A Non-invasive Portable Solution to Estimate Hemoglobin Levels in the Blood

Maythe Mieles Freire[1]([✉]) [iD], Luz María Tobar Subía[1,2],
Brizeida Nohemí Gamez Aparicio[1], and Guillermo Mosquera Canchingre[3]

[1] Universidad Técnica del Norte, Facultad de Ingeniería en Ciencias Aplicadas,
Ibarra, Ecuador
{msmielesf,lmtobarsubia,bngamez}@utn.edu.ec
[2] Universidad de Málaga. Escuela de Ingenierías Industriales, Málaga, Spain
luztobar@uma.es
[3] Universidad Internacional del Ecuador, Facultad de Ciencias Técnicas, Quito,
Ecuador
gmosquera@uide.edu.ec

**Abstract.** Hemoglobin (Hgb) is one of the most essential proteins in the body. Its principal function is to transport oxygen to vital organs and tissues so that they fulfill the necessary functions human life. In order to know the hemoglobin value in the blood, the invasive technique of extracting a blood sample and later evaluating it in a laboratory has traditionally been used. This process can cause discomfort in cases where it is performed repetitively in patients with sensitive skin, children, and the elderly. In addition, due to invasive procedures, there is a high risk of infection, and the analysis of these takes a long time. In this context, a non-invasive portable device capable of obtaining the amount of hemoglobin present in the blood through the implementation of pulse oximetry techniques is presented to provide an alternative for the evaluation of iron deficiency anemia and thus avoid the continuous application of methods that require frequent painful punctures and reduce the risk of infection. The device is based on applying intensity ratios of light absorption of the substance at different wavelengths through an optical pulse oximetry sensor connected to an ESP-32 micro-controller that displays the results on an OLED screen. The electronic system is coupled to a 3D model printed in PLA; its measurement area is based on commercial oximeter designs. Functional tests of the device were carried out with 29 users. The results showed an error of 1.86% when comparing the prototype with a blood chemistry analysis sample.

**Keywords:** Anemia · Absorbance · Beer-Lambert · Hemoglobin · Pulse Oximetry

© The Author(s), under exclusive license to Springer Nature Switzerland AG 2023
J. Maldonado-Mahauad et al. (Eds.): TICEC 2023, CCIS 1885, pp. 365–381, 2023.
https://doi.org/10.1007/978-3-031-45438-7_25

# 1 Introduction

According to statistics compiled by the World Health Organization, in 2019, approximately 24.88%, corresponding to approximately 1620 million people, suffer from anemia [1,11,18]. In Ecuador, this health condition mainly affects women, particularly those of reproductive age. The prevalence rate among this specific group of women is estimated to be 23.9% [2].

Anemia is a condition characterized by low levels of hemoglobin in the blood [27]; which is an iron-carrying glycoprotein responsible for transporting oxygen to the tissues of the body, that is; if there is a large amount of oxygen in the blood, it appears bright red because hemoglobin is a respiratory pigment. This implies that a decrease in color intensity suggests the possible presence of anemic states [3]. The main symptoms observed in individuals with anemia include tiredness, fatigue, weakness, paleness, and headaches [4]. Given the above, it is essential to constantly monitor anemia levels since it allows the treating physician to ensure that the indicated medication generates the desired effect on the patient [6,23]. Normal blood hemoglobin values can vary by age group; a person is generally considered to have anemia when their hemoglobin concentration falls below 13 g/dL for adult men and 12 g/dL for adult women [4]. These reference values identify people who are at risk for this condition. In controlling this condition, invasive methods such as complete hematology analyzers of blood components, blood gas analyzer that measures the amount of arterial gases in the sample, and portable conventional blood gauges that use single-use test strips are used [10]. There are a number of disadvantages to using invasive techniques to measure blood hemoglobin levels: 1) it is painful in patients suffering from chronic anemia, 2) these invasive techniques also require infrastructure (clinical hematology analyzer) and biological reagents, and 3) trained laboratory personnel are required for analysis [28].

Sánchez et al. focus on constructing a device that obtains the concentration of hemoglobin to record and monitor the hemoglobin level through a mobile application. The system uses test tapes, where a drop of blood is placed. Periodic use of these tapes can cause discomfort to the patient [23]. On the other hand, non-invasive devices to measure and evaluate the hemoglobin level in blood are increasingly important in medical care and have attracted much attention as they provide an attractive alternative to traditional invasive methods requiring repeated skin punctures [16]. They can be a valuable tool in pre-diagnosis and self-monitoring, especially in settings where frequent blood hemoglobin readings are needed without the need for invasive procedures [15]. In addition, these devices offer the advantage of being portable, economical, and easy to use [16].

In recent years, significant progress has been noted in the accuracy obtained with non-invasive tools to measure anemia. Researchers have explored various techniques to estimate blood parameters non-invasively. Within these methods are considered imaging, spectrophotometry, optoacoustic spectroscopy, transmission spectroscopy, and spectroscopy of reflection. There is a known mobile application that analyzes the color of the patient's finger blood using the flash of cell phones, called HemaApp [25]. However, not all phones are suitable to run the application since specific features are needed that are available in mid-range or high-end phones. In addition, Choe [6] offers a solution for anemia screening in resource-limited settings, such as rural health centers and remote areas. However, implementing these non-invasive devices in these sectors still faces challenges. Challenges include a need for more trained personnel to operate and interpret the results of these devices, as well as limited financial resources for their acquisition and maintenance. This highlights the potential of non-invasive devices to provide accurate and reliable measurements without needing to pierce the skin repeatedly [25]. However, medical experts emphasize that these non-invasive devices for measuring anemia require validation and clinical evaluation to ensure their accuracy and reliability [22]. Cordova et al., whose device obtains measurements of the amount of hemoglobin, presents an error of 7.5% compared to traditional invasive methods [7]. Therefore, further validation and clinical evaluation is required to ensure the accuracy and reliability of these non-invasive devices. In this context, it is proposed to develop a device that estimates hemoglobin levels in the blood non-invasively, using red and infrared light, as well as spectrum variations, to validate its results with those obtained through complete blood count examinations. This clinical test will determine the accuracy and reliability of the device without the need for invasive procedures.

The rest of this paper is organized as follows: Sect. 2 summarizes the basic principle and the instrument design. Section 3 introduces the extraction dates with the prototype and the clinical experiments. Section 4 introduces the results and comparative analyses of them. Section 5 discusses the advantages and limitations. Finally, Sect. 6 gives final remarks.

## 2 Methods

### 2.1 The Basic Principle of Pulse Oximetry

The Pulse Oximetry method is characterized by determining the absorbance of the substance, which means its ability to capture certain wavelengths [13]. The same one that is based on the Beer-Lambert Law, which establishes that the amount of light that a substance absorbs is proportional to the length or thickness that the light must travel in it, which means that the amount of light absorbed will increase as the path lengthens [7].

The hemoglobin is classified into four types, [9]. The two most abundant types in the blood are oxyhemoglobin ($HbO_2$) and deoxyhemoglobin ($HHb$). The other two types do not present physiological behavior when they interact with oxygen; therefore, they are considered dysfunctional.

Oxyhemogolobin is the one that joins directly with oxygen and it has scarlet red color that characterizes arterial blood, while deoxyhemoglobin named *reduced* manifests when oxygen is loss due to the incomplete saturation, being dark red its characteristic color and it is found in venous blood [9].

To obtain the hemoglobin value, the spectrum absorbance value of the substance study is needed. This value is varies in the range of 600 nm to 1200 nm nm, being this the light absorption register base on the light wavelength that influences the substance. It specifies which wavelengths are the ones absorbed by the sample molecules showing energetic differences of the energetic states [12].

The hemoglobin absorption spectrum is between 600 nm and 1200 nm, therefore, with the value of the amount of light absorbed in a given time, the level of hemoglobin in blood is calculated [21].

The intensity changes produce a form of the photoplethysmographic signal ($PPG$, for its English acronym). It is related to the amount of blood flowing through the veins and arteries. This signal consists of two parts $AC$ (alternating current) and $DC$ (direct current) that will show the interaction of the optical signals that are reflected or transmitted in the acquisition process [12]. In Eq. 1 the relationship of intensities "$R$" between its $AC$ and $DC$ components is presented [21].

$$R = \frac{A_{RED}}{A_{IR}}, \tag{1}$$

where: $A_{RED}$ is the red led light absorption value and $A_{IR}$ is the infrared led light absorption value. Therefore, the hemoglobin level value $Hb$ is determined through the Eq. 2:

$$Hb = \frac{R}{0.645} * A, \tag{2}$$

where: 0.645 is the corelation constant used by medical devices for measurements in health care places [20], A is a value used to calibrate the measurement that depends on the hemoglobin normal values.

## 2.2   Instrument Design

The device design consists of three fundamental components: hardware, software and user. This is shown in Fig 1.

**Hardware.** The system hardware is composed of three electronic components: the $ESP-32$ micro-controller, the $MAX30102$ sensor and the $SSD1306\ OLED$ screen.

The $ESP-32$ microcontroller is used for signal processing and communication since it has built-in Bluetooth and Wi-Fi connection to facilitate the exchange of information over the network. In addition, it has an $I_2C$ communication peripheral and is powered by $3.3V$. The $MAX30102$ pulse oximetry optical sensor is used to measure the light absorption by hemoglobin, using two LEDs (red and infrared LEDs) at different wavelengths ($660nm$ and $880nm$), respectively. The sensor also has a photodetector, a digital-to-analog converter, an amplifier, and a 50 and 60 $Hz$ ambient light filter.

Finally, the $OLED$ screen displays the measurement results. Once the electronic system components are defined, the 3D structure is designed using $CAD$ software (Computer Aided Design). The prototype components are located, taking into account the slots for the photodetector, the measurement LEDs, and the space to receive power from the USB port, see Fig. 2. Additionally, the $3D$ model is observed in the form of a box made up of two removable parts, an upper part (1) for the acquisition and display elements, and a lower part (2) where the control element is located.

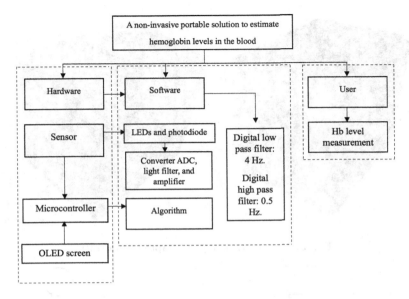

**Fig. 1.** Device structure: Hardware, Software, and User (readapted from [14]).

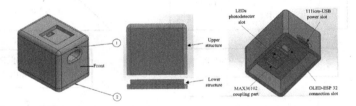

**Fig. 2.** Hemoglobin measurement prototype components (readapted from [14]).

The prototype was $3D$ printed, its dimensions are $72 \times 55 \times 60$ mm, and it weights 56.699 g, see Fig. 3. In the same figure, the yellow arrow indicates the slot where the user has to insert his finger, the green arrow indicates the slot for microcontroller and power supply connection, and the red arrow indicates the OLED screen location.

**Software.** The entire hemoglobin level obtaining procedure is summarized in Fig. 4. The development of the algorithm begins with the libraries definition corresponding to the sensor, screen, and the communication carried out between the electronic components; the finger is detected, and then low-pass and high-pass filters are applied; in the next step, the necessary variables are declared, such as the intensities of the red and infrared LEDs, the r ratio value, and the hemoglobin concentration; the micro-controller attempts to detect the presence of the MAX 30102 sensor; otherwise, a notification is shown on the screen suggesting to check the connection; the *OLED* screen is reset for each measurement, and the hemoglobin value is calculated for each heartbeat using Eq. 2, displaying the result in the display format "Your hemoglobin level is: Hb = ... g/dL".

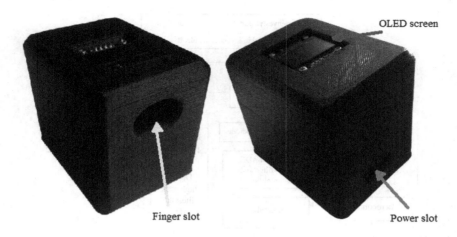

**Fig. 3.** Device 3D model (readapted from [14]).

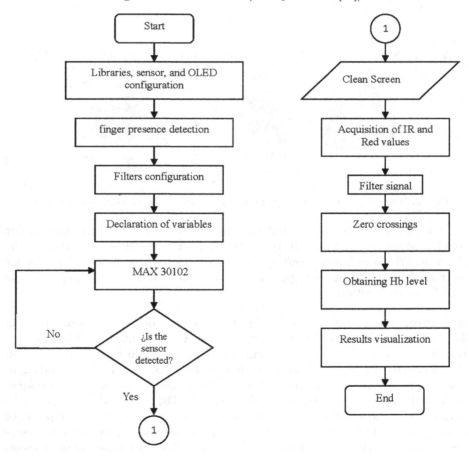

**Fig. 4.** Code flowchart (readapted from [14]).

**User.** According to the World Health Organization, the hemoglobin concentration normal levels in blood are shown in the Table 1.

**Table 1.** Hemoglobin concentration to diagnose anemia at sea level (g/L)± [1].

| Population | No anemia | Anemia Mild | Moderate | Severe |
|---|---|---|---|---|
| Kids from 6 to 59 months old | 110 or higher | 100–109 | 70–79 | less than 70 |
| Kids from 5 to 11 years old | 115 or higher | 110–114 | 80–109 | less than 80 |
| Kids from 12 to 14 years old | 120 or higher | 110–119 | 80–109 | less than 80 |
| Non pregnant women (15 years or older) | 120 or higher | 110–119 | 80–109 | less than 80 |
| Pregnant women | 110 or higher | 100–109 | 70–79 | less than 70 |
| Men (15 years or older) | 130 or higher | 100–129 | 80–109 | less than 80 |

Therefore, for the users participating in the study, normal hemoglobin levels should be considered making an adjustment according to the Table 2; since it is known that people who live at more than 1000 meters above sea level have a higher hemoglobin concentration [1].

**Table 2.** Adjustments of measured hemoglobin concentrations as a function of altitude above sea level.

| Altitude (meters above sea level) | Measured hemoglobin adjustment g/L |
|---|---|
| <1000 | 0 |
| 1000 | −2 |
| 1500 | −5 |
| 2000 | −8 |
| 2500 | −13 |
| 3000 | −19 |
| 3500 | −27 |
| 4000 | −35 |
| 4500 | −45 |

## 2.3   Algorithm: Extraction Dates with the Prototype

The hemoglobin calculation is performed using heartbeats. In each heartbeat, values belonging to the intensities in each one of the LEDs are collected. A thousand samples are read in each time and in two variables the current values of the red and infrared LEDs are assigned.

To avoid unnecessary signals and since the hemoglobin calculation is performed using the pulse oximetry method, it is necessary to work with heartbeat cut frequencies; therefore, two filters are used. A low-pass filter is set to 4 Hz which corresponds to 240 bpm (beats per minute) with means of attenuating high frequency signal components and allowing low frequency signal components to pass through. A high-pass filter that is set to 0.5 Hz or 30 bpm, works without letting low frequencies through. These values were established based on normal heart rate levels in people at rest, which is a range between 60 to 100 bpm, considering abnormal data <50 bpm (bradycardia) and >100 (tachycardia) [15].

If the finger is detected by the sensor, the program identifies the zero crossings, carrying out the calculation operations that are: the $r_{red}$ and $r_{ir}$ intensities average, the $R$ ratio, the oxygen saturation level in the blood $SpO_2$, and the hemoglobin value $Hb$ applying the Eq. 2; otherwise, if the finger is not detected, the program resets the value.

If the heartbeats (bpm) are higher that 50 and lower than 200, which means a normal range, then the results are shown on the OLED screen.

## 3   Experimental Section

A comparative analysis was carried out for functionality verification, meaning that a complete blood chemistry test was performed and compared to the result provided by the device.

To register the results, data-based containing the following information was created: •age, •gender, •ethnicity, •$R$ ratio value, •IR LED Value, •Red LED Value, •Hemoglobin value from laboratory test, and •Hemoglobin value from device test.

To select the patients that participated in the study, the following considerations were taken into account: •The patient should have short nails and no nail polish. •Age range between: 20 to 30 years. •The measurement will be made while the patient is at rest. •The test will be carried out three consecutive times. •Pregnant women are excluded from the study since their hemoglobin values are lower than normal [10]. •People that already were diagnosed or are under treatment are excluded. •People wearing medical devices such as pacemakers and other devices are excluded.

The test with the device followed the next order: 1) The user must be in a comfortable position, preferably seated, with the arm stretched out and placed on a support point to facilitate stability. 2) The user must place the index finger from either hand in the device slot, see Fig. 3. 3) Keeping the finger as still as possible, the sensor reading is obtained for each heartbeat, so the user's breathing must be controlled and calmed. 4) If necessary, the results will be displayed on the arduino IDE serial monitor. 5) The test ends, and then the screen displays the hemoglobin level obtained.

## 4   Result

### 4.1   Clinical Experiments

The results of the 29 people who agreed to participate in the research study are presented. Of which 10 are women, 19 are men, 2 have dark skin pigmentation, and are in an age range between 20 to 30 years; however, a 48-year-old subject was presented in order to test the device functioning at older ages. The tests were carried out in medical laboratories that are located at an altitude of 2.225 meters above sea level.

In Fig. 5, the laboratory results sheet is displayed, obtaining one for each patient, giving a total of 29.

**Informe análisis hematología**

| | | | Sexo: | Edad: |
|---|---|---|---|---|
| Nombre: ▮▮▮▮ | Apellido: ▮▮▮▮ | | | |
| ID muest: 17 | Tipo de paciente: | | ID pac: | 0804580355 |
| Dpt.: | Tiempo de análisis: 24-02-2023 09:55 | | Modo: | WB-CBC+DIFF |

| | Parámet | Result | Unid | Grupo de ref. | |
|---|---|---|---|---|---|
| 1 | WBC | 5.25 | 10^3/uL | 4.00 - 10.00 | |
| 2 | Neu# | 2.74 | 10^3/uL | 2.00 - 7.00 | Mensaje WBC |
| 3 | Lym# | 2.20 | 10^3/uL | 0.80 - 4.00 | |
| 4 | Mon# | 0.28 | 10^3/uL | 0.12 - 1.20 | |
| 5 | Eos# | 0.03 | 10^3/uL | 0.02 - 0.50 | |
| 6 | Bas# | 0.00 | 10^3/uL | 0.00 - 0.10 | |
| 7 | Neu% | 52.1 | % | 50.0 - 70.0 | |
| 8 | Lym% A | 41.9 | % | 20.0 - 40.0 | |
| 9 | Mon% | 5.4 | % | 3.0 - 12.0 | |
| 10 | Eos% | 0.6 | % | 0.5 - 5.0 | |
| 11 | Bas% | 0.0 | % | 0.0 - 1.0 | |
| 12 | RBC | 4.63 | 10^6/uL | 3.50 - 5.50 | |
| 13 | HGB | 14.9 | g/dL | 11.0 - 16.0 | |
| 14 | HCT | 42.2 | % | 37.0 - 54.0 | Mensaje RBC |
| 15 | MCV | 91.3 | fL | 80.0 - 100.0 | |
| 16 | MCH | 32.2 | pg | 27.0 - 34.0 | |
| 17 | MCHC | 35.3 | g/dL | 32.0 - 36.0 | |
| 18 | RDW-CV | 13.3 | % | 11.0 - 16.0 | |
| 19 | RDW-SD | 45.5 | fL | 35.0 - 56.0 | |
| 20 | PLT | 234 | 10^3/uL | 100 - 300 | |
| 21 | MPV | 10.5 | fL | 7.0 - 11.0 | |
| 22 | PDW | 15.8 | | 9.0 - 17.0 | |
| 23 | PCT | 0.246 | % | 0.108 - 0.282 | Mensaje PLT |

**Fig. 5.** Hematology Exam Result (readapted from [14]).

The results of the 29 blood chemistry tests are presented in the Table 3.

The data collected by the device is stored in Table 4, and the three hemoglobin levels obtained from the three samples are shown for each participant; finally, the average Hb is calculated.

Finally, the percentage error is calculated with Eq. 3, and the results standard deviation with Eq. 4, see results in Table 5.

$$Percentage \quad error = \frac{|Measured \quad value - true \quad value|}{|true \quad value|} * 100, \quad (3)$$

where: *Measured value* corresponds to measured value and *true value* corresponds to the real value

$$Standard \quad deviation = \sqrt{\frac{\sum(X - \bar{X})^2}{n - 1}}, \quad (4)$$

where: $X - \bar{X}$ it is the set of all values, and $n$ is the total number of values.

**Table 3.** Laboratory Exam Results.

| User | Sex | *Hb g/dL* Lab |
|------|--------|------|
| 1 | Female | 14.6 |
| 2 | Male | 18.6 |
| 3 | Male | 18.1 |
| 4 | Male | 17.5 |
| 5 | Male | 15.5 |
| 6 | Male | 16.5 |
| 7 | Male | 18.4 |
| 8 | Male | 18.4 |
| 9 | Female | 14.7 |
| 10 | Male | 16.7 |
| 11 | Male | 18.7 |
| 12 | Male | 17.8 |
| 13 | Male | 17.2 |
| 14 | Female | 15.0 |
| 15 | Male | 17.7 |
| 16 | Male | 18.3 |
| 17 | Female | 15.0 |
| 18 | Male | 17.1 |
| 19 | Female | 15.2 |
| 20 | Male | 18.4 |
| 21 | Female | 13.8 |
| 22 | Male | 18.2 |
| 23 | Male | 16.1 |
| 24 | Female | 14.6 |
| 25 | Female | 14.7 |
| 26 | Female | 15.6 |
| 27 | Male | 17.6 |
| 28 | Male | 17.4 |
| 29 | Male | 17.3 |

The mean, median, and outlier values of the results are calculated, see Fig. 6, and it is evident that there is no significant difference between the mean and median data of the values obtained with the device and the blood chemistry test results. Also, no outliers were found.

According to Fig. 7, calculating the normal deviation between the device and hematology examen results, it can be seen that the values do not greatly deviate from the average value 17.575 g/dL in laboratory examination and 17.4275 g/dL

**Table 4.** Device hemoglobin level results $g/dL$.

| User | $Hb_1$ $g/dL$ | $Hb_2$ $g/dL$ | $Hb_3$ $g/dL$ | $Hb$ Average |
|------|------|------|------|------|
| 1 | 14.38 | 14.11 | 14.65 | 14.38 |
| 2 | 18.45 | 18.45 | 18.99 | 18.63 |
| 3 | 16.82 | 16.28 | 18.45 | 17.18 |
| 4 | 18.18 | 18.45 | 17.64 | 18.09 |
| 5 | 15.47 | 14.92 | 13.57 | 14.65 |
| 6 | 14.92 | 16.55 | 16.55 | 16.01 |
| 7 | 17.91 | 18.72 | 18.45 | 18.36 |
| 8 | 18.18 | 16.55 | 17.09 | 17.27 |
| 9 | 14.38 | 14.92 | 14.65 | 14.65 |
| 10 | 16.28 | 16.82 | 17.09 | 16.73 |
| 11 | 17.91 | 18.72 | 18.72 | 18.45 |
| 12 | 17.91 | 17.91 | 18.18 | 18.00 |
| 13 | 16.55 | 17.36 | 17.09 | 17.00 |
| 14 | 14.92 | 15.19 | 14.92 | 15.01 |
| 15 | 17.09 | 17.64 | 18.18 | 17.64 |
| 16 | 18.45 | 18.18 | 18.72 | 18.45 |
| 17 | 14.92 | 13.57 | 15.47 | 14.65 |
| 18 | 17.09 | 16.82 | 17.09 | 17.00 |
| 19 | 15.19 | 14.65 | 15.47 | 15.10 |
| 20 | 18.99 | 17.91 | 18.45 | 18.45 |
| 21 | 13.84 | 14.38 | 14.65 | 14.29 |
| 22 | 18.72 | 18.18 | 18.45 | 18.45 |
| 23 | 16.55 | 16.01 | 16.55 | 16.37 |
| 24 | 14.65 | 14.92 | 15.74 | 15.1 |
| 25 | 14.92 | 15.19 | 14.65 | 14.92 |
| 26 | 14.92 | 15.47 | 15.47 | 15.28 |
| 27 | 17.64 | 17.64 | 16.82 | 17.36 |
| 28 | 17.64 | 17.36 | 18.18 | 17.73 |
| 29 | 17.36 | 16.82 | 16.01 | 16.73 |

in device tests, having a resulting deviation of 0.8735 in laboratory results and 1.0175 in prototype results.

Anemia occurs when the concentration of hemoglobin in the blood falls below 12.0 gm/dL [7]. Understanding the normal deviation of hemoglobin levels in men and women is crucial for detecting, diagnosing, and managing anemia. The variation in hemoglobin levels between sexes is calculated, since, has important implications for clinical practice and the assessment of anemia Fig. 8a, and Fig. 8b.

Mu and sigma values show the average and standard deviation of a variable in a population, respectively. We have found the Mu, and sigma values for the device results and hematology examen results, that means that the average hemoglobin level for men is 17.42 g/dL, with a standard deviation of 1.01 g/dL. On the other hand, for women,indicating that the average hemoglobin level for women is 14.82 g/dL, with a standard deviation of 0.34 g/dL.

## 5  Discussion

The development of a non-invasive hemoglobin measurement device not only benefits patients by improving their comfort and quality of life [19] but also promotes more effective monitoring and prevention of anemia-related complications [24]. By reducing the need for invasive procedures like blood draws, this technology eliminates the discomfort and potential complications associated with such methods, ultimately providing a considerable improvement in the patient's overall well-being.

Moreover, non-invasive hemoglobin measurement devices facilitate frequent and convenient monitoring of hemoglobin levels, which holds particular importance for individuals dealing with chronic conditions like anemia or blood loss. This capability allows these patients to easily track their hemoglobin levels and make informed decisions regarding their health management. This technological advancement presents an opportunity for more proactive and personalized care, contributing to improved health outcomes.

Numerous studies have compared the performance of non-invasive hemoglobin measurement devices to traditional laboratory-based methods [8]. However, managing permits for testing at public health facilities poses several significant challenges. These challenges are related to the burden of red tape, which lengthens and complicates the participant selection process. Furthermore, the use of reagents and modern equipment is vital in order to facilitate the execution of comparative testing. This complex interplay of issues - ranging from obtaining permits to the availability of technical resources - reinforces the inherent difficulty in testing at public health facilities. These challenges prolong the process and highlight the need for careful planning and close collaboration with health institutions.

**Table 5.** Hemoglobin Percentage error and Hemoglobin results standard deviation.

| User | Percentage error | Standard deviation |
|---|---|---|
| 1 | 1.51 | 1.58 |
| 2 | 0.16 | 1.42 |
| 3 | 5.06 | 1.58 |
| 4 | 3.36 | 1.04 |
| 5 | 5.48 | 1.39 |
| 6 | 2.98 | 0.43 |
| 7 | 0.22 | 1.23 |
| 8 | 6.12 | 0.46 |
| 9 | 0.33 | 1.39 |
| 10 | 0.19 | 0.08 |
| 11 | 1.34 | 1.29 |
| 12 | 1.11 | 0.97 |
| 13 | 1.15 | 0.27 |
| 14 | 0.09 | 1.14 |
| 15 | 0.36 | 0.72 |
| 16 | 0.82 | 1.29 |
| 17 | 2.33 | 1.39 |
| 18 | 0.57 | 0.27 |
| 19 | 0.64 | 1.07 |
| 20 | 0.27 | 1.29 |
| 21 | 3.55 | 1.65 |
| 22 | 1.37 | 1.29 |
| 23 | 1.67 | 0.18 |
| 24 | 3.45 | 1.07 |
| 25 | 1.51 | 1.20 |
| 26 | 2.02 | 0.94 |
| 27 | 1.34 | 0.53 |
| 28 | 1.87 | 0.78 |
| 29 | 3.29 | 0.08 |
| **Average** | 1.18 | 0.93 |

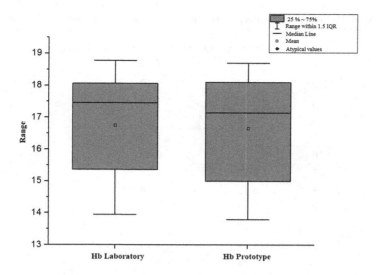

**Fig. 6.** Mean, Median and outlier results deviation (readapted from [14]).

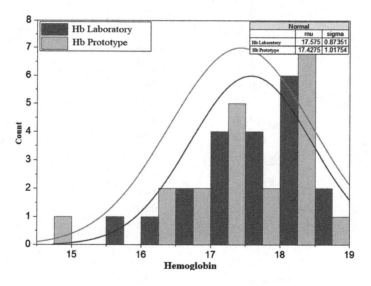

**Fig. 7.** Results normal deviation (readapted from [14]).

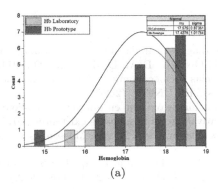
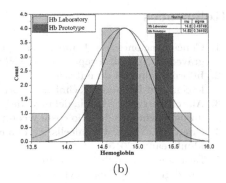

(a)     (b)

**Fig. 8.** a) Men results normal deviation, and b)Women results normal deviation.

## 6   Conclusions

Deoxygenated hemoglobin and oxygenated hemoglobin present higher absorbance for the wavelengths (660 nm and 880 nm), so the application of pulse oximetry through the use of the MAX 30102 sensor was the appropriate non-invasive measurement technique for device development.

According to FDA (Food and Drug Administration), skin pigmentation is one factor that modifies the result [26]. However, based on the performance tests carried out with two dark-skinned volunteers, it is found that the prototype does not present any considerable alteration in the determination of the hemoglobin concentration level.

The device presents low levels of sensitivity due to factors such as the pressure that the person makes when entering the finger into the prototype slot, the micro displacement of the finger in the prototype as the seconds pass, breathing being slower or longer, and the position of the finger that can change when the person moves slightly, making the intensity values close, but not the same.

From the tests carried out, the results of the blood chemistry analysis are compared against the values obtained by the prototype, resulting in an error rate of 1.86% and an average normal deviation of 1.52127.

Extensive research and development have led to the advancement of non-invasive hemoglobin measurement devices, resulting in devices with a relatively high level of technology readiness. The prototype is at technological maturity level 4 [5,17], which implies that the next step will be to conduct tests on sick individuals and compare the measurements with laboratory tests.

In addition, future work is developing a new prototype version that will include Oxygen Saturation and Heart Rate measurements, which are equally fundamental for evaluating human health.

# References

1. Concentraciones de hemoglobina para diagnosticar la anemia y evaluar su gravedad. Technical report, ORGANIZACIÓN MUNDIAL DE LA SALUD (2011)
2. Informe mundial de nutrición: Consecuencias socioeconómicas del embarazo adolescente en Ecuador. Technical report, UNICEF-UNFPA (2020)
3. Alarcó Pérez, J.: Medida del nivel de saturación de oxígeno en sangre: desarrollo de un pulsioxímetro de bajo coste y comparativa con otros sistemas existentes (2015)
4. Prieto, J., Yuste, J.: Balcells. La clínica y el laboratorio. 20 edn. Masson, Issy-les-Moulineaux (2015)
5. Bastogne, T.: IQbD: a technological readiness level-indexed quality-by-design paradigm for medical device engineering. J. Med. Devices **16**(2), 021008 (2022)
6. Chamba, C., et al.: Anaemia in the hospitalized elderly in tanzania: Prevalence, severity, and micronutrient deficiency status. Anemia **2021**, 1–6 (2021). https://doi.org/10.1155/2021/9523836.https://scite.ai/reports/10.1155/2021/9523836
7. Córdova Cárdenas, R.P.: Diseño e implementación de una aplicación móvil basada en android para la evaluación de anemia ferropénica en personas de acuerdo al nivel de hemoglobina. B.S. thesis, Universidad del Azuay (2018)
8. Farooq, F., et al.: Comparison of Masimo total hemoglobin SpHb® continuous non-invasive hemoglobin monitoring device with laboratory complete blood count measurement using venous sample: protocol for an observational substudy of the pregnancy risk and infant surveillance and measurement alliance maternal and newborn health (PRISMA MNH) study. Gates Open Res. **7**(50), 50 (2023)
9. Gómez Vizcaíno, S.R., Suntasig Soria, F.R.: Diseño y construcción de un prototipo de oxímetro de pulso. B.S. thesis (2011)
10. Gonzales, G., Olavegoya, P.: Pathophysiology of anemia in pregnancy: anemia or hemodilution? Revista Peruana de Ginecología y Obstetricia (4) (2019)
11. Kim, Y.J., Han, K.D., Cho, K.H., Kim, Y.H., Park, Y.G.: Anemia and health-related quality of life in South Korea: data from the Korean national health and nutrition examination survey 2008–2016. BMC Public Health **19**, 1–8 (2019)
12. Lorente, C.: Fotofísica y propiedades fotosensibilizadoras de pterinas en solución acuosa. Ph.D. thesis, Universidad Nacional de La Plata (2003). https://doi.org/10.35537/10915/2216
13. Marino, P.: El libro de la UCI. 3rd edn. Wolters Kluwer Health España, S.A. (2008)
14. Mieles Freire, M.S.: Dispositivo para medir la cantidad de hemoglobina en la sangre. B.S. thesis (2023)
15. Miguel, C.M.: Libro de la salud cardiovascular del Hospital Clínico San Carlos y la Fundación BBVA. Fundacion BBVA, 1 edn. (2007)
16. Moshawrab, M., Adda, M., Bouzouane, A., Ibrahim, H., Raad, A.: Smart wearables for the detection of cardiovascular diseases: a systematic literature review. Sensors **23**(2), 828 (2023). https://doi.org/10.3390/s23020828. https://scite.ai/reports/10.3390/s23020828
17. Olechowski, A., Eppinger, S.D., Joglekar, N.: Technology readiness levels at 40: a study of state-of-the-art use, challenges, and opportunities. In: 2015 Portland International Conference on Management of Engineering and Technology (PICMET), pp. 2084–2094. IEEE (2015)
18. Paredes Bautista, E.G.: Prevalencia y factores de riesgo de anemia ferropénica en niños menores de cinco años, en la comunidad Zuleta, provincia de Imbabura, Ecuador. Revista de Ciencias y Seguridad **4**(1), 37 (2019)

19. Ravizza, A., De Maria, C., Di Pietro, L., Sternini, F., Audenino, A.L., Bignardi, C.: Comprehensive review on current and future regulatory requirements on wearable sensors in preclinical and clinical testing. Front. Bioeng. Biotechnol. **7**, 313 (2019)
20. Ryan, M.L., et al.: Noninvasive hemoglobin measurement in pediatric trauma patients. J. Trauma Acute Care Surg. **81**(6), 1162–1166 (2016)
21. Schmitt, J.M., Zhou, G.X., Miller, J.: Measurement of blood hematocrit by dual-wavelength near-IR photoplethysmography. In: Physiological Monitoring and Early Detection Diagnostic Methods, vol. 1641, pp. 150–161. SPIE (1992)
22. Gengo e Silva, R.C., Melo, V.F.A., Lima, M.A.M.: Validity, reliability and accuracy of oscillometric devices, compared with doppler ultrasound, for determination of the ankle brachial index: an integrative review. J. Vasc. Brasileiro **13**(1), 27–33 (2014). https://doi.org/10.1590/jvb.2014.006. https://scite.ai/reports/10.1590/jvb.2014.006
23. Sánchez-Mendel, L.H., Galicia-Galicia, L.A., Molina-García, M., García Ameca, L.A.: Diseño e implementación de un dispositivo electrónico registrador de estados de anemia. Revista de Energías Renovables **1**(3), 22–33 (2017)
24. Sonani, H., et al.: Anemia as a significant predictor of adverse outcomes in hospitalized patients with acute exacerbations of chronic obstructive pulmonary disease: analysis of national (nationwide) inpatient sample database. Cureus **15**(1), e34343 (2023)
25. Wang, E.J., Li, W., Hawkins, D., Gernsheimer, T., Norby-Slycord, C., Patel, S.N.: HemaApp: noninvasive blood screening of hemoglobin using smartphone cameras. In: Proceedings of the 2016 ACM International Joint Conference on Pervasive and Ubiquitous Computing, pp. 593–604 (2016)
26. William, M.: La FDA advierte sobre las limitaciones y la precisión de los oxímetros de pulso. Technical report, Food and Drug Administration, United States (2021)
27. Yang, L., et al.: Allergic disorders and risk of anemia in Japanese children: findings from the japan environment and children's study. Nutrients **14**(20), 4335 (2022)
28. Zhao, X., Meng, L.H., Xie, G., Chen, Y.: Deep-learning-based hemoglobin concentration prediction and anemia screening using ultra-wide field fundus images (2022). https://scite.ai/reports/10.3389/fcell.2022.888268

# Mask R-CNN and YOLOv8 Comparison to Perform Tomato Maturity Recognition Task

Jean Carlo Camacho[ID] and Manuel Eugenio Morocho-Cayamcela[(✉)][ID]

Yachay Tech University, Urcuquí, Ecuador
{jean.camacho,mmorocho}@yachaytech.edu.ec

**Abstract.** This work explores the segmentation and detection of tomatoes in different maturity states for harvesting prediction by using the
laboro tomato dataset to train a mask R-CNN and a YOLOv8 architecture. This work aims to test the mask R-CNN architecture and the
proposed methodology efficiency on the benchmark paper [12]. The evaluation metric intersection over union (IoU) 0.5 showed an average precision of 67.2% with a recall of 78.9% over the laboro tomato dataset
and an IoU average precision of 92.1% with a recall of 91.4% over the
same dataset. The benchmark paper authors perform segmentation and
classification in a separate process using color analysis algorithms and
use the determination coefficient ($R^2$) for how accurately the tomato was
set into the three maturity classes.

The results show that the state-of-the-art YOLOv8 has a $R^2$ of 0.809,
0.897, and 0.968 in the ripe, half-ripe, and green categories, respectively.
However, the Mask R-CNN results are acceptable, with 0.819, 0.809,
and 0.893 in the ripe, half-ripe, and green categories, respectively. The
YOLOv8 model performed better than the one used in the benchmark
paper by detecting, segmenting, and classifying tomatoes. Moreover, the
color-analysis technique used in the benchmark paper results inefficiently
because the classification results showed no linear relation between the
predictions and the real values.

**Keywords:** Object detection · deep learning · precision agriculture ·
maturity recognition · Mask R-CNN · YOLO

## 1 Introduction

This text discusses the industrialization processes in precision agriculture and
their potential applications in recognizing crops, estimating maturity time,
detecting diseases, and nutritional deficiencies using computer vision systems [4,14,19–21]. These applications can reduce manual labor, improve harvesting accuracy, and even be deployed on autonomous robots for picking mature
tomatoes [5]. However, a significant challenge lies in obtaining a suitable dataset
for accurate recognition and instance segmentation. Generating a custom dataset

J. Maldonado-Mahauad et al. (Eds.): TICEC 2023, CCIS 1885, pp. 382–396, 2023.
https://doi.org/10.1007/978-3-031-45438-7_26

may be necessary for crops with limited available information, requiring environmental control, multiple angles, and expert labeling for supervised or semi-supervised tasks.

The laboro dataset, containing multiple classes and diverse images, is chosen for this study [12]. While the original dataset had 160 images, the current version has grown to 804 images.

One of the main challenges while performing this comparison was recreate the original authors methodology, to recreate the results and perform an accurate comparison.

This paper aims to replicate the instance segmentation results using the Mask R-CNN model on the laboro tomato dataset and compare them with YOLOv8, a state-of-the-art model for object recognition and instance segmentation. The proposed approach involves training the models with data augmentation, transfer learning, to improve performance in terms of mean average precision (mAP) and $R^2$ coefficients for predicting tomato instances.

## 2    Related Works

In the work of Sandro Magalh *et al.* [10], the authors performed object detection with the single-shot multi-box detector (SSD) and YOLO architectures to detect tomatoes. They compared some traditional machine learning (ML) techniques that used to work only for ripe tomatoes. However, with the implementation of object detection networks, it was possible to detect green, half-ripe, and ripe tomatoes. The models were trained with the author's own generated dataset on a greenhouse. The images contain tomatoes on the tomato plant collected by the mobile robot AgRob v16, the same robot that performed recognition with the trained model. The authors collected videos to generate the dataset and used a frame every three seconds. They used only the "tomato" class, which included tomatoes in all the ripeness states, and performed data augmentation techniques to give robustness to the model. The results showed that SSD MobileNet v2 was the best generalized and performing model. However, YOLOv4 Tiny also had achievable results with the best prediction times. For future works, the authors mentioned the importance of a regularization mechanism on the models and created sub-classes to detect ripeness states for harvesting procedures.

In the work of Wenli Zhang *et al.* [21] proposed an object recognition architecture for fruit detection in edge computing applications. The problem the authors intend to solve is the speed of the state-of-the-art model's implementation. On the methodology, the authors propose an architecture based on Light-CSPNet as the backbone network, an improved feature extraction model, a down-sampling method, and a feature fusion model to perform real-time fruit detection. The authors trained the model over three different fruits (oranges, tomatoes, and apples) and compared the results against YOLOv3, YOLOv4, YOLOv3-tiny, YOLOv4-tiny, and their own proposed model. The YOLOv3 and YOLOv4 models performed better over precision, recall, and average detection precision (AP) but had a low FPS rate (8.1 and 4.6, respectively) for edge device applications.

On the other hand, the proposed model had a slightly better result than the YOLOv3-tiny and YOLOv4-tiny, with an FPS rate of 24.8 and an AP of 0.93 for oranges, 0.847 for tomatoes and 0.85 for apples.

While some authors present multiple variants of the same architecture, the work of Mobashiru Lawal [9] presented a comparison of the original YOLOv3 and a modified version of it optimized for tomato detection by introducing spatial pyramid pooling and Mish activation function. Three variants of the model were proposed, the A, B, and C versions that used different activation functions. The model YOLO-Tomato-A got an AP of 98.3% with a detection time of 48 ms, YOLO-Tomato-B got an AP of 99.3% with a detection time of 44 ms, and YOLO-Tomato-C got an AP of 99.5% with a detection time of 52 ms. The mish activation function and the SPP combination were the most optimal in this work. The dataset was obtained with a camera in a controlled environment and labeled by an expert.

These previous works show that the YOLO architecture has been a popular option for object detection or instance segmentation [5,16,17]. This is because YOLO architecture performs object detection in a single shot, which results in a very efficient methodology [13,18]. In addition, most state-of-the-art solutions include convolutional neural network use, which performs far better than ML or traditional image processing techniques separately.

However, in the work of Taehyeong Kim *et al.* [8] and Daichi Minagawa *et al.* [11] used a custom deep neural network and Mask R-CNN as the architectures, respectively, to solve the harvest time of the tomatoes. With the Mask R-CNN, they performed object detection to separate the tomato region from the background, removing noise. With the pre-processed images, the authors proposed an image processing methodology of color analysis to calculate the red rate and classify the tomatoes using the image and the red color ratio. The dataset was collected using a robot that uses cameras and takes control of how many days there were until the harvesting day. The classifier was tested with the background and noise images, and against the pre-processed ones, the pre-processed ones showed higher accuracy when predicting the harvest time and days left until harvest time.

## 3    System Model and Methodology

### 3.1    Dataset

The Laboro Tomato: Instance segmentation dataset [1]. It is a dataset containing growing tomatoes in a greenhouse. The dataset separates the tomatoes into three ripening stages, ripe, half-ripe, and green. Furthermore, it contains two different types of tomatoes: cherry and regular. The dataset is designed for object detection and instance segmentation. It contains bounding box annotations and vertices representing the tomato masks to do segmentation tasks for each tomato, along with the class to which it belongs.

Moreover, the images were taken with two cameras, giving different image quality and resolutions. The dataset contains 643 images to train and 161 to test, giving 804. To classify the tomatoes into different categories, the regular (big) and cherry (little) were different species that the experts already knew how to differentiate from the planting phase. Additionally, cherry tomatoes are considerably smaller than regular tomatoes. To classify into the different ripeness states, the authors used the percentage of red the tomato has as one of the criteria. Fully ripened presented a 90% or more, half-ripened was between 30–89% and green was between 0–30% of red color. However, there were other criteria, and experts decided on the final classification. Examples of each category are represented on Fig. 1.

In the benchmark paper [12], the authors mention that they picked up a subset of 60 big and 40 small tomatoes that matches the color criteria initially established to generate an artificial dataset. This carefully selected dataset will be mentioned as the dataset I, and the full laboro dataset will be represented as dataset II.

(a) big green tomato     (b) big half ripen tomato     (c) big full ripen tomato

(d) little green tomato     (e) little half ripen tomato     (f) little full ripen tomato

**Fig. 1.** Illustration that shows an example of each tomato category, where (a), (b), and (c) are big/normal tomatoes, and (d), (e), and (f) represent the little/cherry tomatoes, the images are organized from top to bottom as green, half-ripen, and full-ripen. (Color figure online)

## 3.2  YOLO Architecture

YOLO (you only look once) is a real-time object detection architecture proposed by Joseph Redmon *et al.* [13]. YOLO is a popular option for object detection because it can detect objects from any image in a single shot usin anchor boxes 2 using a single neural network.

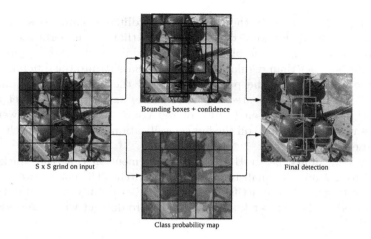

**Fig. 2.** Illustration that shows the basic of how YOLO architecture works [13].

**YOLOv8** is the latest version of the YOLO architecture. However, there are many differences between these versions. On the open access GitHub repository of the roboflow team [2] is publicly available the YOLOv8 implementation, from which scheme is represented in Fig. 3. One of the main differences is that YOLOv8 is the first YOLO version that is an anchor-free model.

The anchor-free model considerably reduces the number of box predictions, which speeds up the non-maximum suppression (NMS) process, in which less likely candidates are sifted until a successful inference. Also, the C2f is implemented as a new convolution layer. In C2f, all the outputs from the bottleneck are concatenated, while in previous versions, only the last bottleneck was used. This details can be found on a bigger depth in [2].

### 3.3   Mask-R CNN Architecture

Mask-R CNN is an object detection and instance segmentation network proposed by Kaiming He *et al.* [7] with the Facebook AI Research group.

The fast R-CNN [6] was extended to process the feature maps into the RoI sections, using the RoI pooling layers, leading to a fast speed and great accuracy. The faster R-CNN has two outputs for each possible object: The class label and a bounding box offset. So the Mask R-CNN included the object mask attached to the object detection as shown in Fig. 4b.

Furthermore, the faster R-CNN contains a extra branch in contrast to the R-CNN, where the information from the pretrained VGG [15] CNN features maps are passed through a Conv layer, then the anchor boxes that are composed by the bounding box and the category, then this is passed through a non-maximum supression layer (NMS) and sent to the RoI pooling layer as in Fig. 4b.

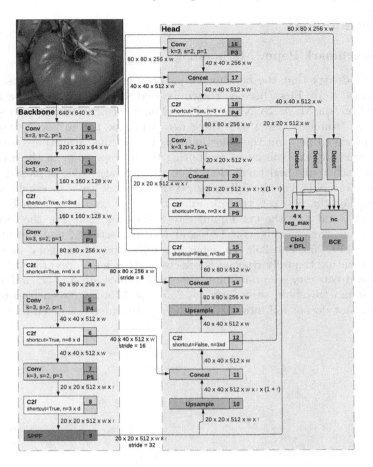

**Fig. 3.** A graphical representation of the YOLOv8 architecture, where the backbone region is composed of successive Conv and C2f layers and an SPPF layer at the end. From the backbone, the P3, P4, and P5 outputs are used as inputs to run inside the head layer, composed of the Unsample, Concat, C2f, and Conv layers. Finally, three outputs are obtained to pass through the Detect layer and separate the bounding box and class loss calculation.

However, Mask R-CNN architecture principal difference from faster R-CNN is that the pooling layer is replaced by a RoI align pooling layers, it predicts in parallel the RoI in a binary mask, which makes the classification independent of the mask prediction.

## 4 Methodology

### 4.1 Benchmark Paper Methodology

The methodology that the benchmark paper authors proposed consists of two fundamental steps. First, because they only used the class tomato to perform the classification, the Mask R-CNN model could only perform instance segmentation of the class "tomato." Then with the generated mask, the authors extracted the tomato pixels to perform the color analysis in the hue-saturation-value (HSV) format. This analysis consist of computing the average color in the area of the mask for each individual prediction, then this average color is passed through multiple thresholds. For the fully ripened category, multiple threshold sets were proposed. For the first set, the minimum threshold values for each HSV value were 0, 140, and 145; the maximum were 5, 255, and 255. For the second set, the minimum threshold is 174, 120, and 135, respectively, and the maximum values are 179, 255, and 255. To define the fully ripened category, one of both sets representing the fully ripened is selected with a logic operator OR. For the half-ripened category, the minimum threshold values are 3, 144, and 155, and the maximum threshold values are 18, 255, and 255. For green tomatoes, any tomatoes that do not fall into this threshold is considered a green tomato.

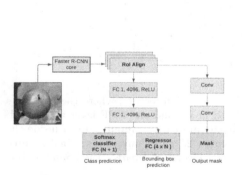

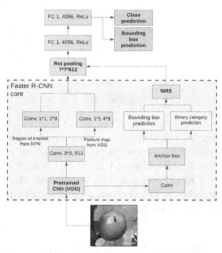

(a) Mask R-CNN architecture scheme. It is an extension from the Faster R-CNN, changing the RoI pooling layer to a RoI align one

(b) Faster R-CNN architecture scheme

**Fig. 4.** Details of the Mask-RCNN architecture in (4a) and its implementation in the Faster R-CNN architecture in (4b).

To evaluate the methodology's performance, the instance segmentation model and the color threshold classification methodology had different metrics to evaluate. Therefore, the mean average precision (mAP) and the recall metrics were used to evaluate the model. The mAP is obtained as the mean of the ratio of correct detections (true positive) over the number of object detections. However, detection is achieved as correct if the intersection over union (IoU) is more than 0.5. The definition of the IoU is in Eq. 1. The mAP equation is defined in Eq. 2, where $N$ is the number of classes, and $AP$ is the average precision. Also, the precision is calculated as the number of true positives over the total detections as in Eq. 3.

$$IoU = \frac{Area(Mask_{groundtruth} \cap Mask_{predicted})}{Area(Mask_{groundtruth} \cup Mask_{predicted})} \tag{1}$$

$$mAP = \frac{1}{N} \sum_{i=1}^{N} AP_i \tag{2}$$

$$P = \frac{true\_positives}{true\_positives + false\_positives} \tag{3}$$

The recall is defined as the number of positive matches over the number of ground truth objects, which is detailed in Eq. 4.

$$recall = \frac{true\_positives}{true\_positives + false\_negatives} \tag{4}$$

Furthermore, to evaluate the classification performed by the color separation, the $R^2$ metric was used and is defined in Eq. 5, where $SS_{res}$ is the sum of the squares of the residual error and $SS_{tot}$ is the total sum of the errors. It works by measuring the amount of variance in the predictions explained by the dataset. The prediction is compared with the expert's labels classifying the tomatoes into different categories. Also is considered that the classes, the half-riped are in the middle, so if a half-riped tomato is a mismatch to any of the other categories, the variance is less than it would be a mismatch between a mature tomato and a green tomato.

$$R^2 = 1 - \frac{SS_{res}}{SS_{tot}} \tag{5}$$

### 4.2  Proposed Methodology

In contrast to the author's work, the tomato classification, as well as the instance segmentation will be performed directly by the Mask R-CNN and YOLOv8 architectures. The color-based classification is removed, which will simplify the pipeline process, the details are represented in the Fig. 5b

Furthermore, as the benchmark paper only uses three labels (ripe, half-ripe, and green) this work will limit to use only three although, specifically the big tomatoes subset.

## 5    Results and Discussions

After training the Mask R-CNN [3] and YOLOv8 [2] models with 309 images
for training and 67 for validating until the loss function was stable and with the
same dataset distribution, both models performed predictions over 66 images.
With the mask obtained from the predicted images, we used the color analysis
technique to classify into the three existing classes. Furthermore, compare this
classification with the obtained by the models-only technique as shown in Table 1.
From this table, we can see that the classification methodology that uses color
analysis to predict the classes performs poorly in contrast to the classification
of the models, even the negative values represent that there is not relationship
between the expected values and the real values. The replicated results on the $R^2$
metric represent a completely different result from what the benchmark paper
authors obtained.

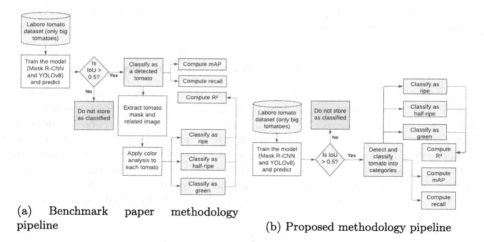

(a)    Benchmark    paper    methodology
pipeline

(b) Proposed methodology pipeline

**Fig. 5.** Authors methodology pipeline in (5a) that will get contrasted with the proposed
methodology that is illustrated in (5b).

When the work was done, the authors used dataset I, which contained specially selected images. Those images fitted well on the thresholds proposed by
the authors and contained only 100 images with tomato samples. Figure 6 shows
a more realistic color intraclass variation between the tomatoes. For example,
on the left image is a half-ripened tomato next to a fully-ripened one that looks
similar to the only one in the right image. Even all half-ripened tomatoes in the
right image could be considered in a similar color range as the fully-ripened one.

Moreover, some tomato masks include a great portion of the tomato plant
and leaves as in the left image from Fig. 6 where a fully-ripened tomato could
be classified as green because it is occluded by the tomato plant, which can
represent a bias in the color analysis, increasing the portion of green in the image

composition. By adding more green values, ripe tomatoes can be misclassified as half-ripened and half-ripened tomatoes as green. The mask accuracy also impacts the quality of the color analysis because the background in most of the samples contains leaves or parts of the tomato plant that also puts additional green color. Also the Mask R-CNN tends to generate duplicated masks for the same element, which is detected two or more times and could represent as an issue to perform the color evaluation technique.

Comparing the YOLOv8 and the Mask R-CNN models as classifiers, both perform well enough, achieving an $R^2$ of 0.809 in the ripe class with the YOLOv8 model as the lowest value. However, YOLOv8 was the best model in the half-ripe and green labels.

**Fig. 6.** Tomatoes images samples from the laboro dataset [1], where the yellow line surrounds fully-ripened tomatoes, the pink line surrounds half-ripened tomatoes, and the purple line surrounds green tomatoes.

(a) Mask R-CNN segmentation and classification sample with a close-up to the boundaries of the generated mask

(b) YOLOv8 segmentation and classification sample with a close-up to the boundaries of the generated mask

**Fig. 7.** YOLOv8 (b) and Mask R-CNN (a) image segmentation and classification with close-up images that highlight the mask quality.

**Table 1.** $R^2$ metric over the three different classes, comparing the Mask R-CNN, YOLOv8 models, and the color analysis in the classification task.

| Dataset | Classification methodology | $R^2$ (ripe) | $R^2$ (half-ripe) | $R^2$ (green) |
|---------|---------------------------|--------------|-------------------|----------------|
| I | Mask R-CNN + color analysis[a] | **0.92** | 0.75 | 0.94 |
| II | Mask R-CNN + color analysis | −0.335 | −0.214 | −0.702 |
| II | YOLOv8 + color analysis | −0.325 | −0.124 | −0.518 |
| II | Mask R-CNN | 0.819 | 0.809 | 0.803 |
| II | YOLOv8 | 0.809 | **0.897** | **0.968** |

[a]images/Original results from the benchmark paper authors [12]

From the $R^2$ metric of the Mask R-CNN and YOLOv8 models presented in the Table 1, it is eventually that both models perform well on the segmentation task. However, the $R^2$ metric is insufficient to choose which model is better for the segmentation and classification task over tomatoes. In the Table 2, it is shown the recall and mAP from both models. Generally, both metrics are inverse as better the precision, worse the recall, and bit-wise. For the YOLOv8 model, both metrics are superior to the Mask R-CNN. The better performance of YOLOv8 could be because of its architecture which could be superior to the Mask R-CNN.

**Table 2.** Recall and mAP from the segmentation task, where the Mask R-CNN and YOLOv8 were trained with the same dataset distribution.

| Dataset | Model | Recall | mAP (IoU 0.5) |
|---------|-------|--------|----------------|
| I | Mask R-CNN + color analysis [a] | 78.9% | 67.2% |
| II | Mask R-CNN | 77% | 75.26% |
| II | YOLOv8 | **83.4%** | **83.7%** |

[a]Original results from the benchmark paper authors [12]

Finally, some examples from the results are shown in Fig. 8 that looks similar, the YOLOv8 and Mask R-CNN models perform equally; however, in the sub-images 8a, 8d, and 8g we can appreciate more mismatches from the original images in the sub-images 8c, 8f, and 8i that the YOLOv8 model in the 8b, 8e, and 8h. Also, the masks from the YOLOv8 model are neater than those from the Mask R-CNN. However, the YOLOv8 masks also include more leaves and sections from the plants than the Mask R-CNN masks, just like in the sub-image 8h and 8g in the inferior right corner.

From Fig. 7, we can appreciate that most of the background is green, and despite this, the green tomato was the most accurate label, but also is very mismatched by the Mask R-CNN that detects tomatoes by similar mismatch on the shape and color of leaves as shown on the Fig. 7a, that can explain the lower value on $R^2$ by the replicated Mask R-CNN model. On the other hand, YOLOv8 has high accuracy in predicting green tomatoes. This accuracy can also be due to the considerably superior amount of green tomatoes in the dataset compared

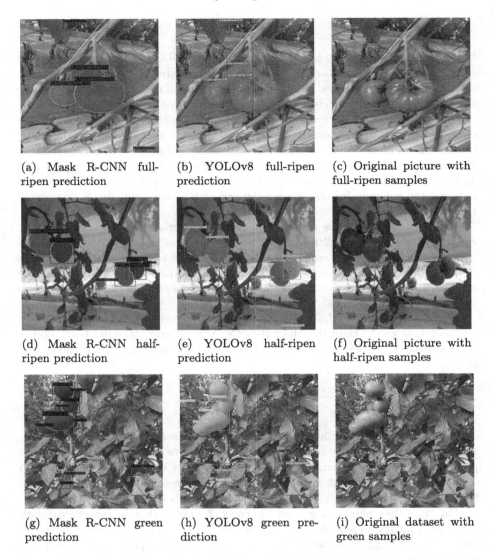

(a) Mask R-CNN full-ripen prediction

(b) YOLOv8 full-ripen prediction

(c) Original picture with full-ripen samples

(d) Mask R-CNN half-ripen prediction

(e) YOLOv8 half-ripen prediction

(f) Original picture with half-ripen samples

(g) Mask R-CNN green prediction

(h) YOLOv8 green prediction

(i) Original dataset with green samples

**Fig. 8.** Illustration that contains in (a), (d), and (g) the Mask R-CNN segmentation and classification, in (c), (f), and (i), the instance segmentation and classification prediction by YOLOv8 model, and in (b), (e), and (h), and the original images from laboro dataset.

to the ripe and half-ripe tomatoes. Furthermore, in Fig. 7b on the right picture, the mask area can be appreciated that covers the tomato area in a sharper way than the Mask R-CNN model on Fig. 7a in the right picture though.

# 6   Conclusions

In this work, we compared the Mask R-CNN and YOLOv8, for instance segmentation and classification task. In addition, we compared the models for classification against a color-based classification technique in the laboro dataset, where the models performed much better in the classification task.

The classification performed by the model is better than the color-based classification due to the number of features the models can extract from the whole image. Not only the color but the contrast, the full illumination of the picture, and the surrounding shapes can be an essential part of the image to proportion an accurate classification. The color thresholds are an inefficient measure that is not scalable not only for the specific dataset of tomatoes but also for detecting ripeness in other crops.

On the other hand, the original benchmark paper results are not consistent when testing on images with different real-world conditions. This inconsistency can be due to the few samples the laboro dataset had when this work was developed and the few images that could be destined for testing. Moreover, the authors apply this methodology to a synthetic dataset that can add biases on the classification.

Furthermore, the YOLOv8 seems to be a better classification and instance segmentation model than the Mask R-CNN. Nevertheless, training both models by changing the hyper-parameters and analyzing the resulting metrics is necessary.

# 7   Future Works

The color analysis methodology to perform classification is inefficient and very inaccurate, and it is better not to consider that to solve maturity recognition task problems. It could be a handful solution as a support to label new data to train a model, and there is not any model that could already do this by classifying the data.

On the other hand, to get an approach to how other architectures work with the maturity recognition task, the results of this work could be replicated, emphasizing those well-known architectures that perform well working with images.

Also, the resultant model of this work could be embedded in a system to detect tomatoes. Then, using a dataset that contains tomato disease labels as well, it could be used for spraying on focused areas, reducing the amount of pesticide.

This work is centered on tomato maturity recognition with images, but a model using real-time video that performs the same object recognition and instance segmentation task is feasible.

# References

1. Laboro tomato: Instance segmentation dataset. https://github.com/laboroai/LaboroTomato. Accessed 5 Jan 2023
2. Ultralytics yolov8. https://github.com/ultralytics/ultralytics. Accessed 20 Jan 2023
3. Chen, K., et al.: MMDetection: Open MMLab detection toolbox and benchmark. arXiv preprint arXiv:1906.07155 (2019)
4. Chiu, M.T., et al.: Agriculture-vision: a large aerial image database for agricultural pattern analysis. In: 2020 IEEE/CVF Conference on Computer Vision and Pattern Recognition (CVPR), pp. 2825–2835 (2020). https://doi.org/10.1109/CVPR42600.2020.00290
5. Ge, Y., et al.: Tracking and counting of tomato at different growth period using an improving YOLO-deepsort network for inspection robot. Machines **10**(6), 489 (2022). https://doi.org/10.3390/machines10060489
6. Girshick, R.: Fast R-CNN. In: 2015 IEEE International Conference on Computer Vision (ICCV). IEEE (2015). https://doi.org/10.1109/iccv.2015.169
7. He, K., Gkioxari, G., Dollár, P., Girshick, R.: Mask R-CNN (2017). https://doi.org/10.48550/ARXIV.1703.06870. https://arxiv.org/abs/1703.06870
8. Kim, T., Lee, D.H., Kim, K.C., Choi, T., Yu, J.M.: Tomato maturity estimation using deep neural network. Appl. Sci. **13**(1), 412 (2022). https://doi.org/10.3390/app13010412
9. Lawal, M.O.: Tomato detection based on modified YOLOv3 framework. Sci. Rep. **11**(1), 1447 (2021). https://doi.org/10.1038/s41598-021-81216-5
10. Magalhães, S.A., et al.: Evaluating the single-shot MultiBox detector and YOLO deep learning models for the detection of tomatoes in a greenhouse. Sensors **21**(10), 3569 (2021). https://doi.org/10.3390/s21103569
11. Minagawa, D., Kim, J.: Prediction of harvest time of tomato using mask R-CNN. AgriEngineering **4**(2), 356–366 (2022). https://doi.org/10.3390/agriengineering4020024
12. Rahim, U.F., Mineno, H.: Highly accurate tomato maturity recognition: combining deep instance segmentation, data synthesis and color analysis. In: 2021 4th Artificial Intelligence and Cloud Computing Conference. ACM (2021). https://doi.org/10.1145/3508259.3508262
13. Redmon, J., Divvala, S., Girshick, R., Farhadi, A.: You only look once: unified, real-time object detection (2015). DOI: https://doi.org/10.48550/ARXIV.1506.02640
14. Shafi, U., Mumtaz, R., García-Nieto, J., Hassan, S.A., Zaidi, S.A.R., Iqbal, N.: Precision agriculture techniques and practices: from considerations to applications. Sensors **19**(17), 3796 (2019). https://doi.org/10.3390/s19173796
15. Simonyan, K., Zisserman, A.: Very deep convolutional networks for large-scale image recognition (2014). https://doi.org/10.48550/ARXIV.1409.1556
16. Su, F., Zhao, Y., Wang, G., Liu, P., Yan, Y., Zu, L.: Tomato maturity classification based on SE-YOLOv3-MobileNetV1 network under nature greenhouse environment. Agronomy **12**(7), 1638 (2022). https://doi.org/10.3390/agronomy12071638
17. Sun, L., et al.: Lightweight apple detection in complex orchards using YOLOV5-PRE. Horticulturae **8**(12), 1169 (2022). https://doi.org/10.3390/horticulturae8121169
18. Wang, C.Y., Bochkovskiy, A., Liao, H.Y.M.: YOLOV7: trainable bag-of-freebies sets new state-of-the-art for real-time object detectors (2022). https://doi.org/10.48550/ARXIV.2207.02696. https://arxiv.org/abs/2207.02696

19. Wang, C., et al.: A review of deep learning used in the hyperspectral image analysis for agriculture. Artif. Intell. Rev. **54**(7), 5205–5253 (2021). https://doi.org/10.1007/s10462-021-10018-y

20. Zhang, N., Wang, M., Wang, N.: Precision agriculture—a worldwide overview. Comput. Electron. Agric. **36**(2–3), 113–132 (2002). https://doi.org/10.1016/s0168-1699(02)00096-0

21. Zhang, W., et al.: Lightweight fruit-detection algorithm for edge computing applications. Front. Plant Sci. **12**, 740936 (2021). https://doi.org/10.3389/fpls.2021.740936

# Software Development

# Development of a Distributed Hydrological Model of Continuous Generation, in a GIS Environment

Fernando Oñate-Valdivieso(✉) , Santiago Quiñones-Cuenca , and Andrés Vallejo

Universidad Técnica Particular de Loja, C/.Marcelino Champagnat S/N, 1101608 Loja, Ecuador
fronate@utpl.edu.ec

**Abstract.** The modeling of hydrological processes is essential for water resource management since it allows us to study the behavior of the hydrological cycle in a precise and detailed manner in scenarios with different characteristics, obtaining vital information for planning. One of the main limitations of a hydrological model is the large volume of information required for its implementation, so a model that requires a reduced volume of information is highly desirable. This paper describes the development of the Continuous Flow Hydrological System (CFHS), a distributed, continuous generation model with minimal information requirements. The model is based on a script written in the Python programming language and executed within the QGIS environment. Through the use of native QGIS tools, the user can delineate a hydrographic basin based on a digital elevation model, visualize the location of weather stations, and use daily precipitation and evapotranspiration data to generate a continuous surface for each variable in the basin. Finally, rainfall runoff calculations are performed using a conceptual hydrological model, resulting in the spatial variation of runoff on a daily basis in the study area. The results are delivered in NetCDF format. The developed model demonstrated great efficiency in the calculations performed and proved to be easy to use, making it an invaluable tool for water resource planning.

**Keywords:** Water resources · Hydrological Model · Phyton · netCDF

## 1 Introduction

The management of water resources is fundamental for the development of a community since water is vital for human activities and survival. In order to effectively manage water resources, it is necessary to study various scenarios, including climate change, increased demand, and changes in land use conditions within a basin, among others. These scenarios can be analyzed through a hydrological model that accurately represents the hydrological cycle in a specific area and provides valuable information for planning purposes.

A hydrological model is essentially a mathematical representation of the water cycle within a particular geographic area, aiming to simulate the processes of rainfall and runoff [1]. Hydrological models have been developed to describe the nonlinear and dynamic transformation of precipitation into runoff, considering processes such as surface and subsurface flows, infiltration, interception, evaporation, transpiration, snowmelt, and more [2]. Such models consist of a set of equations used to estimate runoff as a function of various parameters that express watershed characteristics [3], including geography, geology, and land use [2, 4].

These models can be broadly categorized as either lumped or distributed. A lumped model simplifies the water balance by employing a set of single parameters that capture the average spatial characteristics of a relatively large area. In contrast, distributed models divide the entire basin into smaller subareas, considering the spatial variability of both the data and the model parameters. Notably, a lumped model can also serve as a component within a distributed model [1, 5].

The simulation time scale can range from hourly to daily, weekly, or monthly. Continuous simulation, conducted on a daily basis, is particularly useful for water resource management as it allows the assessment of water availability within a basin and the development of scenarios that offer valuable insights for management decisions. However, when simulation is carried out continuously at an hourly or daily scale, a significant number of parameters and extensive databases containing climatic, topographic, land use, soil type information, among others, are required for most processes involved in the water cycle. This requirement often limits the implementation of hydrological models in many locations. Hence, an accurate hydrological model that demands minimal input information is always highly desirable.

Geographic Information Systems (GIS) are important as common data analysis frameworks in modeling [6] The GIS technique can handle large volumes of spatial data for processing and can combine data types to predict and find additional water resources [7] GIS has made it easier and faster to process data to produce reliable simulation models. Thus, the integration of hydrological processes into a GIS environment has now reached the maturity level to allow a high degree of accuracy in simulating those processes [8].

QGIS is the most popular free geospatial software in the world. It is a powerful open-source Geographic Information System (GIS) tool that not only enables the visualization and analysis of spatial information but also provides an Application Programming Interface (API) in Python, allowing the development of customized applications for specific purposes [9].

This paper presents the development of a continuous-flow distributed hydrological model in a GIS environment that requires the minimum amount of information. The theoretical bases used to model the daily rainfall-runoff process in the basin will be presented, along with a computational solution implemented to develop a fully distributed hydrological model. This model enables the calculation of runoff at the pixel level, utilizing a concentrated hydrological model as its basis.

## 2   Materials and methods

### 2.1   Theoretical bases

The rain-runoff process is modeled using the approach proposed by Perrin et al. [10], with its conceptualization summarized in Fig. 1. The model involves two reservoirs, one for production and one for nonlinear transit, where the water level in each reservoir (S and R) serves as the state variables. The direct runoff (Qd) is obtained by passing through a single unit hydrograph, while the subsurface runoff (Qr) is generated by transiting a different unit hydrograph stored in the nonlinear reservoir. The total runoff is calculated by summing the direct runoff and the subsurface runoff.

The model incorporates four parameters: $x_1$, which represents the maximum water storage capacity in the soil; $x_2$, which represents the exchange coefficient with groundwater; $x_3$, which represents the maximum capacity of the transit reservoir, all measured in millimeters; and $x_4$, which represents the base time of the unit hydrograph in days.

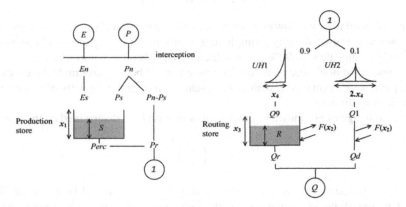

**Fig. 1.** Conceptualization of the hydrological model, adapted from Perrin (2003)

The model inputs are daily precipitation ($P$) and potential evapotranspiration ($E$). The net precipitation ($Pn$) and the net evapotranspiration capacity ($En$) are determined by applying:

$$If\ P \geq E \qquad\qquad P_n = P - E\ and\ E_n = 0 \qquad\qquad (1)$$

$$Otherwise\ P_n = 0 \qquad\qquad and\ E_n = E - P \qquad\qquad (2)$$

$$If\ Pn > 0 \qquad\qquad P_s = \frac{X_1\left(1-\left(\frac{S}{x_1}\right)^2\right)tanh\left(\frac{P_n}{x_1}\right)}{1+\frac{S}{x_1}tanh\left(\frac{P_n}{x_1}\right)} \qquad (3)$$

$$If\ En > 0 \qquad\qquad E_s = \frac{S\left(2-\frac{S}{x_1}\right)tanh\left(\frac{E_n}{x_1}\right)}{1+\left(1-\frac{S}{x_1}\right)tanh\left(\frac{E_n}{x_1}\right)} \qquad (4)$$

So, the water content in the soil is given by:

$$S = S - E_s + P_s \qquad\qquad 0 \le S \le x_1 \ (mm) \qquad\qquad (5)$$

The percolation towards the saturated zone of the soil (*Perc*) is determined as:

$$Perc = S \left\{ 1 - \left[ 1 + \left( \tfrac{4}{9} \tfrac{S}{x_1} \right)^4 \right]^{-1/4} \right\} \qquad\qquad 0 \le Perc \le S \qquad\qquad (6)$$

The water content in the soil (*S*) is updated:

$$S = S - Perc \qquad\qquad (7)$$

The runoff (*Pr*), which is then transited to the outlet of the basin, is calculated with the expression:

$$P_r = Perc + (P_n - P_s) \qquad\qquad (8)$$

*Pr* is divided into two flow components: a) The direct runoff (*Q1*), equivalent to 10% of *Pr*, which is transited using a simple unit hydrograph (*UH2*); and b) The subsurface runoff (*Q9*), equivalent to 90% of *Pr*, which transits through a unit hydrograph (*UH1*) and a subsequent nonlinear reservoir. The base time of both hydrographs is represented by the parameter $x_4$ (in days), with $x_3$ representing the storage capacity of the nonlinear reservoir in millimeters.

The exchange of groundwater or with other basins (*F*) is determined by the equation:

$$F = x_2 \left( \frac{R}{x_3} \right)^{7/2} \qquad\qquad (9)$$

If $x_2 > 0$, there will be water import. If $x_2 < 0$, water will be exported. When $x_2 = 0$, there will be no exchange. $x_2$ is the exchange coefficient with groundwater and represents the maximum amount of water that can be exchanged when $R = x_3$.

The nonlinear transit reservoir (*R*) is determined as:

$$R = max(0; R + Q9 + F) \qquad\qquad (10)$$

The reservoir outlet flow (*Qr*) is calculated by applying the equation:

$$Q_r = R \left\{ 1 - \left[ 1 + \left( \tfrac{R}{x_3} \right)^4 \right]^{-1/4} \right\} \qquad\qquad 0 \le Q_r \le R \qquad\qquad (11)$$

The reservoir level (*R*) is updated by:

$$R = R - Q_r \qquad\qquad (12)$$

Direct runoff is calculated by:

$$Q_d = max(0; Q1 + F) \qquad\qquad (13)$$

Finally, the total runoff $(Q)$ is determined by applying:

$$Q = Q_r + Q_d \tag{14}$$

The described model is a lumped model and will serve as the foundation for developing a fully distributed hydrological model known as the Continuous Flow Hydrological System (CFHS). To achieve this, existing geographic calculation processes were automated in QGIS to delineate the hydrographic basin. Additionally, based on data recorded in weather stations, daily maps of precipitation and evapotranspiration were generated as input data. The calculation of surface runoff at the pixel level within the watershed will be performed by applying the aforementioned model using Python programming.

### 2.2 Computational Solution

CFHS is a free software application that aims to simulate rainfall runoff processes in hydrographic basins. CFHS is based on a script written in the Python programming language and operates within the QGIS environment. By utilizing native QGIS tools, users can delineate a hydrographic basin based on a digital elevation model, visualize geographic coordinate points of climatological stations, and access their daily precipitation and evapotranspiration data, which serve as input variables for the model. The data recorded at the stations are interpolated to generate a continuous surface of each variable across the basin. Subsequently, calculations are performed according to the model proposed in Sect. 2.1, yielding the spatial variation of runoff on a daily basis within the study area. This result is then converted to the NetCDF format, which has the capacity to store a large amount of data and facilitates enhanced visualization.

### Data

*Digital Elevation Model (DEM):* The fundamental basis for the hydrological analysis of an area is the Digital Elevation Model (DEM), which provides detailed information on the topography and distribution of water in the study area. This DEM file makes it possible to identify hydrographic basins, riverbeds, lakes and reservoirs, as well as potential flood zones. Based on this information, surface and groundwater hydrology analyzes can be carried out, water availability estimated, and sustainable water management strategies designed.

*Weather Station Location Coordinates:* The coordinates file is essential for weather analysis, since it allows the weather stations to be accurately located and their location in UTM coordinates. This information is essential to carry out detailed studies on climate and its evolution in different geographical areas and will allow CFHS to generate daily precipitation layers through interpolation.

*Daily Records of Precipitation and Evapotranspiration by Station:* Daily precipitation is recorded in each station considered and must be homogenized by the user, with no information gaps. The daily records of potential evapotranspiration must be calculated by the user prior to entering the model using common methodologies for this purpose, such as those proposed by Thornthwaite [11], Turc [12], Pemnam [13], etc.

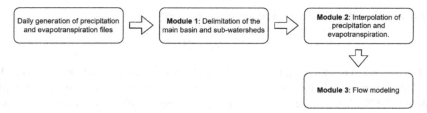

**Fig. 2.** CFHS Operating phases

## Methods

The CFHS implementation process is presented in Fig. 2.

*Generation of Daily Precipitation Files:* The user inputs the daily precipitation and evapotranspiration data in a spreadsheet format. Using this information, daily files for each variable are generated corresponding to each weather station. Python with the Pandas library [14] is employed to implement an algorithm that selects the data within a user-defined date range. Each generated file contains the information specific to a particular weather station.

*Module 1: Delimitation of the Hydrographic Basin and its Sub-basins:* The delimitation of basins is performed based on the digital elevation model (DEM) using QGIS tools. The process commences with the removal of depressions in the DEM file using the Fill Sinks tool. Subsequently, the Channel Network and Basins tool is used to identify water channels, and the Watershed Basins tool is utilized to define the watersheds. The final raster layer is then converted to a vector using the R.to Vect tool, facilitating attribute and value manipulation. The results are saved in various formats for subsequent project steps. The delimited basin serves as a mask to exclude data outside the study area. The process is summarized in Fig. 3.

*Module 2: Precipitation and Evapotranspiration Interpolation:* Since CFHS is a fully distributed model, it is essential to generate continuous daily images depicting the variability of precipitation and evapotranspiration within the study area. To achieve this, the daily data is interpolated using the IDW [15] interpolation tool in QGIS. The input data for interpolation consists of the vector layer representing the weather station locations, determined by their geographic coordinates, along with the corresponding daily precipitation and evapotranspiration data. The information outside the study area is cut using the QGIS Cut Raster tool, employing the delimited basin as a vector mask. The process is illustrated in Fig. 4.

*Module 3: Surface Runoff Modeling:* The rainfall-runoff modeling is implemented by automating the QGIS Raster Calculator tool, as depicted in Fig. 5. Along with the precipitation and evapotranspiration data, the model requires four parameters associated with water infiltration and storage in the soil: maximum water storage capacity in the soil $(x_1)$, exchange coefficient with groundwater $(x_2)$, maximum capacity of the transit reservoir $(x_3)$, and base time of the unit hydrograph $(x_4)$. By applying the model, a daily surface runoff map is generated. All data is converted to the NetCDF format to facilitate storage and visualization of the results. The use of NetCDF format enables the

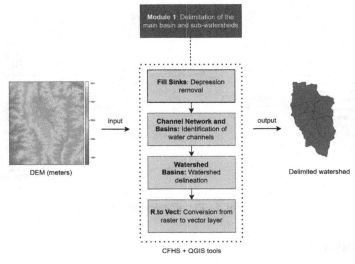

**Fig. 3.** Basin delimitation

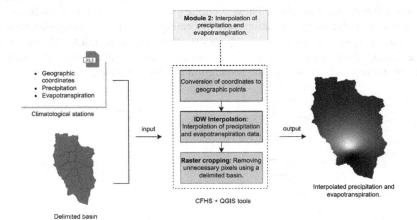

**Fig. 4.** Interpolation of precipitation data

integration of all generated information layers, allowing for the visualization of daily runoff variations in the study area over extended periods. To convert the modeled flow files to the NetCDF format, the Python libraries GDAL (Geospatial Data Abstraction Library) [16] and netCDF4 [17] are utilized, providing the capability to write files in this format. Particularly, netCDF4 serves as a valuable tool for modeling and scientific data storage in domains related to Earth and the environment (refer to Fig. 5).

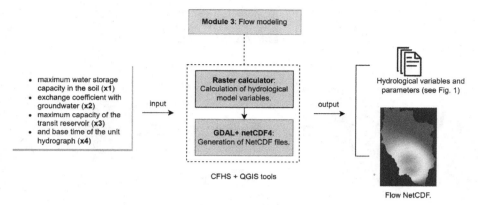

Fig. 5. Runoff calculation

## 2.3 Validation

The validation of the processes conducted by CFHS involved a direct comparison between the model's results and the outcomes obtained through separate processes utilizing GIS software, such as QGIS. These separate processes encompassed basin delimitation, generation of daily precipitation and evapotranspiration maps through interpolation, and the use of spreadsheets to assess the results of numerical modeling. The upper basin of the Zamora River, which traverses the city of Loja, and the data collected from nearby weather stations were chosen as the foundation for this validation (see Fig. 6).

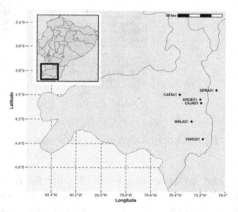

Fig. 6. Study area used for validation

# 3   Results

Figure 7 displays the windows for inputting CFHS parameters. In these windows, you can specify the simulation's date range and the necessary model parameters. By providing the station location information, as well as the precipitation and evapotranspiration data in a project folder, the process of entering the information is straightforward and user-friendly.

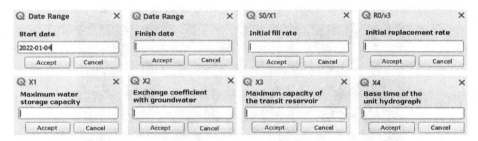

**Fig. 7.**  Input of model parameters

During the execution of CFHS, messages are displayed to inform the user about the progress of the model in each module. This allows for monitoring the execution and detecting any potential errors in data entry and the modeling process in general.

While the CFHS processes are carried out, intermediate maps of the delimited basin and daily values of precipitation and evapotranspiration are obtained using IDW interpolation (Fig. 8). This information is highly valuable as the delimited hydrographic basin defines the study area and serves as the foundation for water resource planning. Similarly, the spatially interpolated precipitation and evapotranspiration data enable us to understand their spatial and temporal variability, identifying areas with moisture deficits or excess.

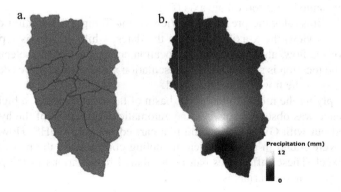

**Fig. 8.**  Basin bounded by CFHS and (b) Interpolated daily precipitation

The final results of the CFHS simulation are presented in Figs. 9, 10, and 11. The extensive amount of information obtained on a daily basis is stored in a netCDF file, requiring the use of Ncview [18], a specialized viewer for this data format. The Main View allows the selection of the variable to be displayed and the desired time period for information presentation (Fig. 9). It is possible to select a particular date for display or a certain period of data, which is presented as an animation. Additionally, the Main View presents the total amount of data and the spatial extent of the information.

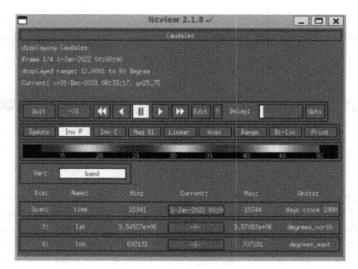

**Fig. 9.** Visualization of the flow in Ncview: Main program.

Figure 10 displays the Ncview Presentation View, which shows the spatial variability of the flows on a specific date determined in the Main View. Moreover, it is possible to select a particular point, thus observing the temporal variability of the flows at that location represented on a coordinate axis (Fig. 11).

Figure 11 illustrates the presentation View of the Temporal Variation of Flows of Ncview. In this view, the x-axis represents the dates, while the y-axis represents the magnitude of the flow, also indicating the location coordinates of the selected point. If more than one location is selected in the presentation view, several curves depicting the time variability of the flow will be displayed.

When applying the model to the upper basin of the Zamora River, a high degree of correspondence was observed between the automatic delimitation of the hydrographic basin carried out with GIS software and that carried out with CFHS. However, slight differences were found in the numerical modeling compared to the modeling carried out using Excel. These differences can be attributed to variations in the precision of significant figures in the variables.

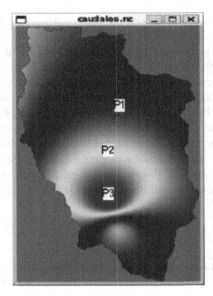

**Fig. 10.** Visualization of the flow in Ncview: Flow map

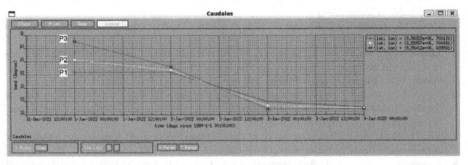

**Fig. 11.** Visualization of the flow in Ncview. Temporal variation of flow values at specific points

## 4  Conclusions

A fully distributed continuous generation hydrological model was developed in a GIS environment. This model, utilizing minimal climatic information and four parameters related to the process of infiltration and water storage in the soil, is capable of calculating surface runoff at the pixel level.

The development of this distributed hydrological model in a GIS environment using Python, GDAL, and NetCDF, based on free software, showcases the significant potential of these tools for water resource management and analysis in various river basins. The integration of these tools with QGIS enables detailed visualization and analysis of the results, which can greatly assist in decision-making processes for water management.

Additionally, storing the results in NetCDF files facilitates data integration with other systems and subsequent analysis.

The creation of an executable Python script in QGIS has proven to be an effective and precise method for the delimitation of hydrographic zones and hydrological calculations. This technological advancement represents a valuable tool for water resource management and planning, as it provides detailed and up-to-date information on hydrological behavior in specific areas. Its accessibility and ease of use make it a practical tool for professionals and decision-makers in the field of water management.

Surface runoff plays a crucial role in water availability for agricultural purposes, human consumption, and the occurrence of extreme flood events that may pose risks to the population. In the context of climate change, rainfall-runoff modeling serves as an essential management tool for studying different scenarios and their impact on water productivity in a basin.

# References

1. Oñate-Valdivieso, F., Bosque Sendra, J., Sastre, A., Ponce, V.M.: Calibration, validation and evaluation of a lumped hydrologic model in a mountain area in southern Ecuador. Agrociencia **50**(8), 945–963 (2016)
2. Ghonchepour, D., Bahremand, A., Croke, B., Jakeman, A.: A methodological framework for the hydrological model selection process in water resource management projects. Nat. Res. Model. **34**, e12326 (2021)
3. Devi, G.K., Ganasri, B.P., Dwarakish, G.S.: A review on hydrological models. Aquat. Procedia **4**, 1001–1007 (2015)
4. Jajarmizadeh, M., Harun, S., Salarpour, M.: A review on theoretical consideration and types of models in hydrology. J. Environ. Sci. Technol. **5**(5), 249–261 (2012)
5. Ponce, V.M.: Engineering Hydrology. Prentice Hall, Englewood Cliffs (1989)
6. Ngoc, A., Kumar, L.: Application of remote sensing and GIS-based hydrological modelling for flood risk analysis: a case study of District 8, Ho Chi Minh city, Vietnam. Geomat. Nat. Hazards Risk **8**(2), 1792–1811 (2017)
7. Yin, H., et al.: A GIS-based model of potential groundwater yield zonation for a sandstone aquifer in the Juye Coalfield, Shangdong. China. J. Hydrol. **557**, 434–447 (2017)
8. Kalogeropoulos, K., et al.: An integrated GIS-hydro modeling methodology for surface runoff exploitation via small-scale reservoirs. Water **12**, 3182 (2020)
9. Rosas-Chavoya, M., Gallardo-Salazar, J.L., López-Serrano, P.M., Alcántara-Concepción, P.C., León-Miranda, A.K.: QGIS a constatly growing free and open-source geospatial software contributing to scientificdevelopment. Cuadernos de Investigación Geográfica **48**, 197–213 (2022)
10. Perrin, C., Michel, C., Andréassian, V.: Improvement of a parsimonious model for streamflow simulation. J. Hydrol. **279**, 275–28911 (2003)
11. Yang, Q., Ma, Z., Zheng, Z., et al.: Sensitivity of potential evapotranspiration estimation to the Thornthwaite and Penman-Monteith methods in the study of global drylands. Adv. Atmos. Sci. **34**, 1381–1394 (2017)
12. Yang, Y., Chen, R., Han, C., Liu, Z.: Evaluation of 18 models for calculating potential evapotranspiration in different climatic zones of China. Agric. Water Manag. **44**, 106545 (2021)
13. Li, Y., Qin, Y., Rong, P.: Evolution of potential evapotranspiration and its sensitivity to climate change based on the Thornthwaite, Hargreaves, and Penman-Monteith equation in environmental sensitive areas of China. Atmos. Res. **273**, 106178 (2022)

14. Data Analysis Library. https://pandas.pydata.org. Accessed 21 June 2023
15. Oñate-Valdivieso, F., Oñate-Paladines, A., Núñez, D.: Evaluation of satellite images and products for the estimation of regional reference crop evapotranspiration in a valley of the Ecuadorian andes. Remote Sens. **14**, 4630 (2022)
16. Geospatial Data Abstraction Library. https://pypi.org/project/GDAL/. Accessed 21 June 2023
17. Python interface to the netCDF library. https://unidata.github.io/netcdf4-python/. Accessed 21 June 2023
18. Ncview. https://cirrus.ucsd.edu/ncview/. Accessed 18 June 2023

# A Domain-Specific Language and Model-Based Engine for Implementing IoT Dashboard Web Applications

Lenin Erazo-Garzon[1]($\boxtimes$) ⓘ, Kevin Quinde[1] ⓘ, Alexandra Bermeo[1] ⓘ,
and Priscila Cedillo[2] ⓘ

[1] Computer Science Research and Development Laboratory (LIDI), Universidad del Azuay,
Cuenca, Ecuador
{lerazo,alexbermeo}@uazuay.edu.ec, kquinde@es.uazuay.edu.ec
[2] Department of Computer Science, Universidad de Cuenca, Cuenca, Ecuador
priscila.cedillo@ucuenca.edu.ec

**Abstract.** The Internet of Things (IoT) has become one of the fundamental pillars of the digital transformation of society, with favorable impacts on people's quality of life. Furthermore, IoT systems generate large volumes of data at very high speeds, which come from diverse sources (heterogeneous sensors), requiring the permanent adaptation of the content and the way of presenting the information to the user; hence, a low-level implementation approach becomes unproductive. In this context, Model-Driven Engineering (MDE) has proven to be an appropriate software development approach to cope with the complexity and evolution of IoT systems. However, there are few proposals for Domain-Specific Languages (DSLs) aimed at building dashboards that synthesize the metrics and fundamental monitoring data of an IoT system. Therefore, this paper proposes a DSL and a model-based transformation engine to design and automatically implement IoT dashboard visualization web applications that combine pages, panels, charts, grids, data filters, hyperlinks, and labels with warnings and prescriptive recommendations. In addition, the proposed solution abstracts implementation details from heterogeneous data sources (physical and virtual sensors), making them transparent to domain experts. The empirical evaluation of the solution through a quasi-experiment based on the Method Evaluation Model (MEM) showed that the participants perceived the solution as useful and easy to use, so they would be willing to use it in the future.

**Keywords:** Dashboard · Domain-Specific Language (DSL) · Internet of Things (IoT) · Model-Driven Engineering (MDE) · Transformation Engine · User Interface (UI)

## 1 Introduction

The Internet of Things (IoT) is one of the fastest-growing areas within information technologies due to its technical, social, and economic impact on society, favorably transforming how we live and work [1]. However, one of the pending problems is the

J. Maldonado-Mahauad et al. (Eds.): TICEC 2023, CCIS 1885, pp. 412–428, 2023.
https://doi.org/10.1007/978-3-031-45438-7_28

development of software for IoT systems since, on the one hand, these systems operate in highly heterogeneous, distributed, scalable and uncertain scenarios; and, on the other hand, traditional Software Engineering methodologies and tools focus mainly on the implementation domain (low-level programming) instead of the problem domain [2].

In particular, IoT systems generate large volumes of data at very high speeds, which come from diverse sources (heterogeneous sensors), requiring permanent adaptation of the content and the way of presenting the information to the user, depending on the context [3]. Hence, a low-level approach to implementing and maintaining an IoT system's data visualization layer (e.g., reports, dashboards) can demand a lot of effort, time, and cost from domain experts, designers, and developers.

Model-Driven Engineering (MDE) has become an appropriate software development approach to bridge the problem-implementation gap. Thus, abstract complexity, automate development, and manage the evolution of modern systems, such as IoT [4]. MDE contemplates the construction of technologies that combine: metamodels, Domain-Specific Languages (DSL), and transformation or generation engines [5].

In their analysis of IoT platform gaps, Mineraud et al. [6] highlight the importance of having DSLs that offer functional primitives to describe the problem and the solution space at a higher abstraction level to speed up the development process of IoT applications. However, the vast majority of existing studies on DSLs focus on the IoT architecture [7], with few DSL proposals oriented towards the visualization of dashboards that synthesize in real-time and in a single site, the metrics and essential monitoring data, coming from the multiple and diverse sources of an IoT system [3, 8, 9].

This paper proposes a visual domain-specific modeling language named Dashboard-IoT, together with a model-based transformation engine that allows stakeholders to design and automatically implement interactive IoT dashboard visualization web applications (viewers) with a high level of abstraction and flexibility. These tools are part of a methodology and supporting infrastructure based on MDE to build self-aware IoT systems [10]. In this sense, the Dashboard-IoT DSL integrates with the Monitor-IoT DSL presented in [7]. The latter focuses on designing IoT architectures that support data collection, transport, processing, and storage with different levels of aggregation, through the Edge, Fog, and Cloud layers. Whereas, from the stored monitoring data, Dashboard-IoT is framed solely in the design of dashboard web viewers that combine pages, panels, charts, grids, data filters, hyperlinks, and labels with warnings and prescriptive recommendations, being the implementation details of heterogeneous data sources (physical and virtual sensors) transparent to domain experts.

The structure of this paper is as follows. Section 2 presents a review of the work related to the study problem. Section 3 describes the metamodel and DSL of IoT dashboards. In turn, Sect. 4 explains the functionalities of the IoT dashboard web application generation engine. Section 5 describes the empirical evaluation of the solution by applying a quasi-experiment. Finally, Sect. 6 presents the conclusions and future work.

## 2   Related Work

Based on a systematic literature review on MDE applied to user interfaces [11], there are few studies within the IoT domain. In particular, only three proposals focus on the visualization of monitoring data in IoT systems, which are analyzed below:

Matos de Morais et al. [3] present a proof-of-concept of a domain-specific modeling language (SiMoNa) built on MetaEdit+ to design interactive infographic presentations for IoT systems. The main limitation is that this solution does not include a transformation engine to generate code from infographic models.

Moreover, De Sanctis et al. [8] propose a framework called MIKADO for the assessment of KPIs over smart cities, composed of: i) a DSL to graphically and textually model a smart city; ii) a textual DSL for modeling KPIs; and iii) two engines that calculate the KPIs and generate a dashboard with their results, based on the specifications contained in the models. However, this proposal offers a reduced type of visual components to present the information in a dashboard. In addition, it presents the impossibility of graphically modeling the structure, organization, and navigation between the components of a dashboard as well as the modeling of interactive dashboards, whose information can be filtered with different levels of aggregation according to the user's needs.

Likewise, Rojas et al. [9] propose Cities-Board, a framework to automate the development of smart city dashboards. This solution includes a DSL to create dashboard models and transformations to generate the corresponding code artifacts. The Cities-Board evaluation focused particularly on measuring generation time and the quality of the generated code compared to other tools. However, as these are front-end solutions, knowing the users' opinions about their usability and usefulness is a priority.

According to the above, several limitations and challenges persist within this field of research, the same ones that are addressed in this document through the proposed solution. The strengths of the related work were harnessed for the construction of the DSL and generation engine of IoT dashboards. Thus, the DSL provides a more complete and intuitive high-level visual modeling language capable of creating interactive dashboards, including various types of information filtering and presentation controls. Likewise, since the Dashboard-IoT DSL is integrated with the Monitor-IoT DSL [7], the complexity and implementation details of the data sources (sensors) are abstracted. Therefore, the modeling of IoT dashboards is reduced to obtaining the information from the monitoring databases and the way of presenting said information. Finally, unlike the existing ones, the proposed solution was the subject of an empirical evaluation based on quasi-experiments to understand users' perceptions of its usefulness and intention for future use.

## 3   Dashboard-IoT DSL

This section describes the Dashboard-IoT DSL for designing IoT dashboard visualization web applications. First, the base metamodel (abstract syntax) of the DSL is explained, including a review of its metaclasses, attributes, and relationships. Then, the graphical notation of the DSL (concrete syntax) is presented.

### 3.1   Dashboard-IoT Metamodel

The IoT dashboards metamodel was built in the standard ECORE format using the Eclipse Modeling Framework (EMF) [12]. First, based on the analysis of related work, the most common and relevant metaclasses among the proposals have been incorporated into the metamodel. Then, additional metaclasses were included to represent essential concepts not previously covered. It should be noted that relationships were defined with the *DataTable* and *DataColumn* metaclasses of the Monitor-IoT metamodel [7] to obtain the specifications on the structure where the monitoring data and metrics are stored (databases, tables, columns). Figure 1 shows the metamodel's metaclasses, attributes, relationships, and enumerations. A number circled in green identifies Dashboard-IoT metaclasses, while a number in blue represents Monitor-IoT metaclasses. The remainder of this subsection describes each of the metamodel metaclasses and attributes.

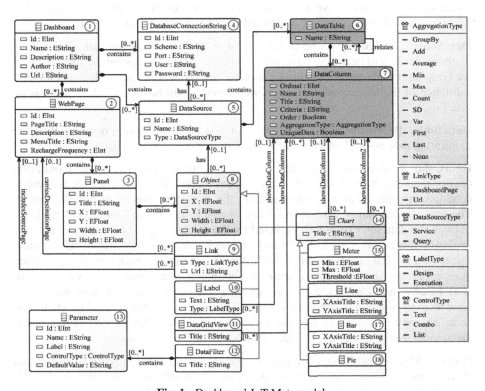

**Fig. 1.** Dashboard-IoT Metamodel.

**Dashboard.** Main metaclass that describes and contains the IoT dashboard model. This metaclass includes the following attributes: id, name, description, and author of the model, and the URL to access the web application that visualizes the modeled IoT dashboards (see Fig. 1(1)).

**WebPage.** Represents a web page in the IoT dashboards metamodel that can contain: panels, charts, grids, labels, hyperlinks, and data filters. This metaclass has the following attributes: id, page title, the title of the main menu option from which the page is called, and page reload frequency (see Fig. 1(2)).

**Panel.** Defines an element to divide a web page into areas or sections in order to display the different objects that an IoT dashboard web application can support in an organized way. First, the panels are drawn inside a web page, defining their size and position. Then, different objects can be included in the panels, such as charts, grids, labels, hyperlinks, and data filters. A panel has the following attributes: title, coordinates (X, Y), width, and height. These attributes are useful for defining the location and size of the panel on the page (see Fig. 1(3)).

**DatabaseConnectionString.** Specifies an object containing the information about the schema, port, user, and password to access the IoT system monitoring databases, from which the data shown in the IoT dashboards will be obtained (see Fig. 1(4)).

**DataSource.** Defines an object containing high-level specifications that indicate how to obtain the data to be displayed in IoT dashboards. Data sources can be specifications for building a SQL query or calling a web service. However, the implementation and validation of the metamodel to support web services will be addressed in future work (see Fig. 1(5)).

**DataTable.** Represents a database table containing the information resulting from the monitoring processes of an IoT system (see Fig. 1(6)).

**DataColumn.** Represents a column of a database table that contains the monitoring data or metadata to be displayed on an IoT dashboard. This metaclass allows setting conditions for the column in order to filter the data to be presented in a dashboard. These conditions can be established during the design of the IoT dashboard model or through the data filter parameters entered by the user during the execution of the web application. In addition, it can be defined whether the data will be sorted by this column. The metaclass also supports configuring different aggregation operations for the column (e.g., group by, sum, average, minimum, maximum, count, standard deviation, first, last). Finally, the metaclass allows specifying a column title, which will be used at the view level to label the column in the corresponding grids or charts (see Fig. 1(7)). The *DataTable* and *DataColumn* metaclasses are part of the high-level specifications of the metamodel used to build the SQL queries to obtain the monitoring data.

**Object.** Abstract metaclass that represents the objects or controls (hyperlink, data filter, chart, label, grid) that can be displayed in an IoT dashboard web application. This metaclass includes the common properties of these objects. The attributes X, Y, height, and width are essential to determine the location and size of objects within a dashboard (see Fig. 1(8)).

**HyperLink.** Defines the navigation flow of an IoT dashboard web application. A hyperlink has the following attributes: URL of the destination web page and type of hyperlink, which can be to a web page internal or external to the IoT dashboard web application (see Fig. 1(9)).

**DataFilter.** This metaclass enables the interaction between the user and the IoT dashboards, allowing the user to set criteria to filter the data to be presented in the charts and controls. A filter includes a set of data input controls (text, combo, list) for the user to enter or select data filtering criteria or conditions. This functional specification, which can be included in an IoT dashboard model, improves the user experience by allowing the user to access information accurately and timely (different levels of aggregation). The *DataFilter* metaclass has an attribute to define the general title of the filter to be displayed on the web page. Whereas the *Parameter* metaclass has the following attributes: i) name, used internally in the programming logic of the web application filters; ii) label, title of the data input control associated to the parameter, which will be displayed on the web page; iii) type of control associated to the parameter (text, combo, list); and iv) default value to be displayed in control associated to the parameter (see Fig. 1(12, 13)).

**Chart.** Abstract metaclass specializing in line, meter, bar, and pie charts. This metaclass contains the common attributes to create a chart as part of a dashboard; that is, it includes the main title of the chart, as well as the columns of the data sources from which the data shown in the chart will be obtained. In particular, the specialized *Line* and *Bar* metaclasses include attributes to set the X-axis and Y-axis titles of the line or bar chart. In contrast, the specialized *Meter* metaclass contains attributes to define the minimum, maximum, and threshold value of a meter chart (see Fig. 1(14–18)).

**Label.** Represents a control that displays data from a column of a data source obtained at run time or from a static value defined in the text attribute of this metaclass at design time (see Fig. 1(10)).

**DataGridView.** Represents a control that displays monitoring data in tabular form on a web page. The data shown in the grid is obtained from the columns specified in the data source (see Fig. 1(11)).

### 3.2  Dashboard-IoT Graphical Designer

The Dashboard-IoT DSL consists of a graphical design tool that simplifies and speeds up the construction and maintenance of IoT dashboard web application models, according to the metamodel presented in the previous subsection. This design tool was built in Obeo Designer Community Edition and Eclipse Sirius [13]; therefore, the EMF (Eclipse Modeling Framework) and GMF (Graphical Modeling Framework) editors are reused for the creation of IoT dashboard web application graphical modeling workbenches. In turn, the graphical designer serializes the IoT dashboard model in XMI format so that the generation engine can interpret it. Figure 2 shows the graphical notation (concrete syntax) for each DSL component (metaclass).

## 4  IoT Dashboard Generation Engine

The goal of the generation engine is to interpret the specifications contained in an IoT dashboard model built on the Dashboard-IoT DSL; and, from these, implement the software artifacts and source code related to web pages, charts, grids, labels, hyperlinks, data filters, connection strings, and SQL queries to retrieve and display information from the respective monitoring databases. The generation engine is developed in Node.js, a cross-platform, open-source, asynchronous event-driven JavaScript runtime environment based on Google's V8 engine [14]. In turn, an IoT dashboard web application, built automatically by the generation engine, has an architecture composed of four layers: client, presentation logic, business logic, and data. These layers are decoupled to contribute to code reuse and improve the application's interoperability, scalability, and maintainability. Figure 3 shows the architecture of the generation engine and the resulting IoT dashboard web applications, including their layers, components, and communication interfaces between them.

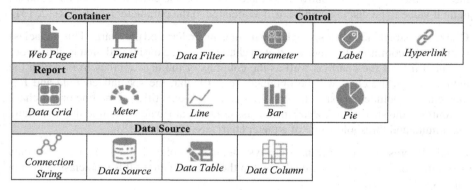

**Fig. 2.** Dashboard-IoT DSL graphical notation.

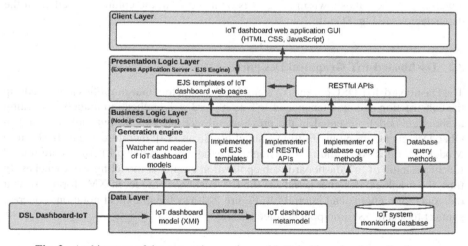

**Fig. 3.** Architecture of the generation engine and IoT dashboard web applications.

**Client Layer:** Depicts the user interface of the IoT dashboard visualization web application generated by the engine. This layer includes web pages in HTML, CSS, and JavaScript that display the charts, grids, and labels containing the IoT system monitoring information as well as the data filters so that the user can interact with the application.

**Presentation Logic Layer:** The Node.js Express application server [14] and the EJS rendering engine [15] are installed in this layer. Hence, it includes two types of software artifacts created by the generation engine: i) the EJS view templates that are rendered to create the web pages with the IoT dashboards to be displayed on the client layer, and ii) the RESTful APIs that are consumed from the EJS templates; and, in their body, they invoke the business layer methods in charge of processing the query requests to the monitoring databases of the IoT system.

**Business Logic Layer:** Contains the generation engine, whose business logic is distributed in four artifacts: i) watcher and reader of IoT dashboard models, which periodically detects the presence of new models or changes in existing models in the subdirectory "./models" located in the engine's root directory; ii) implementer of EJS view templates (web pages) and their parts (panels, graphs, grids, data filters, labels); iii) implementer of RESTful APIs, which link the EJS templates with the database query methods, hiding the latter's code; and iv) implementer of classes that encapsulate the query methods to the monitoring databases. The engine implementer components build the respective software artifacts according to the specifications of the IoT dashboard models.

**Data Layer.** It includes two components. Firstly, the IoT dashboard model in XMI format conforms to the Dashboard-IoT metamodel. Then, the databases referenced in the IoT dashboard model. These databases contain the data and metrics resulting from the IoT system monitoring processes.

## 5   Empirical Evaluation of the Solution

This section presents the empirical evaluation of the DSL and generation engine of IoT dashboard web applications to know the user perception of the ease of use, usefulness, and intention of future use of this technological solution.

As an evaluation strategy, a quasi-experiment was applied with the participation of students from the last semesters of the Systems Engineering College at the Universidad del Azuay, which can be considered as practitioners because there is no great difference with professionals [16–18]. In turn, the Method Evaluation Model (MEM) [19] was used since it integrates user performance and perception variables to predict the usefulness and possible adoption of the solution.

The following subsections describe the IoT scenario used to evaluate the solution, as well as the design, execution, and analysis of the results of the quasi-experiment.

### 5.1   Evaluation IoT Scenario

The IoT scenario used in the quasi-experiment is part of the case study presented in [7], related to an environmental control system for homes where older people live alone. In particular, this evaluation scenario has the scope of designing and implementing an IoT dashboard web application for this environmental control system that displays carbon monoxide (CO) concentration indicators in the home environment. For this, the IoT dashboard model must be made up of two web pages (see Fig. 4).

The first page includes a panel with a meter chart and a label. This chart visualizes the real-time CO concentration level in the home environment, while the label shows the action or recommendation to carry out according to this concentration level.

The second page includes a panel with a line chart and a data filter. This chart shows the daily average CO concentration level over a date range. Therefore, the data filter includes two parameters: the start and end date, allowing the user to set the period (date range) for displaying the data on the chart.

Additionally, the data to be used by the IoT dashboard web viewer is stored in a database that is updated in real-time by the monitoring software artifacts (APIs, applications, web services) built from the Monitor-IoT DSL. These artifacts are responsible for collecting the data from the sensors and storing them in the corresponding databases [7]. Therefore, the IoT dashboard model must include the specifications of the connection string to the database and the data sources (tables, columns, criteria) from which the information to be displayed on the IoT dashboards will be obtained (see Fig. 4). It should be noted that for the rapid deployment of the monitoring software artifacts, databases, and IoT dashboard generation engine required by the evaluation scenario, these were implemented and integrated on the Docker platform, simulating an IoT infrastructure distributed in several computing nodes, at the level of the Edge, Fog and Cloud layers.

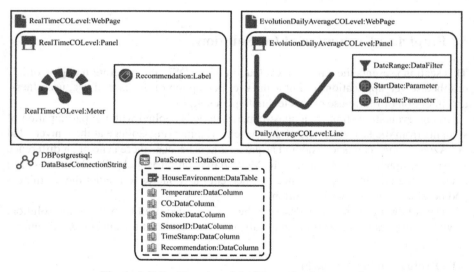

**Fig. 4.** IoT Dashboard model of the evaluation scenario.

Figure 5 presents as an example the web pages designed in the DSL and whose code has been automatically generated by the engine.

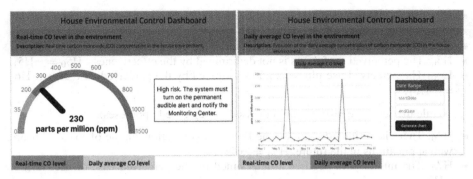

**Fig. 5.** Example of web pages automatically implemented by the generation engine.

## 5.2 Design of the Quasi-experiment

The quasi-experiment was designed following the experimental process proposed by Wohlin et al. [20]. Table 1 presents the *quasi-experiment goal* according to the Goal-Question-Metric (GQM) paradigm proposed by Basili et al. [21].

**Table 1.** Goal-Question-Metric for the quasi-experiment.

| | |
|---|---|
| Evaluate: | The DSL and generation engine of IoT dashboard web applications |
| With the purpose of: | • Determine the user performance (effectiveness and efficiency) using the DSL and generation engine of IoT dashboards<br>• Understand user perception of the ease of use, usefulness, and intended future use of the DSL and generation engine of IoT dashboards |
| From the viewpoint of: | Researcher |
| In the context of: | A group of undergraduate students from the last semesters of the Systems Engineering College |

The *research questions* were formulated based on the user performance and perception variables of the MEM and their causal relationships [19] to respond to the quasi-experiment goal. These questions are listed below:

**RQ1.** Is the DSL and generation engine of IoT dashboard web applications perceived as easy to use and useful? If so, is the user perception the result of their performance when using the proposed solution?

**RQ2.** Is there an intention to use the DSL and generation engine of IoT dashboard web applications in the future? If so, is the intention to use the result of the user perception?

In turn, the research questions were evaluated through hypotheses tests. For its part, the first question was analyzed by the hypotheses:

- $H1_0$: The DSL and generation engine of IoT dashboard web applications is perceived as difficult to use, $H1_0 = \neg H1_1$.

- $H2_0$: The DSL and generation engine of IoT dashboard web applications is not perceived as useful, $H2_0 = \neg H2_1$.
- $H4_0$: The perceived ease of use is not determined by the efficiency, $H4_0 = \neg H4_1$.
- $H5_0$: The perceived usefulness is not determined by the effectiveness. $H5_0 = \neg H5_1$.
- $H6_0$: The perceived usefulness is not determined by the perceived ease of use, $H6_0 = \neg H6_1$.

While the second question was addressed through the hypotheses:

- $H3_0$: There is no intention to use the DSL and generation engine of IoT dashboard web applications in the future, $H3_0 = \neg H3_1$.
- $H7_0$: The intention to use is not determined by the perceived ease of use, $H7_0 = \neg H7_1$.
- $H8_0$: The intention to use is not determined by the perceived usefulness, $H8_0 = \neg H8_1$.

The *quasi-experiment context* was determined by: i) the students from the last semesters of the Systems Engineering College at the Universidad del Azuay, who participated in the quasi-experiment; ii) the IoT scenario described in the previous subsection; and iii) the DSL tools and IoT dashboard generation engine.

The *quasi-experiment tasks* were framed within the established methodological process to design and implement IoT dashboard web applications using the proposed tools. Hence, the main experimental tasks were: i) modeling of data sources (connection strings, tables, relations, columns); ii) modeling of containers (web pages, panels); iii) modeling of controls (charts, grids, labels, data filters); iv) copy the XMI file with the IoT dashboard model, in the subdirectory "./models" that monitors the generation engine; and v) execution and visualization of the IoT dashboards web application generated by the engine.

The *quasi-experiment dependent variables* to evaluate the DSL and generation engine were the user performance (effectiveness and efficiency) and perception (ease of use, usefulness, and intention to use) variables proposed by the MEM [19]. The way of measuring these variables is presented in the following subsection.

The *quasi-experiment material* was provided through a website and included the software tools and documentation required to execute and evaluate the experimental tasks: i) Dashboard-IoT DSL under the Obeo Designer Community Edition platform; ii) Docker Desktop application for running Docker containers, including the monitoring database, software artifacts, and IoT dashboard generation engine; iii) a presentation and an exercise used by the researchers to train the participants in handling the tools of the proposed solution; iv) a bulletin and worksheet with the description and instructions of the experimental exercise; this worksheet includes several fields to collect metrics about the activities performed by the participants and the products obtained; and v) a Google Forms questionnaire to measure the user perception of using the proposed solution.

### 5.3   Adaptation of the MEM for the Evaluation of the solution

Before evaluating the DSL and generation engine of IoT Dashboards, it is necessary to adapt the measurement instruments of the user performance and perception variables of the MEM in the context of these tools. On the one hand, the current effectiveness and efficiency variables were measured according to the following equations:

- **Current Effectiveness.** Degree of the fulfillment of the experimental tasks of the quasi-experiment related to the design and implementation of an IoT dashboard web application; for which, Eq. 1 is used:

$$Effectiveness = \frac{\sum_{i=1}^{n} task\ score_i}{n} \tag{1}$$

where $n$ is the number of experimental tasks, while the *score for each task* is assigned as follows: 1 when the task was performed correctly, 0.5 when the task was partially carried out, and 0 when the task was performed incorrectly.

- **Current Efficiency.** Time spent to complete all the experimental tasks of the quasi-experiment regarding the design and implementation of an IoT dashboards web application; for this, Eq. 2 is used:

$$Efficiency = \sum_{i=1}^{n} task\ duration_i \tag{2}$$

where $n$ is the number of experimental tasks.

On the other hand, the user perception variables were evaluated through an adapted questionnaire presented in Table 2. This questionnaire is made up of twelve questions: i) five questions to measure the perceived ease of use (PEOU); ii) three questions to assess the perceived usefulness (PU); iii) three questions focused on the intention to use (ITU); and iv) an open-ended question to collect suggestions on the technological solution. The questions were evaluated using the Likert scale (5 points), assuming three as a neutral value, from which the solution can be accepted or rejected depending on the perception variables.

**Table 2.** Questionnaire to measure perception.

| No. | Question |
| --- | --- |
| PEOU1 | The graphic designer of the Dashboard-IoT DSL is intuitive and easy to understand? |
| PEOU2 | The graphical notation used by the Dashboard-IoT DSL is intuitive and easy to understand? |
| PEOU3 | The graphic designer of the Dashboard-IoT DSL is easy to use? |
| PEOU4 | The methodological process for designing and implementing an IoT dashboard web application is easy to understand? |
| PEOU5 | The methodological process for designing and implementing an IoT dashboard web application is easy to apply? |
| PU1 | The DSL and generation engine could reduce the time and effort required to implement IoT dashboard web applications? |

(*continued*)

**Table 2.** (*continued*)

| No. | Question |
|-----|----------|
| PU2 | The DSL and generation engine are useful to support the implementation and maintenance activities of IoT dashboard web applications? |
| PU3 | The DSL and generation engine could improve your performance in implementing IoT dashboard web applications? |
| ITU1 | If you need to design and implement a web application to visualize IoT dashboards in the future, would you consider the proposed solution as an alternative? |
| ITU2 | If you need to design and implement a web application to visualize IoT dashboards in the future, would you use the proposed solution? |
| ITU3 | Would you recommend using the DSL and generation engine to implement IoT dashboard web applications? |
| OQ1 | Do you have any suggestions regarding the proposed solution? (open-ended question) |

### 5.4 Execution of the Quasi-experiment

The quasi-experiment was conducted in person with 35 students of the Systems Engineering College at the Universidad del Azuay. The experiment lasted four hours, divided into two sessions (2 h each). The first session was dedicated to the installation of the solution to be evaluated, as well as to the training of the experiment participants. The second session focused on the development of the experimental exercise by the participants. At the end of the experiment, each participant completed the perception questionnaire in Google Forms, and emailed the solved worksheet of the experimental exercise and the XMI file with the IoT dashboard model.

### 5.5 Results of the Quasi-experiment

The data collected in the experiment were evaluated using descriptive statistics, box plots, and hypotheses tests with the support of the SPSS v25 tool (with $\alpha = 0.05$). The significance levels proposed by Moody [22] were used to accept or reject the hypotheses.

**User Perception Analysis.** Figure 6 presents the box plots of the perception variables, having as a common denominator that the mean of each variable is greater than the neutral value (3) of the Likert scale (see Table 3). In addition, the boxplots show outliers belonging to the participant with identifier 4, which have been excluded in order to obtain representative statistical results.

Additionally, using the Shapiro-Wilk test, it was determined that all the perception variables (PEOU, PU, and ITU) do not have a normal distribution ($p < 0.05$). Therefore, the Wilconox one-tailed one-sample test was applied, obtaining a very high level of significance for all the variables ($p < 0.001$) (see Table 3). Consequently, these results allow rejecting the null hypotheses $H1_0$, $H2_0$, and $H3_0$, concluding that the participants perceive the solution as easy to use and useful and would be willing to use it in the future to design and implement IoT dashboard web applications.

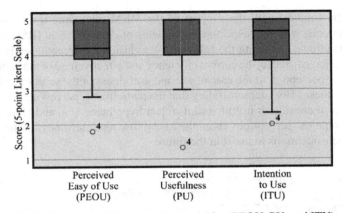

**Fig. 6.** Box plots of the perception variables (PEOU, PU, and ITU).

**Table 3.** Results for user perception variables.

| No. | Min. | Max. | Mean | Std. Dev. | Shapiro-Wilk test p-value | Wilcoxon one-tailed one-sample test p-value |
|-----|------|------|------|-----------|---------------------------|---------------------------------------------|
| PEOU | 2.800 | 5.0000 | 4.3091 | 0.6524 | **0.028 < 0.05** | **0.000 < 0.001** |
| PU | 3.000 | 5.0000 | 4.5455 | 0.6387 | **0.000 < 0.05** | **0.000 < 0.001** |
| ITU | 2.333 | 5.0000 | 4.3788 | 0.7580 | **0.001 < 0.05** | **0.000 < 0.001** |

**User Performance Analysis.** The average effectiveness of the experiment was 96.21%, demonstrating that the vast majority of participants could correctly comply with the experimental tasks. In turn, the efficiency of the participants ranged between 32 and 69 min, with an average time of 49.45 min (see Table 4), which are very favorable results compared to the time required to generate a web application of visualization of IoT dashboards using low-level implementation approaches.

**Table 4.** Results of user performance variables.

| No. | Min. | Max. | Mean | Std. Dev. |
|-----|------|------|------|-----------|
| Effectiveness | 0.8333 | 1.0000 | 0.9621 | 0.0715 |
| Efficiency (minutes) | 32.0000 | 69.0000 | 49.4545 | 12.4966 |

**Causal Relationships Analysis.** In this instance, the structural part of the MEM was validated. For this, the simple linear regression method was applied to verify the existence of causal relationships between the MEM variables as a mechanism to test hypotheses $H4_0$, $H5_0$, $H6_0$, $H7_0$, and $H8_0$. Figure 7 shows a synthesis of the results obtained in evaluating the solution with the support of the MEM, including the resulting linear regression models, with the respective coefficients of determination ($R^2$) and p-values. These results allowed reaching the following conclusions: i) hypotheses $H4_0$ and $H5_0$ could not be rejected; hence, the current efficiency and effectiveness of the participants do not affect their perception of the ease of use and usefulness of the solution, respectively; ii) reject hypotheses $H6_0$, demonstrating that the participants, perceiving the solution as easy to use, also consider it useful; and ii) reject hypotheses $H7_0$ and $H8_0$, evidencing that the participants' perceptions about the ease of use and usefulness of the solution to determine their intentions to use it in the future.

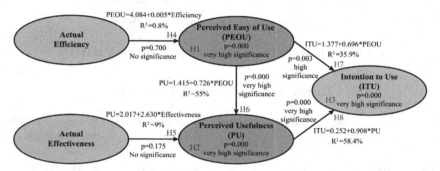

**Fig. 7.** Synthesis of the evaluation results of the solution using the MEM.

### 5.6 Threats to the Validity of the Quasi-experiment

Among the main threats to the reliability of the solution evaluation results, which were observed and mitigated during the quasi-experiment, are:

- The first threat was the selection of the participants of the quasi-experiment. As mentioned, undergraduate students from the last semesters of the Systems Engineering College at the Universidad del Azuay participated. However, according to several studies [16–18], it has been shown that the capacity of this type of student is comparable to that of a junior professional, even more so when students with solid knowledge of the related subject have been selected. Therefore, they are a homogeneous and representative group of participants.
- Additionally, the threat to the participants' experience was reduced through a training phase, based on practical cases to provide a clear understanding of the operation of the solution.
- The threat related to the experimental design was minimized by proposing a complete enough IoT evaluation scenario, with difficulty level according to the time available for the experiment. The biases produced by the researchers and the experimental material were reduced through a pilot experiment with the participation of experts.
- Another threat was the reliability of the perception questionnaire, for which the Cronbach's alpha reliability test [23] was applied to each group of questions on the perception variables. The test results were greater than the minimum accepted threshold

$(\alpha = 0.70)$, obtaining a Cronbach's alpha for perceived ease of use (PEOU) of 0.876, perceived usefulness (PU) of 0.938, and intention to use (ITU) of 0.931, which shows high internal consistency and interrelation between the questions in the questionnaire.

## 6 Conclusions and Future Work

The complexity of IoT systems, characterized by their heterogeneity, dynamism, ubiquity, and scalability, require fast and easy-to-use solutions for managing the visualization of monitoring data and metrics. In particular, there are few DSL proposals aimed at building IoT dashboards, which present functional and evaluation limitations, such as: i) a limited language to model the structure, organization, and navigation between the possible visual components that IoT dashboards may require; ii) lack tools to transform models to code artifacts; and, iii) have not been subjected to rigorous evaluations of their usefulness and usability.

Hence, the main contribution of this work is to provide a more complete and intuitive high-level visual modeling language and a model-based transformation engine for the design and automatic implementation of interactive IoT dashboard web applications, which include various types of information filtering and presentation controls. This solution is part of a comprehensive methodology and infrastructure to build self-aware IoT systems. In addition, this solution gives domain experts the necessary independence to build IoT dashboard web applications, only having to provide high-level visual specifications on how to present the data to the user, without worrying about the implementation and coding details of the data sources (sensors).

The empirical evaluation, based on the Method Evaluation Model (MEM), demonstrated the high efficiency and effectiveness of the participants in using the solution. In addition, the favorable intention of the participants to use the solution in the future was evidenced as a consequence of the fact that they consider it easy to use and useful.

As future work, it is planned to extend the solution's functionalities, incorporating new types of charts, controls, and data sources (e.g., web services, JSON files); and implementing data filters that affect all web page objects. Likewise, more evaluations are planned, through experiments or case studies in industrial contexts with the participation of experienced professionals, including more complex IoT scenarios.

**Acknowledgment.** This work is part of the research project: "Methodology and infrastructure based on models at runtime for the construction and operation of self-aware Internet of Things systems." Hence, we thank the Vice-Chancellor for Research and the Computer Science Research & Development Laboratory (LIDI) of the Universidad del Azuay for their continued support. Additionally, we thank the Vice-Chancellor for Research of the Universidad de Cuenca for their support through the project: "Human-computer interaction based on the senses: case study, measurement of affective response as a tool for nutritionists."

## References

1. Perwej, Y., Haq, K., Parwej, F., Mohamed Hassan, M.M.: The Internet of Things (IoT) and its application domains. Int. J. Comput. Appl. **182**(49), 36–49 (2019)

2. Chen, X., Li, A., Zeng, X., Guo, W., Huang, G.: Runtime model based approach to IoT application development. Front. Comput. Sci. **9**(4), 540–553 (2015)
3. de Morais, C.M., Kelner, J., Sadok, D., Lynn, T.: SiMoNa: a proof-of-concept domain-specific modeling language for IoT infographics. In: IEEE Symposium on Visual Languages and Human-Centric Computing (VL/HCC), pp. 199–203 (2019)
4. Bencomo, N., Götz, S., Song, H.: Models@run.time: a guided tour of the state of the art and research challenges. Softw. Syst. Model. **18**, 3049–3082 (2019)
5. Schmidt, D.C.: Model-driven engineering. Computer **39**(2), 25–33 (2006)
6. Mineraud, J., Mazhelisb, O., Suc, X., Tarkoma, S.: A Gap analysis of Internet-of-Things platforms. Comput. Commun. **89–90**, 5–16 (2016)
7. Erazo-Garzón, L., Cedillo, P., Rossi, G., Moyano, J.: A domain-specific language for modeling IoT system architectures that support monitoring. IEEE Access **10**, 61639–61665 (2022)
8. De Sanctis, M., Iovino, L., Rossi, M.T., Wimmer, M.: MIKADO: a smart city KPIs assessment modeling framework. Softw. Syst. Model. **21**, 281–309 (2022)
9. Rojas, E., Bastidas, V., Cabrera, C.: Cities-board: a framework to automate the development of smart cities dashboards. IoT J. **7**(10), 10128–10136 (2020)
10. Erazo-Garzón, L.: Metodología Basada en Modelos en Tiempo de Ejecución para la Construcción y Operación de Sistemas Autoconscientes de Internet de las Cosas. In: Iberoamerican Conference on Software Engineering (CIbSE), pp. 392–399 (2022)
11. Erazo-Garzón, L., Suquisupa, S., Bermeo, A., Cedillo, P.: Model-driven engineering applied to user interfaces. A systematic literature review. In: Botto-Tobar, M., Zambrano Vizuete, M., Montes León, S., Torres-Carrión, P., Durakovic, B. (eds.) ICAT 2022. CCIS, vol. 1755, pp. 575–591. Springer, Cham (2023). https://doi.org/10.1007/978-3-031-24985-3_42
12. Eclipse Modeling Framework (EMF) Documentation. https://www.eclipse.org/modeling/emf/docs/. Accessed 15 June 2023
13. Obeo Designer Community. https://www.obeodesigner.com. Accessed 15 June 2023
14. Introduction to Node.js. https://nodejs.dev/en/learn/. Accessed 15 June 2023
15. Embedded JavaScript templating - EJS. https://ejs.co/. Accessed 15 June 2023
16. Höst, M., Regnell, B., Wholin, C.: Using students as subjects—a comparative study of students and professionals in lead-time impact assessment. In: 4th Conference on Empirical Assessment and Evaluation in Software Engineering, pp. 201–214 (2000)
17. Kitchenham, B.A., Pfleeger, S.L., Pickard, L.M.: Preliminary guidelines for empirical research in software engineering. IEEE Trans. Softw. Eng. **28**(8), 721–734 (2002)
18. Basili, V.R., Shull, F., Lanubile, F.: Building knowledge through families of experiments. IEEE Trans. Softw. Eng. **25**(4), 456–473 (1999)
19. Moody, D.L.: The method evaluation model: a theoretical model for validating information systems design methods. In: 11th European Conference on Information Systems (ECIS), Naples, Italy (2003)
20. Wohlin, C., et al.: Experimentation in Software Engineering. Springer, Heidelberg (2012). https://doi.org/10.1007/978-3-642-29044-2
21. Basili, V.R., Caldiera, G., Rombach, H.D.: The goal question metric approach. In: Marciniak, J.J. (ed.) Encyclopedia of Software Engineering, vol. 1, pp. 528–532. Wiley, New York (1994)
22. Moody, D.L.: Dealing with complexity: a practical method for representing large entity relationship models. Ph.D. dissertation, Department of Information Systems, University of Melbourne (2001)
23. Cronbach, L.J.: Coefficient alpha and the internal structure of tests. Psychometrika **16**(3), 297–334 (1951)

# Feasibility of Using Serious MIDI-AM Videogames as Resources in Early Childhood Education

Nayeth Solórzano Alcívar[1]([✉]) [ID], Lissenia Isabel Sornoza Quijije[2] [ID],
Gloria Morocho Yunga[1] [ID], Gabriela Pita Quito[1] [ID], and Roberto Poveda Páez[2] [ID]

[1] Escuela Superior Politécnica del Litoral, Campus Gustavo Galindo Km 30.5 Vía Perimetral, Guayaquil, Ecuador
{nsolorza,gnmoroch,gamipita}@espol.edu.ec
[2] Instituto Superior Tecnológico Vicente Rocafuerte, Avenida Quito 506 y Avenida Padre Solano, Guayaquil, Ecuador
{lsornoza,rpoveda}@istvr.edu.ec
http://www.espol.edu.ec, http://www.istvr.edu.ec

**Abstract.** Several studies on educational videogames or serious games applied to early childhood education have been identified. However, there is little research on their use in a controlled manner in the training process of infants (children under four years of age). This article presents the first results, which analyze the feasibility of using the technical and social aspects of a series of educational games called MIDI-AM, monitored by a dashboard to evaluate playability and adoption metrics. This study examines the use of digital games on nutrition and hygiene as evaluation prototypes of the MIDI-AM series. The study was conducted with the intervention of 39 Child Development Centers (CDI and CNH), run by the Ministry of Economic and Social Inclusion in Ecuador. It is analyzed and tested if these educational videogames can be helpful as learning tools in these centers. They are applying qualitative-quantitative mixed methods strategies involving the evaluation of metrics and observational processes with on-site data collection obtained from groups of toddlers attending de CDI and CNH in low-income zones. Then, a survey was conducted on approximately 1365 parents whose children participated in these centers. As a result, a substantial interest in the applicability of these resources was identified despite the technological limitations in the zones involved in this study. Other limits were also determined by the type of application and the games' difficulty levels. Overall, the researchers identify short educational digital games as the most applicable to this age group. However, they should be complemented with physical ludic activities. The application of these tools contributes to consolidating their learning, capturing their attention, and supporting the development of their skills and abilities.

**Keywords:** active learning · serious games · children · dashboard · education

J. Maldonado-Mahauad et al. (Eds.): TICEC 2023, CCIS 1885, pp. 429–447, 2023.
https://doi.org/10.1007/978-3-031-45438-7_29

# 1 Introduction

Training children through educational video games or serious games has become an educational strategy that allows the development of skills and competencies for cognitive development in areas such as reading and mathematics under game-based learning [1]. These focus on the children's interests, as stated in the work of Figueroa-Céspedes, et al. [1], who indicate that play is a spontaneous and natural form of children's behavior, forming an essential part of their development. However, there is little evidence of studies on the evaluation of its implementation in age groups of children under four years to attend care and support services institutions, such as child development centers in Ecuador.

Currently, it is observed that most children are involved in the use of technology and exposed from an early age to interact with it. For example, they can be exposed to educational videogames as an excellent opportunity to strengthen their cognitive schemes because they promote the learning strategy by playing [2]. As mentioned by Raph Koster [3], "fun is just another word for learning" (p.46) as it stimulates various areas of the brain through the interactions made in the game; this can be directly or indirectly.

Conversely, for some age groups, videogames have been considered a bad influence on education for many years due to the high demand for time that children and young people dedicate to them. It is alleged that excessive use of games can cause users to become disconnected from reality and violent behavior. Many theories attempt to explain the increase in violence related to video games using variables that denote aggressiveness and impulsive actions supporting, for example, 'frustration-aggression hypotheses' [4]. However, in recent decades, the importance of digital games has been studied not only in entertainment or free learning but also in academic content, health, and environment, among others; in this context, some studies affirm the existence of video games designed to improve memory, attention, or cognitive resources. An example is the Akili Game, used for medical application activities, which helps to improve concentration and self-control [5].

In 2019, the COVID-19 health emergency began, also affecting the educational system and forcing students and teachers to suddenly adapt to online education, fully supported by the use of technologies and digital pedagogical resources [6]. Educators were challenged to find new ways of learning. Among them, video games have influenced this challenge until today. Thus, the actors involved in the educational system have remained searching for new tools to support the learning process [7]. Considering that video games allow players to learn at their own pace, it is relevant that there is a digital footprint available that makes it easier to know about attempts, successes, and failures, among others. For this reason, some gaming platforms have designed dashboards that generate metrics and other monitoring resources using data collected during their service. The dashboards make it easier for a teacher or tutor to supervise the interactions of their students with video games in a discreet and detailed way, with the aim that these can be used as a controlled support tool in the classroom, as is the case of the MIDI-AM series games [8].

Waweru [9] argues that educational games have been implemented in several sectors, considering that they have a psychological effect concerning motivation, attention, and social integration, depending on the area in which it is focused. They can achieve intrinsic motivation by breaking old learning habits; however, there is evidence that certain video games have generated adverse effects, such as causing violent behavior and stimulating aggression in a competition. However, since certain types of videogames have also evidenced some negative consequences, such as causing violent behavior, it is necessary to consider which types are causing these behaviors, even stimulating aggression in a competition [9]. Therefore, studies on serious, such as the MIDI-AM series, discuss ways of evaluation that allow us to know the positive impact of these, mainly in children [10].

## 1.1  State of Art

The objective of this study is to establish a feasibility analysis of educational video games from the MIDI-AM series (Spanish acronym for Mobile Applications for Children's Educational Interactive Multimedia) in infants attending Child Development Centers (CDI) and Growing with our Children (CNH) of the Ministry of Economic and Social Inclusion in urban-marginal and rural areas of Guayaquil. Ecuador has policies that ensure the comprehensive development of children, which is why it provides various services in specific areas or spaces. Among them are the CDIs for infants between 12 and 36 months of age at the CNHs for children between 0 to 36 months old [11]. According to what was observed during the collection of information for this research, it could be noted that, under the needs of the area, it is sometimes indicated that they work with children up to 48 months old, seeking to include them in the care of these centers until they begin their formal schooling.

Given that, in the first years of life, psychomotricity plays a significant role because it highly influences the intellectual, affective, and social development of the individual, favoring the relationship with the environment and taking into account individual differences, it is argued that educational video games or mobile applications of serious games can positively influence an individual and relate the visual perceptions of these with their environment [12]. These digital games that seek learning also support a child's psychomotor skills, stimulating their intelligence development [12]. In addition, it is identified that studies have promoted teaching practices using ICTs by early childhood educators or educators in the initial training process to stimulate their learning [13]. Therefore, also considering that children are very active, build their understanding, and are possessors of knowledge and interests about the world where they interact [14], the question arises to identify whether, at an early age group, such as infants between one and four years old, who attend child development centers, the use of technologies developed in mobile devices such as serious games are feasible to use for their learning.

**Serious Games.** Serious games are applications for technology-assisted education using video games and animations to investigate learning outcomes [15]. These formative games effectively teach specific skills and cognitive development, such as reading or mathematics [1].

The learning strategy based on a series of formative games positively impacts a student, such as improving their attention and completing learning goals and specific skills through activities with interactive incentives provided by these games. Retaining knowledge in the short, medium, and long term is another advantage that serious games offer. Certain serious games are linked to control platforms that can provide automatic feedback to know the results of what they did. For example, whether they accumulate or decrease points, whether they get rewards or prizes, the status of progress towards completing a goal, or whether they win the game, allowing for active learning. Through an administration and control panel, the teacher can access tracking of data related to interaction, usability, and user experience, which allows them to waste less time knowing which areas or issues need improvement [16]. The videogames development in some platforms makes it feasible for these systems to give feedback on use and automatically recommend a complementary or previous activity that the student can access to complete the learning goal of the session [8, 16].

**MIDI-AM Model.** The MIDI-AM model proposes a structure for the design of educational digital games for children from 4 to 7 years old, using interactive elements that include animated stories and games on academic content to change the traditional teaching model to a model of active learning in the classroom [17]. These applications are linked to a control panel called 'midiapi,' which allows monitoring and presenting results of game usage data stored in a database within a central server [18]. See in Fig. 1 the linking events in the MIDI-AM architecture.

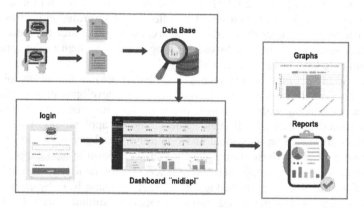

**Fig. 1.** Architecture of MIDI-AM platform

Considering the role played by the image in developing children's thinking, these games highlight the incidence of the image in constructing their culture [19] and learning content. Therefore, the design of these games considers character tendencies according to the content of the stories and with some thematic representation, without ignoring the importance of the graphic line in the fulfillment of their role in the video game, which mainly highlights the connection between a player and video game [20].

The structure for the production or development of educational video games using the MIDI-AM model is presented in four stages that cover the design, development, and control tools:

*Stage 1* – refers to the initial instructions given to the children to explain the game's mechanics.

*Stage 2* – presents productions of animated stories that are used to transmit knowledge or learning to the children about curricular content or teaching value.

*Stage 3* – includes producing short and animated simple interactive games that motivate children with challenges. These can have levels on the same game mechanics, increasing their speed or presenting different elements to identify or move, gradually increasing the difficulty level of story-related content.

*Stage 4* – This phase, of particular interest to educators, presents the design of a control panel (Dashboard), which allows to register and monitor the player's (children's) development during the use of video in a videogame.

**Children Development Centers and Growing with Our Children.** These centers, mnemonically identified as CDI and CNH, are sectorized organizations in urban-marginal. They are born as a social program regulated by the Ministry of Economic and Social Inclusion. The CDIs provide an institutional service to promote integral development through early childhood education. The objective is to improve these infants' quality of life in their social, recreational, nutritional, medical, and other environments.

Meanwhile, the CNHs, according to a technical standard, work lies in reaching levels of development in different areas with activities based on play, focused on their emotional and social bonding, exploration of the body and motor skills, verbal and nonverbal language manifestation, the discovery of the natural and cultural environment [11]. These programs are not part of the regular educational system, and their objective is to promote the integral development of early childhood. Each center serves an average of 30 to 50 children, divided into areas of one to two years, the following group of two to three years, and in some cases, even under four years, seeking to contribute to comprehensive quality development. The people who work as caregivers and tutors in these organizations belong primarily to the same sector where the CDI or CNH is located [11]. The MIES (Spanish acronym Ministry of Economic and Social Inclusion) and SENESCYT (Spanish acronym for Higher Education, Science, Technology and Innovation Secretariat) these two institutions established an agreement to ensure children's professional care and attention in 2014. These two government agencies have different objectives but are in some way related to education.

On the one hand, the MIES guarantees care and attention in early childhood in these social programs, while SENESCYT states that the people who work in these establishments are professionals able to implement comprehensive educational processes. The relationship between the CDIs and the "Instituto Superior Tecnológico Vicente Rocafuerte" (ISTVR) is to develop the academic part of the agreement executing the Dual career of Technology in Integral Development. Therefore, it complies with the professionalization of CDI collaborators, guaranteeing that all the components that govern higher education are fulfilled.

**Casa Hogar Guayaquil.** The "Casa Hogar Guayaquil" is a hosting center managed by the MIES. The objective of this institution is to provide attention to the restoration of children from zero to 12 years under judicial measures due to deprivation of parental care, mistreatment, abuse, or neglect by their parents or guardians [11].

## 1.2 Research Scope

This study aims to determine the feasibility of using mobile applications (apps) in preschoolers, using gamification principles to include serious games in learning activities. For this analysis, the use of the MIDI-AM series apps and their control and metrics management is proposed. For this purpose, it seeks to answer the following questions: What are the age groups within the toddlers who can be reached using serious games? How can kindergartens interact with mobile devices, taking advantage of the serious games that include the presentation of animated stories and basic content video games? Finally, what factors determine the feasibility of using serious digital games in the education of kindergartens that attend the CDI and CNH?

The importance of the study was initially established considering that between 2019 and 2022, we live in a time of the pandemic, leading children and adults to compulsory confinement and virtually perform daily activities, which could be replicated. Therefore, we must be technologically prepared by identifying innovative strategies to support the educational sector. This activity includes the search for activities in favor of the youngest children and evaluating the feasibility of the application and use of technological resources. The execution of this study has been promoted by institutions with educational and social purposes, who expressed their interest in exploring new ways to encourage learning from an early education in playful environments supported by technologies.

## 2  Materials and Methods

### 2.1  Research Design

Framed at an exploratory research level and following guidelines of a mixed qualitative-quantitative method, this research is developed. The study begins with applying qualitative strategies; data on the composition or perception of the games and their applicability are obtained in the first instance through the development of focus groups and observational processes until saturation points on similar results are reached. For data collection and qualitative analysis, a follow-up survey was developed for those directly involved, such as educators who attended the care centers and parents.

In summary, this study works with a representative sample of children, parents, and caregivers in several CDIs or CNHs and an MIES hosting center. For evaluations, the resources of the MIDI-AM series were used as complementary material to the curricular instruction given to the children in their care space. The researcher formed two age groups, the first group from two to three years of age and the second from three to four. The first fieldwork was conducted in spaces and with technological equipment from the reception center, running the pilot tests and initial focus groups for five weeks. Subsequently, we planned and followed up on tests with at least one of the games in the CDIs and CNHs. For this purpose, the children's daily activities included a programmed use of chapters and sections of the game apps. The apps used were selected according to their content, which had to be strictly related to the activities that would complement the development of competencies, knowledge, and skills programmed for each day of

**Table 1.** Videogame associated with skills

| Skill | Learning material | Videogame |
|---|---|---|
| Identify some animals, recognizing the benefits we can have from them | Poster about animals and their benefits | Natural environment: animals |
| Identify sweet and salty foods and the choice for one | Tasting of sweet and savory foods | ÑamiÑam1 |
| Explore some attributes (color, shape) of plants in the environment through the senses | Album of collected leaves | Natural environment: plants |
| Washing hands and face with adult supervision, as well as brushing teeth with adult support, increasing levels of autonomy in personal hygiene | Handwashing video | Loly's precautions |

the week according to the children's age. The skills planned to be reinforced with the video games tested in Table 1.

Next, a cross-sectional quantitative data analysis was made, including all the CDIs and CNHs, run by the MIES in Guayaquil, who work with the ISTVR, an academic institute that professionalizes the caregivers as Child Integral Development Technologists. For this purpose, the ISTVR students working as caregivers in these centers, together with their teachers guided by the research team of this project, carried out the respective data collection (see Fig. 2). The individual questionnaire was designed to conduct a survey directed to the participating children's fathers, mothers, or guardians. The purpose of this instrument was to identify points of view and social and technical aspects that allow evaluation of the feasibility of using the apps according to the criteria and acceptance of those involved. The questionnaire was designed to contain socio-demographic questions and questions related to the application's feasibility.

In parallel, several focus groups were conducted with ISTVR students working in pilot centers. The students, as caregivers in these centers, are the ones who maintain direct contact with the preschoolers during their early preschool years. Therefore, as part of testing MIDI-AM for preschool children, the researchers conducted induction training for the students and the ISTVR educators. Within the proposed methodology, technical factors were also considered to identify new opportunities and needs for enhancement in the MIDI-AM platform and improve the design of its apps as supporting tools for kindergarten teaching.

**Participants.** The research process was carried out through the existing linkage in a research agreement supporting early childhood education involving 36 CDIs, CNHs, 255 students, and 12 educators from ISTVR guided by a team of researchers who carried out this study (see Fig. 2). The educators and students planned and developed practical activities, including using MIDI-AM games to reinforce the learning and skills of the children attending these centers. To create the activities, they planned tasks related to their subject, curricular content, and level of study that would contribute in some way to teachers being able to guide and control the execution of these actions as a classroom project.

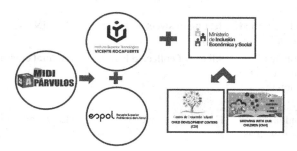

**Fig. 2.** Participating Institutions

Regarding the surveys, these were applied by students from the second to fifth semester of the Technology Integral Child Development career. Some of them work as caregivers or tutors in 39 selected centers. Approximately 35 attended the CDIs or CNHs from zero to four years of age, as appropriate. It is worth mentioning that the students carry out activities with the children as part of their pre-professional internships or their hours of Linking with Society. The caregivers maintain direct contact with the children's parents and legal guardians and perform their daily task activities determined by the MIES.

**Procedures.** For this research, the students/caregivers of the CDIs or CNHs were divided into groups of a maximum of 7 members, who received teacher support for each of the activities requested to be monitored by the research team. In the initial stage, an induction was provided regarding the use of technological tools that would serve as a base for students to create tutorial videos for downloading and recording the games for the CDIs assigned to the tests. These videos were used as an instruction guide so that the families of the children attending the CDIs and CNHs could download and register for the games correctly. Reporting on the platform makes it possible to know how many children entered and the time they spent, among others. This information, stored in the dashboard, allows the presentation of results such as statistical information, graphs, tables, and future interpretation in a natural language [7], as shown in Fig. 1.

Additionally, it is considered that educators play a key and active role in the complete life cycle in the use of serious games: initiation and design, validation, and its application in the classroom, which contributes to obtaining real-time information on their progress, results, and automatic evaluation [21]. Therefore, in this research, it is imperative that students, who in this case take the role of educators and a direct channel with parents of the families or legal guardians of the children in the CDIs and CNHs, must understand how to apply the games in an effective and timely manner.

Once the field tests were completed, the researchers made direct contact with the ISTVR students/caregivers through focus groups that were conducted virtually, seeking to learn about their experience and perspective on the use of the applications. To perform the focus groups, steps suggested by authors such as Rodríguez and Bonilla [22] indicated as follows: establish the objectives, research design, schedule development, selection of participants, selection of the moderator, preparation of stimulus questions, meeting site selection, development of the session, information analysis. Due to the virtual period when this study began, the sessions were conducted online via the Google Meet platform.

## 2.2 Applications and Videogames Analyzed for the Feasibility of Use

In the first stage, two mobile applications of the MIDI-AM series were selected, available on the Play Store for the Android operating system. The chosen applications were ÑamiÑam1 and Loly's Precautions. The first one is related to the contents on food identification and classification, linked to the subject of Child Health and Nutrition. The video game ÑamiÑam1 contains two stories: a short story that allows the user to identify the types of food accompanied by an interactive game with three levels. The second story includes a longer animation to reinforce healthy eating content. The interaction is carried out through the main character named Ñami (see Fig. 3), a friendly rabbit that guides the player through the instructions.

**Fig. 3.** Ñami, the main character of ÑamiÑam game

The second application selected, called 'Loly's Precautions,' is linked to the subject 'Experiences and favorable Environments.' This game aims to create awareness in children about the necessary care to avoid the spread of diseases, emphasizing hand washing, social distancing, and preventive advice. The interaction is made by a character called Loly (see Fig. 4), a friendly parrot from the Ecuadorian coast who guides the player through instructions. Both video games use the structure for children's serious called MIDI-AM [23].

**Fig. 4.** Main character of Loly's Precautions game

## 2.3  Data Collection Plan

**Questionnaires.** The development of the questionnaire to carry out the survey, whose purpose was to obtain specific information from people directly involved with preschool children, was designed after the first demonstrative tests on using the MIDI-AM games. ISTVR students applied the survey to the parents of CDI and CNH families. This procedure aims to know the feasibility of using MIDI-AM educational games in these centers. The survey was developed in Microsoft Forms, whose questionnaire was composed of 14 questions. The first two collected information was obtained from the centers where they worked. The question included demographic variables about the child's gender and age. In the third section of the questionnaire, some questions provide information about the help the parents receive from educators who are ISTVR students. Finally, other questions were asked about the feasibility of using the applications.

**Interview Guide.** In the discussion guide for the focus group interviews, questions were included for the students regarding the experiences they acquired about the induction they received to produce the tutorial aimed at the parents. Also, questions were asked about the experiences they gained in the field work when applying the survey to parents. Fulfilling the information needs a matrix corresponding to Table 2.

**Table 2.** Information requirements matrix.

| Components | Research Questions/Scope |
| --- | --- |
| Determine the age of infants who attend CDI and CNH, apt to use an educational video game, identifying the groups by the students who attend the centers<br>Description of the advantages and disadvantages of the use of video games in kindergartens, made by the students, to determine new criteria for analysis | What are the age groups within toddlers that can be reached with the use of serious games?<br>• Learn about the age groups of children attending childcare centers<br>• Identify the design and Scope of serious games that can operate according to the child's age<br>How can toddlers interact with mobile devices, taking advantage of serious games that include the presentation of animated stories and basic content video games?<br>• To know the students' proposals as caretakers to improve the learning of toddlers using serious games<br>• To rank the efficiency of video games as a complement to education from the educators' and students' points of view |
| To know the perception of parents CDI/CNH on the use of video games in children's education, downloading, and playing feasibility to identify the factors involved | What factors determine the feasibility of using serious digital games in the education of kindergartens attending the CDI and CNH?<br>• Determine the most significant factors that make it difficult for parents to access the applications in the CDI/CNH<br>• Define the level of ease of downloading and using the applications by parents |

**Focus Groups.** The Google Meet videoconferencing platform was used to conduct the focus groups. Four virtual focus groups were held, divided according to the semesters the students/caregivers belonged to, with the intervention of a moderator and an assistant. It began with the objectives and purposes of the session and continued with the questions session, which required participants' intervention. An average of seven students participated per focus group session; all sessions were recorded with the consent of the participants for the subsequent analysis of the information provided.

**Field Tests.** For data collection in the fieldwork, the first on-site tests were carried out in Guayaquil, which takes children in a state of vulnerability. The institution mentioned earlier has tablets as part of its resources. The tablets were not configured with programmed ludic resources but for the children's distraction. Therefore, the MIDI-AM series games selected for the tests were loaded onto the tablets. In each class session, an activity form was filled out, see Fig. 5. The format consists of data to evaluate the skills to be worked on, the associate game, the child data, their expressions, mood, and level of participation in both the playful activities of the story and the video games.

**ACTIVITY REGISTRATION FORM**

Date:                    Skills:                    Game:

| Participant | 1 | 2 | 3 | 4 | 5 | 6 | 7 | 8 | 9 | 10 |
|---|---|---|---|---|---|---|---|---|---|---|
| Gender | | | | | | | | | | |
| Age | | | | | | | | | | |
| Disability | | | | | | | | | | |
| Participation in recreational activities | | | | | | | | | | |
| Level of participation | | | | | | | | | | |
| **Nonverbal Expressions** | | | | | | | | | | |
| Anger | | | | | | | | | | |
| Disinterest | | | | | | | | | | |
| Confusion | | | | | | | | | | |
| Happiness | | | | | | | | | | |
| Enthusiasm | | | | | | | | | | |
| Recognition of didactic material | | | | | | | | | | |
| Participation in serious game | | | | | | | | | | |
| Level of participation | | | | | | | | | | |
| **Nonverbal Expressions** | | | | | | | | | | |
| Anger | | | | | | | | | | |
| Disinterest | | | | | | | | | | |
| Confusion | | | | | | | | | | |
| Happiness | | | | | | | | | | |
| Enthusiasm | | | | | | | | | | |
| Recognition of didactic material | | | | | | | | | | |

**Fig. 5.** Activity registration form

## 3   Results

The qualitative analysis was considered with the preschool children attending the 36 CDIs, CNHs, and one Reception Center in Guayaquil. The researchers observed the children's human-machine interactions from the selected MIDI-AM series game applications downloaded and focus groups held with their caregivers, ISTVR students, and teachers involved in this study. For the collection and analysis of quantitative data, we began by quantifying the results of the parent surveys. Then, the resources of the cloud platform 'midiapi' dashboard were used to analyze metrics on the data obtained from the applications played by the children, seeking consistency between the results.

**Population and Estimated Sample.** A total of 39 CDIs/CNHs were involved in this research, with an average of 35 children for each center. The statistical Eq. (1) was used to calculate a significant sample size for the survey.

$$n = \frac{N * Z^2 * p * q}{d^2 * (N - 1) + Z^2 * p * q} \tag{1}$$

where:

N = Population Size
Z = Confidence Level
p = Probability of Success
q = Probability of Failure
d^2 = Precision (maximum admissible error)

The number of respondents who completed the questionnaire was 1069 since some parents had problems filling out the survey or reflected incomplete data, which were not part of the database. Overall, there was a population of 1365 families, and within them, a sample of 1069 families, reflecting a 99% confidence level, using the formula. Based on these data, the margin of error does not exceed 1.83%.

### 3.1 Focus Groups Results

The NVivo 11 application was used to obtain the results from qualitative data. Coding techniques allow categorizing or forming topics on what was recorded by taking examples of what was expressed as registration units (see Table 3). This technique facilitated the identification of the relationship between the opinions and observations obtained and transcribed from the different participants. The perceptions on using the MIDI-AM evaluated games reflected the following results, according to the interpretative analysis of the comments and observations of the caregivers and teachers with whom the focus groups were developed, considering what they perceived from others involved in testing the games and their perception.

**Parents.** As a result of the information gathered by the students/caregivers who maintain direct contact with the parents, it was highlighted that parents expressed that 'using videogames moderately and appropriately is a significant advance in their children's learning, but they do not know at what age is good for them.'

**Caregivers.** Perception by the ISTVR students in the preschool environment generally reflects that video games are unsuitable for children from 1 to 2 years of age since, at this stage, children are experiencing many skills, which are developed mainly with game use and physical stimuli.

**Teachers.** The feedback related to the interface and design of the applications in the video games used in the research summarizes the need for specific adjustments, such as shortening the histories and level of the games, mainly to stimulate their use but in children older than three years. It was determined that children at an early age (under three years) are partially passive spectators when using simple games with accompaniment. They are not forced to maintain sustained attention and proactivity for long, especially if the games are too extensive. However, these aspects are estimated to improve as they grow older than three years, becoming more active players.

**Table 3.** Record Unit Coded

| Codes | Record Unit example (translated from Spanish) |
|---|---|
| Parents' perception of video games | … the daddies found the game very fun, very didactic, entertaining, and easy to use; they also tell me it is because the mommies supervise them […] |
| Students' perception of the use of video games in the toddlers' environment | … It was a bit complicated for them [the toddlers] since the game is not for the ages of a one-year-old; for the older ones, yes, everything is perfect […] |
| Opinions about the improvements to the application | … I think that apart from increasing levels in the game, you should put a reward at the end of each level so that the child is motivated to continue playing […] |

## 3.2 Pilot Test Results

The first on-site pilot tests, as a part of the cross-sectional analysis, were conducted in a hosting center and three CDIs to examine the child's behavior while playing the MIDI-AM game and doing other ludic activities. The age range for the preschool children in this sample was intended to work with toddlers between two and four years old. However, because the hosting center held children up to five years old, it was decided to include all of them in the sessions of the pilot test. Nursing children under two years old are not considered in this study. Thus, a total group of 54 children were included in the testing group, aged as follows: 20.4% - five years old, 40.7% - four years old, 31.5% - three years old, and 7.4% - two years old.

As part of the field test, several ludic activities were undertaken by ISTVR students, and members of the project developed, such as songs, stories, and didactic material, planning to stimulate learning for complementing the use of the video game to be tested. Each child was accompanied by the action of playing on the Tablet. The level of participation was linked to the level of interaction during the recreational activities. 70.4% of the involvement in playing digital games was registered in children between four and five years old, 29.6% on three years old children, and no participation interest on two years old toddlers was recorded. However, participation using other ludic resources was recorded in all toddlers of all ages included in the test (see Fig. 6).

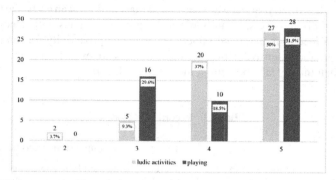

**Fig. 6.** Children's participation in ludic and playing gaming activities

## 3.3 Survey Results

The analysis of the quantitative data obtained from the survey was undertaken by using the SPSS program. This survey was directed to parents to measure the feasibility of using the MIDI-AM games for their toddlers. A question was asked in the first instance about their children's age attending the CDIs or CNHs. The results in this question show that most of the children are in the range of two (44.43%) to three years old (32.09%); this group represents approximately 76.52%, followed by the group of one-year-old children, which represents 17.96% and only 5.52% of 4 years old. Therefore, a representative children population of 82.04% attending these care centers can use these games (see Fig. 7).

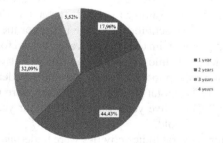

**Fig. 7.** Ages of children who attend the CDI/CNH, according to parents responses

On the other hand, regarding the request to download the selected MIDI-AM games on their devices and to confirm this fact, 92.14% of the sample indicated that they could download the applications without significant problems. However, there is a minority who were unable to download the applications. This group represents 7.86% of the total sample of 1069 respondents. In any case, it was considered relevant to analyze the reason because the remaining 84 families could not access the MIDI applications. One of the most significant causes was the lack of memory in the cell phone or Tablet, followed by unidentified problems in the download process, although, with the help of the caregivers and the project's technical team, they detected incompatibility of the device as it had an outdated Android system.

The respondents also indicated that the connection to which they had internet access was mainly through Wi-Fi; that is, they use fixed internet with reduced data capacity. More than 700 respondents mentioned they have set up internet in their homes, and 264 responded that they have access to a data plan. In addition, 89.06% of the parents or representatives surveyed answered that they use their cell phone to download applications, while 8.91% used a Tablet. A minimal number of respondents, representing 1.78%, could use an emulator on a computer. Finally, only 0.56% responded that they had no device to download (see Fig. 8).

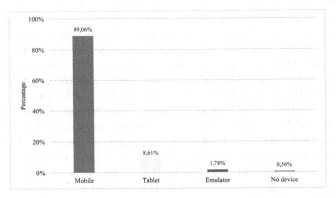

**Fig. 8.** Responses about the type of device used to download the applications

### 3.4  Midiapi Dashboard Results

Analyzing the data obtained from the MIDI-AM platform in the midiapi dashboard, it was identified that the total number of families that could download the applications was 985. This number represents 60.71% of the entire sample. It was detected that 598 parents logged into the apps and generated a user. Regarding the families that downloaded the applications, 446 registered that they played at least one level of the indicated games, representing 74.58% of game apps accessed by those who opened them, see Fig. 9.

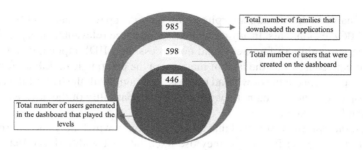

**Fig. 9.** Data obtained from the midiapi dashboard regarding access to MIDI-AM games

## 4  Discussion of Results and Conclusion

The use of technological tools in learning, such as the application of didactic games of the MIDI-AM platform, has been determined as a valuable complementary resource for teaching children in their first year of primary education [10]. However, the objective of this study was focused on the feasibility of using mobile applications such as the MIDI-AM series in early childhood and the possibility of including serious games in their learning activities within the CDIs and CNHs supported by the MIES.

The questions posed were answered based on the results obtained in this investigation. Question 1 indicates: "What age groups of young children can be reached using serious games?" The result from the survey shows that 82.04% of children over two to four years old can reach a level of participation in the use of video games of the application MIDI-AM guided by parents or caregivers (see Fig. 7). From the pilot test, it was identified that 100% of children over three years old were interested in playing the games but not children around two years old; the youngest was more interested in physical ludic games rather than apps (see Fig. 6). Then it can be implied that games such as MIDI-AM are adequate to complement the teaching and learning process more effectively for children aged over three years. However, children under two years old, who represent 7.4%, participated in the pilot test, need to be considered partial spectators. The qualitative analysis implied that the youngest children must be accompanied by an adult who guides them in using a particular digital game resource. Toddlers should not be forced to maintain sustained attention. It is also indicated that the caregivers of these centers must apply a strategy in using digital games for children of early ages. Learning strategies in early childhood must be planned appropriately to select the type and level of a game to be played along with other physical ludic activities and concrete material. Additionally, some games used in early childhood education should require simplifying their routines, shortening their animated content, or recreating them musically for this level of users. These arguments answer Question 2: "How can young children interact with mobile devices, taking advantage of serious games that include the presentation of animated stories and basic content video games?".

In determining the feasibility of using these games in care or reception centers supported by MIES, Question 3 was: "What factors determine the feasibility of using serious digital games in the education of kindergartens that attend the CDI and the CNH?" Based on the statistical results obtained from the parent survey, it can be argued that there is a high percentage of interest in using these games with their children, but considering their children's age. Besides, some studies support these assumptions by promoting teaching practices using ICTs by early childhood educators in the initial training process to stimulate their learning [13]. There is also evidence of parents' interest and curiosity in trying the apps, considering the number of downloads of 92.14% over 1,060 parents, despite the limitation of technological resources, such as Internet access problems, low data access capacity, and high-end mobile devices. It was identified that parents who could use smartphones were able 89.06% to download, install, and use the MIDI-AM apps. This fact also evidence that mobile phones are the devices more used by parents and caregivers for downloading game apps, as shown in Fig. 8. Likewise, it was possible to observe that from 985 families, only 446 of them managed to create a user, and played at least one game (see Fig. 9).

## 4.1 Conclusion

In summary, it was evidenced that caregivers/students (at a technological level), parents, and educators agree on the importance and feasibility of using educational digital games as complementary resources in preschoolers. Nevertheless, pay special attention to the age at which these resources are used. That is why the time of use and the type of game must be planned in detail. In addition, it is confirmed that short educational digital games or serious games are considered essential resources as part of an active learning methodology for toddlers attending CDIs and CNHs. Its marked need is currently justified, adding that in the case of continuing with the possible new needs of virtual environments, educators and tutors of children require alternative tools that allow linking face-to-face activities with some asynchronous teaching tools. In the pilot evaluation, the researchers observed an evident level of interaction of children from the age of three with the games and their interest in seeing all the activities shown in them. Indeed, the results of the dashboard of the MIDI-AM platform corroborated the children's interaction and access to the game, indicating the time spent and the children's successes and failures when playing a game. However, despite the interest and approval of students/caregivers and parents in using these applications for their children, depending on their age, there is a marked limitation in the availability of technological resources that do not guarantee and facilitate their use. Therefore, it is necessary to create achievement support mechanisms that allow the continuity of evaluating these alternative tools for active learning, ensuring their efficient accompaniment by daycare caregivers and their parents.

## 4.2 Future Work

The feasibility of using MIDI serious games as resources in early childhood education in CDIs and CNHs has been confirmed. A roadmap to follow is adopting these serious game tools by including them in the curricular planning activities. Particularly in the training of the technology career for integral child development, they were promoted by the ISTVR with the MIES guidelines. However, to protect the educational digital game apps in favor of toddlers, the necessary technological tools should be considered, such as internet access and the availability of tablets in the centers so that caregivers can carry out these playful activities with the children.

Enhancing human-computer interaction and user experience to generate new educational video games for children can be a field of research to be strengthened. Likewise, the combination of these interaction and design resources can open the area to the development of immersive video games for children as in the field of augmented reality, virtual reality, mixed reality, or with a more significant influence of hardware such as robotics and the internet of things. Nevertheless, always take into consideration the children's age. These new fields in which we can venture should always consider as necessary inputs the insights, pedagogy, contents, and feedback from the most significant number of stakeholders such as parents, teachers, and children.

The feasibility of using MIDI-AM serious games as resources in early childhood education at CDIs and CNHs has been confirmed. Therefore, as a second part of this investigation, a new study to encourage the adoption of improved serious game tools is proposed. The production of any serious game for early childhood should be considered an integral part of the curricular planning activities in the training of the use of technology for a necessary child development career.

**Acknowledgments.** We wish to acknowledge Escuela Superior Politécnica del Litoral (ESPOL) for sponsoring the continuity of this research and publications. Notably, we recognize the contribution of the group of researchers, academics, and students from the Art, Design, and Audiovisual Communication Faculty (FADCOM), mainly to Elizabeth Elizalde as a director of the social link program of the faculty, and the "Instituto Superior Tecnológico Vicente Rocafuerte" (ISTVR) as an academic partner to develop the fieldwork of this research.

# References

1. Figueroa-Céspedes, I., Lambiasi Pérez, R., Cáceres Zapata, P.: Actitud lúdica y rol mediador de aprendizajes en educadoras de párvulos: para aprender jugando se necesitan dos. Revista de estudios y experiencias en educación **21**(47), 371–386 (2022)
2. Alcívar, N.S., Quijije, L.S., Gallegos, D.C.: Adopción de videojuegos educativos infantiles, monitoreada con tableros de control en la nube, pp. 146–160 (2019)
3. Koster, R.: Theory of Fun for Game Design. O'Reilly Media, Inc. (2013)
4. Toribio, M.J.: Videojuegos violentos, violencia y variables relacionadas: Estado del debate. Revista de Psicología Aplicada al Deporte y al Ejercicio Físico **4**(1), 1–12 (2019)
5. Argilés, M., Jurado, L.A., Junyent, L.Q.: Gamification, serious games and action video games in optometry practice. J. Optom. **13**(3), 210–211 (2020)
6. Expósito, C.D., Marsollier, R.G.: Virtualidad y educación en tiempos de COVID-19. Un estudio empírico en Argentina (2020)
7. Solorzano, N.I., Sornoza, L.E., Carrera, D.A.: Adoption of children's educational video games monitored with dashboards in the cloud [Adopción de videojuegos educativos infantiles, monitoreada con tableros de control en la nube]. Iberian J. Inf. Syst. Technol. RISTI [Revista Iberica de Sistemas e Tecnologias de Informacao] **19**, 146–160 (2019)
8. Solórzano, N.I., Gamboa, A.A., Carrera, D.A.: Refined metric interpretation in natural language for educational videogames using fuzzy logic. In: Book Refined Metric Interpretation in Natural Language for Educational Videogames Using Fuzzy Logic, pp. 194–203 (2021)
9. Waweru, B.W., Yap, H.K., Phan, K.Y., Ng, P.J., Eaw, H.C.: Gamesy: how videogames serve as a better replacement for school? In: 2020 IEEE Student Conference on Research and Development (SCOReD), pp. 10–15 (2020)

10. Solórzano, N., Measías, E., Elizalde, E.: MIDI-AM videogame usability in virtual learning as a digital pedagogical tool in emerging economies. Int. J. Online Pedagogy Course Des. (IJOPCD) **12**(2), 1–15 (2022)
11. Ministerio de Inclusión Económica y Social del Ecuador: 'CasaHogarGuayaquil'. https:// www.inclusion.gob.ec/ninas-y-ninos-de-casa-hogar-guayaquil-recibieron-agasajo-del-gob ierno-nacional-durante-dia-conmemorativo/. Accessed 16 June 2023
12. Orellana Lepe, K., Parisi Valladares, G.: Encuesta a educadoras de párvulo sobre el desarrollo de la motricidad gruesa en niños y niñas de 2 a 4 años. UCINF - Information Sciences University (2018)
13. Ferrada-Bustamante, V., González-Oro, N., Ibarra-Caroca, M., Ried-Donaire, A., Vergara-Correa, D., Castillo-Retamal, F.: Formación docente en tic y su evidencia en tiempos de covid-19. Revista saberes educativos (6), 144–168 (2021)
14. Carreño Olave, A., Mena Bastías, C., Lastra Urra, M.J.: Valoración de las tic en el proceso educativo: Una mirada desde los párvulos y sus familias. Revista de Ciencias Sociales Ambos Mundos (1), 55–72 (2020)
15. Zhonggen, Y.: A meta-analysis of use of serious games in education over a decade. Int. J. Comput. Games Technol. **2019** (2019)
16. Chanchí, G.E.G., Vargas, P.A., Campo, W.Y.M.: Construcción de recursos educativos para la temática de accesibilidad en el curso de inter- acción humano computador. Revista Ibérica de Sistemas e Tecnologias de Informação 171–183 (2019)
17. Solórzano, N.I., Elizalde, E.S., Carrera, D.A., Park, D.H., Sornoza, L.I.: MIDI-AM model to identify a methodology for the creation of innovative educational digital games: a proposed serious game methodology based on university research experiences. In: Ariana Daniela Del, P., Nuria Lloret, R. (eds.) Improving University Reputation Through Academic Digital Branding, pp. 133–167. IGI Global (2020)
18. Solorzano, N.I., Carrera, D.G., Sornoza, L.Q., Mendoza, M.: Developing a dashboard for monitoring usability of educational games apps for children. In: 2nd International Conference on Computers in Management and Business, ICCMB 2019, pp. 70–75 (2019)
19. Salvador Sarauz, P.L., Garcés Gutiérrez, L.: Liminalidad: entre la ilustración y la literatura infantil. Ñawi **3**(2) (2019). https://doi.org/10.37785/nw.v3n2.a14
20. Solorzano, N., Moscoso, S., Elizalde, E.: Evolución de Videojuegos y su Línea Gráfica, un enfoque entre la Estética y la Tecnología. Ñawi **3**(2) (2019). https://doi.org/10.37785/nw.v3n2.a10
21. Calvo-Morata, A., Alonso-Fernández, C., Freire-Morán, M., Martínez-Ortiz, I., Fernández-Manjón, B.: Game learning analytics, facilitating the use of serious games in the class. IEEE Revista Iberoamericana de Tecnologias del Aprendizaje **14**(4), 168–176 (2019)
22. Rodríguez Bonilla, L.N., Escobar Ruiz, M.C.: Estrategias desde la ludo matica que permiten el uso y manejo adecuado del internet, en estudiantes del grado 10°. de la i.e. santa cecilia de la ciudad Santiago de Cali (2015)
23. Alcivar, N.I.S., Rios, E.S.E., Gallego, D.A.C., Quijije, L.I.S.: MIDI-AM model to identify a methodology for the creation of innovative educational digital games: a proposed serious game methodology based on university research experiences, pp. 133–167 (2020)

# Search and Visualization of Researcher Networks: Co-authorship in Ecuador

Josué Arias and Lorena Recalde(✉) 🆔

Department of Informatics and Computer Sciences, Escuela Politécnica Nacional,
Ladrón de Guevara, E11-253 Quito, Ecuador
{josue.arias,lorena.recalde}@epn.edu.ec

**Abstract.** The quality of scientific research is based on collaboration among experts. In Ecuador, an increase in scientific production has been observed, which has generated the need for an efficient computer tool to form networks, search for collaborators, and analyze research topics. In response to this, a web application has been developed that utilizes data mining models for searching and visualizing networks of researchers affiliated with Ecuadorian institutions and their academic areas. The project was implemented following the Scrum and CRoss Industry Standard Process for Data Mining (CRISP-DM) methodologies. The two methodologies showed an easy integration by having to not only develop a web application, but also carry out the pre-processing and modeling of data that later feed the functionalities in the platform. The data was extracted from Scopus through the set of APIs offered by Elsevier. The generated retrival models, which were the result of the DM process, were based on TF-IDF (term frequency - inverse document frequency). Finally, these are employed to obtain the best results in the different kinds of searches performed within the application. The architecture of the application consists of three layers: i) the Neo4j graph-oriented database as the data layer, ii) Flask as the backend that supports the business logic, and iii) Angular as the frontend, which utilizes libraries such as Bootstrap for design and D3.js for creating dynamic and interactive graphs. The software prototype offers three types of search: author search, relevant authors search by topic, and relevant articles search by topic.

**Keywords:** Data mining · Graph Databases · Neo4j · Graph Theory · Co-authorship visualization · Information retrieval application

## 1 Introduction

Scientific and quality research is based on the collaboration of experts in a certain academic area [4]. In fact, it is usual for government funding for research projects to be granted when they are i) multidisciplinary, ii) inter-university or iii) proposed by a formally established research group. Therefore, most research projects are carried out by networks of researchers whose objective is collaborative work and obtaining relevant results in order to be more cited [1]. Said

© The Author(s), under exclusive license to Springer Nature Switzerland AG 2023
J. Maldonado-Mahauad et al. (Eds.): TICEC 2023, CCIS 1885, pp. 448–463, 2023.
https://doi.org/10.1007/978-3-031-45438-7_30

scientific production and co-authorship networks have increased throughout the world. In fact, data about published scientific articles show the formation of communities of researchers. For example, Brazil is the central axis of research networks in Latin America and in the last five years it has strengthened its collaborations with Argentina, Mexico and Chile [1].

Something similar happens in Ecuador, which from occupying the 10th place in scientific production in Latin America in 1998 with 148 articles, by 2017 it went on to occupy the 6th place with 3172 articles [10]. In addition, in 2019, the Secretary of Higher Education, Science, Technology and Innovation (SENESCYT) financed 53 scientific research projects, which allowed the participation of researchers in inter-disciplinary and/or inter-university proposals[1]. Consequently, the purpose of collaborations is to carry out a research work focused on different areas or topics of knowledge [10].

Researchers from Ecuadorian universities use different means to be part of these communities. For instance, contacting groups on Facebook and other social networks, searching for official information (names of projects and researchers) through CEDIA[2] or in several indexing databases, and networking at national academic conferences are different strategies to meet peers. All these strategies are "traditional" because Ecuador does not have a computer tool that allows, in an efficient way, to visualize and interact with academic data of researchers to form networks, search for project collaborators who are experts in a certain area, evaluate co-authorships, and analyze research topics, its trends as well as related topics; which, in practice, has become a challenge [4].

This project proposes the development of a Web system that implements a model based on the extraction and presentation of information from the networks of researchers whose affiliation is in Ecuador. The purpose of this model is to facilitate the understanding of scientific research trends (*i.e.* relationships and occurrences between keywords), to help researchers in the search for experts and their research areas, and to discover patterns among scientific articles. Also, in technical terms, we use a data model based on persistence given a graph database. In this way, we can optimize the query time each time the database is accessed from the application and the corresponding transactions are carried out. This is a novel approach in an attempt to manipulate unstructured, massive data that actually forms graph-like data structures and is then visually represented in networks (nodes and edges). This visual form makes interpretation by end users much faster because they invest less cognitive load [15].

The remainder of the paper is structured as follows: Sect. 2 summarizes the theoretical background in terms of the present research; Sect. 3 presents the methodology that builds context and data understanding to define the system develop and its data mining component; in Sect. 4 we detail the web system developed and present its evaluation results; finally, in Sect. 5 conclusions and future work are described.

---

[1] https://www.educacionsuperior.gob.ec/senescyt-y-pnud-premiaran-a-los-53-proyectos-ganadores-de-inedita/.

[2] https://redi.cedia.edu.ec/.

## 2    Background and Related Work

### 2.1    Co-authorship Networks

Co-authorship refers to a collaboration between two or more authors, and this authoring relationship forms a network where the nodes represent the authors, who are linked by edges if they are co-authors in one or more articles [7]. Likewise, the thickness of the edges varies according to the frequency or strength of collaboration between the two authors (relationship strength).

### 2.2    Graph-Oriented Databases

Graph-based databases are a type of NoSQL database. Telecommunication networks, the Web, social networks, recommendation engines and fraud detection are examples of applications. All of these involve a large amount of interconnected information [6]. Unlike relational databases where tables are used, graph-oriented databases store information in nodes and edges. The entities are stored in the nodes and the relationships between entities are stored in the edges. Also, both nodes and relations have properties. The relationships between entities are as important as the entities themselves.

Although relational databases can also store relationships, they are navigated through computationally expensive operations like JOIN. On the other hand, in graph-oriented databases, relationship navigation is very fast because these relationships are not calculated at query times, but are stored natively in the database [11].

### 2.3    Visualization of Academic Data

Academic data contains a lot of information such as authors, affiliations, articles, citations, etc. Similarly, with the rapid growth of digital libraries, how to present this data in a visual way for analysis has become a challenge. With data visualization, it is intended to transform raw data into easy-to-understand graphics, symbols, colors, art, and in the same way, improve the efficiency of data recognition to convey useful information [5]. In other words, the goal of visualization is to create a visual expression rather than complex numerical concepts or results. One of the main areas of data visualization is visual analysis. In fact, visual representations that use graphs can facilitate data processing and analysis by experts in various domains. For example, graph visualization-based analysis is applied today in sources such as online social networks to extract patterns [9]. In terms of the present project, visual analysis is not only important for scientists or researchers, but also for sociologists to analyze the interactions of researchers and the formation of communities, so that private or governmental entities can evaluate the impact of scientists or affiliations and allocate resources to these.

# 3   Methodology

The methodologies that were used to develop this project are Scrum and CRISP-DM (Cross Industry Standard Process for Data Mining) [12]. First, we have Scrum, which, beyond being a methodology, is a lightweight and simple framework that helps people, teams, and organizations generate value through adaptive software solutions to complex problems [13]. On the other hand, we employed CRISP-DM to describe the life cycle of the data mining component of the project [14].

Scrum is capable of involving various processes, techniques, methods, and even methodologies. Therefore, the Scrum framework will embed the CRISP-DM methodology [2]. The latter comprises 6 phases, which will be presented next, and each of these will be included in different *Sprints*. With this in mind, the following is defined.

- *Knowledge of the business and identification of web system requirements.* In this sprint, we work with the Business Knowledge phase of CRISP-DM, which seeks to understand the goals and the data that is available from a particular business case. Understanding the entire business context will serve as support for the definition of the web system requirements.
- *Knowledge of the data for the identification and extraction of academic data.* In this sprint, we determine what is expected to be obtained from the collected data as well as its quality. This phase of CRISP-DM will support the processes of identifying data sources for their corresponding extraction.
- *Data preparation.* In this sprint, activities belonging to the CRISP-DM Data Preparation phase will be carried out, which seeks to process the data, perform cleaning, standardization, categorizations, among others.
- *Entity modeling as author and academic paper for information retrieval.* In this sprint, the results must satisfy what we are hoping to obtain from the modeling or representation of these data.
- *Design and coding of the web system.* In this sprint, we design the interfaces of the web system and code based on the system requirements.

We worked in two more sprints in order to implement and evaluate the tool. These results are presented in Sect. 4.

To start the project, the work that will be carried out during each of the Sprints is established. This process is carried out by the Scrum Team. Regarding the plan, for the user stories that are addressed in each sprint, its duration and the total effort required are estimated. It should be noted that, following the suggestion of the Scrum Guide [13], each Sprint lasts one month or less to maintain consistency in the process.

## 3.1   Knowledge of the Business and Identification of Web System Requirements

We begin with a detailed search on all the resources, limitations, assumptions and other factors, which must be taken into account when developing the project.

Among the software resources necessary to ensure the effective development of the project are Neo4j as a database manager, Python as a programming language and Amazon EC2 and Heroku cloud services for deployment. Concerning the data sources, we identified the feasibility of working with Scopus and/or ScienceDirect. ScienceDirect and Scopus use two different databases. While Scopus indexes almost the entire ScienceDirect database but without the full text of the articles, ScienceDirect contains full text articles from journals and books, mainly published by Elsevier[3]. In addition, ScienceDirect cannot be searched with native Scopus identifiers such as AF-ID, Scopus ID, etc.

Once we have analyzed the restrictions of the Scopus and ScienceDirect APIs, we define the objective of data mining. Thus, our objective is to identify the most relevant keywords for current or historical Ecuadorian authors from their articles extracted from various data sources. To achieve this, the titles, abstracts and, if possible, the full text of each author's articles will be analyzed. The purpose of this task is to establish a relationship between words or terms and authors, and the generated model will be used in the information retrieval process. In this way, it is expected to facilitate access to information related to Ecuadorian authors and improve efficiency in the search for relevant documents. Then, the architecture of the system is established as shown in Fig. 1.

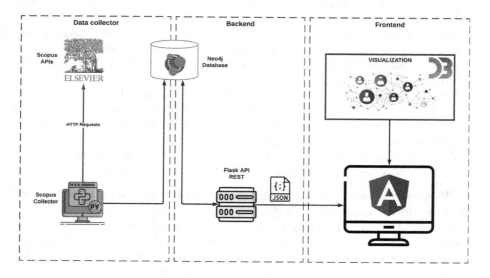

**Fig. 1.** System Architecture.

The architecture of the system is composed of three fundamental layers: i) a graph-oriented database, ii) a backend, and iii) a frontend. In addition, to carry out the data mining process, a set of Python scripts called *data collector* were

---

[3] https://dev.elsevier.com/.

developed. The data collector is the part of the system that is responsible for data extraction, data description, data quality verification, data selection, data cleaning, and data loading into the database through Python. The main sources for data extraction are the Scopus and ScienceDirect bibliographic databases, which consist of a set of APIs for extraction using the Elsevier developer platform.

The Neo4j database is used to store and manage the application data. On the other hand, the backend consists of a REST API built on Flask that provides a programming interface for the application to interact with the database. Finally, the frontend developed in Angular allows users to interact with the application intuitively and view the data stored in the database in a friendly way. In general, the system architecture allows for a clear separation of responsibilities and a high level of modularity in application design. Each part of the system fulfills a specific function and is designed to work independently, which makes it easy to update and maintain the system over time.

**Table 1.** Entities and attributes needed and data sources with their availability.

|  |  | Scopus | Science Direct |
|---|---|---|---|
| Article | Document ID | X | X |
|  | Title | X | X |
|  | Date of Publication | X | X |
|  | Author(s) | X | X |
|  | Affiliation(s) | X | X |
|  | Abstract | X | X |
|  | Complete Text |  | X |
|  | Keywords | X | X |
| Affiliation | Affiliation ID | X |  |
|  | Name | X |  |
|  | City | X |  |
|  | Country | X |  |
|  | Set of Articles with Affiliation | X |  |
|  | Set of Authors with Affiliation | X |  |
| Author | Author ID | X |  |
|  | Name | X |  |
|  | Current Affiliation | X |  |
|  | Past Affiliations | X |  |
|  | Set of Co-authors | X |  |
|  | Set of Articles of Author | X |  |

## 3.2  Knowledge of the Data for the Identification and Extraction of Academic Data

In this phase we identify the information that is necessary and its availability. The Table 1 lists the entities' attributes that are attainable through the data sources. Although ScienceDirect has the "Full Text" field available, which is one of the main fields for the data mining purpose, this data source does not have information for the Affiliation and Author entities. On the other hand, Scopus has at its disposal all the necessary fields, with the exception of the "Full text" field. In addition, Scopus indexes almost the entire ScienceDirect database. Therefore, Scopus is the only data source that will be used for data acquisition.

We developed a module in Python to consume data from the Scopus APIs (ScopusModule). The objective of the module is the automation of the consumption of the Scopus APIs. This module is based on the *ELSAPY* module developed by Elsevier. ScopusModule consists of the several classes. For instance, we developed a class that implements a client interface to api.elsevier.com. The rest of the classes need a client to execute the requests to the Scopus APIs. To initialize a client you must specify an API key and optionally an insttoken and an authtoken. Moreover, the classes to work with the APIs Affiliation Retrieval, Author Retrieval, Abstract Retrieval and Search (Affiliation Search, Author Search and Scopus Search) were specified.

**Data Acquisition.** The ScopusModule was employed in order to extract the data. Before making requests to the Scopus APIs, it is necessary to configure a client. For this task, the ScopusModule Client class is used. Due to the restrictions and quotas that the APIs have for general subscribers, an Institutional Token was requested to be able to extract all the required data. We configured the client with the automatically generated apikey in the Elsevier developer platform and the insttoken provided by the Elsevier integration support team together with the help of our institution's Libraries support team. After this, we proceeded to the extraction of articles.

With the Scopus Search API, all the articles whose affiliation or affiliations belong to Ecuador were extracted. This specification was defined through the search query. Then, 1623 requests were made and a total of 40556 articles were extracted. There were 1232 articles with incomplete authors but they were managed with the Abstract Retrieval API. With this, all articles containing missing information were recovered through the article IDs that were obtained in the previous step. In the same way, the affiliations were obtained from the articles that were previously extracted. In total, 5,372 Ecuadorian affiliations were found. Then, like the affiliations, the authors were extracted from the articles. In total, 39,225 authors with Ecuadorian affiliation were found. Finally, to validate the consistency and quality of the data, we verify completeness, correctness, occurrence of errors, and presence of missing values.

## 3.3  Data Preparation

The database model of this project is graph-oriented, which consists of nodes, edges and properties (Fig. 2). The Article, Author and Affiliation entities of the Scopus model have been parameterized as nodes in the graph-oriented model. Additionally, the Topic node is added, which contains the keywords of the articles. The edges that join the nodes are described as follows.

- An article belongs to an affiliation.
- An author is affiliated to an affiliation.
- An author wrote an article.
- An article uses a topic.
- An author is an expert on a topic.
- An author is co-author of another author, if they wrote an article together.

Finally, there are the properties for nodes to describe them. On the other hand, the only edge with properties (collab_strength) is the one that relates an author to another author.

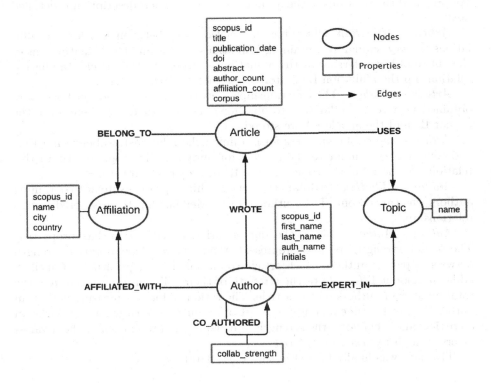

**Fig. 2.** Scopus Data Model.

In this phase, we decide which data will be stored in the database and which data will be used in the corpus for data mining purposes in next phase (text modeling fo Information Retrieval). All articles were stored in the database except for those that did not contain Ecuadorian affiliations. In the identification of the missing attributes and blank fields, 181 articles that did not have authors and/or affiliations were found. In addition, 423 records unrelated to Ecuadorian affiliations were detected. Therefore, the number of articles that were included is 39952. Next, the fields that were included for the articles are identifier, title, publication_date, doi and abstract. All articles in the database were part of the corpus for the purpose of the data mining component, except the articles without abstract, the articles that are corrections to other articles, and duplicate articles based on title and abstract. To identify these articles, the boolean type "corpus" field was used. In total there are 37526 articles that were used in the corpus. Regarding the selection of authors, only those who were related to some Ecuadorian affiliation were included. Therefore, the number of authors is 39225. The attributes included in the authors are identifier, auth_name, last_name, first_name and initials. Concerning the affiliations, only those identified as Ecuadorian will be included. Therefore, the number of affiliations is 5372. The attributes are identifier, affiliation_name, city, and country. We prepared the relations in the data model as well. Their description is detailed next.

*Article - Affiliation.* Obtaining the relationships between articles and affiliations is very similar to obtaining affiliations. While in the Affiliation entity the entire object referring to the affiliation is stored, in the article - affiliation relationship the affiliation ID is stored together with the article ID.

*Article - Author.* The relationships between articles and authors were obtained in a very similar way to obtaining the Author entity; here, only the author ID and the article ID are stored.

*Article - Topics.* The process for obtaining the relationships between article and topic is very similar to the process for obtaining the Topic entity. In this relationship the ID of the topic and the ID of the article are stored.

*Author - Affiliation.* To obtain this relationship, a process similar to obtaining authors was carried out. The Author ID and Membership ID are stored in this relationship.

*Author - Author.* This is the only relation or edge that has properties. The "collab_strength" property represents the measure of collaboration strength between a pair of authors. Each article co-authored by a given pair of authors adds an amount $1/(n-1)$ to the strength of their collaboration, where $n$ is the total number of authors on the article. The rationale for this measure is that an author divides his time among the $n-1$ other authors with whom he works on an article and, therefore, the strength of collaboration with each of them varies inversely with respect to $n-1$ [7].

The data was finally loaded in the Neo4j database.

### 3.4   Entity Modeling as Author and Academic Paper for Information Retrieval

In data modeling, TF-IDF was used to determine how relevant a word or words are in the corpus. TF-IDF is defined as a numerical measure of how relevant a word in a corpus is to a document. It refers to Term Frequency - Inverse Document Frequency. Relevance increases proportionally as the frequency of the word in a document (TF) increases, but is offset by the frequency of the word in the corpus (IDF) [8]. The steps were the following.

*1.* Generate two corpora with the processed text. The first corpus is made up of articles (title, abstract and topics of the article), while the second corpus is made up of authors (list of articles by the author). In the corpus per article, the aim is to determine the relevance of a word in an article. In the corpus by author, the aim is to determine the relevance of a word for an author based on his/her articles.

*2.* Obtain the sparse matrix of TF-IDF for each corpus containing the weights for each word. The columns of the sparse matrix correspond to the words of the corpus and the rows correspond to the articles or authors depending on the corpus established in step 1.

We prepared a strategy of evaluation for the two TF-IDF matrices obtained after training the models: i) get a random topic from the database, ii) in the event that the topic is made up of several words, the weights of each word will be added, iii) extract the documents (articles or authors depending on the corpus) that have the greatest weight for the topic, and iv) determine if the documents obtained are related to the topic.

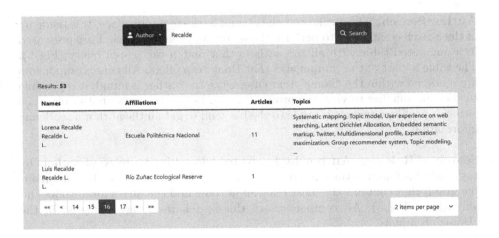

**Fig. 3.** Author Search Results.

## 3.5   Design and Coding of the Web System

This phase covers all aspects related to the structuring, organization and distribution of all the visual components of the system. The prototypes of the system user interfaces were created through the Figma tool. The interfaces were i) Search interface, ii) About interface, iii) Author information interface, iv) Search results of relevant author interface. The final design of the interfaces was evaluated with the Product Owner of the developing team. In general terms, the system is presented in next section.

## 4   Results

In this section, we present the final version of the developed application. It is deployed and ready for its use in the portal https://resnet-frontend.azurewebsites.net/home. Code and other resources are publicly available in terms of reproducibility at the following URLs: https://github.com/jozuenikolas/resnet-frontend, https://github.com/jozuenikolas/resnet-backend, and https://github.com/jozuenikolas/resnet-data-mining. We detail and present some screens of the web system and the results of the app evaluation.

### 4.1   Implementation of a Tool to Build Graphs and Retrieve Information

In this phase, we implement a D3 abstraction layer in Angular. In addition, we coded the author search results interface, the most relevant authors search results interface given a topic as a query, and the most relevant articles search results interface given a topic as a query.

**Author Search.** The author search is found in the main interface. It is made up of the Search component to perform the search and the results that are presented in a paginated table with all the authors that match the search query (Fig. 3). The table is part of the components that Bootstrap offers. All these components are rendered within the "home" template. Once the author is found, it is possible to click on him/her to view the profile (Fig. 4). Before the view that renders the author's profile, a request is made to the backend to get all the author's academic information.

**Search of Relevant Author by Keyword.** Searching for relevant authors by keyword(s) is found in the main interface. It is made up of the Search component, the graph that contains the most relevant authors and the filters for authors and affiliations (Fig. 5). All components of this search result are rendered in the "Home" template.

**Search of Relevant Articles by Keyword.** Like the other two searches, this one is also found in the "home" template. The interface is made up of the Search component, the publication year filter and the paginated table where the most relevant articles are presented (Fig. 6). In this interface there is also the modal to visualize in detail the information of an article.

### 4.2   Acceptability, Functionality and Integration Tests

To assess the acceptance of the system, a survey based on the TAM model (Technology Acceptance Model) was developed. The TAM model provides an

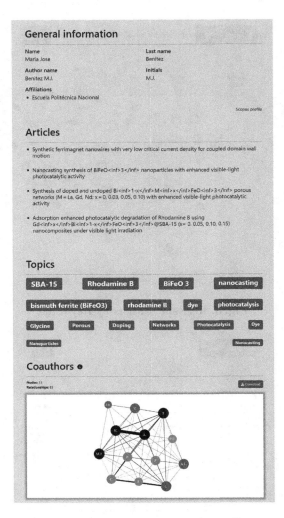

**Fig. 4.** Author Results Detail.

effective methodology to measure the acceptance of a system by focusing on two key aspects 1) ease of use and 2) perceived usefulness. Ease of use refers to the comfort and simplicity that users perceive when interacting with the system. On the other hand, the perceived usefulness focuses on how users value the benefits and advantages that the system offers. The survey was hosted on Google Forms and consisted of 6 questions distributed in the three search types provided by the system. Each type of search included a question to assess ease of use and another to measure perceived usefulness. The survey was structure as follows.

*Author Search:* 1. Was it easy to search for an author? 2. Was the information presented in the author profile useful?

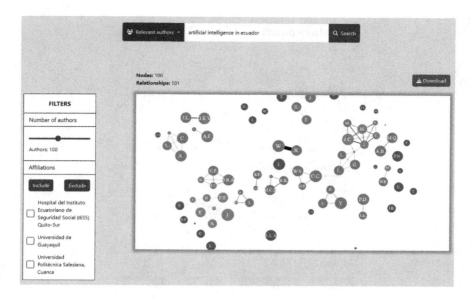

**Fig. 5.** Relevant Authors by Keywords.

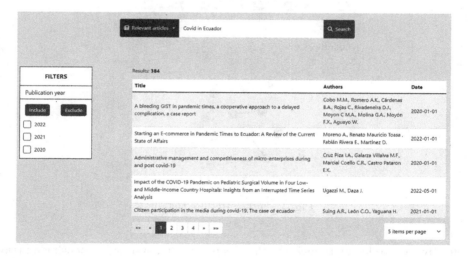

**Fig. 6.** Relevant Articles by Keywords.

*Relevant Authors Search:* 3. Was the graph of relevant authors clear and easy to understand? 4. Was the information presented useful in the search for relevant authors?

*Search for Relevant Articles:* 5. Was the search results table for relevant articles clear and easy to understand? 6. Was the information presented useful in the search for relevant articles?

To analyze the results of the evaluation, the responses of a total of 9 participants were considered, including master's degree students and professors from a University. Questions were rated on a scale of 1 to 5, with a higher score indicating greater ease of use or perceived usefulness. Accordingly, next we show a brief description of results.

**Easy of use.** The average results of the three questions that measure ease of use (Q1, Q3 and Q5) are 4.67, 4.11 and 4.56. These results reinforce the general perception of users about the comfort and simplicity they experienced when using the system.

**Perceived Usefulness.** The average results of the questions that measure perceived usefulness (Q2, Q4 and Q6) were 4.33, 4.89, and 4.78 respectively. These scores indicate that users recognize and value the usefulness that the application offers in various areas, such as finding collaborators, forming networks of researchers and the analysis of research topics.

# 5   Conclusions and Future Work

In terms of collaborative work, the search and selection of academics from different areas of knowledge to produce research is complicated, even more so, when there is no knowledge about their mutual links and their past research work. This project aims to help in the decision-making of Ecuadorian researchers when looking for collaborators in a particular research topic and forming a research network. In addition, it will support users to monitor trends and the latest advances in research topics, as well as meet and obtain information from their researchers. The project focuses on the development of a web tool based on Scrum and CRISP-DM. This platform allows the extraction and presentation of data from the co-authorship networks of researchers with Ecuadorian affiliation. The tool facilitates the visualization of academic information, the search for experts in specific research areas and the analysis of topics, keywords and related topics. In addition, we have implemented Information Retrieval techniques to improve the accuracy and relevance of the results in academic information searches. Indeed, for this task, text modeling with TF-IDF proved to be suitable.

The tool has been designed with the objective of providing an optimal and efficient experience for the end user in the exploration and analysis of academic information. Evaluation results have shown its usefulness and easy of use. It os worth mentioning that at the beginning of the project, there was no tool similar to this in Ecuador, but currently CEDIA has developed the REDI tool, which offers similar features. However, our proposal offers distinctive advantages such as increased output efficiency, the quantification of the strength of co-authorship shown in the edges of the corresponding graph, and a more intuitive interface for users' interaction. As a next step, we propose to carefully evaluate the advantages and functionalities of both tools, and consider possible collaborations or integrations to maximize the benefits and offer an even more complete experience to users and researchers.

For future work we suggest implementing an affiliation search function by topic in the application. This functionality will allow users to enter a topic of interest and visualize a graph that represents the connections between the different affiliations related to that topic. This will facilitate the identification of potential collaborators and will strengthen the capacity to establish academic links between universities. In addition, we are working to develop a reporting module, where a set of data visualizations make up an interactive dashboard that can be used as a decision-making tool. We hope to have some of the reporting attributes like those featured in CiteSpace [3], geared especially for the Ecuadorian audience. Finally, regarding the data used, we consider that research papers indexed in databases other than Elsevier could be used to broaden the academics' profiles.

**Acknowledgements.** The authors gratefully acknowledge the financial support provided by the Escuela Politécnica Nacional, for the registration of the article in the proceedings of the TICEC2023 conference.

# References

1. Adams, J.: The rise of research networks. Nature **490**(7420), 335–336 (2012)
2. Baijens, J., Helms, R., Iren, D.: Applying Scrum in data science projects. In: 2020 IEEE 22nd Conference on Business Informatics (CBI), vol. 1, pp. 30–38. IEEE (2020)
3. Chen, C.: Visualizing and exploring scientific literature with Citespace: an introduction. In: Proceedings of the 2018 Conference on Human Information Interaction & Retrieval, pp. 369–370 (2018)
4. Kumar, S.: Co-authorship networks: a review of the literature. Aslib J. Inf. Manage. **67**, 55–73 (2015)
5. Liu, J., Tang, T., Wang, W., Xu, B., Kong, X., Xia, F.: A survey of scholarly data visualization. IEEE Access **6**, 19205–19221 (2018). https://doi.org/10.1109/ACCESS.2018.2815030
6. Miller, J.J.: Graph database applications and concepts with Neo4j. In: In Proceedings of the Southern Association for Information Systems Conference (SAIS), vol. 2324 (2013)
7. Newman, M.E.J.: Coauthorship networks and patterns of scientific collaboration. Proc. Natl. Acad. Sci. **101**(suppl_1), 5200–5205 (2004). https://doi.org/10.1073/pnas.0307545100
8. Ramos, J., et al.: Using TF-IDF to determine word relevance in document queries. In: Proceedings of the First Instructional Conference on Machine Learning, vol. 242, pp. 29–48. Citeseer (2003)
9. Recalde, L., Baquerizo, G., Zunino, E.: Women in politics and their presence in Twitter: Argentina as a case study. In: 2019 Sixth International Conference on eDemocracy & eGovernment (ICEDEG), pp. 236–241. IEEE (2019)
10. Rodriguez-Morales, A.J., Bonilla-Aldana, D.K., Rodriguez-Morales, A.G.: Publicar desde américa latina.¿ en dónde estamos? - publishing from latin america.¿ Where are we? Revista Ecuatoriana de Neurología **27**(3), 12–14 (2018)
11. Sagar, G., Syrovatskyi, V.: System design: architecting robust, scalable, and modular applications. In: Technical Building Blocks: A Technology Reference for Real-world Product Development, pp. 105–168. Springer, Cham (2022). https://doi.org/10.1007/978-1-4842-8658-6_3

12. Saltz, J.S., Sutherland, A., Hotz, N.: Achieving lean data science agility via data driven Scrum. In: HICSS, pp. 1–10 (2022)
13. Schwaber, K., Sutherland, J.: The Scrum guide, the definitive guide to Scrum: the rules of the game, November 2020 (2022)
14. Wirth, R., Hipp, J.: CRISP-DM: towards a standard process model for data mining. In: Proceedings of the 4th International Conference on the Practical Applications of Knowledge Discovery and Data Mining (2000)
15. Yoghourdjian, V., Yang, Y., Dwyer, T., Lawrence, L., Wybrow, M., Marriott, K.: Scalability of network visualisation from a cognitive load perspective. IEEE Trans. Vis. Comput. Graph. **27**(2), 1677–1687 (2020)

# Visualization Models Applied to Atmospheric Pollutants and Meteorological Variables: A Systematic Literature Review

Andrés Patiño-León(✉) ⓘ, Alexandra Bermeoⓘ, Marcos Orellanaⓘ, and Edisson Andrés Piña-Mejía

Universidad del Azuay, Cuenca, Ecuador
{andpatino,alexbermeo,marore}@uazuay.edu.ec,
Edisson640@es.uazuay.edu.ec

**Abstract.** Air pollution is harmful to human health, which is why it has become a great global concern. Most of the studies analyzed use sensors to monitor air quality and data mining techniques are applied to analyze and identify patterns of air pollutants. However, for these studies, no systematic reviews have been presented that address the use of graphical representations applying models and visualization techniques for air quality. This research presents a systematic review to synthesize primary studies that refer to visualization models and techniques that include data mining techniques, applied to atmospheric pollutants and meteorological variables. 746 articles were extracted, of which only 84 articles were selected after applying the exclusion and inclusion criteria and the quality assessment.

**Keywords:** Atmospheric pollutants · Data mining · Meteorological variables · Visualization models · Visualization techniques

## 1 Introduction

In recent decades, urban and industrial growth has caused an increase in environmental pollution, which represents a serious risk to people's health. To limit the harmful effects of polluting chemicals on the population, tasks such as the identification, classification and control of these elements have become very important.

Studies have also determined that air pollution is directly related to respiratory and cardiovascular pathologies, diabetes, cancer, among others. It has been determined that exposure to a high particulate matter environment has serious consequences on people's health [1]. Furthermore, because of pollution, air quality has decreased considerably, contributing negatively to global warming and ozone layer depletion [2].

Also, to present information on how atmospheric pollutants and methodological variables generate harmful effects on human health, visual and graphic resources are used. Therefore, it is necessary to gather the information generated, by means of an analysis involving visualization techniques [3]. It is important to consider that pollution models of atmospheric variables have a great diversity of variables, so a clear and immediate representation is necessary.

J. Maldonado-Mahauad et al. (Eds.): TICEC 2023, CCIS 1885, pp. 464–481, 2023.
https://doi.org/10.1007/978-3-031-45438-7_31

To determine the current status of models applied to atmospheric pollutants and meteorological variables, a systematic review will synthesize relevant studies. The model proposed by Kitchenham and Charters [4] will be used. The objective is to establish gaps in research on models and visualization techniques applied to atmospheric pollutants and meteorological variables. To carry out this systematic literature review, the most recent articles will be considered due to the scarcity of studies related to the research topic.

## 2 Related Work

Several systematic reviews or mappings can be found in the scientific literature that aim to inquire about the state of the art of models applied to atmospheric pollutants and meteorological variables. The authors of [5] present a systematic review using a bibliometric method to review the status of research related to statistical methods for air pollution predictions. The results indicated that the studies focus on the effects of pollution on diseases, urban pollution exposure models, and land use regression (LUR); while the most investigated pollutants are particulate matter (PM), Nitrogen Oxide (NOx), and Ozone (O3). The artificial neural network (ANN) method is the preferred method in PM and O3 studies, while LUR is widely used in NOx studies.

Also, [6] conducted a systematic review of statistical analyses focused on atmospheric pollutants and meteorological variables. The study focuses on three methods: principal component analysis (PCA), cluster analysis (CA) and path regression analysis (TRA); the same ones applied to pollutants such as PM. Studies that analyze the relationship between meteorological variables and atmospheric pollutants were also included, as well as those that combine the three techniques. The results show that the TRA method is a relevant technique for identifying sources of air pollutant emissions, although it can be improved by incorporating time series. In the future, it is expected that other pollutants can be studied using TRA, as well as including more regions, since there are no studies in Latin America, Asia, Africa or Oceania that use this technique.

Similarly, the authors of [7] present a systematic review on the application of data mining and machine learning methods in the study of air pollution. In the first instance, the most used technique was ANN, however, in recent times decision trees, support vector machines, k-means and the APRIORI algorithm have been widely used. Areas with great potential for future applications include deep learning and geospatial pattern mining.

Finally, [8] present a brief review of air quality models in relation to aspects such as the prediction of pollution health effects. AirQ models were analyzed, the same that use mathematical and numerical approximations to simulate physical and chemical processes of pollutants and their dispersion. As a result, it is observed that most studies focus on the effects of a single pollutant and do not consider their combination, which is why it is necessary to develop evaluation and management methods that consider these scenarios.

# 3   Methodology

A systematic literature review is a research method that allows to obtain, evaluate and construe the information associated with a defined research question or area of interest. For this, it is necessary to follow a methodology; for this paper, the one proposed by Barbara Kitchenham and Stuart Charters [4] is used, which has three stages, planning, execution and presentation of results.

## 3.1   Planning

The first stage in the literature review is planning, where the research questions to be answered, search strategies and inclusion and extraction criteria to obtain the data are defined. An initial search was made in the most representative digital libraries, with the objective of determining the need for this review. The results were not satisfactory, a situation that motivates the development of this review.

**Research Questions.** The following research questions have been defined to extract and organize the information obtained. RQ1: What models and data visualization techniques have been used to present results of air pollutant and meteorological variables? RQ2: How is data processing for the analysis of air pollutants and meteorological variables approached in data science? and RQ3: How are air pollutant and meteorological variable visualization models addressed in the presentation of results?

**Review Protocol.** To define the steps to follow when developing the systematic literature review, a protocol is established, to reduce the possibility of bias when selecting the studies and having an orderly and organized data extraction.

*Selection of Digital Libraries.* For the literature search to answer the questions posed, the study of several primary sources was considered, taking into consideration the most relevant ones in the areas of computer science life sciences. The search methods of each library were researched to make simpler the extraction of information on each engine. The used digital libraries are IEEE, ACM, Science Direct and SpringerLink.

*Search String.* To perform an automatic search in each of the aforementioned libraries, a search string was defined, which was applied to the exact same metadata (title, abstract and keywords) in the chosen libraries. The search string is *(air pollutants OR air quality OR meteorological variables) AND (data visualization OR VIZ) AND models.*

*Inclusion and Exclusion Criteria.* Once the articles have been retrieved from each digital library, it is necessary to decide which ones are definitely going to be part of the review. To do this, criteria for inclusion and exclusion needs to be defined. For the inclusion, any study that meets at least one of the following criteria, is considered: i) Studies that present information on models applied on atmospheric pollutants and/or meteorological variables, ii) Studies presenting information on techniques applied on atmospheric pollutants and meteorological variables, and iii) Accessible articles. Moreover, any article does meet any of the following exclusion criteria, will not be considered: i) Duplicate publications of the same study in different sources, ii) Short articles with less than five pages, iii) Gray literature, which does not have a DOI and iv) Studies that have not been written in English.

## 3.2  Conducting the Review

This is the second stage of the systematic literature review methodology, where the previous stage is executed to obtain data to be analyzed. Once the search was performed, using the string and the initial pool of articles is selected by the authors using the inclusion and exclusion criteria. Then, the quality of the articles must be evaluated, for this, a three-point Likert scale questionnaire is used, which has two subjective closed-questions and two objective closed-questions. The stated questions are: 1) Does the study present issues on visualization models applied on atmospheric pollutants and meteorological variables, 2) Does the study present issues on air quality? 3) Has the study been published in a relevant journal or conference? and 4) Has the study been cited by other authors?

Moreover, to answer each of the research questions, a set of data extraction criteria was defined. The use of this extraction criteria, guarantee that all the data is extracted using the same concepts and criteria by the authors, and the synthesis is easier to perform. The extraction criteria are presented on Table 1.

**Table 1.** Data extraction criteria

| RQ1: What models and data visualization techniques have been used to present results of air pollutant and meteorological variables? | | |
|---|---|---|
| EC02 | Air quality | Particulate matter, ozone, carbon monoxide, sulfur dioxide, nitrogen dioxide |
| EC05 | Types of graphs | Bar, line, circular, area, cone, cylindrical, bubble, heat map, cartogram, grid, box-bigots, histogram |
| EC06 | Dimensionality | One-dimensional, bi-dimensional, three-dimensional |
| EC07 | Visualization techniques | Hierarchical, icon-based, pixel-oriented, graphic-based, hybrid, geometric |
| EC08 | Models | Nested model, pipeline model, ARIMA statistical model, perceptual processing model |
| RQ2: How is data processing for the analysis of air pollutants and meteorological variables approached in data science? | | |
| EC09 | Data processing | Interpolation, sampling, distance measurement |
| EC10 | Data mining techniques | Association rule, classification, prediction, text mining, clustering |
| EC11 | Algorithms | A-priori, FP-growth (frequent growth pattern), RARM (fast association rule mining), decision tree, neural networks, statistics, logistic regression, text data mining, k-Means |
| RQ3: How are air pollutant and meteorological variable visualization models addressed in the presentation of results? | | |
| EC12 | Type of validation | Experiment, proof of concept, case study |
| EC13 | Methodology | New, extension |
| EC14 | Approach scope | Academy, industry |
| EC15 | Type of analysis | Descriptive, predictive, prescriptive |

## 4   Results

The execution of the literature review was divided in phases, as follows:

*Systematic Search.* The search string was applied in the selected digital libraries, applying the filters according to each one. As an initial resulta, there were obtained 746 papers.

*First Screening of Papers.* Due to the number of obtained papers, it is required to filter them based on the title of each paper, so the papers that do not fall into the scope of this review are discarded. At this stage, 621 papers were discarded.

*Second Screening of Papers.* At this stage, the papers were filtered according to the inclusion and exclusion criteria, after the review of the title, abstract and keywords. Each paper was labeled as "Accepted" or "Rejected", accordingly. For use on the next phase, 125 papers were selected.

*Third Screening of Papers.* In this phase, the divergences and doubts in the selection of certain studies from the previous phase were resolved and quality criteria were applied, resulting in 84 selected articles. The applied process is presented in Fig. 1.

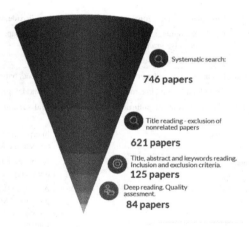

**Fig. 1.** Process for the selection of papers

After the analysis of the variables, it is determined that the following are the parameters to evaluate:

- EC10: Data mining techniques and EC08: Models
- EC07: Visualization techniques, EC02: Air quality, EC05: Types of graphs
- EC11: Algorithms and EC09: Data processing
- EC09: Data processing and EC02: Air quality
- EC15: Type of analysis, EC06: Dimensionality and EC07: Visualization techniques

## 5 Discussion

After the performing of this systematic literature review, the study presents which are the models and data visualization techniques that have been applied for the analysis of atmospheric pollutants and other meteorological variables.

### Comparison of EC10: Data Mining Techniques and EC08: Models

Figure 2 shows the information on the data mining techniques used into different visualization models. The most relevant information is found in the perceptual processing model, where data mining is applied using the classification technique in five articles: [S006, S013, S021, S022, S046] (Appendix A).

Similarly, prediction techniques are used in three articles [S003, S014, S021] and clustering techniques in two articles [S027, S032] (Appendix A). There is a lack of research on the ARIMA statistical model, since there are few studies using data mining with association, prediction or clustering rules. The research that used the ARIMA statistical model with the aforementioned data mining techniques are: [S008, S049, S058] (Appendix A). There are no articles that apply the ARIMA model with text mining.

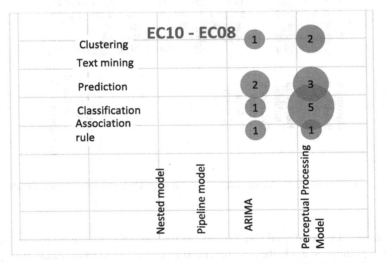

**Fig. 2.** Comparison of EC10: Data mining techniques and EC08: Models

As presented in Fig. 2, the nested and pipeline model have not been used for any study with data mining techniques. Most of the articles collected apply analytical, statistical and predictive models; focusing only on the part of the pipeline model related to data analysis, without considering other stages such as filtering, allocation and representation. A similar case occurs with the nested method, whose processes (target, translation, design and implementation) are not considered in an integral way but are combined with others.

### Comparison of EC07: Visualization Techniques, EC02: Air Quality and EC05: Types of Graphs

The most relevant studies are shown in Fig. 3, in which visualization techniques have been applied to the most relevant air pollutants in the context of air quality analysis. It is evident that icon-based, hybrid and graph-based visualization techniques correspond to 90% of the total number of articles: [S002-S006, S008, S010-S014, S016-S019, S021, S022, S025, S026, S028-S039, S041-S051, S053-S057, S059, S060, S062-S068, S070, S071, S073, S074, S076, S078-S084] (Appendix A).

The other techniques, such as hierarchical, pixel-oriented and geometric; have 10% of the results. Different types of graphs such as bar, line, pie, area, heat maps and cartograms have also been applied; present in 75% of the total studies. Meanwhile, bubble charts, network, histograms and whisker box have 25% of the total number of articles. Finally, it can be evidenced that there are no studies that have applied types of graphs such as cones and cylinders.

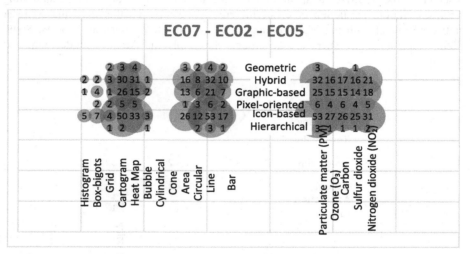

**Fig. 3.** Comparison of EC07: Visualization techniques, EC02: Air quality and EC05: Types of graphs

Moreover, the icon-based visualization technique is the most used to evaluate environmental pollutants, while the pollutant most analyzed in different studies is particulate matter. As for the types of graphics used, the icon-based technique makes use mainly of cartograms, line graphs and heat maps; the first being important because it allows identifying areas where the air quality index is more critical. No important representations have been found for the hierarchical and geometric techniques.

**Comparison of EC11: Algorithms and EC09: Data Processing**

Figure 4 shows that processing has a great impact on the data mining algorithms. It is evident that the statistical algorithm has 10 articles for interpolation, whilst 12 articles are related to the sampling technique and 4 articles linked to distance measurement processing are detected. The mentioned articles correspond to: [S001, S003-S005, S008, S009, S014, S021, S049, S056, S065, S067, S072, S075, S078, S082, S083] (Appendix A).

Also, data processing applied to neural networks has been used in six, nine and four papers, for interpolation, sampling and distance measurement respectively. The related studies are: [S001, S005, S006, S013, S021, S022, S049, S051, S069, S077, S083] (Appendix A). Regarding k-means, logistic regression, decision tree and a-priori algorithms, there are few research results that have applied data processing for the analysis of air pollutants. Similarly, it is evident that there are no studies that employ interpolation, sampling and distance measurement for the FP-growth algorithm, text mining and RARM.

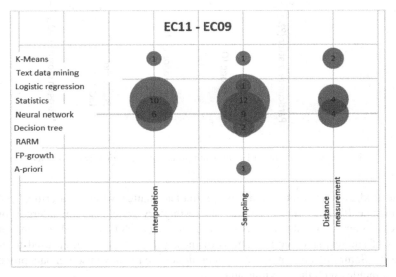

**Fig. 4.** Comparison of EC11: Algorithms and EC09: Data processing

Data sampling used sensors to measure air quality in urban and rural areas, so the data obtained depend on the quality and capacity of the sensor, which could cause anomalous readings in case of malfunctions or calibration errors. Interpolation is the second most used alternative for data processing, since it allows using quantified points to evaluate values at unknown points.

**Comparison of EC09: Data Processing and EC02: Air Quality**
Figure 5 shows the results of the analysis between data processing and air pollutants that affect air quality. The analyzed studies point out that the sampling technique is the most used for the analysis of environmental pollutants, and involves the studies: [S001-S011, S014, S018, S022, S023, S025, S027, S037, S039, S043, S049-S051, S057, S059, S060, S063, S065, S066, S069, S072-S074, S076-S078, S080, S083] (Appendix A).

Additionally, there are several articles that have applied interpolation for data processing: [S001, S003, S013, S016, S021, S026, S041, S044, S049, S050-S052, S056, S059, S066, S067, S071, S073, S075, S078, S079, S083, S084] (Appendix A). The distance measurement technique is only used in a few investigations.

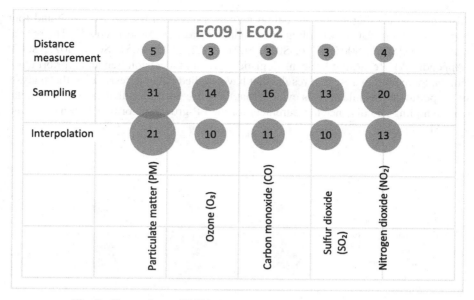

**Fig. 5.** Comparison of EC09: Data processing and EC02: Air quality

The studies concentrate mainly on particulate matter, which is a critical pollutant for human health, since it can penetrate the respiratory system causing allergies or other diseases. Other pollutants such as $O_3$, CO, $SO_2$ and $NO_2$ are analyzed in a similar number of studies, since combinations of these parameters are often used to analyze air quality. Sampling and interpolation techniques are the most used in data processing, which coincides with the previous analysis.

### Comparison of EC15: Type of Analysis, EC06: Dimensionality and EC07: Visualization Techniques

Figure 6 shows that most of the analyzed studies have applied visualization techniques, with graphics of different dimensionality, to apply predictive analysis. For the hybrid type there are 25 articles, for the technique called "graph-based" there are 14 articles, and for the "icon-based" technique there are 36 articles. The articles are: [S001, S002-S006, S008, S010, S011, S014, S019, S021, S022, S025, S028, S038, S043, S046, S049-S052, S054-S056, S059, S060, S065-S069, S072, S073, S075, S076, S078-S080, S082, S083] (Appendix A).

The results obtained for the type of dimensionality indicate that there are several articles that deal with the same type of analysis, these studies are: [S001-S011, S014, S015, S019-S025, S028, S038, S043, S046, S049-S052, S054-S056, S058- S060, S065-S069, S072, S073, S075-S080, S082, S083] (Appendix A). On the other hand, there are few articles that focus on descriptive analysis, employing visualization techniques with different dimensionality. It is evident that there is a deficit of articles with a prescriptive analysis.

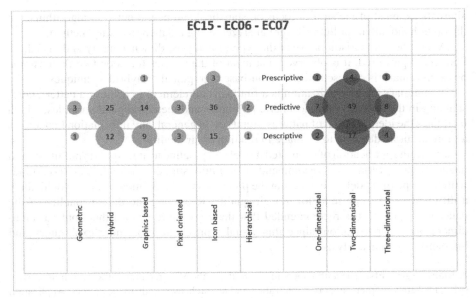

**Fig. 6.** Comparison of EC15: Type of analysis, EC06: Dimensionality and EC07: Visualization techniques

Visualization techniques and graphical dimensionality types have allowed researchers to make predictive analyses based on different patterns of air pollutants over similar time periods. This has allowed the development of recommender systems, which allow the assessment of the health risk associated with air quality when exercising or engaging in outdoor activities.

## 6   Conclusion

This paper presented a systematic literature review on visualization models applied to atmospheric pollutants and meteorological variables, using the methodology proposed by Barbara Kitchenham and Stuart Charters. Based on the results, it was determined that perceptual processing is the most widely used model for the visualization of these elements, followed by the ARIMA model, which is present in only a few articles. As for the data mining techniques used, it is worth mentioning clustering, prediction, classification and association rules, while there are no studies using text mining.

In relation to the comparison of visualization techniques with the types of graphics, all the pollutants established in the criteria have been represented with some technique, mainly with those based on graphs, icons and hybrids. The most referenced graphics in the studies correspond to bar, line, circular, area, heat maps and cartograms.

The analysis of the data processing methods along with the algorithms, or with the atmospheric variables, indicates that all the techniques are applied, with sampling being the most used. As for the referenced algorithms, although there is a diverse range of alternatives, most of the studies focus on statistical and neural network algorithms. On the other hand, all air pollutants were analyzed using a data processing method.

About the comparison between the type of analysis, dimensionality and visualization techniques used, it is observed that most of the articles focus on two-dimensional predictive analysis represented with icon-based, graphical or hybrid techniques.

In summary, data visualization is a fundamental element to achieve a better understanding in the analysis of atmospheric pollutants and meteorological variables, which facilitates the identification of patterns, trends or, in general, any information that allows a more accurate decision to be made in relation to air quality.

Lastly, the application of the nested model and pipeline to atmospheric pollutants and meteorological variables is recommended for future studies, since there are no articles with this type of models. Considering the processes that these models offer would allow a different visual representation for air quality. Regarding the dimensionality of the data visualization, it is recommended that there are more studies that apply a three-dimensional representation, since this visual representation is more exploratory and interactive for data analysis.

**Acknowledgements.** The authors would like to thank the Vice-rectorate of Research of Universidad del Azuay for their support in innovation and research, especially to the project "Application of data mining in the analysis of associations between atmospheric pollutants and meteorological variables, stage VI". As well as the entire staff from the Computer Science Research & Development Laboratory (LIDI).

## Appendix A

| Key | Authors | Title |
| --- | --- | --- |
| S001 | Ma, Rui; Liu, Ning; Xu, Xiangxiang; Wang, Yue; Noh, Hae Young; Zhang, Pei; Zhang, Lin | A Deep Autoencoder Model for Pollution Map Recovery with Mobile Sensing Networks |
| S002 | Chu, Kuo.-Chung.; Xiao, Min.-Yang | A Study on the Correlation between Breast Cancer and Air pollution |
| S003 | Garzon, S; Walther, S; Pang, S; Deva, B; Kupper, A | Urban Air Pollution Alert Service for Smart Cities |
| S004 | Chen, Cheng-Chen; Chen, Li-Hsuan; Guo, Meng-Han | Integration of Building Interface and Smart Sensor Network to Control Indoor Air Pollution through Internet of Things |
| S005 | Abdullah, Samsuri; Ismail, Marzuki; Ahmed, Ali Najah; Mansor, Wan Nurdiyana Wan | Big Data Analytics and Artificial Intelligence in Air Pollution Studies for the Prediction of Particulate Matter Concentration |
| S006 | Schurholz, Daniel; Nurgazy, Meruyert; Zaslavsky, Arkady; Jayaraman, Prem Prakash; Kubler, Sylvain; Mitra, Karan; Saguna, Saguna | MyAQI: Context-aware Outdoor Air Pollution Monitoring System |

*(continued)*

(*continued*)

| Key | Authors | Title |
| --- | --- | --- |
| S007 | R. K. Grace; K. Aishvarya S.; B. Monisha; A. Kaarthik | Analysis and Visualization of Air Quality Using Real Time Pollutant Data |
| S008 | B. U. Kempaiah; B. Charan; R. J. Mampilli | Data Analysis of Air Pollutant Levels in India |
| S009 | K. Verma; S. Mathur; S. K. Khatri | Study on Temperature Variation Pattern Based on Data Analytics |
| S010 | A. Rebeiro-Hargrave; N. H. Motlagh; S. Varjonen; E. Lagerspetz; P. Nurmi; S. Tarkoma | MegaSense: Cyber-Physical System for Real-time Urban Air Quality Monitoring |
| S011 | M. Nurgazy; A. Zaslavsky; P. P. Jayaraman; S. Kubler; K. Mitra; S. Saguna | CAVisAP: Context-Aware Visualization of Outdoor Air Pollution with IoT Platforms |
| S012 | Z. Liao; Y. Peng; Y. Li; X. Liang; Y. Zhao | A Web-Based Visual Analytics System for Air Quality Monitoring Data |
| S013 | Y. Zeng; Y. S. Chang; Y. H. Fang | Data Visualization for Air Quality Analysis on Bigdata Platform |
| S014 | C. Bachechi; F. Desimoni; L. Po; D. M. Casas | Visual analytics for spatio-temporal air quality data |
| S015 | S. Kaur; S. Bawa; S. Sharma | IoT Enabled Low-Cost Indoor Air Quality Monitoring System with Botanical Solutions |
| S016 | N. Ya'acob; A. Azize; N. M. Adnan; A. L. Yusof; S. S. Sarnin | Haze Monitoring based on Air Pollution Index (API) and Geographic Information System (GIS) |
| S017 | A. R. M. Forkan; G. Kimm; A. Morshed; P. P. Jayaraman; A. Banerjee; W. Huang | AqVision: A Tool for Air Quality Data Visualisation and Pollution-free Route Tracking for Smart City |
| S018 | D. Petrova-Antonova; S. Baychev; I. Pavlova; G. Pavlov | Air Quality Visual Analytics with Kibana |
| S019 | V. Rao; M. Singh; P. Mohapatra | SmartAIR: Smart energy efficient framework for large network of air quality monitoring systems |
| S020 | A. Sharma; B. Mishra; R. Sutaria; R. Zele | Design and Development of Low-cost Wireless Sensor Device for Air Quality Networks |
| S021 | T. H. Do; E. Tsiligianni; X. Qin; J. Hofman; V. P. La Manna; W. Philips; N. Deligiannis | Graph-Deep-Learning-Based Inference of Fine-Grained Air Quality from Mobile IoT Sensors |
| S022 | Y. Yang; Z. Bai; Z. Hu; Z. Zheng; K. Bian; L. Song | AQNet: Fine-Grained 3D Spatio-Temporal Air Quality Monitoring by Aerial-Ground WSN |

(*continued*)

(*continued*)

| Key | Authors | Title |
|-----|---------|-------|
| S023 | S. Yarragunta; M. A. Nabi; J. P; R. S | Prediction of Air Pollutants Using Supervised Machine Learning |
| S024 | F. -C. Adochiei; Åž.. -. T. Nicolescu; I. -R. Adochiei; G. -C. Seritan; B. -A. Enache; F. -C. Argatu; D. Costin | Electronic System for Real-Time Indoor Air Quality Monitoring |
| S025 | Z. Deng; D. Weng; J. Chen; R. Liu; Z. Wang; J. Bao; Y. Zheng; Y. Wu | AirVis: Visual Analytics of Air Pollution Propagation |
| S026 | Zhuo Tang; W. Xiong; L. Chen; Ning Jing | A Real-Time System for Air Quality Monitoring Based on Main-Memory Database |
| S027 | D. Engel; K. Greff; C. Garth; K. Bein; A. Wexler; B. Hamann; H. Hagen | Visual Steering and Verification of Mass Spectrometry Data Factorization in Air Quality Research |
| S028 | V. Chang; P. Ni; Y. Li | K-Clustering Methods for Investigating Social Environmental and Natural-Environmental Features Based on Air Quality Index |
| S029 | R. Narango; M. Almeida; R. Zalakeviciute; Y. Rybarczyk; M. Gonzalez | AirQ2: Quito Air Quality Monitoring and Visualization Tool |
| S030 | J. J. Henriques; B. Bojarski; K. W. Byrd; M. Von Wald | Crowd-sourcing Urban Air-quality in Developing Countries through Open Source Technologies |
| S031 | P. Buono; F. Balducci | A Web App for Visualizing Electronic Nose Data |
| S032 | Z. Zhou; Z. Ye; Y. Liu; F. Liu; Y. Tao; W. Su | Visual Analytics for Spatial Clusters of Air-Quality Data |
| S033 | V. Ladekar; R. Daruwala | Indoor Air Quality Monitoring on AWS Using MQTT Protocol |
| S034 | R. A. Myshko; N. I. Kurakina | GIS for Assessment and Modeling Air Pollution by Industrial Facilities |
| S035 | X. Yang; E. Xie; L. Cuthbert | Cluster Segregation for Indoor and Outdoor Environmental Monitoring System |
| S036 | J. MolnÃ¡r; T. Lorinc; O. Slavko | Design and Implementation of an Intelligent Air Quality Sensor |
| S037 | Y. Yang; L. Li | A Smart Sensor System for Air Quality Monitoring and Massive Data Collection |
| S038 | Y. Y. Fridelin; M. R. Ulil Albaab; A. R. Anom Besari; S. Sukaridhoto; A. Tjahjono | Implementation of Microservice Architectures on SEMAR Extension For Air Quality Monitoring |

(*continued*)

(*continued*)

| Key | Authors | Title |
|---|---|---|
| S039 | Y. Ben-Aboud; M. Ghogho; A. Kobbane | A research-oriented low-cost air pollution monitoring IoT platform |
| S040 | G. Vicente; G. Marques | Air Quality Monitoring through LoRa Technologies: A Literature Review |
| S041 | A. I. Prados; G. Leptoukh; C. Lynnes; J. Johnson; H. Rui; A. Chen; R. B. Husar | Access, Visualization, and Interoperability of Air Quality Remote Sensing Data Sets via the Giovanni Online Tool |
| S042 | R. Taborda; N. Datia; M. P. M. Pato; J. M. Pires | Exploring air quality using a multiple spatial resolution dashboard—a case study in Lisbon |
| S043 | I. Gruicin; M. -E. Ionascu; M. Popa | A Solution for Air Quality Monitoring and Forecasting |
| S044 | K. Ren; Y. Wu; H. Zhang; J. Fu; D. Qu; X. Lin | Visual Analytics of Air Pollution Propagation Through Dynamic Network Analysis |
| S045 | A. M. Hussain; S. B. Azmy; A. Abuzrara; K. Al-Hajjaji; A. Hassan; H. Khamdan; M. Ezzin; A. Hassani; N. Zorba | UAV-based Semi-Autonomous Data Acquisition and Classification |
| S046 | Q. Shen; Y. Wu; Y. Jiang; W. Zeng; A. K. H. LAU; A. Vianova; H. Qu | Visual Interpretation of Recurrent Neural Network on Multi-dimensional Time-series Forecast |
| S047 | D. Marquez-Viloria; J. S. Botero-Valencia; J. Villegas-Ceballos | A low cost georeferenced air-pollution measurement system used as early warning tool |
| S048 | D. Ortiz; D. S. Benítez; W. Fuertes; J. Torres | On the Use of Low Cost Sensors for the Implementation of a Real-Time Air Pollution Monitoring System Using Wireless Sensor Networks |
| S049 | S. Iordache; D. Dunea; E. Lungu; L. Predescu; D. Dumitru; C. Ianache; R. Ianache | A Cyberinfrastructure for Air Quality Monitoring and Early Warnings to protect Children with Respiratory Disorders |
| S050 | Noi, Evgeny; Murray, Alan T | Interpolation biases in assessing spatial heterogeneity of outdoor air quality in Moscow, Russia |
| S051 | Ren, Xiang; Mi, Zhongyuan; Georgopoulos, Panos G | Comparison of Machine Learning and Land Use Regression for fine scale spatiotemporal estimation of ambient air pollution: Modeling ozone concentrations across the contiguous United States |

(*continued*)

(*continued*)

| Key | Authors | Title |
|-----|---------|-------|
| S052 | Xu, Chengcheng; Zhao, Jingya; Liu, Pan | A geographically weighted regression approach to investigate the effects of traffic conditions and road characteristics on air pollutant emissions |
| S053 | Yuan, Ye; Chuai, Xiaowei; Zhao, Rongqin; Lu, Qinli; Huang, Xianjin; Xiang, Changzhao; Yuan, Xiaolan; Gao, Runyi; Lu, Yue; Huang, Xianyang; Guo, Xiaomin; Zhuang, Qizhi | Tracing China's external driving sources and internal emission hotspots of export-driven PM10 emission |
| S054 | Díaz, Juan José; Mura, Ivan; Franco, Juan Felipe; Akhavan-Tabatabaei, Raha | aiRe - A web-based R application for simple, accessible and repeatable analysis of urban air quality data |
| S055 | Ren, Chen; Cao, Shi-Jie | Implementation and visualization of artificial intelligent ventilation control system using fast prediction models and limited monitoring data |
| S056 | Reyes, Jeanette M.; Xu, Yadong; Vizuete, William; Serre, Marc L | Regionalized PM2.5 Community Multiscale Air Quality model performance evaluation across a continuous spatiotemporal domain |
| S057 | Collier-Oxandale, Ashley; Feenstra, Brandon; Papapostolou, Vasileios; Polidori, Andrea | AirSensor v1.0: Enhancements to the open-source R package to enable deep understanding of the long-term performance and reliability of PurpleAir sensors |
| S058 | Coulibaly, Lassana; Kamsu-Foguem, Bernard; Tangara, Fana | Rule-based machine learning for knowledge discovering in weather data |
| S059 | Hsieh, Ming-Tsuen; Peng, Chiung-Yu; Chung, Wen-Yu; Lai, Chin-Hsing; Huang, Shau-Ku; Lee, Chon-Lin | Simulating the spatiotemporal distribution of BTEX with an hourly grid-scale model |
| S060 | Ma, Jun; Ding, Yuexiong; Cheng, Jack C. P.; Jiang, Feifeng; Tan, Yi; Gan, Vincent J. L.; Wan, Zhiwei | Identification of high impact factors of air quality on a national scale using big data and machine learning techniques |
| S061 | Singh, Manmeet; Singh, Bhupendra Bahadur; Singh, Raunaq; Upendra, Badimela; Kaur, Rupinder; Gill, Sukhpal Singh; Biswas, Mriganka Sekhar | Quantifying COVID-19 enforced global changes in atmospheric pollutants using cloud computing based remote sensing |
| S062 | Ding, Hui; Cai, Ming; Lin, Xiaofang; Chen, Tong; Li, Li; Liu, Yonghong | RTVEMVS: Real-time modeling and visualization system for vehicle emissions on an urban road network |

(*continued*)

(*continued*)

| Key | Authors | Title |
|-----|---------|-------|
| S063 | Halkos, George; Tsilika, Kyriaki | Understanding transboundary air pollution network: Emissions, depositions and spatio-temporal distribution of pollution in European region |
| S064 | Bachechi, Chiara; Po, Laura; Rollo, Federica | Big Data Analytics and Visualization in Traffic Monitoring |
| S065 | Jin, Ling; Harley, Robert A.; Brown, Nancy J | Ozone pollution regimes modeled for a summer season in California's San Joaquin Valley: A cluster analysis |
| S066 | Isakov, Vlad; Barzyk, Timothy M.; Smith, Elizabeth R.; Arunachalam, Saravanan; Naess, Brian; Venkatram, Akula | A web-based screening tool for near-port air quality assessments |
| S067 | Ahmed, Sara Osama; Mazloum, Reda; Abou-Ali, Hala | Spatiotemporal interpolation of air pollutants in the Greater Cairo and the Delta, Egypt |
| S068 | Salah Eddine SbaiFarida BentayebHao Yin | Atmospheric pollutants response to the emission reduction and meteorology during the COVID-19 lockdown in the north of Africa (Morocco) |
| S069 | R. H. de OliveiraC. de C. CarneiroF. G. V. de AlmeidaB. M. de OliveiraE. H. M. NunesA. S. dos Santos | Multivariate air pollution classification in urban areas using mobile sensors and self-organizing maps |
| S070 | Vlado SpiridonovBoro JakimovskiIrena SpiridonovaGabriel Pereira | Development of air quality forecasting system in Macedonia, based on WRF-Chem model |
| S071 | Dezhan QuXiaoli LinKe RenQuanle LiuHuijie Zhang | AirExplorer: visual exploration of air quality data based on time-series querying |
| S072 | Adriana Simona MihÄƒiÅ£ÄƒMirian Benavides OrtizMauricio CamargoChen Cai | Predicting Air Quality by Integrating a Mesoscopic Traffic Simulation Model and Simplified Air Pollutant Estimation Models |
| S073 | Kiwon Yeom | Development of urban air monitoring with high spatial resolution using mobile vehicle sensors |
| S074 | Tian XiaJames CatalanChris HuStuart Batterman | Development of a mobile platform for monitoring gaseous, particulate, and greenhouse gas (GHG) pollutants |
| S075 | Preciado, M, Vargas, C, Galindez, A, Jamioy, A, Peña,, Quiñonez, E, Solarte, R | Influence of Weather on the Distribution of PM10 Coming from Controlled Sugarcane Burning Events in Colombia |

(*continued*)

(*continued*)

| Key | Authors | Title |
|-----|---------|-------|
| S076 | Turki M. A. Habeebullah | Assessment of ground-level ozone pollution with monitoring and modelling approaches in Makkah, Saudi Arabia |
| S077 | Samaher Al-JanabiMustafa MohammadAli Al-Sultan | A new method for prediction of air pollution based on intelligent computation |
| S078 | Amin MohebbiFan YuShiqing CaiSimin AkbariyehEdward J. Smaglik | Spatial study of particulate matter distribution, based on climatic indicators during major dust storms in the State of Arizona |
| S079 | Kuiying GuYi ZhouHui SunFeng DongLianming Zhao | Spatial distribution and determinants of PM2.5 in China's cities: fresh evidence from IDW and GWR |
| S080 | Daji WuDavid J. LaryGebreab K. ZewdieXun Liu | Using machine learning to understand the temporal morphology of the PM2.5 annual cycle in East Asia |
| S081 | George E. HalkosKyriaki D. Tsilika | Towards Better Computational Tools for Effective Environmental Policy Planning |
| S082 | Paolo BuonoFabrizio Balducci | MonitorApp: a web tool to analyze and visualize pollution data detected by an electronic nose |
| S083 | Omar F. AlThuwayneeSang-Wan KimMohamed A. NajemadenAli AyddaAbdul-Lateef BalogunMoatasem M. FayyadhHyuck-Jin Park | Demystifying uncertainty in PM10 susceptibility mapping using variable drop-off in extreme-gradient boosting (XGB) and random forest (RF) algorithms |
| S084 | Wenwei, Y, Carey, J, Shicheng, L, Che-Jen, L, YuZachariah AdelmanShuxiao WangJia XingLong WangJiabin Li | Development and case study of a new-generation model-VAT for analyzing the boundary conditions influence on atmospheric mercury simulation |

# References

1. Shih, D.H., To, T.H., Nguyen, L.S.P., et al.: Design of a spark big data framework for PM$_{2.5}$ air pollution forecasting. Int. J. Environ. Res. Public Health **18** (2021). https://doi.org/10.3390/ijerph18137087
2. Xilot, J., Benitez-Guerrero, E., Molero-Castillo, G., Barcenas, E.: Sensing of environmental variables for the analysis of indoor air pollution. Int. J. Adv. Comput. Sci. Appl. **11**, 623–630 (2020). https://doi.org/10.14569/IJACSA.2020.0110675
3. Tularam, H., Ramsay, L.F., Muttoo, S., et al.: A hybrid air pollution/land use regression model for predicting air pollution concentrations in Durban South Africa. Environ. Pollut. **274**, 116513 (2021). https://doi.org/10.1016/j.envpol.2021.116513
4. Kitchenham, B.A., Charters, S.: Guidelines for performing Systematic Literature Reviews in Software Engineering. EBSE Technical Report EBSE-2007-01. School of Computer Science and Mathematics, Keele University (2007)

5. Liao, K., Huang, X., Dang, H., et al.: Statistical approaches for forecasting primary air pollutants: a review. Atmosphere (Basel) **12**, 686 (2021). https://doi.org/10.3390/atmos1206 0686

6. Nogarotto, D.C., Pozza, S.A.: A review of multivariate analysis: is there a relationship between airborne particulate matter and meteorological variables? Environ. Monit. Assess. **192**, 573 (2020). https://doi.org/10.1007/s10661-020-08538-1

7. Bellinger, C., Mohomed Jabbar, M.S., Zaïane, O., Osornio-Vargas, A.: A systematic review of data mining and machine learning for air pollution epidemiology. BMC Public Health **17**, 1–19 (2017). https://doi.org/10.1186/s12889-017-4914-3

8. Oliveri Conti, G., Heibati, B., Kloog, I., et al.: A review of AirQ Models and their applications for forecasting the air pollution health outcomes. Environ. Sci. Pollut. Res. **24**, 6426–6445 (2017). https://doi.org/10.1007/s11356-016-8180-1

# Author Index

© The Editor(s) (if applicable) and The Author(s), under exclusive license
to Springer Nature Switzerland AG 2023
J. Maldonado-Mahauad et al. (Eds.): TICEC 2023, CCIS 1885, pp. 483–484, 2023.
https://doi.org/10.1007/978-3-031-45438-7

Printed in the United States
by Baker & Taylor Publisher Services